Global Challenges in the Arctic Region

D0224946

Bringing together interconnected discussions to make explicit the complexity of the Arctic region, this book offers a legal discussion of the ongoing territorial disputes and challenges in order to frame their impact into the viability of different governance strategies that are available at the national, regional and international level.

One of the intrinsic features of the region is the difficulty in the determination of boundaries, responsibilities and interests. Against this background, sovereignty issues are intertwined with environmental and geopolitical issues that ultimately affect global strategic balances and international trade and, at the same time, influence national approaches to basic rights and organizational schemes regarding the protection of indigenous peoples and inhabitants of the region. This perspective lays the ground for further discussion, revolving around the main clusters of governance (focusing on the Arctic Council and the European Union, with the particular roles and interest of Arctic and non-Arctic States, and the impact on indigenous populations), environment (including the relevance of national regulatory schemes, and the intertwinement with concerns related to energy, or migration) and strategy (concentrating in geopolitical realities and challenges analyzed from different perspectives and focusing on different actors, and covering security and climate change related challenges).

This collection provides an avenue for parallel and converging research of complex realities from different disciplines, through the expertise of scholars from different latitudes.

Elena Conde is Associate Professor of Public International Law at the Universidad Complutense de Madrid, Spain.

Sara Iglesias Sánchez is Référendaire at the Court of Justice of the European Union, Luxembourg.

Global Challenges in the Arctic Region

Sovereignty, environment and geopolitical balance

Edited by
Elena Conde and
Sara Iglesias Sánchez

Routledge
Taylor & Francis Group

LONDON AND NEW YORK

First published 2017
by Routledge
2 Park Square, Milton Park, Abingdon, Oxfordshire OX14 4RN
52 Vanderbilt Avenue, New York, NY 10017

Routledge is an imprint of the Taylor & Francis Group, an informa business

First issued in paperback 2019

British Library Cataloguing in Publication Data
A catalogue record for this book is available from the British Library

Library of Congress Cataloging in Publication Data
Names: Conde, Elena, editor. | Iglesias Sanchez, Sara, editor.
Title: Global challenges in the Arctic region : sovereignty,
environment and geopolitical balance / Edited by Elena Conde and
Sara Iglesias Sâanchez.
Description: New York, NY : Routledge, 2016. | Includes
bibliographical references and index.
Identifiers: LCCN 2016007314| ISBN 9781472463258 (hardback) |
ISBN 9781315584768 (ebook)
Subjects: LCSH: Law of the sea–Arctic Ocean. | Sovereignty–Arctic
regions. | Arctic Regions–International status. | Territorial waters–
Arctic regions. | Water boundaries–Arctic regions. | Environmental
law–Arctic regions.
Classification: LCC KZA1667 .G56 2016 | DDC 341.4/5091632–dc23
LC record available at http://lccn.loc.gov/2016007314

ISBN: 978-1-4724-6325-8 (hbk)
ISBN: 978-0-367-28162-5 (pbk)

Typeset in Baskerville
by Wearset Ltd, Boldon, Tyne and Wear

Contents

Contributors

Nuria Arenas-Hidalgo is Associate Professor of Public International Law at the University of Huelva.

Rasmus Gjedssø Bertelsen is Professor and Barents Chair in Politics at the UiT–The Arctic University of Norway, Senior Researcher at Aalborg University and non-resident Senior Research Fellow at the Institute for Security and Development Policy.

Claudia Cinelli is Marie Curie Postdoctoral Fellow at the KG Jebsen Centre for the Law of the Sea, at the University of Tromsø.

Elena Conde is Associate Professor of Public International Law at the Universidad Complutense de Madrid.

Rosa María Fernández Egea is Assistant Professor of Public International Law and International Relations in the Universidad Autónoma de Madrid.

Ángel Gómez de Ágreda is Lieutenant Colonel in the Spanish Air Force.

Mette Højris Gregersen is MSc in Development and International Relations, Aalborg University.

Rob Huebert is Associate Professor in the Department of Political Science at the University of Calgary.

Christoph Humrich is Assistant Professor at the Department of International Relations and International Organization of the University of Groningen.

Marta Iglesias Berlanga is Assistant Professor of Public International Law at the Universidad Pontificia Comillas, Madrid.

Sara Iglesias Sánchez is Référendaire at the Court of Justice of the European Union.

Taisaku Ikeshima is Professor at Waseda University, Japan.

Jens Christian Svabo Justinussen is Associate Professor at the University of the Faroe Islands.

Sven G. Kaufmann is Administrator-lawyer at the Research and Documentation Directorate, Court of Justice of the European Union.

Timo Koivurova is Research Professor and Director of the Arctic Centre and of the Northern Institute for Environmental and Minority Law at the Arctic Centre of the University of Lapland.

Suzanne Lalonde is Professor of Public International Law at the Université de Montreal.

Michał Łuszczuk is Assistant Professor in the International Relations Department at the Maria Curie Skoldowska University in Lublin.

Cécile Pelaudeix is Assistant Professor at Arctic Research Centre, Aarhus University and Research Associate at PACTE-Sciences PO.

François Perreault is Adjunct Research Associate at the Institute of Defense and Strategic Studies in Singapore.

Daria Shapovalova is a PhD researcher at the University of Aberdeen, School of Law.

Marta Sobrido is Associate Professor of Public International Law at the Universidad de A Coruña.

Olav Shram Stokke is Professor in the Department of Political Science at University of Oslo and Fridtjof Nansen Institute.

Soledad Torrecuadrada García-Lozano is Associate Professor of Public International Law and International Relations at the Universidad Autónoma de Madrid.

Li Xing is Professor and Director, Research Center on Development and International Relations, Aalborg University, Denmark and Editor-in-Chief for *Journal of China and International Relations.*

Zhaklin Valerieva Yaneva is a PhD candidate at the Faculty of Political Sciences and Sociology of the Universidad Complutense de Madrid.

Acknowledgments

This collective volume is the most valuable and evident outcome of the research project *The Race for the Arctic: Issues of International Law Arising in the Light of Climate Change* (reference number: DER2012–36026), funded by the Spanish Ministry of Economy and Competitiveness (MEC), led by Elena Conde and composed by eleven research members.

The editors wish to express their gratitude to PhD candidate Zhaklin Valerieva Yaneva for her constant and very valuable support with the preparation of the manuscripts. We also thank Antonella Siliotto for her valuable help with the preparation of the index.

We would also like to extend our thanks to all those friends that gave us their generous advice with some linguistic reviews: Johan Vibe, Mihalis Loizou, Volker Rachold and Zhaklin V. Yaneva.

1 Introduction

Elena Conde and Sara Iglesias Sánchez

Overview

The two polar regions of the planet—the Arctic Ocean and the continent of Antarctica—have traditionally been neglected within international relations, mainly because of their geographical remoteness and inhospitable conditions. Regardless of their common features, each polar space has its own particular traits which have influenced the respective legal regimes applicable in the regions. Antarctica is referred to as a "global common" and is governed by the principle of "Common Heritage of Mankind." Until recently, the Arctic remained a completely frozen maritime space and its legal status had being shaped by different branches of Public International Law—mainly the Law of the Sea, regional regimes—the newly adopted treaties under the auspices of the Arctic Council or the legal framework provided by the European Law for some of the Arctic States, and the domestic law of the eight Arctic States.

The new position of the Arctic as a major issue in the geopolitical, economic and scientific international agenda has been mainly due to the complex process of climate change. Despite the existing uncertainties, it seems undeniable, in the light of existing facts and scientific studies, that the Arctic will soon lose an even greater part of its ice and for even longer periods. This will definitely foster all kinds of human activity in the region, creating a world of opportunities and risks.

The opening of new passages through the Arctic Ocean brings with it trade and tourism in the region. The sea ice retreat makes the exploitation of the extended continental shelf resources easier. But along with these possibilities, there are several risks to be aware of: safe navigation, sustainable exploitation of resources, rights and lifestyle of indigenous populations, the extent of the Arctic Seabed Area and even classic security threats. All these factors may lead to disagreements, even conflict, among the interests of the coastal states—the powerful *Arctic Five*—and those other states interested in using the new ice-free areas. Any such conflict will have to be resolved on the premises of existing international law or by making new regulations. It is therefore likely that new arrangements will have to be made, especially concerning shipping and fishing in the high seas, in order to adapt to the needs of the most powerful Arctic States and which will create a new international balance.

States, international organizations and fora—of which the Arctic Council is a particularly remarkable one—indigenous population and other stakeholders will be the ones to define the political future of this region. As pointed out above, the Arctic is undergoing a process of unprecedented transformation. No state acting alone can address the challenges associated with these changes. The main question therefore is how to enable the existing cooperation mechanisms to continue to protect the critical resources of the Arctic marine environment and the traditional lifestyle of indigenous peoples whilst benefiting from the new opportunities. To achieve this task, international law will be the key instrument to ensure stable Arctic governance.

Considering the current state of affairs in the Arctic, this collective volume is the culmination of work developed by a team of researchers led by Professor Elena Conde (Complutense University of Madrid, Spain) under the auspices of the national research project: *The Race for the Arctic: Issues of International Law Arising in the Light of Climate Change* (reference number: DER2012–36026), funded by the Spanish Ministry of Economy and Competitiveness.

Objective

This book gathers essays written by the members of this research project, including the two editors, as well as valuable studies developed by other renowned academics and practitioners who have devoted their research to the Arctic region. The objective of this book is to provide a genuine representation of the legal and political complexity of the Arctic, bringing together relevant and interconnected discussions about this region. As an academic work, this collection of essays aims to offer an avenue for parallel and converging research on the complex issues arising in different areas and relies on the expertise of scholars from a variety of disciplines.

The volume is divided into five parts. Our goal has been to emphasize the connection between different subjects and academic disciplines in order to highlight the complexity of the Arctic region—a reality that can only be captured through a multidisciplinary study. Part I is devoted to issues of sovereignty in the Arctic, which are strongly linked to environmental and geopolitical issues which are later discussed in Parts IV and V. The discussion of sovereignty in the region lays the ground for further discussion in Part II, which revolves around the main clusters of governance, namely the Arctic Council and the European Union. The human dimension of the challenges which the region is facing is examined in Part III, with particular regard to indigenous peoples and climate induced migration. As is apparent from this description, the structure of the book does not rely on a rigid dogmatic approach, since these five parts are closely intertwined with each other. The different chapters are therefore included in the different parts of the book on the basis of the "center of gravity" of their overall approach to global challenges in the Arctic region.

Structure

Turning towards the specific contents of this volume, Timo Koivurova, offers in his introductory chapter (Chapter 2), a general view of the importance of studying Arctic law from a multidisciplinary perspective. This chapter sets the scene for the remainder of the volume, introducing the wide range of problems affecting the Arctic region.

Part I deals with the legal challenges posed by particular territorial issues that strongly shape the balance of power and coexistence in the Arctic region. The rationale of this part is aimed at providing an overview of some of the legal difficulties that arise when analyzing the region from the point of view of territorial sovereignty and navigation rights. It also offers a legal perspective on the impact of sovereignty issues which relate to environmental protection. The discussion of these issues centers on classical doctrines in Public International Law—sovereign rights over the extended continental shelf (Elena Conde and Zhaklin Yaneva), the disputed status of the oceanic passages (Suzanne Lalonde) and the interpretation of international treaties (Marta Sobrido)—as well as on modern aspects of sovereignty in a multipolar world, considering sustainable development and environmental responsibilities (Claudia Cinelli and Sven G. Kaufmann).

The chapter by Conde and Yaneva (Chapter 3) deals with the very controversial and still present problem of delimitation of maritime boundaries in the Arctic. Maritime delimitation has resulted in disputes over the extension of the outer continental shelf between the Arctic States and between those States and the International Seabed Authority (who acts on behalf of the general interests of all humanity). As this topic has been widely studied, the intention of both authors is to offer a summary of the positions of the Arctic States regarding their extended continental shelves, and to review the legal trends that these developments may hide for future decades. Nevertheless, it is emphasized that besides the difficulties that Arctic States face in tracing the outer limit of their shelves, the correct implementation of Article 76 of the LOS Convention and the remaining uncertainties around some geological features have urged them to participate in a remarkable scientific cooperation which, ultimately, can be used as a diplomatic tool to resolve the existing disputes. Therefore, on the basis of the existing legal provisions—UNCLOS and the Scientific and Technical Guidelines of the Commission on the Limits of the Continental Shelf—and recent state practice in the field, this contribution studies the possibilities offered by scientific cooperation and the different submissions made by the Arctic States, posing questions regarding what will actually remain of the International Seabed Area in the region after the delineation process and what will be its legal status.

The analysis of Public International Law issues in the Arctic continues with Lalonde's chapter (Chapter 4) on navigation routes and oceanic passages. Indeed, Lalonde centers her study on one of the most debated and controversial legal issues posed in the Arctic region as a result of the positions and policies developed by Canada and Russia towards the Northwest Passage and the Northern Sea Route respectively. After a thorough review of the positions of both states, claiming sovereignty over the mentioned maritime passages, the author considers that Canada and Russia regard these routes as part of their national wealth and that, consequently, they should use their authority in a responsible way, taking into consideration the required good governance of the Arctic.

The position of the European Union on the Svalbard waters is carefully analyzed by Sobrido (Chapter 5). The 1920 Treaty of Paris recognized Norwegian sovereignty over Svalbard, imposing numerous conditions, such as the principle of non-discrimination for all vessels and nationals of States which are parties with regard to fishing rights. The progressive expansion of marine coastal states during the 1970s raised doubts on the scope and interpretation of the terms used in the Treaty of Paris, particularly on its applicability to Svalbard's exclusive economic zone and/or continental shelf. Now, the European Union as a whole is not a party to the Treaty of Paris. However, the Union defends and manages the fishing interests in Svalbard waters corresponding to those Member States who are parties. This issue might turn into a legal conflict as the actual debate goes far beyond the scope of fishing and encompasses many other areas.

Part I continues examining modern approaches to sovereignty issues with Kaufmann's chapter (Chapter 6) which offers an in-depth analysis of the principles of sustainable development, stewardship sovereignty and the protection of the Arctic marine environment. This chapter analyses several issues which arise from the commitment of Arctic coastal states to develop their stewardship role under international law. For this purpose, the chapter focuses on the possibilities of resorting to the principle of sustainable development in areas which are effectively or potentially subject to the extended continental shelf regime. First, Kaufmann offers an assessment of the shortcomings of current international law in sovereignty issues. Second, he unveils the potential implications of the stewardship role of Arctic coastal states under International Environmental Law. As a result of the foregoing analysis, the author argues in favor of the possibility to materialize environmental state responsibility on the basis of the principle of sustainable development, therefore highlighting the potential of this principle for resolving the contentious interplay between the principle of state sovereignty and the need to preserve the environment.

Part I concludes with Chapter 7 by Cinelli, who offers a critical analysis of sovereignty from the perspective of sustainable development. The author examines the legal status of ice in the Arctic with a focus on off-shore operations and pollution responses from a European perspective. Cinelli deals also with the stewardship role that Arctic coastal states have in protecting and preserving the Arctic marine environment in cooperation with non-coastal states, non-Arctic States and other stakeholders such as international organizations like the International Maritime Organization or the European Union. She identifies two trends: creeping jurisdiction and creeping cooperation, which give rise to a disordered interaction within the current regulatory framework, composed by soft and hard law instruments, which leads to a governance impasse. In addition, the chapter focuses on the EU's approach towards Arctic ice-covered marine areas, analyzing the applicability of the Offshore Safety Directive 30/2013 in the Arctic.

Part II of the book is devoted to the analysis of the existing international fora and governance mechanisms which function as venues for coexistence and cooperation in the Arctic region. This part brings together, in particular, three contributions which explore the role of the Arctic Council and of the European Union, with a particular focus on fisheries.

Chapter 8 offers an analysis on the Arctic Council, the most prominent regional forum for Arctic governance. Humrich engages with the fundamental question of institutional dynamics and efficiency. Having offered an account of the history of intergovernmental cooperation in the Arctic, he demonstrates how this history can be viewed as efficient and as inefficient. Both perspectives, however, share an important feature, assuming that state governments act on the primary interest of dealing with problems effectively. The second section of this chapter departs from this frame in order to reorient the focus from intergovernmental institutional dynamics towards transnational civil society in the Arctic region.

In Chapter 9, Professor Stokke examines another pressing governance issue: whether international institutions for governing Arctic fisheries are robust enough to cope with the challenges of a warming Arctic, including the withdrawal of ice, unsettled jurisdictional issues, and the possibility that spatial shifts of commercial fish stocks imply greater availability in international waters. The author develops and applies a "bifocal" approach to this subject matter, combining core insights from geopolitical thinking with those of institutionalism, one that highlights the interplay of regime characteristics and the configuration of state interests on contested issues. This bifocal optic, argues Stokke, can better account for the empirical pattern of cooperation and conflict over Arctic fisheries than each of those optics on its own. The chapter goes on to derive certain policy implications for topical Arctic fisheries issues, including the viability of the US initiative for an Arctic high seas fisheries arrangement and how best to combat illegal, unreported or unregulated fisheries in Arctic waters.

The interests of the European Union in the Arctic, regarding navigation routes and maritime governance, are studied in Chapter 10 by Iglesias Berlanga. The first section outlines the different navigation routes and the main legal problems related to each of them, also highlighting the advantages and disadvantages derived from ice navigation and the regulatory measures available. Subsequently, the author examines the applicable legal framework in the polar areas, with special reference to the recently adopted International Code for Ships Operating in Polar Waters (the Polar Code).

Part III brings together three contributions that engage with the human dimension of the Arctic. This part of the book is obviously concerned with the situation of indigenous peoples and with the population of the Arctic. In particular, the three chapters unveil the challenges that climate change and the Arctic peculiarities entail for the legal framework regarding indigenous peoples and migrants.

The first contribution (Chapter 11) examines the challenges for the judicial protection of Arctic Indigenous Peoples within two European judicial systems: the Court of Justice of the European Union and the European Court of Human Rights. This chapter, written by Iglesias Sánchez, offers an overview of the case law of these courts with regard to the rights and interests of Arctic indigenous peoples. Despite the fact that the number of cases that have been brought before these two international/supranational courts on such issues has been relatively low, the author identifies some common points of interest which highlight parallel problems in the European approach to indigenous rights. First, the author examines the situation of Arctic indigenous peoples with regard to their access to justice and, particularly, regarding the protection of collective interests. Second, the chapter analyzes the difficulty in articulating the material claims taking into account the specificity of indigenous rights in the framework of these two legal systems, in which an individualistic conception of rights is strongly embedded.

Fernández Egea and Torrecuadrada explore the interconnection between indigenous rights, the protection of animal life and international trade. Their contribution (Chapter 12) focuses on the issue of the ban on Arctic seals trade in the European Union and the interests and rights of Inuit and explores the tension between the need to safeguard environmental interests and the rights of indigenous peoples, on the one hand, and the imperatives of international law, such as World Trade Organization (WTO) rules. For this purpose, the first part deals with the impact of climate changes on Arctic indigenous peoples. The second is devoted to describing the case study on trade obstacles concerning seal hunt and the EU exception concerning Inuit products before the WTO bodies. As a conclusion, the authors highlight the challenges arising from the difficult combination of moral and environmental interests with the interests of the Inuit.

The chapter by Arenas-Hidalgo (Chapter 13) dwells on the particular issue of climate change induced displacement, questioning the alternative of migration as an adaptation strategy in the Arctic. It is a fact that climate change and the environmental degradation that follows are part of the most important causes that provoke the current phenomenon of population displacement. In this chapter, Arenas-Hidalgo analyzes both the national and international approach to native community relocation in the Arctic. The author carries out a critical examination of the evolution of this issue along the last decades: from the first legal instruments established to protect populations against arbitrary displacement to the current consideration of this subject as a community-based adaptation strategy within the framework of International Environmental Law.

Environmental concerns and the perspective of sustainable development are latent in almost every chapter of this collective volume. However, the three chapters in Part IV offer a closer focus on different topics which revolve around the richness of the natural resources in the Arctic and the delicate balance of its environment: the crucial connection between knowledge and natural resources; the relations between the EU and Greenland from the perspective of sustainable development; and the effectiveness of specific regulatory regimes with regard to the reduction of carbon emissions in this region.

In Chapter 14, Bertelsen and Justinussen explore the links between knowledge and natural resources as a crucial connection for the sustainable development in the Arctic region. The authors focus, in particular, on the Icelandic and Faroese experience with marine resources, renewable energies (geothermal, hydro, tidal and wind power) and offshore oil and gas. This selection is motivated by the fact that these two case studies provide illustrative examples of how human capital of small Arctic societies can contribute to socio-economic and politico-constitutional development.

The specificities of the EU–Greenland relations with regard to Arctic sustainable development are analyzed by Pelaudeix (Chapter 15). The EU is paying significant attention to its relationship with Greenland as an Overseas Territory, and is trying to extend its cooperation with the autonomous island. In this context, the chapter offers an analysis of the efforts that different EU institutions have deployed in order to support this cooperation in the field of sustainable development, as well as the legal framework underpinning this relationship.

The chapter by Shapovalova (Chapter 16) explores the problematic issue of the effectiveness of current regulatory models of gas flaring from the point of view of the reduction of black carbon emissions in the Arctic. The chapter tests the effectiveness of two legal models: the Russian and the Norwegian. For this purpose, after having offered an overview of the actions collectively taken by Arctic States, a second section of the chapter is devoted to the analysis of the regulatory models for gas flaring in Norway and Russia. Finally, a third section outlines a proposal for the improvement of the effectiveness of black carbon regulation in the Arctic by introducing a common gas flaring regime in the region.

Part V is devoted to geopolitical and security concerns in the Arctic. This part brings together a heterogeneous set of analyses, sharing however a focus on the strategic implications of Arctic questions. Thus, they all concentrate on the geopolitical realities and challenges that the Arctic region faces and will face in the years to come. These issues are analyzed from different perspectives and focusing on different actors, and, therefore, cover a wide range of security and climate change related challenges with a strategic implication for the Arctic agenda.

Gómez de Ágreda (Chapter 17) explores the effects of climate change in the Arctic from the geopolitical standpoint and considers that climate change will reconfigure the relationships among nations: local dynamics—related to access to new resources and possible redesign of transit routes—will be of paramount importance in the future balance of power worldwide as the global process of climate change, as any other disruption of the existent status quo becomes eventually trigger for conflicts. Among the negative effects, rising temperatures in polar latitudes, receding ice caps and the redesigning of transit routes are having deeper consequences that surpass the limits of the Polar Circle in our increasingly interconnected world. Geopolitical consequences will, by no means, be limited to the Arctic and its surroundings and will be felt as far as the Tropics.

This perspective is shared by Huebert. His contribution (Chapter 18) is mainly focused on the evolving nature of international security within the circumpolar north. Analyzing recent strategic decisions concerning the perceptions of security in the Arctic region and taken both by Russia and the United States, the Huebert wonders if the Arctic will remain an isolated space in the near future, characterized by political cooperation or, on the contrary, whether it will become part of the greater international security environment.

In their respective contributions, both Ikeshima and Łuszczuk center on the actors, interests and foreign policy roles in the new Arctic political environment modified by climate change. From the perspective of Public International Law, Ikeshima's contribution (Chapter 19) explores the geopolitical dynamics in the Arctic with special reference to the adjustment of national interests of Arctic and non-Arctic States, on one hand, and regional and global interests, on the other. The author considers that traditional geopolitical notions such as the *state as prime actor* and *state interest* have become obsolete in the Arctic region. Departing from this point, Ikeshima discusses the reasons and background for the adjustment mechanism in the context of the dynamics of the actors and the common issues raised by the challenges that will occur in the region. Thanks to the internal and external adjustment, conflicts and disputes that may be caused by the current high profile races concerning the development of resources and energies will be avoided and/or be settled peacefully. This study also evaluates the possibilities and limits of the efforts that need to be made by the actors and relevant institutions in the geopolitical context, as the non-Arctic States—such as the Asian countries (Japan, China and South Korea, among others)—demand to enter the region's governance in order to ensure the compliance with the rule of the law.

From the perspective of globalization and modernization of the International Relations, Łuszczuk (Chapter 20) studies the important transformations taking place in the Arctic region since the beginning of the twenty-first century. Indeed, the multiple consequences of climate change have opened the region for gradually increasing human activities and raise concerns about the region's future. Issues such as sovereignty claims, prospective commercial shipping, resources exploitation, ecological threats and increased political activities have turned the region into a significant arena of the global politics. Therefore, the aim of Łuszczuk's chapter is to present and discuss how these new and important geopolitical aspects have developed the region and how they can affect the interests and capabilities of both Arctic and non-Arctic States in military and non-military spheres.

The role of China in the Arctic governance is examined by Perreault, who offers an analysis of the challenges connected to the status of China as permanent observer of the Arctic Council which shows that China has had an impact on regional policies and on discussions on Arctic governance. Chapter 21, therefore, deals first with China's Arctic interests in the economic, environmental and political spheres. Subsequently, the author engages in the assessment of the different roles and statuses conferred to China and the Arctic States. On this basis, the chapter examines the ensuing power disparities and hierarchies within the evolution of regional policies and governance in the region, concluding with a stimulating discussion on the foreseeable challenges.

Returning to the non-Arctic actors, the contribution of Rasmus Bertelsen, Li Xing and Mette Højris Gregersen explores the use of soft power in China's Arctic policy through the case of science diplomacy and offers us the Chinese perspective on the Arctic governance. This final chapter (22) inserts itself in the general International Relations debate on the rise and accommodation of China in the international system. In this chapter, the authors focus on "the Chinese Dream" for national greatness in the context of the Chinese Arctic policy. The analysis refers to how China uses soft power in its diplomacy (understanding science as a marker of great power status) and in particular to reach goals in Arctic affairs. Thus, the chapter analyzes how China enters the Arctic, creates an image as a legitimate Arctic stakeholder, and builds relations with Arctic nations and beyond through the science field. China's desire to gain a seat at the Arctic table has, however, been clear and has resulted in it having permanent observer status in the Arctic Council. All these efforts can be seen as part of China's aspirations to become accepted as a major power in politics, business and science. Likewise, the authors analyze how Arctic nations deal with the increasing Chinese influence. The case of science diplomacy, therefore, gives the opportunity to explore a broader power concept and to analyze transnational instruments in the management of the rise and accommodation of a new power.

2 Why and how to study Arctic law?

Timo Koivurova[1]

Preliminary remarks

Law and legal systems are organized around well-established political communities. We, legal scholars, are trained to be experts on legal issues related to our nation state. It is the legal system of Finland, China or the United States that gives us our point of departure, and then we usually specialize in some aspect of that legal system, whether that be the Law of Taxation or regulating the protection of the environment. Another alternative is to specialize in international law, regulating the relations between nation states in a number of areas, such as the Law of State Responsibility, Law of the Sea, protection of the environment or human rights. These two legal spaces—national and international—are the main frames for lawyers, in general, and legal scholars, in particular. More recently, we have had to take a stance on whether a specific body of the European Union Law (or European Law) has come into being. Most argue that we now have a *sui generis* body of European Law whereas some still treat European Law as a derivative of international law. Be that as it may, it seems difficult for legal scholars to argue that they are specialists in a multifaceted discipline we have come to call "Arctic law." The purpose of this short introduction is to examine the reasons why there is an increasing focus on Arctic legal issues. Is there added value to focusing on Arctic law as a form of specialization?

It seems evident that we have seen a rapid increase in the legal scholarship covering Arctic issues. There are more and more scholars that focus much of their attention on Arctic legal issues. This is evident for the present author, as when I defended my doctoral dissertation on Environmental Impact Assessment in the Arctic in 2001,[2] there were virtually no organized activities for lawyers and legal scholars around the Arctic. Now there are several journals that have Arctic law as their main focus (such as the Yearbook of Polar Law,[3] and the Arctic Review on Law and Politics[4]), several doctoral dissertations have been defended in recent years on issues relating to Arctic law,[5] the Nordic Council of Ministers has funded the making of two Polar Law Textbooks,[6] and a textbook has even been

written on the international law in the Arctic.[7] In addition, there are conferences that deal with Arctic legal issues, most prominently the Symposium on Polar Law that has already been organized seven times.[8] The
Arctic Law Thematic Network of the University of the Arctic serves as the
foremost association for those legal scholars that conduct Arctic legal
research.[9]

All these activities are spurred on mostly by the opening of the Arctic to
various kinds of economic activities that require legal solutions to ensure
their sustainability in a vulnerable Arctic environment. Another reason is
the climate change which is dramatically transforming the region. The
Arctic warms at twice the rate compared to the rest of the world and feeds
back via various mechanisms (sea ice melting, methane releases) to the
global climate, but it also causes difficult challenges for the region's ecosystems and human communities to adapt.

How to study Arctic law?

What kind of legal research is possible in the region? It is possible to
canvas a few main alternatives as to how Arctic legal research can be done.
It is obviously possible, and for some the ideal method, to apply the
normal legal methodology to the issues of the region, which seems to be
only a peripheral space for larger systems of national and international law
(or European Law). This method entails that one succumbs to the underlying values of these larger legal systems. For instance, the ideal that law
should apply in a similar manner through a nation state might seem inap-
propriate to the peculiar Arctic conditions and specific Arctic problems,
but it does belong to the underlying values of many of the Arctic nation
states' legal systems. But we should not exaggerate the negative effects of
using the normal legal-dogmatic method to take account of the Arctic conditions. Many times law leaves ample room for implementation, interpretation and application, and empowers those who apply the law to make it
fit better for different circumstances, like in the Arctic.

More importantly, perhaps, legal research can always seek to improve
the workings of the law by making *de lege ferenda* argument. It would seem
only natural that legal scholarship that penetrates into Arctic realities will
be able to make suggestions for the improvement of the law to better take
account of the unique Arctic conditions.

A stronger option is to start creating more autonomous principles for
the region. This is part of everyday life in legal scholarship. In national or
international law, scholars construct existing legal norms in a new way if
they see a need for it. Often, as a result, a label is given to such a newly distinguished discipline, which may attract the energies of young scholars
thereby creating a new discipline of law. One example is Indigenous Law,
which emerged initially from the developments in both national legal
systems around the world and in international law, in particular human

rights law. It currently draws from various levels of law, together with customary law systems of indigenous peoples, and covers practically all legal issues related to indigenous peoples (from labor and environmental protection to protecting their land rights and self-determination). If this kind of disciplinary development is to take place, scholars are commonly expected to provide consistency to the emerging discipline by arguing that principles can be teased out from the existing norms that support the underlying values of that discipline.

In international law, this is often seen through its regionalization. Whenever there is a regional legal framework created, such as the European Union, the Antarctic Treaty System or the Mediterranean legal regime, it is possible for scholars to support its development by interpreting its norms in a way that makes it a more coherent and autonomous whole. Even if there is no overarching legal treaty framework for the Arctic, a viable argument has been made that it is possible for a type of Arctic Treaty system to come into existence. Erik Molenaar suggests that we may already be witnessing the emergence of an Arctic Council System, which leads to a more coordinated approach to Arctic governance. As put by Molenaar:

> This article proposes the notion of the ACS [Arctic Council System] to rationalize that the Arctic SAR [Search and Rescue] Agreement and the Meetings of the Parties established by it can be part of the Council's output even though it was not, and in fact could not be, formally adopted by it ... The ACS notion can also be put in a broader context. The two-tiered approach of negotiating non-legally binding international instruments under the auspices of the Council, thereby giving rise to the ACS as well as strengthening the Arctic Council through, inter alia, a standing Arctic Council secretariat, shapes the evolving international regime for the governance and regulation of the marine Arctic. This two-tiered approach is preferred by the Arctic eight and in particular the Arctic five over a new regional framework instrument, at least for now and the immediate future. There are several domains which require or would benefit from enhanced regional co-operation in the marine Arctic, and the ACS may expand to fill these gaps and shortcomings.[10]

This type of scholarly work can provide thought structures that enable further regionalization of Arctic governance.

Still another possibility is to examine how law functions in reality. The remoteness of the region means that it is of utmost importance to know how law works (or not) in the region. We cannot be sure whether the law in our Western law books actually influences the reality, which then leads us to suggest improvements for the enforcement and supervision of systems in these regions or, alternatively, forces us to think what type of law may best function in these regions. This latter path comes close to customary law systems of the region's indigenous peoples, for whom law is co-constitutive with their established practices, not something that has been ordered from a distant place by a given law-making procedure.

Concluding words

However one chooses to study law in the Arctic, it does seem to contain properties that make us better lawyers, whether as practitioners or legal scholars. The fact that we have to deal with national, European and international law increases our ability to navigate a world that is becoming multi-layered from the viewpoint of governance. But it is important to point out that by focusing on Arctic law as one general whole, it is possible to better understand the legal arrangements in the Arctic.

If we want to understand the very specific legal arrangement of the territory of Nunavut in Canada, it is clear that we need not only be knowledgeable of the evolving international indigenous law and human rights law in general, but also of the Law of the Sea, not to even mention the national framework of law in Canada. We cannot understand the Finnish northern environmental protection law without a strong understanding of how EU Law expects Member States to protect the environment, nor can we fully understand it without comprehending the protection the Saami indigenous peoples enjoy via the International Covenant on Civil and Political Rights over their traditional livelihood, reindeer herding, vis-à-vis the adverse effects from industrial activities. Added to this must be a good understanding of the complex national environmental legal system of Finland. Many of these legal developments on different levels are fully interacting and it is often impossible to understand one without understanding all the normative forces that have a bearing on the issue. This is evidently the added value by focusing on Arctic law, given that one needs to understand all these diverse forces of law and regulation, the understanding of which will enable better understanding of normative developments in the region.[11]

Yet, if we want to understand how these legal and other norms function in the reality of the Arctic, it is imperative to cooperate with other neighboring sciences, for example with colleagues working in the fields of international relations, political science and anthropology. This is what any legal scholar will find out when (s)he commences work in the Arctic, where the "implementation machinery" of law may very well be far away and under-resourced.

Perhaps we can create an analogy to how the natural scientists treat the Arctic as a natural laboratory. We social scientists, legal scholars included, can also use the Arctic as a unique place where legal innovations are needed. But in this day and age of globalization, it would be futile not to admit that the Arctic is part and parcel of global governance. The Arctic clearly has much to contribute in terms of legal innovations to global governance,[12] but we who are interested in Arctic governance also need to be aware that the region is well integrated into the global multi-layered governance framework.

Notes

1 The author wants to thank Adam Stepien for his insightful comments to this introductory chapter. The usual disclaimer, of course, applies.
2 Timo Koivurova, "Environmental Impact Assessment in the Arctic: A Study of International Legal Norms" (PhD diss., University of Lapland, 2001), Ashgate Publishing, 2002. The doctoral defense version was published earlier: "Environmental Impact Assessment in the Arctic: A Study of the International Legal Norms Applicable to the Planning Stage of Environmentally Harmful Activities," *Acta Universitatis Lapponiensis* 42 (2001), 440 pages. The final version was published by Lambert Publishing, 2015.
3 See the website of the *Yearbook of Polar Law*, accessed January 20, 2015, www.brill.com/publications/yearbook-polar-law.
4 See the website of the *Arctic Review on Law and Politics*, accessed January 20, 2015, http://site.uit.no/arcticreview/f.
5 See, among others, Md. Waliul Hasanat, "Soft-law Cooperation in International Law: The Arctic Council's Efforts to Address Climate Change" (PhD diss., University of Lapland, 2012), *Acta Universitatis Lapponiensis* 234 (Rovaniemi: Lapland University Press, 2012); Leena Heinämäki, "The Right to Be a Part of Nature: Indigenous Peoples and the Environment" (PhD diss., University of Lapland, 2010), (Rovaniemi: Lapland University Press, 2010); Tanja Joona, "ILO Convention No. 169 in a Nordic Context with Comparative Analysis: An Interdisciplinary Approach" (PhD diss., University of Lapland, 2012), *Juridica Lapponica* 37 (Rovaniemi: Lapland University Press, 2012); Natalia Loukacheva, Autonomy and Indigenous Peoples in the Arctic: Case Study of Greenland and Nunavut (S.J.D. diss., University of Toronto, 2004).
6 See the website of the Polar Law Textbooks, accessed January 20, 2015, http://norden.diva-portal.org/smash/record.jsf?pid=diva2%3A701555&dswid=-6175.
7 Michael Byers, *International Law and the Arctic* (Cambridge: Cambridge University Press, 2013).
8 See the website of the Polar Law Institute in the University of Akureyri, accessed January 20, 2015, www.polarlaw.is/en/previous-symposiums.
9 See the websites of the University of the Arctic, as well as the Northern Institute for Environmental and Minority Law, accessed January 20, 2015, www.uarctic.org/organization/thematic-networks/arctic-law/ and www.arcticcentre.org/EN/RESEARCH/NIEM/thematic-network, respectively.
10 See Erik J. Molenaar, "Current and Prospective Roles of the Arctic Council System within the Context of the Law of the Sea," in Tom Axworthy, Timo Koivurova and Waliul Hasanat (eds), *The Arctic Council: Its Place in the Future of Arctic Governance* (Toronto: Walter and Duncan Gordon Foundation, 2012), 179–80, accessed January 20, 2015, http://gordonfoundation.ca/sites/default/files/publications/The%20Arctic%20Council_FULL.pdf.
11 Moreover, we have to challenge our very notions of what law is or is not, when dealing with customary law systems of region's indigenous peoples.
12 See, forthcoming, Timo Koivurova, Paula Kankaanpää and Adam Stepien, "Innovative Environmental Protection: Lessons from the Arctic," *Journal of Environmental Law* 2 (2015).

References

Byers, Michael. *International Law and the Arctic*. Cambridge: Cambridge University Press, 2013.

Hasanat, Waliul. "Soft-law Cooperation in International Law: The Arctic Council's Efforts to Address Climate Change." PhD diss., University of Lapland, 2012. *Acta Universitatis Lapponiensis* 234. Rovaniemi: Lapland University Press, 2012.

Heinämäki, Leena. "The Right to Be a Part of Nature: Indigenous Peoples and the Environment." PhD diss., University of Lapland, 2010.

Joona, Tanja. "ILO Convention No. 169 in a Nordic Context with Comparative Analysis: An Interdisciplinary Approach." PhD diss., University of Lapland, 2012. *Juridica Lapponica* 37. Rovaniemi: Lapland University Press, 2012.

Koivurova, Timo "Environmental Impact Assessment in the Arctic: A Study of International Legal Norms." PhD diss., University of Lapland, 2001.

Loukacheva, Natalia. "Autonomy and Indigenous Peoples in the Arctic: Case Study of Greenland and Nunavut." S.J.D. diss., University of Toronto, 2004.

Molenaar, Erik J. "Current and Prospective Roles of the Arctic Council System within the Context of the Law of the Sea." In *The Arctic Council: Its Place in the Future of Arctic Governance*, edited by Tom Axworthy, Timo Koivurova and Waliul Hasanat. Toronto: Walter and Duncan Gordon Foundation, 2012, 139–90. Accessed January 20, 2015, http://gordonfoundation.ca/sites/default/files/publications/The%20Arctic%20Council_FULL.pdf.

Part I

Sovereignty issues and international law

3 Arctic outer continental shelf

Elena Conde and Zhaklin Valerieva Yaneva

Introduction

Recently, there have been many studies on the outer continental shelf in the light of the United Nations Convention on the Law of the Sea (UNCLOS or the LOS Convention),[1] mainly because the deadline for submitting enlargement proposals to the Commission on the Limits of the Continental Shelf (CLCS) is approaching. Considering the growing interest in the rich natural resources that are currently lying undiscovered beyond the 200 nautical miles (nm) limit, it is not surprising that states are becoming more and more interested in expanding their respective continental shelves.

There are two important premises to be taken into account in order to understand this article's special focus on the Arctic: first, the effects of climate change; and second, the growing state demands for sovereign rights over this frozen region. Hence, the outer continental shelf, especially the determination of its limits beyond 200 nm, has become one of the most important aspects in the aspirations of all the bordering states laying claims to the Arctic, because of the increasing impact of climate change on the ocean and the need for diversification and exploitation of new energy sources. Furthermore, many studies have been optimistic about the natural resources in the Arctic seabed, which have turned the region into a kind of "promised land," open for state appropriation.[2] The combination of a melting sea where abundant resources are expected to be found and, in particular, the high prices of energy sources have led to constant media alerts on the approaching "race for the Arctic," focused mainly on its resources.

This is even more alarming given the bold statements of some of the Arctic States and the wish to extend their respective continental shelves. Accordingly, Russia—one of the most influential Arctic States—was the first to submit an application to extend its Arctic continental shelf early in 2001. After the Commission on the Limits of the Continental Shelf replied asking Russia to provide more information on the proposed extension of its continental shelf, the controversial *Arktika* expedition took place with Russia planting its flag on the Lomonosov Ridge. This unilateral act caused vehement reactions and certain fears among the rest of the circumpolar states, in particular, and the international community, in general.[3]

Nevertheless, all the changes that the Arctic is experiencing nowadays—increasing global economic and political relevance, as well as strategic implications—"have placed the region within a new geostrategic framework in which non-Arctic States are eager to play a greater role and gain open access to resources (e.g., fisheries, bio-prospecting, new sea routes, and minerals),"[4] alongside traditional Arctic stakeholders. In fact, although climate change has opened the door to potential conflicts and tensions in the region, which must not be forgotten, the reality has proved otherwise: the region seems to be an area of cooperation, mainly in the scientific, technological and legal spheres. Likewise, two of the Arctic giants, Russia and Canada, collaborate closely, while Russia and Norway concluded a treaty in 2010 on the delimitation of maritime areas in the Barents Sea, a geologically rich area in gas and oil, which is an example of peaceful cooperation to be followed.

Considering the very abundant and solid scientific studies already made around the outer continental shelf in the Arctic Ocean, it is not the authors' aim to reproduce ideas which have already been well expressed and established by many outstandingly fine colleagues in the Arctic field. Therefore, there will only be a brief mention of some general aspects concerning the topic. On the other hand, the object of this analysis is a highly scientific and technical issue that explains why many of the details included in the general provisions on the continental shelf (Article 76 and Annex II of UNCLOS) are often scarcely understood by legal writers, which is why they can often be characterized as "believers" in the sense that they believe in the evidence presented by geologists and physicists.

Therefore, the basic interest of this study would be: in examining and explaining the political reasons behind the Arctic submissions for extended continental shelves; in the assessment of the economic data relating to the exploitation of submerged Arctic resources; and in the forecast on what might be hidden behind the renewed "*Mare Nostrum*" campaign and what remains untouched, if any, of the international seabed area. Other points will also be dealt with, or at least pointed out, such as some of the terminology used by UNCLOS ("the limits [...] will be legally binding and definitive" [Article 76.8]) or the possibility of enhancing the role of the CLCS (a legal body or a technical one?). Therefore, the present contribution can be described as a political study of the legal submissions made by the circumpolar states to the CLCS in pursuit of an enlargement of their respective continental shelves in the Arctic Ocean.

The continental shelf under the UNCLOS regime

Before delving deep into the topic of the extended Arctic continental shelf, the general legal regime provided by the LOS Convention deserves some explanation.[5]

Basically and from a geographical point of view, the continental shelf is a natural prolongation of the land territory and comprises the seabed and subsoil areas that extend underwater from the edge of the continental mass[6] or, from a geological point of view, it is "a broad, relatively shallow submarine terrace of continental crust forming the edge of a continental landmass,"[7] where the depth of the superjacent water is approximately between 100 and 200 meters. For quite some time, this definition was sufficient, but then, in the mid-twentieth century, many states began to unilaterally declare sovereign rights for exploration and exploitation of the resources situated in their continental shelves,[8] although the exact extension of this maritime space was not yet clearly defined in the legal doctrine.

Undoubtedly, the development of science and technology played an essential role in the establishment of the current legal concept of "continental shelf" and its inclusion in the customary as well as conventional law, as it helped reveal that part of the continents are submerged as a result of rising sea levels flooding the continental land masses after the last ice age and that most of the platform is at a depth of about 200 meters, which also meant that the length of the seabed was gradually being reduced in favor of this new maritime zone.

Therefore, UNCLOS, the last legal general instrument on the Law of the Sea, defines the continental shelf in legal terms as the stretch of the seabed adjacent to the shores of a particular country to which it belongs. Likewise, the LOS Convention establishes that every coastal nation has a continental shelf extending 200 nm from the baseline of the nation's coastline and stipulates the criteria for a possible prolongation up to 350 nm when the continental mass can be proved before the Commission on the Limits of the Continental Shelf to naturally extend that far. Two important facts contributed to the content of these norms: on the one hand, those states that were not naturally favored with wide continental shelves wanted to match the length of the platform with that of the exclusive economic zones (200 nm); and on the other hand, those states that already had wide platforms wanted to assert the possibility that, under certain conditions, the platform and corresponding rights over it could be extended.

Hence, the LOS Convention provides several sovereign rights, but not full sovereignty, for the coastal states to exercise in their respective continental shelves, mainly relating to the exploration and exploitation of the natural resources that are independent of any occupation or express proclamation (Article 77.3 UNCLOS).[9] However, delimitation and usage of the continental shelves "does not result in the coastal state 'owning' new territory. It results only in exclusive exploration and exploitation rights, and in the state receiving the imprimatur of the CLCS if they see eye-to-eye on every detail of those limits."[10] Those rights are exclusive in the sense that if the coastal state does not execute them, no other country may undertake these activities without the express consent of the coastal state.

To sum up, according to the UNCLOS norms, "[t]he continental shelf would no longer be linked to the exploitability criterion [and] [g]iven the natural prolongation perspective, the continental shelf may be extended ... depending on geological criteria (article 76.5)."[11] As a consequence we may conclude that, strictly speaking, the concept of a continental platform refers to the continent submerged under seawater. But, in a broad legal sense, the concept refers to:

> the seabed and subsoil of the submarine areas that extend beyond its territorial sea throughout the natural prolongation of its land territory to the outer edge of the continental margin, or to a distance of 200 nautical miles from the baselines from which the breadth of the territorial sea is measured where the outer edge of the continental margin does not extend up to that distance.
>
> (Article 76 UNCLOS)

Therefore, the provision tries to reconcile the interests of both the states with naturally large continental shelves and those that have small ones.

All in all, Article 76 UNCLOS, through its complex ten paragraphs, determines the procedure that a coastal state must follow in order to delineate the outer limits of its extended continental shelf beyond 200 nm. To do so, the state must demonstrate to the Commission on the Limits of the Continental Shelf that those areas claimed as part of the extended continental shelf are a natural prolongation of the continental mass, which would mean implementing a long and expensive procedure for collecting scientific data.

The Commission on the Limits of the Continental Shelf: criteria for the enlargement of the coastal states' continental shelves

To address the need of attending the coastal states' demands for the prolongation of the outer limits of their continental shelves beyond 200 nm from the baselines, the UNCLOS has created a specific body, the Commission on the Limits of the Continental Shelf, where states must submit their claims no later than ten years after the LOS Convention for that state comes into force.[12] Likewise, states must demonstrate to the CLCS that the areas claimed as part of the extended continental shelf actually belong to the land mass. Providing such evidence entails a long and costly process of collecting scientific data, which explains why many states tend to conduct joint missions to collect the necessary information. Thus far, the CLCS has received sixty-five submissions and has issued recommendations on eighteen, a fact that implies the Commission will need a considerable amount of time to deal with the rest. Among the positive resolutions that allow the establishment of final and binding limits in accordance with Article 76.8 is the submission of one Arctic state: Norway.

However, before turning attention to Arctic matters, we should briefly summarize the procedure the CLCS uses. Once the Commission has received submissions from a coastal state,[13] it starts analyzing the proposed delineation and, eventually, issues recommendations. Therefore, only those outer limits that are established "on the basis of" such recommendations will become "final and binding"[14] in a legal sense.

Nevertheless, it still remains rather unclear whether the Commission uses information other than that provided by the coastal state in its submission. Also, given the direct interest of other states in the extent of the international seabed area, we should ask what realistic options are available for bringing the issue of delineating the outer limits before an international dispute settlement body for re-examination.[15] In this respect, Franckx points out correctly that the CLCS should be the natural ally of the Common Heritage of Mankind, as it was created to ensure that states do not inflate their requests. However, its mandate for doing so has proved to be limited, as is the case of the Seabed Disputes Chamber of the International Tribunal for the Law of the Sea.[16] This will soon require dialogue between the Commission on the Limits of the Continental Shelf and the other bodies created by UNCLOS.

While being aware of the problems and ambiguities that might appear when determining the outer edge of the continental margin, we should recognize that, from a legal perspective, this is an extremely complex task that requires scientific support.[17] Article 76 of UNCLOS contains both the basis for entitlement to delineate the outer limits of an extended continental shelf and the methods that coastal states should follow in order to establish the delineation beyond 200 nm. Hence, according to Article 76.4 a, there is the *test of appurtenance,* which is used to:

> determine the legal entitlement of a coastal State to delineate the outer limits of the continental shelf throughout the natural prolongation of its land territory to the outer edge of the continental margin, or to a distance of 200 nautical miles from the baselines from which the breadth of the territorial sea is measured where the outer edge of the continental margin does not extend up to that distance.[18]

However, what happens if a state can or cannot demonstrate to the Commission that the natural prolongation of its submerged land territory extends beyond 200 nm? If it cannot do so, the outer limit is automatically delineated up to the distance stipulated in Article 76.1 and, therefore, it is not obliged to submit information to the Commission, nor is the Commission entitled to make recommendations. On the contrary, if a state is able to prove that the continental margin extends naturally beyond 200 nm, then its limits can be delineated by applying the rules described in paragraphs 4–10.

There are two alternative lines that can be used in a complementary way: *the rule of the thickness of sedimentary rocks* (Article 76.4 a.i, known as the Irish formula) or *the morphological rule*, based on the situation of the foot of the continental slope, which is the point of maximum change in gradient at its base (Article 76.4 a.ii, known as the Hedberg formula). Nevertheless, when the foot of the continental slope is difficult to determine—"in the absence of evidence to the contrary" is the exact terminology in Article 76.4 b—the coastal state can use other geological and geophysical means to locate it. Finally, the maximum extension is determined by one or both formulas that give rise to a line of 350 nm measured from the baselines of the territorial sea (*distance rule*) or by a line at 100 nm from the 2,500 meter isobaths (*bathymetric rule*).[19]

Therefore, if all these methods are satisfied, according to Article 76.8, a coastal state has an obligation to submit information on the limits of the extended continental shelf to the Commission:

> Information on the limits of the continental shelf beyond 200 n.m. from the baselines from which the breadth of the territorial sea is measured shall be submitted by the coastal State to the Commission on the Limits of the Continental Shelf set up under Annex II on the basis of equitable geographical representation. The Commission shall make recommendations to coastal States on matters related to the establishment of the outer limits of their continental shelf. The limits of the shelf established by a coastal State on the basis of these recommendations shall be final and binding.
>
> (Article 76.8, UNCLOS)[20]

Reading the provisions above, it is quite clear that the terminology is fairly ambiguous. Notwithstanding, the implications of the interpretation of the concepts might have important legal effects, as they can influence the final delineation of the outer edge of the continental margin. Therefore, we may conclude that the application of the methods embedded into Article 76 has proved to be a difficult task, as the LOS Convention makes use of scientific terms in a legal context and this supposes the need for close cooperation between scientific and technical experts, mainly from the fields of geology, geophysics, hydrology and geodesy, on the one hand, and legal advisors, on the other, in order to rigorously apply the norms relating to the continental shelf. Article 76 is thus a key example of the necessary relationship between science and law. Nevertheless, being a legal requirement above all, its legal sense should not be sacrificed in favor of scientific sense, but rather complemented by it.

Undoubtedly, some questions are arising in relation to Article 76 and the answers given will be important for understanding how the Commission functions in delimiting the extended continental shelf, despite the obvious difficulties it is facing:

1   What meaning shall be given to the phrase "the limits of the shelf established by a coastal state on the basis of these recommendations shall be final and binding" (Article 76.8)? Ultimately, the coastal state is the only sovereign able to establish final limits of its platform and there is also the possibility that a state might decide to not abide by those recommended. Therefore, should there be a dispute with the Commission's recommendations, it seems that the only option left for the CLCS is to request the advisory jurisdiction of the International Tribunal for the Law of the Sea to settle the problem according to Article 138 of the Rules of the Tribunal.

2   For whom are these limits "final and binding?" Logically, for the state requesting them and perhaps for the other parties to UNCLOS. But, what about the non-parties?

3   What happens with the delimitation of the continental shelf between states with opposite or adjacent coasts? In accordance with Article 76.10 UNCLOS and Article 9 of the Annex II to the LOS Convention, the provisions "are without prejudice to the question of delimitation of the continental shelf between states with opposite or adjacent coasts." This issue has been also addressed in the Commission's rules of procedure (see Rule 44) and in Annex I so that it could safeguard the rights of third parties. However, it seems quite doubtful that CLCS recommendations would not cause disputes at some time, with undoubted political consequences.

4   What happens if disputes arise between states concerning the delimitation of their extended continental shelves, even when states are following the recommendations of the Commission exactly? What happens if there is a dispute over the requested marine zones between the coastal states and the International Seabed Authority? It can definitely be seen that there are some legal uncertainties surrounding the extended continental shelf and the powers of the CLCS. Therefore, decisions will be required from the Commission on what space is to be left for the international seabed area once extended platforms have been set (especially valid in the case of the Arctic). Hence, it seems possible that in the future the area might disappear from the Arctic as a result of the gradual "sovereignization" of the seabed (which is reminiscent of a resurgence of the "theory of sectors").[21]

Arctic outer continental shelf

In the last few decades, concerns have been growing over the pernicious effects of climate change, which vary across the planet as a whole, but have particularly strong repercussions in the fragile Arctic ecosystem. It is evident that due to melting of the ice caps, changes are occurring in the Arctic marine ecosystem which, in turn, determine alterations in the patterns of human use of this ecosystem. Thus, the thaw opens the door: to easier, but not less dangerous, maritime navigation (related to commercial navigation, tourism, usage for military purposes); to the opportunity to explore and exploit the vast living and non-living resources of the region; to the construction of facilities and structures; and to cabling and scientific research, among others. As a matter of fact, the Arctic Ocean is:

> richly endowed with biological resources, both marine living and terrestrial [...]; renewable energy flow resources, such as hydropower, wind, geothermal, solar, bio and ocean energy, etc., and non-renewable resources such as oil, natural gas, uranium, coal and various minerals, including rare earth minerals which, in the current geopolitical context, have strategic significance.[22]

Moreover, the Arctic Ocean is one of the least studied parts of the planet and contains more than a quarter of the Earth's continental shelves.[23] With the favorable expectations of resource exploitation, there is nothing surprising in that all the states bordering the Arctic Ocean are trying to extend their continental shelves according to Article 76 UNCLOS and are currently engaged in gathering the required data to submit to the CLCS in compliance with the applicable legal framework.

Therefore, we can say that delimitations in the Arctic region deal with a classic dilemma of international law: on the one hand, it addresses individual state interests in the Arctic, and on the other hand, it is concerned with safeguarding the Arctic commons—or the Arctic in itself as a global common—which currently seems to be resolved in favor of particular interests.[24]

Nevertheless, the delimitation of the Arctic outer continental shelf turns out to be an especially complex matter as state demands seem to overlap, mainly in the following regions: Lomonosov and Alpha-Mendeleev Ridges, since Canada, Denmark/Greenland and the Russian Federation consider them to be wholly part of their continental shelves. Russia was the first ever to make a submission for prolongation of its Arctic continental shelf before the CLCS back in 2001, claiming territory situated all the way to the North Pole and, thereby, encompassing the above-mentioned ridges.[25] The CLCS requested the Russian Federation to submit further geological data and research, which it did by submitting a partially revised claim on August 3, 2015, which, if approved, will considerably expand Russia's Arctic territory.[26]

On the other hand, Canada and Denmark have conducted or are currently conducting explorations of the Arctic seabed in order to provide further evidence that Lomonosov should be considered a natural prolongation of their continental shelves. In its 2014 submission, while referring to the previous Russian submission, Denmark pointed out that the future CLCS recommendations would be "[...] without prejudice to the delimitation of the continental shelf between the two States."[27] It also notes that the Greenland shelf is likely to overlap with a future continental shelf submission by Canada, and probably also with a submission by the USA.

Additionally, Finland and Sweden do not have a continental shelf beyond 200 nm. Moreover, Iceland's shelf is located in the Norwegian Sea, not the Arctic Ocean, and in 2006 the State reached an agreement (Agreed Minutes) with Norway and Denmark/Faroe Islands on how to deal with their overlapping claims.[28] However, this last agreement is not the only example of bilateral agreement between Arctic States in regard to the delineation of their shelves. Also deserving mention is the landmark treaty between Norway and the Russian Federation concerning maritime delimitation and cooperation in the Barents Sea and the Arctic Ocean, signed on September 15, 2010,[29] which refers to the continental shelf beyond 200 nm in the Barents Sea and the Western Nansen Basin in the Arctic Ocean. Apart from this agreement, Norway submitted its application to the CLCS on November 27, 2006 regarding three areas in the Northeast Atlantic and the Arctic: the Loophole in the Barents Sea, the Western Nansen Basin in the Arctic and the Banana Hole in the Norwegian Sea. In April 2009, Norway was the first Arctic State to have defined its platform following the relevant recommendations of the Commission, but it must be highlighted that close scientific cooperation with its neighboring states, especially the Russian Federation and Denmark, was essential to achieve this.[30]

Thus far, Canada's only submission, made on December 6, 2013, has affected the Atlantic Ocean. However, it is very extensive and this fact makes it highly probable that the future Canadian submission concerning the Arctic will be huge, possibly overlapping with those of Russia, Denmark/Greenland and the USA.[31]

The USA is a different case, as it is not a party to the LOS Convention (only to the 1958 Geneva Convention on the Continental Shelf) and, therefore, does not have the right to submit information concerning its extended continental shelves to the CLCS. Nevertheless, the American policy implies that the USA considers all the relevant requisites of Article 76 UNCLOS as part of customary law. This means that the USA may delimit its extended continental shelf, but it would not count with the approval of the CLCS and such unilateral delimitation may cause disputes with other states as they are not obliged to respect such a unilateral act, and certainly will not attach the same recognition as if it was supported by the Commission.[32] Accordingly, the USA has been seriously thinking about the need to adhere to the LOS Convention in order to apply Article 76 and submit the question of the outer limit of their Arctic continental shelf to the CLCS. Such a position would also suppose equal negotiating power with the other states with claims on the Arctic continental shelf such as Canada, Russia, Norway and Denmark. Another way to avoid possible delimitation conflicts for the USA would be to negotiate the outer limits directly with its counterparts.

Finally, the process of determining the outer limits of the continental shelf in the Arctic Ocean has shown that states do adhere to the UNCLOS norms in contrast to the "media frenzy speculating over possible conflicts in respect of overlapping claims."[33] Nevertheless, we should reflect on whether the established time limits for implementing current international law of this importance are adequate, especially bearing in mind the extreme conditions in the Arctic Ocean. On the one hand, it is very difficult to collect and analyze data that describe the geophysical characteristics of the seabed and subsoil in ice-covered waters and, on the other, establishing the outer continental shelf beyond 200 nm will have little significance for the near future as "conventional oil and gas technology still lacks capacity to operate effectively and safely in the extreme Arctic conditions."[34]

The "science-law-technology" ratio as a basis for further Arctic cooperation

The significance of the Arctic Ocean for understanding the global climate is indisputable and, therefore, international scientific cooperation and free access for researchers become of key importance. Hence, "the characteristics of the Arctic Ocean provide a rationale for a more liberal regime for marine scientific research than that applicable to other parts of the globe."[35]

The type of marine scientific research involved should be taken into consideration when research concerning the outer continental shelf is at stake. Provisions of Part XIII of UNCLOS refer mainly to "pure or fundamental marine scientific research," or that which is undertaken for the benefit of humankind and whose results are to be made generally known.[36] This assumption strongly contrasts with the secrecy surrounding marine scientific research on extended continental shelves made by coastal states, as they seem to be more interested in the forecast for exploration and exploitation of (un)known resources or with possible military and strategic uses of the seabed.[37]

Oude Elferink states that in the last couple of years the Arctic coastal states have been meeting on a multi- and bilateral basis and discussing scientific and technical issues related to the prolongation of the continental shelves in the Arctic Ocean beyond the 200 nm limit, as well as providing legal expertise on the preparation of the submissions to the CLCS.[38] In fact, it was thanks to a scientific and political approach that a rapprochement between the positions of the United States and Russia on the Arctic continental shelf, clearly impossible in 2001, has been in progress since 2008. Another example of scientific cooperation is that between Canada and the United States. As of September 2011, both countries have been relying on one another and sailed together in the Beaufort Sea and Canada Basin, with scientists bundling information from various national databases to produce the International Bathymetric Chart of the Arctic Ocean in 2002.[39] A good example of Arctic cooperation can also be found in the 2010 agreement between Russia and Norway in the Barents Sea and the Arctic, which resolves their maritime boundary dispute and creates optimal conditions for oil and gas activity in the regulated zone, as well as assurances that the countries will jointly develop any shared hydrocarbon deposits that straddle the newly agreed boundary. Similarly, Russia, Canada and Denmark are exchanging scientific data on the Arctic outer continental shelf. All these actions point to scientific research and cooperation being vital to promote state interests in the Arctic region.

Therefore, we share Oude Elferink's opinion that science-law-technology cooperation among the Arctic States is quite logical because:

> Weather and ice-conditions in the Arctic make data gathering much more difficult and costly than in other regions [...] [where the] same geographical features may be relevant for defining the outer limit of the continental shelf of two states [Alpha-Mendeleyev and Lomonosov Ridges] [...] agreement in the scientific community on the interpretation of data may reinforce the position of a State in arguing its case before the CLCS.[40]

In addition, the existing science-law-technology cooperation on delimiting the Arctic outer continental shelves matches with the provisions of Part XIII of UNCLOS on marine scientific research, because provided the Commission does not issue any recommendations, the requested parts of the seabed continue to be regulated by Part XI of UNCLOS: "all States, irrespective of their geographical location, and competent international organizations have the right, in conformity with the provisions of Part XI, to conduct marine scientific research in the Area" (Article 256 UNCLOS). On the other hand, the provisions of Articles 242, 243 and 244 UNCLOS deal specifically with marine scientific research cooperation which is intrinsically related to Part XIV of UNCLOS on "Development and transfer of marine technology."[41]

Hidden interests

The extended continental shelf has turned out to be one of the most controversial issues under the current regime of the LOS Convention. It is of primary importance because if a state *cannot* prove before the Commission on the Limits of the Continental Shelf that a certain area of the adjacent seabed is part of its continental shelf, it will continue to be part of the international seabed area, where the natural resources are to be managed on behalf of mankind according to the regime established by Part XI of UNCLOS and later amended by the 1994 Agreement on implementation of Part XI.[42] On the contrary, if a coastal state *does* prove that the zone is part of its continental shelf, it *alone* enjoys sovereign rights to exploit and explore its resources, as established in Part VI of UNCLOS.[43] Indeed, it must be taken into account that the non-determination of the outer continental shelves means the non-determination of the international seabed area. The differences between the two spaces are remarkable and of pivotal importance in determining the rights of the states or contractors interested in the exploration or exploitation of the bottom of the oceans.[44]

Even though high seas freedoms remain over waters and sea ice superjacent to the extended continental shelf, possible restrictions on marine scientific research and other unintended consequences increase with the size of the shelf over which each coastal state may exercise sovereign rights.[45] As has been pointed out, some states—this could be the case of Spain as a fishery power[46]—fear that these continental shelf extensions might hide creeping sovereign claims of the coastal states, gradually reducing traditional freedoms of the high seas, such as freedom of fishing.

Concerns about the extension of the outer continental shelf in the Arctic and its possible consequences also inspired some of the most controversial decisions taken by the European Union after the Russian flag planting at the Lomonosov Ridge, namely, the European Parliament's resolution of October 2008. The repeated refusal of some Arctic States to accept the EU among the observers at the Arctic Council (it has been accepted as "observer in principle" status at 2013 Kiruna Ministerial Meeting) as well as the internal disagreements among EU institutions and Member States on Arctic politics, have resulted in a more cautious European approach to the region.[47]

The sovereign rights for the exploration and exploitation of the resources derived from enlarging continental shelves should also be considered from the perspective of the indigenous people's rights of the Arctic region. Their declarations (especially, the 2009 Circumpolar Inuit Declaration on Sovereignty in the Arctic) usually point to international law—the Law of the Sea and the human rights law being the most important—as a basis for any Arctic activity.[48] Concerning resource exploration by indigenous groups, Baker states, not without reason, that:

> [i]ndeed, even if indigenous rights in continental shelf mineral resources per se do not exist (a matter of domestic law that varies from state to state), development there may still affect, in the words of article 32, "[indigenous] lands or territories and other resources."[49]

This important issue and that of the self-determination of peoples might be critical in the future developments of some territories, such as Greenland, whose most likely evolution from the self-rule agreed with Denmark in 2009, seems to be independence from Denmark. The legal background that supports self-determination as an imperative principle of public international law, points out that the peoples who exercise the right of self-determination should have permanent sovereignty over their riches and natural resources, as stated by General Assembly Resolution 1803 (XVII).[50]

Conclusion

Who owns the North Pole seems to be a question that will be repeated for many years into the future. With the progressive melting of the Arctic Ocean, the five coastal states have been submitting their claims over adjacent marine areas, seeking to protect their national interests in exploring and exploiting the existing natural resources. As a consequence, various potential disputes have arisen in the region over maritime delimitation, with the issue on the outer limits of the Arctic continental shelf beyond 200 nm being the most problematic of all and a possibility endorsed under Article 76 of the LOS Convention. In this regard, if the coastal state is able to provide enough scientific data that demonstrates that their continental mass extends naturally to the "outer edge of the continental margin," in the terms used by the Convention, then its own sovereign rights can be legally extended to 350 nm with the only limitation resulting from the payments that are to be made to the International Seabed Authority under Article 82 UNCLOS. Nevertheless, questions on the management of natural resources beyond the areas under national jurisdiction of one of the Arctic States—for example, the central Arctic Ocean—will continue to be decided mainly between the traditional Arctic stakeholders, but these will need to balance their interests with those of the interested non-Arctic actors.

The Commission on the Limits of the Continental Shelf comprises scientists from various fields and is the technical body that makes recommendations to states on their respective submissions, which if accepted by the state, become "final and binding." However, these recommendations made by the Commission must be parallel and not intercept in any way any negotiation processes over maritime delimitation or any judicial decisions in this regard, something that seems rather hypothetical.

The difficult implementation of Article 76 UNCLOS as well as the Arctic realities (harsh climate, darkness, ice, high costs of any development, among others) have highlighted the importance of "science-law-technology" cooperation for the collection of data on the continental shelves of neighboring states, as well for improvement of the respective positions on overlapping regions in the continental shelves claims. In some cases, the process of jointly gathering information has prompted a resolution for hitherto unsettled maritime boundaries disputes, as was the case of the 2010 treaty between Norway and the Russian Federation concerning maritime delimitation and cooperation in the Barents Sea and the Arctic Ocean. Therefore, UNCLOS has emerged as a means through which international scientific cooperation for the collection of data on the Arctic continental shelf and the seabed is channeled.

Hence, through scientific cooperation, for which there are multiple callings throughout the entire LOS Convention, not only the resources of the states involved in the search for data are being shared, but it also seeks a rapprochement between the contrasting opinions among neighbors. How this cooperation will be developed in future depends mainly on the willingness of the Arctic States to engage with others and mainly with the "outsiders" in the region.

The future in the Arctic remains the answer to the general question "who owns the Arctic?"[51] The final outcome of the process of extending continental shelves, seems to be a renaissance of the *Mare Nostrum* concept, whose consequences are still to be determined. The future of this creeping activity might turn into a progressive "sovereignization" of the seas where the rights of self-determination of indigenous populations should be taken into account, as most probably some of them could become new sovereign states in the near future.

Notes

1 Alex G. Oude Elferink and Constance Johnson, "Outer Limits of the Continental Shelf and 'Disputed Areas': State Practice Concerning Article 76.10 of the LOS Convention," *The International Journal of Marine and Coastal Law* 21 (2006): 461–87; Alex G. Oude Elferink, "The Establishment of Outer Limits of the Continental Shelf Beyond 200 Nautical Miles by the Coastal State: The Possibilities of Other States to Have an Impact on the Process," *The International Journal of Marine and Coastal Law* 4 (2009): 535–56.

2 One of the most influential studies is the U.S. Geological Survey "*Circum-Arctic Resource Appraisal: Estimates of Undiscovered Oil and Gas North of the Arctic Circle*," U.S. Department of the Interior (2008), according to which the Arctic could hold about 13 percent of the world's undiscovered oil reserves and as much as 30 percent of the natural gas reserves that can be found mainly north of the Arctic Circle—located offshore in the high seas—or within the exclusive economic zones of the Arctic States. Meanwhile, inshore exploration and exploitation have been happening for a long time now. However, a 2009 analysis of this survey—Donald L. Gautier et al., "Assessment of Undiscovered Oil and Gas in the Arctic," *Science* 324 (2009): 1175–79, accessed November 6, 2015, http://oceans.mit.edu/wp-content/uploads/oil_gas_arctic.pdf—concluded that the majority of the reserves are located within the 200 nm of the territorial sea baselines. For more on the Arctic resources, see Charles Emmerson and Glada Lahn, "Arctic Opening: Opportunity and Risk in the High North," *Chatham House Report* (2012): 18–35, accessed November 6, 2015, www.chathamhouse.org/publications/papers/view/182839; Natalia Loukacheva, "Resource Developments and Polar Law," in *Polar Law and Resources*, edited by Natalia Loukacheva (Copenhagen: Norden, 2015). Loukacheva further considers the problems of possible pressures on Arctic ecosystems caused by offshore and inshore drilling and the existence of different legal systems and lists some of the recent measures taken to resolve the problem. For the EU vision on Arctic resources, see Sandra Cavalieri et al., *EU Arctic Footprint and Policy Assessment: Final Report* (Berlin: Ecologic Institute, 2010).

3 The 2008 Ilulissat Declaration, signed by the five Arctic coastal States, tries to put an end to these fears. The States have reaffirmed that the Law of the Sea is and should remain the legal framework for resolving all emerging issues, including the delimitation of the outer limits of the Arctic continental shelf. The Declaration goes further implying the need for regional cooperation (much appreciated in the science field and with an important implication on

the continental shelf issues) and encouraging the coastal States to cooperate more actively. Nevertheless, the Declaration was criticized for not including the other three Arctic States—Finland, Iceland and Sweden.

4 Loukacheva, "Resource Developments and Polar Law," 30.

5 The definition and the criteria for the establishment of the outer limits of continental shelves are set out in Article 76 of UNCLOS. In addition, the Third UN Conference on the Law of the Sea adopted on August 29, 1980 a "Statement of Understanding" which was later included as Annex II to the Final Act of the Conference. The Scientific and Technical Guidelines of the CLCS from 1999 are also important to help States determine their extended continental shelves.

6 The presumption that land dominates the sea can be also found in the *North Sea Continental Shelf* cases (*Federal Republic of Germany* v. *Denmark* and *Federal Republic of Germany* v. *Netherlands*), Judgment, *ICJ Reports* (1969).

7 Encyclopædia Britannica (eds), "Continental shelf," in *Encyclopædia Britannica*, accessed November 4, 2015, http://global.britannica.com/science/continental-shelf.

8 To cite some of them, Declaration of the President Truman of United States of America (1945) and the President of Mexico (1945) as well as those that followed from Chile, Ecuador and Peru with the Declaration of Santiago from 1952.

9 Even before the signature of the UNCLOS, there were international norms accepting sovereign rights over their continental shelves up to 200 meters or to a distance where the depth of waters admitted of resource exploitation: *The 1958 Convention on the Continental Shelf*. The 1982 LOS Convention in a way reaffirmed the pre-existing rules with the creation of the 200 nm exclusive economic zone and the extended continental shelf rights for states with continental shelves that extend beyond that distance.

10 Betsy Baker, "Oil, Gas, and the Arctic Continental Shelf: What Conflict?," *Oil, Gas and Energy Law* 2 (2012): 6–7, accessed November 4, 2015, https://www.ogel.org/article.asp?key=3251.

11 Danilo Comba, "The Polar Continental Shelf Challenge: Claims and Exploitation of Mineral Sea Resources–An Antarctic and Arctic Comparative Analysis," *Yearbook of International Environmental Law* 20.1 (2009): 158. It was the 1958 Geneva Convention on the Continental Shelf that established the uncertain criterion of exploitability for delimitation of the continental shelves. This had been increasingly criticized by the human sciences as technology soon made the exploitability of this area more and more possible at greater depths.

12 Øystein Jensen, "Limits of the Continental Shelf in the Arctic Ocean," *European Society of International Law Reflections* 2.4 (2013): 1–4, accessed November 5, 2015, www.esil-sedi.eu/sites/default/files/Jensen%20-%20ESIL%20Reflection.pdf.

13 It is important to remember that sometimes the delineation of a land and maritime territory involves a pre-existing dispute among the interested states. Therefore, along its large practice, the CLCS has created the means to deal with such disputes which can be found in the Annex I of the Rules of Procedure of the Commission on the Limits of the Continental Shelf (adopted April 17, 2008). The options are the following: a coastal State cannot submit information on part of its continental shelf; joint submissions, or the Commission may not consider the submission for the time being, implying that it is not going to make recommendations.

14 Jensen, "Limits of the Continental Shelf in the Arctic Ocean."

15 Ibid.

16 Erik Franckx, "The International Seabed Authority and the Common Heritage of Mankind: The Need for States to Establish the Outer Limits of their Continental Shelf," *The International Journal of Marine and Coastal Law* 25.4 (2010):

559–60; Marta Abegón Novella, "Las opiniones consultivas de la Sala de controversias de los Fondos Marinos del Tribunal Internacional del Derecho del Mar
como un instrumento para la protección del interés general," paper presented
at the XXV Jornadas Ordinarias de Profesores de Derecho Internacional y
Relaciones Internacionales "La Gobernanza del Interés Público Global," Universitat Pompeu Fabra, Barcelona, Spain, September 19–20, 2013, accessed
December 8, 2015, www.upf.edu/dipri/_pdf/Comunicaciones_presentadas.
pdf. The Seabed Disputes Chamber is a separate judicial body within the International Tribunal for the Law of the Sea (ITLOS), whose primary function is to
interpret Part XI of UNCLOS, its annexes and other relevant regulations (see
Articles 186–191 of the Convention and 35–40 of the Statute of the ITLOS).
Both the Assembly and the Council of the Authority may request the Chamber
to issue advisory opinions on legal questions arising within the scope of their
activities. The first advisory opinion was issued on February 1, 2011 on request
of the Republic of Nauru.

17 In this regard the international jurisprudence has been repeatedly stating that
the concept of "natural prolongation" is essential for the demands of an
extended continental shelf. See *North Sea Continental Shelf* cases, Judgment, *ICJ
Reports* (1969): 3; *Continental Shelf (Tunisia v. Libya Arab Jamahiriya)*, Judgment,
ICJ Reports (1982): 18; *Continental Shelf (Libya Arab Jamahiriya v. Malta)*, Judgment, *ICJ Reports* (1985): 13.

18 Commission on the Limits of the Continental Shelf, *Scientific and Technical
Guidelines of the Commission on the Limits of the Continental Shelf*, May 13, 1999,
consulted November 5, 2015, www.un.org/Depts/los/clcs_new/documents/
Guidelines/CLCS_11.htm#2.2.%20%20Test. It is important to define the
concept of "continental margin." According to Article 76.3 UNCLOS, the
"continental margin" is the natural prolongation of the land mass, and consists
of the bed and subsoil of the shelf, slope and continental rise, but does not
include the ocean floor. In other words, the LOS Convention makes a geomor-
phological definition of the concept which, eventually, gives the coastal State
the necessary title to extend its continental shelf.

19 Tomas H. Heidar, "Legal Aspects of Continental Shelf Limits," in *Legal and Sci-
entific Aspects of Continental Shelf Limits*, edited by Myron H. Nordquist, John
Norton Moore and Tomas H. Heidar (Leiden and Boston, MA: Martinus
Nijhoff Publishers, 2004), 24–28.

20 For a critical analysis on the application of Article 76.8 in relation to paragraph
10 of the same article, see Elena Conde Pérez, "El papel de la investigación
científica marina en la delimitación de la plataforma continental de los Estados
Árticos," in *La contribution de la Convention des Nations Unies sur le Droit de la Mer à
la bonne gouvernance des mers et des océans* vol. 1, edited by José Manuel Sobrino
Heredia (Naples: Editoriale Scientifica, 2014), 290–92. The following problems
are pointed out: absence of legal experts at the CLCS; ambiguous rules on the
interpretation of the Article 76 (*state parties* v. *the Scientific and Technical Guidelines
of the Commission on the Limits of the Continental Shelf*); uncertainty surrounding the
possibility that State does not present its submission to the Commission in
the established period; what happens if a state discords with the final decision of
the CLCS, etc. Similarly, critics and possible solutions—especially whether or not
a coastal State is entitled to exercise its rights over the continental shelf beyond
200 nm before final and binding limits have been established (also in relation to
the Arctic) and whether is it possible to define provisionally such extension—can
be found in Alex G. Oude Elferink, "The Outer Limits of the Continental Shelf
in the Polar Regions," in *The Law of the Sea and the Polar Regions: Interactions between
Global and Regional Regimes*, edited by Erick J. Molenaar, Alex G. Oude Elferink
and Donald R. Rothwell (Leiden and Boston, MA: Martinus Nijhoff Publishers,

2013), 61–84; Alex G. Oude Elferink, "The Regime for Marine Scientific Research in the Arctic: Implications of the Absence of Outer Limits of the Continental Shelf beyond 200 Nautical Miles," in *Arctic Science, International Law and Climate Change: Legal Aspects of Marine Science in the Arctic Ocean*, edited by Susanne Wasum-Rainer, Ingo Winkelmann and Katrin Tiroch (Berlin and Heidelberg: Springer, 2012), 189–207. On the lack of a rule on delimitation of the continental shelf between states with opposite or adjacent coasts, see Danilo Comba, "The Polar Continental Shelf Challenge," 161–62.

21 Elena Conde Pérez, "Geopolítica del Ártico: el Derecho Internacional ante los retos del cambio climático en la región," *Cursos de Derecho Internacional y Relaciones Internacionales de Vitoria-Gasteiz 2014* (Cizur Menor, Navarra: Thomson Reuters-Aranzadi, 2015), 139–40.

22 Loukacheva, "Resource Developments and Polar Law," 19.

23 Conde Pérez, "Geopolítica del Ártico," 137.

24 Claudia Cinelli, "The Delimitation Process in the Central Arctic Seabed: Sovereign Rights or a *condominium* or *res communis omnium?*," paper presented at the ESIL 5th Biennial Conference Regionalism and International Law, Valencia, Spain, September 13–15, 2012, accessed November 5, 2015, http://eu-arctic-forum.org/publications/the-delimitation-process-in-the-central-arctic-seabed-sovereign-rights-or-a-condominium-or-res-communis-omnium/.

25 In its request of 2001, Russia sustained, among other things, that the Lomonosov and Alpha-Mendeleyev Ridges were underwater elevations and, therefore, natural components of the continental margin of the country under Article 76.6 UNCLOS. As Manero notes, the question would then be whether the two ridges are "oceanic ridges" which, therefore, would not be countable in the concept of an extended continental shelf (Article 76.3) or if they are "submarine ridges" which can be part of the extended continental shelf under Article 76.6. Ana Manero Salvador, *El deshielo del Ártico: retos para el Derecho Internacional. La delimitación de los espacios marinos y la protección y preservación del medio ambiente* (Cizur Menor, Navarra: Aranzadi, 2011), 58–67. Furthermore, as Jensen remarks, the distinction between "submarine ridges" and submarine "elevations" is critical, as the latter category confers a more favorable maximum limitation on the extent of the continental shelf under the LOS Convention. And indeed, if the said sea floor highs were to be legally classified as elevations, this would indicate that in the entire Arctic Ocean only two relatively small enclaves would remain part of the international seabed area: the Gakkel Ridge, and a smaller seabed area in the Canada Basin. Jensen, "Limits of the Continental Shelf in the Arctic Ocean."

26 Heather A. Conley and Caroline Rohloff, "The New Ice Curtain: Russia's Strategic Reach to the Arctic," *Report of the CSIS Europe Program* (2015): XII.

27 Ted McDormand and Clive Schofield, "Maritime Limits and Boundaries in the Arctic Ocean: Agreements and Disputes," in *Handbook of the Politics of the Arctic*, edited by Leif Christian Jensen and Geir Hønneland (Cheltenham: Edward Elgar, 2015), 220.

28 Oude Elferink, "The Outer Limits of the Continental Shelf in the Polar Regions," 68. The Agreed Minutes indicate that in the area concerned, the three States have resolved their outer continental shelf boundaries, but they are provisional until the Commission completes its work. See McDormand and Schofield, "Maritime Limits and Boundaries in the Arctic Ocean," 219.

29 Legislative bodies in both countries have approved the treaty and it entered into force on July 7, 2011, see www.regjeringen.no/globalassets/upload/SMK/Vedlegg/2010/avtale_engelsk.pdf. Apart from the maritime delimitation, the treaty also ensures the continuation of the extensive and fruitful Russian–Norwegian cooperation on fisheries, and governs cooperation on the exploitation

of any petroleum deposits that extends across the delimitation line. Actually, this treaty was first envisioned in the comments sent by Norway to the CLCS regarding the Russian submission before the Commission as Norway believed that the existence of an overlapping area between the two countries in the central part of the Barents Sea—situated at no more than 350 nm from the baselines—could be delimited according to Articles 76.3, 76.4 and 76.5 by the signature of a bilateral agreement without the need of any scientific or technical evaluation by the Commission.

30 Denmark (January 24, 2007), Iceland (January 29, 2007) and the Russian Federation (February 21, 2007) presented their responses to the Norwegian proposal at the CLCS, as did Spain (March 3, 2007, in relation to the marine areas adjacent to the Svalbard Archipelago).

31 McDormand and Schofield point out that there will be an interesting scenario in the Central Arctic Ocean as there will have to be agreements for boundary "trijunction" points involving Canada/Russia/USA and Canada/Denmark (Greenland)/Russia. See McDormand and Schofield, "Maritime Limits and Boundaries in the Arctic Ocean," 222.

32 Oude Elferink, "The Outer Limits of the Continental Shelf in the Polar Regions," 63–64. Oude Elferink states further that the USA might be right in defending that the provisions of Article 76 have become customary law as they are widely accepted by the international community and there seems to be no state objecting to them. In regard to the US position, we might highlight the 2009 US Arctic Region Policy, which begins by stressing its legal foundations:

> [t]his directive shall be implemented in a manner consistent with the Constitution and laws of the United States, with the obligations of the United States under the treaties and other international agreements [...], and with customary international law as recognized by the United States, including [...] the law of the sea.

In a section devoted to the extended continental shelf, the policy specifies: "the most effective way to achieve international recognition and legal certainty for our extended continental shelf is through the procedure available to States Parties to the U.N. Convention on the Law of the Sea." See Baker, "Oil, Gas, and the Arctic Continental Shelf," 14.

33 Loukacheva, "Resource Developments and Polar Law," 29. The author states further that "the real question is not per se about the 'race' for resources among the Arctic States but rather about their 'competition' over the collection of scientific data relating to the continental margin in the Arctic Ocean." To this we should add the growing concerns over the consequences that the resource development might have on the fragile Arctic ecosystem and the traditional livelihoods of the Arctic indigenous peoples.

34 Jensen, "Limits of the Continental Shelf in the Arctic Ocean," 3.

35 Oude Elferink, "The Regime for Marine Scientific Research in the Arctic," 207.

36 Article 245.3 UNCLOS says:

> Coastal States shall, in normal circumstances, grant their consent for marine scientific research projects by other States or competent international organizations in their exclusive economic zone or on their continental shelf to be carried out in accordance with this Convention exclusively for peaceful purposes and in order to increase scientific knowledge of the marine environment for the benefit of all mankind. To this end, coastal States shall establish rules and procedures ensuring that such consent will not be delayed or denied unreasonably.

37 Elena Conde Pérez, *La investigación científica marina: Régimen jurídico* (Madrid: Marcial Pons, 1998), 21–37.

38 Oude Elferink, "The Outer Limits of the Continental Shelf in the Polar Regions," 68 and 71–72. He believes that the cooperation was, on the one hand, to gather scientific data, but, on the other, it also helped to improve the respective positions on the overlapping regions in the claims. See also Elizabeth Riddell-Dixon, "Meeting the Deadline: Canada's Arctic Submission to the Commission on the Limits of the Continental Shelf," *Ocean Development and International Law* 42 (2011): 368–82; Thomas Winkler, "Danish Interests in the Arctic," in *Changes in the Arctic Environment and the Law of the Sea*, edited by Myron H. Nordquist, John Norton Moore and Tomas H. Heidar (Leiden: Martinus Nijhoff Publishers, 2010), 477–86; Elizabeth Riddel-Dixon, "Canada and Arctic Politics: The Continental Shelf Extension," *Ocean Development and International Law* 39 (2008): 343–60; Betsy Baker, "Law, Science, and the Continental Shelf: The Russian Federation and the Promise of Arctic Cooperation," *American University International Law Review* 25.2 (2010): 251–83; Ronald Macnab et al., "Cooperative Preparations for Determining the Outer Limit of the Juridical Continental Shelf in the Arctic Ocean: A Model for Regional Collaboration in Other Parts of the World?," *Boundary and Security Bulletin* 9.1 (2001): 86–96; Roderick Kefferpütz, "On Thin Ice? (Mis)interpreting Russian Policy in the High North," *Policy Brief* 205 (Center for European Policy Studies, 2010), accessed November 7, 2015, www.ceps.eu/publications/thin-ice-misinterpreting-russian-policy-high-north; Deana Arsenian and Andrey Kortunov, "The U.S. and Russia: Reinventing a Relationship," *World Politics Review*, December 1, 2010, accessed November 7, 2015, www.worldpoliticsreview.com/articles/7195/the-u-s-and-russia-reinventing-a-relationship; Baker, "Oil, Gas, and the Arctic Continental Shelf: What Conflict?"

39 Baker, "Oil, Gas, and the Arctic Continental Shelf: What Conflict?," 4.

40 Oude Elferink, "The Outer Limits of the Continental Shelf in the Polar Regions," 71–72.

41 Conde Pérez, *La investigación científica marina*, 67–74 and 185–249.

42 Briefly explained, the general framework that governs the Area and the resources therein is established under the "revolutionary" principle of Common Heritage of Mankind as ruled out by Part XI of UNCLOS and its Annexes III and IV, amended by 1994 Agreement on implementation of Part XI of UNCLOS. Even after this legislative process, inspired by the idea of free trade and liberal exploitation of the resources of the Area, the concept of Common Heritage of Mankind survived, as Article 311.6 of UNCLOS demonstrates. The regime of the Seabed Area is considered to be the best expression of the idea of Common Heritage of Mankind as it creates a real institutionalization of the concept through the Seabed Authority, an international organization. As delegate of Humankind, the Authority must provide for a responsible and sustainable exploration and exploitation of the resources therein and it has elaborated a set of rules, regulations and procedures (the so-called Mining Code) to regulate those activities. See Elena Conde Pérez, "España, la Unión Europea y los espacios de interés internacional," paper presented at the XXVI Jornadas Ordinarias de la Asociación de Profesores de Derecho Internacional y Relaciones Internacionales "España y la Unión Europea en el orden internacional," Sevilla, Spain, October 15–16, 2015, forthcoming.

43 Notwithstanding, the sovereign rights in the extended continental shelf are exercised with some limitations: even when a State has sovereign rights over the seabed beyond the 200 nm, it has to contribute a percentage of the revenues from the exploitation of non-living resources in that seabed to the International Seabed Authority (which will distribute that contribution to the States which are

Party to the United Nations Convention on the Law of the Sea on the basis of equitable sharing criteria, taking into account the interests and needs of developing States, particularly the least developed and the land-locked).

44 Conde Pérez, "España, la Unión Europea y los espacios de interés internacional."
45 Baker, "Oil, Gas, and the Arctic Continental Shelf: What Conflict?," 8.
46 On March 28, 1995, Spain made a claim against Canada before the International Court of Justice—which the Court itself properly defined as relating to "jurisdiction over fisheries"—insisting to the Court to declare the Canadian law unenforceable to Spain; to incite Canada to repair, and to declare that the exercise of jurisdiction and enforcement measure constituted a violation of the principles and norms of international law. Spain invoked as a basis for the Court's jurisdiction the declarations of acceptance of jurisdiction made by both States according to Article 36.2 of the Statute. The judgment came out of December 4, 1998, stating that the Court has no jurisdiction to rule on the dispute as it considered the dispute basis covered by paragraph 2d of the Canadian declaration of May 2, 1994. *Case concerning fisheries jurisdiction (Spain v. Canada)* Judgment, *ICJ Reports* (1998).
47 Elena Conde Pérez and Zhaklin Valerieva Yaneva, "The European Union has its Eye on the Arctic," *The Yearbook of Polar Law* (unpublished); Elena Conde Pérez and Zhaklin Valerieva Yaneva, "The European Arctic Policy in progress: a review," *Polar Science* (2016).

> The EU pillars of actions can be summarized in three words: "Knowledge, Responsibility, Engagement" which support the ratio behind of several initiatives that contribute, *inter alia*, to research and sustainable development in the Arctic and promote environmentally friendly technologies that could be used for sustainable activities, including oil and gas prospection, exploration and production.
>
> (Claudia Cinelli, "The Delimitation Process in the Central Arctic Seabed," 5–6)

48 In this sense, Betsy Baker points out that the Circumpolar Declaration names specifically *The 2007 UN Declaration on the Rights of Indigenous Peoples*, which is supported by all the Arctic States except Russia. Article 32 of UNDRIP calls for *the free and informed consent* of indigenous peoples "prior to the approval of any project affecting their lands or territories and other resources, particularly in connection with the development, utilization or exploitation of mineral, water or other resources." Baker, "Oil, Gas, and the Arctic Continental Shelf: What Conflict?," 15–16. On the consequences of the different marine disputes on the indigenous peoples' rights—the dispute concerning the sovereignty in the Beaufort Sea between the USA and Canada or the case concerning the delimitation of Hans Island, between Denmark and Canada—see Asim Zia, Ilan Kelman and Michael Glantz, "Arctic Melting Tests the United Nations Convention on the Law of the Sea," in *Diplomacy on Ice: Energy and the Environment in the Arctic and Antarctic*, edited by Rebecca Pincus and Saleem H. Ali (New Haven, CT and London: Yale University Press, 2015), 131–35.
49 Baker, "Oil, Gas, and the Arctic Continental Shelf: What Conflict?," 15–16.
50 This question has received renewed interest in Spain: it submitted its request for an extended continental shelf in the Atlantic around the Canary Islands, in 2014, and this submission has created a dispute not only against Morocco but also in reference to the sovereign rights of Sahara population which still does not enjoy its right of self-determination.
51 Michael Byers uses this question as a title of his well-known monography *Who Owns the Arctic? Understanding Sovereignty Disputes in the North* (Vancouver, BC: Douglas & McIntyre, 2010).

Bibliography

Allain, Monique Andree. "Canada's Claim to the Arctic: A Study in Overlapping Claims to the Outer Continental Shelf." *Journal of Maritime Law and Commerce* 42.1 (2011): 1–47.

Arctic Ocean Conference. *The Ilulissat Declaration.* May 28, 2008. Accessed November 6, 2015, www.regjeringen.no/globalassets/upload/ud/080525_arctic_ocean_conference_outcome.pdf.

Arsenian, Deana and Andrey Kortunov. "The U.S. and Russia: Reinventing a Relationship." *World Politics Review,* December 1, 2010. Accessed November 7, 2015, www.worldpoliticsreview.com/articles/7195/the-u-s-and-russia-reinventing-a-relationship.

Baker, Betsy. "Law, Science, and the Continental Shelf: The Russian Federation and the Promise of Arctic Cooperation." *American University International Law Review* 25.2 (2010): 251–83.

Baker, Betsy. "Oil, Gas, and the Arctic Continental Shelf: What Conflict?" *Oil, Gas and Energy Law* 2 (2012). Accessed November 4, 2015, www.ogel.org/article.asp?key=3251.

Byers, Michael. *Who Owns the Arctic? Understanding Sovereignty Disputes in the North.* Vancouver, BC: Douglas & McIntyre, 2010.

Carleton, Chris. "Article 76 of the UN Convention on the Law of the Sea: Implementation Problems from the Technical Perspective." *International Journal of Marine and Coastal Law* 21 (2006): 287–308.

Cavalieri, Sandra et al. *EU Arctic Footprint and Policy Assessment: Final Report.* Berlin: Ecologic Institute, 2010.

Cinelli, Claudia. "The Delimitation Process in the Central Arctic Seabed: Sovereign Rights or a *condominium* or *res communis omnium*?." Paper presented at the ESIL 5th Biennial Conference Regionalism and International Law, Valencia, Spain, September 13–15, 2012. Accessed November 5, 2015, http://eu-arctic-forum.org/publications/the-delimitation-process-in-the-central-arctic-seabed-sovereign-rights-or-a-condominium-or-res-communis-omnium/.

Comba, Danilo. "The Polar Continental Shelf Challenge: Claims and Exploitation of Mineral Sea Resources—An Antarctic and Arctic Comparative Analysis." *Yearbook of International Environmental Law* 20.1 (2009): 158–87.

Commission on the Limits of the Continental Shelf, *Scientific and Technical Guidelines of the Commission on the Limits of the Continental Shelf,* May 13, 1999, accessed November 5, 2015, www.un.org/Depts/los/clcs_new/documents/Guidelines/CLCS_11.htm#2.2.%20%20Test.

Conde Pérez, Elena. *La investigación científica marina. Régimen jurídico.* Madrid: Marcial Pons, 1998.

Conde Pérez, Elena. "El papel de la investigación científica marina en la delimitación de la plataforma continental de los Estados Árticos." In *La contribution de la Convention des Nations Unies sur le Droit de la Mer à la bonne gouvernance des mers et des océans* vol. 1, edited by José Manuel Sobrino Heredia, 285–303. Naples: Editoriale Scientifica, 2014.

Conde Pérez, Elena. "España, la Unión Europea y los espacios de interés internacional." Paper presented at the XXVI Jornadas Ordinarias de la Asociación de Profesores de Derecho Internacional y Relaciones Internacionales "España y la Unión Europea en el orden internacional." Sevilla, Spain, October 15–16, 2015 (forthcoming publication).

Conde Pérez, Elena. "Geopolítica del Ártico: el Derecho Internacional ante los retos del cambio climático en la región." In *Cursos de Derecho Internacional y Relaciones Internacionales de Vitoria-Gasteiz 2014*, 99–159. Cizur Menor, Navarra: Thomson Reuters-Aranzadi, 2015.

Conde Pérez, Elena and Zhaklin Valerieva Yaneva. "The European Arctic Policy in Progress." *Polar Science* (unpublished, pending acceptation).

Conde Pérez, Elena and Zhaklin Valerieva Yaneva. "The European Union has its Eye on the Arctic." *The Yearbook of Polar Law* (unpublished, pending acceptation).

Conley, Heather A. and Caroline Rohloff. "The New Ice Curtain: Russia's Strategic Reach to the Arctic." *Report of the CSIS Europe Program* (2015).

Emmerson, Charles and Glada Lahn. "Arctic Opening: Opportunity and Risk in the High North." *Chatham House Report* (2012): 18–35. Accessed November 6, 2015, www.chathamhouse.org/publications/papers/view/182839.

Encyclopædia Britannica. "Continental Shelf." In *Encyclopædia Britannica.* Accessed November 4, 2015, http://global.britannica.com/science/continental-shelf.

Franckx, Erik. "The International Seabed Authority and the Common Heritage of Mankind: The Need for States to Establish the Outer Limits of their Continental Shelf." *The International Journal of Marine and Coastal Law* 25.4 (2010): 543–67.

Gautier, Donald L. et al. "Assessment of Undiscovered Oil and Gas in the Arctic." *Science* 324 (2009): 1175–79. Accessed November 6, 2015, http://oceans.mit.edu/wp-content/uploads/oil_gas_arctic.pdf.

Golitsyn, Vladimir. "Continental Shelf Claims in the Arctic Ocean: A Commentary." *International Journal of Marine and Coastal Law* 24 (2009): 401–08.

Heidar, Tomas H. "Legal Aspects of Continental Shelf Limits." In *Legal and Scientific Aspects of Continental Shelf Limits*, edited by Myron H. Nordquist, John Norton Moore and Tomas H. Heidar, 19–41. Leiden and Boston, MA: Martinus Nijhoff Publishers, 2004.

Heininen Lassi, Alexander Sergunin and Gleb Yarovoy. *Russian Strategies in the Arctic: Avoiding a New Cold War*. Moscow: Valdai Discussion Club, 2014. Accessed November 7, 2015, www.uarctic.org/media/857300/arctic_eng.pdf.

Jares, Vladimir. "The Continental Shelf Beyond 200 Nautical Miles: The Work of the Commission on the Limits of the Continental Shelf and the Arctic." *Vanderbilt Journal of Transnational Law* 42.4 (2009): 1265–305.

Jensen, Øystein. "Limits of the Continental Shelf in the Arctic Ocean." *European Society of International Law Reflections* 2.4 (2013): 1–4. Accessed November 5, 2015, www.esil-sedi.eu/sites/default/files/Jensen%20-%20ESIL%20Reflection.pdf.

Kefferpütz, Roderick. "On Thin Ice? (Mis)interpreting Russian Policy in the High North." *Policy Brief* 205. Center for European Policy Studies, 2010. Accessed November 7, 2015, www.ceps.eu/publications/thin-ice-misinterpreting-russian-policy-high-north.

Kunoy, Björn. "A New Arctic Conquest: The Arctic Outer Continental Margin." *Nordic Journal of International Law* 76 (2007): 465–80.

Loukacheva, Natalia. "Resource Developments and Polar Law." In *Polar Law and Resources*, edited by Natalia Loukacheva, 17–37. Copenhagen: Norden, 2015.

Macnab, Ronald et al. "Cooperative Preparations for Determining the Outer Limit of the Juridical Continental Shelf in the Arctic Ocean: A Model for Regional Collaboration in Other Parts of the World?" *Boundary and Security Bulletin* 9.1 (2001): 86–96.

Manero Salvador, Ana. *El deshielo del Ártico: retos para el Derecho Internacional. La delimitación de los espacios marinos y la protección y preservación del medio ambiente.* Cizur Menor, Navarra: Aranzadi, 2011.

McDormand, Ted and Clive Schofield. "Maritime Limits and Boundaries in the Arctic Ocean: Agreements and Disputes." In *Handbook of the Politics of the Arctic,* edited by Leif Christian Jensen and Geir Hønneland, 207–27. Cheltenham: Edward Elgar, 2015.

Nordquist, Myron H., John Norton Moore and Tomas H. Heidar (eds). *Legal and Scientific Aspects of Continental Shelf Limits.* Leiden and Boston, MA: Martinus Nijhoff Publishers, 2004.

Novella, Marta Abegón. "Las opiniones consultivas de la Sala de controversias de los Fondos Marinos del Tribunal Internacional del Derecho del Mar como un instrumento para la protección del interés general." Paper presented at the XXV Jornadas Ordinarias de Profesores de Derecho Internacional y Relaciones Internacionales "La Gobernanza del Interés Público Global." Universitat Pompeu Fabra, Barcelona, September 19–20, 2013. Accessed December 8, 2015, www.upf.edu/dipri/_pdf/Comunicaciones_presentadas.pdf.

Oude Elferink, Alex G. "The Establishment of Outer Limits of the Continental Shelf Beyond 200 Nautical Miles by the Coastal State: The Possibilities of Other States to Have an Impact on the Process." *The International Journal of Marine and Coastal Law* 4 (2009): 535–56.

Oude Elferink, Alex G. "The Outer Limits of the Continental Shelf in the Polar Regions." In *The Law of the Sea and the Polar Regions: Interactions between Global and Regional Regimes,* edited by Erick J. Molenaar, Alex G. Oude Elferink and Donald R. Rothwell, 61–84. Leiden and Boston, MA: Martinus Nijhoff Publishers, 2013.

Oude Elferink, Alex G. "The Regime for Marine Scientific Research in the Arctic: Implications of the Absence of Outer Limits of the Continental Shelf beyond 200 Nautical Miles." In *Arctic Science, International Law and Climate Change: Legal Aspects of Marine Science in the Arctic Ocean,* edited by Susanne Wasum-Rainer, Ingo Winkelmann and Katrin Tiroch, 189–207. Berlin and Heidelberg: Springer, 2012.

Oude Elferink, Alex G. and Constance Johnson. "Outer Limits of the Continental Shelf and 'Disputed Areas': State Practice Concerning Article 76 (10) of the LOS Convention." *The International Journal of Marine and Coastal Law* 21 (2006): 461–87.

Riddell-Dixon, Elizabeth. "Canada and Arctic Politics: the Continental Shelf Extension." *Ocean Development and International Law* 39 (2008): 343–60.

Riddell-Dixon, Elizabeth. "Meeting the Deadline: Canada's Arctic Submission to the Commission on the Limits of the Continental Shelf." *Ocean Development and International Law* 42 (2011): 368–82.

U.S. Geological Survey. "*Circum-Arctic Resource Appraisal: Estimates of Undiscovered Oil and Gas North of the Arctic Circle.*" U.S. Department of the Interior (2008).

Winkler, Thomas. "Danish Interests in the Arctic." In *Changes in the Arctic Environment and the Law of the Sea,* edited by Myron H. Nordquist, John Norton Moore and Tomas H. Heidar, 477–86. Leiden: Martinus Nijhoff Publishers, 2010.

Zia, Asim, Ilan Kelman and Michael Glantz, "Arctic Melting Tests the United Nations Convention on the Law of the Sea." In *Diplomacy on Ice: Energy and the Environment in the Arctic and Antarctic,* edited by Rebecca Pincus and Saleem H. Ali, 128–41. New Haven, CT and London: Yale University Press, 2015.

4 The Northwest Passage and Northern Sea Route[*]

Sovereignty and responsibilities

Suzanne Lalonde

Introduction

In the past few decades, Canada's sovereign control of the Northwest Passage has been the subject of government protests and academic criticism. One of the most compelling arguments has been that Canada has broken faith with its own commitment to multilateralism.[1] According to this particular view, Canada's stated concern for the Arctic environment and its indigenous population is but window dressing for what amounts to a nationalistic and unilateralist policy.

On the other side of the globe, Russia's Arctic policy, including developments along the Northern Sea Route, has increasingly been denounced as aggressive and militaristic. Speaking to a sold-out crowd in Montreal in March 2014, the former Secretary of State, Hillary Rodham Clinton urged Canada to present a unified front with the USA to counter what she portrayed as "heightened aggression by Russia in the Arctic."[2] In May 2014, Norway's defense minister stated that "NATO needs to become more watchful about defending its members' security, including in the Arctic, because of the 'completely new' situation created by Russia's behaviour."[3]

The aim of this chapter is to consider these harsh assessments of the Canadian and Russian positions and policies in respect of the Northwest Passage (NWP) and Northern Sea Route (NSR). It will begin by setting out the nature of the disagreement as to the legal status of the two waterways. The following section will then focus very specifically on recent Canadian and Russian actions in regards to the Northwest Passage and Northern Sea Route. This section will not presume to analyze, justify or rationalize the two countries' overarching Arctic policies and all the various measures adopted by Canada and Russia in support of their national strategies. Rather, it will try and determine whether in light of recent initiatives, the two Arctic neighbors, while claiming important rights and prerogatives over the seaways, are also attempting to live up to the obligations and responsibilities that weigh on territorial sovereigns.

The debate over the legal status of the Northwest Passage and the Northern Sea Route

Canada and Russia's respective positions regarding the Northwest Passage[4] and the Northern Sea Route[5] are well established. Successive Canadian governments have declared that all of the waters within Canada's Arctic Archipelago are Canadian historic internal waters over which Canada exercises full sovereignty.[6] Indeed, "exercising sovereignty" over Canadian "Arctic lands and waters" is the first of four pillars underpinning Canada's 2012 Northern Strategy.[7] This assertion of sovereignty necessarily includes the right to govern and control access to the various routes that make up the Northwest Passage. For its part, the Soviet government claimed early in the 1960s that a number of the strategic straits that make up the Northern Sea Route (notably the Vil'kitskii, Dmitrii Laptev and Sannikov Straits) belonged historically to the Soviet Union, now the Russian Federation.[8] More recently, both the 2008 "Russian Federation's Policy for the Arctic to 2020"[9] and the 2013 "Russian Strategy for the Development of the Arctic Zone and the Provision of National Security until 2020"[10] have emphasized Russia's sovereignty over the Northern Sea Route and the need to protect the country's national interests.

Washington, in contrast, has consistently maintained that the Northwest Passage and critical straits along the Northern Sea Route are "international straits" through which the ships and aircraft of all nations enjoy a right of transit passage.[11] Indeed, though Canadian Arctic governance measures have in the past been the object of protests by other States[12] and recent European Union policy documents have emphasized freedom of navigation in the newly opened Arctic routes,[13] the United States has been the most vocal and persistent objector to Canada's and Russia's sovereignty claim.[14]

A number of reasons explain the long-standing stalemate over the strategic waterways: decades of public pronouncements reiterating the official Canadian, Russian and American positions have severely limited the governments' political *marge de manoeuvre*. But perhaps most importantly, ambiguities in the legal regime, including the very definition of an international strait, have also allowed the Arctic neighbors to craft solid, reasonable and persuasive arguments.

As Vincent explains, a coastal State's powers and prerogatives diminish as the distance from shore increases.[15] For this reason, a State exercises the greatest degree of control over its internal waters, defined in Article 8 (1) of the UN Law of the Sea Convention (LOSC) as "waters on the landward side of the baseline of the territorial sea."[16] While the Convention does not set out a detailed set of international rules governing internal waters, State sovereignty is the key concept, as confirmed by Article 2 (1) of the Convention[17] and by the International Court of Justice's 1986 *Nicaragua* decision:

> The basic concept of State sovereignty in customary international law, expressed in, *inter alia*, Article 2, paragraph 1 of the United Nations Charter, extends to the *internal waters* and territorial sea of every State and to the air space above its territory.[18]

Recognized as an integral part of a State's territory, international law thus provides that internal waters are subjected to the full force of the coastal State's legislative, administrative, judicial and executive powers. Foreign ships benefit from what has been termed a presumptive right of entry into the internal waters of a coastal State but as Gidel insists, "the presumption is in favour of a right of access to ports; but [it is a] presumption and not [an] obligation."[19] This right to control foreign access to internal waters, which necessarily implies a right to deny access if national imperatives so dictate, is at the heart of the dispute surrounding the status of the North-west Passage and the Northern Sea Route.

It is the official Canadian Government's position that all of the waters within its Arctic archipelago are Canadian *historic internal* waters.[20] And while according to Rothwell a similar claim has never been officially sanctioned by the Soviet or Russian Governments, "there is no denying that a strong view has been presented that not only are certain bays properly classified as historic but also that the various seas which make up the Russian Arctic waters can also be so classified."[21] The aide-mémoire sent by the Soviet government to the US embassy in Moscow in July 1964 certainly appears to invoke the concept of history in regards to its northern seaway.[22]

Under international law, a State may validly claim title over a maritime zone on historic grounds if it can demonstrate that it has, for a considerable length of time, effectively exercised its exclusive authority over the maritime area in question. In addition, it must show that, during that same period of time, the exercise of authority has been acquiesced in by other countries, especially those directly affected by it.[23] This third criterion is widely considered a fatal flaw in both Canada's and Russia's position in light of the United States' sustained protests, particularly as one of the States most directly concerned by the claims.

In the absence of a historic title, the LOS Convention provides that "waters on the landward side of the baseline of the territorial sea form part of the internal waters of the State."[24] Whereas Article 5 of the LOS Convention provides that the normal baseline, in the absence of specific geographical circumstances, should be "the low-water line along the coast," many States have instead relied on the use of straight baselines as defined in Article 7 of the Convention. Reliance on such an "exceptional" baseline is authorized only where "the coastline is deeply indented and cut into, or if there is a fringe of islands along the coast in its immediate vicinity."

Following the transit of the American ice-breaker *Polar Sea* in 1985, Canada acted to consolidate its legal position by drawing lines around the outer perimeter of its Arctic archipelago. It should be emphasized that in making the announcement, Joe Clark, the then Canadian Minister for External Affairs, stated that "these baselines define the outer limit of Canada's *historic* internal waters."[25] However, although the Canadian Government's intention may have been to simply draw lines so as to better identify the extent of Canada's historic internal waters, there is no doubt that most States and commentators assess the Canadian lines according to the legal rules that govern the drawing of *straight baselines.*[26]

Earlier that same year, by a January 15, 1985 Declaration of its Council of Ministers,[27] the Soviet Union drew straight baselines connecting its Arctic island groups of Novaya Zemlya, Severnaya Zemlya and the New Siberian Islands to the mainland.[28] Michael Byers speculates that:

> the move may have been prompted by the negotiation of the UN Convention on the Law of the Sea, which the Soviet Union had signed but not yet ratified, since the UNCLOS provisions on straight baselines are less favourable to coastal states than the pre-existing customary international law.[29]

Several commentators have questioned whether the Canadian and Russian northern coastlines present the particular geographical circumstances defined in paragraph 1 of Article 7 in the LOS Convention and which alone can justify reliance on straight baselines.[30] Doubts have also been raised as to whether Canada's and Russia's Arctic baseline systems respect the construction criteria laid out in paragraph 3 of Article 7, particularly the requirement that the "drawing of straight baselines must not depart to any appreciable extent from the general direction of the coast."[31]

However, even if a case can be made in favor of the legal validity of Canada's and Russia's straight baselines and even if they are considered the legal basis (rather than historic title) for the claim that the waters they enclose are Canadian or Russian internal waters, the Northwest Passage and certain key segments of the Northern Sea Route may not have the same status. For an international strait cannot be closed off by new baselines. Rothwell confirms this interpretation of the interplay between the different regimes defined by the LOS Convention: "UNCLOS clearly implies that transit passage through international straits can be enjoyed where the waters have only become 'internal' following the establishment of straight baselines under the Convention."[32] Thus the crux of the matter, if neither country can satisfy the criteria establishing a historic title, is whether the Northwest Passage and certain key straits of the Northern Sea Route were "international straits" when Canada and Russia drew their straight baselines in 1985.

The LOS Convention contains a separate section—Part III—dealing exclusively with the rules governing "Straits used for international navigation." While Part III reflects the consensus ultimately reached during the

Third UN Law of the Sea Conference (UNCLOS III) on the scope and nature of the legal regime applicable to international straits, no precise definition of what constitutes an "international strait" could be agreed upon. Consequently, the principal source of law on this central issue remains today the International Court of Justice's (ICJ) ruling in the 1949 *Corfu Channel* case.[33]

In one of the key passages of its decision, the ICJ identified the twin criteria which together define an international strait: "one pertaining to geography and the other to the function or use of the strait" to borrow Pharand's words.[34] In answering the question "whether the test is to be found in the volume of traffic passing through the Strait or in its greater or lesser importance for the international navigation," the Court stated that "the decisive criterion is rather its geographical situation as connecting two parts of the high seas and the fact of its being used for international navigation."[35]

On the basis of the *Corfu Channel* case, most commentators today agree that both a geographical and a functional element must be satisfied for a body of water to qualify as an international strait. Indeed, the Court's deliberate use of the coordinative conjunction "and" gives equal weight to both criteria. The first criterion pertaining to geography has not been the subject of much discussion and it was simply updated in Article 37 of the LOS Convention to reflect the creation of the exclusive economic zone: "This section applies to straits which are used for international navigation between one part of the high seas or an exclusive economic zone and another part of the high seas or an exclusive economic zone."

It is rather the second, functional criterion, which has fueled some debate among Law of the Sea specialists. Some commentators, primarily American, have argued that so long as the body of water can, potentially, be used for international navigation, the ICJ's definition or test is satisfied.[36] Others, including Canada's foremost expert on the Northwest Passage, Donat Pharand,[37] have argued that before a strait can be defined as an "international strait," it must be a "useful route for international maritime traffic,"[38] that it must have a history of usage, as of right, by the ships of foreign nations.[39] Some support for this view, which insists on actual use, can be gathered from the various references to straits in Part III of the LOS Convention. Indeed, Part III is titled "Straits *Used* for International Navigation" and this reference is subsequently repeated in Articles 34, 36 and 37. Reference can also be made to the UK government's pleadings in the 1951 *Norwegian Fisheries* case wherein an international strait was defined as "any legal strait to which a special regime as regards navigation applies under international law because the strait is *substantially used* by shipping proceeding from one part of the high seas to another."[40]

In the absence of a clear, widely accepted definition of an "international strait" subject to the right of transit passage, the question of the legal status of the Northwest Passage and the Northern Sea Route has attracted much academic and expert commentary.[41] While there are diverging opinions, most commentators seem to agree that in light of the absence of any *non-consensual* transits by foreign vessels through the two Arctic seaways, they do not *at present* meet the definition of an international strait subjected to the right of transit passage. For example, Byers concludes that the "Vil'kitskii, Shokal'skii, Dmitrii Laptev, and Sannikov Straits are almost certainly Russian internal waters, given the absence of any non-consensual transits by foreign surface vessels."[42] He cites Brubaker[43] and Rothwell[44] in support of his conclusion as well as Churchill and Lowe.[45] And in her 2010 volume *International Straits: Concept, Classification and Rules of Passage*, Ana G. López Martín concludes: "Today the majority doctrine excludes the whole of the Northwest Passage from the classification of an international strait because it cannot be used for international navigation."[46]

However, as Pharand warned in his final published contribution on the question of the legal status of the Northwest Passage, it could well become "internationalized" in the future as the Arctic region becomes increasingly accessible as a result of climate change:

> Given the current thinning and shrinking of the ice pack that is presently taking place, Canada must envisage an eventual use of its Passage for foreign commercial navigation ... Because of special factors such as the remoteness of the region, the difficulties of navigation, and the absence of alternative routes, comparatively little use for international navigation might be required. A pattern of international shipping across the Passage, developed over relatively few years, might be considered sufficient to make it international.[47]

It must be emphasized that Pharand was envisaging increased commercial use of the NWP by ships that might not recognize Canada's dominion over the Passage. Increased maritime activity, if respectful of Canadian authority, would not itself jeopardize the legal status of the Northwest Passage. However, the changing circumstances underlined by Pharand are very real and are also affecting access to Russia's Northern Sea Route. Consequently, Pharand's warning that the legal status of the Northwest Passage could at some point in the future change is also of real relevance for the Russian waterway.

Responsible management and control of the Arctic passages

One of the best explanations of the fundamental concept of territorial sovereignty remains today Max Huber's arbitral award in the *Island of Palmas* case in 1928.[48] In what is probably the most cited passage of the decision, the sole arbitrator declared:

> Sovereignty in relations between States signifies independence. Independence in regard to a portion of the globe is the right to exercise therein, to the exclusion of any other State, the functions of a State … The development … of international law, [has] established this principle of the exclusive competence of the State in regards to its territory…[49]

However, what is often overlooked is the care Huber took to stress that territorial sovereignty does not only confer rights and prerogatives upon the State but also imposes obligations:

> Territorial sovereignty, as has already been said, involves the exclusive right to display the activities of a State. This right has as corollary a duty: the obligation to protect within the territory the rights of other States … Without manifesting its territorial sovereignty in a manner corresponding to circumstances, the State cannot fulfill this duty. Territorial sovereignty cannot limit itself to its negative side, i.e. to excluding the activities of other States…[50]

The aim of this section is to try and evaluate whether Canada and Russia, while claiming the Northwest Passage and the Northern Sea Route as part of their national territory, have also taken steps to fulfill their fundamental duty to act as responsible and responsive sovereigns over those waters.

The Northwest Passage

As the introduction to Canada's Arctic Foreign Policy proclaims, "[t]he Arctic is fundamental to Canada's national identity," it is "embedded in Canadian history and culture, and in the Canadian soul."[51] To meet the challenges and opportunities created by changing conditions in the "new North," the Canadian Government adopted in 2009 a "Northern Strategy" and in 2010, released "Canada's Arctic Foreign Policy." Both documents inevitably identify the exercise of sovereignty as the first and most important pillar of Canada's Arctic strategy but they also emphasize as a key priority, promoting the economic and social development of the region. Indeed, Prime Minister Harper speaking in Iqaluit Nunavut in August 2009 referred to the Canadian North as having "the potential to be a transformative economic asset for the country."[52]

Marine transportation plays a vital role in the sustainability of the region and will also play a critical role in the responsible development of the North's economic potential. This fact was explicitly acknowledged by Canada when it chose "development for the people of the North" as the theme of its recent chairmanship of the Arctic Council and identified safe Arctic shipping as an essential element in reaching that goal.

According to the Government of the Northwest Territories, the number of transits of the Northwest Passage has increased from four per year in the 1980s to 20–30 per year in the period 2009–2013. However, only seventeen vessels managed a full transit in 2014 due to a short and cold summer.[53] Although this volume of vessel traffic is quite low compared with more southern Canadian waters, the 2014 report of the Commissioner of the Environment and Sustainable Development[54] also confirms that Arctic voyages have been on the increase since 1990.[55] And according to the same report, this trend is expected to continue in coming years, "driven largely by growing northern communities, expanding resource development projects, and increasing tourism."[56]

Though the 2009 Arctic Marine Shipping Assessment (AMSA) indicated that the Northwest Passage was not expected to become a viable trans-Arctic route through 2020 due to variable ice conditions and other operational challenges,[57] any increase in shipping activities, including destinational traffic through segments of the Northwest Passage, brings with it increased risks for marine safety and the environment. For even with a significant decrease in sea ice extent and thickness, marine operations within the Canadian Arctic archipelago including along the various routes of the Northwest Passage will continue to take place in a hostile environment, with variable climatic and ice conditions, across vast distances.

Various Canadian federal departments share the responsibility for managing risks to the marine environment and for supporting safe and efficient navigation in the Arctic.

- Transport Canada is the lead authority for implementing and enforcing the *Arctic Waters Pollution Prevention Act*[58] and its Regulations as well as the *Canada Shipping Act, 2001.*[59]

  In order to discharge its enforcement mandate, Transport Canada is responsible for monitoring Arctic waters and conducting inspections to prevent vessels from entering zones they cannot navigate safely, as well as detecting and deterring spills and illegal discharges of pollution by ships.[60]

- Pursuant to the *Oceans Act*[61] and the *Canada Shipping Act, 2001*, the Canadian Coast Guard is responsible for providing marine communications and for supporting safe navigation by providing ice-breaking services and aids to navigation. These responsibilities include implementing the *Northern Canada Vessel Traffic Services Zone Regulations (NORDREG)*[62] which require vessels of 300 gross tonnage or more and those carrying pollutants or dangerous goods as cargo to report information about the vessel and its intended route.

- The Canadian Hydrographic Service [CHS] under the federal Department of Fisheries and Oceans is responsible for providing hydrographic services and products such as nautical charts.

- Environment Canada provides weather and ice information services.

The recent 2014 Auditor General's report (AG Report) reviewed the actions and programs of these various Canadian government departments and made a number of recommendations for the more effective coordination of their respective strategies and activities. Two issues in particular were flagged by the Auditor General as threatening Canada's capacity to act as a responsible steward of the Arctic waters: a reduction in Canadian Coast Guard (CCG) ice-breaker presence and the inadequacy of existing surveys and nautical charts.

Under Canada's *Oceans Act*, the Canadian Coast Guard is the designated authority for the provision of ice-breaking services in support of the safe, economical and efficient movement of ships in Canadian waters. Every year, the CCG deploys six ice-breakers in support of marine navigation and other programs in the Canadian Arctic,[63] with the *Amundsen* dedicated to scientific research. As detailed in the AG Report, ice-breaking services in the Canadian Arctic include:

- providing ice information in partnership with the Canadian Ice Service and ice routing advice to other vessels;
- harbor breakout;
- providing supplies for Arctic communities when commercial services are not available; and
- escorting individual vessels and convoys, freeing ships beset in ice and maintaining shipping channels and tracks through ice.[64]

The CCG "Central and Arctic Region" website also identifies "boating safety," "search and rescue," "aids to navigation" and "environmental protection and response" as part of its mandate.[65]

A more accessible Arctic will increase the demands on the CCG to ensure environmental protection and response, effective monitoring of increased shipping as well as ice-breaking and escort services for commercial vessels. Indeed, though a warming climate has boosted the prospect for increased shipping through the NWP and NSR, a number of significant challenges will continue to pose a threat to the safety of navigation: Arctic storms, shallow waters, icing, icebergs and growlers (small chunks of icebergs difficult to spot).

In August 2010, the cruise ship *MV Clipper Adventurer* ran aground near Kugluktuk Nunavut when it hit a rock shelf in the Coronation Gulf. The CCG's *Amundsen* had to travel 500 miles to rescue the 200 passengers and crew from the beleaguered vessel.[66] During the 2012 shipping season, ice conditions in Frobisher Bay along the route used to supply Iqaluit in Nunavut were particularly severe and led to several incidents where vessels became trapped in pressured ice. In four cases, the vessels were trapped for several days and each had to be freed by Coast Guard ice-breakers. In September 2013, the *Nordic Orion*, an ice-strengthened sea freighter became the first bulk carrier to use the Northwest Passage as a transit trade lane.

The Danish-owned, Panamanian-flagged vessel relied on an escort by the CCG's most capable ice-breaker, the *Louis St-Laurent*, for a substantial part of the route.

Despite its increasing responsibilities, the Auditor General of Canada recently reported that "the Canadian Coast Guard's icebreaking presence in the Arctic is decreasing while vessel traffic is increasing."[67] He also stated:

> The Canadian Coast Guard has decreased the number of days it operates icebreakers in the Arctic. Since 2011, the Coast Guard has decreased by 33 ship days the total time it planned to deploy icebreakers in the Arctic. In addition, in two of the last four years, the Coast Guard operated one less icebreaker in the Arctic than intended due to maintenance issues, and it did not meet its planned deployment times for those two years … In each year since at least 2007, commercial vessels have entered the Arctic earlier and left later than Coast Guard icebreakers.[68]

The six vessels providing ice-breaking services in the Canadian Arctic are on average thirty years old and are approaching the end of their operational lives. As a 2014 media report underlined, "recent incidents have shown that Canada's small and aging fleet is at the limits of its capabilities."[69] In 2011, the 42-year-old *Louis St-Laurent*, Canada's most powerful ice-breaker, was disabled when one of its propellers broke, cutting short her Arctic mission and requiring assistance from the USCGC *Healy*.[70] The following year, the CCG's research ice-breaker, the 34-year-old *Amundsen*, missed the summer navigation season while cracks in four of her six engines were being repaired.[71]

According to the Auditor General, "[f]unded plans are in place to extend the operations of five of these vessels by between 8 and 15 years."[72] However, the report acknowledges that there are "no other icebreakers of equal capability to replace the vessels undergoing refit, which will leave at most five icebreakers available for service nearly every season until 2021."[73] Perhaps most importantly, the two most capable ice-breakers in the Canadian fleet, the CCGS *Terry Fox* and *Louis St-Laurent*, are scheduled to be decommissioned in 2020 and 2022 respectively.

During a trip to the Canadian Arctic in 2008, Prime Minister Stephen Harper announced the government's plans to build a new heavy ice-breaker. Shipyards Co. Ltd in North Vancouver was scheduled to begin construction of the *Diefenbaker* in 2015 so it could be in the water in time to replace the *Louis St-Laurent*, originally slated to be decommissioned in 2017. But a scheduling conflict at the shipyard with the Canadian Navy's new resupply ships pushed the start of construction back to at least 2018 with an expected delivery date in 2022. Government officials have indicated that it will cost an extra $55 million to keep the *Louis St-Laurent* operational until that time.[74] In addition, the original 2008 price tag of $720 million for the new ice-breaker has been drastically revised to reflect the new delivery date and is estimated at $1.3 billion.[75] As the Auditor General warns in his recent report, the arrival of the *Diefenbaker* "will not result in an increase in the number of icebreakers in the fleet since the new vessel will replace only one of the two icebreakers to be decommissioned."[76]

In March 2004, the Chairman of the Standing Committee on Fisheries and Oceans tabled in the House of Commons a unanimous report on the Canadian Coast Guard titled "Safe, Secure, Sovereign: Reinventing the Canadian Coast Guard."[77] In presenting the report, the Chairman emphasized that the CCG "has been chronically underfunded and has never had the resources to fully meet the goals it was intended to attain."[78] Ten years later, the Canadian Coast Guard appears to be facing the same challenge: how to fulfill its multifaceted mandate in the face of growing maritime activity without the necessary assets and insufficient funding.

Another critical issue flagged by the Auditor General's 2014 audit was the inadequacy of existing hydrographic surveys and nautical charts. As the report notes, "[n]autical charts are essential to safe marine navigation: they provide critical information on water depths and hazards such as shoals and hidden rocks."[79] They are also important for emergency response and search and rescue activities in Arctic waters. Indeed, during the *MV Clipper Adventurer* rescue operation in August 2010, the Canadian Hydrographic Service (CHS) was brought in to survey the area to ensure the safety of rescue vessels and to provide safe routes to local ports.[80]

The Canadian Hydrographic Service estimates that about one percent of Canadian Arctic waters are surveyed to modern standards.[81] The CHS does not have vessels dedicated to data collection in the Arctic and therefore conducts its surveys mainly based on opportunity. It relies on CCG vessels as platforms from which to deploy its survey launches and also collaborates with other federal departments, territorial governments and academic organizations for data collection. The Auditor General found that while demands for charting in the Arctic are growing, the CHS's resources to do hydrographic work in the region have recently declined. "This is an additional challenge on top of a lack of dedicated vessels for conducting surveys, the size and remoteness of the Arctic waters, and the short season in which to carry out the work."[82]

Scientists have been urging the federal government to step up its efforts to chart northern Canadian waters for fear of more near-disastrous incidents like the groundings of the *Hanseatic* (1996), *Nanny* (2010 and 2012) and *Clipper Adventurer* (2010). In August 1996, the *Hanseatic* ran aground in Simpson Strait, perforating two of the ship's fuel reservoirs and all 153 passengers had to be evacuated by helicopter.[83] The *Clipper Adventurer* had at least a dozen watertight compartments breached when it hit the underwater shoal in August 2010 and came perilously close to sinking.

"[Had] the weather been bad when the Clipper Adventurer first grounded, the incident might have resulted in loss of the ship, loss of life and damage to the environment from escaping fuel and ballast water" according to Hughes Clark, head of the University of New Brunswick's ocean mapping group.[84] In October 2012, the oil tanker *Nanny* ran aground in Chesterfield Narrows. No injuries or pollution were reported; the double-hulled ship was badly damaged on its hull and rudder but not the tanks. It was, however, the second time that the *Nanny* had run aground in Nunavut waters. In September 2010, the *Nanny* was lodged in Simpson Strait near Gjoa Haven while carrying more than 9 million liters of diesel.[85]

Of course Canada's Arctic waters are vast (covering approximately 7 million square kilometers of marine area north of 60 degrees latitude) and its coastlines are among the longest in the world. Even with unshakeable political will and a limitless budget, it is not possible to envisage that the entire Canadian Arctic marine area could be surveyed to modern standards. As Canadian Coast Guard deputy commissioner, Jody Thomas, asserted in a 2014 interview, "[t]hat's not a reasonable use of money or resources."[86] In recognition of this reality but also in response to the need to guarantee safe navigation in Canadian Arctic waters, the Canadian Coast Guard has launched the "Northern Marine Transportation Corridors Initiative."

Working with industry, territorial governments, northern communities and other federal departments (including Transport Canada and the CHS), the Coast Guard initiative will identify a number of Arctic sea lanes that will bear the brunt of shipping and other marine transits as the region becomes more accessible. "Replicating the wide range of corridors, marine services and aids to navigation that exist in the south isn't reasonable from a fiscal perspective or from a service perspective," the CCG deputy commissioner declared.[87] "It's going to be a very analytical approach to ensure that there is good value for money, and ensure the safe stewardship of vessels in the Arctic."[88] Indeed, according to a CCG brief, the concept of corridors must be understood as a pragmatic framework to enhance marine navigation safety in the North and to guide future Arctic investments.[89]

Using Arctic marine traffic data for 2011–2013, as well as traditional knowledge on marine ecosystems, the CCG has already designated a network of preliminary transportation corridors.[90] According to the Coast Guard, 77 percent of the 2011–2013 Arctic marine traffic was captured by the designated corridors. The CCG brief also provides statistical information in respect of the percentage of ice-breaking services (escorts), pollution and SAR incidents as well as the number of aids to navigation within the corridors or within a distance of five nautical miles.[91] The establishment of "safe marine corridors" and the statistics gathered are intended to provide the CHS and CCG with a useful guide as to where it should focus their mapping activities and invest in new infrastructure. As John Higginbotham, a former assistant deputy minister for Transport Canada now a senior fellow with the Centre for International Governance Innovation stresses: "the concept [transportation corridors] forces you to make strategic choices of where you're going to invest very limited resources so that it meets strategic objectives."[92]

Increased navigation opportunities in the Northwest Passage come with increased risks to safety and the environment. The CCG's "Northern Marine Transportation Corridors Initiative" is a vital first step in meeting those daunting challenges. Rather than a "scatter-gun approach,"[93] which would be incredibly inefficient and prohibitively expensive, the project will help focus Canada's investments in the North and ensure the safety of cruise ships, commercial vessels, sealift vessels and local traffic. At present, Canada lacks a single port along the Northwest Passage in which a crippled ship might obtain mechanical assistance or seek refuge from extreme weather conditions.[94] After several hiccups and delays, work however has begun on the refurbishment of the wharf at Nanisivik on Baffin Island with an expected completion date in 2018. The Nanisivik facility's main goal will be to refuel the Royal Canadian Navy's new Arctic patrol ships during the open water season. It will house storage tanks for naval fuel, a site office and a wharf operator's shelter. There will also be a helicopter landing pad and the facility will provide the CCG with a space to store cargo during Arctic resupply missions.[95] Nanisivik is located on what is at present identified as a "secondary" corridor in the CCG initiative. As Byers urges, the Canadian Government should also consider other ports[96] along the primary corridors which will bear the brunt of increased shipping (e.g., Tuktoyaktuk, Resolute and Cambridge Bay).

Work has also begun on the Canadian High Arctic Research Station (CHARS) in Cambridge Bay, a community along one of the CCG's designated primary corridors, and is scheduled to open its doors on July 1, 2017.[97] The Station, which will be a world-class hub for science and research, will no doubt strengthen Canada's position internationally as a leader in polar science and technology and make a vital contribution to improving the quality of life of Northerners.[98] However, it will not provide any essential services to help Canada manage the increased risks and stresses posed by navigation in nearby waters. Byers' assessment that "Canada's Arctic search-and-rescue capabilities are desperately poor" seems unassailable:

> Our long-range helicopters are based in British Columbia, Nova Scotia and Labrador; each aircraft would take more than a day to fly the 2.500 kilometers to the Northwest Passage, stopping to refuel along the way. C-130 Hercules planes can be sent from southern Canada, but unlike helicopters, cannot hoist people on board. Worse yet, the Hercules used for search and rescue are nearly half a century old and often undeployable for maintenance reasons.[99]

And though the CBC reported on April 1, 2015 that Canada's Department of National Defense has put out a tender to buy new search and rescue aircraft with improved technology, past tenders would seem to suggest that the new planes are likely years away.[100]

While scientists predict that the Northwest Passage will be the last of the Arctic shipping lanes to become commercially viable, it is time for the Canadian government to make adequate investments into the Coast Guard Arctic fleet lest its Arctic neighbors and other interested stakeholders conclude that Canada is all talk and no action. As Byers insists, "[t]he best way to promote Canada's legal position is to provide infrastructure and essential services."[101] The CCG Marine Transportation Corridors Initiative should guide substantial investments in search and rescue capabilities and the construction of new ports along the main routes of the Northwest Passage. As Joe Clark famously said in 1985, Canada must demonstrate that it can "afford the Arctic."[102]

Northern Sea Route

As Ekaterina Klimenko emphasizes in the very first sentence of her policy paper "Russia's Evolving Arctic Strategy," "[t]he Russian Federation has made the development of the Arctic a strategic priority."[103] For President Vladimir Putin, the Arctic is "a concentration of practically all aspects of national security—military, political, economic, technological, environmental and that of resources."[104] Russia's long-standing engagement with the North is also identified as the first key finding in regards to Russia's Arctic strategy in a 2011 report prepared by the Defence Academy of the United Kingdom:

> Russia has a very long and involved history with the Arctic, stretching over centuries, which can neither be ignored nor put to one side. This historical record is important for a number of reasons, not least because the current political leadership in the Kremlin—both the President (D Medvedev) and the PM (V Putin)—have openly talked about a "generational debt" being owed by the present generation of Russians to those in the past, who spared no effort in exploring and exploiting the wealth of the Arctic for the benefit of the country, as a whole. Similarly, they both see it as incumbent on them that the Arctic will still provide and ensure the future well-being and prosperity for the country in the years ahead and will strive to maintain their country's hold on the region.[105]

Russia is undoubtedly the dominant player in the region in many critical respects:

> Geographically, it encompasses half of the Arctic coastline, 40% of the land area beyond the Arctic Circle, and three quarters of the Arctic

population—about three million of the total four million. Economically, as much as 20% of Russia's gross domestic product (GDP) and of its total exports is generated north of the Arctic Circle. In terms of resources, about 95% of its gas, 75% of its oil, 96% of its platinum, 90% of its nickel and cobalt, and 60% of its copper reserves are found in Arctic and sub-Arctic regions. To this must be added the riches— often estimated but rarely proven—of the continental shelf, seabed, and the water itself, ranging from rare earth minerals to fish stocks.[106]

Russia's current Arctic policy rests on two key documents, "The fundamentals of state policy of the Russian Federation in the Arctic for the period up to 2020 and beyond" adopted by President Medvedev in September 2008 (Russian State Policy) and "The Strategy for the Development of the Arctic Zone of the Russian Federation and National Security up to 2020" adopted by President Putin in November 2013 (Russian Strategy). As Barbora Padrtova explains, the documents were drafted under the guidance of the influential Russian Security Council,

> whose permanent members include the most important centers of power, such as the president, prime minister, ministers of interior, foreign affairs, and defense, and the directors of the Federal Security Service of the Russian Federation ... and the Foreign Intelligence Service.[107]

After an initial section of general provisions, the 2008 Russian State Policy lists the "National Interests of the Russian Federation in the Arctic." The first national interest identified is the "use of the Arctic zone of the Russian Federation as a strategic resource base of the Russian Federation providing the solution of problems of social and economic development of the country."[108] According to Alexander Pelyasov, the 2013 Russian Strategy is also essentially preoccupied with the challenges that Russia faces in its Arctic Zone because of "the deep restructuring of its industrial economy" and the "imperative of innovative modernization."[109] Marlene Laruelle concurs, stating that "the Arctic offers theoretically unique opportunities that would enable the Russian economy to guarantee itself several decades of ample revenues."[110] Both Laruelle and Pelyasov stress that Russia's strategies for the Arctic do not only reflect "its relationship with the major international powers or regional institutions"[111] but are also oriented internally:[112]

> The Arctic is above all a domestic issue: it is an economic resource, a strategy for Siberian regional development, and an opportunity for new population settlement and human capital formation. Russia's reading of the Arctic is therefore based on *potentialities*: seen from Moscow, the Arctic is not the country's back door, but rather its potential twenty-first-century front door.[113]

To unlock the economic potential of the Russian Arctic Zone, both the State Policy and Strategy emphasize the need to modernize and develop the infrastructure of its Arctic transport system. In fact, the "use of the Northern Sea Route [NSR] as a national single transport communication of the Russian Federation in the Arctic" is identified as the fourth national interest of the Russian Federation in the 2008 State Policy.

Russia's prime minister envisages a bright future for the Northern Sea Route claiming that it could well become the "Suez of the North."[114] Speaking at the second International Arctic Forum in September 2011, President Putin stressed Russia's intentions "to turn the Northern Sea Route into a key transport route of global importance ... capable of being a competitor to more traditional routes, both when it comes to price, safety and quality."[115] And since 2010, a number of important initiatives have been launched and massive investments have been made to reach this goal.

In 2013, a legal and administrative agency was created to oversee the revitalization of the NSR, the "Northern Sea Route Administration" (NSRA) which began operations and launched its highly informative website on April 15, 2013. According to the Administration's website, its primary goal is to ensure safe navigation and the protection of the marine environment in the waters of the NSR. It lists a number of important functions under its mandate including:

- Obtaining and considering the submitted applications and issuing the permissions for navigation through the NSR;
- Assistance in the organization of search and rescue operations in the water areas of the NSR;
- Assistance in eliminating the consequences of pollution from vessels, of harmful substances, sewage or garbage; and
- Making recommendations about development of routes of navigation and using ice-breaking fleet in the water area of the NSR, ice and navigational conditions there.[116]

As Nataliya Marchenko reports,[117] in 2013, Russian legislation also officially defined the NSR boundaries as extending "from Novaya Zemlya in the west (68°35'E) to the Bering Strait in the east (168°58'37"W)."[118] Within these boundaries, all vessels are required to follow updated rules known as the "Rules of navigation on the water area of the Northern Sea Route" and comply with the newly adopted "Federal Law of Shipping on the Water Area of the Northern Sea Route."[119] Under the new federal law, "insurance requirements, shipping fees, and icebreaking assistance fees have been, to some degree, standardized."[120]

Recognizing that ice-breakers will play a vital role in support of increased Arctic navigation, "a key factor [in the] rise and development of the Russian North,"[121] President Putin pledged in September 2011

38 billion rubles ($1.2 billion) to expand Russia's fleet of atomic ice-breakers.[122] Although Russia already boasted the largest fleet of ice-breakers, with six nuclear-powered[123] and several diesel-electric ice-breakers, some of the Russian vessels were nearing the end of their service life and were slated to be decommissioned three to five year period. Vijay Sakhuja reports that in August 2014, Rosatomflot, a subsidiary company of Rosatom, the Russian agency responsible for managing nuclear-powered vessels, announced that three next-generation nuclear-powered Russian ice-breakers, the *Arctic*, the *Siberia* and the *Ural* would enter into service in 2017–2021.[124] According to Marchenko, construction of the *Arctic*, the world's largest and most powerful nuclear-powered ice-breaker, was already underway at the Baltic Shipyard in St. Petersburg in November 2013 and is expected to become operational in 2017.[125]

Marchenko also reports that in 2014, five Russian nuclear ice-breakers were deployed along the Northern Sea Route: "three Arktika-type ice-breakers, the *Sovetsky Soyuz* (1989), the *Yamal* (1992) and the *50 let Pobedy* (2007), and two Taymyr-type ice-breakers, the *Taymyr* (1989) and the *Vaygach* (1990)."[126] The atomic nature of the Russian ice-breakers allows for months of independent navigation and tremendous ice-breaking capacity contributing heavily to the success of their mission: leading and breaking ice for ships along the Northern Sea Route, rescuing ships trapped in ice, and supporting scientific expeditions. The *Arctic* is being built to generate 175 MWe which will allow it to crack ice fields three meters thick.[127] It is anticipated that the new ice-breaker will be granted the highest ice class—9—meaning that the ship will be able to break ice in the Arctic all year round. As a 2013 news report proclaimed: "the unique vessel will further increase Russia's dominance in the region."[128]

In 2009, Russia authorities also pledged 910 million rubles (€21.8 million) for the creation of ten search and rescue (SAR) centers along the Northern Sea Route:[129] in Murmansk, Arkhangelsk, Naryan-Mar, Vorkuta, Nadym, Dudinka, Tiksi, Pevek, Providarniya and Anadyr.[130] The first of the new SAR centers was officially opened in Naryan-Mar in August 2013 and includes a fire department as well as a department for search and rescue equipped with vehicles, boats, a berth and training facilities.[131] A second center has since been opened in Dudinka and the *BarentsObserver* reported in October 2014 the opening of the third Russian center in Arkhangelsk.[132] The latest center has the necessary capacity for fire-fighting, diving and oil spill clean-up. It is equipped with boats for search and rescue operations, fire-fighting vessels, RIBs, off-road vehicles and snow scooters.

In addition, the website of the Northern Sea Route Administration, under the tab "Search and Rescue, Prevention of Pollution by Oil," provides a map and detailed information in regards to:

• The Dikson maritime rescue coordination center;
• Two maritime rescue subcenters: Pevek and Tiksi;

- The ice-breakers operating in the water area of the Northern Sea Route; and
- The forward operational locations with emergency and rescue equipment and oil spill equipment.[133]

Information is provided on the assets positioned at the various locations. For example, the Dikson coordination center and Pevek and Tiksi subcenters each have a rescue boat, a rescue vessel and long-range aircraft. Both the Pevek and Tiksi subcenters have, in addition, a light helicopter. The *BarentsObserver* also reported in 2012 that extra aircraft (ten helicopters and eight aircraft) were being deployed in the Arctic Zone to stations in Murmansk, Novaya Zemlya, Dikson and Mys Shmidta.[134]

The Northern Sea Route Information Office website provides additional information in regards to Russia's seventeen Arctic ports via an interactive map.[135] The website also contains a host of other relevant information (e.g., ice pilot services, ice concentration in the NSR and transit statistics) as well as access to all relevant Russian legislation. The website, under the tab "Books and Charts," provides a list of Pilot books and other relevant publications for the NSR. In addition, it also provides access to the ninety-eight navigational charts in existence for NSR transit passage.[136] A 2012 article published on the ArcticEcon website, citing a Russian author (Клюев), claimed that "[b]y 2015–2016, Russia plans to have sorted out all navigational blank spots, and upgraded all navigation maps with route depth data."[137]

After an in-depth review of the amounts budgeted for the renewal of the Northern Sea Route and the activities underway, Jared Allen concludes: "with … plans to construct yet more powerful nuclear icebreakers, and ambitious development plans for NSR emergency/rescue centers Russia will, at least into the foreseeable future, continue to discover and advance the Arctic world."[138] At the very least, they signal Russia's determination to assume efficient and responsible leadership over increasing polar navigational activities.

Conclusion

In the concluding remarks to his 2012 article, Allen writes: "The intensification of the Northern Sea Route transit will depend on Russia's ability to portray an image of Arctic dominance. This is meant in the sense of trust and punctuality, as opposed to that of military strength."[139]

Both Canada and Russia's legal claim to exercise full and exclusive sovereignty over the waters of the Northwest Passage and the Northern Sea Route is contested. While opposition has traditionally been centered in Washington, other nations are waking up to the potential of the two Arctic seaways and the benefits to be gained from a regime of free transit through their waters.

The Canadian and Russian Governments invoke vital national interests as the fundamental justification for their control of the NWP and NSR. Whereas Canada has traditionally insisted on concerns of an environmental nature and the need to protect its vulnerable Northern populations, like Russia, it is increasingly envisioning the Arctic has an important reservoir of national wealth. But Canadian and Russian dominion over waters considered to be part of their national heritage cannot be envisaged solely as a source of power or authority. As Huber famously declared, "[t]erritorial sovereignty cannot limit itself to its negative side."[140] Rather, it must be exercised responsibly, in recognition of the many duties that flow from sovereign control.

Both Arctic neighbors have made important strides in living up to those responsibilities, particularly Russia. Commitments, translated into real and concrete actions and programs are absolutely vital for the future governance of the Northwest Passage and the Northern Sea Route. For, in the absence of decisive and sustained involvement in the development of both Arctic seaways, Canada and Russia cannot hope to convince an increasingly wide array of interested stakeholders that they remain the best possible stewards and managers of the Northwest Passage and the Northern Sea Route.

Notes

* This chapter takes into account development up to May 4, 2015.
1 See for example, Jean-François Bélanger, "Canada and the Arctic: The Case for Deeper Cooperation with Washington." *Canadian Naval Review* 8.4 (2013): 3; and Marie-Pierre Busson, "Le discours sur l'Arctique, rhétorique d'exception?" (Masters thesis, École Nationale d'Administration Publique, 2008).
2 Ingrid Peritz, "Hillary Clinton Warns Montreal Crowd of Russia's Increased Activity in Arctic." *The Globe and Mail,* March 18, 2014, accessed February 12, 2015, www.theglobeandmail.com/news/politics/clinton-warns-montreal-crowd-of-russias-increased-activity-in-arctic/article17560676/.
3 Gwladys Fouche, "Wary of Russia, Norway Urges NATO Vigilance in Arctic." *Reuters,* May 20, 2014, accessed February 12, 2015, www.reuters.com/article/2014/05/20/us-norway-defence-russia-idUSBREA4J0HE20140520.
4 The Northwest Passage spans the waters within the Canadian Arctic Archipelago between Baffin Bay in the east and the Beaufort Sea in the west. As Rothwell explains, the Northwest Passage is in reality a series of connected straits passages.

> Given the large number of islands that make up the Arctic Archipelago, there exist many potential shipping routes from east to west and west to east. The practical reality, however, is that because of the heavy ice found in these polar waters, and the shallow draught that exists in some of the straits, there are only a handful of viable combinations of straits and channels which can be used to make the complete crossing.
>
> (Donald R. Rothwell, "The Canadian–U.S. Northwest Passage Dispute: A Reassessment." *Cornell International Law Journal* 26 (1993): 352)

According to Pharand, the Northwest Passage consists of five basic routes: Route 1, through Prince of Wales Strait; Route 2, through the M'Clure Strait;

Route 3, through Peel Sound and Victoria Strait; Route 3A, through Peel Sound and James Ross Strait; Route 4 through Prince Regent Inlet; Route 5, through Fury and Hecla Strait; and Route 5A, through Fury and Hecla Strait and Prince Regent Inlet. However, at present, only Routes 1 and 2, referred to as the northern routes, are known to be suitable for deep-draft ships: Donat Pharand, *Canada's Arctic Waters in International Law* (Cambridge: Cambridge University Press, 1988), 189–201 (see map of the various routes at 190–91).

5 According to the authors of the recent study *Shipping in Arctic Waters*,

> a minimum definition of the NEP [Northeast Passage] is that it is made up of all the marginal seas of the Eurasian Arctic, i.e., the Chukchi, the East Siberian, the Laptev, the Kara and the Barents Sea. As such, the NSR makes up approximately 90 percent of the NEP.
>
> (Willy Østreng et al., *Shipping in Arctic Waters: A Comparison of the Northeast, Northwest and Trans Polar Passages* (London: Springer-Praxis, 2013), 18)

The NSR was designated as a separate part of the NEP and as an administered, legal entity under full Soviet jurisdiction and control by the Council of People's Commissars of the USSR on December 17, 1932. According to the official Russian definition, the NSR stretches from Novaya Zemlya in the west to the Bering Strait in the east and its different sailing lanes cover 2,200 to 2,900 nautical miles of ice-infested waters. Ibid, 13.

6 Government of Canada, "Canada's Arctic Foreign Policy." *Department of Foreign Affairs, Trade and Development*, last modified June 3, 2013, accessed February 12, 2015, www.international.gc.ca/arctic-arctique/arctic_policy-canada-politique_arctique.aspx?lang=eng.

7 Government of Canada, "Canada's Northern Strategy". last modified December 21, 2012, accessed February 12, 2015, www.northernstrategy.gc.ca/index-eng.asp.

8 Office of Ocean Affairs, *Limits in the Seas No. 112: United States Responses to Excessive National Maritime Claims* (Washington, DC: US State Department, 1992), 71.

9 Russian Federation, "Basics of the State Policy of the Russian Federation in the Arctic for the Period till 2020 and for a Further Perspective." *The Arctic Governance Project*, September 18, 2008, accessed February 12, 2015, www.arctis-search.com/Russian+Federation+Policy+for+the+Arctic+to+2020.

10 Russian Federation, "Russian Strategy of the Development of the Arctic Zone and the Provision of National Security until 2020." *The International Expert Council on Cooperation in the Arctic*, February 8, 2013, accessed February 12, 2015, www.iecca.ru/en/legislation/strategies/item/99-the-development-strategy-of-the-arctic-zone-of-the-russian-federation.

11 In his January 2009 "National Security Presidential Directive and Homeland Security Presidential Directive." President George W. Bush emphasized that freedom of the seas was a top national priority for the United States. "The Northwest Passage is a strait used for international navigation, and the Northern Sea Route includes straits used for international navigation; the regime of transit passage applies to passage through those straits." The White House, Section III "Policy," sub-section B "National Security and Homeland Security Interests in the Arctic," at paragraph 5, January 9, 2009, accessed February 12, 2015, www.fas.org/irp/offdocs/nspd/nspd-66.htm. See also President Obama's "National Strategy for the Arctic Region" of May 2013:

> Accession to the Convention [1982 United Nations Law of the Sea Convention] would protect U.S. rights, freedoms, and uses of the sea and airspace throughout the Arctic region, and strengthen our arguments for freedom

of navigation and overflight through the Northwest Passage and the Northern Sea Route.

The White House, Section 3 "Strengthen International Cooperation," third bullet point "Accede to the Law of the Sea Convention." May 10, 2013, accessed February 12, 2015, www.whitehouse.gov/sites/default/files/docs/nat_arctic_strategy.pdf.

12 For example, in 1978, a Canadian official acknowledged that a "drawer full of protests" had been received following the adoption of Canada's 1970 *Arctic Waters Pollution Prevention Act.* Erik Wang, director of legal operations, Department of External Affairs, Canada, House of Commons, Standing Committee on External Affairs and National Defence, Proceedings No. 16, April 27, 1978, 16, cited in Ted L. McDorman, "The New Definition of 'Canada Lands' and the Determination of the Outer Limit of the Continental Shelf." *Journal of Maritime Law and Commerce* 14 (1983): 215. Willy Østreng reports that Russia's regulatory powers are challenged by the European Union in "The Northeast and Northern Sea Route." Arctic Knowledge Hub website, accessed March 11, 2015, www.arctis-search.com/The+Northeast+Passage+and+Northern+Sea+Route+2.

13 Reference can be made to the 2008 Communication of the European Communities to the European Parliament and the Council, "The European Union and the Arctic Region," in which Member States and the Community were exhorted to "defend the freedom of navigation and the right of innocent passage in the newly opened routes and areas." See section 3.3, "Transport." EUR-Lex website, accessed February 14, 2015, http://eur-lex.europa.eu/legal-content/EN/ALL/?uri=CELEX:52008DC0763. This call was repeated in paragraph 48 of the recent "European Parliament Resolution of 12 March 2014 on the EU Strategy of the Arctic," which also calls on:

> the states in the [Arctic] region to ensure that any current transport routes—and those that may emerge in the future—are open to international shipping and to refrain from introducing any arbitrary unilateral obstacles, be they financial or administrative, that could hinder shipping in the Arctic, other than *internationally agreed measures* aimed at increasing security or protection of the environment.
>
> (Emphasis added. European Parliament website, accessed February 23, 2015, www.europarl.europa.eu/sides/getDoc.do?type=TA&language=EN&reference=P7-TA-2014–0236)

14 It should be noted however that the "Guidelines of the Germany Arctic Policy" released by the Federal Foreign Office in September 2013 announced that the German Federal Government is "campaigning for freedom of navigation in the Arctic Ocean (Northeast, Northwest and Transpolar Passages) in accordance with high safety and environmental standards." Auswärtiges Amt, *Guidelines of the Germany Arctic Policy: Assume Responsibility, Seize Opportunities* (Berlin: Federal Foreign Office, September 2013), accessed March 11, 2015, www.bmel.de/SharedDocs/Downloads/EN/International/Leitlinien-Arktispolitik.pdf?__blob=publicationFile.

15 "Au fur et à mesure que l'on s'éloigne de ses côtes, les compétences de l'État diminuent, pour disparaître presque totalement dans la haute mer": Philippe Vincent, *Droit de la mer* (Bruxelles: Éditions Larcier, 2008), 12.

16 United Nations Law of the Sea Convention, adopted December 10, 1982, entered into force November 16, 1994, 1833 *U.N.T.S.* 397.

17 Article 2 (1) states: "[t]he sovereignty of a coastal State extends, beyond its land territory and *internal waters* and, in the case of an archipelagic State, its archipelagic waters, to an adjacent belt of sea, described as the territorial sea." Emphasis added.

18 *Military and Paramilitary Activities In and Against Nicaragua (Nicaragua v. United States of America), ICJ Reports* 1986, 14 at 111, paragraph 212. Emphasis added.

19 Gilbert Gidel, "La présomption est dans le sens de l'ouverture des ports; mais présomption et non obligation." *Le droit international public de la mer,* tome II (Châteauroux: Établissements Mellottée, 1932), 45, quoted in Laurent Lucchini and Michel Voelckel, *Droit de la mer,* tome 2, volume 2 (Paris: Pédone, 1990), 287.

20 As the UN Secretariat explained in its 1962 study:

> In principle, the scope of historic title emerging from the continued exercise of sovereignty should not be wider in scope than the scope of the sovereignty actually exercised. If the claimant State exercised sovereignty as over internal waters, the area claimed would be internal waters, and if the sovereignty exercised was sovereignty as over the territorial sea, the area would be territorial sea.
>
> (UN Secretariat, "Juridical Regime of Historic Waters, Including Historic Bays." Document A/CN.4/SER.A/1962/Add.1, *Yearbook of the International Law Commission* 2 (1962): 23, paragraph 164)

This principle was later confirmed by the International Court of Justice in its 1982 judgment in the Tunisia/Libya case:

> It seems clear that the matter continues to be governed by international law which does not provide for a *single* "régime" for "historic waters" or "historic bays," but only for a particular régime for each of the concrete, recognized cases of "historic waters" or "historic bays."
>
> (Continental Shelf (*Tunisia/Libyan Arab Jamahiriya*), *ICJ Reports* 1982, 18 at 74. Emphasis in the original)

21 Donald Rothwell, *The Polar Regions and the Development of International Law* (Cambridge: Cambridge University Press, 1996), 209.

22 *Aide mémoire from the Soviet Ministry of Foreign Affairs to American Embassy Moscow,* July 21, 1964, reproduced in R. Douglas Brubaker, "The Legal Status of Straits in Russian Arctic Waters – Internationality." *INSROP Working Paper* 57, September 11, 1996, accessed February 12, 2015, www.arctis-search.com/tiki-download_wiki_attachment.php?attId=104.

23 UN Secretariat, "Juridical Regime of Historic Waters," 18, paragraph 119. See more generally, Donat Pharand, "Historic Waters in International Law with Special Reference to the Arctic." *University of Toronto Law Journal* 21 (1971): 1; and Clive R. Symmons, *Historic Waters in the Law of the Sea: A Modern Re-Appraisal* (Leiden: Brill, 2007).

24 Article 8 (1) of the LOS Convention.

25 Statement in the House of Commons by Secretary of State for External Affairs, Joe Clark, September 10, 1985, *Canadian Yearbook of International Law* 24, (1986): 326, reprinted in Franklyn Griffiths (ed.), *Politics of the Northwest Passage* (Kingston & Montreal: McGill-Queen's University Press, 1987), 269. Emphasis added.

26 J. Ashley Roach and Robert W. Smith, *Excessive Maritime Claims* 3rd edn (Boston, MA: Martinus Nijhoff Publishers, 2012), 111.

27 Office of Ocean Law and Policy, "Bureau of Oceans and International Environmental and Scientific Affairs." *U.S. Department of State, Limits in the Seas* 109, September 29, 1988, accessed February 12, 2015, www.state.gov/documents/organization/58383.pdf.

28 Tullio Scovazzi, "New Developments Concerning Soviet Straight Baselines." *International Journal of Estuarine and Coastal Law* 3 (1988): 37; and Vladimir

Golitsyn, "The Arctic – On the Way to Regional Cooperation." *Marine Policy Report* 1 (1989): 91.

29 Michael Byers, *International Law and the Arctic* (Cambridge: Cambridge University Press, 2013), 87, citing Donat Pharand, "The Arctic Waters and the Northwest Passage: A Final Revisit." *Ocean Development and International Law* 38 (2007): 15.

30 See among others J. Ashley Roach and Robert W. Smith, *Excessive Maritime Claims*, 97 and 111–12; Rothwell, *The Polar Regions*, 273–74; and Erik Franckx, *Maritime Claims in the Arctic: Canadian and Russian Perspectives* (Dordrecht: Martinus Nijhoff, 1993), 101–07 and 192–93.

31 The other criterion imposed by paragraph 3 is that: "the sea areas lying within the lines must be sufficiently closely linked to the land domain to be subject to the régime of internal waters."

32 Rothwell, *The Polar Regions*, 208.

33 *Corfu Channel Case*, ICJ Reports 1949, 4.

34 Pharand, "The Arctic Waters and the Northwest Passage," 30.

35 *Corfu Channel Case*, 28.

36 Richard J. Grunawalt, "United States Policy on International Straits." *Ocean Development and International Law* 18 (1987): 445–56; and James Kraska, "The Law of the Sea Convention and the Northwest Passage." *International Journal of Marine and Coastal Law* 22 (2007): 257, 274.

37 Pharand, "The Arctic Waters and the Northwest Passage," 35.

38 *Corfu Channel Case*, 28.

39 See among others Richard R. Baxter, *The Law of International Waterways* (Cambridge, MA: Harvard University Press, 1964), 3; Daniel Patrick O'Connell, *The International Law of the Sea*, edited by Ivan Anthony Shearer, (Oxford: Clarendon Press, 1982), 497; and Robin Churchill and Vaughan Lowe, *The Law of the Sea* 3rd edn (Manchester: Manchester University Press, 1999), 106.

40 Reply of the United Kingdom, *Fisheries Case (United Kingdom* v. *Norway)*, ICJ Pleadings 1951, vol. II, at 555.

41 See among many other scholarly contributions: Rothwell, *The Polar Regions*, 273–74; Franckx, *Maritime Claims in the Arctic*, 101–07 and 192–93; Pharand, *Canada's Arctic Waters in International Law*, 187–257; Anatoly L. Kolodkin and Marlen E. Volosov, "The Legal Regime of the Soviet Arctic: Major Issues." *Marine Policy* 14 (1990): 163; Kraska, "The Law of the Sea Convention and the Northwest Passage," 257.

42 Byers, *International Law and the Arctic*, 149.

43 R. Douglas Brubaker, *Russian Arctic Straits* (Dordrecht: Martinus Nijhoff, 2004), 41 and 189.

44 Rothwell, *The Polar Regions*, 206.

45 Churchill and Lowe, *The Law of the Sea*, 138.

46 Ana Gemma López Martín, *International Straits: Concept, Classification and Rules of Passage* (Heidelberg: Springer, 2010), 59.

47 Pharand, "The Arctic Waters and the Northwest Passage," 44.

48 "The *Island of Palmas Case* (*United States of America* v. *The Netherlands*)." Award of the Tribunal, April 4, 1928, *Reports of International Arbitral Awards* II (2006): 829.

49 Ibid., 838.

50 Ibid., 839.

51 Government of Canada, introduction to "Canada's Arctic Foreign Policy." *Department of Foreign Affairs, Trade and Development*. Accessed May 6, 2016, www.international.gc.ca/arctic-arctique/arctic_policy-canada-politique_arctique.aspx?lang=eng.

52 Quoted under the "Promoting Economic and Social Development" section of Ibid.

53 Government of the Northwest Territories, "7.3 Trends in Shipping in the Northwest Passage and the Beaufort Sea," Department of the Environment and Natural Resources, last modified January, 2015, accessed February 12, 2015, www. enr.gov.nt.ca/state-environment/73-trends-shipping-northwest-passage-and-beaufort-sea. These shipping statistics are in stark contrast to the low level of maritime activity in the first half of the twentieth century: "Since the first crossing of the Northwest Passage by *Amundsen* in 1906, few ships (less than 1 every 10 years on average) had successfully completed the full passage until 1969."

54 Office of the Auditor General, "Marine Navigation in the Canadian Arctic," in Report of the Commissioner of the Environment and Sustainable Development—hereinafter AG Report—(October 7, 2014), accessed February 12, 2015, www.oag-bvg.gc.ca/internet/docs/parl_cesd_201410_03_e.pdf. The objective of the audit was to determine whether key federal departments adequately support safe marine transportation in Canada's Arctic waters.

55 The graphic in Exhibit 3.2 "Vessel Voyages in the Canadian Arctic Since 1990," shows approximately 125 voyages in 1990 compared to 350 voyages in 2013. Much of this increase is attributed to fishing vessels as well as tug boats, pleasure craft, research vessels and passenger vessels.

56 AG Report, see supra note 54.

57 Arctic Council, AMSA 2009 Report, 2nd printing, (2009): 5. At: www.arctic. noaa.gov/detect/documents/AMSA_2009_Report_2nd_print.pdf.

58 Arctic Waters Pollution Prevention Act (R.S.C., 1985, c. A-12), Canada Justice Laws website, last modified April 1, 2014, accessed February 12, 2015, http:// laws-lois.justice.gc.ca/eng/acts/A-12/page-1.html.

59 Canada Shipping Act, 2001 (S.C. 2001), c. 26, Canada Justice Laws website, last modified February 26, 2015, accessed March 11, 2015, http://laws-lois. justice.gc.ca/eng/acts/C-10.15/page-1.html.

60 AG Report, paragraph 3.51.

61 Oceans Act (S.C. 1996, c. 31), Canada Justice Laws website, last modified February 26, 2015, accessed March 11, 2015, http://laws-lois.justice.gc.ca/eng/ acts/o-2.4/page-1.html.

62 Northern Canada Vessel Traffic Services Zone Regulations (SOR/2010–127), Canada Justice Laws website, last modified July 1, 2010, accessed February 12, 2015, http://laws-lois.justice.gc.ca/eng/regulations/SOR-2010-127/Full Text.html.

63 For information on Canada's ice-breaker fleet, see "Icebreaking Operations Services." *Canadian Coast Guard* website, last modified April 16, 2015, accessed June 27, 2015, www.ccg-gcc.gc.ca/Icebreaking/home.

64 AG Report, paragraph 3.40.

65 "Who We Are and What We Do," in *Canadian Coast Guard* website, last modified June 24, 2013, accessed February 12, 2015, www.ccg-gcc.gc.ca/eng/ Central_Arctic/About_Us.

66 Tobi Cohen, "Canadian Rescue Capacity Questioned in Wake of Arctic Ship Grounding." *Postmedia News*, August 29, 2010, accessed April 21, 2014, www. canada.com/technology/Canadian+rescue+capacity+questioned+wake+Arctic +ship+grounding/3457291/story.html.

67 AG Report, paragraph 3.42.

68 Ibid., paragraphs 3.45 and 3.46.

69 Brian Kingston, "When it Comes to the Arctic, Canada is Unprepared," *Huffington Post*, September 18, 2014, accessed February 14, 2015, www.huffington-post.ca/global-shapers-community-ottawa/arctic-canada_b_5838640.html.

70 "Icebreaker's Mission Cut Short Due to Broken Propeller." *CBC News*, October 12, 2011, accessed April 21, 2015, www.cbc.ca/news/canada/north/icebreaker-s-mission-cut-short-due-to-broken-propeller-1.1088902.

71 "Amundsen Icebreaker Dry-Docked for the Year." *CBC News*, January 31, 2012, accessed April 21, 2015, www.cbc.ca/news/canada/north/amundsen-icebreaker-dry-docked-for-the-year-1.1139458.
72 AG Report, paragraph 3.47.
73 Ibid.
74 Lee Berthiaume, "Coast Guard's New Icebreaker to Cost Twice as Much as Originally Estimated." *Ottawa Citizen*, November 13, 2013, accessed April 21, 2015, http://o.canada.com/news/coast-guards-new-icebreaker-to-cost-twice-as-much-as-originally-estimated.
75 Ibid.
76 AG Report, paragraph 3.48.
77 Standing Committee on Fisheries and Oceans, House of Commons, "Safe, Secure, Sovereign: Reinventing the Canadian Coast Guard." *Parliament of Canada* website, March 2014, accessed April 21, 2015, www.parl.gc.ca/House Publications/Publication.aspx?DocId=1263626&Mode=1&Parl=37&Ses=3& Language=E.
78 Standing Committee on Fisheries and Oceans, House of Commons, Parliament of Canada, "Committee Calls for an Expanded National Security Mandate for the Canadian Coast Guard." *News Release*, March 31, 2004, accessed April 21, 2015, www.parl.gc.ca/HousePublications/Publication.aspx? DocId=1279763&Language=E&Mode=1&Parl=37&Ses=3.
79 AG Report, paragraph 3.14.
80 Jane George, "Experts: Canada Must Step Up Arctic Charting." *Nunatsiaq Online*, December 17, 2010, accessed April 21, 2014, www.nunatsiaqonline.ca/ stories/article/171210_experts_canada_must_step_up_arctic_charting/.
81 AG Report, paragraph 3.17 and exhibit 3.14.
82 Ibid., paragraph 3.22.
83 Emma J. Stewart and Jackie Dawson, "A Matter of Good Fortune? The Grounding of the *Clipper Adventurer* in the Northwest Passage, Arctic Canada," *Arctic* 64.2 (2011): 263, accessed April 21, 2015, http://pubs.aina.ucalgary.ca/ arctic/Arctic64–2–263.pdf.
84 George, "Experts: Canada Must Step Up Arctic Charting."
85 "Grounded Arctic Tanker Tries to Lighten Load." *CBC News*, September 13, 2010, accessed April 21, 2015, www.cbc.ca/news/canada/north/grounded-arctic-tanker-tries-to-lighten-load-1.961697; "Oil Tanker Off Course When it Ran Aground in Nunavut." *CBC News*, February 4, 2014, accessed April 21, 2015, www.cbc.ca/news/canada/north/oil-tanker-off-course-when-it-ran-aground-in-nunavut-1.2522730.
86 Lee Berthiaume, "Coast Guard to Scope Out Arctic Shipping Lanes." *Ottawa Citizen*, January 21, 2014, accessed April 21, 2015, http://o.canada.com/news/ coast-guard-to-scope-out-arctic-shipping-lanes.
87 Ibid.
88 Ibid.
89 Canadian Coast Guard, "Northern Marine Transportation Corridors Initiative," accessed May 6, 2016, https://umanitoba.ca/faculties/management/ ti/media/docs/ALVARO__NMTC_Presentation.pdf.
90 See map, ibid., 8.
91 Ibid., 7.
92 Berthiaume, "Coast Guard to Scope Out Arctic Shipping Lanes."
93 Ibid.
94 Michael Byers, "Canada's Arctic Nightmare Just Came True: The Northwest Passage is Commercial." *The Globe and Mail*, September 20, 2013, accessed April 21, 2015, www.theglobeandmail.com/globe-debate/canadas-arctic-nightmare-just-came-true-the-northwest-passage-is-commercial/article14432440/.

95 Sarah Rogers, "Nanisivik Naval Fuel Station Postponed until 2018: National Defense." *Nunatsiaq Online*, March 6, 2015, accessed April 24, 2015, www. nunatsiaqonline.ca/stories/article/65674nanisivik_refueling_port_wont_open_until_2018_national_defence/.

96 Byers, "Canada's Arctic Nightmare Just Came True."

97 "PM Launches Construction of the New Canadian High Arctic Research Station." *Prime Minister of Canada* website, August 23, 2014, accessed June 27, 2015, http://pm.gc.ca/eng/tnews/2014/08/23/pm-launches-construction-new-canadian-high-arctic-research-station.

98 Government of Canada, "Canadian High Arctic Research Station (CHARS)." *Aboriginal Affairs and Northern Development Canada*, last modified April 7, 2015, accessed June 27, 2015, www.aadnc-aandc.gc.ca/eng/1314731268547/131473 1373200.

99 Byers, "Canada's Arctic Nightmare Just Came True."

100 "New Search and Rescue Aircraft in Canada's North Likely Years Away." *CBC News*, April 1, 2015, accessed April 24, 2015, www.cbc.ca/news/canada/north/new-search-and-rescue-aircraft-in-canada-s-north-likely-years-away-1.3017513.

101 Byers, "Canada's Arctic Nightmare Just Came True."

102 House of Commons, *Debates*, 1st Session, 33rd Parliament, September 10, 1985, 6464, quoted in Elizabeth B. Elliot-Meisel, "Still Unresolved after Fifty Years: The Northwest Passage in Canadian-American Relations, 1946–1998," *The American Review of Canadian Studies* 29.3 (1999): 416.

103 Ekaterina Klimenko, *Russia's Evolving Arctic Strategy – Drivers, Challenges and New Opportunities*. Policy Paper 42 (Solna, Sweden: Stockholm International Peace Research Institute, 2014), 1, accessed April 24, 2015, http://books.sipri. org/files/PP/SIPRIPP42.pdf.

104 Vladimir Putin, "Meeting of the Security Council on State Policy in the Arctic." *The Kremlin* website, April 22, 2014, accessed April 5, 2015, http://en.kremlin.ru/events/president/news/20845.

105 Steven J. Main, "If Spring Comes Tomorrow ... Russia and the Arctic." *Defence Academy of the United Kingdom* (May 2011), accessed April 5, 2015, www.da. mod.uk/Research-Publications/category/64/if-spring-comes-tomorrow-russia-and-the-arctic-2011–19150. © Crown Copyright 2016.

106 Marlene Laruelle, *Russia's Arctic Strategies and the Future of the Far North* (Armonk, NY: M.E. Sharpe, 2014), xxi. Footnote omitted.

107 Barbora Padrtova, "Russian Approach Towards the Arctic Region," in *Panorama of Global Security Environment*, edited by Marian Majer et al. (Bratislava: CENAA, 2012), accessed March 19, 2015, http://cenaa.org/analysis/russian-approach-towards-the-arctic-region/.

108 Russian Federation, "Basics of the State Policy of the Russian Federation."

109 Alexander Pelyasov, "The Strategy for the Development of the Arctic Zone of the Russian Federation and National Security up to 2020." Adopted by the President of the Russian Federation, *Arctic Yearbook*, No Pr-232, (February 8, 2013), accessed March 11, 2015, www.arcticyearbook.com/index.php/commentaries-2013/74-russia...y-the-president-of-the russian-federation-on-february-8–2013-pr-232.

110 Laruelle, *Russia's Arctic Strategies*, xxii.

111 Ibid.

112 Pelyasov, "Russian Strategy of the Development of the Arctic Zone."

113 Laruelle, *Russian Arctic Strategies*, xxii–xxiii.

114 Marco Evans, "Northeast Passage: Russia Moves to Boost Arctic Shipping," trans. Christopher Sultan, *Der Spiegel*, August 22, 2013, accessed February 14, 2015, www.spiegel.de/international/world/russia-moves-to-promote-northeast-passage-through-arctic-ocean-a-917824.html. After four years of increased use of the NSR by vessels transiting between Europe and Asia, the amount of cargo transported

in 2014 dropped 77 percent compared to 2013 (274,000 tons of cargo in 2014 compared to 1,355,897 in 2013). According to the Head of the Northern Sea Route Administration, the negative development can be attributed to a change in patterns by two important clients: EvroKhim and Novatek. However, in June 2013, Prime Minister Medvedev insisted that "[a] figure around 10 million tons is absolutely normal, it may even be more." Trude Pettersen, "Northern Sea Route Traffic Plummeted." *BarentsObserver*, December 16, 2014, accessed March 14, 2015, http://barentsobserver.com/en/arctic/2014/12/northern-sea-route-traffic-plummeted-16–12.

115 Pettersen, "Northern Sea Route Traffic Plummeted."
116 Federal State Institution, "Object of Activity and Functions of NSRA." under the "Home" tab, *The Northern Sea Route Administration* website, accessed March 11, 2015, www.nsra.ru/en/celi_funktsii/.
117 Nataliya Marchenko, "Northern Sea Route: Modern State and Challenges," paper presented at the 33rd annual conference of the American Society of Mechanical Engineers, San Francisco, California, June 8–13, 2014, accessed March 10, 2015, www.unis.no/20_RESEARCH/2050_Arctic_Technology/Smida/PDF/2014/OMAE2014–23626_Nataly.pdf.
118 See map on the NSRA website, accessed March 11, 2015, www.nsra.ru/en/pso.
119 Available under the "Official Information" tab, NSRA website, accessed March 11, 2015, www.nsra.ru/en/celi_funktsii/.
120 Jared Allen, "The Northern Sea Route as a Viable Development: Russia's Fleet of Atomic Icebreakers." *ArcticEcon*, October 1, 2012, accessed February 14, 2015, https://arcticecon.wordpress.com/tag/icebreaker/.
121 Ibid.
122 Gleb Bryanski, "Russia's Putin says Arctic Trade Route to Rival Suez." *Reuters Canada*, September 22, 2011, accessed April 15, 2015, http://ca.reuters.com/article/topNews/idCATRE78L5TC20110922.
123 The seventh ice-breaker, the *Sevmorput*, is a container vessel.
124 Vijay Sakhuja, "Russia Commits to Building Northern Sea Route Infrastructure." *Valdai International Discussion Club*, August 20, 2014, accessed March 12, 2015, http://valdaiclub.com/economy/71280.html.
125 Marchenko, "Northern Sea Route."
126 Ibid.
127 Alexei Danichev, "Russia Lays Down World's Largest Icebreaker." *Ria Novosti*, November 5, 2013, accessed April 23, 2015, http://rt.com/news/world-biggest-icebreaker-russia-275/.
128 Ibid.
129 Andrey Vokuev, "Russia Opens First Arctic Search and Rescue Center." *Barents-Observer*, August 27, 2013, accessed April 24, 2015, http://barentsobserver.com/en/arctic/2013/08/russia-opens-first-arctic-search-and-rescue-center-27–08.
130 Trude Pettersen, "Russia to have Ten Arctic Rescue Centers by 2015." *Barents-Observer*, November 18, 2011, accessed April 24, 2015, http://barentsobserver.com/en/topics/russia-have-ten-arctic-rescue-centers-2015.
131 Vokuev, "Russia Opens First Arctic Search and Rescue Center."
132 Thomas Nilsen, "Russia: Third of 10 Arctic Search and Rescue Centre Opens on Northern Sea Route." *BarentsObserver*, October 15, 2014, accessed April 24, 2015, http://barentsobserver.com/en/arctic/2014/10/third-arctic-search-and-rescue-center-opened-15–10.
133 "Search and Rescue, Prevention of Pollution by Oil," *NSRA* website, accessed April 24, 2015, www.nsra.ru/en/pso/.
134 Trude Pettersen, "Russia Deploys 18 Emergency Aircraft to the Arctic." *Barents-Observer*, March 15, 2012, accessed April 24, 2015, http://barentsobserver.com/en/arctic/russia-deploys-18-emergency-aircraft-arctic.

135 "Arctic Ports," *Northern Sea Route Information Office* website, accessed April 24, 2015, www.arctic-lio.com/arcticports.
136 "Books and Charts," *NSR* tab on the *Northern Sea Route Information Office* website, accessed 24 April, 2015, www.arctic-lio.com/nsr_booksandcharts.
137 Allen, "The Northern Sea Route as a Viable Development."
138 Ibid.
139 Ibid.
140 *The Island of Palmas Case (United States of America v. The Netherlands)*, 839.

References

Allen, Jared. "The Northern Sea Route as a Viable Development: Russia's Fleet of Atomic Icebreakers." *ArcticEcon*, October 1, 2012, accessed February 14, 2015, https://arcticecon.wordpress.com/tag/icebreaker/.
Arctic Council, AMSA 2009 Report, 2nd printing, (2009): 5. At: www.arctic.noaa.gov/detect/documents/AMSA_2009_Report_2nd_print.pdf.
Arctic Waters Pollution Prevention Act (R.S.C., 1985, c. A-12). Canada Justice Laws website, last modified April 1, 2014, accessed February 12, 2015, http://laws-lois.justice.gc.ca/eng/acts/A-12/page-1.html.
Auswärtiges Amt. *Guidelines of the Germany Arctic Policy: Assume Responsibility, Seize Opportunities*. Berlin: Federal Foreign Office, September 2013, accessed March 11, 2015, www.bmel.de/SharedDocs/Downloads/EN/International/Leitlinien-Arktispolitik.pdf?__blob=publicationFile.
Baxter, Richard R. *The Law of International Waterways*. Cambridge, MA: Harvard University Press, 1964.
Bélanger, Jean-François. "Canada and the Arctic: The Case for Deeper Cooperation with Washington." *Canadian Naval Review* 8.4 (2013): 4–8.
Berthiaume, Lee. "Coast Guard's New Icebreaker to Cost Twice as Much as Originally Estimated." *Ottawa Citizen*, November 13, 2013, accessed April 21, 2015, http://o.canada.com/news/coast-guards-new-icebreaker-to-cost-twice-as-much-as-originally-estimated.
Berthiaume, Lee. "Coast Guard to Scope Out Arctic Shipping Lanes." *Ottawa Citizen*, January 21, 2014, accessed April 21, 2015, http://o.canada.com/news/coast-guard-to-scope-out-arctic-shipping-lanes.
Brubaker, R. Douglas. "The Legal Status of Straits in Russian Arctic Waters – Internationality." *INSROP Working Paper* 57, September 11, 1996, accessed February 12, 2015, www.arctis-search.com/tiki-download_wiki_attachment.php?attId=104.
Brubaker, R. Douglas. *Russian Arctic Straits*. Dordrecht: Martinus Nijhoff, 2004.
Bryanski, Gleb. "Russia's Putin says Arctic Trade Route to Rival Suez." *Reuters Canada*, September 22, 2011, accessed April 15, 2015, http://ca.reuters.com/article/topNews/idCATRE78L5TC20110922.
Bush, George W. "National Security Presidential Directive and Homeland Security Presidential Directive." The White House, January 9, 2009, accessed February 12, 2015, www.fas.org/irp/offdocs/nspd/nspd-66.htm.
Busson, Marie-Pierre. "Le discours sur l'Arctique, rhétorique d'exception?" Master's thesis, École Nationale d'Administration Publique, 2008.
Byers, Michael. "Canada's Arctic Nightmare Just Came True: The Northwest Passage is Commercial." *The Globe and Mail*, September 20, 2013, accessed April 21, 2015, www.theglobeandmail.com/globe-debate/canadas-arctic-nightmare-just-came-true-the-northwest-passage-is-commercial/article14432440/.

Byers, Michael. *International Law and the Arctic.* Cambridge: Cambridge University Press, 2013.

Canada Shipping Act, 2001 (S.C. 2001), c. 26, Canada Justice Laws website, last modified February 26, 2015, accessed March 11, 2015, http://laws-lois.justice. gc.ca/eng/acts/C-10.15/page-1.html.

Canadian Coast Guard website, last modified June 24, 2013, accessed February 12, 2015, www.ccg-gcc.gc.ca/eng/Central_Arctic/About_Us.

CBC News. "Grounded Arctic Tanker Tries to Lighten Load." *CBC News*, September 13, 2010, accessed April 21, 2015, www.cbc.ca/news/canada/north/grounded-arctic-tanker-tries-to-lighten-load-1.961697.

CBC News. "Icebreaker's Mission Cut Short Due to Broken Propeller." *CBC News*, October 12, 2011, accessed April 21, 2015, www.cbc.ca/news/canada/north/icebreaker-s-mission-cut-short-due-to-broken-propeller-1.1088902.

CBC News. "Oil Tanker Off Course When it Ran Aground in Nunavut." *CBC News*, February 4, 2014, accessed April 21, 2015, www.cbc.ca/news/canada/north/oil-tanker-off-course-when-it-ran-aground-in-nunavut-1.2522730.

CBC News. "Amundsen Icebreaker Dry-Docked for the Year." *CBC News*, January 31, 2012, accessed April 21, 2015, www.cbc.ca/news/canada/north/amundsen-icebreaker-dry-docked-for-the-year-1.1139458.

CBC News. "New Search and Rescue Aircraft in Canada's North Likely Years Away." *CBC News*, April 1, 2015, accessed April 24, 2015, www.cbc.ca/news/canada/north/new-search-and-rescue-aircraft-in-canada-s-north-likely-years-away-1.3017513.

Cohen, Tobi. "Canadian Rescue Capacity Questioned in Wake of Arctic Ship Grounding." *Postmedia News*, August 29, 2010, accessed April 21, 2014, www. canada.com/technology/Canadian+rescue+capacity+questioned+wake+Arctic+ship+grounding/3457291/story.html.

Churchill, Robin and Vaughan Lowe. *The Law of the Sea*, 3rd edn. Manchester: Manchester University Press, 1999.

Danichev, Alexei. "Russia Lays Down World's Largest Icebreaker." *Ria Novosti*, November 5, 2013, accessed April 23, 2015, http://rt.com/news/world-biggest-icebreaker-russia-275/.

Elliot-Meisel, Elizabeth B. "Still Unresolved after Fifty Years: The Northwest Passage in Canadian-American Relations, 1946–1998." *The American Review of Canadian Studies* 29.3 (1999): 407–30.

European Parliament. "European Parliament Resolution of 12 March 2014 on the EU Strategy of the Arctic." European Parliament website, accessed February 23, 2015, www.europarl.europa.eu/sides/getDoc.do?type=TA&language=EN&reference=P7-TA-2014–0236.

Evans, Marco. "Northeast Passage: Russia Moves to Boost Arctic Shipping," trans. Christopher Sultan, *Der Spiegel*, August 22, 2013, accessed February 14, 2015, www.spiegel.de/international/world/russia-moves-to-promote-northeast-passage-through-arctic-ocean-a-917824.html.

Federal State Institution, "Object of Activity and Functions of NSRA." *The Northern Sea Route Administration* website, accessed March 11, 2015, www.nsra.ru/en/celi_funktsii/.

Fouche, Gwladys. "Wary of Russia, Norway Urges NATO Vigilance in Arctic." *Reuters*, May 20, 2014, accessed February 12, 2015, www.reuters.com/article/2014/05/20/us-norway-defence-russia-idUSBREA4J0HE20140520.

Franckx, Erik. *Maritime Claims in the Arctic: Canadian and Russian Perspectives.* Dordrecht: Martinus Nijhoff, 1993.

George, Jane. "Experts: Canada Must Step Up Arctic Charting." *Nunatsiaq Online*, December 17, 2010, accessed April 21, 2014, www.nunatsiaqonline.ca/stories/article/171210_experts_canada_must_step_up_arctic_charting/.

Gidel, Gilbert. *Le droit international public de la mer* (tome II). Châteauroux: Établissements Mellottée, 1932.

Golitsyn, Vladimir. "The Arctic – On the Way to Regional Cooperation." *Marine Policy Report* 1 (1989): 91–99.

Government of Canada, "Canada's Northern Strategy," last modified December 21, 2012, accessed February 12, 2015, www.northernstrategy.gc.ca/index-eng.asp.

Government of Canada, "Canada's Arctic Foreign Policy," *Department of Foreign Affairs, Trade and Development*, last modified June 3, 2013, accessed February 12, 2015, www.international.gc.ca/arctic-arctique/arctic_policy-canada-politique_arctique.aspx?lang=eng.

Government of Canada. "Canada's Arctic Foreign Policy." *Department of Foreign Affairs, Trade and Development*. Accessed May 6, 2016, www.international.gc.ca/arctic-arctique/arctic_policy-canada-politique_arctique.aspx?lang=eng.

Government of Canada. "Canadian High Arctic Research Station (CHARS)." *Aboriginal Affairs and Northern Development Canada*, last modified April 7, 2015, accessed June 27, 2015, www.aadnc-aandc.gc.ca/eng/1314731268547/1314731373200.

Government of the Northwest Territories. "7.3 Trends in Shipping in the North-West Passage and the Beaufort Sea." *Department of the Environment and Natural Resources*, last modified January, 2015, accessed February 12, 2015, www.enr.gov.nt.ca/state-environment/73-trends-shipping-northwest-passage-and-beaufort-sea.

Griffiths, Franklyn (ed.). *Politics of the Northwest Passage*. Kingston and Montreal: McGill-Queen's University Press, 1987.

Grunawalt, Richard J. "United States Policy on International Straits." *Ocean Development and International Law* 18 (1987): 445–56.

Kingston, Brian. "When it Comes to the Arctic, Canada is Unprepared." *Huffington Post*, September 18, 2014, accessed February 14, 2015, www.huffingtonpost.ca/global-shapers-community-ottawa/arctic-canada_b_5838640.html.

Klimenko, Ekaterina. *Russia's Evolving Arctic Strategy – Drivers, Challenges and New Opportunities*. Policy Paper 42. Solna: Stockholm International Peace Research Institute, 2014. Accessed April 24, 2015, http://books.sipri.org/files/PP/SIPRIPP42.pdf.

Kolodkin, Anatoly L. and Marlen E. Volosov. "The Legal Regime of the Soviet Arctic: Major Issues." *Marine Policy* 14.2 (1990): 158–68.

Kraska, James. "The Law of the Sea Convention and the Northwest Passage." *International Journal of Marine and Coastal Law* 22 (2007): 257–81.

Laruelle, Marlene. *Russia's Arctic Strategies and the Future of the Far North*. Armonk, NY: M.E. Sharpe, 2014.

López Martín, Ana Gemma. *International Straits: Concept, Classification and Rules of Passage*. Heidelberg: Springer, 2010.

Lucchini, Laurent and Michel Voelckel. *Droit de la mer* (tome 2, volume 2). Paris: Pédone, 1990.

Main, Steven J. "If Spring Comes Tomorrow … Russia and the Arctic." *Defence Academy of the United Kingdom* (May 2011), accessed April 5, 2015, www.da.mod.uk/Research-Publications/category/64/if-spring-comes-tomorrow-russia-and-the-arctic-2011-19150. © Crown Copyright 2016.

Marchenko, Nataliya. "Northern Sea Route: Modern State and Challenges." Paper presented at the 33rd annual conference of the American Society of Mechanical

Engineers, San Francisco, California, June 8–13, 2014, accessed March 10, 2015, www.unis.no/20_RESEARCH/2050_Arctic_Technology/Smida/PDF/2014/ OMAE2014–23626_Nataly.pdf.

McDorman, Ted L. "The New Definition of 'Canada Lands' and the Determination of the Outer Limit of the Continental Shelf." *Journal of Maritime Law and Commerce* 14 (1983): 195–221.

Nilsen, Thomas. "Russia: Third of 10 Arctic Search and Rescue Centre Opens on Northern Sea Route." *BarentsObserver*, October 15, 2014, accessed April 24, 2015, http://barentsobserver.com/en/arctic/2014/10/third-arctic-search-and-rescue-center-opened-15-10.

Northern Canada Vessel Traffic Services Zone Regulations (SOR/2010–127). Canada Justice Laws website, last modified July 1, 2010, accessed February 12, 2015, http://laws-lois.justice.gc.ca/eng/regulations/SOR-2010-127/FullText.html.

Obama, B. "National Strategy for the Arctic Region." The White House, May 10, 2013, accessed February 12, 2015, www.whitehouse.gov/sites/default/files/docs/nat_arctic_strategy.pdf.

Oceans Act (S.C. 1996, c. 31). Canada Justice Laws website, last modified February 26, 2015, accessed March 11, 2015, http://laws-lois.justice.gc.ca/eng/acts/o-2.4/page-1.html.

O'Connell, Daniel Patrick and Ivan Anthony Shearer. *The International Law of the Sea*. Oxford: Clarendon Press, 1982.

Office of the Auditor General, "Marine Navigation in the Canadian Arctic," in *Report of the Commissioner of the Environment and Sustainable Development*. October 7, 2014, accessed February 12, 2015, www.oag-bvg.gc.ca/internet/docs/parl_cesd_201410_03_e.pdf.

Office of Ocean Affairs, *Limits in the Seas No. 112: United States Responses to Excessive National Maritime Claims*. Washington, DC: US State Department, 1992.

Office of Ocean Law and Policy, "Bureau of Oceans and International Environmental and Scientific Affairs." *U.S. Department of State, Limits in the Seas* 109, September 29, 1988, accessed February 12, 2015, www.state.gov/documents/organization/58383.pdf.

Østreng, Willy. "The Northeast and Northern Sea Route." *Arctic Knowledge Hub* website, accessed March 11, 2015, www.arctis-search.com/The+Northeast+Passage+and+Northern+Sea+Route+2.

Østreng, Willy et al. *Shipping in Arctic Waters: A Comparison of the Northeast, Northwest and Trans Polar Passages*. London: Springer-Praxis, 2013.

Padrtova, Barbora. "Russian Approach Towards the Arctic Region." In *Panorama of Global Security Environment*, edited by Marian Majer et al., 339–51. Bratislava: CENAA, 2012. Accessed March 19, 2015, http://cenaa.org/analysis/russian-approach-towards-the-arctic-region/.

Pelyasov, Alexander. "The Strategy for the Development of the Arctic Zone of the Russian Federation and National Security up to 2020." Adopted by the President of the Russian Federation, *Arctic Yearbook*, No Pr-232 (February 8, 2013), accessed March 11, 2015, www.arcticyearbook.com/index.php/commentaries-2013/74-russia...y-the-president-of-the-russian-federation-on-february-8-2013-pr-232.

Peritz, Ingrid. "Hillary Clinton Warns Montreal Crowd of Russia's Increased Activity in Arctic," *The Globe and Mail*, March 18, 2014, accessed February 12, 2015, www.theglobeandmail.com/news/politics/clinton-warns-montreal-crowd-of-russias-increased-activity-in-arctic/article17560676/.

Pettersen, Trude. "Russia to have Ten Arctic Rescue Centers by 2015." *Barents-Observer*, November 18, 2011, accessed April 24, 2015, http://barentsobserver.com/en/topics/russia-have-ten-arctic-rescue-centers-2015.

Pettersen, Trude. "Russia Deploys 18 Emergency Aircraft to the Arctic." *Barents-Observer*, March 15, 2012, accessed April 24, 2015, http://barentsobserver.com/en/arctic/russia-deploys-18-emergency-aircraft-arctic.

Pettersen, Trude. "Northern Sea Route Traffic Plummeted." *BarentsObserver*, December 16, 2014, accessed March 14, 2015, http://barentsobserver.com/en/arctic/2014/12/northern-sea-route-traffic-plummeted-16-12.

Pharand, Donat. "Historic Waters in International Law with Special Reference to the Arctic." *University of Toronto Law Journal* 21 (1971): 1–14.

Pharand, Donat. *Canada's Arctic Waters in International Law*. Cambridge: Cambridge University Press, 1988.

Pharand, Donat. "The Arctic Waters and the Northwest Passage: A Final Revisit." *Ocean Development and International Law* 38 (2007): 3–69.

Prime Minister of Canada. "PM Launches Construction of the New Canadian High Arctic Research Station." *Prime Minister of Canada* website, August 23, 2014, accessed June 27, 2015, http://pm.gc.ca/eng/news/2014/08/23/pm-launches-construction-new-canadian-high-arctic-research-station.

Putin, Vladimir. "Meeting of the Security Council on State Policy in the Arctic." *The Kremlin* website, April 22, 2014, accessed April 5, 2015, http://en.kremlin.ru/events/president/news/20845.

Roach, J. Ashley and Robert W. Smith. *Excessive Maritime Claims* 3rd edn. Boston, MA: Martinus Nijhoff Publishers, 2012.

Rogers, Sarah. "Nanisivik Naval Fuel Station Postponed until 2018: National Defense." *Nunatsiaq Online*, March 6, 2015, accessed April 24, 2015, www.nunatsiaqonline.ca/stories/article/65674nanisivik_refueling_port_wont_open_until_2018_national_defence/.

Rothwell, Donald R. "The Canadian-U.S. Northwest Passage Dispute: A Reassessment." *Cornell International Law Journal* 26 (1993): 331–72.

Rothwell, Donald R. *The Polar Regions and the Development of International Law*. Cambridge: Cambridge University Press, 1996.

Russian Federation, "Basics of the State Policy of the Russian Federation in the Arctic for the Period till 2020 and for a Further Perspective." *The Arctic Governance Project*, September 18, 2008, accessed February 12, 2015, www.arctis-search.com/Russian+Federation+Policy+for+the+Arctic+to+2020.

Russian Federation, "Russian Strategy of the Development of the Arctic Zone and the Provision of National Security until 2020." *The International Expert Council on Cooperation in the Arctic*, February 8, 2013, accessed February 12, 2015, www.iecca.ru/en/legislation/strategies/item/99-the-development-strategy-of-the-arctic-zone-of-the-russian-federation.

Sakhuja, Vijay. "Russia Commits to Building Northern Sea Route Infrastructure." *Valdai International Discussion Club*, August 20, 2014, accessed March 12, 2015, http://valdaiclub.com/economy/71280.html.

Scovazzi, Tullio. "New Developments Concerning Soviet Straight Baselines." *International Journal of Estuarine and Coastal Law* 3 (1988): 37–43.

Stewart, Emma J. and Jackie Dawson. "A Matter of Good Fortune? The Grounding of the *Clipper Adventurer* in the Northwest Passage, Arctic Canada." *Arctic* 64.2 (2011): 263–67.

Standing Committee on Fisheries and Oceans, House of Commons, Parliament of Canada, "Committee Calls for an Expanded National Security Mandate for the Canadian Coast Guard." *News Release*, March 31, 2004, accessed April 21, 2015, www.parl.gc.ca/HousePublications/Publication.aspx?DocId=1279763&Language=E&Mode=1&Parl=37&Ses=3.

Standing Committee on Fisheries and Oceans, House of Commons, "Safe, Secure, Sovereign: Reinventing the Canadian Coast Guard." *Parliament of Canada* website, March 2014, accessed April 21, 2015, www.parl.gc.ca/HousePublications/Publication.aspx?DocId=1263626&Mode=1&Parl=37&Ses=3&Language=E.

Symmons, Clive R. *Historic Waters in the Law of the Sea: A Modern Re-Appraisal.* Leiden: Brill, 2007.

Vincent, Philippe. *Droit de la mer.* Bruxelles: Éditions Larcier, 2008.

Vokuev, Andrey. "Russia Opens First Arctic Search and Rescue Center." *BarentsObserver*, August 27, 2013, accessed April 24, 2015, http://barentsobserver.com/en/arctic/2013/08/russia-opens-first-arctic-search-and-rescue-center-27-08.

5 The position of the European Union on the Svalbard waters[1]

Marta Sobrido[2]

Introduction

Svalbard is an archipelago in the Arctic Ocean, between mainland Norway and the North Pole, flanked to the west by Denmark (Greenland), and to the east by Russia (Franz Josef Land). In 1920, the Treaty Concerning the Archipelago of Spitsbergen (hereinafter, Treaty of Paris[3]) was adopted, and came into force in 1925. It put an end to Svalbard's status as *terra nullius* or no man's land. Since then Norway has exercised sovereign rights over the archipelago, but such sovereignty must be understood as necessarily limited by a number of conditions set out in the treaty itself.

Currently, there is no doubt that the Svalbard archipelago belongs to Norway, nor is it in dispute that the Treaty of Paris still applies. However, certain problems concerning the scope of the restrictions that limit the Norwegian sovereignty over the archipelago are arising, such as the territorial scope of the Treaty.[4]

So far, the European Union has experienced two types of crises concerning the waters of Svalbard, both relating to fishing. The first crisis took place about ten years ago when several Spanish and Portuguese vessels were captured. These flag states did not recognize Norway taking coercive and punitive measures, a national position which was initially supported by the European Commission. More recently, a second crisis was triggered when Norway adopted discriminatory measures in relation to haddock fishing, which resulted in protests by the European Commission.

The issue underlying these crises is the legal nature of the maritime areas of Svalbard. The divergent positions taken by Norway and the EU on this issue explain many of the problems faced by the EU fishing fleet in these waters. Moreover, differences between EU Member States seem to condition the Union's response to this situation.

Against this background, this chapter examines the position of the EU concerning the legal status of the waters of Svalbard.[5] First, it refers to the Treaty of Paris, and then analyzes the maritime delimitation of Svalbard established by Norway as well as the Norwegian actions that provoked the EU to react.

The Treaty of Paris

This chapter takes as a starting point the Treaty of Paris and will not, therefore, examine the claims made on Svalbard by different states prior to its adoption.[6]

The Treaty of Paris acknowledges "the full and absolute sovereignty" of Norway over the Archipelago of Svalbard, including both land masses and territorial waters. However, this sovereignty is subject to several conditions.

In order to define the "land" that forms the Archipelago of Svalbard, the treaty uses the formula of drawing an imaginary rectangle, where land is the surface left inside the rectangle, the so-called Svalbard Box.[7] This formula, quite common in old treaties, could include undiscovered or yet unnamed islands. Taking into account the fact that only the land, not the water, is the object of delimitations, the Svalbard Box does not outline any maritime borders.

As regards the "waters," the treaty simply speaks of "territorial waters"[8] without giving a precise definition. At that time, the waters of the States were limited to—using current terminology—internal waters and territorial sea, and waters beyond that were considered the high seas. It is important to note that with the Treaty of Paris, Norway acquired sovereignty over Svalbard waters for four miles, which at that time was the general distance of the territorial waters of Norway.[9] The waters that currently comprise the Svalbard Fisheries Protection Zone, including much of the water that now constitutes the territorial sea of the island up to the twelve-mile limit, were considered high seas at that time.

Regarding the "conditions" that limit Norwegian sovereignty, it is important to note that the purpose of the Treaty of Paris was twofold. On the one hand, it attempted to eliminate inconveniences derived from the status of Svalbard as a no man's land: drawbacks such as the legal uncertainty for the economic operators in the area, or even international tensions among states. On the other hand, it aimed to maintain Svalbard's demilitarization and the benefits of economic exploitation—hunting, fishing, mining—for those who had previously benefited from the regime of freedom. For these reasons, the Treaty of Paris recognizes the sovereignty of Norway, thus putting an end to the disadvantages, but subject to certain limitations, thus maintaining the advantages.

The conditions imposed on Norway in the Treaty of Paris limit the exercise of Norwegian sovereignty through fiscal and military constraints[10] and enshrine the principle of non-discrimination in relation to the nationals of all the contracting parties: equal rights of fishing and hunting; equal freedom of access and entry; and equal exercise and practice of all maritime, industrial, mining or commercial enterprises.[11]

The holders of this right to non-discrimination are persons, but only those who are nationals of states recognizing Norwegian sovereignty. Both issues are discussed below.

Holders of the right to non-discrimination: natural or legal persons

The holders of the right to non-discrimination recognized by the Treaty of Paris are persons, both natural and legal.[12] The idea is that people can still enter and reside in Svalbard and continue to benefit from the exploitation of living natural resources—fishing and hunting—and may also exercise all maritime, industrial, mining or commercial enterprises. Without that condition imposed on Norway in the Treaty of Paris, the competence of Norway as a sovereign state that can regulate such activities, could result in a more beneficial treatment of Norwegians and/or nationals of a country or countries in particular.

However, although that right to non-discrimination is recognized for natural and legal persons and not States, it is enshrined in an international treaty (Treaty of Paris). Therefore, the violation of that right gives both the persons in question and the States of which they are nationals a right to react, but on different levels: national or international, respectively.

First, the person who considers that his or her right to enter, reside and/or perform such activities under the same conditions as Norwegian nationals and/or nationals of other State parties to the Treaty of Paris has not been respected must present the case to a national court; however, not to one under the jurisdiction of their own country, but in Norway, the country violating the treaty.[13] This has already happened on several occasions, and a problem arises in cases relating to events that have taken place in the waters of the Fisheries Protection Zone around Svalbard. The problem is that Norway does not recognize the application of the Treaty of Paris in those waters,[14] and, so far, the Norwegian judicial system have avoided ruling on this specific issue; some judgments have been handed down, but not from the Supreme Court of Norway, the highest court of appeal.[15] Once legal remedies in the Norwegian system have been exhausted without a favorable result, the person concerned can seek assistance from his own State in order to make an international claim for compliance with the provisions of the Treaty of Paris through diplomatic protection.[16] However, it must be noted that although individuals can invite their State to react internationally, the fact is that, unless national law provides otherwise, the State is free to exercise that protection at its own discretion. Diplomatic protection is a right of the State to enforce international law in the person of its nationals, rather than a right of its nationals. Indeed, the State may decide not to exercise diplomatic protection in a given case.[17]

As regards the States that are party to the Treaty of Paris, as just noted, if Norway does not respect the right to non-discrimination, such States can exercise diplomatic protection for their nationals, once all the domestic remedies have been exhausted.[18] Additionally, States that are a party to the Treaty of Paris can challenge Norway in connection with the determination of the geographical scope of the Treaty, regardless of whether actions by Norway are affecting a national of this State. To date, no State has denounced the violation of the Treaty of Paris before an international court,[19] even though Iceland has repeatedly threatened to turn to the International Court of Justice.[20]

Holders of the right to non-discrimination: nationals of all the high contracting parties

In the articles relating to the principle of non-discrimination, the Treaty of Paris refers to "nationals of all the High Contracting Parties,"[21] so the right of non-discrimination is recognized only for nationals of the States which are party to this treaty.[22]

The purpose is not to reduce the scope of the beneficiaries, since the Treaty of Paris is open and any State can accede and become a party to it. The aim is rather to strengthen Norwegian sovereignty and prevent future territorial claims as the States acceding to the treaty recognize Norwegian sovereignty.

In any case, at this point, and moving on to the issue of the delimitation of its territorial waters, it seems that Norwegian sovereignty over Svalbard is not being challenged, and, on this basis, Norway also affirms the same for States that are not party to the Treaty of Paris (according to the doctrine of acquiescence).[23]

The maritime boundaries of Svalbard established by Norway

In 1925, Norway acquired sovereignty over Svalbard waters for a distance of four miles. However, since then the International Law of the Sea has evolved. This chapter does not describe in detail this evolution and only uses as a reference the current situation, recognized by the United Nations Convention on the Law of the Sea from 1982 (UNCLOS), of which both Norway and the EU (and its Member States) are parties. UNCLOS recognizes the right of islands to have internal waters, territorial sea, a contiguous zone, an exclusive economic zone and a continental shelf.[24]

Waters of Svalbard

As mentioned before, according to UNCLOS, every island has the right to several different spaces. First, internal waters and a territorial sea of up to twelve nautical miles both measured from the baselines; these are waters that are part of the territory of the state. Second, a contiguous zone of up to twenty-four nautical miles from the baselines, which are waters where the coastal State can exercise the control necessary to prevent or punish the infringement of certain regulations within its territory. Third, the exclusive economic zone of up to 200 nautical miles from the baselines, where the coastal State has certain rights and jurisdiction.[25] The distances of 12, 24 and 200 miles are considered as potential maximum distances, unless they collide with another State's territorial sea, contiguous zone or exclusive economic zone, respectively.

Under the provisions of Norwegian law, Svalbard currently has internal waters, territorial sea and the so-called Fishery Protection Zone around Svalbard.

Unlike the rest of Norway, which in 1961 expanded its jurisdiction over fisheries to the twelve-mile limit,[26] the territorial sea of Svalbard continued to extend for four miles[27] until 2004, at which point it was also increased to twelve miles.[28] Moreover, the internal waters are the waters on the landward side of the baselines, established for Svalbard in 1970.[29] There is a single regulation for internal waters and the territorial sea for Svalbard and the rest of Norway, but in Svalbard waters the Treaty of Paris only applied.

In the absence of a contiguous zone,[30] the next possible space for a distance of 200 miles is an exclusive economic zone. Norway could have followed the same pattern for these waters as for internal waters and the territorial sea: recognize an exclusive economic zone for all of Norway, with the particularity of implementing the Treaty of Paris in the exclusive economic zone of Svalbard. Since Norway does not recognize the application of the Treaty of Paris beyond the territorial sea it first established an economic zone in 1976 by a regulation known as the Zone Act,[31] which stipulated that, unless stated otherwise, the right to fish in this area was reserved for Norwegians. The reaction of the States which are party to the Treaty of Paris, who opposed the establishment of a discriminatory regime in the waters of Svalbard,[32] led Norway to establish a specific regime for Svalbard waters in 1977:[33] the Svalbard Fishery Protection Zone.[34]

Based on the regulation of the economic zone (Zone Act, 1976),[35] the regulation that establishes the Fisheries Protection Zone around Svalbard (Royal Decree, 1977) is an exception, since it explicitly states that the Norwegian economic zone discriminatory fisheries regime is not applicable in these waters. According to the Royal Decree of 1977, the Norwegian Ministry of Fisheries is competent to stipulate the fishing regime to apply to Svalbard waters; thus, and with regard to the allocation of quotas, a regime based on historical catches has been established. Although Norway acknowledges having taken into account the position of the States which are party to the Treaty of Paris, Norway endeavors to make clear that the Svalbard non-discriminatory fishing regime is justified by conservation needs and that, therefore, the difference between the exclusive economic zone of the Norwegian mainland and the Fisheries Protection Zone around Svalbard is an "administrative distinction" established for "considerations of practicality and effectiveness."[36] However, this formula (recognition of the same fishing regime as would be applied by the Treaty of Paris) allows an understanding between Norway and the parties to the

Treaty of Paris, despite maintaining different positions with regards to the legal basis for that non-discriminatory regime. Norway considers that the legal basis is its competence to establish the fishing regime as a coastal State. The remaining States, more specifically those that have expressed their opinion and recognize the jurisdiction of Norway to adopt conservation and management measures for fishery resources in the Fisheries Protection Zone around Svalbard, claim that the legal basis is the principle of non-discrimination enshrined in the Treaty of Paris.

The delimitation of the Svalbard Fisheries Protection Zone follows the same delimiting criteria as the Norwegian exclusive economic zone (200 miles, except where this distance abuts another State's sovereign area), but there is an important difference between the two: should there be an overlap, it seems that the exclusive economic zone of the Norwegian mainland prevails.[37]

Since 2010, the year in which Norway signed the maritime delimitation treaty with Russia, the delimitation of the waters of the Fisheries Protection Zone around Svalbard has been completed. Svalbard waters delimit with the waters of the Norwegian mainland in the south (Royal Decree, 1977), and with the waters of other countries: Denmark-Greenland in the west (Agreement of 2006),[38] Russia-Novaya Zemlya and Franz Josef Land in the east (Agreements of 1957 and 2010).[39] Moreover, Svalbard waters are adjacent to international waters: Nansen Basin in the northwest, Banana Hole in the east and Loop Hole in the west.[40]

Continental shelf of Svalbard

The UNCLOS[41] provides for the continental shelf to be determined by two criteria: one is geological and establishes a maximum extension for all cases; and a distance criterion of 200 miles, should the continental shelf not exceed that distance.[42] Norwegian legislation stipulates that the continental shelf must follow both criteria: distance in areas where the Norwegian continental shelf is equal to or less than 200 miles; and the geological in areas where the Norwegian continental shelf exceeds 200 miles (extended continental shelf).

In areas where Norway opts for the distance criterion, its continental shelf has an extension of 200 miles. However, this extension is reduced in cases where the Norwegian continental shelf would overlap with that of another neighboring State; in such cases the delimitation must be set by agreement between the two States concerned. As regards the continental shelf of Svalbard, this has been Denmark's stance with respect to Greenland, and Russia's with regard to Novaya Zemlya and Franz Josef Land, through the agreements of 2006 and 2010, respectively, as referenced in the previous section. In addition there is the question, still pending, of delimiting Svalbard's continental shelf with that of the Norwegian mainland.

In areas in which Norway has chosen the geological criteria, in 2006 it submitted to the Commission on the Limits of the Continental Shelf (CLCS)[43] information for the three enclaves in international waters bordering the waters of Svalbard. In these three zones, Norway takes into consideration the outer limits of the continental shelf of Svalbard.[44] The CLCS issued its recommendations in March 2009.[45] However, the competence of the CLCS does not affect matters relating to delimitation of boundaries between States. In this regard, the delimitation with Russia's continental shelf is relevant to Svalbard (Agreement of 2010 *supra*). However, as regards Denmark, the Agreement of 2006 does not delimit the respective continental shelves beyond 200 miles and, in December 2014, Denmark submitted to the CLCS information on the limits of the continental shelf of northern Greenland and the outer limits on the Eurasian side of the Lomonosov Ridge extending to the 200-mile line of Svalbard. As a consequence, the northern continental shelf of Greenland overlaps with the continental shelf of Svalbard.[46]

For decades, Norway assimilated the geological and legal concepts of continental shelf, claiming that the continental shelf of Svalbard was an extension of the continental shelf of the Norwegian mainland and therefore the Treaty of Paris was not applicable.[47] In addition to contravening the UNCLOS,[48] this strategy has the disadvantage of limiting the extent of the Norwegian continental shelf, because it only took the baselines of the Norwegian mainland as its points of reference.[49] The information submitted by Norway to the CLCS (2006), and the treaties with Denmark (2006) and Russia (2010) make it clear that Norway has changed its strategy and claims the right for Svalbard to generate a continental shelf of its own, different from the continental shelf generated by Norwegian mainland,[50] although the distinction between the two continental shelves of Svalbard and the mainland has not been determined.

The position of the European Union

The Treaty of Paris is an open treaty, meaning that states that did not participate in its creation can accede to it. Currently, forty-two States are party to the Treaty of Paris, mostly, but not all, European.[51] Since only States, not international organizations, can be party to the Treaty the EU is excluded from membership. However, twenty of the twenty-eight EU Member States have signed the Treaty of Paris,[52] and further accessions in the future cannot be ruled out.[53]

The issue of the geographical scope of the Treaty of Paris is not only relevant from the point of view of the fishing industry, concerned about conservation and management of living resources of the waters beyond the territorial sea to a distance of 200 miles. Indeed, it is also important in other areas, most notably in relation to hydrocarbons—exploration and exploitation of non-living resources of the continental shelf—because of the principle of non-discrimination, but also particularly because of the fiscal constraints imposed by the Treaty of Paris.[54] Even if there is currently no political debate on this issue[55] due to the lack of activity on the Svalbard continental shelf, it still conditions the general debate about the geographical scope of the Treaty of Paris, the "elephant in the room."[56]

To date the legal and political "noise" comes mainly from fisheries. This refers to various Norwegian legal instruments that have provoked reaction from third states and even the EU. The problems regarding fisheries in the Fisheries Protection Zone around Svalbard are essentially twofold. One refers to Norway's competence to adopt conservation and management measures and/or appropriate enforcement and sanctioning, and the other is the principle of non-discrimination. The EU as an important player in international fishing[57] has been involved in both debates. However, the situation is delicate, politically and legally. From the political point of view because the EU is dealing with its most important partner in fisheries and a very important partner in other areas.[58] This must be taken into account in understanding the lack of forcefulness, as will be seen below, that the EU seems to display in relation to offenses committed by Norway, which are denounced by the European Commission, but Norway does not desist. There is also the lack of diligence on other issues, such as the possible adverse effects of the maritime delimitation between Norway and Russia,[59] and from a legal point of view because of the difficulties faced by the EU in acting as an official interlocutor on the issues of Svalbard. Unlike other areas such as energy, where the EU shares competences with Member States,[60] the EU has exclusive competence over fisheries. However, Norway seems not to accept it as a competent contact in regards to fishing in Svalbard waters, since is not party to the Treaty of Paris[61] and the Member States of the EU themselves have expressed their concern at various times on the EU's management of the issue.[62]

Nature and extent of Norway's competence in the waters of the Fisheries Protection Zone around Svalbard

A first discussion concerned the possibility of Svalbard having its own exclusive economic zone and continental shelf. It should be remembered that the Treaty of Paris was signed in 1920 (in force since 1925) and, at that time, the International Law of the Sea only identified the territorial sea as territorial waters of the coastal State, but did not recognize rights to the continental shelf situated beyond these waters.

The first confrontations occurred in the 1970s,[63] and some of the then Member States of the EU, and the European Commission, made statements, if only to record their reservations concerning Norway's actions. The disagreements began over the continental shelf, especially after a Norwegian statement declaring the Svalbard continental shelf as an extension of the Norwegian mainland continental shelf, thus assimilating the legal and geological definition, as mentioned before, so that the Treaty of Paris did not apply to it (1974, statement). Opposition from the then Soviet Union was clear, while Norway's allies, such as the United States of America or the United Kingdom (a member of the EU since 1973) reserved their positions. Soon thereafter, a disagreement arose over the waters beyond the Svalbard territorial sea and up to a distance of 200 miles. As indicated in a previous section, the first reactions were triggered by Norway's establishment of an economic zone in which the fishing rights were reserved for Norwegians (1976, Zone Act). Later, there were new reactions to the establishment of a Svalbard Fisheries Protection Zone, in which the discriminatory fisheries regime of the Norwegian economic zone would not apply, but in which Norway does not recognize the application of the Treaty of Paris. Moreover, Norway confirmed its competence to adopt conservation and fisheries management measures in the new zone, referring to general rules of the economic zone on willful or negligent violation of these provisions (1977, Royal Decree). Again, the United States and the United Kingdom reserved their position; but now so also did France and Germany (founding members of the EU), and the European Commission regarding the fishing rights of its Members States.[64] However, the Netherlands (also founding member of the EU) was in favor of Svalbard generating an exclusive economic zone and a continental shelf, but they also stated that the Treaty of Paris should remain applicable in such spaces. Other States that are currently part of the EU, but that were not at the time, such as Spain (a member since 1986), the then Czechoslovakia,[65] Poland and Hungary (all members since 2004), disagreed with Norway's adoption of unilateral measures in these waters. The Soviet Union, meanwhile, once again clearly expressed its opposition.

From the 1980s, although some Norwegian measures relating to the continental shelf stirred up reactions from certain States,[66] the cause of contention has been in the field of fisheries. The application of a non-discriminatory fisheries regime in the Fisheries Protection Zone around Svalbard, articulated by Norway with a reference to historical catches,[67] allowed for coexistence. However, it did not prevent certain confrontations arising from the adoption of coercive and punitive measures by Norway against vessels of other States which are party to the Treaty of Paris, primarily Russia, Iceland and Spain.[68]

The most challenging incidents have not taken place with regard to EU vessels, but with Icelanders (use of force in the case of the seizure of the Icelandic fishing vessel *Hagangur II* in 1994) and Russians (sending the anti-submarine warfare destroyer *Severomorsk* to Svalbard waters in 2002; the flight of the Russian vessel *Elektron* with two Norwegian inspectors on board in 2005).[69] However, the arrests of Spanish and, to a lesser extent, Portuguese vessels were strongly contested by their flag States—an attitude of rejection that was supported by the European Commission at first. In all these cases, Norway did not formally react internationally.[70] Norway acted firmly, but nationally[71] by arresting and imposing sanctions in cases in which it was able to do so.[72]

As regards the arrests of EU vessels (Spanish and Portuguese), the first arrests took place in 2004. The reason for these was the failure to comply with Norwegian legislation. The problem that arises is not Norwegian competence to adopt such legislation, but Norway's powers to adopt coercive and punitive measures for the breach of such legislation. Norway asserts its competence through legislation and practice (boardings and penalties), but these powers are not recognized by the affected States.[73] Spain and Portugal requested the support of the European Commission.[74] The Commission, which does not question the competence of Norway to adopt such rules and supports its powers on inspection, declared that:

> Norway has a full right and responsibility to carry out inspection activities on all vessels in this area. However, the Commission believes that any follow-up action against the vessels should be carried out by the flag state and that it is the responsibility of the flag state to ensure that appropriate action is taken against any vessels infringing the conservation provisions for this area.[75]

However, the European Commission received calls to attention from other Member States of the EU for its pronouncements on this subject.[76] The Treaty of Paris not only affects fisheries, but also areas where the EU does not have an exclusive competence. At the time, the United Kingdom openly ruled on this issue, stating that maritime zones generated by Svalbard are subject to the provisions of the Treaty of Paris[77] and expressing its concern over the exploitation of the continental shelf (2006).[78] Now the European Commission admits that its actions at the time were precipitate and that it is not competent to rule on this issue alone.[79] The fisheries sector, in any case, wants the European Commission to clarify its position.[80] With regard to Spain, it does not seem to seek either direct or public confrontation on this issue.[81]

Russia, which in a moment of tension came to testify that the Svalbard waters constituted the high seas (2001),[82] seems to have abandoned this position with the treaty of maritime delimitation of 2010 between Norway and Russia. The treaty of 2010 does not affect the Treaty of Paris[83] but, as already explained, takes into account the maritime spaces of Svalbard that is, the Fisheries Protection Zone and continental shelf, to establish the delimitation. However, Russia continues to show its opposition.[84]

Non-discriminatory fishing regime

Norway maintains a non-discriminatory fishing regime in the waters of the Fisheries Protection Zone around Svalbard. For this reason, the debate on whether some specific measures established by Norway are discriminatory in regard of the fleet of another State, does not require the basis of the principle of non-discrimination to be addressed. However, given the lack of understanding between the parties as to whether or not there is discrimination, the next step could be to address the following reasoning: if the legal basis of the Fisheries Protection Zone around Svalbard is domestic law (as maintained by Norway), then the judicial route will be only in Norwegian courts; but if the Treaty of Paris applies to the Fisheries Protection Zone around Svalbard (as argued by many States which are party to the treaty), then the route may not end in the Norwegian courts; once the internal remedies are exhausted, the State concerned may exercise diplomatic protection of its nationals.

So far, three cases—relating to vessels of Iceland (Judgment, May 7, 1996), Spain (Judgment, November 27, 2006) and Germany (Judgment, March 21, 2014)—have reached the Supreme Court of Norway,[85] which has avoided ruling on the legal basis of the Fisheries Protection Zone around Svalbard, because it considered that Norway did not violate the principle of non-discrimination.

The principle of non-discrimination does not mean offering the same treatment to all parties, but allows for certain differences to be established. Discrimination occurs when dealing differently with similar situations. The differences must be based on objective criteria other than nationality, which is often not easy. For example, what would happen if Norway banned bottom trawls in the Fisheries Protection Zone around Svalbard? Could that possibly end Russian fishing there?[86]

With respect to the three cases on which the Supreme Court of Norway has ruled, the most controversial are the second and the third, where EU vessels were involved. However, it is interesting to refer to all three cases.

First, in 1996, the Supreme Court of Norway stated that the fact that the allocation of fishing quotas in the Fisheries Protection Zone around Svalbard was done by reference to traditional fishing in these waters—a criterion that left out Iceland—was not contrary to the principle of non-discrimination. Reference to historical catches is also the method used by the EU for allocating fishing quotas among Member States of the EU (known as relative stability).[87] In any case, it should also be noted that Europêche (Association of National Organizations of Fishery Enterprises in the EU) deems it appropriate to review the historic track records to reflect the "right" reference periods for allocation—thus avoiding repeating past mistakes—as well as the current state and migration patterns of the fish stocks.[88]

Second, in 2006, the Supreme Court of Norway adopted a controversial decision[89] which addressed the issue of reporting requirements for fishing in the Svalbard Fisheries Protection Zone.[90] The Supreme Court stated that the treatment Norway gave to Russia in connection with a breach of reporting requirements (warnings without enforcement), which differed from the treatment of the remaining States (warnings with enforcements), did not constitute a violation of the principle of non-discrimination and should be understood in the context of the broader fisheries-relations between Norway and Russia.[91]

Finally, in 2014, the Supreme Court of Norway had to deal with a matter on which the European Commission itself had formally protested: the regulation of fishing for haddock in the Fisheries Protection Zone around Svalbard. In 2011, Norway applied different conditions for Norwegian, Russian and Greenlandic vessels (quotas) and for EU and Faroese vessels (by-catches). The EU delegation in Oslo delivered a *note verbale* on July 8, 2011 to the Norwegian Ministry of Foreign Affairs indicating that these new regulations had been applied in a discriminatory manner and that they disregarded the specific provisions of the Treaty of Paris of 1920.[92] However, Norway has not changed the regulation (2012, 2013, 2014, and 2015).[93] The case on which the Supreme Court of Norway ruled in 2014 concerned the arrest of a German ship by the Norwegian authorities in 2012 for exceeding the percentage of by-catches conceded to EU vessels in the waters of the Svalbard Fisheries Protection Zone. In this case, the Supreme Court recognized that the conditions imposed on vessels from the EU causes a major economic loss, which is not justified by conservation requirements, but the court admitted it for reasons of immediacy: in 2010 the presence of haddock increased, EU vessels did not have a haddock quota in the Fisheries Protection Zone around Svalbard, there was a risk of overfishing and the by-catch regulation, in contrast to a quota arrangement, could be decided quickly and unilaterally by Norway. However, as mentioned before, this type of regulation has remained in force, a situation that continues to be criticized by Europêche[94] and also in the framework of the Long Distance Advisory Council (EU advisory council constituted in 2007 for the long-distance fleet).[95] In addition, a situation somewhat similar to that of the haddock, and which is also reported by the fishing industry, is that of the Greenland halibut.[96]

Conclusions

The main question that arises in connection with the Treaty of Paris is its geographic scope beyond the Svalbard territorial sea. However, so far, none of the parties involved have turned to international courts for resolution, even though Iceland has repeatedly threatened to go to the International Court of Justice.

The Norwegian Government is firm in its position: a clear and consistent statement about the non-application of the Treaty of Paris in maritime areas beyond the territorial sea. And its highest judicial body, the Supreme Court of Norway, avoids taking a position. This strategy is possible because so far in none of the cases has the violation of the principle of non-discrimination been considered, which was the argument put forward by the parties in reporting a violation of the Treaty of Paris in the Svalbard Fisheries Protection Zone.

However, it seems that the government of Norway, although standing firm, does not want the matter to reach the International Court of Justice (ICJ) and avoids major provocations that could cause such actions from the other parties to the Treaty of Paris. In any case, given that other States do not seem interested, for now, in litigation before the ICJ, Norway has not avoided tense situations, such as those generated by the regulation of haddock resulting in the formal protest of the EU. This regulation has been maintained by Norway since 2011, although its Supreme Court recognized its validity only as a preliminary measure.

For its part, the EU faces a complex legal situation regarding Svalbard. On the one hand, the Union is not a party to the Treaty of Paris, and although it has exclusive competence in the conservation and management of fishery resources, Norway does not seem to fully accept its competence in regards to the fishery in Svalbard waters. EU Member States are concerned about how the EU is handling this question. Furthermore, the Treaty of Paris does not only affect fishing; specifically, one of the most important issues is the exploitation of resources of the continental shelf, and the EU's competence in the area of energy is shared with the Member States.

At first, the EU accepted the competence of Norway to adopt conservation measures in the Fisheries Protection Zone around Svalbard, but rejected its competence to take coercive and punitive measures against any infringement of such measures by EU vessels as, according to the EU, such powers belonged to the flag State. That was the case in 2006 when the European Commission supported the Spanish and Portuguese claims. But, after the wake-up call that the European Commission received immediately from some EU Member States, especially the United Kingdom, it avoided further pronouncements on Norwegian competence on coercive measures and sanctions. Currently, the European fisheries sector is calling on the European Commission to clarify its position, although the Commission still maintains that it alone is not competent to rule on the issue.

However, the EU has steadily affirmed that the Treaty of Paris applies in the Fisheries Protection Zone around Svalbard. Does the EU have competence to take position on this issue (geographical scope of the treaty) and not on the previous one (extent of Norwegian powers)? As for the EU Member States which are parties to the Treaty of Paris, do they have to express their position if they do not want to be bound by this EU statement concerning the geographical scope? Do other States which are party to the Treaty of Paris have to accept this statement as part of the *acquis communautaire* if they join the EU at a future date?

In any case, despite the clarity and forcefulness of this statement by the EU on the geographical scope of the Treaty of Paris, its reaction to possible Norwegian infringements does not seem to be sufficiently strong (formal protest of the EU in 2011 in connection with the Norwegian haddock regulations, regulations that Norway has since maintained), or even sufficiently diligent (in 2014 the European Commission recognized that it was still studying the possible adverse effects of the maritime delimitation treaty of 2010 between Norway and Russia). The European Commission appears to act on these fishery issues in response to pressure rather than taking the initiative, and somehow it is understandable considering the debate on its competence to represent the interests of the EU States that are party to the Treaty of Paris. The pressure on the European Commission to act or not to act is exerted from within the structure of the EU, mainly by the European Parliament (Fisheries Commission) and the Regional Advisory Council (Long Distance Advisory Council), and from outside lobbying by the fishery sector, especially Europêche.

Finally, it should be remembered that the EU and Norway have excellent relations. Norway is a major economic partner of the EU and forms the European Economic Area together with Iceland and Liechtenstein. Where fisheries are concerned, even if the EEA does not apply to fishery products, it turns out that both at present and in the past, Norway has been the EU's most important partner.

The approach to this problem, therefore, requires taking account of both legal and policy considerations.

Annex

Regulations regarding the Fisheries Protection Zone around Svalbard*

Adopted by Royal Decree. June 3, 1977 pursuant to the Act of December 17, 1976 No. 91 relating to the Norwegian Economic Zone §1. Proposed by the Norwegian Ministry of Foreign Affairs. Modified August 12, 1994, No. 802, September 16, 1994, No. 874, July 13, 1995, No. 643, July 19, 1996, No. 704, March 2, 2001, No. 225.

§1 A fisheries protection zone is created in the waters off Svalbard for the conservation of the living resources of the sea and the regulation of fishing and hunting.

The outer limit of the Fisheries Protection Zone shall be at a distance of 200 nautical miles (one nautical mile = 1.852 meters) from the defined baselines, or where baselines are not established, from lines connecting the outermost points of the archipelagos.

The Fisheries Protection Zone is further limited by the limits of the exclusive economic zone off the Norwegian mainland, as determined by the Royal Decree of December 17, 1976.

Where the fisheries protection zone abuts another state's sovereign area, the boundary shall be drawn in accordance with agreement.

§2 The provisions of §3 of the Act of December 17, 1976, No. 91, relating to the Norwegian Economic Zone, are not yet applicable in the Fisheries Protection Zone.

§3 The Norwegian Ministry of Fisheries is authorized to determine:

1 Prohibitions to fish in specific areas in order to protect the growth of young fish and ensure the maintenance of stocks. The ban may be applied during the whole year or part of the year.
2 Provisions on equipment regulations and minimum sizes for fish.
3 Highest annual total allowable catch and fishing effort for each species. Catches and fishing effort can be appropriately distributed throughout the year, and to countries that can participate in the fishery.
4 Provisions concerning which countries' vessels are allowed to fish.
5 Provisions concerning the registration and other requirements to be satisfied before being allowed to participate in the fishery.
6 Provisions concerning the mesh size, dimensions and design of fishing gear.
7 Provisions concerning permitted by-catches.
8 Prohibition or regulation of catching methods and the use of tools.
9 Prohibition of specific uses of the catch.
10 Prohibition of having particular gear on board, and of storing fishing gear that cannot be used in the area in which the vessel is located.
11 Provisions concerning the duty and obligation to report catches, species, catching period, fishing ground, fishing gear, etc.
12 Provisions concerning the implementation of controls, including obligations for the vessel/owner.
13 Provisions concerning the duty to have and to use specific equipment for control, reporting and position determination. The ministry may determine the extent to which vessels should cover the cost of acquisition, installation and use of such equipment.

Amended by regulations August 12, 1994, No. 802, September 16, 1994, No. 874, July 19, 1996, No. 704, March 2, 2001, No. 225.

§4 Willful or negligent violation of the provisions laid down in or pursuant to this regulation are subject to penalties and forfeiture under the provisions of §8 and §9 of the Act of December 17, 1976, No. 91, relating to the economic zone.

Amended by Regulations of August 12, 1994, No. 802, September 16, 1994, No. 874 (formerly §6), July 13, 1995, No. 643.

§5 These regulations come into force on June 15, 1977.
Amended September 16, 1994, No. 874 (formerly §7).

* Non-official translation by Eric Eikrem.

Notes

1 Research carried out within the project MARSAFENET—NETwork of experts on the legal aspects of MARitime SAFEty and security (COST ACTION IS 1105)—and the Jean Monnet Centre of excellence of the University Institute for European Studies "Salvador de Madariaga" (University of A Coruña, Spain).

2 The author wishes to express her appreciation for the review and valuable comments made by Dr. Elena Conde, Complutense University of Madrid, and Dr. Sara Iglesias, Court of Justice of the European Union.

3 The treaty is officially titled "Treaty Concerning the Archipelago of Spitsbergen." However, the name of this Archipelago changed to become "Archipelago of Svalbard." The EU still uses the former name (more precisely, "Spitzbergen and Bear Island") to refer to the possibilities of cod catches in the 1987 Decision on the allocation of cod in the area (Council Decision of May 18, 1987, OJ L 135, May 23, 1987, 29) or in the annual distributions (Council Regulation 2015/104 of January 19, 2015; OJ L 22, January 28, 2015, 90, Cod in zones I and II B, n. 2). The official versions of the Treaty of Paris (in English and French) are available in the Norwegian Lovdata legal database, accessed July 20, 2015, http://emeritus.lovdata.no/traktater/texte/tre-19200209–001.html. There is also an unofficial abridged version in Spanish in José Manuel Sobrino, *Recopilación de Textos internacionales y de la Unión Europea* (A Coruña: Netbiblo, 2012), 684–85.

4 Other debates also arise, regarding the right of free and non-discriminatory access and entry to the archipelago by air. See Claudia Cinelli, "Spain in the Arctic," *Spanish Yearbook of International Law* 16 (2010): 7–8, accessed July 20, 2015, www.sybil.es/documents/ARCHIVE/vol. 16/Cinelli.pdf. More recently, the issue of entry restrictions during the visit to Svalbard of the Russian Deputy Prime Minister Dmitry Rogozin, blacklisted by Norway—in line with the EU—in response to Russia's actions undermining or threatening the territorial integrity, sovereignty and independence of Ukraine. Rogozin's visit took place in April 2015 and caused the reaction from Norway. See, among others, "Norway in Arctic Dispute with Russia over Rogozin Visit," *BBC News*, April 20, 2015, accessed July 20, 2015, www.bbc.com/news/world-europe-32380101.

5 For interpretation of the Treaty of Svalbard in the light of UNCLOS, see Marta Sobrido, "Interpretation of Conventional Regimes Prior to UNCLOS: Fishing Rights Recognized in the Svalbard Treaty (1920)," in *The Contribution of the United Nations Convention on the Law of the Sea to Good Governance of Seas and Oceans*, edited by José Manuel Sobrino (Naples: Scientifica, 2014), 197–222.

6 José Luis Meseguer, "Régimen jurídico de los espacios marítimos de Spitzberg (Svalbard). Posición de Noruega, España y otros Estados." *Revista Española de Derecho Internacional* 2 (2007): 632–35; Geir Ulfstein, *The Svalbard Treaty: From Terra Nullius to Norwegian Sovereignty* (Oslo: Scandinavian University Press, 1995).

7 Treaty of Paris, Article 1.

8 Treaty of Paris, Article 2, paragraph 1.

9 The Royal Decree of 22 February 1812 provided that:

> it shall be an established rule that in all cases where Our Majesty's territorial frontier at sea falls to be determined, it shall be reckoned according to the customary distance in nautical miles from the outermost island or islet not swept over by the sea,
>
> (www.un.org/depts/los/LEGISLATIONANDTREATIES/PDFFILES/
> NOR_1812_Decree.pdf, accessed July 20, 2015)

In accordance with the Counter-Memorial Submitted by the Government of Norway in the case of Maritime Delimitation in the Area Between Greenland

and Jan Mayen, *Denmark* v. *Norway* (hereinafter, Norwegian Counter-Memorial 1990), "the 1812 Decree fixed a limit of four nautical miles." International Court of Justice (ICJ), *Maritime Delimitation in the Area Between Greenland and Jan Mayen* (*Denmark* v. *Norway*) from May 11, 1990, volume I, paragraph 207, accessed July 20, 2015, www.icj-cij.org/docket/files/78/6615.pdf.

10 Treaty of Paris, Articles 8 and 9.

11 Treaty of Paris, Articles 2 and 3.

12 Generally speaking, nationals, but in relation to fisheries, Article 2 of the treaty speaks of "ships and nationals."

13 Many countries are contracting parties of the Treaty of Paris, but Norway is the state that while exercising its sovereignty over Svalbard must respect and ensure the non-discrimination principle.

14 As will be discussed later in the text, Norwegian law recognizes a non-discriminatory fishery regime in the Fisheries Protection Zone around Svalbard, but on the basis of Norwegian sovereignty.

15 Language problems prevent comprehensive monitoring of Norwegian case law (the author does not speak Norwegian). However, in the case of the vessel *Kiel*, the judgment of the Supreme Court, translated into English, refers to the lower courts saying that the District Court and the Court of Appeals based its reasoning on the Treaty of Paris not applying to the Svalbard Fisheries Protection Zone, but this Court also avoided ruling on the issue. Supreme Court of Norway, Judgment on the case 2013/1772, March 21, 2014, points 6 (District Court), 7 (Court of Appeals), 20, and 62, accessed July 20, 2015, www.domstol.no/en/Enkelt-domstol/-Norges-Hoyesterett/Summary-of-Recent-Supreme-Court-Decisions/Summary-of-Supreme-Court-Decision-2014/.

16 A set of nineteen Draft Articles on Diplomatic Protection was adopted by the International Law Commission (ILC) in 2006, accessed July 20, 2015, http://legal.un.org/ilc/texts/instruments/english/commentaries/9_8_2006.pdf. The question whether to adopt a convention on the basis of these articles is still being discussed at the General Assembly. In this chapter, those articles (hereinafter, Draft Articles on Diplomatic Protection) are taken as reference. According to Article 1:

> diplomatic protection consists of the invocation by a State, through diplomatic action or other means of peaceful settlement, of the responsibility of another State for an injury caused by an internationally wrongful act of that State to a natural or legal person that is a national of the former State with a view to the implementation of such responsibility.

17 The current stage of the codification is not going in the direction pointed out by the Special Rapporteur who proposed that in case of violations of *jus cogens*, the State should be responsible to some extent, but it has been formulated as a recommendation to States especially when there has been a serious injury (Draft Articles on Diplomatic Protection, Article 19). On this question, see John Dugard, "Articles on Diplomatic Protection," in *United Nations Audiovisual Library of International* (United Nations, 2013), 4, accessed July 20, 2015, http://legal.un.org/avl/ha/adp/adp.html.

18 Draft Articles on Diplomatic Protection, Article 14.

19 What does exist is a simulation: Model Court of Justice—"ModelCJ"—of FLAUMUN (Faculty of Law, Ankara University Model United Nations Club) is a student based activity where committees and commissions of the United Nations are simulated (http://modelcj.org/). On Svalbard, see the simulation case no. 24 of the International Tribunal for the Law of the Sea, Dispute concerning Svalbard Islands (*United Kingdom* v. *Norway*); Judgment of February 6, 2015, accessed July 20, 2015, http://modelcj.org/itloscase/.

20 The problem arises in connection with Icelandic vessels fishing for herring. See Geir H. Haarde, Minister for Foreign Affairs and External Trade of Iceland to the Althing on Foreign Affairs, *Report to the Althing on Foreign Affairs*, November 17, 2005, accessed July 20, 2015, www.mfa.is/news-and-publications/nr/2879:

> preparations for Iceland's legal proceedings against Norway before the International Court of Justice in the Hague on the Svalbard issue are well under way, as this appears to be the only way to protect Icelandic interests in the Svalbard region.

More recent, "Iceland Threatens Court Action Over Norwegian Herring Issue." *Fishupdate.com*, September 22, 2014, accessed July 20, 2015, www.fishupdate.com/iceland-threatens-court-action-over-norwegian-herring-issue-fishupdate-com/.

21 As it was noted above, in relation to fisheries, Article 2 of the treaty refers to "ships and nationals of all the High Contracting Parties."

22 In the past there was an exception. In view of the political situation at that time, the Treaty of Paris (Article 10) stated that: "until the recognition by the High Contracting Parties of a Russian Government shall permit Russia to adhere to the present Treaty, Russian nationals and companies shall enjoy the same rights as nationals of the High Contracting Parties." The Soviet Union (1922–1991, Russian Federation since 1991) did not become party to the Treaty of Paris until 1935.

23 In this regard, the website of the Norwegian Ministry of Justice and Public Security states that:

> [t]he effective exercise of authority [in Svalbard] over a long period of time combined with the fact that Norwegian sovereignty has not been challenged by other states forms an independent basis in public international law for Norwegian sovereignty over the area. This is of importance in international law in relation to states other than those that are parties to the Svalbard Treaty.

See www.regjeringen.no/en/find-document/dep/JD/reports-to-the-storting/19992000/report-no-9-to-the-storting-/4/id456892/, accessed December 29, 2014.

24 Rocks are an exceptions to this ruling. Since they cannot sustain human habitation or economic life on their own, they shall not have exclusive economic zone or continental shelf according to Article 121 UNCLOS. Further on islands, see Erik Frankx, "The Regime of Islands and Rocks," in *The IMLI Manual on International Maritime Law, Volume I, The Law of the Sea*, edited by David Attard, Malgosia Fitzmaurice and Norman Martínez (Oxford: Oxford University Press, 2014), 99–124.

25 Spaces regulated in Parts II (internal waters, territorial sea) and V (exclusive economic zone) of UNCLOS.

26 Act of March 24, 1961 relating to Norway's Fishery Limit, applied to mainland Norway and Jan Mayen. See also, Norwegian Counter-Memorial 1990, paragraph 211 and Act of June 17, 1966 No. 19 relative to the prohibition for foreigners to fish within the Norwegian territorial sea (http://faolex.fao.org/docs/pdf/nor13949E.pdf, accessed July 21, 2015) which states that "the fishery limit off Norway and Jan Mayen shall run at a distance of 12 nautical miles … outside and parallel to the baselines…," section 1.

27 When the Treaty of Paris came into force, the distance of the Norwegian territorial sea was about four miles (Royal Decree of February 22, 1812, customary distance). Subsequently, the distance of four miles is specified in other royal decrees (1970, 2001) in which the baselines of Svalbard are set for the purpose of delimiting the territorial sea. Royal Decree of September 25, 1970 (www.un.org/depts/los/LEGISLATIONANDTREATIES/PDFFILES/NOR_1970_DelimitationDecree.

pdf) was repealed by the Royal Decree of 1 June 2001; see *The Law of the Sea Bulletin* 46 (2001): 72–82, accessed July 21, 2015, www.un.org/depts/los/doalos_publications/LOSBulletins/bulletinpdf/bulletinE46.pdf.

28 The Royal Decree of February 22, 1812 was repealed by the Act of June 27, 2003 No. 57 relating to Norway's territorial waters and contiguous zone. This Act of 2003 stipulates, *inter alia*, that the breadth of Norway's territorial sea is twelve nautical miles measured from the baselines and entered into force on January 1, 2004 for mainland Norway, Svalbard and Jan Mayen. *The Law of the Sea Bulletin* 54 (2004): 94–98, accessed July 21, 2015, www.un.org/depts/los/doalos_publications/LOSBulletins/bulletinpdf/bulletin54e.pdf.

29 Royal Decree of September 25, 1970.

30 The Act No. 57 of June 27, 2003, which applies to all Norwegian waters, provides in paragraph 4 for the establishment of a contiguous zone. In relation to Svalbard, this has not been established. It has to be recalled that in the contiguous zone:

> the coastal State may exercise the control necessary to: (a) prevent infringement of its customs, fiscal, immigration or sanitary laws and regulations within its territory or territorial sea; (b) punish infringement of the above laws and regulations committed within its territory or territorial sea.
>
> (Article 33.1 UNCLOS)

Under the Treaty of Paris, Svalbard has a special status with regards to customs and tax (Article 8 states that collected taxes, dues and fees may only benefit Svalbard) and immigration (Article 3 states that citizens and companies from all treaty nations enjoy the same right of access to and residence in Svalbard).

31 Act No. 91 of December 17, 1976 relating to the Norwegian Economic Zone, accessed July 21, 2015, www.un.org/Depts/los/LEGISLATIONANDTREATIES/PDFFILES/NOR_1976_Act.pdf. The Zone Act was supplemented, on the same date, by a royal decree. Zone Act, paragraph 1: "An economic zone shall be established in the seas adjacent to the coast of the Kingdom of Norway. The King shall determine the date for the establishment of the economic zone and the waters to which it shall apply." Royal Decree of December 17, 1976 relating to the establishment of the Economic Zone of Norway: "(1) Pursuant to the Act of 17 December 1976 relating to the economic zone of Norway, the economic zone shall be established in the waters off the Norwegian mainland with effect from 1 January 1977," accessed July 21, 2015, www.un.org/depts/los/LEGISLATIONANDTREATIES/PDFFILES/NOR_1976_Decree.pdf.

32 According to different authors. See, for example, Meseguer, "Régimen jurídico," 654.

33 Laid down by Royal Decree of June 3, 1977 pursuant to the Act No. 91 of December 17, 1976 relating to the Norwegian Economic Zone §1. The author has not found any version in English. For an (unofficial) translation in English by Eric Eikrem, see Annex.

34 Norway has established three zones of 200 nautical miles: an exclusive economic zone around the Norwegian mainland (with effect from January 1, 1977), a Fisheries Protection Zone around Svalbard (with effect from June 15, 1977) and a fishery zone around Jan Mayen (with effect from May 29, 1980). All three zones were created pursuant to the Zone Act.

35 In fact, in case of violation, the Royal Decree that establishes the Fisheries Protection Zone around Svalbard refers to the Zone Act. This matter will be approached again later in the text when analyzing the adoption of coercive and punitive measures by Norway against vessels of other States which are party to the Treaty of Paris that were fishing in the Fisheries Protection Zone around Svalbard.

36 Norwegian Counter-Memorial 1990, paragraphs 229–31.
37 Royal Decree of June 3, 1977, paragraph 1:

> §1 … The outer limit for the Fisheries Protection Zone shall be at a distance of 200 nautical miles … The Fisheries Protection Zone is further limited by the limits of the exclusive economic zone off the Norwegian mainland, as determined by the Royal Decree of December 17, 1976. Where the fisheries protection zone abuts another state's sovereign area, the boundary shall be drawn in accordance with agreement.

Royal Decree of December 17, 1976, paragraph 1: "…The outer limit of the economic zone shall be drawn at a distance of 200 nautical miles … but not beyond the median line in relation to other States."

38 In February 2006, Norway, Denmark and Greenland signed an agreement on the delimitation of the continental shelf and fishing areas between Greenland and Svalbard (with effect from June 2, 2006). The agreement concerns the delimitation of the waters and continental shelf which are located within 200 miles of both parties. The midline principle was used to establish the delimitation. For the text of the treaty (and attached chart), see: Division for Ocean Affairs and the Law of the Sea Office of Legal Affairs, *Law of the Sea Bulletin* 75 (New York: United Nations, 2011): 18–21.
39 In 1957, Norway and the then USSR agreed on the maritime delimitation of their mainland territories in the waters of the fjord Varangerfjord. But beyond that area, they failed to agree: Norway claimed delimitation based on the midpoint; the USSR claimed delimitation based on the theory of the sectors, only corrected to respect the "Svalbard box." In 2007, the maritime delimitation of Varangerfjord was extended 73 km offshore. In 2010 Norway and Russia finally established the maritime delimitation of their waters and continental shelf in the Barents Sea and the Murmansk Treaty entered into force on July 7, 2011. The English text and the chart are available on the Norwegian Government's website: https://www.regjeringen.no/en/aktuelt/treaty/id614254/. The treaty has been studied by different authors: Pål Jakob Aasen, *The Law of Maritime Delimitation and the Russian-Norwegian Maritime Boundary Dispute*, FNI Report 1 (2010), accessed July 21, 2015, www.fni.no/doc&pdf/FNI-R0110.pdf; Tore Henriksen and Geir Ulfstein, "Maritime Delimitation in the Arctic: The Barents Sea Treaty," *Ocean Development & International Law* 42.1 (2011): 1–21; Øystein Jensen, "Current Legal Developments in the Barents Sea," *The International Journal of Marine and Coastal Law* 26 (2011): 151–68.
40 Nansen Basin is located in the Arctic Ocean; Banana Hole is an international enclave in the Norwegian Sea; and Loop Hole is an international enclave in the Barents Sea. See the chart (Figure 1) contained in the "Executive Summary of the Submission" of the "Continental Shelf Submission of Norway in Respect of areas in the Arctic Ocean, the Barents Sea and the Norwegian Sea," accessed July 21, 2015, www.un.org/depts/los/clcs_new/submissions_files/submission_nor.htm.
41 On continental shelf, see Part VI (Articles 76–85) of UNCLOS.
42 UNCLOS, Article 76 (1):

> 1. The continental shelf of a coastal State comprises the seabed and subsoil of the submarine areas that extend beyond its territorial sea throughout the natural prolongation of its land territory to the outer edge of the continental margin, or to a distance of 200 nautical miles from the baselines from which the breadth of the territorial sea is measured where the outer edge of the continental margin does not extend up to that distance.

43 The UNCLOS provides that the State that intends to establish the outer limits of its continental shelf beyond the 200 nautical miles, must submit to the CLCS characteristics of that limit with scientific and technical support information. The CLCS will make recommendations to the State; continental shelf limits finally determined by the State, based on the recommendations of the CLCS, will be final and binding.

44 The continental shelf of Norway in the Western Nansen Basin is based on the continental shelf of Svalbard. The continental shelf of Norway in the Banana Hole consists of two parts: the continental shelf of Svalbard and mainland Norway to the east; and the continental shelf of Jan Mayen to the west. The continental shelf of Norway in the Loop Hole is based on the continental shelf of Svalbard and mainland Norway.

45 "Commission on the Limits of the Continental Shelf, Recommendations of the Commission on the Limits of the Continental Shelf in Regard to the Submission made by Norway in Respect of Areas in the Arctic Ocean, the Barents Sea and the Norwegian Sea," on November 27, 2006, adopted on March 27, 2009, accessed July 21, 2015, www.un.org/Depts/los/clcs_new/submissions_files/submission_nor.htm.

46 Kingdom of Denmark, Submission, December 15, 2014, accessed July 21, 2015, www.un.org/depts/los/clcs_new/submissions_files/submission_dnk_76_2014.htm.

47 In this regard, Churchill and Ulfstein point out that this argument, as well as the argument that the Treaty of Paris only applies to the territorial sea, has been developed in detail by two Norwegian writers who have close connections with the Norwegian Ministry of Foreign Affairs, but who write in a personal capacity: Professor Carl August Fleischer, at the time special consultant to the Ministry, and Mr. Rolf Einar Fife, at that time Director General of the Legal Affairs Department of the Ministry. Robert Churchill and Geir Ulfstein, "The Disputed Maritime Zones around Svalbard," paper presented at Panel XI, Changes of the Arctic Environment and the Law of the Sea, Martinus Nijhoff Publishers, October 2011, 566, accessed July 21, 2015, http://papers.ssrn.com/sol3/papers.cfm?abstract_id=1937583. Most detailed writings of Fleischer and Fife on this issue are in Norwegian, but they also have written in English and French. For example, Fleischer wrote in 1976:

> To which areas do the provisions of the Treaty concerning mineral rights and, further, the mining regulations apply? The answer is the islands plus their territorial waters, which go out to 4 nautical miles from the baselines as for other parts of Norway. The continental shelf is subject to the ordinary Norwegian legislation on the shelf ... There are two legal grounds for this position, both of which are sufficient. First, there is nothing in the Treaty which gives Norway special obligations in respect of the continental shelf ... Even if there should be a special "Spitzbergen continental shelf" it would fall under article i of the Treaty, which would retain the full freedom of the Norwegian legislature. Second, there is a single continuous continental shelf which stretches from the Northern coast of Norway up to and around Svalbard. The provisions of international law for delimitation of the shelf by a median line or by agreement apply only to the case where the continental shelf is adjacent to two different states. Svalbard is not "another state" in relation to Norway.
> (Carl August Fleischer, "Oil and Svalbrd." *Nordisk Tidsskrift for International Ret* 45 (1976): 7–13)

In 2007, Fleischer still stated that "the continental shelf and the 200 miles zones have not been included in the specific restrictions agreed to in the Treaty; which means that there is no basis for applying the restrictions in those areas" but he was no longer defending the existence of a single continuous continental shelf as argument against the application of the Treaty of Paris. Carl August Fleischer, "The New International Law of the Sea and Svalbard," (paper presented at the symposium *Politics and Law – Energy and Environment in the Far North* organized by The Norwegian Academy of Science and Letters, January 25, 2007), 6, accessed July 21, 2015, www.dnva.no/binfil/download.php?tid=27095.

48 As Churchill and Ulfstein note (*supra* note 47, 567–68), the proposition that Svalbard has no continental shelf contradicts Article 121 of UNCLOS, under which every island, apart from an uninhabitable rock, has a continental shelf.

49 On the maximum distance of the outer limit of the continental shelf, see Article 76 of UNCLOS.

50 Now Norway clearly distinguishes the geological perspective:

> In Svalbard's case, it is also clear from all maps of the seabed that a continuous continental shelf extends north from mainland Norway and around and past Svalbard. The geological situation is therefore not significantly different from that of the Shetland Islands on the United Kingdom shelf, or that of Novaya Zemlya and Franz Josef Land on the Russian shelf. In geological terms, it would therefore not be appropriate to talk about Svalbard having its own, continental shelf,

> from the legal perspective: "Like all land areas, Svalbard's coasts generate continental shelf." "The Continental Shelf—Questions and Answers." Norwegian Government website, October 30, 2009, accessed July 21, 2015, www.regjeringen.no/no/dokumenter/the-continental-shelf-questions-and-an/id583774/.

51 Countries of Europe (25), Asia (7), America (6), Africa (2) and Oceania (2). The full list can be consulted on the website of the Governor of Svalbard, Svalbard Treaty, June 14, 2012, accessed July 21, 2015, www.sysselmannen.no/en/Toppmeny/About-Svalbard/Laws-and-regulations/Svalbard-Treaty/.

52 Until 2004, the date of entry into force of the fifth enlargement of the EU, only three of the fifteen EU countries were not parties to the Treaty of Paris (Luxembourg, Ireland and Austria). With the successive enlargements of the EU, this situation has been changing. Some of the States that have joined the EU were already parties to the Treaty of Paris at the time of joining the EU (Estonia, Poland, Bulgaria and Romania) or achieved such status later (the Czech Republic in 2006, Lithuania in 2013). Currently, the following countries are not parties to the Treaty of Paris: Cyprus, Croatia, Slovakia, Slovenia, Ireland, Latvia, Luxembourg and Malta.

53 Joining the treaty has clear advantages for States with interests in the area. For instance, in relation to the adhesion of Lithuania to the Treaty of Paris in 2013, Evaldas Ignatavičius, the acting Vice-Minister of Foreign Affairs, said when introducing the draft law on the ratification:

> In respect of the Lithuanian interests, it is a truly important treaty, because we have already had cases when our ships, having crossed the territorial boundaries of the Archipelago, were seized and were requested to pay fines. Thus, we will be able to avoid such incidents in the future once we ratify the treaty and it comes into effect.
> ("Seimas Ratified International Documents." Press Release of Seimas of the Republic of Lithuania, December 4, 2012, accessed July 21, 2015, http://www3.lrs.lt/pls/inter/w5_show?p_r=9252&p_d=131064&p_k=2)

54 According to Article 8 of the Treaty of Paris,

> Norway undertakes to provide for the territories ... [of the Archipelago of Spitsbergen] mining regulations which, especially from the point of view of

imposts, taxes or charges of any kind … shall exclude all privileges, mono-
polies or favours for the benefit of the State or of the nationals of any one
of the High Contracting Parties, including Norway … Taxes, dues and
duties levied shall be devoted exclusively to the said territories and shall not
exceed what is required for the object in view. So far, particularly, as the
exportation of minerals is concerned, the Norwegian Government shall
have the right to levy an export duty which shall not exceed 1% of the
maximum value of the minerals exported up to 100.000 tons, and beyond
that quantity the duty will be proportionately diminished.

55 As will be seen later, there were some controversies over the continental shelf of
Svalbard in the 1970s (as a result of the Norwegian statement considering the continental shelf of Svalbard as extension of the mainland continental shelf) and in
the 1980s (as a result of the Norwegian extension of the area for petroleum
exploration, from the waters of mainland Norway towards Svalbard). More
recently, in January 2015, the opening of three blocks for oil drilling in the
Barents Sea announced in the 23rd licensing round provoked Russian diplomatic
protest (Note from the Russian Embassy to Norway to the Norwegian Foreign
Ministry, dated March 3). Russia believes these blocks belong to the Svalbard continental shelf and that production of oil and gas there should be regulated by the
Treaty of Paris. As the Head of the environmental organization Bellona notice,
"[i]n order not to increase the tension between Norway and Russia, Norway
should let the disputed blocks lie." Trude Petterson, "Russia Protects Drilling in
Svalbard Zone." *BarentsObserver*, May 5, 2015, accessed July 21, 2015, http://barent-
sobserver.com/en/energy/2015/05/russia-protests-drilling-svalbard-zone-05-05.

56 As noted by Geir Ulfstein at a conference "Petroleum Activities in the Disputed
Areas around Svalbard?" (Arctic Frontiers, January 22, 2013, *Tromsø*, Norway), the
issue of implementing the Treaty of Paris in the continental shelf is "the elephant
in the room": everyone sees it but nobody talks about it. Accessed May 6, 2016,
http://webtv.uit.no/Mediasite/Play/8e883eda3aba4e1b9546a13feca3df0b1d.

57 With regard to the importance of the EU in international fishing, among other
studies, see Belén Sánchez Ramos, "El papel de Unión Europea en la institucionalización de las relaciones marítimas internacionales," in *The Contribution of
the United Nations Convention on the Law of the Sea to Good Governance of Seas and
Oceans*, edited by José Manuel Sobrino (Naples: Scientifica, 2014), 407–28; José
Manuel Sobrino and Gabriela Oanta, "Los Acuerdos Internacionales de Pesca
instrumentos indispensables de la Política Pesquera Común de la Unión
Europea," *Noticias de la Unión Europea* 326 (2012): 51–65.

58 Janez Potočnik, Member of the EU Commission:

> I would like to deliver this answer on behalf of my colleague, Commissioner
> Damanaki … Let me underline the sensitivity of this important fishery-
> related issue. It concerns delicate aspects of international law and, more
> importantly, has a bearing on our relations with Norway which, at present
> and historically, has been our most important partner in fisheries and also
> other marine-related, including Arctic, issues.
>
> (Janez Potočnik, "Svalbard Archipelago and its Fisheries Resources,"
> (debate at the meeting of the Fishery Commission of the European
> Parliament on February 26, 2014), accessed July 21, 2015, www.europarl.
> europa.eu/sides/getDoc.do?pubRef=-//EP//TEXT+CRE+20140226+ITEM-
> 019+DOC+XML+V0//EN)

59 In 2014, the EU was still studying the possible adverse effects of the maritime
delimitation treaty of 2010 between Norway and Russia.

> The Commission is currently investigating whether the single delimitation
> line has any adverse effect for Union fishing vessels operating in the waters

in question, and whether it is in any way contestable under applicable international law and the relevant provisions of the United Nations Convention on the Law of the Sea in particular.

(Potočnik, "Svalbard Archipelago.")

60 As we will see later, the attitude of certain EU Member States, who showed their displeasure when a few years ago the European Commission acted on its own in relation to the Treaty of Paris. On the scope of the EU Law concerning the continental shelf (of the Members States of the EU) in the light of the jurisprudence of the EU Court of Justice, see Jorge A. Quindimil, "La plataforma continental como ámbito de aplicación del derecho de la Unión Europea a la luz de la jurisprudencia del Tribunal de Justicia." *Revista de Derecho Comunitario Europeo* 48 (2014): 529–49.

61 Carmen Fraga Estévez, member of the European Parliament,

Keep in mind that the uncompromising stance of Norway is based on the fact that the Commission is not a signatory to the Treaty of Paris. For this reason, Norway would only negotiate with the Member States; in turn, the Commission prevents these states from negotiating bilaterally [with Norway] fishing quotas, because it is an exclusive competence of the EU.

(Carmen Fraga, "Svalbard Archipelago and its fisheries resources" (speech at the meeting of the Fishery Commission of the European Parliament, February 26, 2014), trans. the author)

62 Meseguer, for example, refers to the document that Netherlands circulated in 1986 between the Permanent Missions of the Member States to the European Commission. Among other things, Meseguer notes that in this document the Netherlands clearly stated that issues relating to fishing activities in Svalbard should be treated separately and, consequently, the EU could not accept in any way an association with other issues related to the relationship between Norway and the EU. The Netherlands declared that exchanging Svalbard areas for something else (eventually market concessions) was not acceptable. Meseguer, "Régimen jurídico," 659–60.

63 Torbjørn Pedersen, "The Dynamics of Svalbard Diplomacy." *Diplomacy & Statecraft* 19.2 (2008): 238–43.

64 EC Commission note verbale No. 00146 to Norway on July 19, 1977, quoted in Pedersen, "The Dynamics of Svalbard Diplomacy," note 41.

65 Since 1993, it has been divided into two states: the Czech Republic and Slovakia.

66 Especially the tension arising in the 1980s when Norway extended the area for petroleum exploration into the Barents Sea from the waters of mainland Norway towards the Svalbard archipelago, which caused the reaction of the United Kingdom and the Soviet Union. Pedersen, "The Dynamics of Svalbard Diplomacy," 243–45.

67 Allocation of fishing possibilities taking into account the history of catches. This formula leads to an unequal distribution (not everyone can fish the same) but it is not necessarily discriminatory. This issue will be addressed in the section "Non-Discriminatory Fishing Regime" of this chapter.

68 Conde states that Spanish interests on the exploitation of the living resources of the Arctic are or may be susceptible to a clash with the same interests on the part of two major Arctic States, Canada and Norway. About Spanish interests v. Norwegian interests, Conde focuses on Svalbard. Elena Conde Pérez, "Geopolítica del Ártico. Especial referencia a los intereses de España en la región ártica," in *Geopolítica del Ártico: Dos visiones complementarias. España–Singapur* (Madrid: Ministerio de Defensa, 2014), 27–28, accessed July 21, 2015, www.defensa.gob.es/ceseden/Galerias/destacados/publicaciones/docSegyDef/ficheros/066_LA_GEOPOLITICA_DEL_ARTICO._DOS_VISIONES_COMPLEMENTARIAS._ESPANA-SINGAPUR.pdf.

69 Kristian Åtland and Torbjørn Pedersen, "Cold War Legacies in Russia's Svalbard Policy," in *Environmental and Human Security in the Arctic*, edited by Gunhild Hoogensen Gjørv, Dawn Bazely, Marina Goloviznina and Andrew Tanentzap (London: Routledge, 2014), 28–31; Roger Howard, *The Arctic Gold Rush: The New Race for Tomorrow's Natural Resources* (London and New York: Continuum, 2009), 99–101.

70 On sovereign rights and jurisdiction of the coastal state in the exclusive economic zone, see Article 56.1.b UNCLOS.

71 According to Milano and Papanicolopulu,

> in the case of real uncertainty concerning entitlement to a specific area, the presence of good faith joined with the objective impossibility of establishing beforehand who will be awarded the area in question, makes it particularly difficult for one State to claim the international responsibility of the other for breach of its sovereignty or sovereign rights.
>
> (Enrico Milano and Irini Papanicolopulu, "State Responsibility in Disputed Areas on Land and at Sea." *Heidelberg Journal of International Law* 71 (2011): 637, accessed July 21, 2015, www.zaoerv. de/71_2011/71_2011_3_a_587_640.pdf)

72 Norway considered that these vessels were carrying out illegal fishing. On illegal fishing, Gabriela A. Oanta, "Illegal Fishing as a Criminal Act at Sea," in *La criminalité en mer/Crimes at Sea*, edited by Efthymios D. Papastavridis and Kimberley N. Trapp (Leiden and Boston, MA: Martinus Nijhoff Publishers, 2014), 149–97. On illegal fishing in the Barents Sea, see Olav Schram Stokke, "Barents Sea Fisheries: The IUU Struggle." *Arctic Review of Law and Politics* 2 (2010): 207–24.

73 In this regard, the intervention of the Spanish Government before the Spanish parliament in 2006 is very illustrative. The Spanish government stated that:

> Spain considers that although Norway has powers to establish fishing regulations…, this Government rejects that the fisheries protection zone around Svalbard is equivalent to the exclusive economic zone of Norway, and thus this Government rejects that Norway has the competence neither to assume nor execute measures with regards to ships flying the Spanish flag. Thus, if evidence of infringement has been found following an inspection of the Norwegian Coast Guard, Norway should transfer the resulting inspection report to the Spanish fisheries administration for it to apply measures accordingly. However, this approach is not shared by Norway, which considers that these waters are comparable to its exclusive economic zone, which would entitle it to arrest vessels which have allegedly violated the fishing regulations in force.
>
> (Martin Fragueiro, Secretary General of Marine Fisheries, Hearing of the Spanish Government before the Parliament, September 13, 2006, trans. the author, accessed July 21, 2015, www.congreso.es/ public_oficiales/L8/CONG/DS/CO/CO_643.PDF)

74 Session 2692 of the Council of the European Union "Agriculture and Fisheries," November 22–24, 2005.

75 EU Commission, Answer to the parliamentary question E-4303/06 of December 11, 2006, in *Parliamentary Questions Addressed by Members of the European Parliament to other EU Institutions and Bodies, and their Answers*, accessed July 21, 2015, www.europarl.europa.eu/plenary/en/parliamentary-questions.html.

76 Erik J. Molenaar, "Fisheries Regulation in the Maritime Zones of Svalbard." *The International Journal of Marine and Coastal Law* 27 (2012): 25.

77 In this note verbale of March 11, 2006 to the Government of Norway, the British Government states,

> [t]he United Kingdom considers that the Svalbard archipelago ... generates its own maritime zones, separate from those generated by other Norwegian territory, in accordance with the United Nations Convention on the Law of the Sea. It follows therefore that there is a continental shelf and an exclusive economic zone which pertain to Svalbard ... the United Kingdom considers that maritime zones generated by Svalbard are subject to the provisions of the Treaty of Paris.
>
> > (Reproduced in Letter on the Fisheries Regulation in the Maritime Zones of Svalbard of July 18, 2014 sent by Europêche and Copa-Cogeca to the Fisheries Commissioner (hereinafter, Letter Europêche 2014), accessed July 21, 2015, http://chil.me/download-file/b1cd1e46-58e2-4662-be86-74bdf45b837f)

78 Further:

> the United Kingdom considers that maritime zones generated by Svalbard are subject to the provisions of the Treaty of Paris, in particular article 7, which requires that Svalbard should be open on a footing of equality to all parties to the Treaty and article 8, which inter alia specifies the tax regime which applies to the exploitation of minerals in Svalbard. The United Kingdom expects that the Norwegian authorities will fully comply with the obligations of Norway under the Treaty of Paris, as set out above,
>
> > (Letter Europêche 2014)

79 The author of this work attended a meeting in 2013 where a representative of the Commission admitted this to representatives of the fisheries sector.

80 Letter Europêche 2014:

> Europêche takes note of past notifications issued by the Commission challenging the restricting and enforcement measures over non-Norwegian vessels adopted by this country in the maritime zone of the Svalbard [Notes Verbales No. 26/04, 32/09]. However, this position seems to be altered in the recent Note Verbale 19/11 [in line with the UK's position above] where the European Commission accepts the regulations proposed by Norway subject to: 1. The application of the non-discrimination principle; 2. Based on scientific advice; 3. Respected by all interested Parties. We are extremely interested to know whether the aforementioned position is indeed the new approach adopted by the European Commission on the subject.

81 The Press Release of the Spanish Ministry of Agriculture, Food and Environment, states:

> The [Spanish] Secretary General of Fisheries ... signed ... a Memorandum of understanding with the Norwegian fisheries authorities in connection with monitoring, control and surveillance of fisheries.... During the meeting that preceded the signing, delegations from both countries have addressed other issues of interest such as fisheries in the waters of Svalbard.... The talks aim to facilitate the access of Spanish vessels to waters governed by the Treaty of Paris of 1920 and the continuation of Spanish investigations to determine the status of the populations of Greenland halibut.
>
> > (Spanish Ministry of Agriculture, Food and Environment, Press release, January 9, 2013, trans. Marta Sobrido, accessed July 21, 2015, www.magrama.gob.es/ca/prensa/13.01.09%20Carlos%20Dominguez%20memor%C3%A1ndum%20Noruega_tcm8–243105.pdf)

82 Pedersen, "The Dynamics of Svalbard Diplomacy," 247.

83 Article 6 of the Treaty between Norway and Russia concerning Maritime Delimitation and Cooperation in the Barents Sea and the Arctic Ocean states:

> The present Treaty shall not prejudice rights and obligations under other international treaties to which both the Kingdom of Norway and the Russian Federation are Parties, and which are in force at the date of the entry into force of the present Treaty.

84 Valery Konyshev and Alexander Sergunin, "Russia's Policies on the Territorial Disputes in the Arctic." *Journal of International Relations and Foreign Policy* 2.1 (2014): 75, accessed July 21, 2015, http://aripd.org/journals/jirfp/Vol_2_No_1_March_2014/4.pdf.

85 On the 1996 Decision of 1996 (Rt-1996–624), R. Churchill, "Norway: Supreme Court Judgment on Law of the Sea Issues." *International Journal of Marine and Coastal Law* 11 (1996): 576. Summaries of the Decisions adopted in 2006 (case 2006/871; ref. HR-2006–1997-A – Rt-2006–1498) and 2014 (case 2013/1772; ref. HR-2014–00577-A) are available on the official website of the Supreme Court of Norway (hereinafter, Summary of Supreme Court decisions): www.domstol.no/en/Enkelt-domstol/-Norges-Hoyesterett/The-Supreme-Court-of-Norway-/. On the last case, Tore Henriksen, "Norwegian By-Catch Regulations Alleged to Violate the Svalbard Treaty." *The JCLOS Blog*, March 18, 2014, accessed July 21, 2015, http://site.uit.no/jclos/2014/03/18/norwegian-by-catch-regulations-alleged-to-violate-the-svalbard-treaty/; and Irene Dahl, "Norwegian By-Catch Regulations are Not Discriminatory." *The JCLOS Blog*, June 2, 2014, accessed July 21, 2015, http://site.uit.no/jclos/2014/06/02/norwegian-by-catch-regulations-are-not-disciminatory/.

86 As noted by Zilanov, deputy head of the Federal Russian Fishery's Agency public chamber, the fishery industries of Russia and Norway are asymmetric. Russia catches 95 percent of its fish with bottom trawls and 5 percent by line. The Norwegians use lines to catch 70 percent; trawling only accounts for 30 percent. Therefore, Norway could introduce new rules on trawlers or could even ban bottom trawls; this second measure would end the Russian fishing in the Fisheries Protection Zone around Svalbard. Cited in Anna Korppoo, Nina Tynkkynen and Geir Hønneland, *Russia and the Politics of International Environmental Regimes: Environmental Encounters or Foreign Policy?* (Cheltenham: Edward Elgar, 2015), 105.

87 In fact, the EU has not adequately taken into account the historical catches of its Member States. But that is a matter which goes beyond the subject of this chapter.

88 Letter Européche 2014.

89 For a critical review, see Churchill and Ulfstein, "The Disputed Maritime Zones around Svalbard," 587.

90 Two Spanish fishing vessel captains were fined for failing to keep catch logbooks for cod in the Fisheries Protection Zone around Svalbard. One of them was also fined for incorrect reporting of cod caught in the same area. The appellants' argument that they have been unfairly discriminated was related to the reporting obligation in the "Regulations of 21 September 1994 No 880 relating to Regulatory Measures for Fishing in the Fisheries Protection Zone around Svalbard." This argument was based particularly in the fact that Russian vessels consistently fail to comply with the reporting rules, but Norwegian authorities only issued warnings to the ship owning companies in such cases. According to the appellants, foreign policy considerations were the reason why the Norwegian authorities had not taken stronger measures against these violations of regulations.

91 The Supreme Court has noted that Norway and Russia agree on an annual total quota for the northeast Arctic cod fishery, and Russian vessels' catches are thereby included in Russia's part of the total quota irrespective of whether the fishing takes place in the Fisheries Protection Zone around Svalbard, in the Norwegian exclusive economic zone or in the Russian exclusive economic zone. It is therefore the Russian, not the Norwegian, authorities that carry out quota controls in relation to both individual Russian vessels and shipowning companies and that carry out controls of fishing under the Russian part of the total quota.

92 Information contained in the answer given by the Commission to the parliamentary question E-P-006711/2011 of August 5, 2011.

93 The quotas and percentages of by-catches have been amended, but not the difference in treatment based on nationality.

94 Letter Europêche 2014.

95 Long Distance Advisory Council, Letter R-04–13/WG2 to the Fisheries Committee of the European Parliament regarding Svalbard. Subsequently, the organization has continued to address the issue, see, Working group 2, Draft agenda of the meeting of November 4, 2014. Both letter and draft agenda can be accessed on www.ldrac.eu/.

96 The letter states:

> Concerning the Greenland halibut, Norway has issued a general prohibition of catching this species both in the territorial waters of Svalbard (Reg. No 1518) and in its Fisheries Protection Zone (Reg. No 1524). However, it contains an exception allowing vessels which have a license to catch this species in the Norwegian exclusive economic zone, to fish in the territorial waters and Fisheries Protection Zone of Svalbard in order to complete their quota. These regulations aimed to protect the good state of the stock, yet, at the same time, become a legal use provoking a de facto exclusion of the EU fishing fleet from those waters (even from the territorial waters where there is no controversy on the scope of the Spitsbergen Treaty, i.e. it fully applies); while allowing the Russian and Norwegian fleet to catch up to 96% of the quota available,
>
> (Letter Europêche 2014)

References

Aasen, Pål Jakob. *The Law of Maritime Delimitation and the Russian-Norwegian Maritime Boundary Dispute.* FNI Report 1 (2010), accessed July 21, 2015, www.fni.no/doc&pdf/FNI-R0110.pdf.

Åtland, Kristian and Torbjørn Pedersen. "Cold War Legacies in Russia's Svalbard Policy." In *Environmental and Human Security in the Arctic,* edited by Gunhild Hoogensen Gjørv, Dawn Bazely, Marina Goloviznina and Andrew Tanentzap. London: Routledge, 2014, 17–36.

BBC News. "Norway in Arctic Dispute with Russia over Rogozin Visit." April 20, 2015, accessed July 20, 2015, www.bbc.com/news/world-europe-32380101.

Churchill, Robert. "Norway: Supreme Court Judgment on Law of the Sea Issues." *International Journal of Marine and Coastal Law* 11 (1996): 576–580.

Churchill, Robert and Geir Ulfstein. "The Disputed Maritime Zones around Svalbard." Paper presented at Panel XI, *Changes of the Arctic Environment and the Law of the Sea,* Martinus Nijhoff Publishers (October 3, 2011), accessed July 21, 2015, http://papers.ssrn.com/sol3/papers.cfm?abstract_id=1937583.

Cinelli, Claudia. "Spain in the Arctic." *Spanish Yearbook of International Law* 16 (2010): 7–8, accessed July 20, 2015, www.sybil.es/documents/ARCHIVE/vol.16/Cinelli.pdf.

Conde Pérez, Elena. "Geopolítica del Ártico: Especial referencia a los intereses de España en la región ártica." In *Geopolítica del Ártico: Dos visiones complementarias. España-Singapur.* Madrid: Ministerio de Defensa, 2014, 15–33, accessed July 21, 2015, www.defensa.gob.es/ceseden/Galerias/destacados/publicaciones/doc SegyDef/ficheros/066_LA_GEOPOLITICA_DEL_ARTICO._DOS_VISIONES_COMPLEMENTARIAS._ESPANA-SINGAPUR.pdf.

Dahl, Irene. "Norwegian By-Catch Regulations are Not Discriminatory." *The JCLOS Blog,* June 2, 2014, accessed July 21, 2015, http://site.uit.no/jclos/2014/06/02/norwegian-by-catch-regulations-are-not-disciminatory/.

Division for Ocean Affairs and the Law of the Sea Office of Legal Affairs. "Executive Summary of the Submission" of the "Continental Shelf Submission of Norway in Respect of Areas in the Arctic Ocean, the Barents Sea and the Norwegian Sea," accessed July 21, 2015, www.un.org/depts/los/clcs_new/submissions_files/submission_nor.htm.

Division for Ocean Affairs and the Law of the Sea Office of Legal Affairs. *Law of the Sea Bulletin* 46 (New York: United Nations, 2001): 72–82, accessed July 21, 2015, www.un.org/depts/los/doalos_publications/LOSBulletins/bulletinpdf/bulletin E46.pdf.

Division for Ocean Affairs and the Law of the Sea Office of Legal Affairs. *Law of the Sea Bulletin* 54 (New York: United Nations, 2004): 94–98, accessed July 21, 2015, www.un.org/depts/los/doalos_publications/LOSBulletins/bulletinpdf/bulletin 54e.pdf.

Division for Ocean Affairs and the Law of the Sea Office of Legal Affairs. *Law of the Sea Bulletin* 75 (New York: United Nations, 2011): 18–21, accessed July 21, 2015, www.un.org/depts/los/doalos_publications/LOSBulletins/bulletinpdf/bullet-in75e.pdf.

Dugard, John. "Articles on Diplomatic Protection." *United Nations Audiovisual Library of International* (2013): 1–9, accessed July 20, 2015, http://legal.un.org/avl/ha/adp/adp.html.

EU Commission. Answer to the parliamentary question E-4303/06 of December 11, 2006, in *Parliamentary Questions Addressed by Members of the European Parliament to other EU Institutions and Bodies, and their Answers,* accessed July 21, 2015, www.europarl.europa.eu/plenary/en/parliamentary-questions.html.

Fishupdate. "Iceland Threatens Court Action Over Norwegian Herring Issue." *Fishupdate.com,* September 22, 2014, accessed July 20, 2015, www.fishupdate.com/iceland-threatens-court-action-over-norwegian-herring-issue-fishupdate-com/.

Fleischer, Carl August. "Oil and Svalbard." *Nordisk Tidsskrift for International Ret* 45 (1976): 7–13.

Fleischer, Carl August. "The New International Law of the Sea and Svalbard." Paper presented at the symposium *Politics and Law – Energy and Environment in the Far North* organized by The Norwegian Academy of Science and Letters, January 25, 2007, 6, accessed July 21, 2015, www.dnva.no/binfil/download.php?tid=27095.

Fragueiro, Martin. Secretary General of Marine Fisheries, Hearing of the Spanish Government before the Parliament, September 13, 2006, trans. the author, accessed July 21, 2015, www.congreso.es/public_oficiales/L8/CONG/DS/CO/CO_643.PDF.

Frankx, Erik. "The Regime of Islands and Rocks." In *The IMLI Manual on International Maritime Law, Volume I, The Law of the Sea,* edited by David Attard, Malgosia Fitzmaurice and Norman Martínez. Oxford: Oxford University Press, 2014, 99–124.

Governor of Svalbard. Svalbard Treaty, June 14, 2012, last updated April 25, 2016, accessed May 6, 2016, www.sysselmannen.no/en/Toppmeny/About-Svalbard/Laws-and-regulations/Svalbard-Treaty/.

Haarde, Geir H. *Report to the Althing on Foreign Affairs.* November 17, 2005, accessed July 20, 2015, www.mfa.is/news-and-publications/nr/2879.

Henriksen, Tore. "Norwegian By-Catch Regulations Alleged to Violate the Svalbard Treaty." *The JCLOS Blog,* March 18, 2014, accessed July 21, 2015, http://site.uit.no/jclos/2014/03/18/norwegian-by-catch-regulations-alleged-to-violate-the-svalbard-treaty/.

Henriksen, Tore and Geir Ulfstein. "Maritime Delimitation in the Arctic: The Barents Sea Treaty." *Ocean Development & International Law* 42.1 (2011): 1–21.

Howard, Roger. *The Arctic Gold Rush: The New Race for Tomorrow's Natural Resources.* London and New York: Continuum, 2009.

International Court of Justice (ICJ). *Maritime Delimitation in the Area Between Greenland and Jan Mayen (Denmark v. Norway)* from May 11, 1990, volume I, paragraph 207, accessed July 20, 2015, www.icj-cij.org/docket/files/78/6615.pdf.

International Law Commission (ILC). Draft Articles on Diplomatic Protection, 2006, accessed July 20, 2015, http://legal.un.org/ilc/texts/instruments/english/commentaries/9_8_2006.pdf.

Jensen, Øystein. "Current Legal Developments in the Barents Sea." *The International Journal of Marine and Coastal Law* 26 (2011): 151–68.

Kingdom of Denmark. Submission, December 15, 2014, accessed July 21, 2015, www.un.org/depts/los/clcs_new/submissions_files/submission_dnk_76_2014.htm.

Konyshev, Valery and Alexander Sergunin, "Russia's Policies on the Territorial Disputes in the Arctic." *Journal of International Relations and Foreign Policy* 2.1 (2014): 55–83, accessed July 21, 2015, http://aripd.org/journals/jirfp/Vol_2_No_1_March_2014/4.pdf.

Korppoo, Anna, Nina Tynkkynen and Geir Hønneland. *Russia and the Politics of International Environmental Regimes: Environmental Encounters or Foreign Policy?.* Cheltenham: Edward Elgar, 2015.

Letter Europêche 2014. British Government note verbale to the Government of Norway, March 11, 2006, reproduced in Letter on the Fisheries Regulation in the Maritime Zones of Svalbard of July 18, 2014 sent by Europêche and Copa-Cogeca to the Fisheries Commissioner, accessed July 21, 2015, http://chil.me/download-file/b1cd1e46-58e2-4662-be86-74bdf45b837f.

Meseguer, José Luis. "Régimen jurídico de los espacios marítimos de Spitzsberg (Svalbard). Posición de Noruega, España y otros Estados." *Revista Española de Derecho Internacional* 2 (2007): 631–63.

Milano, Enrico and Irini Papanicolopulu. "State Responsibility in Disputed Areas on Land and at Sea." *Heidelberg Journal of International Law* 71 (2011), 587–640, accessed July 21, 2015, www.zaoerv.de/71_2011/71_2011_3_a_587_640.pdf.

Model Court of Justice of FLAUMUN (Faculty of Law, Ankara University Model United Nations Club). Simulation case no. 24 of the International Tribunal for the Law of the Sea, Dispute concerning Svalbard Islands (*United Kingdom* v. *Norway*), Judgment of February 6, 2015, accessed July 20, 2015, http://modelcj.org/itloscase/.

Molenaar, Erik J. "Fisheries Regulation in the Maritime Zones of Svalbard." *The International Journal of Marine and Coastal Law* 27 (2012): 3–58.

Norwegian Counter-Memorial 1990, Act of June 17, 1966, No. 19, accessed July 21, 2015, http://faolex.fao.org/docs/pdf/nor13949E.pdf.

Norwegian Economic Zone. Act No. 91 of December 17, 1976 relating to the Norwegian Economic Zone, accessed July 21, 2015, www.un.org/Depts/los/LEGISLATIONANDTREATIES/PDFFILES/NOR_1976_Act.pdf.

Norwegian Government. "The Continental Shelf—Questions and Answers." Norwegian Government website, October 30, 2009, accessed July 21, 2015, www.regjeringen.no/no/dokumenter/the-continental-shelf-questions-and-an/id583774/.

Norwegian Ministry of Justice and Public Security. accessed December 29, 2014, www.regjeringen.no/en/find-document/dep/JD/reports-to-the-storting/19992000/report-no-9-to-the-storting-/4/id456892/.

Oanta, Gabriela A. "Illegal Fishing as a Criminal Act at Sea." In *La criminalité en mer/Crimes at Sea*, edited by Efthymios D. Papastavridis and Kimberley N. Trapp. Leiden and Boston, MA: Martinus Nijhoff Publishers, 2014, 149–97.

Pedersen, Torbjørn. "The Dynamics of Svalbard Diplomacy." *Diplomacy & Statecraft* 19.2 (2008): 236–62.

Petterson, Trude. "Russia Protects Drilling in Svalbard Zone." *BarentsObserver*, May 5, 2015, accessed July 21, 2015, http://barentsobserver.com/en/energy/2015/05/russia-protests-drilling-svalbard-zone-05-05.

Potočnik, Janez. "Svalbard Archipelago and its Fisheries Resources." Debate at the meeting of the Fishery Commission of the European Parliament on February 26, 2014, accessed July 21, 2015, www.europarl.europa.eu/sides/getDoc.do?pubRef=-//EP//TEXT+CRE+20140226+ITEM-019+DOC+XML+V0//EN.

Quindimil, Jorge A. "La plataforma continental como ámbito de aplicación del derecho de la Unión Europea a la luz de la jurisprudencia del Tribunal de Justicia." *Revista de Derecho Comunitario Europeo* 48 (2014): 529–49.

Sánchez Ramos, Belén. "El papel de Unión Europea en la institucionalización de las relaciones marítimas internacionales." In *The Contribution of the United Nations Convention on the Law of the Sea to Good Governance of Seas and Oceans*, edited by José Manuel Sobrino. Naples: Scientifica, 2014, 407–28.

Seimas, Republic of Lithuania. "Seimas Ratified International Documents." Press Release, December 4, 2012, accessed July 21, 2015, http://www3.lrs.lt/pls/inter/w5_show?p_r=9252&p_d=131064&p_k=2.

Sobrido, Marta. "Interpretation of Conventional Regimes Prior to UNCLOS: Fishing Rights Recognized in the Svalbard Treaty (1920)." In *The Contribution of the United Nations Convention on the Law of the Sea to Good Governance of Seas and Oceans*, edited by José Manuel Sobrino. Naples: Scientifica, 2014, 197–222.

Sobrino, José Manuel and Gabriela Oanta. "Los Acuerdos Internacionales de Pesca instrumentos indispensables de la Política Pesquera Común de la Unión Europea." *Noticias de la Unión Europea* 326 (2012): 51–65.

Spanish Ministry of Agriculture, Food and Environment, Press release, January 9, 2013, trans. Marta Sobrido, accessed July 21, 2015, www.magrama.gob.es/ca/prensa/13.01.09%20Carlos%20Dominguez%20memor%C3%A1ndum%20Noruega_tcm8–243105.pdf.

Stokke, Olav Schram. "Barents Sea Fisheries: The IUU Struggle." *Arctic Review of Law and Politics* 2 (2010): 207–24.

Supreme Court of Norway. Judgment on the case 2013/1772, March 21, 2014, points 6 (District Court), 7 (Court of Appeals), 20, and 62, accessed July 20, 2015, www. domstol.no/en/Enkelt-domstol/-Norges-Hoyesterett/Summary-of-Recent-Supreme-Court-Decisions/Summary-of-Supreme-Court-Decision-2014/.

Treaty of Paris (in English and French). Norwegian Lovdata legal database, accessed July 20, 2015, http://emeritus.lovdata.no/traktater/texte/tre-19200209–001.html.

Treaty of Paris (in Spanish). Unofficial abridged version in José Manuel Sobrino, *Recopilación de Textos internacionales y de la Unión Europea.* A Coruña: Netbiblo, 2012, 684–85.

Ulfstein, Geir. *The Svalbard Treaty: From Terra Nullius to Norwegian Sovereignty.* Oslo: Scandinavian University Press, 1995.

Ulfstein, Geir. "Petroleum Activities in the Disputed Areas around Svalbard?." Arctic Frontiers conference, January 22, 2013, Tromsø, Norway, accessed May 6, 2016, http://webtv.uit.no/Mediasite/Play/8e883eda3aba4e1b9546a13feca3df0b1d.

6 Stewardship sovereignty, sustainable development and the protection of the Arctic marine environment

Injecting environmental values in international sovereignty law

Sven G. Kaufmann

Introduction

The Ilulissat Declaration of May 15, 2008,[1] signed by the five Arctic coastal states—Canada, Denmark, Norway, the Russian Federation and the United States of America—has been widely discussed and criticized. The main catalyst for this debate was the potential challenge the said Declaration poses to the existing Arctic cooperation system as core Arctic issues, such as climate change, were to be dealt with outside the existing fora such as the Barents Forum or, most notably, the Arctic Council.[2] Regardless of the accuracy of such an assumption, the Ilulissat Declaration constitutes a clear statement in favor of the legal status quo of the Arctic Ocean under International Law.[3] Whereas the same states have without question, committed themselves both prior to and since the Ilulissat Declaration to an effective protection of the Arctic marine environment[4]—an ecologically highly sensitive ecosystem particularly vulnerable to human interferences and accidents such as oil spills[5]—the fact that the declaration was the result of a multilateral meeting of the five coastal states only, taking place on an ad hoc basis outside the established framework by any intergovernmental forum (including the Arctic Council), stresses the notion of territorial sovereignty of coastal states.

Nevertheless, the Declaration also delineates a further statement, which has attracted less attention among legal scholars, but the five Arctic coastal states have explicitly recognized: "the Arctic Ocean is a unique ecosystem, which [the Arctic five] have a stewardship role in protecting."[6] In the preceding decades, the international legal system has slowly turned away from its primary objective of securing and strengthening state sovereignty, thus opening itself to the integration of what has been coined as "common interests." Such interests tend to transcend the interests of individual states and rather aim to protect the public goods of the international community as a whole. It is widely agreed that the protection of the environment is a common interest of the international community as a whole and constitutes the core of modern International Environmental Law.[7]

As Judge Weeramantry declared in his separate opinion in the Gabcikovo-Nagymaros Case almost twenty years ago,

> we have entered an era of International Law in which International Law subserves not only the interests of individual States, but looks beyond them and their parochial concerns to the greater interests of humanity and planetary welfare [...] international environmental law will need to proceed beyond weighing the rights and obligations of parties within a closed compartment of individual State self-interest, unrelated to the global concerns of humanity as a whole.[8]

In the end, the reasoning poses the question as to whether environmental protection should, as a core value under international law, prevail over state interests. In the affirmative, the matter of limitations to state sovereignty, justified under ecological considerations, seems to be a valid issue warranting reflection.

The aim of this contribution is to highlight several elements that could arise from the Arctic coastal states' commitment to their stewardship role under international law, with a special focus on a possible recourse to the principle of sustainable development in areas which are effectively or potentially subject to the extended continental shelf regime. After assessing the shortcomings of current International Sovereignty Law, the potential implications of the stewardship role endorsed by the Arctic coastal states under International Environmental Law will be examined. With regard to the limited scope of this contribution, it will focus on the general prospect of restricting the sovereign rights of exploitation under environmental considerations and the obligation to conduct environmental impact assessments (EIAs) for exploitation activities on the marine subsoil.

Coastal state sovereignty under international law and shortcomings concerning the exploitation and protection of Arctic marine hydrocarbon resources

The existing legal framework

The international legal framework applicable in the Arctic Ocean has been abundantly described. However, in order to examine any issue of potential limitations to the exercise of coastal state territorial sovereignty and sovereign rights, the relevant exploitation and protection regimes applicable to Arctic waters under international law require depiction so as to allow for an examination of the appropriateness of such limitations.

Coastal state sovereignty: exploitation and protection regimes

The United Nations Convention on the Law of the Sea (UNCLOS)[9] provides a comprehensive exploitation regime of seabed resources. As a specific mechanism of allocation of natural resources, the extended continental shelf regime is of special interest in discussing the issue of potential sovereignty limitations.

GENERAL RULES

Under Article 193 UNCLOS, states have the sovereign right to exploit their natural resources pursuant to their environmental policies and in accordance with their duty to protect and preserve the marine environment.[10] Articles 2 and 3 UNCLOS state that the sovereignty of coastal states extends to encompass its territorial sea up to a limit not exceeding twelve nautical miles, measured from the baselines. As for the area beyond this limit and up to 200 nautical miles—the continental shelf—Article 77 (1) UNCLOS provides that coastal states exercise sovereign rights for the purpose of exploring it and exploiting its natural resources. Under Article 81 UNCLOS, the coastal state shall have the exclusive right to authorize and regulate drilling on the continental shelf for all purposes.

Notwithstanding the semantic but eventually insubstantial distinction between sovereignty and sovereign rights,[11] UNCLOS grants coastal states a sovereign right to exploitation, as far as the territorial sea is concerned, and an exclusive right to exploitation in terms of the continental shelf. Therefore, coastal states are thus able to decide whether and to what extent resources shall be exploited. The fact that the United States is not a party to UNCLOS does not significantly alter its obligations under international law, as most of UNCLOS' provisions reflect Customary Law.[12]

Beyond the continental shelf lies the Area, which is qualified as Common Heritage of Mankind under Article 136 UNCLOS. According to Article 137 (1) UNCLOS, no state shall claim or exercise sovereignty or sovereign rights over any part of the Area or its resources, nor shall any state or natural or juridical person appropriate any part thereof. Consequently, the Area is subject to an internationalized exploitation regime under the auspices of the International Seabed Authority (the Authority).[13]

As recognized under Customary Law, territorial sovereignty allows states within the aforementioned limits to conduct or authorize such activities as they choose within their territory, including activities that may have adverse effects on their own environment, insofar as said activities within their jurisdiction and control respect the environment of other states or of areas beyond national control.[14]

THE EXTENDED CONTINENTAL SHELF REGIME

The apportionment of the seabed and subsoil of the submarine areas extending beyond the territorial sea is subject to a regime known as the extended continental shelf regime. Under Article 76 (4)–(6) UNCLOS, a coastal state whose outer limits of the continental shelf extend beyond 200 nautical miles from the baselines is entitled to claim a continental shelf of up to 350 nautical miles.[15] The coastal state can assert its sovereign rights for the purpose of exploring and exploiting natural resources on the extended continental shelf, as provided for in Article 77 (1) UNCLOS.[16]

Approximately one-third of the whole continental shelf in the Arctic Ocean could be subject to coastal states' claims under the extended continental shelf regime, hence reducing the Area to a mere 10 percent of the Arctic Ocean.[17] The exercise of state jurisdiction over the continental margin beyond 200 nautical miles substantially consistent with Article 76 UNCLOS is widely seen as a rule of Customary Law.[18] The only compensatory provision for this encroachment is provided for in Article 82 UNCLOS, according to which coastal states exploiting resources on their continental shelf beyond 200 nautical miles are bound to make payments and contributions through the Authority.

The environmental protection regime

Both UNCLOS and Customary Law as well as International Environmental Law provide the relevant international rules concerning marine environmental protection in the Arctic Ocean.

REQUIREMENTS UNDER UNCLOS

Under Article 192 UNCLOS, states have the general obligation to protect and preserve the marine environment. Article 194 UNCLOS lays down the specifications of this general obligation. Under Article 194 (1) UNCLOS, states shall take, individually or jointly as appropriate, all measures that are necessary to prevent, reduce and control pollution of the marine environment from any source, using for this purpose the best practicable means at their disposal. Of particular interest is paragraph 2 which provides that states shall take all measures necessary to ensure that activities under their jurisdiction or control are so conducted as not to cause damage by pollution to other states and their environment, and that pollution arising from incidents or activities under their jurisdiction or control does not spread beyond the areas where they exercise sovereign rights in accordance with this Convention. In addition, Article 196 (1) UNCLOS stipulates that states shall take all measures necessary to prevent, reduce and control pollution of the marine environment resulting from the use of technologies under their jurisdiction or control.

In relation to pollution stemming from seabed activities subject to national jurisdiction, Article 208 UNCLOS stipulates that: (1) Coastal states shall adopt laws and regulations to prevent, reduce and control pollution of the marine environment arising from or in connection with seabed activities subject to their jurisdiction and from artificial islands, installations and structures under their jurisdiction; and (2) States shall take other measures as may be necessary to prevent, reduce and control such pollution. Despite a number of international environmental agreements in the field of marine protection, International Environmental Law does not provide for notable, legally binding regulatory mechanisms concerning exploration and exploitation activities within the territorial sea or the continental shelf.

Article 206 UNCLOS puts a general obligation on states to assess, as far as is practicable, the potential effects of activities under their jurisdiction or control on the marine environment when they have reasonable grounds for believing that planned activities may cause substantial pollution of or significant and harmful changes to the marine environment.

REQUIREMENTS UNDER CUSTOMARY LAW

In addition to the requirements under UNCLOS, coastal states are also subject to substantial or procedural environmental obligations imposed by Customary Law, this fact being especially relevant with regard to the United States, who is not a party to UNCLOS and therefore is exclusively bound by customary rules.

Customary International Law provides substantial rules and places several obligations on coastal states in order to counterbalance the fact that they have complete jurisdiction over their natural resources. In this vein, we ought to particularly note the no-harm principle, which forbids states from causing significant transboundary environmental harm and obliges them to take adequate measures to control and regulate in advance sources of potential significant transboundary harm.[19] The precautionary principle is also generally considered Customary Law, requiring that, where there are reasonable grounds for concern that serious or irreversible damage might occur, effective and proportional measures should be taken to prevent environmental degradation even in the absence of scientific certainty.[20] Furthermore, the obligation to use best environmental practices could also be taken into consideration, although its binding nature is still doubtful due to lack of state practice. Among the relevant procedural obligations, one can note the requirement to undertake an environmental impact assessment where there is a risk that the proposed industrial activity may have a significant adverse impact in a transboundary context[21] as well as the requirement to inform potentially concerned states in case of activities and incidents that may have transboundary effects.[22]

It has to be noted that the obligation to conduct environmental impact assessments (EIAs), as embodied in Article 206 UNCLOS, does not yet represent a rule of Customary Law.[23]

REQUIREMENTS UNDER INTERNATIONAL ENVIRONMENTAL LAW

Several global multilateral environmental agreements place substantial obligations on coastal states in the field of shipping security and the prevention of marine pollution from ships, notably the MARPOL Convention,[24] the SOLAS Convention,[25] the STCW Convention[26] and the London Convention 72/96.[27] However, these conventions have been designed for ship navigation and provide only very limited, non-mandatory regulations for offshore activities.[28] Regulations drafted in international fora such as the Arctic Council, notably the Arctic Offshore Oil and Gas Guidelines,[29] are not legally binding. No mandatory requirements concerning navigation in ice-covered waters have yet been adopted, as the existing regulations (the *Polar Shipping Guidelines*[30] and the *Arctic Shipping Guidelines*),[31] adopted under the auspices of the International Maritime Organization (IMO), contain only legally non-binding provisions.

A mandatory International Code for Ships Operating in Polar Waters (Polar Code) is due to enter into force in January 2017 subsequent to its adoption by IMO's Maritime Safety Committee in November 2014 and its Marine Environment Protection Committee on May 15, 2015.[32]

On a regional level, the OSPAR Convention[33] delineates provisions aimed at both maritime security and offshore activities. However, it covers only Arctic waters belonging to the North-East Atlantic. The only regional Arctic conventions concluded so far are the Agreement on the Conservation of Polar Bears and their Habitats of November 15, 1973[34] and, drafted within the frame of the Arctic Council, the Arctic Search and Rescue Agreement of May 12, 2011[35] and the Agreement on Cooperation on Marine Oil Pollution Preparedness and Response in the Arctic of May 15, 2013.[36] The latter two provide no substantial obligations relevant to the permissibility of exploration or exploitation activities in the Arctic Ocean.

Territorial sovereignty of Arctic coastal states and the protection of the marine environment

The wide recognition of coastal states' territorial sovereignty over the natural resources on the continental shelf underlies the five Arctic coastal states' statement in the Ilulissat Declaration. It has thus been described as a "pre-emptive strike against growing global in the Arctic, and a determination to re-territorialize the Arctic Ocean."[37] UNCLOS mainly seeks to achieve an equitable balance between economic and environmental interests. In this respect, UNCLOS favors the economic interests of coastal states over environmental interests of the international community, in the sense that the adoption of provisions concerning environmental protection is left to international state cooperation or national legislation. Even if this is consistent with the nature of UNCLOS' environmental provisions in Part XII as a mere framework,[38] environmental protection is subject to the states' willingness to cooperate and, eventually, legislate. Furthermore, effective international cooperation in this field requires clear determination of territorial jurisdiction over Arctic waters, which it seems is not the case.[39] This may be one of the main reasons for the lack of comprehensive, legally binding international provisions governing navigational and off-shore activities in Arctic waters. The exact scope and effectiveness of the mandatory Polar Code remains to be seen.

On the one hand, the best solution may indeed be to allocate jurisdiction over marine resources to coastal states that are actually able and incentivized to control them, as they would be among the first to be exposed to any harm caused by exploitation activities. On the other hand, this approach simultaneously implies that the rights to exploitation concerning potentially vulnerable areas are thus given exactly to those states who may also have the least interests in actually protecting and preserving marine resources if they have the actual ability to exploit them.[40] Regulations and limitations to the exploitation activities under international law focus on the potential transboundary effects of activities, which is in fact a valid criteria in order to fix delimitations of two or more sovereign states' interests, but falls short in terms of effective environmental protection. This is also true as far as the Common Heritage of Mankind regime over the Area is concerned, because this regime has no direct environmental purpose and rather aims at the collective use of resources as opposed to the actual protection of the marine environment and its resources.[41] What is even more disturbing is that the extended continental shelf regime allows coastal states to impede on the common heritage regime, clearly placing coastal states' sovereign interests above conservation, not to mention long-term protection of the Area.

Nonetheless, even if the Common Heritage of Mankind regime does not aim at the preservation of the marine environment, but rather at the temporary preservation of its resources in view of its future exploitation, taking into account the interests and needs of, *inter alia*, developing states,[42] the prohibition of state activities outside of the frame of Part XI of UNCLOS[43] shows that international law has developed towards the recognition of limitations to state sovereignty for the sake of superior interests.[44] At the same time, the weight apportioned to an effective protection of the environment under international law, even if it appears in opposition to state interests recognized by traditional international law, will have to increase with the passing of time. Indeed, the understanding of the environment as a "living system, rather than a storehouse of commodities to be extracted,"[45] may lead lawyers who are more interested in protection than exploitation of marine resources to argue in favor of further limitations of state sovereignty. This might seem even more plausible as far as the Arctic Ocean is concerned, where coastal states maintain traditional territorial sovereignty over a highly vulnerable area of international interest while high ecological risks cannot be dismissed.

Regarding specific substantial obligations on behalf of coastal states, UNCLOS largely refers to the cooperation duty incumbent on states (Article 197), thereby leaving it to the states acting alone or through competent international organizations, notably the IMO, to elaborate relevant provisions concerning the prevention, reduction and control of pollution in the marine environment. Environmental protection of the Arctic Ocean thus falls to the coastal states themselves, with the exception of "The Area," which is subject to an international body, the International Seabed Authority (Article 145 UNCLOS).

Although the Arctic has been, for years, considered in need of a comprehensive legal regime, tailored to its specific needs,[46] no specific mandatory regime has emerged so far, and any substantial development seems most improbable in light of the Ilulissat Declaration.[47] Consequentially, as coastal states are the main actors of international marine environmental protection, the very concept of territorial sovereignty will have to be challenged.[48] Hereinafter, the Arctic coastal states' commitment to their stewardship role over the Arctic Ocean as a potential limitation to their territorial sovereignty will be examined.

Environmental obligations entailing restrictions on its discretionary power to use the territory under its jurisdiction, do exist as far as risks or pollutions have a transboundary impact or an impact on areas outside national jurisdiction. However, states enjoy wide discretionary power as long as such risks or pollutions remain limited to its sovereign territory. Functional sovereignty of coastal states over their marine resources is awarded regardless of the actual need for protection of the marine environment.

Stewardship role, stewardship sovereignty and limitations to territorial sovereignty of coastal states

Stewardship and sovereignty of coastal states

As important as territorial sovereignty is to the current international legal order, the graduation of the possibility of individual state appropriation over marine areas in the sense of a functional sovereignty is at the core of UNCLOS. Indeed, the Law of Sea differentiates, as far as the seabed and subsoil of the submarine areas are concerned, between the territorial sea, the continental shelf[49] and the Area, thus providing a differentiated allocation of resources by balancing coastal states' interests and the interests of the international community as a whole through an interweaving of national jurisdiction and international competences.[50]

The notion of (ocean) stewardship is profoundly linked to the notion of responsibility[51] and often connected to other "legal metaphors,"[52] all describing, essentially, a special commitment to the preservation and protection of a marine area, involving both rights and duties. Under UNCLOS, the International Seabed Authority can been seen as having stewardship over the Area, as it watches over activities being carried out for the benefit of mankind as a whole (Article 140 [1]) and acts on behalf of mankind as a whole (Article 137 [2]). It thus upholds a collective interest in a legally protected entity. If this understanding of stewardship over resources or an area is to be broadened, the steward, being either an international body or a state, would merely be administering an area placed under its stewardship, which necessarily excludes control in the sense of full jurisdiction by virtue of territorial sovereignty. The steward would therefore have, to a certain extent, control and rights over resources or an area, but said control or rights must be exercised for the benefit of specific others, be it mankind or the international community, or, more extensively, for the benefit—in the sense of preservation—of the resources or the area themselves. Hence, a state's stewardship over resources or a defined area put, in any form, under its jurisdiction under international law, must entail restrictions to its sovereignty, which may coincide with functional restrictions under specific legal regimes. However, its substantive content cannot be limited to the environmental obligations that follow, as a counterbalance, from the sovereignty itself, because the notion of stewardship would be utterly meaningless. A strict distinction between, on the one hand, territorial sovereignty and, on the other, a Common Heritage of Mankind regime, is not necessarily the only way of looking at the management of areas, especially since international environmental law is given more and more weight in the shaping of international law. The power exercised by a steward state over resources or an area put under its jurisdiction under international law could therefore be coined as "stewardship sovereignty,"[53] entailing substantial restrictions to the freedom of action of the steward state under international law.

Such an understanding could not only encompass the possibility of a stewardship regime such as the Common Heritage of Mankind, where the beneficiary is mankind, but also an understanding of stewardship for the benefit of the environment itself. It is evident that this does not entail prohibition of state activities by negating its sovereignty as such. However, it would entail a more conceptual understanding of state sovereignty in the sense of the obligation to protect the marine environment, put on coastal states under Articles 192 and the following. UNCLOS and Customary Law were not considered only as a mere obligation under International (Environmental) Law. The protection of the marine environment should also be considered to be a value inherent to coastal state sovereignty, amounting to a general inherent limitation to its scope and extent. This limitation can be seen as the consequence of a coastal state's stewardship obligation (duty) of environmentally sustainable development. Thus understanding would mark a step towards the transformation of the role of steward states into a role akin to that of actual trustees which must protect and augment the object of the trust for its own sake.[54]

Stewardship sovereignty of coastal states and environmental stewardship obligations

The stewardship obligation (duty) of environmentally sustainable development can be based on a combination of the public trusteeship doctrine and the principle of sustainable development.

Elements of the public trust doctrine: responsibility towards humanity and the environment itself

The notion of stewardship sovereignty is generally considered to be closely linked to the Anglo-American doctrine of public trust, whose application on an international level has been widely debated since the 1970s. More recently however, the debate has turned its attention to principle of trusteeship as applied specifically to earth resources under international law.[55] In the context of environmental protection, the concept of Common Heritage of Mankind, as enshrined by UNCLOS regarding the Area, has been described as one of the most developed applications of a trusteeship—mankind as a whole as the beneficiary of the trusteeship obligations.[56] The public trust doctrine is generally regarded as encompassing two core elements, namely the obligation to use natural resources with due regard to intra- and intergenerational equity and the observation of the principle of sustainable development.[57] In the absence of an international institution, states could be considered as trustees through the idea of a functional dual role, thus administering an area not only with their own interests in mind but also as a representative of humanity as a whole.[58] To fail in the protection, conservation and prudential management of the heritages would violate the trust and legal obligations implicit in responsibly supervising the Earth's heritage for future generations.[59] Hence, in order to give substance, a trustee—or, as it might seem, a steward—state would have substantial obligations to refrain from any action that is inconsistent with sustainable development.

Regardless of the actual appropriateness of the public trust doctrine for ensuring an effective framework of state sovereignty under environmental considerations,[60] this doctrine appears to have several weaknesses. First, one of the major flaws is that it is likely to permit state sovereignty both to be restricted and broadened.[61] There have been examples of legal implementation of their stewardship role by coastal states, mostly through the establishment of maritime protection zones involving restrictions to the design, construction, equipment and manning of passing vessels.[62] Even though such initiatives may yield environmental benefits, the trust doctrine risks, however, being misused. Second, application of the trust doctrine is generally considered as covering resources that ought to belong to the commons and, consequently, they are placed beyond state jurisdiction, such as the Area as Common Heritage of Mankind.[63] This ultimately conditions any potential trusteeship to the common decision of one or more states to subject a certain area to a certain protection regime. Potentially then, this could lead to a particular coastal state appointing itself as guardian of the marine environment. Third, the beneficiary of public trusteeship on an international level is generally considered to be mankind or the international community, not the environment as such, which weakens the scope of environmental protection.

However, it could be argued that the marine environment as such is both an object and beneficiary of the trusteeship relation.[64] The admissibility of curtailing state sovereignty on environmental grounds has also been discussed from alternative angles, such as the lawfulness of environmental intervention of one state on another state's territory for the sake not only of the said state's population or the international community, but also for the sake of the protection of the environment as such.[65] Such an understanding of a trusteeship relationship, would, however, entail the need to disconnect the trustee condition of a coastal state over its marine environment, considered a global common, both from its own decision and from the question whether this environment is located within or beyond state jurisdiction. This would eventually mean that the coastal state cannot exercise full sovereignty on grounds of its trusteeship—or stewardship—relationship over its marine environment.

Stewardship sovereignty and the principle of sustainable development

If an inherent limitation to sovereignty under a trusteeship relation between state and its marine environment is to be recognized, the question arises concerning the adequate justification and scope of such a legal implementation of a stewardship relationship. Since the core of the question touches upon the need to reconcile economic development with protection of the environment[66] within state jurisdiction, the principle of sustainable development would seem to be a fitting legal instrument.

The principle of sustainable development is, foremost, a guiding principle of state action of a general scope. The normative content of the principle of sustainable development has been discussed for quite some time. Critics have argued that sustainable development is a mere objective of state action, lacking normative content as every state would be entitled to shape it under its own national law to a large extent.[67] It is generally accepted that the sustainable development principle encompasses four legal elements, namely the principle of intergenerational equity, the principle of sustainable use, the principle of equitable use or intragenerational equity and the principle of integration.[68] The last element is generally understood as the need for policy makers to take into account the inter-dependencies and importance of nature and to consider the impacts and implications of proposed policies.[69] These elements are also, to a certain extent, reflected in the ecosystem-based management approach, advocated by many marine experts in order to address environmental issues related to ocean governance.[70]

Regardless of the actual normative value of the sustainable develop-ment principle in the sense of the conventional sources of international law, as stated in Article 38 (1) of the ICJ-Statute, the sheer evidence of state commitment to sustainable development on a global and regional level[71] could entail a link between the exercise of state sovereignty and the sustainable principle. This link could take the shape of balancing-test norm, in the sense that it establishes the relationship between different primary norms,[72] or regulates the implementation of one single primary norm. It is therefore a normative instrument in the sense that it not only serves as a tool of interpreting existing agreements,[73] but it also shapes the discretionary power inherent in state action itself.[74] It permits the integra-tion of environmental considerations in the design and implementation of economic development activities, which, eventually, are nothing more than the exercise of sovereignty and sovereign rights by a state. Eventually, the principle of sustainable development comes down to the acceptance, on foremost environmental grounds, of limits placed upon the use and exploitation of natural resources.[75]

When considering the principle of sustainable development as a limita-tion to coastal state sovereignty, it is a matter of shaping the sovereign right to exploit natural resources in accordance with a state's duty to protect and preserve the marine environment.[76] In other words, sover-eignty is eroded by a duty of environmentally sustainable resource use. Hence, one could argue in favor of the emergence of a general limitation of coastal state sovereignty under International Environmental Law, essen-tially giving rise to a "sustainability test" to be applied when sovereignty and sovereign rights are being exercised. Obligations of coastal states under the principle of sustainable development, which could be labeled as environmental stewardship obligations, could be seen not as deriving from a rule of Customary Law, but rather as a requirement of the exercise of territorial sovereignty. Such an approach, based on a modern reflection on the significance given to the effective protection of the marine environ-ment for its own sake under international law and the awareness of the necessity of ecosystem-based management techniques, could be justified under trusteeship and sustainable development principles, linked with the principle of sovereignty of coastal states over their natural resources as expressed in Article 193 UNCLOS.

Sustainable development could, at the global level, encompass a concept of stewardship according to which the power of states to exploit natural resources would be curtailed in terms of potential environmentally hazardous activities regardless of transboundary requirements. Consequently, it would reach beyond the prevention principle, which is still partially rooted in the no-harm principle and subject to a continuous debate in terms of its normative value and substantial content.[77] In this sense, the protection of the marine environment for its own sake would be promoted as an expression of environmental values under international sovereignty law.

Environmental stewardship obligations as restrictions to coastal state sovereignty

A whole set of environmental obligations could be discussed in the light of the above-mentioned understanding of stewardship sovereignty. However, as this would go beyond the scope of this contribution, only two aspects will be briefly addressed: the obligation to conduct EIAs before proceeding to offshore activities and the possible restrictions to state sovereignty concerning activities on the extended continental shelf.

IMPLICATIONS FOR EXPLOITATION ACTIVITIES WITHIN STATE JURISDICTION (TERRITORIAL SEA AND CONTINENTAL SHELF): THE EXAMPLE OF EIAS

With regard to a, thus far endorsed "sustainability test" of offshore activities within state jurisdiction, and bearing in mind that one of the main elements of sustainable development is an effective consideration of potential environmental impacts and the use of ecosystem-based management techniques, stewardship sovereignty could be read as satisfying two main criteria in the search for a suitable legal framework.

On the one hand, stewardship sovereignty would entail an obligation to conduct comprehensive EIAs for any hazardous activity[78] on the marine subsoil, regardless of the risk of transboundary harm. The embedding of stewardship obligations in the principle of state sovereignty would mark a substantial difference in terms of the obligation to conduct environmental impact assessments under Article 206 UNCLOS, which is widely regarded as an expression of the prevention principle. First, it would uphold an integrative approach to state activities under the sustainable development principle. Therefore, corresponding stewardship obligations would not be seen as a simple paraphrase of the prevention principle, as it would not only aim to minimize environmental impacts so that an acceptable threshold could be reached while balancing economic activities, but it would also consider the protection of the marine environment for its own sake. Second, the prevention principle as articulated in Article 206 UNCLOS cannot generally be regarded as a rule of Customary Law yet. Third, Article 206 UNCLOS, even though it maintains an objective standard for the determination of the relevant threshold,[79] grants a considerable measure of discretion to the coastal state in assessing the need to conduct an EIA. Last, the absence of an EIA would amount not only to a breach of an obligation under international treaty law, but also to an exceedance of state sovereignty itself.

On the other hand, stewardship sovereignty would necessarily entail a shift in the burden of proof, in the sense that coastal states would have to establish, in the form of a prior justification procedure, that the intended activity will not lead to environmental harm.[80] As a matter of fact, the proof of lawful exercise of sovereign rights is, in contrast to the breach of a rule of treaty or Customary Law, incumbent on the state conducting or authorizing the relevant activity.

PARTICULARITIES RELATING TO ACTIVITIES ON THE EXTENDED CONTINENTAL SHELF

Certain particularities under stewardship sovereignty of coastal states could apply as far the exploitation of the extended continental shelf—the continental shelf beyond 200 nautical miles from the baselines, claimed according to Article 76 UNCLOS—is concerned. As a matter of fact, the extended continental shelf regime constitutes a major encroachment on the Area and in turn on the Common Heritage of Mankind. It therefore undermines the very idea of placing a submarine area outside national jurisdiction so as to create space for a higher ranked interest.[81] This raises the question of a potential continuity of the Common Heritage of Mankind regime and possible repercussions on the "sustainability test" as applied to deep seabed mining activities. Restrictions to functional state sovereignty over the extended continental shelf could be bolstered by considerations directly linked to the Common Heritage of Mankind, if this regime is not to be considered as entirely discarded by the extended continental shelf regime.

In this respect, an analogous application of Area-related provisions to coastal states, provided for under Article 150 UNCLOS, could be advocated for in terms of certain development policies relating to activities in the Area. As the Authority acts on behalf of mankind, any coastal state conducting activities on the extended continental shelf could be regarded as acting "on behalf" of the Authority. Environmental stewardship obligations as, for example, the above-mentioned mandatory assessment of environmental risks, would therefore also counterbalance the "territorial temptation"[82] of coastal states. Furthermore, the protection regime applied to the extended continental shelf should not be less comprehensive than the one provided for under Article 145 UNCLOS and implemented by the Authority. Regarding exploitation activities in the Area, the obligation of the contractor to conduct an environmental impact assessment is explicitly set out in the annex to the Agreement relating to the implementation of Part XI of UNCLOS and the sponsoring state is under a due diligence obligation to ensure compliance by the sponsored contractor with this obligation.[83]

Conclusion

The protection of the Arctic marine environment from risks arising from exploitation activities on the marine subsoil has been on the international agenda for several years. That being said, legal provisions remain confined to state cooperation within the existing framework provided by UNCLOS and International Environmental Law, which struggles to lead to actual agreements. This contribution argues in favor of the possibility to materialize environmental state responsibility and contribute to resolving the problem of the interplay between the still dominant principle of state sovereignty and the necessity of environmental safeguards under international law, regardless of questions related to the Customary Law status of a principle or not. The principle of sustainable development has significant potential to contribute to an integrated management of Arctic waters by establishing not only objectives, but also a legal threshold aimed at governing the economic actions of the five Arctic coastal states on their marine subsoil. This could substantially contribute to the shaping of stewardship sovereignty of coastal states as an environmental "protection vision."[84] It is a thought for future evolution of requirements under the sustainable development principle as a modern expression of International Environmental Law.[85]

According to Koivurova, the Arctic is not only a place for imagination in general, but also a source of inspiration for legal innovation.[86] Admittedly, the Arctic coastal states' reference, in the Ilulissat Declaration of May 2008, to their stewardship role in protecting the marine environment was not intended to summon any additional environmental obligations upon themselves beyond those directly stemming from UNCLOS and Customary Law. Yet, in the light of the increasing weight attributed to environmental protection under international law as well as growing environmental concerns about high-risk exploration and exploitation activities in Arctic waters, this status quo might not be satisfactory. The Ilulissat Declaration also contains a commitment of the five Arctic coastal states to "take steps in accordance with International Law [...] to ensure the protection and preservation of the fragile marine environment of the Arctic Ocean." What if they were already one step further than they thought?

Notes

1 See www.oceanlaw.org/downloads/arctic/Ilulissat_Declaration.pdf.
2 See, among others, Waliul Hasanat, "Towards Model Arctic-Wide Environmental Cooperation Combating Climate Change." *Yearbook of International Environmental Law* 20 (2009): 122–57.

3 The Arctic coastal states underlined "their sovereignty, sovereign rights and jurisdiction in large areas of the Arctic Ocean," Ilulissat Declaration of May 15, 2008.

4 See the Iqaluit Declaration, adopted at the 9th Ministerial Meeting of the Arctic Council on April 24, 2015, point 31: "…that effective prevention measures are critical to ensuring the protection of the Arctic marine environment from potential incidents [and] that marine oil pollution prevention, preparedness and response remain a long-term commitment of the Arctic Council."

5 For an assessment of environmental risks, see Arctic Council's Protection of the Arctic Marine Environment (PAME) Working Group, *Arctic Ocean Review – Final Report* (May 2013): 69ff.; the Agreement on Cooperation on Marine Oil Pollution Preparedness and Response in the Arctic of May 15, 2013.

6 Ilulissat Declaration of May 15, 2008.

7 See, among others, Alexandre Kiss and Dinah Shelton *International Environmental Law* 2nd edn (New York: Transnational Publishers, 2000), 144ff.

8 Separate Opinion of Judge Weeramantry in *Gabcikovo-Nagymaros Project* (*Hungary* v. *Slovakia*), Judgment, I.C.J. Reports 1997: 88 at 118.

9 United Nations Convention on the Law of the Sea, signed at Montego Bay on December 10, 1982, 1833 UNTS.

10 See also United Nations General Assembly (UNGA) Resolution 1803 (XVII) on Permanent Sovereignty over Natural Resources, December 14, 1962.

11 Jean-Francois Pulvenis, "Le plateau continental, définition et régime," in *Traité du nouveau droit de la mer*, edited by René-Jean Dupuy and Daniel Vignes (Paris: Editions Economica, 1985), 323.

12 Budislav Vukas, "United Nations Convention on the Law of the Sea and the Polar Marine Environment," in *Protecting the Polar Marine Environment: Law and Policy for Pollution Prevention*, edited by Davor Vidas (Cambridge: Cambridge University Press, 2000), 34–56.

13 Article 153 (1) UNCLOS: "Activities in the Area shall be organized, carried out and controlled by the Authority on behalf of mankind as a whole."

14 *Legality of the Threat or Use of Nuclear Weapons*, Advisory Opinion, I.C.J. Reports 1996: 226 at 241, paragraph 29. See also Philippe Sands and Jacqueline Peel, *Principles of International Environmental Law* 3rd edn (Cambridge: Cambridge University Press, 2012), 191.

15 According to Article 76 (6) UNCLOS, the limit of 350 nautical miles does not apply to submarine elevations.

16 Article 77 (1) UNCLOS; see also *Dispute Concerning Delimitation of the Maritime Boundary between Bangladesh and Myanmar in the Bay of Bengal (Bangladesh* v. *Myanmar)*, Judgment of March 14, 2012, International Tribunal on the Law of the Sea (ITLOS), paragraphs 362ff.

17 For claims before the Commission on the Limits of the Continental Shelf pursuant to Article 76 (8) UNCLOS, see www.un.org/depts/los/clcs_new/commission_submissions.htm. For a comprehensive study of this regime, see Ron Macnab, "The Outer Limit of the Continental Shelf in the Arctic Ocean," in *Legal and Scientific Aspects of the Continental Shelf Limits*, edited by Myron H. Nordquist, John N. Moore and Tomas H. Heidar (Leiden: Martinus Nijhoff Publishers, 2004), 301–11.

18 See J. Ashley Roach and Robert W. Smith, *Excessive Maritime Claims* 3rd edn (Leiden: Martinus Nijhoff Publishers, 2012): 187ff.

19 Ulrich Beyerlin and Thilo Marauhn, *International Environmental Law* (Oxford: Hart, 2011). 40ff.

20 Daniel Kazhdan, "Precautionary Pulp: Pulp Mills and the Evolving Dispute between International Tribunals over the Reach of the Precautionary Principle." *Ecology Law Quarterly* 38 (2011): 527–52, at 533ff.

21 *Pulp Mills on the River Uruguay* (*Argentina* v. *Uruguay*), Judgment, I.C.J. Reports 2010: 14 at 82 paragraph 204; Advisory Opinion of February 1, 2011 on Responsibilities and Obligations of States Sponsoring Persons and Entities with Respect to Activities in the Area (No 17), ITLOS, paragraphs 146ff.
22 International Law Commission (ILC) Draft Articles on Prevention of Transboundary Harm from Hazardous Activities, Articles 8 and 9.
23 Neil Craik, *The International Law of Environmental Impact Assessment: Process, Substance and Integration* (Cambridge: Cambridge University Press, 2008), 120ff.
24 International Convention for the Prevention of Pollution From Ships (MARPOL 73/78), ILM 12 (1973) 1319 and ILM 17 (1978) 546; all Arctic coastal states are parties to all annexes.
25 International Convention for the Safety of Life at Sea (SOLAS) of November 1, 1974, 1184 UNTS 2, as modified by protocol of October 11, 1988.
26 International Convention on Standards of Training, Certification and Watchkeeping for Seafarers, 1361 UNTS 2, as modified on July 9, 1995.
27 Convention on the Prevention of Marine Pollution by Dumping of Wastes and Other Matter, ILM 11 (1972) 1294, and Protocol of November 7, 1996, ILM 36 (1997) 1; only Canada, Norway and Denmark are parties to the Protocol.
28 Sergei V. Vinogradov and Jay P. Wagner, "International Legal Regime for the Protection of the Marine Environment Against Operational Pollution from Offshore Petroleum," in *Environmental Regulation of Oil and Gas*, edited by Zhiguo Gao (London: Kluwer Law International 1998), 93ff.
29 Protection of the Arctic Marine Environment (PAME)Working Group, Arctic Council, Arctic Offshore Oil and Gas Guidelines (AOOGG), March 2014.
30 IMO Resolution A.1024 (26) of December 2, 2009 "Guidelines for Ships Operating in Polar Waters."
31 IMO MSC/Circ.1056-MEPC/Circ.399 "Guidelines for Ships Operating in Arctic Ice-covered Waters."
32 Resolution MSC.385 (94) of November 26, 2014.
33 Convention for the Protection of the Marine Environment of the North-East Atlantic, September 22, 1992, 2354 UNTS 67, spec. annex II.
34 ILM 13 (1974) 13.
35 ILM 50 (2011) 1119.
36 For a description of both agreements, see Michael Byers, *International Law and the Arctic* (Cambridge: Cambridge University Press, 2013), 278ff.
37 Klaus Dodds, "The Ilulissat Declaration (2008): The Arctic States, 'Law of the Sea,' and Arctic Ocean." *SAIS Review of International Affairs* 33 (2013): 45, at 45.
38 Pierre-Marie Dupuy, "La préservation du milieu marin," in *Traité du nouveau droit de la mer*, edited by René-Jean Dupuy and Daniel Vignes (Paris: Éditions Economica, 1985), 1012.
39 For a recent account, see Isabelle Mandraud, "La Russie déploie des troupes en Russie." *Le Monde*, October 13, 2014, 6.
40 See also John E.D. Larkin, "UNCLOS and the Balance of Environmental and Economic Resources in the Arctic." *Georgetown International Environmental Law Review* 22 (2010): 325.
41 Kemal Baslar, *The Concept of the Common Heritage of Mankind in International Law* (Leiden: Martinus Nijhoff Publishers, 1998), 232; Kiss also describes its purpose in guaranteeing a "rendement continu maximal." See Alexandre Kiss, "La notion de patrimoine commun de l'humanité." *Recueil des Cours de l'Académie de droit international de la Haye* 172 II (1982): 228–383.
42 Article 140 (1) UNCLOS.
43 Article 134 (2) UNCLOS.
44 It is interesting to notice that this regime has been considered as binding Customary Law even before its entering into force, *The Coast of St. Pierre and Miquelon Arbitration* (*Canada* v. *France*), June 10, 1992, ILM 31 (1992), 1149ff.

45 Richard N.L. Andrews, *Managing the Environment, Managing Ourselves: A History of American Environmental Policy* (New Haven, CT: Yale University Press, 1999), 202.

46 Rob Huebert and Brooks Yeager, *A New Sea: The Need for a Regional Agreement on Management and Conservation of the Arctic Marine Environment.* WWF Report (2008): 28ff.

47 Kristin N. Casper, "Oil and Gas Developments in the Arctic: Softening of Ice Demands Hardening of Law." *Natural Resources Law* 49 (2009): 825–81. It is described as a "Do-Nothing-Declaration."

48 For the interplay of state obligations under international law and state sovereignty, see Geoffrey Palmer, "An International Regime for Environmental Protection." *Washington University Journal of Urban and Contemporary Law* 42 (1992): 5–19.

49 According to Article 56 (3) UNCLOS, rights set out under the exclusive economic zone regime with respect to the seabed and subsoil shall be exercised in accordance with Part VI, relating to the continental shelf.

50 On the concept of functional sovereignty, see Nico Schrijver, *Sovereignty Over Natural Resources: Balancing Rights and Duties* (Cambridge: Cambridge University Press, 2008), 394ff.

51 Nicole Graham, "Dephysicalisation and Entitlement: Legal and Cultural Discourses of Place as Property," in *Environmental Discourses in Public and International Law*, edited by Brad Jessup and Kim Rubenstein (Cambridge: Cambridge University Press, 2012), 96–119, at 117.

52 For a comprehensive account of this topic, see Peter H. Sand, "Public Trusteeship for the Oceans," in *Law of the Sea, Environmental Law and Settlement of Dispute, Liber Amicorum Judge Thomas A. Mensah*, edited by Tafsir M. Ndiaye and Rüdiger Wolfrum (Leiden: Martinus Nijhoff Publishers, 2007), 521–44, at 535ff., who raises the question whether it could be seen as a "wider fiduciary commitment to protect the ocean as a whole, regardless of its national or international subdivisions."

53 For what seems to be the first account of that notion, see Dan Tarlock, "Stewardship Sovereignty: The Next Step in Former Prime Minister Palmer's Logic." *Washington University Journal of Urban and Contemporary Law* 42 (1992): 21–29, at 24, 26.

54 Kiss and Shelton, *International Environmental Law*, 26, who underline that such an understanding amounts to a "good faith" approach.

55 Separate Opinion of Judge Weeramantry in *Gabcikovo-Nagymaros Project* (*Hungary* v. *Slovakia*), Judgment, I.C.J. Reports 1997: 88 at 110; for a detailed account of the Public Trust doctrine, see Sand, "Public Trusteeship for the Oceans," 521ff.

56 Patricia Birnie, Alan Boyle and Catherine Redgwell, *International Law and the Environment* (Oxford: Oxford University Press, 2009), at 134.

57 Ved P. Nanda and William K. Ris, "Public Trust Doctrine: A Viable Approach to International Environmental Protection." *Ecology Law Quarterly* 5 (1976): 291–319.

58 Peter H. Sand, "Global Environmental Change and the Nation State," in *Multilevel Governance of Global Environmental Change*, edited by Gerd Winter (Cambridge: Cambridge University Press, 2011), 519–38, at 526.

59 Christopher C. Joyner, "Legal Implications of the Concept of Common Heritage of Mankind." *International and Comparative Law Quarterly* 35 (1986): 190, at 195.

60 Judge McNair already challenged the compatibility of an international trusteeship system with the concept of sovereignty in 1950, see ICJ, Separate Opinion Judge McNair, Advisory Opinion of July 11, 1950, on the International Status of South West Africa, *ICJ Reports* (1950): 128, Separate Opinion Judge McNair, 146, at 150; for a critical appraisal, see Hong S. Cho, *The Public Trust Doctrine and Global Commons* (Berkeley, CA: Berkeley Press, 1995), at 332, 337.

61 Scott J. Shackelford, "Was Selden Right?: The Expansion of Closed Seas and its Consequences." *Stanford Journal of International Law* 47 (2011): 1–50, at 35ff.

62 US-Presidential Proclamation N.8031 of June 15, 2006 on the Establishment of the Northwestern Hawaiian Islands Marine National Monument. For a French example, Decree N.2004–33 of January 8, 2004 on the Establishment of a protection zone in the Mediterranean.

63 Jutta Brunnée, "Common Areas, Common Heritage, and Common Concern," in *Oxford Handbook of International Environmental Law*, edited by Daniel Bodansky, Jutta Brunnée and Ellen Hey (Oxford: Oxford University Press, 2008), 551–73, at 561ff.

64 Dan Tarlock, "Ecosystems," in *Oxford Handbook of International Environmental Law*, edited by Daniel Bodansky, Jutta Brunnée and Ellen Hey (Oxford: Oxford University Press, 2008), 574–94. The author, at 593, argues around the notion of "ecosystem." See also Kerstin Odendahl, *Die Umweltpflichtigkeit der Souveränität* (Berlin: Duncker and Humblot, 1999), at 361ff.

65 Martin Nettesheim, "Die ökologische Intervention." *Archiv des Völkerrechts* 33 (1996): 168–217, at 168ff.

66 *Gabcikovo-Nagymaros Project* (*Hungary* v. *Slovakia*), Judgment, *I.C.J. Reports* (1997): 140. At that time the ICJ spoke of a mere concept, not a principle.

67 Birnie et al., *International Law and the Environment*, 55; Günther Handl, "Sustainable Development: General Rules vs. Specific Obligations," in *Sustainable Development and International Law*, edited by Wilfried Lang (Leiden: Martinus Nijhoff Publishers, 1995), 35–54, at 43.

68 Sands and Peel, *Principles of International Environmental Law*, 215.

69 Daniel Barstow Magraw and Lisa D. Hawke, "Sustainable Development," in *Oxford Handbook of International Environmental Law*, edited by Daniel Bodansky, Jutta Brunnée and Ellen Hay (Oxford: Oxford University Press, 2008), 613–38.

70 H.J. Diamond, "The Need for Ecosystem-Based Management," in *Changes in the Arctic Environment and the Law of the Sea*, edited by Myron H. Nordquist, John N. Moore and Tomas H. Heidar (Leiden: Martinus Nijhoff Publishers, 2010), 389–96, at 392ff.

71 Rio Declaration on Environment and Development, June 14, 1992, principle 4, and Agenda 21, Chapter 17; for the Arctic States in particular, see the Iqaluit Declaration, point 4.

72 Vaughan Lowe, "Sustainable Development and Unsustainable Arguments," in *International Law and Sustainable Development–Past Achievements and Future Challenges*, edited by Alan Boyle and David Freestone (Oxford: Oxford University Press, 1999), 19–37, where is used the expression "modifying norm."

73 See the catchy wording in WTO Appellate Body, October 12, 1998, WT/DS58/AB/R, Import Prohibition of Certain Shrimp and Shrimp Products (India, Pakistan, Malaysia and Thailand/USA), at paragraph 154: "[...] add colour, texture and shading to our interpretation of the agreements."

74 A parallel could be drawn with the principle of proportionality, which arguably is an international peremptory norm. See Alexander Orakhelashvili, *Peremptory Norms in International Law* (Oxford: Oxford University Press, 2006), at 53ff.

75 Sands and Peel, *Principles of International Environmental Law*, 217; on the social aspects of the sustainability principle, see Samantha J. Fow, "Arctic Sustainability Principle." *Vermont Journal of Environmental Law* 13 (2012): 537–51.

76 Tarlock, "Ecosystems," 593.

77 Beyerlin and Marauhn, *International Environmental Law*, 53.

78 Principle 2 of the ILC Draft principles on the allocation of loss in the case of transboundary harm arising out of hazardous activities (2006) defines a "hazardous activity" as an activity which involves a risk of causing significant harm.

79 Craik, *International Law of Environmental Impact Assessment*, 98.

80 The existence of such a procedural element under the precautionary principle has been rejected by the ICJ in the Pulp Mills-Judgment, supra note 21, at 164.

81 Sven Kaufmann, "Le régime juridique de l'océan Arctique: un paradoxe entre exploitation souveraine et protection internationale," in *Marché et environnement: le marché: menace ou remède pour la protection internationale de l'environnement,* edited by Jochen Sohnle and Marie-Pierre Camproux-Duffrène, (Brussels: Bruylant, 2014), 177–97.
82 On that expression, see Helmut Tuerk, *Reflections on the Contemporary Law of the Sea* (Leiden: Martinus Nijhoff Publishers, 2012), 159ff.
83 See Section 1 (7) of the Annex to the Agreement relating to the implementation of Part XI of UNCLOS and Advisory Opinion of February 1, 2011 on Responsibilities and Obligations of States Sponsoring Persons and Entities with Respect to Activities in the Area (No 17), ITLOS, 141.
84 Tarlock, "Ecosystems," 592–94.
85 As a matter of fact, the UNEP Governing Council stressed in 1989 that the principle of sustainable development, as stated in the Brundtland Report, does not imply any encroachment upon national sovereignty, see UNEP/GC.15/2, May 1989, annex II.
86 Timo Koivurova, "Alternatives for an Arctic Treaty–Evaluation and a New Proposal." *RECIEL* 17 (2008): 14–26, at 14.

References

Andrews, Richard N.L. *Managing the Environment, Managing Ourselves: A History of American Environmental Policy.* New Haven, CT: Yale University Press, 1999.

Arctic Council. Protection of the Arctic Marine Environment (PAME) Working Group, *Arctic Ocean Review – Final Report* (May 2013).

Baslar, Kemal. *The Concept of the Common Heritage of Mankind in International Law.* Leiden: Martinus Nijhoff Publishers, 1998.

Beyerlin, Ulrich and Thilo Marauhn. *International Environmental Law.* Oxford: Hart, 2011.

Birnie, Patricia, Alan Boyle and Catherine Redgwell. *International Law and the Environment.* Oxford: Oxford University Press, 2009.

Brunnée, Jutta. "Common Areas, Common Heritage, and Common Concern." In *Oxford Handbook of International Environmental Law,* edited by Daniel Bodansky, Jutta Brunnée and Ellen Hey, 551–73. Oxford: Oxford University Press, 2008.

Byers, Michael. *International Law and the Arctic.* Cambridge: Cambridge University Press, 2013.

Casper, Kristin N. "Oil and Gas Developments in the Arctic: Softening of Ice Demands Hardening of Law." *Natural Resources Law* 49 (2009): 825–81.

Cho, Hong S. *The Public Trust Doctrine and Global Commons.* Berkeley, CA: Berkeley Press, 1995.

Craik, Neil. *The International Law of Environmental Impact Assessment: Process, Substance and Integration.* Cambridge: Cambridge University Press, 2008.

Diamond, H.J. "The Need for Ecosystem-Based Management." In *Changes in the Arctic Environment and the Law of the Sea,* edited by Myron H. Nordquist, John N. Moore and Tomas H. Heidar, 389–96. Leiden: Martinus Nijhoff Publishers, 2010.

Dodds, Klaus. "The Ilulissat Declaration (2008): The Arctic States, 'Law of the Sea,' and Arctic Ocean." *SAIS Review of International Affairs* 33 (2013): 45–55.

Dupuy, Pierre-Marie. "La préservation du milieu marin." In *Traité du nouveau droit de la mer,* edited by René-Jean Dupuy and Daniel Vignes. Paris: Éditions Economica, 1985.

Fow, Samantha J. "Arctic Sustainability Principle." *Vermont Journal of Environmental Law* 13 (2012): 537–51.

Graham, Nicole. "Dephysicalisation and Entitlement: Legal and Cultural Discourses of Place as Property," in *Environmental Discourses in Public and International Law*, edited by Brad Jessup and Kim Rubenstein, 96–119. Cambridge: Cambridge University Press, 2012.

Handl, Günther. "Sustainable Development: General Rules vs. Specific Obligations." In *Sustainable Development and International Law*, edited by Wilfried Lang, 35–54. Leiden: Martinus Nijhoff Publishers, 1995.

Hasanat, Waliul. "Towards Model Arctic-Wide Environmental Cooperation Combating Climate Change." *Yearbook of International Environmental Law* 20 (2009): 122–57.

Huebert, Rob and Brooks Yeager. *A New Sea: The Need for a Regional Agreement on Management and Conservation of the Arctic Marine Environment.* WWF Report (2008).

Joyner, Christopher C. "Legal Implications of the Concept of Common Heritage of Mankind." *International and Comparative Law Quarterly* 35 (1986).

Kaufmann, Sven. "Le régime juridique de l'océan Arctique: un paradoxe entre exploitation souveraine et protection internationale." In *Marché et environnement: le marché: menace ou remède pour la protection internationale de l'environnement*, edited by Jochen Sohnle and Marie-Pierre Camproux-Duffrène, 177–97. Brussels: Bruylant, 2014.

Kazhdan, Daniel. "Precautionary Pulp: Pulp Mills and the Evolving Dispute between International Tribunals over the Reach of the Precautionary Principle." *Ecology Law Quarterly* 38 (2011): 527–52.

Kiss, Alexandre. "La notion de patrimoine commun de l'humanité." *Recueil des Cours de l'Académie de droit international de la Haye* 172 II (1982): 228–383.

Kiss, Alexandre and Dinah Shelton. *International Environmental* Law 2nd edn. New York: Transnational Publishers, 2000.

Koivurova, Timo. "Alternatives for an Arctic Treaty–Evaluation and a New Proposal." *RECIEL* 17 (2008): 14–26.

Larkin, John E.D. "UNCLOS and the Balance of Environmental and Economic Resources in the Arctic." *Georgetown International Environmental Law Review* 22 (2010): 307–36.

Lowe, Vaughan. "Sustainable Development and Unsustainable Arguments." In *International Law and Sustainable Development – Past Achievements and Future Challenges*, edited by Alan Boyle and David Freestone, 19–37. Oxford: Oxford University Press, 1999.

Macnab, Ron. "The Outer Limit of the Continental Shelf in the Arctic Ocean." In *Legal and Scientific Aspects of the Continental Shelf Limits*, edited by Myron H. Nordquist, John N. Moore and Tomas H. Heidar, 301–11. Leiden: Martinus Nijhoff Publishers, 2004.

Magraw, Daniel Barstow and Lisa D. Hawke. "Sustainable Development." In *Oxford Handbook of International Environmental Law*, edited by Daniel Bodansky, Jutta Brunnée and Ellen Hay, 613–38. Oxford: Oxford University Press, 2008.

Mandraud, Isabelle. "La Russie déploie des troupes en Russie." *Le Monde*, October 13, 2014.

Nanda, Ved P. and William K. Ris. "Public Trust Doctrine: A Viable Approach to International Environmental Protection." *Ecology Law Quarterly* 5 (1976): 291–319.

Nettesheim, Martin. "Die ökologische Intervention." *Archiv des Völkerrechts* 33 (1996): 168–217.

Odendahl, Kerstin. *Umweltpflichtigkeit der Souveränität*. Berlin: Duncker and Humblot, 1999.

Orakhelashvili, Alexander. *Peremptory Norms in International Law*. Oxford: Oxford University Press, 2006.

Palmer, Geoffrey. "An International Regime for Environmental Protection." *Washington University Journal of Urban and Contemporary Law* 42 (1992): 5–19.

Pulvenis, Jean-François. "Le plateau continental, définition et régime." In *Traité du nouveau droit de la mer*, edited by René-Jean Dupuy and Daniel Vignes. Paris: Éditions Economica, 1985.

Roach, J. Ashley and Robert W. Smith. *Excessive Maritime Claims* 3rd edn. Leiden: Martinus Nijhoff Publishers, 2012.

Sand, Peter H. "Public Trusteeship for the Oceans." In *Law of the Sea, Environmental Law and Settlement of Dispute, Liber Amicorum Judge Thomas A. Mensah*, edited by Tafsir M. Ndiaye and Rüdiger Wolfrum, 521–44. Leiden: Martinus Nijhoff Publishers, 2007.

Sand, Peter H. "Global Environmental Change and the Nation State." In *Multilevel Governance of Global Environmental Change*, edited by Gerd Winter, 519–38. Cambridge: Cambridge University Press, 2011.

Sands, Philippe and Jacqueline Peel. *Principles of International Environmental Law* 3rd edn. Cambridge: Cambridge University Press, 2012.

Schrijver, Nico. *Sovereignty Over Natural Resources: Balancing Rights and Duties*. Cambridge: Cambridge University Press, 2008.

Shackelford, Scott J. "Was Selden Right?: The Expansion of Closed Seas and its Consequences." *Stanford Journal of International Law* 47 (2011): 1–50.

Tarlock, Dan. "Stewardship Sovereignty: The Next Step in Former Prime Minister Palmer's Logic." *Washington University Journal of Urban and Contemporary Law* 42 (1992): 21–29.

Tarlock, Dan. "Ecosystems." In *Oxford Handbook of International Environmental Law*, edited by Daniel Bodansky, Jutta Brunnée and Ellen Hey, 574–96. Oxford: Oxford University Press, 2008.

Tuerk, Helmut. *Reflections on the Contemporary Law of the Sea*. Leiden: Martinus Nijhoff Publishers, 2012.

Vinogradov, Sergei V. and Jay P. Wagner. "International Legal Regime for the Protection of the Marine Environment Against Operational Pollution from Offshore Petroleum." In *Environmental Regulation of Oil and Gas*, edited by Zhiguo Gao. London: Kluwer Law International, 1998.

Vukas, Budislav. "United Nations Convention on the Law of the Sea and the Polar Marine Environment." In *Protecting the Polar Marine Environment: Law and Policy for Pollution Prevention*, edited by Davor Vidas. Cambridge: Cambridge University Press, 2000.

7 Legal status and environmental protection of the Arctic sea ice

European perspectives

Claudia Cinelli[1]

Introduction

The Arctic coastal states bordering the Arctic Ocean—Canada, Denmark/Greenland, Norway, Russian Federation and the United States[2]—have internationally recognized sovereignty over Arctic lands and islands and, consequently, sovereignty and jurisdiction over the Arctic maritime zones generated by their relevant coasts. They have a stewardship role in protecting and preserving the Arctic marine environment by taking steps both nationally and in cooperation among them and the non-coastal Arctic States (Finland, Iceland and Sweden)—namely, within the Arctic Council—and other interested states and/or international entities (Arctic and non-Arctic) particularly, within the International Maritime Organization (IMO) and the European Union (EU).

Indeed, current economic and political developments of the Arctic ice-covered marine areas are not taking place in a legal vacuum. There are several legal rules that govern the behavior of states and non-state actors in the Arctic and their interplay between regulation levels (international, EU, regional, national and local) is often complex.

Two different, but complementary, trends are here identified: that is, creeping jurisdiction *versus* creeping cooperation. As far as creeping jurisdiction is concerned, the Law of the Sea has evolved towards granting coastal states an ever larger set of sovereign rights and broader jurisdiction over marine areas. The five Arctic coastal states are indeed challenging each other on the mapping of maritime jurisdiction.

The second trend is manifested in an increased need for Arctic governance and international cooperation to ensure environmental protection, reinforced by the great changes due to global warming and ice melting. The regional cooperation process inaugurated by Gorbachev in 1987, advanced through the Rovaniemi Process in 1991, and culminated in 1996 with the creation of the Arctic Council, is now progressing with a certain openness to other states and non-state actors. According to Byers, "regions dominated by realist thinking—as was the case in the Arctic during the Cold War—are susceptible to 'creeping cooperation': a momentum-generating process of institutionalization and legalization."[3]

The aforementioned trends are moving towards a disordered interaction between the existing regulatory framework composed by *hard law* and *soft law*. This interaction seems to lead to a *governance impasse*: on the one hand, there is the existing patchwork of general *hard law* which, while binding, does not always deal with the specific characteristics of the Arctic region and mostly ensures states' sovereignty, sovereign rights and jurisdiction. On the other hand, the *impasse* is embodied in the *soft law* approach towards common concerns which, while specifically dealing with the new conditions and needs of the Arctic region and their impact at a global level, is not legally binding. The impasse calls upon governance innovation in the Arctic, towards the strengthening of international cooperation between Arctic and non-Arctic States, and the setting up of environmental provisions common to all actors, including safety measures for offshore operations.

However, despite the legal impasse, or because of it, the international significance of the *soft law* approach lies in the fact that it provides immediate instruments of different regulation which, to some extent, lead to the proliferation of international actors, including non-Arctic actors, under a "de-formalized" law in different plans of actions. In this sense, a good example would be the emerging role of the European Union (EU) in the Arctic. The EU's evolving policy on the Arctic aims to establish a coherent and comprehensive approach on matters where the Arctic region has an impact on the EU and vice versa. However, European institutions—the European Parliament and the European Commission jointly with the Council—seem to have different perspectives on how to deal with Arctic ice-covered marine areas.

This study briefly addresses the legal status of the ice in international law, to then focus on the European perspectives related to the ongoing development of the EU Arctic Policy, while making a special reference to the environmental protection of the Arctic Ocean through EU laws and regulations. In this sense, the study focuses on the applicability of the Offshore Safety Directive 30/2013 in the Arctic sea ice (before reaching some concluding reflections.

Arctic ice-covered waters in international law: a brief overview

Arctic sea ice is governed by the general framework of the Law of the Sea. Currently there appears to be no doubt about the fact that sea ice has the same legal status as sea water. From a historical perspective, this was supported by those scholars who argued that the de facto presence of ice-covered marine areas in the Arctic Ocean does not produce any change *de jure* of its legal regime. They simply found that, despite the presence of the ice, the Arctic Ocean was, like any other ocean, divided into two regimes under the general international law then in force: state sovereignty in territorial seas and international freedom in high seas.[4]

Years later, this doctrine was confirmed by international practice. During the Cold War, the American nuclear-powered submarine *Nautilus* crossed the Arctic Central Ocean through the geographical point of the North Pole for the first time. This historic event clearly demonstrated the strategic-military advantages of the Arctic marine basin. In response, the Soviets were not to be outdone, and soon the Arctic seas were filled with nuclear submarines from both sides. Accordingly, the legal status of the ice-covered area around the geographic point of the North Pole, that is the polar cap, was given the same status as that of the high seas where freedom of navigation applies.

At the same time, Arctic States significantly contributed to the development and codification of the Law of the Sea through unilateral acts;[5] general, regional or bilateral agreements or otherwise, and by submitting maritime disputes to international courts.[6] The presence of ice itself had no relevant impact on the placement of the maritime boundary.[7]

Thus, in international practice—past and present—the Arctic Ocean and its ice-covered marine areas have been treated like any other marine area.[8] The exception that proves the rule is contained in the UNCLOS. Its Part XII is devoted to the protection and preservation of the marine environment and specifically contains Section 8 on ice-covered areas, composed by only one Article: the so-called "Arctic exception" of Article 234 (also known as "the Canadian clause")[9] concerning the protection and preservation of the marine environment in ice-covered areas within the Exclusive Economic Zone (EEZ). This allows Arctic States to unilaterally enforce a strict pollution-prevention regime in the Arctic EEZs. Each of the five states bordering the Arctic Ocean have claimed an EEZ—or analogous zones such as fishery protection zones which are generally called *sui generis* zones[10]—where they have the sovereign rights to exploit, preserve and manage resources such as fish, gas and oil.

More recently, the legal status of Arctic sea ice as sea water of any other ocean was clearly set out by the 2008 Ilulissat Declaration adopted by the five Arctic coastal states.[11] This Declaration is divided into two sections. In the first section, the states seem to minimize the impact of Arctic changes in terms of environmental concerns and business opportunities, relying on the fact that changes are only a possibility. They emphasize the fact that:

[b]y virtue of their sovereignty, sovereign rights and jurisdiction in large areas of the Arctic Ocean the five coastal [s]tates are in a unique position to address these possibilities and challenges. Notably, the law of the sea provides for important rights and obligations concerning the delineation of the outer limits of the continental shelf, the protection of the marine environment, including ice-covered areas, freedom of navigation, marine scientific research, and other uses of the sea.[12]

Far from adopting an ad hoc regime for the Arctic, much less an *ad modum* of the Antarctic Treaty, the Declaration specifically does not explore the possibility of applying Part IX of UNCLOS on enclosed and semi-enclosed seas. As it is commonly known, Part IX of UNCLOS is composed by Articles 122 and 123. Article 122 provides the definition of enclosed or semi-enclosed seas which is relevant as it provides for direct cooperation or cooperation through "an appropriate regional organization" of states bordering enclosed or semi-enclosed seas. There is no consensus about the exact meaning of the definition and the extent of the obligations it establishes. In any case, it cannot be denied that the Arctic is a regional sea.

The second section of the Ilulissat Declaration does not seem to be in conflict with this conclusion as it refers to cooperation through international and regional entities. After affirming that Arctic coastal states "have a stewardship role in protecting,"[13] they decide to take:

> steps in accordance with international law both nationally and in cooperation among the five states and other interested parties to ensure the protection and preservation of the fragile marine environment of the Arctic Ocean [...] including through the International Maritime Organization to strengthen existing measures and develop new measures to improve the safety of maritime navigation and prevent or reduce the risk of ship-based pollution in the Arctic Ocean.[14]

In this sense, the International Code for Ships Operating in Polar Waters (Polar Code) was adopted by the IMO in November 2014. And finally, the Arctic coastal states declare that they "will continue to contribute actively to the work of the Arctic Council and other relevant international fora."[15]

Therefore, the Declaration considers the Arctic iced waters like any other marine areas. In addition, the Declaration does not exclude the Arctic States to further contribute to the work of the EU in developing its Arctic Policy.

The legal status of the Arctic ice-covered waters in European Law

A few months after the adoption of the 2008 Ilulissat Declaration, in September 2008, the Nordic Council of Ministers, together with its Arctic actors and European Union experts, hosted in the same town of Ilulissat the Conference *Our Common Concern for the Arctic*, in which Arctic and non-Arctic entities participated. The Conference adopted a different perspective from the Ilulissat Declaration: that is, a general interests approach to the Arctic challenges. The Conference did not make conclusive findings for facing the new conditions or specificities of the Arctic and ended up drafting a list of common concerns related to macro-areas, such as climate change and environment, sustainable development and the use of resources. It made a valid contribution towards the increasing role of the EU in the Arctic. The EU is actually the only non-Arctic international actor that is laying the groundwork for a process of defining a policy for the Arctic from a global perspective, based primarily on the legal framework of UNCLOS to which the EU (succeeding to the European Community) has been a Party since 1994. Therefore, one might deduct that, the EU being a party to UNCLOS, the legal framework applicable to the Arctic Ocean, including ice-covered marine areas, is the Law of the Sea. However, the positions of EU institutions—European Parliament and European Commission—have been and still are, to some extent, opposed.

The European Arctic

In 1997, the European Environmental Agency (EEA) in its report "The State of the European Arctic Environment," underlined that:

> [t]here is no single geographical definition of the extent of the Arctic, and even less so of the European Arctic. There is also no political agreement on the definition of the concept. The definition used in this report is therefore deliberately imprecise, as the geographical distribution of the various phenomena, species, impacts, characteristics, etc. of importance to the region do not always coincide. For the purpose of this report, the European Environment Agency has identified the European Arctic as follows: Iceland, Svalbard archipelago, Franz Joseph Land, and Novaja Zemlja; Scandinavia and Finland north of the Arctic Circle; Murmansk oblast and northern Arkhangelsk oblast, northern Karelia, and Nenets east to Yamal; the seas of these land areas as well as the international waters between them.[16]

Geographical uncertainties are also shown by several Arctic international research programs, which have chosen different definitions for the geographical boundaries according to the requirements set by the study subjects.[17] In addition, regulatory instruments apply to different Arctic scope coverages, which is relevant *ratione loci* in terms of scope of application of rules,[18] including EU law and politics.

In 1998, the EU opened the "Arctic Windows" making the European Arctic areas a priority of Northern Dimension Policy.[19] The EU has continued to be involved in external matters as well as to actively move forward to other issues entailing an internal dimension, including maritime affairs, environment, energy and transport policy areas. The previous interest, mainly focused on the European Arctic, has been expanded to the entire Arctic region due to the awareness about the Arctic's importance in a global context. According to the circle line, today the EU considers that:

the notion of "Arctic region" [...] covers the area around the North Pole north of the Arctic Circle. It includes the Arctic Ocean and territories of the eight Arctic states: Canada, Denmark (including Greenland), Finland, Iceland, Norway, Russia, Sweden and the United States.[20]

It is according to this notion that EU does not have a coastline on the Arctic Ocean. Therefore, the Arctic geographical coverage does not include European Arctic waters, but only land territories. Indeed, it includes the Arctic territories of Member States such as Finland and Sweden, as well as the territories of States of the European Economic Areas (EFTA EEA) as Iceland and Norway.[21] Finally, as for Denmark, Greenland is one of the Oversees Countries and Territories of the EU,[22] while Canada, Russia and the United States are strategic partners of the EU.

Towards the EU Arctic policy: different perspectives

By the beginning of the new millennium, the potential and actual geopolitical consequences of Arctic warming have urged the EU to consider new strategy for the Arctic. Its Arctic Climate Change Policy *has indeed become* a challenge for its Integrated Maritime Policy. Its Arctic Climate Change Policy was indeed integrated into a challenge for its Integrated Maritime Policy.[23] At first glance, this seems to be a paradox since the EU does not have a coastline in the Arctic. Nevertheless, the EU policies in areas such as environment, climate change, energy, research, transport and fisheries have a direct bearing on the Arctic. This is a fundamental premise of the EU's Integrated Maritime Policy, which is based on the fundamental premise that each sea region is unique and needs individual solutions in order to maximize the sustainable use of its resources. Therefore, the Arctic is no different, and so it is in this respect that the EU has an interest in securing a sustainable future for the Arctic Ocean. In addition, the Arctic Ocean contains areas beyond national jurisdiction that is high seas and deep seabed in the event that the International Seabed Area (Area) is eventually delimited. The EU is the only international non-Arctic actor that is laying the groundwork for a process of defining and developing an EU Arctic Policy. However, European institutions—the European Parliament and the European Commission—seem to have different perspectives on how to deal with resource exploitation management and environmental protection.

The European Parliament position

The European Parliament (EP) in its 2008 Resolution on Arctic Governance focused on the fact that UNCLOS "was not formulated with specific regard to the current circumstances of climate change and the unique consequences of melting ice in the Arctic Seas."[24] The EP appealed, although with some nuances, to the legal instrument of analogy, proposing a system of governance for the Arctic *ad modum* of Antarctica: system of governance based on the interest of humankind. The EP did not provide the legal basis on how to develop and make this "analogy Antarctica–Arctic" effective. It concludes with the suggestion to the European Commission (EC) "to pursue the opening of international negotiations designed to lead to the adoption of an international treaty for the protection of the Arctic, having as its inspiration the Antarctic Treaty, as supplemented by the Madrid Protocol signed in 1991."[25] In this sense, clarifies, that "as a minimum starting-point such a treaty could at least cover the unpopulated and unclaimed area at the center of the Arctic Ocean."[26]

Among other ambiguities, it is unclear whether the EP suggests applying the prohibition of exploiting mineral resources *ex* Article 7 of the 1991 Madrid Protocol to the Antarctic Treaty. And, if so, in the case that the Area will be finally delimited in the center of the Arctic Ocean, the problem would be how to combine such prohibition with the application of Part XI of UNCLOS and its 1994 Implementation Agreement regarding the legal regime of the Common Heritage of Mankind.

Three years later, the new EP, elected in 2009, adopted another resolution, where it changed its perspective for the Arctic governance. In its Resolution on a "Sustainable EU policy for the High North,"[27] the EP only stresses the need for a united, coordinated EU policy on the Arctic region, in which both the EU's priorities and the potential challenges should be clearly defined.[28] This Resolution seems to show the difficulties to accommodate competing interests and positions where the emphasis seems to be put on opportunities for resource exploitation rather than on environmental protection. Different from the previous 2008 Resolution, the EP affirmed that:

> the Arctic region is not to be regarded as a legal vacuum, but as an area with well-developed tools for governance; nevertheless, [...] due to the challenges of climate change and increasing economic development, those existing rules need to be further developed, strengthened and implemented by all parties concerned.[29]

As a last development, on March 2014, the EP adopted a Resolution on an "EU strategy for the Arctic."[30] It was adopted shortly before the legislative term as the new election took place in 2014. In comparison with the previous 2011 Resolution, it appears to give a more prominent place to environmental considerations.[31] There were several motions by different political groups. Particularly, the motion by the "European Free Alliance Greens" group was adopted on March 5, 2014 and called on the EU "to promote strict precautionary regulatory standards in the field of environmental protection and safety for oil exploration, prospection and production internationally."[32] In the same document, the motion goes further calling for "a ban on oil drilling in the icy Arctic waters of the EU and the EEA and for promotion by the EU of comparable precautionary standards in the Arctic Council and for Arctic coastal states."[33] Therefore, it seems that this motion had the aim to give to the Arctic sea ice waters of the EU and EEA an ad hoc status. However, it seems to present legal and political uncertainties. First, the legal meaning of the "icy Arctic waters of the EU" is not clear as EU does not have a coastline in the Arctic Ocean. Second, "the icy Arctic waters of the EEA" refers to those of Norway and Iceland, which are associated countries and are submitted to EEA regime. However, not all EU regulations and legislation are EEA-relevant as will be analyzed below with regard to the application of Offshore Safety Directive.

On March 12, 2014 the Resolution was adopted without taking into consideration the explicit ban proposed by the Verts/ALE group.[34] However, it was reiterated that the serious environmental concerns relating to the Arctic waters require special attention to ensure the environmental protection in relation to any offshore oil and gas operations in the Arctic. Indeed, the 2014 Resolution calls for a binding instrument for pollution prevention,[35] without specifying the EU legal basis and its application *ratione loci*. It seems that the EP still supports, although in a less ambitious manner than that of 2008 Resolution, the idea of an ad hoc legal status for the ice-covered areas.

The European Commission position

In its Communication "The European Union and the Arctic Region," the European Commission (EC) put forward a structured and coordinated approach towards Arctic matters as the first layer of the EU Arctic policy,[36] based, in principle, on the application of the UNCLOS legal framework. The priority goal of the EU is to find the right balance between preserving the Arctic environment and the need for the sustainable use of resources.

On June 26, 2012, the European Commission and the EU High Representative for Foreign Affairs and Security Policy adopted the document "Developing a European Union Policy towards the Arctic Region: Progress since 2008 and Next Steps."[37] It is accompanied by two other documents: first, "The inventory of activities in the framework of developing a European Union Arctic Policy"[38] and, second, "Space and the Arctic."[39]

As concerns the most recent developments at the time of writing, according to the EP's plenary debate which was held in Strasbourg on April 17, 2013, the current pillars of the EU Arctic action carried out by the EC can be summarized in three words: "Knowledge, Responsibility, Engagement." Starting with "knowledge," the EU's new Horizon 2020 Programme—which tackles societal challenges by helping to bridge the gap between research and global market—will enhance the EU external actions in the Arctic in order to establish closer links with third countries and their economic activities in the Arctic. It seems very pertinent to consider the EU's external relations with international entities which are increasing their research activities in the Arctic (particularly the World Meteorological Organization, the IMO and the Food and Agriculture Organization as well as the Barents-Euro Arctic Council and the Council of the Baltic Sea States). However, it must be noted that there is still no direct presence of the EU in the Arctic circumpolar cooperation either at or within the Arctic Council. Turning to "responsibility," the EU aims to work with Arctic partners and with the private sector to develop environmentally-friendly, low-risk technologies that could be used by the extractive and shipping industries. Finally, on "engagement," the EU steps up its dialogue with all Arctic States and stakeholders.[40] The EC underlines that the future Arctic policy should be consistent with the strategy of each Arctic State, so that Arctic governance can be developed and implemented on the basis of effective cooperation with countries and key partners, in particular the industry sector.

The EC position is supported also by other European entities. As said by Filip Hamro-Drotz, Member of the European Economic and Social Committee: "we should make the best of the opportunities the Arctic brings, but at the same time we should strive at limiting to the minimum the negative consequences of human activities in the region."[41]

As a major consumer, importer and technology provider of energy and raw materials, the EU has a growing interest in the resource policy developments in the Arctic States. However, the existing EU regulatory framework does not represent an exhaustive answer to the severe pressures from industry's activities at sea—including offshore drilling by European companies—which may be qualified as "threat multipliers," facing the concurrent need for ensuring safety and security within cross-sectoral and ecosystem-based approach to a sustainable maritime governance.

Even the important role played by the EU specialized agency on integrated maritime affairs has recently shown the weakness of the international fragmented system of action and intervention in the several maritime issues concerned, as well as energy supply. Moreover, maritime public administrations should steadily, in cooperation with the maritime industry and other private stakeholders in the chain of responsibility, make serious efforts to ensure safekeeping public and private actions at sea. From this perspective, the recent practice has shown the weakness of the EU ecosystem approach to Arctic security, safety and sustainability of the regulatory framework in dealing with new challenges and in adjudicating colliding interests in the Arctic, including those related to offshore drilling. The Arctic environment remains the cornerstone of the EU Arctic Policy as supported by the 2014 Council Conclusion which calls for further development of an integrated and coherent Arctic Policy by December 2015.[42]

The EU and environmental protection of Arctic ice-covered area: special reference to the Offshore Safety Directive 30/2013

According to the International Energy Agency, the global energy demand will grow by 56 percent between 2010 and 2040. Non-renewable fossil fuels serve as the dominant source of energy for humanity, powering over four-fifths of the world's utilities.[43] This implies that oil and gas will continue to have the same relevance in the global energy supplies in the years to come as they have today. There is huge potential as well as risks associated with energy-related operations in the Arctic. The energy industry sector has proved that the Arctic can be drilled, but it has not proved that these activities can be developed entirely safely yet having not demonstrated, for example, their ability to clean up a petroleum spill in ice-choked waters. Environmental groups, as NGOs (like Greenpeace)[44] or as the aforementioned Verts/ALE group in the EP, bitterly oppose drilling in such fragile ecosystem.

The EC has reacted to the incident in the Gulf of Mexico of April 2010, launching an in-depth analysis of current environmental standards adopted throughout the EU and its Member States. The study resulted in the drafting of the document "Addressing the challenge of the safety of offshore oil and gas"[45] which shows that, although the EU already has examples of national regulatory practices, harmonization "upwards" of the current framework could further improve the safety of such activities. On the basis of these findings, on October 27, 2011 the EC has adopted the Proposal for a Regulation of the European Parliament and of the Council on the safety of offshore oil and gas prospection, exploration and production in the hydrocarbon sector (Offshore Rules).[46] Offshore Rules aimed to set minimum safety standards for prospection, exploration and production of hydrocarbons offshore, reducing the likelihood of serious accidents, limiting the consequences, and at the same time increasing the protection of the marine environment.[47] Under the Irish Presidency, the Directive proposal was approved by the Council of the EU in the first reading, then by the EP in the second reading.[48]

The legal basis of the Offshore Safety Directive is Article 191 of the Treaty on the Functioning of the EU (TFUE), which establishes the objectives of preserving, protecting and improving the quality of the environment as well as prudent and rational utilization of natural resources. It reflects the EU obligation to ensure a high level of protection, taking into account the diversity of situations in the various regions of the EU. The EU considers the Arctic region as a region of the EU to which the Offshore Safety Directive makes explicit reference. In the preamble, the Directive underlines that the Arctic waters require special attention in relation to any offshore oil and gas operations and encourages Member States, who are members of the Arctic Council to actively promote the highest standards with regards to environmental safety in such a vulnerable and unique ecosystem.[49] In this sense, the Directive promotes a coordinated approach towards the safety of offshore oil and gas operations at international level in relevant global and regional fora, including those related to Arctic waters.[50]

Starting from the premise that all EU actions are based on the precautionary principle and on the principles that preventive action should be taken, the main part of the Directive concerns rules, such as the establishment of emergency plans, and requirements for risk management to be complied by the private sector. It aims at establishing minimum requirements for preventing major accidents in offshore oil and gas operations and limiting the consequences of such accidents.[51] In particular, it focuses on the legal aspects related to private actors and risk assessment documentation, that is, private actors' primary responsibility for controlling the risks, while implementing prevention policy in and outside the Union.[52] A primary role is given to the Competent National Authority for carrying out regulatory functions related to the conducting of offshore oil and gas operations.[53]

Applicability: is the offshore safety directive EEA-relevant?

Article 2 (2) of the Directive defines its geographical scope where the term "offshore" means situated in the territorial sea, economic exclusive zone (EEZ) or continental shelf of any EU Member States as defined by UNCLOS. As mentioned before, no Member States are Arctic coastal states and, therefore, no Arctic waters are European waters in legal terms. Despite the fact that Article 2 (2) does not refer to maritime zones of EEA Arctic States—Norway and Iceland—the Directive was adopted as relevant for the whole EEA. During the ordinary legislative procedure, it was considered indeed that the Directive needs to be respected by all concerned Parties, including EEA States, in their actions since its entry into force.

As regards the EEA States, in principle, the Directive obliged them to bring into force the laws, regulations and administrative provisions necessary to comply with the Directive by July 19, 2015. For private actors, such as owners and operators of installations, additional transitional periods are to be applied.[54] However, there is a common EFTA position (shared by all three EEA EFTA States, in particular Iceland and Norway as Arctic States) that the Offshore Safety Directive is only binding upon the EU States and it is not EEA relevant. The rationale behind this is twofold: first, the geographical scope; and second, the material scope. As far as the Directive's geographical scope is concerned, EEA EFTA States argue that it is wider than the geographical scope of the EEA Agreement. The Offshore Safety Directive applies to oil and gas operations in the waters of the Member States, including their territorial sea, EEZ and on their continental shelves. However, as it follows from Article 126 of the EEA Agreement, the

Agreement applies to the "territories of the EFTA States," being considered "territories" the lands and the territorial sea. Therefore, the EEZ and continental shelf, where the Norwegian oil and gas operations take place, fall outside the geographical scope of the EEA Agreement. The EEA EFTA States are accordingly not obliged to make the Directive applicable outside the territorial sea and, on the other hand, it does not give meaning to the Directive to be applied within the land territory alone.

As far as the material scope is concerned, the main objective of the Offshore Safety Directive is—as the EEA EFTA States interpret it—to ensure safety in the offshore petroleum sector and not a well-functioning internal market. The main part of the Directive concerns rules, such as the establishment of emergency plans and requirements for risk management, which will not affect the functioning of the internal market. Hence, they also consider the Directive to fall outside the material scope of the EEA Agreement. Currently, the EU is aware of the EEA EFTA position and continues its dialogue with concerned states on this matter.

Applicability outside Europe: specific reference to the Arctic waters and its interaction with MOPPR Agreement

The applicability of the Offshore Safety Directive outside Europe is related to the regulation of operations conducted by EU-based companies—registered in the territory of Members States—acting at territorial sea, EEZ and continental shelf of non-EU Members States. The EU-based companies operating outside Europe have an obligation to report circumstances of any major accident in which they have been involved.[55] Details of the information required are specified by the relevant Member States in line with the Regulations adopted on October 13, 2014.[56]

Reports by EU-based companies are also a tool for cooperation between Member States in what concerns knowledge, information and experience in the offshore sector. In particular, cooperation is envisaged to ensure better functioning of the measures of the risk management, major accident prevention, verification of compliance, and emergency response related to offshore oil and gas operation within and, when appropriate, outside the Union.[57] In addition, in order to avoid major accidents or imminent threat thereof, which has or is capable of having transboundary effects, measures relating to areas outside of the Union have to be coordinate between Member States.

More specifically, the Offshore Safety Directive makes direct reference to the Arctic waters. The Preamble stresses the importance of Arctic waters as adjacent water to the EU. In this sense it states that:

> Member States who are members of the Arctic Council are encouraged to actively promote the highest standards with regard to environmental safety in this vulnerable and unique ecosystem, such as through the

creation of international instruments on prevention, preparedness and response to Arctic marine oil pollution, and through building, inter alia, on the work of the Task Force established by the Arctic Council and the existing Arctic Council Offshore Oil and Gas Guidelines.[58]

In addition, Article 33 on the coordinated approach at international level underlines that "the Commission shall promote high safety standards for offshore oil and gas operations at international level in relevant global and regional fora, including those relating to Arctic waters."[59]

The encouragement of EU to Member States that are members of the Arctic Council have been already (partially) satisfied. The Offshore Safety Directive was indeed adopted after the 2013 Kiruna ministerial meeting of the Arctic Council where the Agreement on Cooperation on Marine Oil Pollution Preparedness and Response in the Arctic (MOPPR Agreement) was adopted.[60] The MOPPR Agreement reflects the growing relevance of the Arctic Council in filling legal *lacunae* and it is open to seeking cooperation with non-Parties of the Agreements (non-Arctic States) that may be able to contribute to achieve the scope of oil pollution response.

Analogously to the Directive, the MOPPR Agreement has the specific objective to strengthen cooperation, coordination and mutual assistance among the Parties through their Competent National Authorities if an oil spill occurs. With regard to the geographical scope of application, it applies to oil pollution incidents that occur in, or may pose a threat to, any marine area over which Arctic States exercise sovereignty, sovereign rights or jurisdiction, including its internal waters, territorial sea, EEZ and continental shelf.[61] Therefore, the geographical scope of MOPPR Agreement does not overlap with that of the Offshore Safety Directive for two reasons. First, as said before, no EU Member States are Arctic coastal States, and, second, it seems that the EEA EFTA position is to consider the Directive as non-EEA relevant.

In addition, the MOPPR Agreement also includes monitoring activities in order to identify oil pollution incidents not only in areas under national jurisdiction, but also, "to the extent feasible," beyond it.[62] What does "the extent feasible" mean? To what extent are the monitoring activities consistent with the scope of application of the Agreement? To what extent might it be relevant for the applicability of the Offshore Safety Directive outside Europe?

Differently from the Offshore Safety Directive and its Regulation, the Agreement includes the non-binding Operational Guidelines, which set out provisions to guide oil pollution preparedness and response in the Arctic. In its Section 4, titled "Response Operations in Areas Beyond National Jurisdiction," the Guidelines go further than the application scope of the Agreement and underline that actions (without specifying "monitor actions" as the text of the Agreement) in areas beyond national jurisdiction (such as the high seas) should be undertaken in accordance with national and international law.[63] At this point, it seems that the "extent of feasibility" might be given by the consistence of (monitoring) activities with national and international law.

However, the application scope of the Agreement is not clear yet. Definition of jurisdictional issues through the analysis of the emerging mosaic of national jurisdictions is still far from complete. But complementing the sovereignty approach, it is apparent that the Arctic Council is opening access and presenting roles for relevant global actors, such as the EU, in the near future.[64] In the meantime, while considering that the 2013 MOPPR Agreement adopted by the Arctic States does not include specific binding common standards, the EP is still calling for a binding ad hoc instrument for Arctic pollution prevention.[65]

Conclusion

Ice does not have an ad hoc legal status either in International or in EU law. The only specific regulation is the IMO's Polar Code. Therefore, the presence of ice does not change the legal status of the Arctic Ocean. The Law of the Sea is fitted to be applied to the dynamic evolution of Arctic environmental challenges and threats. UNCLOS, generally considered the Constitution for Oceans, is based on both sovereignty-based approach and general interests approach, thus responding to all the current trends in the Arctic (creeping jurisdiction v. creeping cooperation, as defined in the introduction). The sovereignty-based approach, which reflects the creeping jurisdiction trend, is regulated mainly by Parts II–VIII of UNCLOS in which the maritime delimitation process is also taken into consideration. As Parts of the same "Constitution," they have to be applied harmoniously with Part XIII which is based on the general interests approach (reflecting, to some extent, the creeping cooperation trend) and especially dedicated to the protection and preservation of the marine environment. By considering the Arctic Ocean as a (regional) semi-enclosed sea, Part IX of UNCLOS, also calls for inviting, where appropriate, other interested states or international organizations (such as the EU) to cooperate with the Arctic Council. In terms of future developments, it is desirable that such cooperation would lead to the adoption of binding instruments (*hard law*) which include compliance mechanisms and better indicate the interaction between the MOPPR Agreement and Offshore Safety Directive in the field of offshore operations. Otherwise, there would be questioning over the *governance impasse* and the effectiveness of further increasing mechanisms of cooperation, where the standpoint of common interests among and between the Arctic States and other entities will mainly be identified through *soft law*, non-binding instruments.

Any further development of the EU role in the Arctic will depend on the internal coherence at an institutional level, between the EP and EC. Despite of the EP position, the premise seems to be that EC and the

Council are developing the EU Arctic Policy with a high degree of external vertical coherence with international instruments like UNCLOS, as well as horizontal coherence related to environmental and energy policies, as proves the Offshore Safety Directive.

Notes

1 This publication is the result of collaboration within the framework of MC-IEF Project EU_ARCTYCA and, complementary, of the COST Action IS1105, network of experts on the legal aspects of maritime safety and security (MARSAFENET).
2 All of them, except the United States, are Parties to the 1982 UN Convention on the Law of the Sea (UNCLOS). UNCLOS (adopted on December 10, 1982; entered into force on November 16, 1994) 1833 UNTS 396; the Agreement relating to the Implementation of Part XI of the United Nations Convention of the Law of the Sea of December 10, 1982 (adopted on July 28, 1994; entered into force on July 28, 1996) 1836 UNTS 4, and the Agreement for the Implementation of the Provision of the United Nations Convention of the Law of the Sea of December 10, 1982 relating to the Conservation and Management of Straddling Fish Stocks and Highly Migratory Fish Stocks (adopted on August 4, 1995 and entered into force on December 11, 2001) 2167 UNTS 88.
3 Michael Byers, *International Law and the Arctic* (Cambridge: Cambridge University Press, 2013), 283.
4 James Brown Scott, "Arctic Exploration and International Law." *AJIL* 3.4 (1909): 928–41. Thomas Willing Balch, "The Arctic and Antarctic Regions and the Law of Nations." *AJIL* 4.2 (1910): 265–75; Thomas Willing Balch, "Les Régions Arctiques et Antarctiques et le droit international." *RDI* XII (1910): 434–42.
5 The first Arctic State to claim EEZ was Norway. It established three zones of 200 nautical miles pursuant to the Act of December 17, 1976 relating to the exclusive economic zones of Norway (also called the Zone Act). Three years later, the USA proclaimed their EEZ through a Statement by the President of March 10, 1983. Other coastal States claimed their EEZ years later.
6 Claudia Cinelli, *El Ártico ante el Derecho del Mar Contemporáneo* (Valencia: Tirant lo Blanch, 2012).
7 Judgment on Maritime Delimitation in the Area between Greenland and Jan Mayen, *ICJ Reports* (1993).
8 Donat Pharand, "The Legal Status of the Arctic Regions." *RCADI* II (1979): 49–116.
9 Olav Schram Stokke, "A Legal Regime for the Arctic? Interplay with the Law of the Sea Convention." *Marine Policy* 31 (2007): 402–08. Rob Huebert, "Article 234 and Marine Pollution Jurisdiction in the Arctic," in *The Law of the Sea and Polar Maritime Delimitation and Jurisdiction*, edited by Alex G. Oude Elferink and Donald R. Rothwell (London: Martinus Nijhoff, 2001), 249–62.
10 Gemma Andreone, "The Exclusive Economic Zone," in *The Oxford Handbook of the Law of the Sea*, edited by Donald R. Rothwell, Alex G. Oude Elferink, Karen N. Scott and Tim Stephens (Oxford: Oxford University Press, 2015), 159–81; Gemma Andreone and Giuseppe Cataldi, "Sui generis zones," in *The IMLI Manual on International Maritime Law Volume I: The Law of the Sea*, edited by David Attard, Malgosia Fitzmaurice and Norman A. Martinez Gutierrez (Oxford: Oxford University Press, 2014), 217–93.
11 The Ilulissat Declaration "Arctic Ocean Governance." May 28, 2008. www.ocean law.org/downloads/arctic/Ilulissat_Declaration.pdf (accessed March 15, 2015).

12 Ibid., paragraph 3.
13 Ibid., paragraph 5.
14 Ibid.
15 Ibid., paragraph 8.
16 The report *The State of the Arctic Environment* (October 22, 1997) has been prepared for the European Environment Agency by the Norwegian Polar Institute with support from GRID Arendal and several other institutions. At: www.eea.europa.eu/es accessed May 6, 2016).
17 See UArctic Atlas "Defining the Arctic," on the University of Arctic website: http://old.uarctic.org/AtlasTheme.aspx?m=642 (accessed May 6, 2016).
18 International Maritime Organization (IMO) Guidelines for Ships Operating in Arctic Ice-Covered Waters (December 23, 2002) IMO Doc. MSC/Circ. 1056-MEPC/Circ. 399, that is, the forerunner of International Code for Ships Operating in Polar Waters (Polar Code) was adopted by the IMO in November 2014. For the FAO Arctic Fisheries Zone—Zone No. 18, www.fao.org/fishery/area/Area18/en (accessed May 6, 2016).
19 The Northern Dimension is a joint policy between EU, Russia, Norway and Iceland. The ND Policy was initiated in 1999 and renewed in 2006. Its main objectives are to provide a common framework for promotion of dialogue and concrete cooperation; strengthen stability and well-being; intensify economic cooperation, and promote economic integration, competitiveness, and sustainable development in Northern Europe. At: www.eeas.europa.eu/north_dim/ (accessed May 6, 2016).
20 COM(2008) 763 final, at 1.
21 Provisions of the EEA Agreement ensure full participation of the EFTA EEA countries in the internal market, and, in this respect, allows for cooperation in fields such as environment, research, tourism and civil protection, all of great importance for the Arctic.
22 Between 1973 and 1985 Greenland was part of the EU. Following a referendum in 1982, it withdrew and is now associated to the EU under the Overseas Association Decision (Council Decision 2013/755/EU of November 25, 2013).
23 Green Paper "Towards a future Maritime Policy for the Union: A European Vision for the Oceans and Seas." COM(2006) 275 final, at 14.
24 Resolution on Arctic Governance (October 8, 2008) paragraph D.
25 Ibid., paragraph 15.
26 Ibid.
27 Resolution on a Sustainable EU policy for the High North (January 20, 2011).
28 The Parliament expresses its position on all relevant policy areas: new transport routes (paragraphs 9–14), natural resources (paragraphs 15–23), climate change (paragraphs 31–41) and governance (paragraphs 42–55).
29 Ibid., paragraph 42.
30 Indrek Tarand, Isabella Lövin, Carl Schlyter, Margrete Auken, Satu Hassi and Iñaki Irazabalbeitia Fernández on behalf of the Verts/ALE Group Doc. 2013/2595(RSP).
31 Ibid., paragraph 38.
32 Ibid., paragraph 35.
33 Ibid.
34 Resolution on EU strategy for the Arctic (March 12, 2014).
35 Ibid., paragraph 18.
36 COM(2008) 763 final (November 20, 2008).
37 JOIN(2012) 19 final.
38 SWD(2012) 182 final.
39 SWD(2012) 183 final.
40 SPEECH/13/329.

41 CES/13/7.
42 Council Conclusions on Developing a European Union Policy towards the Arctic Region (May 12, 2014), paragraph 15.
43 Ping Zhou, "Fossil Fuels Petroleum, Coal, and Natural Gas Power Much of the Planet." At: http://geography.about.com/od/economic-geography/a/Fossil-Fuels.htm (accessed May 6, 2016).
44 See www.greenpeace.org/international/en/Ai (accessed May 18, 2015). Also, the recent news about the crew of the Greenpeace ship *Arctic Sunrise* that took part in a peaceful protest at Gazprom's oil rig to call attention to the threat of oil drilling and climate change. For more information, see "Meet the Arctic 30," www.greenpeace.org/international/en/campaigns/climate-change/arctic-impacts/Peace-Dove/Arctic-30/ (accessed May 6, 2016).
45 COM(2010) 560 final (October 12, 2010).
46 COM(2011) 688 final (October 27, 2011).
47 During three different EU presidencies (Poland, Denmark and Cyprus), the Council, through its Working Party on Energy (EWP), analyzed the Draft Regulation and presented several amendments. Subsequently, the Proposal for a Regulation has become "Proposal for a Directive" following the resolution of the EWP Council and, in parallel, also from the Committee on Industry, Research and Energy (ITRE) of the European Parliament.
48 It was published in the Official Journal of the European Union on June 28, 2013 as Directive 2013/30/EU of June 12, 2013 on the safety of operations at sea in the hydrocarbons sector (Offshore Safety Directive) and amending Directive 2004/35/EC. The ordinary legislative procedure (Article 294 TFEU) gives the same weight to the European Parliament and the Council of the European Union on a wide range of areas, including environment, which is the legal basis of the Offshore Safety Directive.
49 Preamble, paragraph 52, Offshore Safety Directive.
50 Article 33, Offshore Safety Directive.
51 Article 1, Offshore Safety Directive.
52 Articles 19 and 20, Offshore Safety Directive.
53 Articles 8 and 9, Offshore Safety Directive.
54 Article 41, Offshore Safety Directive.
55 Preamble, paragraphs 36, 38, 39, 41 and 61, and, more precisely, Article 20, Offshore Safety Directive.
56 Regulation (EU) No. 1112/2014 (October 13, 2014).
57 Article 27, Offshore Safety Directive.
58 Preamble, paragraph 52, Offshore Safety Directive.
59 Article 33.3, Offshore Safety Directive.
60 "Agreement on Cooperation on Marine Oil Pollution, Preparedness and Response in the Arctic," signed on May 15, 2013; not yet in force. At: www.arctic-council.org/eppr/agreement-on-cooperation-on-marine-oil-pollution-preparedness-and-response-in-the-arctic/ (accessed May 6, 2016).
61 Article 3, MOPPR Agreement.
62 Article 7, MOPPR Agreement.
63 Appendix IV to the MOPPR Agreement, *Operational Guidelines.*
64 In the meantime, individual State applications for permanent Observer Status to the Arctic Council have been accepted. In contrast to previous ministerial meetings, the Kiruna ministerial meeting welcomed six new Observer States: China, India, Italy, Japan, the Republic of Korea and Singapore. During the Kiruna ministerial meeting, on May 15, 2013, the Arctic Council deferred a final decision on EU application until the Arctic ministers are agreed by consensus. In other words, the EU's application for Observer Status was received affirmatively but has not yet been approved. It seems that the possible reason

for this delay may be related to the EU bid, which includes concerns on the EU ban on seal fur and other products from Canada, the country that took over the chairmanship of the Arctic Council from Sweden. The next ministerial meeting was held in April 2015. It has to be noted that the EU has not yet obtained formal status of permanent observer of the Arctic Council according with the Iqaluit Ministerial Meeting in 2015.

65 See note 34 *supra*.

References

Andreone, Gemma. "The Exclusive Economic Zone." In *The Oxford Handbook of the Law of the Sea*, edited by Donald R. Rothwell, Alex G. Oude Elferink, Karen N. Scott, and Tim Stephens, 159–81. Oxford: Oxford University Press, 2015.

Andreone, Gemma and Giuseppe Cataldi. "Sui generis zones." In *The IMLI Manual on International Maritime Law Volume I: The Law of the Sea*, edited by David Attard, Malgosia Fitzmaurice and Norman A. Martinez Gutierrez, 217–93. Oxford: Oxford University Press, 2014.

Balch, Thomas Willing. "The Arctic and Antarctic regions and the Law of Nations." *AJIL* 4.2 (1910): 265–75.

Balch, Thomas Willing. "Les Régions Arctiques et Antarctiques et le droit international." *RDI* XII (1910): 434–42.

Byers, Michael. *International Law and the Arctic.* Cambridge: Cambridge University Press, 2013.

Cinelli, Claudia. *El Ártico ante el Derecho del Mar Contemporáneo.* Valencia: Tirant lo Blanch, 2012.

Huebert, Rob. "Article 234 and Marine Pollution Jurisdiction in the Arctic." In *The Law of the Sea and Polar Maritime Delimitation and Jurisdiction*, edited by Alex G. Oude Elferink and Donald R. Rothwell, 249–62. London: Martinus Nijhoff Publishers, 2001.

Oude Elferink, Alex G. and Donald R. Rothwell. *The Law of the Sea and Polar Maritime Delimitation and Jurisdiction.* London: Martinus Nijhoff Publishers, 2001.

Pharand, Donat. "The Legal Status of the Arctic Regions." *RCADI* II (1979): 49–116.

Scott, James Brown. "Arctic exploration and International Law." *AJIL* 3.4 (1909): 928–41.

Stokke, Olav Schram. "A Legal Regime for the Arctic? Interplay with the Law of the Sea Convention." *Marine Policy* 31 (2007): 402–08.

Zhou, Ping. "Fossil Fuels Petroleum, Coal, and Natural Gas Power Much of the Planet." At: http://geography.about.com/od/economic-geography/a/Fossil-Fuels.htm (accessed May 6, 2016).

Part II
The governance of the Arctic region

8 The Arctic Council at twenty

Cooperation between governments in the global Arctic

Christoph Humrich

Introduction

At the time of writing this chapter, the Arctic Council (AC) is in its nineteenth year of existence.[1] Looking back on the development of the AC in the preceding years, it is surely fair to say that intergovernmental cooperation in the Arctic region has come of age. Still, in the face of the "transformative change now occurring," as the Conference of Parliamentarians of the Arctic Region (CPAR) states, there seems to be a need for developing this cooperation further.[2] To that end the CPAR is calling for an Arctic Summit on occasion of the AC's twentieth anniversary in 2016.

Such a summit could become an important catalytic event for the debate over the AC and the form and functioning of regional intergovernmental cooperation in the Arctic. Ever since the idea of a regional governance institution was first entertained seriously in the 1980s, this debate has provided accounts of the institutional dynamics of Arctic politics and policies. The present chapter joins in this debate and concurs with Timo Koivurova's remark that reflecting on the "limits and possibilities of the Arctic Council" makes it "important to examine the past of Arctic intergovernmental cooperation."[3] However, examining the past and reconstructing institutional dynamics can be done in more than one way and the different ways to write histories determine the respective lessons drawn. As James March and Johan Olsen maintain, there is "a grand issue" dividing students of institutional dynamics: "the question of institutional efficiency."[4] The answers to this question make the distinction between two general perspectives on institutional dynamics: the latter are either viewed as *efficient* or as *inefficient* histories.

The following first main section briefly sketches the history of intergovernmental cooperation in the Arctic from both general perspectives. The section aims at demonstrating how the differences between efficient and inefficient histories show in evaluations of past achievements *of* and future directions *for* the AC. Those appraising the history of Arctic governance as efficient mostly recommend and foresee incremental adjustments in the *functions* of the AC as sufficient adaptation to emerging challenges from transformative change in the region. By contrast, those seeing the history as inefficient, urgently call for fundamental alterations in the institutional *form* of regional intergovernmental cooperation.

But the two perspectives also share an important characteristic. They both frame "nation-state governments [...] as actors primarily interested in dealing with problems as effectively as possible."[5] Efficient histories merely assume the actors manage to achieve just this, while the inefficient histories' gist is that they do not. Klaus Dieter Wolf claims that, in the end, this frame furthers a limited appreciation of the *government* dimension of the actors. To correct for this, Wolf proposes to consider a different frame: the *new raison d'état.*[6] The second main section of this chapter accordingly substitutes the frame of the *new raison d'état* for the state as problem-solving actor. This changes the historical perspective again and thus also the lessons drawn for the future. Recommendations derived from inefficient histories to fundamentally alter the institutional form of intergovernmental cooperation appear as neither effective nor desirable. The efficient views of history by contrast place too high hopes for functional adjustments on the intergovernmental institutional dynamics.

The chapter will conclude by directing the view away from intergovernmental institutional dynamics to transnational civil society in the Arctic region and its deliberative processes. Increasing their relevance for and impact on regional governance seems to be the best option in dealing with the challenges the region is facing.

Two histories of institutional dynamics and their lessons for the future of Arctic intergovernmental cooperation

This section portrays the institutional dynamics of Arctic intergovernmental cooperation in two ways: as an efficient and as an inefficient history. The efficient history perspectives impute functional rationality to the actors. Actors know what they want, what they can get in interaction with other relevant actors and the latters' prevailing interests, and how to get it. Over a series of interactive encounters, actors manage to realize potential mutual gains. According to March and Olsen, for efficient histories "the presumption is that political bargains adjust quickly and in a necessary way to exogenous changes."[7] If at first sight institutional dynamics defy this presumption, the analyst searches for external constraints or changes in interests or resources still unaccounted for in the efficient history.

Inefficient histories by contrast "emphasize the slow pace of historical adaptation."[8] An inefficient history has no difficulty in admitting that institutional dynamics at rare times might adapt to exogenous change efficiently, but it sees "the match between political institutions and their environments as less automatic, less continuous and less precise."[9] Rather than being surprised by institutional slack, analyses from this perspective demonstrate how endogenous constraints like path dependencies or pertinacious identities interfere with the dynamics of institutional adaptation, limit the ability to realize potential gains to the full extent, and lead to inconsistencies between actual institutional form and functional requirements.

While the perspectives do not necessarily disagree about environmental changes and challenges to the institutions, their role vis-à-vis the practice of institutional adaptation itself is different. An analyst from the efficient history perspective is optimistic by default that actors and institutions eventually adapt well to environmental change. The analyst at best can spare the actors some time and troubles by making creative suggestions for optimal bargains or by working out the details of specific institutional adjustments. Inefficient history perspectives do not expect actors or institutions to meet environmental changes adequately. Therefore, analysts here point out unrecognized internal limits to the realization of potential gains and issue wake-up calls to the actors.

An efficient history of Arctic intergovernmental cooperation

In histories of Arctic intergovernmental cooperation it is generally agreed that Mikhail Gorbachev's famous speech at Murmansk in 1987 can count as a catalytic event, which set in motion a *first phase* of institutional dynamics in the Arctic.[10] Gorbachev proposed extensive intergovernmental cooperation in the Arctic region, which before had simply been unthinkable due to the Cold War politics.[11] The speech not only created momentum for the general rapprochement between the East and the West but also opened a large window of opportunity for Arctic intergovernmental cooperation. Finland was quick to seize this opportunity and responded positively to the proposal the next day. Already the following year informal talks on the possibility of Arctic intergovernmental cooperation were held. The USA was at first reluctant to enter into any regional cooperation, but was finally convinced by external events to adapt its policy: the environmental disaster of the *Exxon Valdez* oil spill and the sinking of the Russian nuclear-powered submarine *Komsomolets* both occurring in spring 1989.[12] Right after that an official Finnish initiative was launched for a circumpolar intergovernmental cooperation on environmental protection. Thomas S. Axworthy's account of the Finnish initiative characterizes it as "an excellent illustration" of an efficient strategy, acknowledging limited resources and political feasibility and thus successfully "aiming at attainable results."[13] In the so-called Rovaniemi Process, the initiative lead in 1991 to the signing of the Arctic Environmental Protection Strategy (AEPS) by all eight states with territory above the Arctic Circle.[14] The AEPS institutional form consisted of regular ministerial meetings and four working groups.[15] The issue-scope of the working groups was an aggregate of the particular interests of the Arctic Eight, and thus the structure constituted an effective bargain.[16]

However, Gorbachev's momentum eventually carried even further because it was used by Canada to promote its idea for a more institutionalized cooperation in a regional body. Shortly after the announcement of the Finnish initiative and not even a month after the Berlin Wall's fall in 1989, the Canadian Prime Minister Brian Mulroney spoke in Leningrad and asked "why not a council of Arctic countries...?"[17] The Finnish initiative had been conceived by most as a confidence-building exercise, thus the narrow environmental focus made sense. With the now apparent end of the Cold War a more comprehensive and institutionalized intergovernmental cooperation to realize mutual gains in the Arctic became possible.

Yet, a *second phase* of Arctic intergovernmental cooperation could only start when another exogenous change occurred. While the USA had given up resistance against such cooperation, it was initially unwilling to invest in a new institutional structure. Negotiations on the AC could not begin before the US government changed and the new administration adapted its Arctic policy in line with its generally supportive view of multilateralism. It announced willingness to negotiate the terms of a regional forum in 1995.[18] The Arctic States finished negotiations in just a year and delivered the founding declaration of the AC in 1996.[19] The four initial working groups of the AEPS were smoothly transferred to the environmental protection pillar of the AC at the fourth and last AEPS ministerial in Alta, Norway the year after. Thus, a change of institutional form "from a strategy [...] to an organization [...] happened in a relatively short time frame."[20]

Beside the change in institutional form, changes in terms of actor inclusion and issue-scope were part of the institutional dynamics in the second phase. Both changes can be seen as an adaptation to the changes in global environmental politics, which had already left its mark on Arctic intergovernmental cooperation. The 1992 UN Conference on Environment and Development in Rio de Janeiro, Brazil (UNCED) had not only established sustainable development as a principle of multilateral environmental cooperation, but it also emphasized the indigenous peoples' crucial role in its blueprint for global sustainable development, the *Agenda 21*. This had been reflected in the declaration of the AEPS second ministerial meeting in Nuuk, 1993, which had been strongly influenced by the Rio Declaration. Since Nuuk a new AEPS working group on sustainable development was in preparation. It was eventually realized and incorporated under the sustainable development pillar of the AC as the council's fifth working group (SDWG). Moreover, during the Rovaniemi Process and the AEPS work, indigenous peoples' organizations (IPOs) had progressively played a stronger role.[21] Their contributions to the effectiveness and legitimacy of the intergovernmental cooperation was acknowledged in the AC by giving IPOs the status of Permanent Participants. A creative solution was found to define IPOs eligible for this status, which neither endangered the interests of the existing participants nor closed the door for new.

It was in fact encouraging indigenous peoples to organize more effectively nationally and transnationally and worked to enhance their contributions to the tasks of the AC.[22]

To conclude, it may be stated that in the second phase the AC efficiently built on the existing AEPS structure and adapted it to a new situation in multilateral environmental cooperation.

The institutional set-up of the AC was finalized during the first and second ministerial meetings of the AC in Iqaluit, Canada, 1998 and Barrow, Alaska, 2000.[23] The Barrow meeting can be seen as the entrance into the *third phase* of the Arctic States' intergovernmental cooperation. Institutional dynamics refocused from form change to actual functioning. In Barrow, two comprehensive and consequential programs were initiated: the *Arctic Climate Impact Assessment* (ACIA) and the *Arctic Council Action Plan to Eliminate Pollution of the Arctic* (ACAP). ACIA published a much acclaimed report in 2004 and ACAP became the foundation for the sixth and so far last addition to the Council's working group roster at the 2006 ministerial meeting in Salekhard, Russia. Moreover, the Barrow declaration makes several explicit references to institutional dynamics outside the Arctic: multilateral environmental policies related to the control of persistent organic pollutants (POPs) and mercury, the IMO guidelines for polar shipping, and the preparations for the Rio+10 conference from 2002.[24]

With these activities, the Barrow meeting set the tune for the coming years: ACIA was not to remain the only landmark publication based on working group output of the AC, and the Arctic States were increasingly recognized as a group in other multilateral environmental policy settings and could gain influence there. The SDWG increasingly focused on social and economic topics important to indigenous peoples. Mobilization and the active involvement of IPOs increased. In the efficient history perspective, the AC successfully found its institutional niche in intergovernmental cooperation relevant to the Arctic. First, it focused on regional knowledge production. As Olav Stokke concludes, the AC thereby successfully "exploits the particular edge ... [it] has over other bodies," and thus "took advantage of its circumpolar scope and the priority given by its member states to polar science."[25] Second, it managed to serve as a catalyst for global initiatives on norm-setting beneficial to the Arctic.[26] Third, it gave a boost to perceiving the Arctic as a distinct region. Knowledge production about the "common North" provided articulations of the Arctic as a region and thus effectively contributed to a regionalization process.[27] Finally, the AC provided a venue for indigenous peoples and transnational civil society, which empowered further "even indigenous organizations with a strong tradition of transnational work."[28]

During 2007 through 2009, however, several developments reached their culmination and the *fourth phase* of the Arctic intergovernmental cooperation began. The establishment of the Arctic States as a distinct group and the landmark reports of the AC had already incited much renewed interest in the region in non-Arctic quarters. But three developments put the Arctic at the center of global media attention: A Russian expedition planted a flag on the sea floor at the North Pole, which it claimed to belong to her extended continental shelf; the US Geological Survey produced estimates of significant undiscovered hydrocarbon deposits in the region; and climate change hit the Arctic with record low ice covers. These developments were quickly linked with prophesies about looming conflict between the Arctic States and a resource bonanza to the detriment of the fragile Arctic environment, which was threatened by climate change anyway.[29] As all three developments pertained mostly to the Arctic Ocean, the five coastal states met in Ilulissat, Greenland, in 2008 without the other three Member States of the AC, to discuss sovereignty and governance issues of the Arctic. Many observers thus saw the AC "faced" with "potential marginalization" as the prime venue for intergovernmental cooperation in the Arctic.[30] As Takei notes, these developments and their political response may thus have "cast doubt on the ability of the Arctic Council to effectively address problems in the Arctic." However, as he goes on, "responses by Arctic Council member states led to successive actions aimed at strengthening the Council."[31] The Arctic Five met separately to boost the efforts to strengthen the AC. These efforts had begun at the AC's sixth ministerial meeting in Tromsø, Norway (2009), and continued through subsequent meetings in Nuuk, Greenland (2011) and Kiruna, Sweden (2013).[32]

Through these three meetings, questions regarding inclusion, issue-scope as well as implementation drove the institutional dynamics. The increased interest in the region and the work of the AC had made it necessary to revise the observer rules for non-Arctic States.[33] Moreover, the developments mentioned above had made it clear that the AC was also facing new regulatory challenges from traffic and hydrocarbon-related activities in the region and needed increased organizational capacity. Thus, the Arctic States established a permanent secretariat in Tromsø,[34] negotiated two legally binding agreements on Search and Rescue (SAR) and Marine Oil Pollution Preparedness and Response (MOPPR),[35] and broadened the scope of Arctic regional cooperation by facilitating the creation of an Arctic Economic Council as a business venue thereby confirming that "economic cooperation will be on the top of our agenda."[36]

Therefore the efficient history perspective concludes that, confronted with exogenous challenges, institutional dynamics adapted promptly. All in all, participants and observers of Arctic intergovernmental cooperation who view institutional dynamics as efficient histories agree that "the AC has exceeded the expectations."[37]

An inefficient history of Arctic intergovernmental cooperation

An analysis from the inefficient histories perspective sees the *first phase* of Arctic intergovernmental cooperation much less like a quickly seized opportunity. It points to the potential that had been there in existing ideas for comprehensive Arctic intergovernmental cooperation and the political opportunities to realize it: already in the mid-1980s Canadian academics, environmentalists, and IPOs had begun to develop and promote plans for intergovernmental cooperation in the Arctic. When Gorbachev made his proposal for the region, these plans did not seem merely theoretical anymore. After Mulroney had spoken in Leningrad, blueprints for a council proliferated.[38] Yet, when launching its initiative after the Murmansk speech, the Finnish government was "picking up on perhaps the least contentious of Gorbachev's suggestions."[39] It cut down the broad issue-scope of Gorbachev's speech to the environmental aspect which seemed to work well enough as a confidence-building measure, served the specific pollution-related interests of the Scandinavian states, and bore little risk in political and security terms.

The Canadian proposal for a more comprehensive regional body by contrast was stranded on the remnants of Cold War caution and skepticism vis-à-vis any idea traceable to Soviet origin—particularly in the USA. Despite the fact that the other seven Arctic States had already reached an agreement on the desirability of an Arctic regional body early on, "the intergovernmental discussions almost petered out [...] in the face of continuing US uneasiness."[40] Until that changed in 1995, the geopolitical outlook of the USA still was one of the Cold War superpower for which regional engagement beyond narrow functional cooperation seemed unsuitable.[41] Yet, as the USA had finally agreed to join the AEPS and the idea of a regional body was discussed in this context, the seven others shied away from the possibility of endeavoring to have stronger and more comprehensive cooperation without the USA.

Even after US policies had changed, this cast a shadow on the *second phase* of Arctic intergovernmental cooperation, because it gave the USA a "take-it-or-leave-it" bargaining chip and the final council arrangement came out as a "minimalist version of what had been envisaged back in the early 1990s."[42] It was minimalist in two regards: the issue-scope and the institutional form. Regarding institutional form, Koivurova concludes that between AEPS and AC, "the fundaments of the cooperation have remained very much the same."[43] The issue-scope of the AC became somewhat broader than that of the initial AEPS cooperation through the addition of sustainable development as one of the two AC pillars. However, not only was security explicitly banned as an issue from the AC's portfolio,[44] sustainable development was also given as narrow a focus as the concept permitted. By contrast to the environmental protection pillar, sustainable development got one working group only, which was not even agreed at the AC's inauguration.[45] In a sense, the Arctic States failed to tap the potential of the worldwide embrace of the concept.

When Finland launched the Rovaniemi process in 1989, environmental policy makers from all states were already busy in planning UNCED.

However, the concept entered Arctic intergovernmental cooperation only at the Nuuk ministerial meeting in 1993, one year after the Rio conference. It then took the Arctic Eight five more years to include the corresponding working group in the new high-level forum, and then even two more years to decide on a minimalist sustainable development framework document. When the world was reviewing a decade of implementing Agenda 21 on the occasion of the Rio+10 conference in 2002, the Arctic Council's SDWG had only managed to produce operating guidelines for its projects. "Effective governance," an inefficient history of the AC's early years pointed out, "is more of a distant goal than a present reality."[46]

The landmark reports, which the AC produced in the *third phase* of its intergovernmental cooperation, can also be acknowledged from the perspective of inefficient histories. Paradoxically, such acknowledgement makes the inefficient history perspective's account even stronger in at least two respects.

First, landmark reports from the second phase of the Arctic intergovernmental cooperation were already providing clear evidence of the "potentially serious consequences of transboundary environmental issues in the Arctic" but the AC "continued the 'talk and study mentality' of the AEPS" and even made it the specific niche of the AC.[47] In other words, institutional dynamics did not adjust. The policy or regulatory responses of the AC remained "sluggish and weak."[48] Since then, more reports have produced more evidence of dramatic environmental change in the region, but not even non-binding technical guidelines were sufficiently implemented.[49] Insofar as this is due to the soft law character of the AC's output, Koivurova states that "the assessments the council has sponsored seem increasingly to challenge the very fundament of the cooperation."[50]

Second, all the AC landmark reports are still mainly insular achievements in a largely unsystematic and fragmented project-driven conduct of the individual working groups. Depending on voluntary commitment, projects largely follow the momentary interests of individual Arctic States, and thus make it difficult to steer the institutional dynamics towards efficient adjustment: "the very structure of the council's working arrangement, divided as it is [...] places limits on the ability of the council to grapple with the complex and interrelated problems posed by the new development opportunities in the region."[51]

It is no surprise then that inefficient histories are not much impressed by the measures implemented in the *fourth phase* of Arctic intergovernmental cooperation either. To begin with, they point out that a reorganization of working groups with the objective of creating more coherence through issue-integration has not even been considered at this stage. The newly established permanent secretariat's competences are restricted and its funding is limited. As Nikolas Sellheim thus foresaw, "the impacts of the secretariat on the normative environment of the

Arctic Council related governance are likely to be low."[52] While it is true that in regard to implementation the two legally binding regulatory responses to challenges are a step forward, this step is not a huge one. The agreements "reaffirm and implement [...] preexisting treaty obligations in the Arctic, without bringing any new obligations to any of the Parties."[53] Moreover, the negotiations on the more important oil pollution *prevention* will, in all likelihood, end with a soft law document only.[54] Finally, the agreements did not use the opportunity to include a wider array of important stakeholders and parties to realize the respective aims. They remained exclusively regional as did the structure of participation in the AC. The new observer rules reaffirm the AC as a forum for Arctic States only.[55] They do not even consider the root cause of the increasing interest in the AC's work—the globalization of the Arctic—but still, observers already outnumber the members and permanent participants, and there are more to follow.[56] Thus, the new rules seem to only defer the problem of inclusion.

Looking back on the institutional dynamics of Arctic intergovernmental cooperation, inefficient histories must conclude like a review of the AC's achievements already did after its early infancy: the states at best engage in "institutional tinkering" while the region "totters."[57]

Lessons drawn from histories of Arctic intergovernmental cooperation

If, as inefficient histories assume, the causes for institutional slack are internal, it is logical to propose a change in institutional *form* as proper remedy. For the inefficient histories of Arctic intergovernmental cooperation therefore the belief is sensible "that with its current weak institutional structure [...] there is not much the Arctic Council can do" to meet the challenges the region is facing head on.[58] The wake-up calls remain the same throughout the decades the debate on Arctic governance has accompanied the actual institutional dynamics. In one way or the other they suggest a shift from a soft law to a hard law arrangement for regional intergovernmental cooperation.

From the efficient history perspective the quest for a hard law fundament for Arctic intergovernmental cooperation is dismissed. Efficient histories doubt that the form change will be functional as hard law might decrease the ability to adjust. Moreover, in their opinion, hard law proposals rely on a rather blue-eyed view of law's obligatory effect. Efficient histories instead lead to suggestions detailing functional adjustments, because "the existing capacity to address matters of governance in the Arctic is substantial."[59] Yet, the optimism that institutional dynamics will efficiently adapt to environmental change through incremental adjustments might rely on a somewhat blue-eyed reading of the institutional history. The next section thus questions the common assumption of both historical perspectives in regard to the state as actor.

The *new raison d'état* and the form and functions of the Arctic Council

As indicated in the introduction, both ways of accounting for institutional dynamics assume that states are interested in effective problem-solving. Otherwise neither the wake-up calls emerging from inefficient histories, nor efficient histories' hope for proper institutional coping with environmental change would make sense. However, according to Klaus Dieter Wolf, this particular assumption about states as actors "led to a complete neglect of the 'government' dimension which is also inherent in intergovernmental cooperation."[60] Governments are interested in self-assertion and in maximizing their autonomy as necessary preconditions for the exercise of governance. Governments have "an *a priori* interest in themselves."[61]

Government autonomy is dependent on ideational and material resources. The main ideational resource is authority based on legitimacy, which usually needs to be produced through the constituencies' opportunity to participate in governance processes (input legitimacy/self-determination) or by the constituencies' satisfaction with the government's performance (output legitimacy). Revenues from taxes are the main material resources. They need to be spent to increase output legitimacy or to protect self-determination and government autonomy domestically and internationally through means of violence. Wolf argues that before the age of globalization, "posing military threats to one another" paradoxically was producing "the greatest possible degree of autonomy" domestically.[62] The threat of war was the justification for levying taxes and at the same time lowered the constituencies' demands in regard to input and output legitimacy. With the decreasing relevance of military threats posed against Western states, however, this source of government autonomy more or less dried out.[63] In addition, globalization is undermining the resource base of government autonomy in at least two regards.

Economic globalization limits the ability to generate revenues by taxes because of the increased mobility of capital and production, that can threaten to leave or does not come if government regulations impose costs unacceptable to them. Governments get into a competition for capital and production, which reduces their ability to generate the resources they need for the production of output legitimacy.[64] Decreasing output legitimacy creates increasing demand for input legitimacy, which limits the autonomy of the government to the degree that competition for capital and production goes against interests of constituencies.[65] This latter effect is aggravated by *societal* globalization, which entails the emergence of trans- and subnational spheres of authority, which compete with the government's national legitimacy base.

Political globalization entails the internationalization of decision-making as yet another threat to government autonomy.[66] Wolf, however, rather sees it as a strategy of governments to regain some autonomy: "Intergovernmental self-commitment enables them to reestablish their claim to regulate economic activities and to manipulate the domestic context."[67] Economic and societal globalization might push the states to trade in international for domestic autonomy and thus further political globalization. The governments' practice to strategically commit internationally to maximize autonomy is what Wolf calls the *new raison d'état*. He sees multilateral, hard law institutions as uniquely providing the opportunity for an autonomy trade-off. However, he also emphasizes that states aim at maximizing their autonomy. The particular form of intergovernmental commitments that maximizes autonomy might depend on the domestic and international context. Therefore, governments might not necessarily always prefer the hard law option. Quite on the contrary, if the context is different, soft law arrangements might serve to maximize autonomy.

This is the case in the Arctic where the *new raison d'état* emerges from different conditions than in the European context Wolf mainly refers to. As *governments*, the Arctic States' political administrations are confronted with economic and societal globalization. But they face globalization as *Arctic* state governments too. While they are subject to the general loss of autonomy, they also have to cope with the particulars of the Arctic context. For output legitimacy, governments need revenues *for* the development of the Arctic. But they also need revenues *from* the Arctic as a resource. Conflicting interests between indigenous peoples, environmentalists and business make it hard to rely on input legitimacy. At the same time, it has become more difficult to generate legitimacy, as spheres of authority in the Arctic States have increasingly *devolved* to a subnational level (local governments and indigenous self-determination) and *evolved* at a transnational level (transnational civil society organizations, IPOs).[68] Moreover, the Arctic is not a regional market like the EU. It does not have a much developed business structure. Neither is it an integrated economic area, nor does it attract capital and production by sheer seize. Moreover, the lack of infrastructure and the harsh environmental conditions impose high costs for production and high risk for capital.[69]

From the perspective of the *new raison d'état*, this creates a situation where the Arctic governments pursue three strategies to maintain or regain autonomy for the exercise of governance in the region. First, they have an incentive to regain control over alternative spheres of authority in regard to legitimacy as a resource. Furthermore, rather than regaining regulatory power by intergovernmental self-commitment, they need to exploit intergovernmental synergies to establish conditions for luring capital and production into the Arctic while at the same time remain flexible enough to keep regulatory costs low. Finally, the Arctic States' governments still have a high degree of control over their Arctic periphery in terms of political globalization. They have thus little incentive to invite non-Arctic States in regional intergovernmental cooperation.

In the remainder of this section, institutional dynamics in regard to the problems of inclusion, issue-scope and integration illustrate that the present governance arrangement serves the *new raison d'état* just fine in the Arctic.[70]

Inclusion

Reviewing the two histories of institutional dynamics in Arctic intergovernmental cooperation yields at least two puzzling questions in regard to inclusion.

First, if the IPOs were crucial contributors to intergovernmental cooperation, why are the states so hesitant to improve their input by providing respective infrastructure and funding? Or vice versa: if the IPOs' participation is not to the benefit of intergovernmental cooperation, why were they included in the first place?

Second, while the Arctic States acknowledged the substantial input of non-Arctic States, "it is fair to say that observers were rather marginalized during the AEPS implementation period."[71] The Nuuk observer rules clarified who can become an observer, but did not change much in regard to the observers' possibilities of active involvement. This is strange, if, as Nord put it, the one thing one should have learned in the history of Arctic intergovernmental cooperation "is that the needs of the Arctic are best served when there is an ongoing dialogue among all who feel that they are participants in the future of the region."[72]

From the perspective of the *new raison d'état*, it is not difficult to see why governments are not too keen to enable IPOs to better participate in intergovernmental institutions.[73] But it must seem odd that the governments included IPOs in the realm where they usually can act autonomously in the first place. However, the particular situation in the Arctic regarding the domestic increase of indigenous self-determination delivers a respective explanation together with the transnational organization of Arctic indigenous peoples. As one observer succinctly put it, Arctic intergovernmental cooperation provided the means for the governments "to take the initiative back from different Arctic organizations and movements representing the civil society."[74] Jyrki Käkönen thus argued that the Rovaniemi process could "be understood as a counter act of the unified states" and "environmental protection as a southern means of control."[75] This interpretation seems to have been shared at least by some Arctic inhabitants who were "leery of the intervention of national governments claiming authority over issues involving the Arctic as a whole."[76] While this gives a domestic autonomy reason why the governments started Arctic intergovernmental cooperation, it does not yet explain the innovative inclusion of the IPOs in the AC. Yet, the inclusion arrangement involved the governments in the emerging transnational spheres of authority and gave them back part of their control. The permanent participant status determined whom the states would accept at the table and thus gave the governments even some structuring influence over the transnational organization of indigenous peoples.

Non-Arctic States by contrast have not been accepted to any comparable degree at the Arctic table. This is despite the fact that environmental change in the Arctic is mostly caused outside the region. It appears odd because one of the reasons for the Scandinavian governments to start Arctic intergovernmental cooperation was precisely the inclusion of the USSR as the outside cause to some of their environmental problems. Why not include non-Arctic States as well? With this background, the statement by Piotr Graczyk and Timo Koivurova that "Arctic states' reluctance to engage with external entities stems from a preoccupation with own interests" is not immediately convincing.[77] It becomes convincing when it is narrowed to the interest of the governments in their autonomy and refers to the degree that the Arctic governments fear the loss of autonomy when they have to cope with additional actors. When the AC set-up was discussed, the Scandinavian states committed to the inclusion of the USA because it was the inner balance against the USSR. But there cannot be a proper balance against the inclusion of all relevant non-Arctic States and entities (such as China or the EU). The Arctic governments therefore maximize their autonomy through a different arrangement. On the one hand, they have an observer regime which gives the AC members full control, generates additional resources through observer contributions and obliges the observers in regard to the Arctic Eight's regional interests. On the other hand, the AC has intensified its outreach and international visibility policy and its engagement in global multilateral environmental policies. This increases the Arctic governments' ability to pursue their interests in relation to the outside causes of Arctic environmental change in the relevant intergovernmental contexts outside the region as the cases of persistent organic pollutants and mercury show.

Issue-scope and integration

The problems of issue-scope and integration provide two other examples of *new raison d'état* practices in the Arctic. The first example relates to the question whether security should be included into the issue-scope of the AC. From the *new raison d'état* perspective such an inclusion is not to be expected. Security is the realm where government autonomy is still least impaired.[78] On the one hand, that provides an incentive for the governments to securitize issues, which is also the case—to some degree—in the Arctic context.[79] On the other hand, however, at the current stage of institutional dynamics, the Arctic governments would limit their room for maneuver considerably by sharing security affairs with IPOs and observers. The private meeting of the Arctic Five in Ilulissat illustrates this: if there is a need to discuss security related issues, this is done as exclusively as possible.

But why then do security related statements appear in the AC declarations and why did the AC negotiate the clearly security related SAR agreement under its auspices? Again, this can be explained as an autonomy maximizing move because the security related vocabulary appeared as soon as non-Arctic organizations like EU and NATO took an interest in the Arctic.[80] While the reference to peace and security signaled to these organizations that the Arctic governments can handle such matters alone, Arctic governments were at the same time not committing themselves to such an extent that IPOs or observers would get involved. The separately negotiated SAR agreement was also providing a venue for exclusively intergovernmental and regional defense diplomacy while *not* including security under the AC issue-scope.[81]

The second example in regard to issue-scope is the introduction of sustainable development in Arctic intergovernmental cooperation. On a global scale, committing to Agenda 21 made sense for the developed countries because it was a potential opportunity for comprehensive environmental regulation programs vis-à-vis the global economy while it gave some flexibility and leeway to developing countries. In the AC context, it was the other way round. Here, the AEPS had already established environmental protection as an issue, and sustainable development reopened a way to boost development. The Russian government saw it that way explicitly, but Canada and Scandinavian governments also concurred and had the additional reason that sustainable development could channel the IPOs' participation and thus linked it to the question of IPO inclusion.[82] It also explains why the USA was so much against its inclusion, because at that time Washington could gain more by giving in to environmentalists, who were strictly opposed to economic development in the Arctic. The intergovernmental commitment in turn gave leeway vis-à-vis the Alaskan government, which was more pro-development.

However, at the same time, Arctic governments needed to remain flexible and to avoid regulatory costs for Arctic businesses where necessary. Adopting sustainable development in a fragmented and narrow way instead of introducing it wholesale in the Arctic context achieved this aim. The more recent role the concept played in Arctic intergovernmental cooperation confirms one thing: rather than integrating environment and development, it served to isolate economic activities from the environmental core of the AC's activities and make the former the top priority.

If Arctic intergovernmental cooperation is influenced by the *new raison d'état*, the prospects for adaptations of institutional dynamics—be they in form or in function—remain low as long as environmental change does not provide different incentives in regard to the *new raison d'état*. Moreover, the perspective also suggests that even if a binding treaty were feasible, it might not be desirable. It would strengthen executives' control of the Arctic and the exclusionary character of its intergovernmental cooperation structure.

But having rejected both optimism about functional adjustment potential and blueprints for a fundamental change in institutional form, what remains? The following concluding part takes up Wolf's ideas again. The logic of the *new raison d'état* can be escaped by realizing that "we do not have to rely on the intergovernmental arena alone when we think about the reorganization of governance beyond the state."[83]

Conclusion: reconnecting the Arctic Council with the global Arctic

To escape the *new raison d'état*, Wolf sees particular potential in two guiding principles: functional differentiation and embedded degovernmentalization. The former aims at "mobilizing additional problem-solving and power-controlling resources at the same time" by shifting attention away from spatial to sectoral organization of governance.[84] The latter of the two principles calls for "associative and parliamentary arenas [...] to be conceived of primarily as deliberative forums" engaged in "policy formulation, agenda setting, and public debate."[85] Fragmentation resulting from functional differentiation could be avoided through the integrating capacities of deliberating publics. These embed traditional intergovernmental cooperation within a broader conception of governance. While the governments would retain their decision-making power "intergovernmental diplomacy would indeed lose its singular authority to run the political process beyond the state."[86]

If the only hope for institutional dynamics in the Arctic lies with transnational civil society, it is not just a faint hope. Along with intergovernmental institutional dynamics in the Arctic, a transnational civil society and an indeed remarkable deliberative periphery of intergovernmental cooperation emerged: be it in network associations—such as the Parliamentarians of the Arctic, the Northern Forum, and the transnational indigenous peoples organizations or their big conferences—or at events like the Arctic Frontier or newly created Arctic Circle congresses, the region has numerous deliberative arenas. The University of the Arctic is a forum, which certainly provides a node between these networks as do the AC and its working groups. Their events are crystallization points both for the functionally differentiated and for the broader publics.

If transnational civil society associations manage to initiate networks reaching from local rights holders to global stakeholders, "national governments would no longer be the gatekeepers to decide on inclusion or exclusion."[87] If transnational civil society used deliberative arenas to find compromises or even consensus which bridges conflicting interests and came up with an integrated vision of the region, government discretion to pick and choose their issue agenda could be limited. In a true bottom–up process these arenas could for instance serve to compile a regional Agenda 21 by reviewing all the knowledge and recommendations already produced in Arctic intergovernmental cooperation. It could serve as a new blueprint for the institutional adaptation to environmental change in the region. It would revive the strategic approach envisioned rudimentarily and not very ambitiously by the AEPS and which eventually got lost in the AC's division of labor. Finally, such a strategic approach could make it easier for the forums providing nodes between civil society networks to coordinate a critical monitoring and appraisal of the implementation of a comprehensive strategy.

In this sense it might not be a bad idea to take up the CPAR's call for an Arctic Summit to celebrate the twentieth anniversary of the Arctic Council. While not much should be expected from the gathered heads of state or government, such a summit could work as a catalytic event for transnational civil society in the Arctic as did UNCED globally in 1992 after twenty years of global environmental politics.

Notes

1 The Council was inaugurated on September 19, 1996 at a meeting of the eight Arctic States in Ottawa.
2 The 11th Conference of Parliamentarians of the Arctic Region. "Conference Report." (2014):, 29. Accessed March 29, 2015, www.arcticparl.org/files/cpar conference2014-e.pdf.
3 Timo Koivurova, "Limits and Possibilities of the Arctic Council in a Rapidly Changing Scene of Arctic Governance," *Polar Record* 46.2 (2010): 146.
4 James G. March and Johan P. Olsen, "The Institutional Dynamics of International Political Orders," *International Organization* 52.4 (1998): 954.
5 Klaus Dieter Wolf, "The New Raison d'état as a Problem for Democracy in World Society," *European Journal of International Relations* 5.3 (1999): 334.
6 Ibid., 344–50.
7 March and Olsen, "Institutional Dynamics," 954.
8 Ibid., 954.
9 Ibid., 954–55.
10 See, for instance, Thomas S. Axworthy and Ryan Dean, "Changing the Arctic Paradigm from Cold War to Cooperation: How Canada's Indigenous Leaders Shaped the Arctic Council," *Yearbook of Polar Law* 5.1 (2013): 7–43; Eva Carina Helena Keskitalo, "International Region-Building: Development of the Arctic as an International Region," *Cooperation and Conflict* 42.2 (2007): 187–205; David Scrivener, *Gorbachev's Murmansk Speech: The Soviet Initiative and Western Response* (Oslo: Norwegian Atlantic Committee, 1989); Oran R. Young, *Creating Regimes: Arctic Accords and International Governance* (Ithaca, NY: Cornell University Press, 1998).
11 Kristian Åtland, "Mikhail Gorbachev, the Murmansk Initiative, and the Desecuritization of Interstate Relations in the Arctic," *Cooperation and Conflict* 43.3 (2008): 289–311. The article also contains a comprehensive account of the speech's content.
12 Young, *Creating Regimes*, 54–5.
13 Axworthy and Dean, "Changing the Arctic Paradigm," 18.
14 Arctic Environmental Protection Strategy (1991) 30 I.L.M. 1624 [AEPS].
15 A comprehensive explanative account is provided by Young, *Creating Regimes*. A comprehensive description and evaluation of the working groups is found in Håken R. Nilson, "Arctic Environmental Protection Strategy (AEPS): Process and Organization, 1991–97. An Assessment" (Norwegian Polar Institute, 1997).

16 Young, *Creating Regimes*.

17 Quoted in Axworthy and Dean, "Changing the Arctic Paradigm," 26.

18 David Scrivener, *Environmental Cooperation in the Arctic: From Strategy to Council* (Oslo: The Norwegian Atlantic Committee, 1996); Oran R. Young, "Institutional Linkages in International Society: Polar Perspectives," *Global Governance* 2.1 (1996): 1–23.

19 See Joint Communiqué and Declaration on the Establishment of the Arctic Council (1996) 35 I.L.M. 1382 [Arctic Council Declaration].

20 Linda Nowlan, "Arctic Legal Regime for Environmental Protection," *IUCN Environmental Policy and Law Paper* No. 44, The World Conservation Union, (2001): x.

21 Sébastien Duyck, "Polar Environmental Governance and Non-State Actors," in *Diplomacy on Ice: Energy and the Environment in the Arctic and Antarctic*, edited by Rebecca H. Pincus and H. Ali Saleem (New Haven, CT: Yale University Press, 2015), 23.

22 For a comprehensive treatment of the status, see Timo Koivurova and Leena Heinamäki, "The Participation of Indigenous Peoples in International Norm-Making in the Arctic," *Polar Record* 42.1 (2006): 101–09.

23 For an overview of the meeting outcomes, see Timo Koivurova and David L. Vanderzwaag, "The Arctic Council at 10 Years: Retrospect and Prospects," *UBC Law Review* 40 (2007): 121–94.

24 Ibid., 132.

25 Olav Schram Stokke, "International Institutions and Arctic Governance," in *International Cooperation and Arctic Governance. Regime Effectiveness and Northern Region Building*, edited by Olav Schram Stokke and Geir Hønneland (London: Routledge, 2007), 167.

26 Olav Schram Stokke, Geir Hønneland and Peter Johann Schei, "Pollution and Conservation," in *International Cooperation and Arctic Governance: Regime Effectiveness and Northern Region Building*, edited by Olav Schram Stokke and Geir Hønneland (London: Routledge, 2007), 95–99.

27 Sebastian Knecht and Kathrin Keil, "Arctic Geopolitics Revisited: Spatialising Governance in the Circumpolar North," *The Polar Journal* 3.1 (2013): 178–203.

28 Stokke, "International Institutions and Arctic Governance," 175.

29 A now rather infamous example of this attention is Scott G. Borgerson, "Arctic Meltdown: The Economic and Security Implications of Global Warming," *Foreign Affairs* 87.2 (2008): 63–77.

30 Douglas C. Nord, "The Shape of the Table, the Shape of the Arctic," *International Journal* 65.4 (2010): 827–36; Torbjørn Pedersen, "Debates over the Role of the Arctic Council," *Ocean Development and International Law* 43.1 (2012): 153.

31 Yoshinobu Takei, "The Role of the Arctic Council from an International Law Perspective: Past, Present and Future," *Yearbook of Polar Law* 6 (2014): 359.

32 For an overview, see Takei, "The Role of the Arctic Council."

33 Piotr Graczyk and Timo Koivurova, "A New Era in the Arctic Council's External Relations? Broader Consequences of the Nuuk Observer Rules for Arctic Governance," *Polar Record* 50.3 (2014): 225–36; Piotr Graczyk, "Observers in the Arctic Council—Evolution and Prospects," *Yearbook of Polar Law* 3 (2011): 575–633.

34 Nikolas Sellheim, "The Establishment of the Permanent Arctic Council Secretariat: Challenges and Opportunities," in *The Arctic Council: Its Place in the Future of Arctic Governance*, edited by Thomas S. Axworthy, Timo Koivurova and Waliul Hasanat (Toronto: The Gordon Foundation, 2012), 60–83.

35 For an account of both agreements, see Svein Vigeland Rottem, "A Note on the Arctic Council Agreements," *Ocean Development & International Law* 46.1 (2015): 50–59.

36 Arctic Council Secretariat, *Kiruna Vision for the Arctic* (Kiruna: Arctic Council, 2013), 2.
37 Paula Kankaanpää and Oran R. Young, "The Effectiveness of the Arctic Council," *Polar Research* 31 (2012), 17176, http://dx.doi.org/10.3402/polar.v31i0.17176.
38 For a comprehensive account of proposals from the mid-1980s, see Axworthy and Dean, "Changing the Arctic Paradigm."
39 Keskitalo, "International Region-Building," 196.
40 Scrivener, *Environmental Cooperation in the Arctic*, 21.
41 Young, "Institutional Linkages in International Society," 12; Young *Creating Regimes*, 63.
42 David Scrivener, "Arctic Environmental Cooperation in Transition," *Polar Record* 35.192 (1999): 6.
43 Koivurova, "Limits and Possibilities of the Arctic Council," 148.
44 Arctic Council Declaration, footnote to Article 1(a).
45 David L. Vanderzwaag, Rob Huebert and Stacey Ferrara, "The Arctic Environmental Protection Strategy, Arctic Council and Multilateral Environmental Initiatives. Tinkering While the Arctic Marine Environment Totters," *Denver Journal of International Law and Policy* 30.2 (2002): 153.
46 Ibid., 166.
47 Ibid., 167.
48 Ibid., 132.
49 Koivurova and Vanderzwaag, "The Arctic Council at 10 Years," 157.
50 Koivurova, "Limits and Possibilities of the Arctic Council," 153.
51 Rob Huebert and Brooks B. Yeager, *A New Sea: The Need for a Regional Agreement on Management and Conservation of the Arctic Marine Environment* (Report, WWF International Arctic Programme, 2008), 23. Similar observations had been made earlier: Nilson, "Arctic Environmental Protection Strategy"; Vanderzwaag et al., "The Arctic Environmental Protection Strategy," 121–94.
52 Sellheim, "Establishment of Permanent Arctic Council Secretariat," 77.
53 Shih-Ming Kao, Nathaniel S. Pearre, and Jeremy Firestone, "Adoption of the Arctic Search and Rescue Agreement: A Shift of the Arctic Regime toward a Hard Law Basis?," *Marine Policy* 36.3 (2012): 837.
54 Arctic Council, *Arctic Council SAO Meeting. Final Draft Report* (Yellowknife, Canada, October 22–23, 2014), 8.
55 Nord, "The Shape of the Table," 834–35; Philip E. Steinberg and Klaus Dodds, "The Arctic Council after Kiruna," *Polar Record* 51.1 (2015): 108–10.
56 Switzerland seems to be the most recent applicant for observer status: Kevin McGwin, "Swiss in the Arctic. Like Ice for Chocolate," *The Arctic Journal*, February 20, 2015, accessed April 10, 2015, http://arcticjournal.com/politics/1343/ice-chocolate.
57 Vanderzwaag et al., "The Arctic Environmental Protection Strategy," 131.
58 Timo Koivurova, "Alternatives for an Arctic Treaty. Evaluation and a New Proposal," *RECIEL* 17.1 (2008): 14.
59 Arctic Governance Project, *Arctic Governance in an Era of Transformative Change: Critical Questions, Governance Principles, Ways Forward* (Report of the Arctic Governance Project, 2010), 13.
60 Wolf, "The New Raison d'état," 334.
61 Ibid., 334.
62 Ibid., 335.
63 Andrew Linklater, "Citizenship and Sovereignty in the Post-Westphalian State," *European Journal of International Relations* 2.1 (1996): 83.
64 Ibid.
65 David Held, *Democracy and the Global Order: From the Modern State to Cosmopolitan Governance* (Cambridge: Polity Press, 1995), 127–34.

66 Ibid., 107–13.
67 Wolf, "The New Raison d'état," 335.
68 See Monica Tennberg, Harto Hakovirta and Lassi Heininen (eds), *Regional and Transnational Cooperation in the North* (Rovaniemi: University of Lapland, 1994).
69 See the contributions in Lassi Heininen and Chris Southcott (eds), *Globalization and the Circumpolar North* (Fairbanks, AK: University of Alaska Press, 2010).
70 For similar conclusions from a different perspective, see Valur Ingimundarson, "Managing a Contested Region: The Arctic Council and the Politics of Arctic Governance," *The Polar Journal* 4.1 (2014): 183–98.
71 Graczyk and Koivurova, "A New Era in the Arctic Council's External Relations?," 228.
72 Nord, "The Shape of the Table," 835.
73 Ingimundarson, "Managing a Contested Region," 183–98.
74 Jyrki Käkönen, "Democracy and Sustainable Development in the Arctic," in *Nordic Arctic Research on Contemporary Arctic Problems*, edited by Lise Lyck (Aalborg: Aalborg University Press, 1992), 238.
75 Ibid.
76 Oran Young, quoted in Keskitalo, "International Region-Building," 200.
77 Graczyk and Koivurova, "A New Era in the Arctic Council's External Relations?," 225–36.
78 Wolf, "The New Raison d'état," 340.
79 Ingimundarson, "Managing a Contested Region," 183–98.
80 Timo Koivurova, "Gaps in International Regulatory Frameworks for the Arctic Ocean," edited by Paul Arthur Berkman and Alexander N. Vylegzhanin, *Environmental Security in the Arctic Ocean* (Dordrecht: Springer, 2014), 145.
81 Heather Exner-Pirot, "Defence Diplomacy in the Arctic: The Search and Rescue Agreement as a Confidence Builder," *Canadian Foreign Policy Journal* 18.2 (2012): 195–207.
82 Monica Tennberg, *The Arctic Council: A Study in Governmentality* (Rovaniemi: University of Lapland, 1998), 156–65; Young, *Creating Regimes*, 159–62.
83 Wolf, "The New Raison d'état," 355.
84 Ibid., 356.
85 Ibid.
86 Ibid.
87 Ibid.

References

Arctic Council. *Arctic Council SAO Meeting. Final Draft Report*. Yellowknife, Canada, October 22–23, 2014.

Arctic Council Secretariat. *Kiruna Vision for the Arctic*. Kiruna: Arctic Council, 2013.

Arctic Governance Project. *Arctic Governance in an Era of Transformative Change: Critical Questions, Governance Principles, Ways Forward*. Report of the Arctic Governance Project, 2010.

Åtland, Kristian. "Mikhail Gorbachev, the Murmansk Initiative, and the Desecuritization of Interstate Relations in the Arctic." *Cooperation and Conflict* 43.3 (2008): 289–311.

Axworthy, Thomas S. and Ryan Dean. "Changing the Arctic Paradigm from Cold War to Cooperation: How Canada's Indigenous Leaders Shaped the Arctic Council." *Yearbook of Polar Law* 5 (2013): 7–43.

Borgerson, Scott G. "Arctic Meltdown: The Economic and Security Implications of Global Warming." *Foreign Affairs* 87.2 (2008): 63–77.

Duyck, Sébastien. "Polar Environmental Governance and Non-State Actors." In *Diplomacy on Ice: Energy and the Environment in the Arctic and Antarctic,* edited by Rebecca H. Pincus and H. Ali Saleem, 13–40. New Haven, CT: Yale University Press, 2015.

Exner-Pirot, Heather. "Defense Diplomacy in the Arctic: The Search and Rescue Agreement as a Confidence Builder." *Canadian Foreign Policy Journal* 18.2 (2012): 195–207.

Graczyk, Piotr. "Observers in the Arctic Council—Evolution and Prospects." *Yearbook of Polar Law* 3 (2011): 575–633.

Graczyk, Piotr and Timo Koivurova. "A New Era in the Arctic Council's External Relations?: Broader Consequences of the Nuuk Observer Rules for Arctic Governance." *Polar Record* 50.3 (2014): 225–36.

Heininen, Lassi and Chris Southcott (eds). *Globalization and the Circumpolar North.* Fairbanks, AK: University of Alaska Press, 2010.

Held, David. *Democracy and the Global Order: From the Modern State to Cosmopolitan Governance.* Cambridge: Polity Press, 1995.

Huebert, Rob and Brooks B. Yeager. *A New Sea: The Need for a Regional Agreement on Management and Conservation of the Arctic Marine Environment.* WWF Report, International Arctic Programme, 2008.

Ingimundarson, Valur. "Managing a Contested Region: The Arctic Council and the Politics of Arctic Governance." *The Polar Journal* 4.1 (2014): 183–98.

Käkönen, Jyrki. "Democracy and Sustainable Development in the Arctic." In *Nordic Arctic Research on Contemporary Arctic Problems,* edited by Lise Lyck, 235–42. Aalborg: Aalborg University Press, 1992.

Kankaanpää, Paula and Oran R. Young. "The Effectiveness of the Arctic Council." *Polar Research* 31, (2012), 17176, http://dx.doi.org/10.3402/polar.v31i0.17176.

Kao, Shih-Ming, Nathaniel S. Pearre and Jeremy Firestone. "Adoption of the Arctic Search and Rescue Agreement: A Shift of the Arctic Regime toward a Hard Law Basis?" *Marine Policy* 36.3 (2012): 832–38.

Keskitalo, Eva Carina Helena. "International Region-Building: Development of the Arctic as an International Region." *Cooperation and Conflict* 42.2 (2007): 187–205.

Knecht, Sebastian and Kathrin Keil. "Arctic Geopolitics Revisited: Spatialising Governance in the Circumpolar North." *The Polar Journal* 3.1 (2013): 178–203.

Koivurova, Timo. "Alternatives for an Arctic Treaty. Evaluation and a New Proposal." *RECIEL* 17.1 (2008): 14–26.

Koivurova, Timo. "Limits and Possibilities of the Arctic Council in a Rapidly Changing Scene of Arctic Governance." *Polar Record* 46.2 (2010): 146–56.

Koivurova, Timo. "Gaps in International Regulatory Frameworks for the Arctic Ocean." In *Environmental Security in the Arctic Ocean,* edited by Paul Arthur Berkman and Alexander N. Vylegzhanin Dordrecht: Springer, 2014.

Koivurova, Timo and Leena Heinämäki. "The Participation of Indigenous Peoples in International Norm-Making in the Arctic." *Polar Record* 42.1 (2006): 101–09.

Koivurova, Timo and David L. Vanderzwaag. "The Arctic Council at 10 Years: Retrospect and Prospects." *UBC Law Review* 40 (2007): 121–94.

Linklater, Andrew. "Citizenship and Sovereignty in the Post-Westphalian State." *European Journal of International Relations* 2.1 (1996): 77–103.

March, James G. and Johan P. Olsen. "The Institutional Dynamics of International Political Orders." *International Organization* 52.4 (1998): 943–69.

McGwin, Kevin. "Swiss in the Arctic. Like Ice for Chocolate." *The Arctic Journal,* February 20, 2015, accessed April 10, 2015, http://arcticjournal.com/politics/1343/ice-chocolate.

Nilson, Håken R. "Arctic Environmental Protection Strategy (AEPS): Process and Organization, 1991–97. An Assessment." Norwegian Polar Institute, 1997.

Nord, Douglas C. "The Shape of the Table, the Shape of the Arctic." *International Journal* 65.4 (2010): 827–36.

Nowlan, Linda. "Arctic Legal Regime for Environmental Protection." *IUCN Environmental Policy and Law Paper* No. 44. The World Conservation Union (2001).

Pedersen, Torbjørn. "Debates over the Role of the Arctic Council." *Ocean Development and International Law* 43.1 (2012): 146–56.

Rottem, Svein Vigeland. "A Note on the Arctic Council Agreements." *Ocean Development & International Law* 46.1 (2015): 50–59.

Scrivener, David. *Gorbachev's Murmansk Speech: The Soviet Initiative and Western Response.* Oslo: Norwegian Atlantic Committee, 1989.

Scrivener, David. *Environmental Cooperation in the Arctic: From Strategy to Council.* Oslo: Norwegian Atlantic Committee, 1996.

Scrivener, David. "Arctic Environmental Cooperation in Transition." *Polar Record* 35.192 (1999): 51–59.

Sellheim, Nikolas. "The Establishment of the Permanent Arctic Council Secretariat: Challenges and Opportunities." In *The Arctic Council: Its Place in the Future of Arctic Governance*, edited by Thomas S. Axworthy, Timo Koivurova and Waliul Hasanat, 60–83. Toronto: The Gordon Foundation, 2012.

Steinberg, Philip E. and Klaus Dodds. "The Arctic Council after Kiruna." *Polar Record* 51.1 (2015): 108–10.

Stokke, Olav Schram. "International Institutions and Arctic Governance." In *International Cooperation and Arctic Governance: Regime Effectiveness and Northern Region Building*, edited by Olav Schram Stokke and Geir Hønneland, 164–85. London: Routledge, 2007.

Stokke, Olav Schram, Geir Hønneland and Peter Johann Schei. "Pollution and Conservation." In *International Cooperation and Arctic Governance: Regime Effectiveness and Northern Region Building*, edited by Olav Schram Stokke and Geir Hønneland, 78–111. London: Routledge, 2007.

Takei, Yoshinobu. "The Role of the Arctic Council from an International Law Perspective: Past, Present and Future." *The Yearbook of Polar Law Online* 6.1 (2014): 349–74.

Tennberg, Monica. *The Arctic Council: A Study in Governmentality.* Rovaniemi: University of Lapland, 1998.

Tennberg, Monica, Harto Hakovirta and Lassi Heininen (eds). *Regional and Transnational Cooperation in the North.* Rovaniemi: University of Lapland, 1994.

Vanderzwaag, David L., Rob Huebert and Stacey Ferrara. "The Arctic Environmental Protection Strategy, Arctic Council and Multilateral Environmental Initiatives. Tinkering While the Arctic Marine Environment Totters." *Denver Journal of International Law and Policy* 30.2 (2002): 131–72.

Wolf, Klaus Dieter. "The New Raison d'état as a Problem for Democracy in World Society." *European Journal of International Relations* 5.3 (1999): 333–63.

Young, Oran R. *Creating Regimes: Arctic Accords and International Governance.* Ithaca, NY: Cornell University Press, 1998.

Young, Oran R. "Institutional Linkages in International Society: Polar Perspectives." *Global Governance* 2.1 (1996): 1–23.

9 Geopolitics, governance and Arctic fisheries politics

Olav Schram Stokke

Introduction

Are we experiencing a resurgence of geopolitical competition over Arctic living resources, and if so, how robust are the institutional means for coping with this? The rapid retreat of the Arctic ice cap, combined with higher water temperatures in the region, has fueled expectations of greater availability of valuable fish species, also in waters beyond national jurisdiction. Pointing to the risk of uncontrolled harvesting operations, the USA has obtained support from the other coastal states for a declaration that they will abstain from high seas fisheries in the Arctic until a regulatory regime can be put in in place. An arrangement confined to the Arctic coastal states is unlikely to find acceptance among other states hoping to benefit from harvesting operations in high seas parts of Arctic waters. Areas beyond national jurisdiction are not the only Arctic waters on which views differ as to the appropriate locus of authority for making and enforcing fisheries rules. For instance, Canada has yet to settle its northwestern maritime boundary with the USA in the Beaufort Sea, or its northeastern boundary with Denmark–Greenland in the Lincoln Sea. The Russian Duma has failed to ratify the treaty drawn up with the USA on the Bering Sea boundary. And although Norway and Russia succeeded in closing forty years of negotiations in the 2010 Barents Sea Delimitation agreement, they still do not see eye to eye on who has enforcement competence over Russian vessels in the 200 nm Fisheries Protection Zone around Svalbard.

This chapter examines whether these various shifts and disputes justify worries that the Arctic region is set for interstate fisheries controversy in the years ahead, with geopolitical rivalry undermining the basis for sound resource management. I outline three core propositions in geopolitical thinking, revolving around the causal weight of coercive power, certain geographic properties and global rivalries when explaining regional developments. This geopolitical optic is then contrasted with an institutionalist or governance approach, more sensitive to the interplay of institutional characteristics and the configuration of state interests. The subsequent sections explore whether a bifocal optic, combining core insights from geopolitical thinking with those of institutionalism, can better account for the empirical pattern of cooperation and conflict over Arctic fisheries than each of those optics on its own. I conclude by deriving some policy implications for current Arctic governance.

Two optics

Geopolitical analysis has regained currency in studies of international affairs, apace with increasingly troubled relations between Russia and the West over such issues as NATO expansion, Iraq, and Ukraine, and with the rising economic and political weight of powers like China and India.[1] Variants of the geopolitical optic are increasing applied also in analyses of Arctic international relations, as is evident in recent studies by Borgerson,[2] Dodds,[3] Tamnes and Offerdal[4] and, in the fisheries sector, Huebert.[5] This tradition is marked by considerable diversity,[6] but three propositions are salient and jointly distinguish it from other realist traditions *and* from the institutionalist approach sketched below. The three propositions are as follows: that a shift in coercive-power relationships will undermine existing institutions; that certain geographic characteristics are major determinants of international outcomes; and that global rivalries shape regional international affairs.

Geopolitics

The geopolitical approach to international relations involves examining the connections between geographic space and power politics,[7] sensitive to expansionist inclinations and to interstate rivalry over finite territories and resources. Towards the end of the nineteenth century, geopolitical thinking emerged as a distinct subset of the much larger, long-standing realist tradition in studies of international affairs.

Like all scholars in the realist tradition, geopoliticians narrow in on *power* relationships, viewing international institutions as relatively marginal to interstate competition over territories, sea lanes and natural resources. They see states as the key players in world politics; and, unlike some early contributors, like Swedish Rudolf Kjellén and German Klaus Haushofer, geopolitical scholars typically model states as unitary, boundedly rational actors within an international system marked by anarchy, here meaning the absence of centralized authority. Agreed allocations of regulatory competence or behavioral prescriptions may play a role, but one that is highly sensitive to changes in underlying relationships of power and interests.[8] In particular, "[w]e must study the problem of boundaries," noted geopolitical theorist Haushofer, calling for special attention to "population pressure, living space, and [...] shifts and transfers of power throughout the world."[9] An important proposition in geopolitical thinking, held jointly among all political realists, is that international boundaries and institutions in general are essentially fluid, subject to revision if rising powers perceive them as unduly constraining.

A far more distinctive geopolitical proposition is that *geographic characteristics* are essential factors to consider in seeking to predict or explain the outcomes of international rivalries. This idea was famously articulated by Halford Mackinder in his program article with the telling title "The Geographic Pivot of History:"[10] "[f]or the first time we can perceive [...] certain aspects, at any rate, of geographical causation in universal history." Some three decades later, the causal language of Nicholas Spykman was more cautious, encouraging a view on geography "as a conditioning rather than as a determining factor."[11] For both authors, state size is crucial because it tends to correlate with population and abundance of natural resources, which in turn typically translate into power-projection capacity. *Location* is of equal interest, as Spykman went on to note:

> Location with reference to the equator and to oceans and land masses determines nearness to centers of power, areas of conflict, and established routes of communication, and location with reference to immediate neighbors defines position in regard to potential enemies, thereby determining the basic problems of territorial security.[12]

Other geographic characteristics that come into focus with the geopolitical optic are topography and climatic conditions, since both affect the basis for a state's economic production and political cohesion, as well as its physical accessibility to a possible intruder.

From the outset, geopoliticians pointed out how the constraining as well as the enabling effect of those geographic properties could be modified by technological advances. Thus, Alfred Mahan in his classic *The Influence of Sea Power upon History, 1660–1783* encouraged Washington DC to push for the construction of the Panama Canal, so that US naval capabilities in the Atlantic could be projected into the Pacific.[13] Conversely, Mackinder warned that Russia's ambitious development of railway infrastructure, allowing better use of its natural resources for industrialization purposes and rapid transport of troops from one part of the empire to another, made Russia a far more credible contender for global primacy, ultimately calling for reassessment of Britain's alliance policies.[14]

The third constitutive part of geopolitical thinking is *holism*, implying that global processes shape regional politics and that security concerns define interstate relations also in other issue areas. In his discussion of Mackinder's classic, Ó Tuathail highlights the "god's eye global view [...] seeing international politics as a unified worldwide scene."[15] That global view of regional issues also marks modern varieties of geopolitical thinking, as evident in the Cold War doctrines associated with Truman and with Brezhnev. In declaring that "the very existence of the Greek state is today threatened by the terrorist activities of several thousand armed men, led by Communists," US President Truman offered an early statement of the domino theory: "[s]hould we fail to support Greece and Turkey in this fateful hour, the effect will be far reaching to the West as well as to the East."[16] No less sensitive to global interconnectedness, Soviet leader Brezhnev warned, after the allied invasion of Czechoslovakia that had put an end to the Prague Spring, that "the socialist countries and the Communist Parties [...] must damage neither socialism in their country nor the fundamental interests of the other socialist countries nor the worldwide workers' movement."[17]

Not included in this brief sketch of geopolitical thinking is a heterogeneous set of contributions to "critical geopolitics" which, in the words of one prominent figure, "seeks to reveal the hidden politics of geopolitical knowledge"[18] by examining how various discourses on key concepts like "national security" or "civilizations" promote the interests of some states or societal groups at the expense of others.[19] Such reflection on the implicit assumptions and the social or political implications of concepts and theories applied in studying international relations is valuable also to the development of geopolitical thinking, but its object of analysis is vastly broader than that addressed by the geopolitical mainstream considered here.

For sure, even the mainstream of geopolitical thinking is diverse, as evident in stark differences between the early contributions of Mahan, Haushofer and Mackinder, with their social Darwinist assumptions, imperialist aspirations, and broad-brush analyses, and the far more disciplined explanatory schemes developed by Spykman, Kissinger or others. However, they all fit the general description of "geopolitical thinking" as that part of the power-oriented realist tradition that insists on the causal force of geographic properties and on the need to examine regional rivalries as parts of a global whole.

International governance

The variant of institutionalism that highlights international governance shares important characteristics with geopolitical thinking, yet differs on two of the three propositions highlighted above. The term "governance" derives ultimately from the Greek *kybernan*, "to steer." At the international level, such hierarchic connotations can be misleading, since a government with recognized control over its territory enjoys considerable autonomy in regulating conduct within that territory. Young defines governance as the "establishment and operation of [...] rules of the game that serve to define practices, assign roles and guide interaction" in order to reap common benefits or avoid reciprocal threats, also in the security domain.[20]

Whereas the term "global governance" is intended to capture what many see as the rising significance of various non-state actors in the making and implementation of behavioral norms,[21] *international* governance is about rules established and operated mainly by states.[22] Like the typical geopolitician, an international-governance scholar sees states as key players in world affairs and the system of states as essentially anarchic, in the specific sense that each state retains its right to withdraw acceptance of an overarching authority.[23] However, where geopoliticians portray those states as compelled to seeking dominance over others, governance scholars warn that maintaining such dominance is costly and vulnerable to setbacks and therefore typically less desirable than cooperative patterns of interaction,[24] especially where the coordination of behavior is necessary if parties are to reap common goods or avoid common "bads."[25] Where geopoliticians consider international institutions as fluid and causally marginal, governance scholars accord them a central position, precisely because such institutions can help to realize such joint gains.[26] Finally, where the geopolitical view is "the god's eye" holist one, viewing regional issues as reflections of global rivalries filtered through geographic properties relevant to power projection, the international governance approach starts out more narrowly from the specific configuration of interests among states concerning the issue in question.

Bifocal optics and Arctic fisheries

The geopolitical and the international-governance optics bring into focus the same set of actors but different aspects of their interaction. As any user of bifocal glasses knows, to scrutinize a distant object through the reading segment yields a blurred picture, and likewise if one tries to read a book through the primary lens. Those lenses are ground for different purposes, allowing their wearer to alternate between the lenses, able to see the text and the distant object with equal clarity.

The remainder of this chapter is structured in terms of the three geopolitical propositions. For each of those propositions, I ask first whether adding the international-governance optic improves the ability to account for important developments in Arctic fisheries politics, especially concerning resource access and allocation. Then I derive some implications relevant to a topical Arctic fisheries issues: respectively, the robustness of the legal framework for Arctic fisheries governance; the viability of the US initiative for an Arctic high seas fisheries arrangement; and combatting illegal, unreported or unregulated fisheries in Arctic waters.

Institutions yielding to power?

The geopolitical claim that today's institutions are shaped by yesterday's geopolitics, and will tomorrow be shaped by today's geopolitics, was echoed by the Canadian Prime Minister Harper when commenting on his government's Arctic policies: "Canada has a choice when it comes to defending our sovereignty over the Arctic. We either use it or lose it."[27] However, the way in which states have allocated Arctic marine living resources among themselves shows that regional or global power differentials are poor predictors of outcomes, and that allocative solutions, once established, tend to remain fairly stable even when power relations change significantly. That observation has certain implications for the robustness of the overarching framework for Arctic governance.

Power differentials and the allocation of Arctic stocks

Changing power relations have influenced the broad contours of international fisheries law, but once in place, rules of access or allocation have proven sticky. The current division of competence for managing fisheries among coastal states and others, centered on 200 nm exclusive economic zones (EEZs), has emerged through processes of commercial and political rivalry, legal arguments backed by power capabilities, and the deliberate use of resource crises to legitimize changes in existing rules.[28] Thus, power has certainly influenced the outcome, but in ways that cannot be discerned without an optic capable of narrowing in on the specific configuration of interests characteristic of Arctic fisheries.

International allocations of Arctic fishing rights do not mirror power differentials between neighbors, as the geopolitical optic would lead us to expect. In the European segment, where large-scale fishing has the longest history, Russia has for centuries been the most powerful state by far, yet there is little evidence of successful Russian attempts to dominate the neighbors on allocative issues. Quite the contrary: already in the 1700s Norwegian and Russian fishermen enjoyed de facto mutual access to each other's waters on the northernmost coasts of Norway and Russia's Kola Peninsula,[29] just as they do today.[30] Relatively small size appears to have promoted economic opportunities for Norwegian resource users in the Russian Arctic. Historians argue that steep increases in Norwegian sealing activities in the White Sea and on Novaya Zemlya during the nineteenth century, when lower temperatures had left Russian competitors ice-locked, were accepted by Russian authorities precisely because their smaller neighbor posed no real threat to Russian sovereignty in the region.[31] And in the 1970s, Iceland was similarly able to turn its relatively small size, combined with an economy dependent on fisheries, into a bargaining chip in its struggle for extended coastal-state jurisdiction. That struggle included physical encounters between the Icelandic Coast Guard and British naval vessels, and, during the most heated period, severed diplomatic relations between the two NATO allies.[32] Historically, therefore, there is little to indicate that might is readily converted to right in international fisheries politics—neither in Arctic nor in sub-Arctic waters.

A closer look at Russo–Norwegian fisheries relations after the emergence of EEZs can shed additional light on how international institutions, once established, may undermine the tenability of geopolitical predictions.[33] Among the nations with a history of cod and haddock harvesting in the Barents Sea, Norway and the Soviet Union benefited hugely from the stepwise extension of coastal state jurisdiction that peaked with the global acceptance of EEZs, but there, as in many other places, such extension also fueled partly overlapping claims. The disputed maritime boundary between Norway and Russia, which was resolved only in 2010,[34] separated members of two competing military alliances but did not prevent the emergence, and gradual strengthening, of an international fisheries regime that has come to involve not only the two coastal states but also several non-regional user states, including Spain, Portugal and other members of the European Union. That regime is based on a number of bilateral and multilateral agreements, but centers on the Norwegian–Russian Joint Commission on Fisheries, which helps to coordinate scientific investigation, to adopt agreed quotas and technical regulations, and to maintain direct contact and close collaboration among the various fisheries compliance agencies. Among the shared stocks managed under this regime is Northeast Arctic cod, today the world's biggest cod stock, and the regime as a whole stands out as one of the world's most successful international fisheries regimes.[35]

The governance optic explains this cooperative pattern of interaction by identifying the specific configuration of interests that characterizes fisheries management. Fish stocks are scarce common properties, implying that access to exploitation is open to many users—a situation capable of generating individual incentives that threaten to undermine collective rationality. A "tragedy of the commons"[36] looms because some of the costs involved in harvesting disappear from the harvester's cost-benefit calculations, and such "externalities" typically generate *more* of the activity than is collectively desirable.[37] Each harvester enjoys the full benefit from the catch hauled on board, whereas any cost of that activity in terms of reduced availability will be shared by many, even future generations. International fisheries regimes, like that centered on the Joint Commission, aim at breaking the link between "commons" and "tragedies" by building scientific knowledge, placing normative constraints on harvesting operations, and altering incentives to encourage behavior that can better align individual and collective rationality.[38]

A particularly thorny issue of fisheries management in the Barents Sea concerns the Fisheries Protection Zone around Svalbard that Norway established in 1977.[39] Norway's regulations in this zone are disputed by some states due to differing interpretations of the 1920 Svalbard Treaty, which grants to Norway sovereignty over the archipelago, with some specified limitations. According to the treaty, Norway must give equal access to, and equal treatment of, nationals of any signatory state to specified economic activities; it must refrain from collecting more tax than is needed for administering the archipelago; and it may not establish naval bases there.[40] According to Norway, those limitations apply only onshore and in the territorial sea, not to the continental shelf or to waters beyond the territorial sea. The Soviet Union (and later Russia) has openly rejected Norway's right to establish unilaterally any zone beyond Svalbard's territorial waters; and several other states have reserved their opinion on whether such a zone falls within the ambit of the limitations specified in the Svalbard Treaty.[41] In terms of fisheries management, the challenge has been to find procedures for exercising enforcement authority that touch as lightly as possible on such a contested jurisdictional issue.

The *modus vivendi* that Norway has achieved with other states with fishing rights in the Fisheries Protection Zone involves a combination of coastal-state restraint in the exercise of management authority and practical acceptance of such authority by all user states, with some differences in their degree of acceptance.[42] Norwegian restraint is evident in rather mild responses when rule violations committed by foreign vessels are exposed,[43] usually no more than written warnings. In return, most other regime participants have instructed their fishers to follow Norwegian information as well as conservation measures in the zone, and to accept at-sea inspections. Although Russian captains are instructed not to sign inspection papers—which Moscow considers would be too much of an acceptance of Norwegian jurisdiction—they rarely obstruct at-sea inspectors. Despite a few incidents that have required hectic diplomacy,[44] the larger picture is that Norway has gradually strengthened its regulation and enforcement activities in the Fisheries Protection Zone around Svalbard.[45]

The gradual strengthening of this coastal-state dominated fisheries regime, and Norway's ability to sharpen its regulatory and enforcement activities in the waters around Svalbard, reflect the underlying reality that uncontrolled fishing in a large area where Northeast Arctic cod is highly available is simply not in the interest of any user state with fishing rights to this valuable stock. That reality emerges far more clearly through the issue-specific and institutional-sensitive governance part of our bifocal optics than through the geopolitical lens.

Implications for the present governance framework

Whether one applies a geopolitical or an international-governance optic, today's overarching legal framework for Arctic fisheries governance as laid out in the United Nations Law of the Sea Convention (UNCLOS) appears quite robust despite the deterioration of general relations between Russia and the West and despite the steady relative economic and political decline of those states most influential in shaping it.

The basis for the present allocation of regulatory competence in Arctic fisheries stands firm, legally as well as politically. The legal foundation is evident in the universal acceptance of the division of regulatory competence codified in UNCLOS, notably the extension of coastal-state jurisdiction over oil, gas and other mineral deposits in the continental shelf and the living resources found in the water column within the outer boundaries of the exclusive economic zones. A corresponding political stabilizer is the alignment of this division of competence to the self-interests of the world's leading states. The Arctic regional powers, including the USA and Russia, were major proponents of the balance that was struck between coastal states and maritime interests—notably through the EEZ concept—and changing it would certainly not be in their interest.[46]

Satisfaction among leading powers with the legal state of play is evident at the declaratory level as well as in the actions of Arctic States. In their 2008 Ilulissat Declaration, the five regional coastal states made it clear that they see no reason to cede any of the regulatory leeway conferred upon them by international law as regards management of natural resources and the environment simply because the waters in question are located to the north of the Arctic Circle: "[b]y virtue of their sovereignty, sovereign rights and jurisdiction in large areas of the Arctic Ocean the five coastal states are in a unique position to address these possibilities and challenges [and] [. . .] have a stewardship role in protecting" Arctic ecosystems.[47] Their body language too has indicated eagerness to avoid conflict over potentially contentious issues. Around half of the Arctic maritime boundary delimitations called for in the Arctic by the extension of coastal-state jurisdiction have been settled already: a proportion well above the global average.[48] This high rate of Arctic boundary settlement, and the manner in which powerful Arctic States have managed their non-settled boundaries, indicates firm support of the existing legal framework.

Those who warn against jurisdictional fluidity in Arctic affairs often point to outside actors as potential challengers of the legal order. Borgerson, for instance, relates what he sees as "coming anarchy" in the Arctic to "energy-hungry newcomers, such as China."[49] It is true that several leading Asian states have been taking increasing interest in Arctic affairs;[50] and the larger geopolitical backdrop, with several emerging economies raising their share of the world's trade, production, and military potency, has made some Arctic States wary of revisionist statements on the legal order.[51] A much-cited example are the remarks of retired Chinese Rear Admiral, Yin Zhuo: "the North Pole and the sea area around the North Pole belong to all the people in the world," and "China must play an indispensable role in Arctic exploration as we have one-fifth of the world's population."[52] Variants of the "global commons" argument are reportedly pervasive also in India's discourses on the Arctic.[53] If the perception that coastal-state sovereign rights to Arctic natural resources are up for revision were widely shared among decision makers in ascending world powers like China and India, that would clearly call for a geopolitical optic.

However, no such revisionism is traceable in any official statement issued by an Asian government. On the contrary, in accordance with the Arctic Council's formal criteria for observer applications, China, India, Japan and the Republic of Korea have explicitly pledged recognition of:

Arctic States' sovereignty, sovereign rights and jurisdiction in the Arctic [...] [and that] an extensive legal framework applies to the Arctic Ocean including, notably, the Law of the Sea, and that this framework provides a solid foundation for responsible management of this ocean.[54]

Such explicit support of the existing legal order in the Arctic is reinforced by the fact that China and India were among those who championed the division of competence that became codified in UNCLOS. Just like the Arctic States, these emerging powers were among the greatest winners from the extension of coastal-state jurisdiction.[55]

In summary, the geopolitical proposition that international institutions are little more than clotted power relationships, vulnerable to even small shifts in relative power capabilities, receives scarce empirical support from this brief review of how states have allocated scarce fish resources in the Arctic. Certainly, military means have occasionally been used, and the prevailing allocative rules do reflect the views of the most powerful states, but those rules have proven difficult to change, and they are applied also when they benefit weaker states at the expense of powerful ones. Adding the governance optic allows us to examine the specific interest configuration typical of fisheries management and to see how international institutions may help states to overcome collective-action problems. Applying both optics to the question of whether the overarching framework for Arctic fisheries governances is robust, yields an affirmative answer, as that framework is upheld by a potent blend of might and right.

Geographical causation?

The geographic properties highlighted in geopolitical thinking, such as location and topography, are relevant to Arctic fisheries but have hitherto been far from decisive as regards distributive outcomes. As this section shows, one explanation is that geopoliticians were correct in pointing out that technological advances intervene in the relationship between geography and interstate rivalry. Another explanation is that geographic properties affect not only the physical basis for military power projection but also the legal basis for claiming fisheries jurisdiction or a share of specific stocks. Jointly, as will be argued here, those observations indicate that the US initiative for an Arctic high seas fisheries management body set up by the five Arctic coastal states will need to open up for non-Arctic state participation in order to provide effective means for conservation and management.

Location, climate and topography in Arctic fisheries politics

Technological dynamism and institutional circumstances have conspired to compound the straightforward relationship that geopoliticians expect to see between certain geographical properties and important determinants of international rivalry—including the region's political salience, the number of players competing for its natural resources, and the acceptance of international norms on fisheries access.

In the Arctic region, physical diversity and dramatic seasonal changes prohibit sweeping statements on resource accessibility, yet early geopolitical writers depicted this region as uniformly inaccessible. Mackinder argued that remoteness from competing centers of power combined with the thick polar ice served to shelter polar regions from military competition.[56] In the same vein, the otherwise technology-sensitive Spykman predicted that "location on the North Polar Sea will remain for a long period of time a tremendous obstacle notwithstanding the heroic efforts of the Soviet government to open up the North Siberian coast."[57] Yet, not so many years after that prediction, long-range bombers and nuclear submarines equipped with long-range ballistic missiles had placed Arctic waters centrally in the strategic deterrence between the two superpowers, triggering vast investments in extensive early-warning systems in the region.[58] The strategic bombers acted on the geographical property that the Arctic offers the shortest distance from own territory to the opponent's largest population centers, whereas the submarines utilized the noisy ice cover as a shield from aerial as well as sonar surveillance. In both cases, technological advance had turned what the geopolitical optic had identified as operational constraints into strategic opportunities.

The general point, that spatial remoteness from economic and political centers and apparently forbidding climate are challenges which human ingenuity tends to overcome, had been rubbed in centuries earlier by extensive distant-water harvesting operations in the high north. Whaling ships from Britain and Holland had sought out whaling grounds around Svalbard already in the 1600s, often outcompeting harvesters from ports closer at hand.[59] Long distances and rough climatic conditions were soon overcome also by the much smaller vessels that coastal fishers in the Barents region have used, for many centuries, in their harvesting of Northeast Arctic cod. In late medieval times, the Hanseatic trading network linked these cod fisheries to a Europe-wide market for dried and salted fish. Even today this cod is by far the most valuable marine stock taken north of Arctic Circle, feeding harvesting, processing and distribution networks around the globe. Fishermen would concentrate on the large amounts of mature cod—*skrei* in Norwegian—that aggregate for spawning around the North Norwegian Lofoten archipelago during late winter and spring. Gradually, however, operations spread to the feeding areas in the Barents Sea, and a summer fishery at the Svalbard banks emerged already in the second half of the 1800s.[60]

Similarly, technological and institutional circumstances and not geographic characteristics determined the spatial deployment of the Soviet trawler fleet, with its main port in Murmansk. The Soviet emphasis on proteins and production volume, coupled with subsidized fuels, made distant-water pelagic species highly attractive. In the final years of the Soviet Union, the Murmansk-based fishing fleet was taking between half and two-thirds of its catches *outside* the Barents Sea, mostly in the North-west and Central Atlantic.[61] As with size and power differentials among regional states, distance from major population centers and harsh climatic conditions have never been decisive factors for the allocation of Arctic fish resources.

In fact, geographic characteristics of the Arctic may have influenced regional and global fisheries politics more profoundly by a process of international governance than by posing physical constraints to outside players. In focus here is the configuration of Norway's Arctic coastline, which together with Norway's relative smallness and dependence on fisheries, helped to trigger a decisive advance in coastal-state efforts to extend their fisheries jurisdiction. Central to this development was the bitter and long-standing fisheries conflict that arose not from the presence of Russian coastal fishers in Norwegian waters but with the arrival of British trawlers in 1906—"expensive boats with expensive gear which could only pay their way by making large catches of fish and by using possibly more ruthless methods."[62] Two key characteristics of Norway's Arctic coastline— its islands and its fjords—were prominent in the subsequent forty-year dispute between the world's primary naval power and that small coastal state that had obtained independence only the preceding year. Yet, the significance of those geographic properties was not, as a geopolitical ana-lysis would hold, to provide operational conditions that support or impede military advance but rather as a basis for arguing the appropriateness of competing solutions on regulatory competence.

Responding quickly to complaints from local fishers that the foreign trawlers were "stealing" their fish and destroying their gear, in 1906 Norway banned foreign harvesting within its territorial waters, which Norway defined more extensively than the UK was prepared to accept. The former justified arrests of British trawlers in what the UK considered high seas by measuring Norway's fisheries boundary from a number of straight baselines that followed the "outer coastline," including islands and islets, and crossed the fjords that indent the mainland.[63] Neither the process nor the outcome of this dispute matches the pattern we would expect from a geopolitical analysis. It was the small state that sent its naval vessels to board and arrest, whereas the global power merely filed diplo-matic protests, "usually ineffectual."[64] No agreed solution was found even under circumstances that dramatically boosted the existing power asym-metry between the parties, as is evident in the new round of negotiations called during World War II, at a time when the Norwegian government was in exile in London.[65] In the end, it was the great power that decided to let legal arguments trump material capabilities by filing a complaint to the International Court of Justice. The Court upheld Norway's procedure for drawing straight baselines across the fjords to the low-water marks of the outer islands[66]—thereby triggering the process of stepwise extensions of coastal-state fisheries jurisdiction that culminated in 1982 with the adoption of UNCLOS. Because the Court ruled the straight baselines as legitimate also for the territorial sea, the implications went far beyond fisheries.[67]

In summary, geographic properties have affected Arctic fisheries politics, but not quite in the way a geopolitician would expect. Technological as well as institutional factors intervene in this relationship, which would indicate that analysts equipped with bifocal optics are better placed to account for who gets what. This finding has implications for the ongoing process that might create a new institution for management of stocks occurring outside national jurisdiction in the Arctic Ocean.

Geographic properties and Arctic high seas fisheries governance

Geographic properties are highly relevant for evaluating the US initiative aimed at creating a regional high seas fisheries management organization for the Arctic Ocean. As noted, this initiative has come in response to a northward shift in the migratory patterns of some valuable fish stocks, expected to make them more available in waters beyond national jurisdiction. Those efforts met with some success with the 2014 agreement among the Arctic coastal states on "the need for interim precautionary measures to prevent any future commercial fisheries without the prior establishment of appropriate regulatory mechanisms."[68] However, constructing a regional high seas fisheries regime on the basis of five Arctic coastal states would ignore not only the limits that international law imposes on coastal-state fisheries jurisdiction but also the impacts that sea floor topography and climatic conditions have on fish availability.

True, conservation and use of fisheries resources that cross national boundaries are among the issues where the UNCLOS encourages regional management regimes (Articles 63–64 and 116–19); for stocks straddling the high seas and coastal-state zones, parties to the 1995 UN Fish Stocks Agreement are obliged to create or join a regional fisheries regime. Unlike in the EEZ, however, that obligation does not come with the right to exclude non-regional states that might claim a "real interest" in the stock based on one or more of a long list of criteria (Article 8), with zonal attachment and historical catches as the most weighty.[69] Given the vast expanses of the Arctic Ocean, a fish stock that adapts to rising temperatures by moving northward is unlikely to have been exploited by all the Arctic States and also unlikely to have avoided exploitation by states outside the region. Thus, several non-Arctic States now members of the European Union were among the founders of the North East Atlantic Fisheries Commission (NEAFC), which has regulatory competence with respect to high seas areas in the European segment of the Arctic Ocean. Under such circumstances, a regime with a membership confined to

Arctic coastal states would run counter to the spirit as well as the letter of international fisheries law.

The conclusion that success is unlikely with any high seas fisheries arrangement tailored solely to the interests of five coastal states stands firm, also if we replace the governance optic with that of geopolitics. The most valuable stocks harvested in the Arctic are groundfish, whose migratory patterns are spatially confined to the relatively shallow continental shelves. Those shelves include some pockets of high seas, however, including the "Loophole," located between the EEZs of Norway and Russia. In periods with high water temperatures, Northeast Arctic cod has been available here, triggering challenges to the management authority claimed by the coastal states.[70] In the first half of the 1990s, the most recent period of good availability in the Loophole, vessels owned by Icelanders, Faroese and Greenlanders predominated, sometimes but not always registered under flags of convenience. All of those neighboring states and territories are small and lacking in material power, so vessels flying flags of convenience, awarded by registers located far away and low in follow-up aspiration as well as ability, would seem particularly vulnerable to the employment of coercive means by a mighty coastal state such as Russia. Seen through the geopolitical lens, such vulnerability can only have been sharpened by the fact that the major Arctic power, the USA, had recently experienced similar problems with large-scale unregulated or illegal harvesting operations by foreign vessels, at the time perceived as a major contributor to the collapse of the valuable Alaska pollack fisheries in the high seas portion of the Bering Sea.[71]

Despite these apparently favorable circumstances for coastal-state activism in the Loophole, no stretching of international fisheries law in terms of unilateral inspection or detention of foreign vessels was undertaken by Russia or by Norway. Instead, just as the USA had refrained from using coercive power outside national jurisdiction in the Central Bering Sea, the coastal states proceeded in ways compatible with the expectations of a governance scholar: Acknowledging that the legal basis for applying force is weak and aware of how the norm against such force is nested in a complex web of jurisdictional competence that generally serves their own interests, the coastal states granted the neighboring states and territories quotas in the Norwegian and Russian EEZs in exchange for keeping their vessels out of the Loophole.[72]

Thus we see that none of the geographic characteristics in focus for geopolitical analysis have been strong predictors of Arctic fisheries developments and to the extent that they have influenced interstate relations, the effect has mostly been to stimulate cross-boundary cooperation, strengthen coastal-state jurisdiction and induce the coastal states to keep within the bounds of international fisheries law. The implication for Arctic high seas fisheries management is that, should the US-initiated process for creating a regional fisheries body reach the negotiation stage, such a proposed body should be open to participation from non-Arctic States with a real interest in Arctic stocks.

Holism?

The insistence that regional developments be examined as parts of broader processes is perhaps the greatest value that the geopolitical optic adds to a governance-oriented study of Arctic fisheries politics. Neither the shape of present Arctic institutions nor the pressures for change in those institutions can be understood without keen attention to global processes. That observation also sheds light on the institutional means that are relevant to Arctic States when seeking to deal with illegal, unreported or unregulated fisheries in the Arctic.

The external dependency of Arctic affairs

Variation in political attention to Arctic issues derives largely from processes and developments that originate outside the region. Up until the late 1980s, international institutions operating across the East–West divide were few and far between.[73] In the European part of the Arctic Ocean, fisheries was the only issue-area with a track record of in-depth, institutionalized East–West collaboration, with the Norwegian–Russian Joint Commission on Fisheries as the prime example.[74] Then, in 1987, the Soviet leader Gorbachev launched an initiative for a broader and deeper collaboration with his nation's Arctic neighbors, triggering a wave of collaborative initiatives in the North.[75] Western states as well as NGOs were quick to note these cooperative signals, viewing improvements in general East–West relations as a window of opportunity for creating an institutional infrastructure that had been largely lacking. Thus, dependency on global processes generated not conflict but incentives to exploit a window of political opportunity. The result was a web of cooperative institutions like the Barents Euro–Arctic Region and the Arctic Council, which have continued to operate in relative insulation from the recent decline in East–West relations.

Today's commercial interest in Arctic natural resources is fueled by the rising demand for certain commodities produced in large quantities in the North, notably petroleum, minerals and seafood. Arctic resource extraction depends on high commodity prices, since harsh environmental conditions and remoteness from major markets entail operational costs typically higher than for corresponding activities undertaken further south. During the past few decades, the main driver of demand for Arctic commodities has been the geo-economic rise of certain Asian and Latin American emergent economies, especially China, India and Brazil. The expanding role of these countries in world production and consumption, and their dependence on natural resources found in other parts of the world, also account for the interest in new sea lanes for transport, like the Northern Sea Route that links Europe with Asia and Pacific America.[76]

Similar comments apply as regards Arctic environmental challenges. Most of the changes currently underway in the region derive from a rise in average temperatures that is roughly twice the global mean, driven by greenhouse gases emitted chiefly in industrial and urban centers further south.[77] The same is true for the hazardous substances that bio-accumulate in Arctic food chains and threaten regional ecosystems. The Pole-bound atmospheric and oceanic circulation systems, as well as rivers emptying into the Arctic seas, transport a range of toxic substances that originate or volatilize further south, including heavy metals like mercury and persistent organic pollutants (POSs).[78] As with variation in levels of conflict in the international system and in global demand for Arctic natural resources, this dependence on processes outside the region serves to drive international cooperation. Since Arctic-specific institutions cannot deal with these environmental problems without engaging other international institutions with broader participation, various UN-based regulatory processes have come to the fore in regulating the use, production and trade of hazardous substances that end up in the Arctic, notably the 2001 Stockholm Convention on POPs[79] and the 2013 Minamata Convention on Mercury.[80]

Major drivers for the creation of Arctic institutions are located outside the region; this is true of the demand for Arctic commodities as well as the discharges of pollutants and greenhouse gases that generate its major environmental challenges. The remainder of this section focuses on the upshot of these external dependencies for efforts to improve fisher adherence with Arctic fisheries rules.

External dependency and Arctic institutional interplay

In the European segment of the Arctic, the two major international fisheries bodies are the Norwegian–Russian Joint Commission on Fisheries, composed of representatives of the two coastal states in the Barents Sea, where most of the fish is taken; and the much broader NEAFC, which has acquired a crucial role in the system for improving compliance with Northeast Arctic cod regulations.[81]

The bilateral Joint Commission meets annually to adopt and allocate total quotas and other regulations for several shared stocks, including Northeast Arctic cod.[82] Also non-coastal states participate in the regime by accepting, in separate bilateral and trilateral agreements, the quotas and technical regulations established by Norway and Russia, in return for gaining access to coastal-state waters. The system for ensuring compliance with these rules has evolved from being largely decentralized, relying heavily on national systems for cross-checking target group catch reports, to one with significant contributions from international cooperative bodies at bilateral and especially multilateral levels.

Such multilateralization of the compliance system, centered on the NEAFC Scheme of Control and Enforcement, came in response to a dramatic drop in fisher compliance due to a change in the system of activities.[83] When, in around 2000, Russian vessels began to trans-ship their catches for final delivery in EU Member States rather than landing them in one of the coastal states,[84] they undermined the fit between the regime's compliance system and the activities to be monitored. Illegal harvesting of Northeast Arctic cod came to account for 20–25 percent of the total catches in some years.[85] Such levels of quota overfishing jeopardized the stock as well as the legitimacy of regional management measures, and shifted wealth from legal fishers to cheaters, while promoting corrupt practices in fish production and distribution in Europe and beyond.[86]

Combating this huge compliance deficit required the mobilization of NEAFC to support rule-enforcement activities under the bilateral Joint Commission, achieved by amending the NEAFC Scheme of Control and Enforcement to apply beyond its regulatory area (the high seas) and include also frozen fish taken in the regional EEZs.[87] The extension of the NEAFC scheme obliged all members, including every major port state in the Northeast Atlantic, to prohibit any NEAFC vessel from landing or trans-shipping frozen fish in its port unless the flag state confirms that the catch has been taken under its quota. This mobilization of the NEAFC scheme for enforcing non-NEAFC rules was possible because the key members in the regime centered on the bilateral Joint Commission—Norway and Russia—successfully pressed for complementary measures in another, broader and therefore better equipped regime.

As this section shows, geopolitical thinkers are correct in holding that Arctic politics is strongly influenced by the region's interconnectedness with global political, economic and bio-geophysical processes, but they are mistaken when they indicate that such external dependency has a natural propensity to drive interstate conflict. Just like the most severe environmental challenges, managing Arctic fisheries requires keen attention to how regional states can induce synergistic interplay with broader institutions.

Conclusions

No, we are not experiencing a resurgence of geopolitical conflict over Arctic fisheries. Regional as well as non-Arctic States are adhering to the existing allocation of competence, and for good reasons. Marine living resources are found preponderantly within regional EEZs and altering the basic deal underlying today's legal order for the Arctic would go counter to the interests of not only the leading Arctic powers but those of the geopolitically ascendant Asian states as well. Firm and pervasive interest in the existing legal structure also explains why ongoing efforts to create a high seas fisheries management body for the Arctic will have to open up for non-Arctic participation if it is to provide the means for avoiding a tragedy-of-the-commons outcome should fish stocks become more available outside the regional EEZs. Similarly, the enmeshment of Arctic fisheries in broader and sometimes global production and distribution chains poses challenges to governance efforts that can be met only by mobilizing broader institutions.

These findings emerge from the development and use of a bifocal optic that combines insights from two distinct traditions in the study of international relations. On its own, the geopolitical optic yields rather blurred explanatory pictures of Arctic fisheries politics. However, if molded into a primary lens ground to international-governance specifications, both optics improve in specificity and tenability. Changes in international fisheries law have been slow. Although the general direction has usually been compatible with, or has promoted, the interests of powerful states, important counter-examples do exist, and greater powers have rarely succeeded in depriving weak states of any benefit deriving from an agreed allocation of competence. Similarly, geographic characteristics like physical location and topography have been influential in shaping regional fisheries institutions, and their effects on power politics have been modified by technological advances that have often altered the number of states engaging in Arctic fisheries affairs, precluding any attempt to exclude non-regional players. The third core element of geopolitical thinking—its holistic insistence that regional issues be studied in a global context—provides a particularly valuable corrective to the international governance approach, which otherwise tends to narrow in on specific issue areas within a limited spatial scope.

Notes

1 Walter Russell Mead, "The Return of Geopolitics," *Foreign Affairs* 93.3 (2014): 69–79.
2 Scott G. Borgerson, "Arctic Meltdown: The Economic and Security Implications of Global Warming," *Foreign Affairs* 87.2 (2008): 63–77.
3 Klaus Dodds, "Flag Planting and Finger Pointing: The Law of the Sea, the Arctic and the Political Geographies of the Outer Continental Shelf," *Political Geography* 29.2 (2010): 63–73, accessed October 17, 2015, doi: http://dx.doi.org/10.1016/j.polgeo.2010.02.004.
4 Rolf Tamnes and Kristine Offerdal, *Geopolitics and Security in the Arctic: Regional Dynamics in a Global World* (London: Routledge, 2014).
5 Rob Huebert, "Security Threats in the Arctic, Still Present?," paper presented at the I Spanish Symposium on the Arctic Region: The Arctic Facing International Law, Politics and Research, Madrid, Spain, November 13, 2014; Rob Huebert, "Security Challenges in the Arctic," in *Global Challenges in the Arctic Region: Sovereignty, Environment and Geopolitical Balance*, edited by Elena Conde and Sara Iglesias Sánchez (London: Routledge, 2015).
6 Gearóid Ó Tuathail, "Thinking Critically about Geopolitics," in *Geopolitics Reader*, edited by Gearóid Ó Tuathail, Simon Dalby and Paul Routledge (London: Routledge, 1998), 1–14.
7 Rolf Tamnes and Kristine Offerdal, "Introduction," in *Geopolitics and Security in the Arctic: Regional Dynamics in a Global World*, edited by Rolf Tamnes and Kristine Offerdal (London: Routledge, 2014), 6.

8 Susan Strange, "Cave! hic dragones: A Critique of Regime Analysis," *International Organization* 36.2 (1982): 419–96; John J. Mearsheimer, "The False Promise of International Institutions," *International Security* 19.3 (1995): 5–49.

9 Klaus Haushofer, "Why Geopolitik?," in *Geopolitics Reader*, edited by Gearóid Ó Tuathail, Simon Dalby and Paul Routledge (London: Routledge, 1998), 34. Originally published in Andreas Dorpalen, *The World of General Haushofer* (New York and Toronto: Farrar & Rinehart, 1942).

10 The term "geopolitics" had been introduced a few years earlier by Kjellén; Mackinder reportedly detested it. See Halford J. Mackinder, "The Geographical Pivot of History," in *The Geographical Journal* 23.4 (1904): 422, accessed October 17, 2015, doi: 10.2307/3451460; Gearóid Ó Tuathail, "Putting Mackinder in his Place: Material Transformations and Myth," *Political Geography* 11.2 (1992): 102.

11 Nicholas J. Spykman, "Geography and Foreign Policy, I," in *The American Political Science Review* 32.1 (1938): 28–50, accessed October 17, 2015, doi: 10.2307/1949029. Spykman was Professor of International Relations at Yale University, while Mackinder became the first Professor of Geography at Oxford University.

12 Spykman, "Geography and Foreign Policy, I," 31.

13 Alfred Mahan, *The Influence of Sea Power upon History, 1660–1783* (Boston, MA: Little, Brown and Company, 1890), 34.

14 Mackinder, "The Geographical Pivot of History," 436.

15 Gearóid Ó Tuathail, Simon Dalby and Paul Routledge (eds.), *Geopolitics Reader* (London: Routledge, 1998), 16.

16 Harry Truman, "The Truman Doctrine," in *Geopolitics Reader*, edited by Gearóid Ó Tuathail, Simon Dalby and Paul Routledge (London: Routledge, 1998), 58–60. Originally published in *Public Papers of the Presidents of the United States*, 1947.

17 Leonid Brezhnev, "The Brezhnev Doctrine," in *Geopolitics Reader*, edited by Gearóid Ó Tuathail, Simon Dalby and Paul Routledge (London: Routledge, 1998), 74–77. Originally published in *Pravda*, September 25, 1968.

18 Ó Tuathail, "Thinking Critically about Geopolitics," 3.

19 Examples in the context of Arctic affairs include Jason Dittmer, Sami Moisio, Alan Ingram and Klaus Dodds, "Have You Heard the One about the Disappearing Ice?: Recasting Arctic Geopolitics," *Political Geography* 30.4 (2011): 202–14, accessed October 17, 2015, doi: http://dx.doi.org/10.1016/j.polgeo.2011.04.002; Ola Tunander, "Geopolitics of the North: Geopolitik of the Weak: A Post-Cold War Return to Rudolf Kjellén," *Cooperation and Conflict* 43.2 (2008): 164–84, accessed October 17, 2015, doi: 10.1177/0010836708089081.

20 Oran R. Young, *International Governance: Protecting the Environment in a Stateless Society* (Ithaca, NY: Cornell University Press, 1994), 15.

21 For example, James N. Rosenau, "Governance in the Twenty-First Century," *Global Governance* 1.1 (1995): 16–19.

22 Olav Schram Stokke, "Regimes as Governance Systems," in *Global Governance: Drawing Insights from the Environmental Experience*, edited by Oran R. Young (Cambridge, MA: MIT Press, 1997), 28.

23 Among others, Robert O. Keohane, "Theory of World Politics: Structural Realism and Beyond," in *Neo-Realism and its Critics*, edited by Robert O. Keohane (New York: Columbia University Press, 1986), 158–204; Young, *International Governance*.

24 G. John Ikenberry, "The Illusion of Geopolitics: The Enduring Power of the Liberal Order," *Foreign Affairs* 93.3 (2014): 80–91.

25 Arild Underdal, "International Cooperation: Transforming 'Needs' into 'Deeds,'" *Journal of Peace Research* 24.2 (1987): 167–83.

26 Marc A. Levy, Oran R. Young and Michael Zürn, "The Study of International Regimes," *European Journal of International Relations* 1.3 (1995): 267–330, accessed October 17, 2015, doi: 10.1177/1354066195001003001.

27 Cited in Klaus J. Dodds, "We are a Northern Country: Stephen Harper and the Canadian Arctic," *Polar Record* 47.243 (2011): 371.

28 Olav Schram Stokke, "Fisheries and Whaling," in *Encyclopedia of Global Environmental Governance and Politics* (Cheltenham: Edward Elgar, 2015), 364–73.

29 Jens Petter Nielsen, "The Barents Region in Historical Perspective: Russian–Norwegian Relations 1814–1917 and the Russian Commitment in the North," in *The Barents Region: Cooperation in Arctic Europe*, edited by Olav Schram Stokke and Ola Tunander (London: Sage Publications, 1994), 89.

30 Olav Schram Stokke, *Disaggregating International Regimes: A New Approach to Evaluation and Comparison* (Cambridge, MA: MIT Press, 2012).

31 Nielsen, "The Barents Region in Historical Perspective," 90. Those long-standing sealing operations were even allowed to continue after the Russian Revolution had brought an end to nearly 200 years of "Pomor trade," the exchange of fish taken off the Norwegian coast for Russian agricultural products stocked by Archangelsk merchants: Rolf Tamnes and Sven G. Holtsmark, "The Geopolitics of the Arctic in Historical Perspective," in *Geopolitics and Security in the Arctic: Regional Dynamics in a Global World*, edited by Rolf Tamnes and Kristine Offerdal (London: Routledge, 2014), 12–48.

32 Jón Th. Thór, *British Trawlers and Iceland 1919–1976, Publications of the Department of Economic History of the University of Göteborg 69* (Gothenburg: Department of Economic History of the University of Göteborg, 1995).

33 Olav Schram Stokke, Lee G. Anderson and Natalia Mirovitskaya, "The Barents Sea Fisheries," in *The Effectiveness of International Environmental Regimes: Causal Connections and Behavioral Mechanisms*, edited by Oran R. Young (Cambridge, MA: MIT Press, 1999), 91–155. Olav Schram Stokke, "International Environmental Governance and Security in the Arctic," in *Geopolitics and Security in the Arctic: Regional Dynamics in a Global World*, edited by Rolf Tamnes and Kristine Offerdal (London: Routledge, 2014), 121–46.

34 Arild Moe, Daniel Fjærtoft and Indra Øverland, "Space and Timing: Why was the Barents Sea Delimitation Dispute Resolved in 2010?," *Polar Geography* 34.3 (2011): 145–62, accessed October 17, 2015, doi: 10.1080/1088937X.2011.597887.

35 Geir Hønneland, *Making International Fisheries Agreements Work: Post-Agreement Bargaining in the Barents Sea* (Cheltenham: Edward Elgar, 2012); Stokke, *Disaggregating International Regimes*.

36 Garrett Hardin, "The Tragedy of the Commons," *Science* 162 (1968): 1243–48.

37 Underdal, "International Cooperation."

38 Stokke, "Fisheries and Whaling."

39 Stokke, "International Environmental Governance and Security in the Arctic."

40 Treaty concerning the Archipelago of Spitsbergen, and Protocol (Paris, February 9, 1920), Articles. 1, 3, 8 and 9.

41 Geir Ulfstein, *The Svalbard Treaty: From terra nullius to Norwegian Sovereignty* (Oslo: Aschehoug, 1995), 422.

42 Stokke, "International Environmental Governance and Security in the Arctic."

43 Torbjørn Pedersen, "The Constrained Politics of the Svalbrd Offshore Area," *Marine Policy* 32 (2008): 917.

44 On the "Elektron" case in 2006, see Kristian Åtland and Kristin Veen Bruusgaard, "When Security Speech Acts Misfire: Russia and the Elektron Incident," *Security Dialogue* 40.3 (2009): 333–53.

45 Pedersen, "The Constrained Politics of the Svalbrd Offshore Area;" Stokke, *Disaggregating International Regimes*.

46 Stokke, "International Environmental Governance and Security in the Arctic."
47 Ilulissat Declaration, May 28, 2008, accessed March 15, 2015, http://oceanlaw.org/downloads/arctic/Ilulissat_Declaration.pdf.
48 Olav Schram Stokke, "The Promise of Involvement: Asia in the Arctic," *Strategic Analysis* 37.4 (2013): 474–79, accessed October 17, 2015, doi: 10.1080/09700161.2013.802520.
49 Borgerson, "Arctic Meltdown," 71.
50 Among others, Gang Chen, "China's Emerging Arctic Strategy," *Polar Journal* 2 (2011): 358–71; Aki Tonami, "Future-Proofing Japan's Interests in the Arctic: Scientific Collaboration and a Search for Balance," *Asia Policy* 18 (2014): 52–58.
51 Stokke, "The Promise of Involvement."
52 J. Juo, *China News Service*, March 5, 2010, translated and cited by Linda Jakobson and Jingchao Peng, "China's Arctic Aspirations," *SIPRI Policy Paper* 34 (2012): 15.
53 Vijay Sakhuja, "India and the Changing Arctic," presentation at the Arctic Frontiers conference in Tromsø, Norway, January 24, 2013.
54 Arctic Council Rules of Procedure (Revised at the 8th Arctic Council Meeting in Kiruna, May 15, 2013), Annex 2, item 6; accessed March 15, 2015, www.arctic-council.org/index.php/en/document-archive/category/425-main-documents-from-kiruna-ministerial-meeting?download=1781:rules-of-procedure.
55 Stokke, "The Promise of Involvement."
56 Mackinder, "The Geographical Pivot of History," 430.
57 Spykman, "Geography and Foreign Policy, I," 4.
58 Tamnes and Holtsmark, "The Geopolitics of the Arctic in Historical Perspective."
59 Sune Dalgård, *Dansk–norsk hvalfangst 1615–1660: En studie over Danmark-Norges stilling i europæisk merkantil ekspansjon* (Copenhagen: G.E.C. Gad, 1962).
60 Odd Nakken, "Past, Present and Future Exploration and Management of Marine Resources in the Barents Sea and Adjacent Areas," *Fisheries Research* 37 (1998): 23–24.
61 G. Matishov et al., *Barents Sea: Global International Water Assessments (GIWA) Regional Assessment 11 (UNEP)* (Kalmar: University of Kalmar, 2004), 25.
62 Richard O. Wilberforce, "Some Aspects of the Anglo–Norwegian Fisheries Case," *Transactions of the Grotius Society* 38 (1952): 151–68, accessed October 17, 2015, doi: 10.2307/743164. Wilberforce was among the legal experts representing the UK in the Anglo–Norwegian Fisheries Case in 1951.
63 Jens Evensen, "The Anglo–Norwegian Fisheries Case and Its Legal Consequences," *The American Journal of International Law* 46.4 (1952): 609–30, accessed October 17, 2015, doi: 10.2307/2194293.
64 Wilberforce, "Some Aspects of the Anglo–Norwegian Fisheries Case," 154.
65 Ragnhild Hystad-Kjelle, "Like fra is-tiden har befolkningen i det nordlige Norge levet av fiske. Noregs argumenter for torskeførekomstane i internasjonale forhandlingsfora 1949–1994," Master's thesis (Bergen: University of Bergen, 2014), 23.
66 Evensen, "The Anglo–Norwegian Fisheries Case and Its Legal Consequences," 620.
67 Details in Evensen, "The Anglo–Norwegian Fisheries Case and Its Legal Consequences" and Wilberforce, "Some Aspects of the Anglo–Norwegian Fisheries Case." The corresponding kick-off event with respect to the continental shelf had occurred three years earlier as part of a political process examined better under a geopolitical optic: the 1948 Truman Declaration that unilaterally extended the US continental shelf.

68 Government of Greenland, "Consensus to Protect the Central Arctic Ocean from Unregulated Fisheries," *Press Release*, February 25, 2014, accessed November 5, 2014, http://naalakkersuisut.gl/~/media/Nanoq/Images/Nyheder/250214/press%20release%20english.docx.

69 Olav Schram Stokke, "Managing Straddling Stocks: The Interplay of Global and Regional Regimes," *Ocean and Coastal Management* 43.2/3 (2000): 205–34.

70 Robin R. Churchill, "The Barents Sea Loophole Agreement – a 'Coastal State' Solution to a Straddling Stock Problem," *International Journal of Marine and Coastal Law* 14.4 (1999): 467–90; Olav Schram Stokke, "Managing Fisheries in the Barents Sea Loophole: Interplay with the UN Fish Stocks Agreement," *Ocean Development and International Law* 32.3 (2001): 241–62.

71 David A. Balton, "The Bering Sea Doughnut Hole Convention: Regional Solution, Global Implications," in *Governing High Seas Fisheries: The Interplay of Global and Regional Regimes*, edited by Olav Schram Stokke (New York: Oxford University Press, 2001), 143–79. Today, it is widely held that the extensive foreign fishing had in fact been conducted inside poorly monitored Russian EEZs, implying that "collapse" of the high-seas fishery was in fact a reduction of illegal fisheries.

72 Stokke, "Managing Fisheries in the Barents Sea Loophole."

73 Oran R. Young, "The Age of the Arctic," *Foreign Policy* 61 (1985): 160–79; Olav Schram Stokke, "The Northern Environment: Is Cooperation Coming?," *Annals of the American Academy for Political and Social Science* 512 (1990): 58–69.

74 Hønneland, *Making International Fisheries Agreements Work*; Stokke, *Disaggregating International Regimes*.

75 Olav Schram Stokke and Ola Tunander, *The Barents Region: Cooperation in Arctic Europe* (London: Sage Publications, 1994); Olav Schram Stokke and Geir Hønneland. *International Cooperation and Arctic Governance: Regime Effectiveness and Northern Region Building* (London: Routledge, 2007).

76 Stokke, "Fisheries and Whaling."

77 Robert Harriss, "The Arctic: Past or Prologue?," *Environment: Science and Policy for Sustainable Development* 54.5 (2012): 3–13, accessed October 17, 2015, doi: 10.1080/00139157.2012.711663.

78 Olav Schram Stokke, "Environmental Security in the Arctic: The Case for Multilevel Governance," *International Journal* 66 (2011): 835–48.

79 Henrik Selin, *Towards International Chemical Safety: Taking Action on Persistent Organic Pollutants (POPs)* (Linköping: Linköping University, 2000), 133.

80 Steinar Andresen, Kristin Rosendal and Jon Birger Skjærseth, "Why Negotiate a Legally Binding Mercury Convention?," *International Environmental Agreements: Politics, Law and Economics* 13.4 (2013): 425–40, accessed October 17, 2015, doi: 10.1007/s10784-012-9198-6.

81 Olav Schram Stokke, "Trade Measures and the Combat of IUU Fishing: Institutional Interplay and Effective Governance in the Northeast Atlantic," *Marine Policy* 33.2 (2009): 339–49.

82 Stokke, *Disaggregating International Regimes*.

83 Stokke, "Trade Measures and the Combat of IUU Fishing."

84 Geir Hønneland, *Kvotekamp og kyststatssolidaritet: Norsk-russisk fiskeriforvaltning gjennom 30 år* (Bergen: Fagbokforlaget, 2006), 80.

85 Advisory Committee on the Marine Environment and Advisory Committee on Ecosystems, *Report of the ICES Advisory Committee on Fisheries Management* (ICES Advice 2008), Book 3.

86 Stokke, "Trade Measures and the Combat of IUU Fishing."

87 Ibid.

References

Advisory Committee on the Marine Environment and Advisory Committee on Ecosystems. *Report of the ICES Advisory Committee on Fisheries Management* (ICES Advice 2008). Book 3.

Andresen, Steinar, Kristin Rosendal and Jon Birger Skjærseth. "Why Negotiate a Legally Binding Mercury Convention?." *International Environmental Agreements: Politics, Law and Economics* 13.4 (2013): 425–40. Accessed October 17, 2015. doi: 10.1007/s10784-012-9198-6.

Åtland, Kristian and Kristin Veen Bruusgaard. "When Security Speech Acts Misfire: Russia and the Elektron Incident." *Security Dialogue* 40.3 (2009): 333–53.

Balton, David A. "The Bering Sea Doughnut Hole Convention: Regional Solution, Global Implications." In *Governing High Seas Fisheries: The Interplay of Global and Regional Regimes*, edited by Olav Schram Stokke, 143–79. New York: Oxford University Press, 2001.

Borgerson, Scott G. "Arctic Meltdown: The Economic and Security Implications of Global Warming." *Foreign Affairs* 87.2 (2008): 63–77.

Brezhnev, Leonid. "The Brezhnev Doctrine." In *Geopolitics Reader*, edited by Gearóid Ó Tuathail, Simon Dalby and Paul Routledge, 74–77. London: Routledge, 1998. Originally published in *Pravda*, September 25, 1968.

Churchill, Robin R. "The Barents Sea Loophole Agreement – A 'Coastal State' Solution to a Straddling Stock Problem." *International Journal of Marine and Coastal Law* 14.4 (1999): 467–90.

Chen, Gang. "China's Emerging Arctic Strategy." *Polar Journal* 2 (2011): 358–71.

Dalgård, Sune. *Dansk–norsk hvalfangst 1615–1660: En studie over Danmark-Norges stilling i europæisk merkantil ekspansjon.* Copenhagen: G.E.C. Gad, 1962.

Dittmer, Jason, Sami Moisio, Alan Ingram and Klaus Dodds. "Have You Heard the One about the Disappearing Ice? Recasting Arctic Geopolitics." *Political Geography* 30.4 (2011): 202–14. Accessed October 17, 2015. doi: http://dx.doi.org/10.1016/j.polgeo.2011.04.002.

Dodds, Klaus. "Flag Planting and Finger Pointing: The Law of the Sea, the Arctic and the Political Geographies of the Outer Continental Shelf." *Political Geography* 29.2 (2010): 63–73. Accessed October 17, 2015. doi: http://dx.doi.org/10.1016/j.polgeo.2010.02.004.

Dodds, Klaus J. "We are a Northern Country: Stephen Harper and the Canadian Arctic." *Polar Record* 47.243 (2011): 371–82.

Evensen, Jens. "The Anglo–Norwegian Fisheries Case and Its Legal Consequences." *The American Journal of International Law* 46.4 (1952): 609–30. Accessed October 17, 2015. doi: 10.2307/2194293.

Hardin, Garrett. "The Tragedy of the Commons." *Science* 162 (1968): 1243–48.

Harriss, Robert. "The Arctic: Past or Prologue?" *Environment: Science and Policy for Sustainable Development* 54.5 (2012): 3–13. Accessed October 17, 2015. doi: 10.1080/00139157.2012.711663.

Haushofer, Klaus. "Why Geopolitik?" In *Geopolitics reader*, edited by Gearóid Ó Tuathail, Simon Dalby and Paul Routledge, 33–35. London: Routledge, 1998. Originally in Dorpalen, Andreas. *The World of General Haushofer*. New York and Toronto: Farrar & Rinehart, 1942.

Huebert, Rob. "Security Threats in the Arctic, Still Present?" Paper presented at the I Spanish Symposium on the Arctic Region: The Arctic Facing International Law, Politics and Research. Madrid, Spain, November 13, 2014.

Huebert, Rob. "Security Challenges in the Arctic." In *Global Challenges in the Arctic Region: Sovereignty, Environment and Geopolitical Balance*, edited by Elena Conde and Sara Iglesias Sánchez. London: Routledge, 2017.

Hystad-Kjelle, Ragnhild. "Like fra is-tiden har befolkningen i det nordlige Norge levet av fiske. Noregs argumenter for torskeførekomstane i internasjonale forhandlingsfora 1949–1994." Master's thesis (Bergen: University of Bergen, 2014).

Hønneland, Geir. *Kvotekamp og kyststatssolidaritet: Norsk-russisk fiskeriforvaltning gjennom 30 år*. Bergen: Fagbokforlaget, 2006.

Hønneland, Geir. *Making International Fisheries Agreements Work: Post-Agreement Bargaining in the Barents Sea*. Cheltenham: Edward Elgar, 2012.

Ikenberry, G. John. "The Illusion of Geopolitics: The Enduring Power of the Liberal Order." *Foreign Affairs* 93.3 (2014): 80–91.

Juo, J. *China News Service*, March 5, 2010. Translated and cited by Linda Jakobson and Jingchao Peng, "China's Arctic Aspirations." *SIPRI Policy Paper* 34 (2012).

Keohane, Robert O. "Theory of World Politics: Structural Realism and Beyond." In *Neo-Realism and its Critics*, edited by Robert O. Keohane, 158–204. New York: Columbia University Press, 1986.

Levy, Marc A., Oran R. Young and Michael Zürn. "The Study of International Regimes." *European Journal of International Relations* 1.3 (1995): 267–330. Accessed October 17, 2015. doi: 10.1177/1354066195001003001.

Mackinder, Halford J. "The Geographical Pivot of History." *The Geographical Journal* 23.4 (1904): 421–44. Accessed October 17, 2015. doi: 10.2307/3451460.

Mahan, Alfred T. *The Influence of Sea Power upon History, 1660–1783*. Boston, MA: Little, Brown and Company, 1890.

Matishov, G., N. Golubeva, G. Titova, A. Sydnes and B. Voegele. *Barents Sea: Global International Water Assessments (GIWA) Regional Assessment 11 (UNEP)*. Kalmar: University of Kalmar, 2004.

Mead, Walter Russell. "The Return of Geopolitics." *Foreign Affairs* 93.3 (2014): 69–79.

Mearsheimer, John J. "The False Promise of International Institutions." *International Security* 19.3 (1995): 5–49.

Moe, Arild, Daniel Fjærtoft and Indra Øverland. "Space and Timing: Why was the Barents Sea Delimitation Dispute Resolved in 2010?" *Polar Geography* 34.3 (2011): 145–62. Accessed October 17, 2015. doi: 10.1080/1088937X.2011.597887.

Nakken, Odd. "Past, Present and Future Exploration and Management of Marine Resources in the Barents Sea and Adjacent Areas." *Fisheries Research* 37 (1998): 23–36.

Nielsen, Jens Petter. "The Barents Region in Historical Perspective: Russian–Norwegian Relations 1814–1917 and the Russian Commitment in the North." In *The Barents Region: Cooperation in Arctic Europe*, edited by Olav Schram Stokke and Ola Tunander, 87–100. London: Sage Publications, 1994.

Ó Tuathail, Gearóid. "Thinking Critically about Geopolitics." In *Geopolitics Reader*, edited by Gearóid Ó Tuathail, Simon Dalby and Paul Routledge, 1–14. London: Routledge, 1998.

Ó Tuathail, Gearóid. "Putting Mackinder in his Place: Material Transformations and Myth." *Political Geography* 11.2 (1992): 100–18.

Pedersen, Torbjørn. "The Constrained Politics of the Svalbrd Offshore Area." *Marine Policy* 32 (2008): 913–19.

Rosenau, James N. "Governance in the Twenty-First Century." *Global Governance* 1.1 (1995): 16–19.

Sakhuja, Vijay. "India and the Changing Arctic." Presentation at the Arctic Frontiers conference in Tromsø, Norway, January 24, 2013.

Selin, Henrik. *Towards International Chemical Safety: Taking Action on Persistent Organic Pollutants (POPs)*. Linköping: Linköping University, 2000.

Spykman, Nicholas J. "Geography and Foreign Policy, I." *The American Political Science Review* 32.1 (1938): 28–50. Accessed October 17, 2015. doi: 10.2307/1949029.

Stokke, Olav Schram. "The Northern Environment: Is Cooperation Coming?" *Annals of the American Academy for Political and Social Science* 512 (1990): 58–69.

Stokke, Olav Schram. "Regimes as Governance Systems." In *Global Governance: Drawing Insights from the Environmental Experience*, edited by Oran R. Young, 27–65. Cambridge, MA: MIT Press, 1997.

Stokke, Olav Schram. "Managing Straddling Stocks: The Interplay of Global and Regional Regimes." *Ocean and Coastal Management* 43.2/3 (2000): 205–34.

Stokke, Olav Schram. "Managing Fisheries in the Barents Sea Loophole: Interplay with the UN Fish Stocks Agreement." *Ocean Development and International Law* 32.3 (2001): 241–62.

Stokke, Olav Schram. "Trade Measures and the Combat of IUU Fishing: Institutional Interplay and Effective Governance in the Northeast Atlantic." *Marine Policy* 33.2 (2009): 339–49.

Stokke, Olav Schram. "Environmental Security in the Arctic: The Case for Multilevel Governance." *International Journal* 66 (2011): 835–48.

Stokke, Olav Schram. *Disaggregating International Regimes: A New Approach to Evaluation and Comparison*. Cambridge, MA: MIT Press, 2012.

Stokke, Olav Schram. "The Promise of Involvement: Asia in the Arctic." *Strategic Analysis* 37.4 (2013): 474–79. Accessed October 17, 2015. doi: 10.1080/09700161.2013.802520.

Stokke, Olav Schram. "International Environmental Governance and Security in the Arctic." In *Geopolitics and Security in the Arctic: Regional Dynamics in a Global World*, edited by Rolf Tamnes and Kristine Offerdal, 121–46. London: Routledge, 2014.

Stokke, Olav Schram. "Fisheries and Whaling." In *Encyclopedia of Global Environmental Governance and Politics*, 364–73. Cheltenham: Edward Elgar, 2015.

Stokke, Olav Schram and Geir Hønneland. *International Cooperation and Arctic Governance: Regime Effectiveness and Northern Region Building*. London: Routledge, 2007.

Stokke, Olav Schram and Ola Tunander. *The Barents Region: Cooperation in Arctic Europe*. London: Sage Publications, 1994.

Stokke, Olav Schram, Lee G. Anderson and Natalia Mirovitskaya. "The Barents Sea Fisheries." In *The Effectiveness of International Environmental Regimes: Causal Connections and Behavioral Mechanisms*, edited by Oran R. Young, 91–155. Cambridge, MA: MIT Press, 1999.

Strange, Susan. "Cave! hic dragones: A Critique of Regime Analysis." *International Organization* 36.2 (1982): 419–96.

Tamnes, Rolf and Sven G. Holtsmark. "The Geopolitics of the Arctic in Historical Perspective." In *Geopolitics and Security in the Arctic: Regional Dynamics in a Global World*, edited by Rolf Tamnes and Kristine Offerdal, 12–48. London: Routledge, 2014.

Tamnes, Rolf and Kristine Offerdal. *Geopolitics and Security in the Arctic: Regional Dynamics in a Global World*. London: Routledge, 2014.

Tamnes, Rolf and Kristine Offerdal. "Introduction." In *Geopolitics and Security in the Arctic: Regional Dynamics in a Global World*, edited by Rolf Tamnes and Kristine Offerdal, 1–11. London: Routledge, 2014.

Thór, Jón Th. *British Trawlers and Iceland 1919–1976, Publications of the Department of Economic History of the University of Göteborg 69*. Gothenburg: Department of Economic History of the University of Göteborg, 1995.

Tonami, Aki. "Future-Proofing Japan's Interests in the Arctic: Scientific Collaboration and a Search for Balance." *Asia Policy* 18 (2014): 52–58.

Truman, Harry. "The Truman Doctrine." In *Geopolitics Reader*, edited by Gearóid Ó Tuathail, Simon Dalby and Paul Routledge, 58–60. London: Routledge, 1998. Originally published in *Public Papers of the Presidents of the United States*, 1947.

Tunander, Ola. "Geopolitics of the North: Geopolitik of the Weak: A Post-Cold War Return to Rudolf Kjellén." *Cooperation and Conflict* 43.2 (2008): 164–84. Accessed October 17, 2015. doi: 10.1177/0010836708089081.

Ulfstein, Geir. *The Svalbard Treaty: From terra nullius to Norwegian Sovereignty*. Oslo: Aschehoug, 1995.

Underdal, Arild. "International Cooperation: Transforming 'Needs' into 'Deeds.'" *Journal of Peace Research* 24.2 (1987): 167–83.

Wilberforce, Richard O. "Some Aspects of the Anglo–Norwegian Fisheries Case." *Transactions of the Grotius Society* 38 (1952): 151–68. Accessed October 17, 2015. doi: 10.2307/743164.

Young, Oran R. "The Age of the Arctic." *Foreign Policy* 61 (1985): 160–79.

Young, Oran R. *International Governance: Protecting the Environment in a Stateless Society*. Ithaca, NY: Cornell University Press, 1994.

10 The Arctic development

New navigational routes and maritime governance

Marta Iglesias Berlanga

Introduction

The Arctic, whose name derives from a Greek word meaning "bear"[1] is an area located around the North Pole comprising the Arctic Ocean and adjacent lands within the Arctic Polar Circle (66° 33' N). This includes the Canadian Arctic Archipelago and Greenland, namely the areas remaining within the +10°C isotherm of the warmest month, and exclude the northern section of Scandinavia, which is affected by the North Stream of the Atlantic and enjoys significantly better weather conditions than other territories located at the same latitude.

Arctic lands do not constitute a continent or a land unit on their own, as in the case of the Antarctic continent, but form part of the adjacent continental masses. Therefore, we can distinguish between European,[2] Asiatic[3] and American[4] polar land. Although it is populated by human groups adapted to the harsh living conditions imposed by the environment, in particular the Lapps in Europe, the communities of North Siberia in Asia and the Eskimo in America, the Arctic is, for the most part, a large ocean covered by ice floes surrounded by treeless land and frozen underground. From a physical, chemical and biological perspective, the Arctic is particularly important, as it is especially sensitive to changes in climate and is considered by scientists and researchers as an "early warning system" or the "barometer" of global climate change, according to the United Nations Environment Program (UNEP).

Apart from the current concerns they are raising, the polar regions are little known. Exploration began in times of geographical discoveries, in the sixteenth and seventeenth centuries. Indeed, when it was found that those lands discovered by Christopher Columbus were not East Asia but a new continent, the need arose to overcome this obstacle between Europe and Asia. Thus, expeditions were organized in search of a possible passage to the Northwest through the Canadian Arctic Archipelago, or to the Northeast, bordering European and Asiatic territories bathed by the Arctic Ocean. Those attempts, although not achieving the expected results, did provide knowledge about this huge isolated world, which except for

Greenland (due to fishery) and the Svalbard or Spitsbergen islands (due to the rich and abundant coal deposits) remain uninhabited due to their once precarious economic use and the sometimes impossible living conditions.

In the world we live in today, governed by immediacy, it seems hard to step back and observe from a distance events that, despite being less visible in the short term, will soon be part of an essentially different planetary scenario. One of the most dramatic consequences of climate change is the melting of the Arctic ice caps (reduction of the frozen part of the Arctic Ocean and melting of Greenland's ice sheet) which is accelerating access to new natural resources (especially hydrocarbons) and is opening new shipping routes that were inaccessible not so long ago. Thus, while mankind looks towards this region with concern, due to what may be irreversible damage to the environment caused by global warming, the five costal Arctic States—United States, Canada, Norway, Russia and Denmark (through Greenland)—as well as other countries and international organizations such as the European Union (EU), do not seem willing to miss this unprecedented opportunity to extract oil, gas, diamonds and living resources from waters that were previously unreachable, but will probably be accessible in the fairly near future.

Focusing on this last aspect, we will begin by analyzing the Arctic navigation routes, their geographical characteristics, the main states interested in their navigability and the reason for any international legal problems this may pose. On a secondary level, we will highlight the advantages and disadvantages derived from ice navigation to finally consider if the current range of regulatory measures is able to respond to climate change in the Arctic, paying special attention to the newly adopted International Code for Ships Operating in Polar Waters (known as *Polar Code*).

Arctic navigation routes

Northeast Passage (Northern Sea Route) and the legendary Northwest Passage: characteristics and states' interests

There are basically three Arctic navigation routes: (1) the Northeast Passage or Northern Sea Route (NSR); (2) the legendary[5] Northwest Passage; and (3) the Transpolar Sea Route, which will be analyzed in Section 3, and which can also be divided into two: (a) the central route under the ice sheet, suitable for military submarines but not for commercial use; and (b) the central route on the surface, only navigable by icebreakers during the melting season.

The Northeast Passage/NSR is a shipping route that connects the Atlantic and Pacific Oceans along the Russian coasts. Although it was in 1525 when the diplomat Gerasimov suggested for the first time the possible existence of a maritime passage between the Atlantic and the Pacific, the

NSR was not officially opened until 1935.[6] In the 1990s, with the disintegration of the Soviet Union, commercial navigation from the main Russian port in the Arctic, Arkhangelsk, to the Bering Strait separating Siberia and Alaska began to decline and some stretches of the route became impracticable. Nowadays, Russian interest in the Arctic melting is partly based on the idea of mobilizing natural resources, boosting economic growth and developing Siberia, especially timber and coal exports. Indeed, in January 2014 the Russian Minister of Defence emphasized that one of the priorities of the country was to "revive" the abandoned stations of the 1990s, taking into account that Russia has a significant fleet of vessels specialized in Arctic navigation, namely ice-breakers and, particularly, the nuclear-powered versions.[7] On the other hand, we should also point out that maritime traffic is mainly concentrated in the Northeast Passage (August and September are the most suitable months for navigation), as the Northwest Passage was only open for the first time to maritime traffic during the boreal summer of 2007 and later in August of 2011.

However, Russia is not the only state interested in the viability of the Northern Sea Route. Japan imports 80 percent of its energy supplies through the South China Sea, whose pirate plagued waters are under dispute among China, Taiwan, Vietnam and the Philippines. The idea of accessing an alternative navigational route that would avoid Somalian piracy and would also shorten the distance between Japan and Hamburg by 27 percent is especially attractive.

The Northwest Passage is a maritime route bordering North America in the north that goes through the Arctic Ocean and connects the Davis and the Bering Straits (the Atlantic and Pacific Oceans). The route flows through a set of straits located in the Canadian Arctic Archipelago, which includes ninety-four major islands and 34,469 minor ones. It must be remembered that islands such as Ellesmere, Victoria and Baffin, are among the ten largest in the world. As we are about to see below, Canada is the country most interested in obtaining undisputed administrative control of navigation through this route.

Legal problems related to the Northwest Passage and the Northern Sea Route

International straits or inland waters?

The legal problems associated with commercial ship navigation in Arctic waters are mainly twofold. On the one hand, from a legal point of view there is a need to determine whether the Northwest Passage and the Northern Sea Route flow freely through international straits or inland waters. On the other hand, it is unclear whether the rights provided to coastal states by Article 234 of the United Nations Convention on the Law of the Sea (UNCLOS) of 1982 can be applied to their territorial seas.

Taking into account that Article 35 of Part III of UNCLOS has a limited scope and distinguishes between two types of straits—that is, straits formed by inland waters and straits regulated by long-standing international conventions—to which Part III is not applicable, some states have long demanded that the maritime zones comprising some of their straits be classified as historic waters. This is the case of Canada and Russia in relation to the Northwest Passage and the Northern Passage respectively,[8] along with the demands regarding the establishment of straight baselines.

Straits comprising waters that have always been inland waters fall outside the scope of the application of Part III of UNCLOS. According to Article 35.a:

> Nothing in this Part affects:
> a. any areas of internal waters within a strait, except where the establishment of a straight baseline in accordance with the method set forth in article 7 has the effect of enclosing as internal waters areas which had not previously been considered as such.

The most important legal consequence generated by this provision is that the rights of transit passage or those of innocent passage, enjoyed by vessels or aircraft in areas of the strait that are considered territorial sea, do not extend to inland waters. These zones are governed by Part II of the convention and, therefore, are subject to exclusive sovereignty of the coastal state. In these straits there is no right of passage of any kind and they cannot be considered as international straits.

When is it possible to talk about inland waters that have not emerged as a consequence of drawing straight baselines in accordance with Article 7 of UNCLOS? The possibility of a strait which encompasses inland waters that have never been transformed into such by drawing straight baselines can occur, according to Pharand,[9] due to the existence of historic titles. Therefore, we will be tackling the hypothesis of historic waters that will create historic straits similar to historic bays, referred to in Article 10.6 of UNCLOS.[10] Although there are generally recognized historic bays (such as the Chesapeake, Delaware or the Gulf of Fonseca), the situation is not the same when referring to the existence of historic inland waters in straits. All in all, if the Indreleia of Norway is excluded, there is no general recognition of the existence of other straits that enclose historic waters.[11]

However, Canada and Russia maintain that the different straits included in the Northeast and the Northwest Passages enclose historic inland waters. Such a statement is to be understood as follows: the maritime routes described are not international straits, there is no right of free navigation of any kind, and they are subject to the exclusive jurisdiction of the coastal state. De facto, according to this claim, Canada issued a Territorial Sea Geographic Coordinates Order of September 10, 1986,[12] claiming all the waters of the Canadian Arctic Archipelago to be part of the

Canadian inland waters and deemed them to be historic waters.[13] Meanwhile, Russia has done likewise in its Decree of July 20, 1957 and in its Memory of July 21, 1964.[14]

In order to qualify as historic waters international law states that the waters must comply with two requirements: (a) the effective and continued exercise of sovereignty by the coastal state or the coastal states over the waters at issue; and (b) the recognition of this situation by other states. Thus, even though for the situations described above there is little doubt the first condition has been met, we cannot say the same for the second requirement if we take into account the protests of the Member States of the European Union (EU) and those of the United States of America, which refuse to recognize the existence of a historic title that justifies the Canadian and Russian delimitations and considers them to contravene international law.[15]

In this context, in 1985 the US ice-breaker USCGC *Polar Sea* went through the Northwest Passage without asking permission from Canada, alleging that it was a profitable way of sailing the ship from Greenland to Alaska and that there was no need for permission to navigate through an international strait. In 1986, the Canadian government made a statement strengthening Canadian rights in those waters, a statement that has never been recognized by the United States. However, in 1988 Canada and the United States signed an agreement on Arctic Cooperation that, despite the fact that it does not solve the problems of sovereignty, affirms that American ice-breakers have to seek permission from the Canadian government in order to navigate through Canadian Arctic waters. Despite the agreement, in 2005 Canada reported unauthorized navigation through its waters by several American nuclear submarines. Indeed, the United States has reiterated its position through different acts, such as the US National Security and Homeland Security Presidential Directive of 2009,[16] by which an Arctic policy is being established. In any case, to defend this position it would be essential for the United States to be bound by UNCLOS.[17] If it achieved the status of a party to the LOS Convention, the American government could also benefit from the possibility of submitting a claim before the commission on the limits of the extended continental shelf in the Beaufort and Chukchi Seas. Furthermore, if we take into account that 90 percent of the European Union's foreign trade is carried out by sea, the organization's strong defense of an international strait and its legal status seems logical, as well as its interest in avoiding alleged discriminatory practices of Arctic coastal states towards merchant ships of third countries, such as the establishment of special fees, compulsory services, special provisions, etc.[18]

Article 234 of the United Nations Convention on the Law of the Sea of 1982

Going back to the classification of the Canadian Arctic Archipelago as inland waters, due to Canada's perception of those waters as historic, another provision that raises significant problems of interpretation and scope of application is Article 234 of UNCLOS:

> Coastal States have the right to adopt and enforce non-discriminatory laws and regulations for the prevention, reduction and control of marine pollution from vessels in *ice-covered areas within the limits of the exclusive economic zone*, where particularly severe climatic conditions and *the presence of ice-covering such areas for most of the year* create obstructions or exceptional hazards to navigation, and pollution of the marine environment could cause major harm to or irreversible disturbance of the ecological balance. Such laws and regulations shall have due regard to navigation and the protection and preservation of the marine environment based on the best available scientific evidence.

Considering the fact that the article recognizes the right of Arctic coastal states to adopt and apply stricter rules than those provided for (leaving aside IMO regulations) in order to prevent and control pollution in areas covered by ice *within the limits of the exclusive economic zone* (EEZ), there are some questions that are not answered by Article 234 of UNCLOS: What does the presence of ice in those areas during most part of the year mean? Can it be interpreted that the presence of partial ice cover over the waters poses an exceptional risk for navigation? What is the meaning of "the limits of the exclusive economic zone"? Is the outer limit of the EEZ not exceeding 200 nautical miles, measured from the baselines determined in accordance with the UNCLOS? Or is the EEZ an area beyond and adjacent to the territorial sea and, consequently, an area of 188 nautical miles?

An analysis of the national legislation of Canada, Denmark, Iceland, Norway, Russia and the United States shows that the final outcome is that only Canada and Russia have adopted more rigorous standards than GAIRAS (Generally Accepted International Rules and Standards) as regards building, design, equipment and navigation patterns. The most important Canadian law about this is the *Arctic Waters Pollution Prevention Act* (AWPP, 1970), the act which inspired Article 234 of the UNCLOS and which has two main parts: the Arctic Shipping Pollution Prevention Regulation (ASPPR)[19] and the Arctic Waters Pollution Prevention Regulation (AWPPR, 1972).[20] From this perspective, Canada and Russia do not distinguish between territorial sea and exclusive economic zone (EEZ). In their opinion they have the right to exercise in the territorial sea the competences attributed to them by Article 234 of UNCLOS in the exclusive economic zone[21] and can, therefore, limit the right of innocent passage in the territorial sea. Furthermore, could it be feasible to enforce Article 234 of the UNCLOS in international straits, thus limiting the right of transit passage or the right of innocent passage in those waters?[22] To avoid the recognition of those rights, have the other states made claimed against this particular aspect? Not yet.

Transpolar Route or Central Arctic Ocean Route: characteristics and interests of the states

The Transpolar Route or Central Arctic Shipping Route is a maritime route that crosses the Arctic through its most temperate zone and runs directly over the North Pole, avoiding the Northeast and the Northwest Passages.

China is one of the states most interested in this route. Six of the ten ports with the heaviest traffic in the world are located in China. Exploitation of this route would allow China to save on fuel, stopover costs and the transit charges of the Suez Canal (used by approximately 17,000 vessels each year). It would also be a much safer route than the Somali one in the Gulf of Aden (plagued, as mentioned above, with pirates). Indeed, China has already made approaches to some Nordic countries and in 2014 it signed its first free trade agreement with Iceland. The idea of the Chinese is to invest in the construction of transpolar ports in Iceland and the vicinity of the Bering Strait. China has invested around €1.7 billion in the exploitation of an iron mine in Greenland containing one-tenth of the world's rare earth deposits (seventeen metals essential to manufacturing the high technology equipment, which is nowadays monopolized by China).[23] Furthermore, in Murmansk in April 2011, discussions were held with Russia on a general agreement for maritime transport through the Northern Sea Route, according to the agreement signed in October 2010 between the Chinese National Petroleum Corporation and Sovcomflot, the biggest Russian company in the maritime transport field. In this respect, we should not forget that nearly half of the Chinese gross domestic product (GDP) is directly related to maritime transport.[24]

Moreover, China has obtained observer status on the Arctic Council, the intergovernmental forum created in 1996 to promote cooperation in the Arctic and of which the eight Arctic States are members (the so-called Arctic Eight are: Canada, Denmark, Finland, Iceland, Norway, Russia, Sweden and the United States). Apart from the Arctic Eight, there are other states participating as observers on the Arctic Council: France, Germany, the Netherlands, Poland, Spain, United Kingdom, China, Italy, Japan, Republic of Korea, Singapore and India. Although three members of the Council (Denmark, Finland and Sweden) are also Member States of the EU and two others (Norway and Iceland), though not members, are currently part of the European Economic Area (EEA), the European Union itself has not yet been admitted as an observer on the Arctic Council. At present, the question of whether the European Union should be granted observer status is likely to be overshadowed by the recent deterioration of Europe's relations with Russia over the Ukrainian conflict. Given Russia's importance to the region, the Arctic States have more interest in maintaining relations with the Kremlin concerning Arctic issues than in supporting the EU's bid. However, Finland and Sweden consider that the role of the EU in the Arctic Council would be very beneficial to promote, for example, the Northern Dimension. Indeed, on the basis of the practical work of the Barents Euro-Arctic Council (BEAC),[25] the European Council[26] has confirmed the need to boost the Northern Dimension's environmental activities and development of transport links in the region, including new navigation routes.[27] In this context, it should not be forgotten that Iceland, "next member state of the European Union," will have a geostrategic position relative to Arctic navigation routes.

This reality proves that the Arctic dispute is not only limited to the five coastal states of the Arctic Ocean (Norway, Canada, the United States, Russia and Denmark). Other countries and international organizations, apart from China, Japan and the EU, that are also interested in this remote part of the planet are South Korea,[28] India, Singapore and Spain.[29] The Central Arctic, which is an area the size of the Mediterranean Sea,[30] is the last refuge of untouched fisheries in the world and this could open up significant new opportunities for the Spanish fishing fleet. The area from the 200-mile limit to the North Pole is considered international waters (a maritime space where it is possible to fish freely within the limitations established by the UNCLOS of 1982) and these resources can be exploited by everyone. Furthermore, the energy company REPSOL has already obtained licenses to exploit oil and gas in Alaska, Canada and Norway.[31]

Advantages and disadvantages of opening Arctic Routes to maritime navigation

As discussed above, the main advantages derived from opening new Arctic navigation routes to maritime traffic are reduced distances (leading to large savings in time and fuel) and the chance to avoid passage through the Suez Canal or Panama Canal. However, navigation in the Arctic is not easy, as it requires a significant economic outlay. The following aspects must also be considered:

- Important investments are needed to adapt vessel hulls to ice navigation;
- Ice-breaker fees;
- The increased cost of insurance policies;
- The lack of ports or infrastructure in some areas. For example, the Northwest Passage has no infrastructure at all, as it had been permanently covered by ice until the boreal summer of 2007. As pointed out previously, most traffic is concentrated in the Northeast Passage, but if international maritime transport increases in the Arctic and new ports are created, it might be necessary to coordinate the Port State Control (PSC)[32] through a new specific Memorandum of Understanding (MOU).[33] In this regard, can the existing MOUs ensure high standards for the Arctic? Nowadays the Paris MOU applies to twenty-five countries, including all the Arctic States. The Tokyo MOU is the only

other agreement affecting the coastal states of the Arctic and maritime authorities in Canada and Russia are parties to this MOU;

- Information is needed on varying ice conditions;
- Issues such as the draught restrictions in some points of the Northeast Passage, the jurisdictional problems not yet solved in the Arctic (delimitation of maritime borders) and the risks of ice navigation (such as icebergs). Indeed, when a cargo ship takes the Northern Sea Route, a Russian pilot must be on board. Sometimes ships sail alongside a Russian atomic nuclear ice-breaker, which increases navigation costs and makes the traditional Panama and Suez Canal routes look more attractive.

Applicable legal framework in polar zones: special reference to the Polar Code

General framework

Receding ice as a consequence of climate change has extended the navigable season in the Arctic, which until recently was practicable only in summer. Considering this and advances in naval technology, it is not absurd at all to think that maritime traffic in the polar region could increase in the short term. Although we still do not know exactly the extent of energy resources in the Arctic, as they are discovered the demand for maritime transport will rise to facilitate the movement of staff and building material or to export the extracted products to Western markets. However, an increase in maritime transport can also multiply the risk of maritime pollution.

From a legal point of view, the most urgent need is to develop a shipping regime that minimizes any impact on security and the environment from an increase in maritime traffic in the Arctic or due to an increase in the industrial use of Arctic waters (such as exploiting hydrocarbons or fishing).

The new applicable legal framework for polar zones is heterogeneous, as it is made up of: (a) international standards which includes, in essence, the provisions of the 1982 UNCLOS and a wide range of international treaties and other non-binding directives adopted in the framework of the IMO; (b) regional standards mainly created by the Arctic Council; (c) national standards of coastal states, as a consequence of international and regional standards that do not sufficiently provide the appropriate levels of security and environmental protection in polar waters; and (d) standards created by some private organisms such as classification societies.

Although this may initially seem very complete, this multifaceted regulation can bring with it confusion and may even call into question the effectiveness of its different instruments. In addition, during the creation of this legal framework no reference has been made to international agreements on liability and compensation for maritime accidents, or to contracting marine insurance (which will undoubtedly play a major role in the navigation of polar areas).

The creation of a strong, harmonized system, adapted to the nature and risks of maritime navigation in the Arctic, depends on the willingness of states to cooperate,[34] as nowadays no country is strong enough to exploit and preserve the Arctic region unilaterally. In this context, the adoption on November 21, 2014 of the International Code for Ships Operating in Polar Waters (the so called Polar Code)[35] by the Maritime Safety Committee (MSC) of the International Maritime Organization (IMO) is definitely a positive sign of this good will.

The Polar Code

The idea of creating a Polar Code dates back to the *Exxon Valdez* oil spill on the coasts of Alaska in March 1989. As is well known, of the 41 million liters of oil which the ship was transporting, 37,000 were dumped in the sea, causing the biggest ecological tragedy that Alaska has ever suffered. More recently, the origin of the Polar Code is related to the AMSA (Arctic Marine Shipping Assessment) report of 2009, drafted under the auspices of the Arctic Council.[36] Among other issues, the report recommends that certain provisions of the 2009 Polar Guidelines be made obligatory.

Created in response to the recent climate changes in the Arctic and Antarctic region, the objective of the Polar Code is to adapt the existing IMO provisions to the peculiar polar climate, in order to provide it with the same level of security and environmental protection in polar waters that exists in other regions covered by the instruments of the IMO. All in all, the idea is to guarantee a harmonized international framework for navigation in the Arctic and Antarctic regions.

It is important to bear in mind that the Polar Code does not aim to overlap with other legal documents, but to include new aspects and additional requirements which do not appear in other legal instruments. For this reason, it is structured into two parts:

- *Part A*, taking into consideration the specific risks linked to polar waters (environmental risks, remote location, human risks, etc.), includes obligatory provisions intended to complement prescriptions established in the International Convention for the Safety of Life at Sea (SOLAS), in the International Convention for the Prevention of Pollution from Ships (MARPOL), and in some other relevant international treaties adopted under IMO aegis;
- *Part B* includes non-binding additional guidelines intended to facilitate the application of the obligatory requirements of Part A.

Focusing on Part A of the Polar Code, in November 2014, the MSC (Maritime Safety Committee) adopted both the draft of the Code, presented at its 93rd session, and a new Chapter XIV of the SOLAS Convention titled "Safety Measures for Ships Operating in Polar Waters," which makes the

Introduction and Part I-A of the Polar Code obligatory. Chapter XIV regulates the construction and adequacy of the vessel and its equipment, guidelines for ice navigation and the rules on rescue and crew training in polar waters. Generally speaking, the amendments to the SOLAS Convention will enter into force on January 1, 2017. Any new ships built after that date, as well as older vessels that are to operate in polar waters, must meet Polar Code prescriptions in order to obtain renewal certificates. The Polar Ship Certificate[37] must also be complemented by the Polar Water Operational Manual (PWOM) to provide the owner, operator, master and crew with sufficient information regarding the ship's operational capabilities and limitations to support their decision-making process. The PWOM must be approved by a recognized organism or body. However, the Polar Code does not refer to the costs of those adaptations.

Consequently, the demands of the Polar Code regarding design, shipbuilding, equipment and machinery offer an excellent business opportunity for Spanish naval, engineering and auxiliary industries, as they are sectors of recognized prestige and solvency in the global market. In this context, taking into account that the "imminent" opening of new shipping routes in the Arctic will probably contribute to the development of the tourist sector, one of the types of vessels which will have to adjust to Polar Code conditions (resistance to low temperatures and to the presence of ice) will be cruise ships, some of which are already arriving at Spanish shipyards for repairs and to obtain a wide range of supplies.[38]

At the same time, faced with the possibility of an increase in maritime traffic in the Arctic, which would multiply risks of marine pollution, the 68th session of the Marine Environment Protection Committee (MEPC) of the IMO (which was held May 11–15, 2015 in London) adopted the environmental part of the Polar Code and relevant amendments under the MARPOL Convention to make the code mandatory. The agreed provisions prohibit the discharge of sewage into the sea (unless performed in line with MARPOL Annex IV and requirements in the Polar Code), noxious liquid substances or mixtures containing such substances, and oil or oil mixtures; require fuel tanks be separate from the outer shell; and restrict garbage discharge, except when permitted in accordance with MARPOL Annex V and requirements in the Polar Code. Those amendments are in line with the response instrument to the dumping of hydrocarbons into Arctic waters that is currently being developed by the Emergency Prevention, Preparedness and Response Working Group (EPPR) of the Arctic Council, more specifically, the Agreement on Cooperation on Marine Oil Pollution, Preparedness and Response in the Arctic, including Appendix IV Operational Guidelines.[39]

However, there are some aspects that are not yet resolved and need to be refined. Thus, although the Polar Code covers Arctic and Antarctic polar waters, there has been progress on the idea of distinguishing both spaces due to their remarkable differences.[40] Amongst others, while the Arctic is an ocean surrounded by continents, the Antarctic is a continent surrounded solely by the Antarctic Ocean. Moreover, while in the Arctic there are sovereignty conflicts,[41] in the Antarctic states' demands are "frozen" and there is no sovereignty, as the Madrid Protocol to the Antarctic Treaty of 1991 restated. Furthermore, indigenous people have lived in the Arctic from time immemorial, developing human activity that does not take place in the Antarctic, where, except for researchers and tourists, there is no stable population. Finally, as scientists have determined, the glacier discharge is between 3.5 and 4 times greater in the Arctic than in the Antarctic.[42] These differences may contribute to supporting the position of the Arctic coastal states, which reject the idea of any kind of analogy between the Arctic and the Antarctic that could create a system of global governance or an Arctic Treaty.

There are issues pending in the Polar Code and the lack of development of a traffic control system in polar waters should be highlighted. Though the flag state would usually be the one in charge of controlling traffic, the question is how it would do so. Vessel Traffic Services (VTS) could be useful for this purpose. VTS are services for controlling and monitoring maritime traffic and are designed to improve security and environmental protection. There can be two types of VTS:

- Surveyed VTS, where one or more land-based sensors or AIS (automatic identification system) send their signals to a central location where operators monitor and manage vessel traffic movement. However, an AIS alone may not be enough for the Arctic; it might be necessary to use LRIT (long-range identification and tracking), which can receive information from vessels within 1,000 miles. However, installing LRIT should be a requirement of the Polar Code;
- Non-surveyed (consisting on different reporting points where ships are required to report their identity, course and speed).

The scope of application of the Polar Code is another aspect that still needs to be resolved. Thus, the first phase will only apply to SOLAS vessels, which means to passenger and cargo ships, (although chapters referring to environmental protection will apply to all types of vessels according to the provisions of the various annexes of MARPOL); and a second phase will be applied to non-SOLAS vessels, including fishing vessels and recreational crafts (yachts). Depending on the presence and type of ice, the Polar Code divides vessels into three categories: category A (ships designed for operation in polar waters at least in medium first-year ice, which may contain old ice inclusions); category B (ships not included in category A, designed for operation in polar waters in at least thin first-year ice, which may contain old ice inclusions); and category C (ships designed to operate in open waters or in ice conditions less severe than those included in categories A and B). Regarding category C, however, it should be taken into account that 10 percent of ice can be a risk for non-strengthened vessels.[43]

Conclusion

Every cloud has a silver lining, and that seems to be the understanding of the adjacent and non-adjacent states to the Arctic Ocean, since the melting of the Land of Midnight Sun appears to bring economic benefits that were unimaginable only a short while ago. Beyond the claims for residual continental shelves and the scope of the Treaty of Spitsbergen, the main navigation problems that merchant vessels must deal with are those related to the territorial dispute between Canada and Denmark regarding Hans Island (Kennedy Channel of Nares Strait) and the various maritime delimitation conflicts. At this point, there are two issues pending: (1) deciding whether the Northwest and the Northeast Passages flow across international straits or across inland waters, in order to draft the corresponding legal framework; and (2) deciding the spatial scope of the application of Article 234 of UNCLOS and identifying if, according to the behavior of states, it is possible that the right conferred on coastal states by the article can also be exercised in the territorial sea. Regarding the difficulties that have to be solved within the framework of the IMO (for example, the IMO is not a suitable forum for pronouncing on Law of the Sea controversies as well as the applicable legal regime for navigation in the Northwest Passage and the NSR), the objective is now to determine if the Polar Code really is the instrument the Arctic region needs to respond to climate change and if the potential of the region will be looked after and exploited on a co-operational basis, which Mikhail Gorbachev mentioned in a speech in Murmansk way back in 1987. Beyond these considerations, there are obviously many options for multilateral reform and cooperation on Arctic shipping that have to be dealt with by the states or pursued outside the IMO. Significant among these complementary actions are: the approach of a multifaceted strategy regarding the jurisdiction of a port state, which should extend from coordination of the port state control to the development of a specific MOU for the Arctic Ocean; the development of marine contingency planning (preparedness and response for pollution incidents, search and rescue, places of refuge, etc.) and/or the exchange of state information on Arctic navigation in the Northwest and Northeast Passages (considering that the Transpolar Arctic Passage is currently frozen and therefore closed to navigation).

We can use the Arctic or we can lose it. The challenge is to use it responsibly.

Notes

1 The etymological origin of the word "Arctic" makes clear reference to constellations Ursa Major and Ursa Minor, which, as widely known, are very close to the Polar Star (a star which at the same time is part of the Ursa Minor constellation). The term "Antarctic," on the contrary, comes from the word *ant-arkos* and means "without bears."

2 These include Jan Mayen and Svalbard islands, Bear Island, Kong Karls Land, Kvitöya and Hopen, which belong to Norway and Franz Josef Land and Novaya Zemlya archipelagos belonging to Russia.

3 Asiatic polar lands include: Severnaya Zemlya archipelago, conformed by four major islands (Bolshevik Island, October Revolution Island, Komsomolets Island and Pioneer Island) and many islets and reefs; the islands of Maly Taimar and Schmidt, respectively located in the southeast and the northwest of the Severnaya Zemlya; East Falkland island and the islands of Wiese and Usakov, New Siberian islands, comprising nine islands (Kotellni, Fadievskii, New Siberia, MalliLiajovsk o Ljahov, BolsoiiLiajovsk, Belkov; Stolbovoi, Semenov and Vilkitzki) located between the Laptev Sea and the East Siberian Sea; De Long Islands; Henriette located in the northeast of New Siberian islands; Vrangel or Wrangel Islands and Herald or Gerald Island, separated by the De Long Strait from the Soviet Far East.

4 Polar American lands comprise Greenland and the American Arctic Archipelago, which belongs completely to Canada. It is formed by a huge extension of islands that constitute the enlargement, mainly under water, of the Canadian Shield. The main islands are Baffin Island, Ellesmere Island, Victoria Island, Banks Island, Prince of Wales Island, Somerset Island, the Parry Archipelago (consisting of the islands of Melville, Bathurst, Prince Patrick, Cornwallis and Devon) and Sverdrup archipelago (Axel Heiberg Island, Ellef Ringnes Island and Amund Ringnes Island, located in the north of McClure Strait, Melville Sound and Barrow Strait).

5 As long ago as the Age of Discovery, European explorers dreamed of a northern sea route to the Pacific. This "Northwest Passage" would not be successfully transited, though, until the legendary adventurer Roald Amundsen did it between 1903 and 1906—spending nearly two of those years immobilized by ice.

6 After the Russian Revolution of 1917, the Soviet Union was isolated from the Western powers and the use of the route became indispensable, a circumstance which was enormously helped by the arrival of ice-breakers.

7 Alberto Trillo Barca, "El conflicto en el Ártico: ¿hacia un tratado internacional?," *Documento de Trabajo, Serie Unión Europea (UE) y Relaciones Internacionales* 54/2011 (Madrid: CEU Ediciones, 2012), 41. Accessed July 7, 2015, www.idee. ceu.es/Portals/0/Publicaciones/SerieUE_54_2012_El_conflicto_en_el_artico. pdf; Mariene Laruelle, *Russia's Arctic Strategies and the Future of the Far North.* New York: Routledge, 2014.

8 Ana Gemma López Martín, *La navegación por los estrechos internacionales: Geoestrategia y derecho* (Madrid: Dykinson, 2008), 134–37.

9 Donat Pharand and Leonard H. Legault, *The Northwest Passage: Arctic Straits* (Dordrecht, Boston, Lancaster: Martinus Nijhoff Publishers, 1984), 98, cited in López Martín, *La navegación por los estrechos internacionales*, 136–37.

10 In accordance with this article "The foregoing provisions do not apply to so-called 'historic' bays or in any case where the system of straight baselines provided for in article 7 is applied."

11 Although it has been discussed, if the Long Island Sound comprises historic waters, this maritime way should be considered a bay and not a strait. North American jurisprudence, in the cases of *Mahler* v. *Transportation Co.* in 1986 and *US* v. *Maine* in 1983, pronounced it a bay, as pointed out by López Martín, *La navegación por los estrechos internacionales*, 137.

12 See www.un.org/Depts/los/LEGISLATIONANDTREATIES/regionlist.htm.

13 Tullio Scovazzi, "La ligne de base de la mer territoriale dans l'arctique canadien," *Annuaire Français de Droit International (AFDI)* XXXIII (1987): 663;

Jacques-Yvan Morin "Le progrès technique, la pollution et l'évolution récente du Droit de la Mer au Canada, particulièrement à l'égard de l'Arctique," *Canadian Yearbook of International Law (CYBIL)* VIII (1970): 158.

14 See: www.un.org/Depts/los/LEGISLATIONANDTREATIES/regionlist.htm.

15 Julio D. González Campos, Luis I. Sánchez Rodríguez and Paz Andrés Sáenz de Santa María, *Curso de Derecho Internacional Público* 3rd edn (Madrid: Civitas, 2003), 638.

16 NSPD-66, National Security Presidential Directive and Homeland Security Presidential Directive. The White House, January 9, 2009, accessed May 6, 2016, www.fas-org/irp/offdocs/nspd/nspd-66.html. According to Part B. 5 in Section III of the Directive:

> Freedom of the seas is a top national priority. The Northwest Passage is a strait used for international navigation, and the Northern Sea Routes include straits used for international navigation; the regime of transit passage applies to passage through those straits. Preserving the rights and duties relating to navigation and overflight in the Arctic region supports our ability to exercise these rights throughout the world, including through strategic straits.

17 Steven Groves "LOST in the Arctic: The US Need Not Ratify the Law of the Sea Treaty to Get a Seat at the Table," *Heritage Foundation,* June 16, 2008, accessed July 7, 2015, www.heritage.org/research/reports/2008/06/lost-in-the-arctic-the-us-need-not-ratify-the-law-of-the-sea-treaty-to-get-a-seat-at-the-table.

18 Trillo Barca, "El conflicto en el Ártico," 50; Claudia Cinelli, "La cuestión ártica y la Unión Europea," *Revista Española de Relaciones Internacionales* 1 (2009): 138–63, accessed July 7, 2015, http://reri.difusionjuridica.es/index.php/RERI/article/view/9/9.

19 *Arctic Shipping Pollution Prevention Act,* C.R.C., C 353.

20 *Arctic Waters Pollution Prevention Regulation,* C.R.C., C 354.

21 European Commission. *Legal Aspects of Arctic Shipping.* Framework Service Contract. No. FISH/2006/09-LOT 2. Summary Report submitted to DG Maritime Affairs & Fisheries, (February 2010).

22 Cintia Bosch Lozano, "Régimen jurídico de la navegación en aguas polares. Especial referencia al Código Polar" (Proyecto Fin de Carrera para la obtención del Título de Licenciado en Náutica y Transporte Marítimo, Universitat Politécnica de Catalunya, 2012): 28–29; Claudia Cinelli, *El Ártico ante el Derecho del Mar contemporáneo* (Valencia: Tirant lo Blanch, 2012), 157–58, accessed July 7, 2015. www.peacepalacelibrary.nl/ebooks/files/343075628.pdf.

23 Blanca Palacián De Inza and Ignacio García Sánchez, "Geopolítica del deshielo en el Ártico," *Estudios de Política Exterior* 154, July–August 2013, accessed July 7, 2015, www.politicaexterior.com/articulos/politica-exterior/geopolitica-del-deshielo-en-el-artico.

24 Atle Staalesen, "China's New Foothold on Northern Sea Route," *BarentsObserver,* November 26, 2010, accessed July 7, 2015, http://barentsobserver.com/en/sections/business/chinas-new-foothold-northern-sea-route.

25 BEAC is the forum for intergovernmental and interregional cooperation in the Barents Region, established in 1983 in order to "provide impetus to existing cooperation and consider new initiatives and proposals."

26 The European Council defines the European Union's general political direction and priorities. It consists of the heads of state or government of the European Union's Member States, together with its President and the European Commission President.

27 Council of the European Union, *Council Conclusions on Developing a European Union Policy Towards the Arctic Region. Foreign Affairs Council Meeting,* Brussels, May 12, 2014.

28 South Korea bought in 2007 the Finnish Company AkerFinnyard, which has developed promising technology for research in areas with ice.

29 Paul Arthur Berkman "Arctic Ocean State-Changes: Self Interests or Common Interests," *Yearbook of International Law* (2009): 527–41.

30 Klaus Dodds, "A Polar Mediterranean? Accessibility, Resources and Sovereignty in the Arctic Ocean," *Global Policy* 1 (2010): 303–11.

31 Fernando Goitia, "La batalla por el Ártico. ¿Guerra Fría? No, helada." *XL Semanal*, April 27, 2014, accessed May 6, 2016, www.finanzas.com/xl-semanal/magazine/20140427/batalla-artico-guerra-fria-7144.html.

32 PSC is the inspection of foreign ships in other national ports by PSC officers (inspectors) for the purpose of verifying the competency of the Master and officers on board and the condition of the ship and its equipment to comply with the requirements of international conventions (SOLAS, MARPOL, STCW, etc.) and that the vessel is manned and operated in compliance with applicable international law.

33 In 1978, a number of European countries agreed in The Hague on a Memorandum to audit the labor conditions on board following ILO rules and recommendations. After the *Amoco Cádiz* disaster, it was decided by IMO to audit on safety and pollution prevention. Following the foundation built by the Paris MOU (1982), several other regional MOUs have been signed, including the Tokyo MOU (Pacific Ocean), Acuerdo Latino or Acuerdo de Viña del Mar (South and Central America), the Caribbean MOU, the Mediterranean MOU, the Indian MOU, the Abuja MOU (West and Central Atlantic Africa), the Black Sea MOU and the Riyadh MOU (Persian Gulf). The United States is not a member of any Port State Control MOU. However, the United States Coast Guard verifies that all foreign vessels operating in United States waters are in substantial compliance with international conventions, as well as all applicable US laws, regulations and treaties.

34 Pablo Pareja Alcaraz, "El Ártico como espacio de cooperación: evolución, contenido y límites," in *Mares y Océanos en un mundo en cambio: Tendencias jurídicas, actores y factores*, coordinated by José Manuel Sobrino Heredia (Valencia: Tirant lo Blanch, 2007): 883–903; Oran R. Young, "Governing the Arctic: From Cold Water Theatre to Mosaic of Cooperation," *Global Governance* 11, no. 1, (2005): 9–15.

35 Resolution of the Maritime Safety Committee of the IMO 386 (94), as provided in Article VIII (b) (iv) of SOLAS Convention.

36 Arctic Council, Arctic Marine Shipping Assessment 2009 Report. Accessed May 6, 2016, www.arctic.noaa.gov/detect/documents/AMSA_2009_Report_2nd_print.pdf.

37 The Code would require ships intending to operate in the defined waters of the Antarctic and Arctic to apply for a Polar Ship Certificate, which would classify the vessel into one of three categories (A, B or C). The issuance of a certificate would require an assessment, taking into account the range of operating conditions and hazards the ship may encounter in polar waters. The assessment would include information on identified operational limitations, and plans or procedures or additional safety equipment necessary to mitigate incidents with potential safety or environmental consequences.

38 Markus Gómez Dabic, "Código Polar: Retos para el sector naval," *Garrigues*, December 1, 2014, accessed July 7, 2015, www.garrigues.com/es/Publicaciones/Articulos/Paginas/Codigo-Polar-retos-para-el-sector-naval.aspx.

39 The website for the Emergency Prevention, Preparedness and Response Working Group (EPPR) is at: www.arctic-council.org/eppr.

40 Efrén Gustavo Marqués Rueda, "La condición jurídica del Ártico y la Antártida: un asunto pendiente en la agenda jurídico-política de las Relaciones Internacionales," *Revista de Relaciones Internacionales de la UNAM* 107 (2010): 39–65.

41 For example, the Beaufort Sea dispute between the United States and Canada concerning the delineation of the international maritime boundary between the Yukon and Alaska or the dispute between Canada and Denmark about Hans Island. Jessica M. Shadian, *The Politics of Arctic Sovereignty.* Routledge Advances in International Relations and Global Politics, 2014.
42 Staalesen, "China's New Foothold on Northern Sea Route," 60–61.
43 Bosch Lozano "Régimen jurídico de la navegación en aguas polares," 83–105.

References

Berkman, Paul Arthur. "Arctic Ocean State-Changes: Self Interests or Common Interests." *Yearbook of International Law* (2009): 527–41.

Bosch Lozano, Cintia. "Régimen jurídico de la navegación en aguas polares. Especial referencia al Código Polar." *Proyecto Fin de Carrera para la obtención del Título de Licenciado en Náutica y Transporte Marítimo.* Universitat Politécnica de Catalunya, 2012.

Cinelli, Claudia. "La cuestión ártica y la Unión Europea." *Revista Española de Relaciones Internacionales* 1 (2009): 138–63. Accessed July 7, 2015, http://reri.difusion-juridica.es/index.php/RERI/article/view/9/9.

Cinelli, Claudia. *El Ártico ante el Derecho del Mar contemporáneo.* Valencia: Tirant lo Blanch, 2012. Accessed July 7, 2015, www.peacepalacelibrary.nl/ebooks/files/343075628.pdf.

Dodds, Klaus. "A Polar Mediterranean? Accessibility, Resources and Sovereignty in the Arctic Ocean." *Global Policy* 1 (2010): 303–11.

Goitia, Fernando. "La batalla por el Ártico. ¿Guerra Fría? No, helada." *XL Semanal,* April 27, 2014. Accessed May 6, 2016, www.finanzas.com/xl-semanal/magazine/20140427/batalla-artico-guerra-fria-7144.html.

Gómez Dabic, Markus. "Código Polar: retos para el sector naval." *Garrigues,* December 1, 2014. Accessed July 7, 2015, www.garrigues.com/es/Publicaciones/Articulos/Paginas/Codigo-Polar-retos-para-el-sector-naval.aspx.

González Campos, Julio D., Luis I. Sánchez Rodríguez and Paz Andrés Sáenz de Santa María. *Curso de Derecho Internacional Público* 3rd edn. Madrid: Civitas, 2003.

Groves, Steven. "LOST in the Arctic. The US Need Not Ratify the Law of the Sea Treaty to Get a Seat at the Table." *Heritage Foundation,* June 16, 2008. Accessed July 7, 2015, www.heritage.org/research/reports/2008/06/lost-in-the-arctic-the-us-need-not-ratify-the-law-of-the-sea-treaty-to-get-a-seat-at-the-table.

Iglesias Berlanga, Marta. "La 'Guerra del Ártico' y los intereses españoles. Geoestrategia y Derecho." In *Economía Pesqueira: Achegas desde un curso universitario,* coordinated by Mª Carme García Negro 605–26. Santiago de Compostela: Sotelo Blanco, 2010.

Laruelle, Mariene, *Russia's Arctic Strategies and the Future of the Far North.* New York: Routledge, 2014.

López Martín, Ana Gemma. *La navegación por los estrechos internacionales: Geoestrategia y derecho.* Madrid: Dykinson, 2008.

Marqués Rueda, Efrén Gustavo. "La condición jurídica del Ártico y la Antártida: un asunto pendiente en la agenda jurídico-política de las Relaciones Internacionales." *Revista de Relaciones Internacionales de la UNAM* 107 (2010): 39–65.

Morin, Jacques-Yvan. "Le progres techique, la pollution et l'évolution récente du Droit de la mer au Canada, particulièrement à l'égard de l'Arctique." *Canadian Yearbook of International Law* VIII (1970): 158–249.

National Security Presidential Directive and Homeland Security Presidential Directive. The White House, January 9, 2009, accessed May 6, 2016, www.fas-org/irp/offdocs/nspd/nspd-66.html.

Østreng, Willy, Karl Magnus Eger, Brit Fløistad, Arnfinn Jørgensen-Dahl, Lars Lothe, Morten Mejlaenda-Larsen and Tor Wergeland. *Shipping in Arctic Waters: A Comparison of the Northeast, Northwest and Trans Polar Passages*. Berlin and Heidelberg: Springer Praxis Books, 2013.

Palacián De Inza, Blanca and Ignacio García Sánchez. "Geopolítica del deshielo en el Ártico." *Estudios de Política Exterior* 154, July–August 2013. Accessed July 7, 2015, www.politicaexterior.com/articulos/politica-exterior/geopolitica-del-deshielo-en-el-artico.

Pareja Alcaraz, Pablo. "El Ártico como espacio de cooperación: evolución, contenido y límites." In *Mares y Océanos en un mundo en cambio. Tendencias jurídicas, actores y factores*, coordinated by José Manuel Sobrino Heredia, 883–903. Valencia: Tirant lo Blanch, 2007.

Pharand, Donat and Leonard H. Legault. *The Northwest Passage: Arctic Straits*. Dordrecht, Boston, Lancaster: Martinus Nijhoff Publishers, 1984.

Scovazzi, Tullio. "La ligne de base de la mer territoriale dans l'arctique canadien." *Annuaire Français de Droit International* XXXIII (1987): 663–80.

Shadian, Jessica M. *The Politics of Arctic Sovereignty: Oil, Ice, and Inuit Governance*. Abingdon: Routledge, 2014.

Speth, James Gustave. "Foreword." *Diplomacy on Ice: Energy and the Environment in the Arctic and Antarctic*, edited by Rebecca H. Pincus and Saleem H. Ali. New Haven, CT: Yale University Press, 2015.

Staalesen, Atle. "China's New Foothold on Northern Sea Route." *BarentsObserver*, November 26, 2010. Accessed July 7, 2015, http://barentsobserver.com/en/sections/business/chinas-new-foothold-northern-sea-route.

Trillo Barca, Alberto. "El conflicto en el Ártico: ¿hacia un tratado internacional?." *Documento de Trabajo, Serie Unión Europea (UE) y Relaciones Internacionales* 54/2011. Madrid: CEU Ediciones, 2012. Accessed July 7, 2015, www.idee.ceu.es/Portals/0/Publicaciones/SerieUE_54_2012_El_conflicto_en_el_artico.pdf.

Witschel Georg, Ingo Vinkelmann, Kathrin Tiroch and Rüdiger Wolfrum. *New Chances and New Responsibilities in the Arctic Region*. Berlin: Berliner Wissenschafts, 2010.

Young, Oran R. "Governing the Arctic: From Cold Water Theater to Mosaic of Cooperation." *Global Governance*, Vol. 11, no. 1 (2005): 9–15.

Part III
The human dimension

11 Arctic indigenous peoples at European courts*

Issues concerning their effective judicial protection at the CJEU and the ECtHR

Sara Iglesias Sánchez

Introduction

This chapter aims to offer an overview of the case law of the Court of Justice of the European Union (CJEU) and of the European Court of Human Rights (ECtHR) with regard to the rights and interests of Arctic indigenous peoples. Of course, the procedures and issues they deal with differ greatly. Moreover, the number of cases that have been brought before these two international/supranational courts on these issues has been relatively low. It must also be taken into account that national systems play the most important role in the protection of the rights and interests of Arctic peoples and the individuals belonging to those groups. The study of this case law does not, therefore, offer a basis for general conclusions on the status of legal protection for Arctic indigenous peoples in Europe.

Nevertheless, a parallel look at the case law from these two courts can offer some elements for discussion on the way in which the unique vulnerability of indigenous peoples and their particular legal status in international law permeates the examination of specific situations by the European judiciary. In this regard, despite the differences between procedures, objectives and jurisdiction, the small number of decisions handed down by the ECtHR and the CJEU that affect the rights and interests of Arctic indigenous peoples raise some common points of interest and offer a unique view of the European approach to indigenous rights. Indeed, in the particular European framework, the development of indigenous rights and its interconnection with the protection of fundamental rights is essentially connected with the Arctic.[1]

In this regard, this chapter does not intend to uncover all the complexities of the legal status of indigenous peoples in Europe.[2] The aim here is more modest: to offer an account of the case law of the Court of Justice of the European Union and the European Court of Human Rights, identifying two sets of connected issues. First, the situation of Arctic indigenous peoples with regard to their access to justice in the two jurisdictional systems mentioned above and, particularly, regarding the protection of collective interests. Second, the difficulty in articulating the material claims taking into account the specificity of indigenous rights in the framework of these two systems, in which an individualistic conception of rights is strongly embedded. In this last regard, special attention will be devoted to the right to property and the correlative specific indigenous interest in preserving the use and immemorial possession of their lands and the right to exploit natural resources, particularly, in the case law of the ECtHR. Before examining, in two different sections, the case law of the ECtHR and the CJEU, a brief account of the international legal venues available for the defense of indigenous rights and interests is offered below.

A variety of legal venues

Alongside the internal institutions and mechanisms set up by the States in which Arctic indigenous peoples are located, there are different international legal fora available—general and specific—for defending indigenous rights and interests.

In the universal international arena, the Human Rights Committee of the United Nations, despite not being a specialized organ in indigenous rights, has become central in setting some very important precedents on indigenous rights within the general human rights framework. Particularly relevant is its interpretation of Article 27 of the International Covenant on Civil and Political Rights (ICCPR), which, according to the Committee, requires States to respect the sense of identity of indigenous peoples in connection with their traditional lands.[3] In the same vein, the Committee on the Elimination of Racial Discrimination can also be considered an important venue for indigenous peoples.[4]

Additionally, international law has progressed in recognizing the particular need to protect indigenous peoples through specific treaties[5] and the creation of mechanisms aimed at providing expertise. Within the UN system, three important specific monitoring mechanisms that work at different levels have been set up:[6] the UN Permanent Forum on Indigenous Issues,[7] the Expert Mechanism on the Rights of Indigenous Peoples[8] and the Special Rapporteur on the Situation of Human Rights and Fundamental Freedoms of Indigenous Peoples,[9] which has been actively involved in several situations related to Arctic indigenous peoples.[10]

Notwithstanding the enormous value of the above-mentioned universal mechanisms for the protection of indigenous peoples' rights, none of them offers the solid protection of a judicial body. Even the pronouncements of quasi-judicial mechanisms that contemplate the possibilities of individual claims have a lesser degree of normative force and, therefore, of effective protection in terms of enforceability.

Besides these universal mechanisms, the controversy on the Arctic seals has brought to the fore the relevance of the mechanism for settling commercial disputes for the protection of indigenous interests. Indeed, and as explained elsewhere in this volume,[11] the World Trade Organization's (WTO) mechanism for dispute settlement has proven to be a challenge for safeguarding some indigenous interests that are directly linked to international trade. This mechanism does not focus on the protection of fundamental or individual rights, and peoples or individuals do not have legal standing to bring their cases or complaints directly before this inter-state system. Therefore, the interests of indigenous peoples are only considered indirectly and in a limited way; only inasmuch as the States involved in the controversy are prepared to claim these rights and invoke them before the WTO bodies.

In this connection, the Court of Justice of the European Union and the European Court of Human Rights offer access to fully fledged judicial bodies in which the protection of individual rights plays a paramount role, albeit with substantial differences.

In the framework of the European Union, there are several procedures through which the interests of indigenous peoples can be brought before the CJEU. The EU acts and national measures within the scope of EU law have to respect fundamental rights, particularly, as recognized in the Charter of Fundamental Rights of the European Union. Despite the fact that this instrument does not contain specific rights for indigenous peoples, several rights contained in the Charter can be relevant for the protection of Arctic peoples. National courts dealing with cases that concern the rights of Arctic peoples in which the interpretation of EU law is at issue always have the possibility of asking for a preliminary ruling. This avenue, however, is not open to individuals or private parties as an individual right, but is a prerogative of the referring court, which remains free not to refer a case to the CJEU even if the parties so desire.[12] Private parties can also resort to the annulment procedure to challenge the legality of an EU act: this is the most direct way in which Arctic peoples have sought access to the CJEU, although they have encountered some problems due to the limitations on the legal standing of private parties in annulment procedures.[13]

Procedural hurdles also exist when initiating proceedings in the framework of the European Court of Human Rights. Here the problems encountered are linked to the definition of victim, which is one of the prerequisites to gain access to the ECtHR. Besides this procedural perspective, another point of interest in the framework of the case law of the ECtHR is the material approach to certain specific rights which are of particular interest for Arctic peoples. Indeed, the Convention does not contain specific rights regarding minorities or indigenous peoples, and case law has shown how difficult it is to include the collective perspective in the traditional understanding of Convention rights.

These perspectives will be explored, subsequently, in the following sections.

Arctic peoples in the European Court of Human Rights

As Koivurova rightly put it, despite the fact that the ECtHR has jurisdiction over various Arctic indigenous peoples from Denmark, Norway, Finland, Sweden and Russia, its case law has been modest in number and relevance.[14] Two important sets of hurdles might explain this fact: the procedural difficulties associated with bringing a case before the ECtHR for members of Arctic indigenous peoples, and the difficulties of subsuming the particular claims of indigenous peoples within the scope of Convention rights.

Admissibility of claims

The criteria for the admissibility of claims before the ECtHR are laid down in Article 35 of the European Convention on Human Rights (ECHR). First, the Court will only deal with a case after all domestic remedies have been exhausted and within a period of six months after the final decision in the domestic system has been taken. Second, the applications should not be anonymous, nor should they have substantially the same matter as another claim already submitted to another procedure of international investigation or settlement. Third, the application should not be incompatible with the provisions of the Convention or its Protocols, manifestly ill-founded or entail an abuse of the right of individual application, and the applicant should have suffered a significant disadvantage.[15] Moreover, according to Article 34 of the Convention, individual applications can only be submitted by persons, non-governmental organizations or groups of individuals who claim to be the victim of a violation by one of the State parties.

The concept of who is to be considered a victim, which is autonomously defined by the ECtHR,[16] has an important impact on the access of Arctic indigenous peoples to the ECtHR. Indeed, this is the most important element related to the *ius standi* in the Convention system and, as it is common in human rights protection systems, it is based on the underlying rationale of protection of individual rights. Therefore, the protection of collective rights and of some rights which present specific features with regard to indigenous peoples can encounter difficulties at the very preliminary stages, when it comes to determining the victim status of the collectivities or the associations that intend to bring actions to protect their common goods.[17]

In the case *Könkämä and other 38 Saami villages against Sweden*,[18] the respondent government claimed that the applicant Saami villages could not be regarded as victims of the alleged violations, relating to their exclusive fishing, hunting and herding rights under Article 1 of Protocol 1 to the Convention, because the rights at issue were not afforded to the villages but to their members. The European Commission of Human

Rights did not accept the exception put forward by Sweden. Indeed, the Commission considered that, since the villages did have competences which were connected to the herding rights and therefore were able to represent the inhabitants of the villages with regard to this issue, the Saami villages were regarded as a non-governmental organization. However, the application was considered inadmissible because the applicants had not exhausted all the domestic remedies available to them. Even if some of the villages had exhausted remedies before the Supreme Court, their applications before the Commission had not been presented within the six months period required as a condition of admissibility.

On the contrary, in *Johtti Sapmelccat against Finland*,[19] the legal standing of the applicant association was denied the qualification of victim. Indeed, the ECtHR compared it with the case of *Könkämä and other 38 Saami villages v. Sweden* and concluded that the association was not responsible for fishing rights in the area concerned, that it did not represent its members in such matters and that the rights concerned could only be exercised by a Saami as a private individual.

These two cases highlight the importance of the competences and responsibilities of entities, organizations or bodies when it comes to determining the status of victim under the Convention. Indeed, their role is central in this regard, since the rights affected are often rights to be enjoyed collectively and that can only with difficulty be brought before the courts by single individuals.[20] However, the fact that an organization is devoted to the protection of the interests and culture of Arctic indigenous peoples is not sufficient, since it is necessary to prove that the organization at issue is endowed with competences and powers directly related to exercising the rights concerned. This makes their status as a victim dependent on the competences that are granted to them under national systems and it represents an important hurdle for indigenous peoples in their search for the correct way to gain access to the ECtHR.

The interpretation of Convention rights

One of the challenges that has most often been put forward by the literature with regard to the protection of the human rights of indigenous peoples is precisely the unsuitability of the systems that are based mainly on the protection of individual rights to protect claims that are associated to common goods and interests which are to be enjoyed by a collectivity of individuals.[21]

However, the fact that the European Convention on Human Rights is considered to be a living instrument that can be interpreted in a flexible and progressive way, makes it a very valuable tool to grant protection to indigenous rights through different Convention rights, such as the right to respect for private and family life; the freedoms of thought, conscience and religion, of expression and of assembly and association; the right to education, or the prohibition of discrimination. Beyond the general consideration of human rights as a suitable vehicle to protect indigenous peoples in their capacity as minorities, indigenous rights present very relevant specificities, which are to a considerable extent related to their profound and strong connection to their lands.[22] This explains the particular significance of the right to property in the case law of the ECtHR with regard to Arctic indigenous peoples.

In this regard, the challenges posed by the collective dimension of indigenous rights have been catalyzed in several cases in relation to the application of Article 1 of Protocol 1 to the Convention. According to this article,

> every natural or legal person is entitled to the peaceful enjoyment of his possessions. No one shall be deprived of his possessions except in the public interest and subject to the conditions provided for by law and by the general principles of international law.

The main challenge in this regard is to adjust the traditional interpretation of the Convention right to property to the interests and rights of indigenous peoples relating to their lands, as well as to their rights related to the exploitation of natural resources, such as fishing and herding rights. This very particular problem has been the object of specialized analysis, bringing to the fore the development of the concept of property in the framework of the Convention to show how this instrument could potentially evolve and provide a more suitable response to the specific situation of indigenous peoples and their rights arising from immemorial use.[23] Indeed, it is difficult to bring common and ancestral possession within the traditional conceptions of private property as recognized by States. The recognition of ancestral indigenous property has nonetheless already been recognized in the area of international human rights.

Primarily, the ILO Convention (no 169) on Indigenous and Tribal Peoples of 1989 contains the most advanced position in this regard. In its the second part, related to land rights, there is a specific reference to:

> the special importance for the cultures and spiritual values of the peoples concerned of their relationship with the lands or territories, or both as applicable, which they occupy or otherwise use, and in particular the collective aspects of this relationship.[24]

In particular, Article 14, paragraph 1 establishes that:

> the rights of ownership and possession of the peoples concerned over the lands which they traditionally occupy shall be recognized. In addition, measures shall be taken in appropriate cases to safeguard the right of the peoples concerned to use lands not exclusively occupied

by them, but to which they have traditionally had access for their subsistence and traditional activities. Particular attention shall be paid to the situation of nomadic peoples and shifting cultivators in this respect.

However, this Convention has not been widely ratified within Europe: only Norway, Denmark, the Netherlands and Spain have ratified it, and the two last States have declared that they do not have indigenous peoples in their territories.

The United Nations Declaration on the Rights of Indigenous Peoples (UNDRIP), adopted in 2007 by the General Assembly, also contains an approach which explicitly takes into account the specific relationship of indigenous peoples with their lands. Whereas its Article 10 recognizes the right not to be forcibly removed from their lands or territories, Articles 25 and 26 establish the specific rights to their lands, territories and resources.[25]

However, despite these developments at the international level, the low ratification of the 169 ILO Convention and the declaratory nature of the UNDRIP entail that the specific approach to indigenous rights to lands and resources is not universally adopted by all regional systems and by all States.[26]

Against this background, the approach of the Strasbourg system to the rights to land and resources of Arctic indigenous peoples is also profoundly influenced by the dogmatic challenges connected with the debate on the self-determination of indigenous peoples and the correlative claim to State sovereignty over their lands.[27] The difficulty to subsume these specific rights in the traditional categories of public sovereignty and private property rights is moreover increased by the challenges posed by the collective nature of the rights at issue and by other practical hurdles, such as the difficulty to prove ancestral origin in the framework of the claims made by indigenous peoples.

Despite all these difficulties, the ECtHR has succeeded to a certain extent in progressively finding room for the application of Article 1 of Protocol 1 to the Convention to the specific situation of Arctic indigenous peoples. Most of the cases, which will be briefly addressed in order to map the evolution of the case law, have their origin in applications introduced by members of or associations representing the Saami people.

The first case in which the Strasbourg system addressed the right to land of Arctic indigenous peoples is *G. and E. against Norway*,[28] also known as the "Alta case." This case deals with the decision by the Norwegian government to start a construction project in the Alta valley to build a hydroelectric power plant, which as a consequence would leave some parts of the valley under water. Among other claims, the Saami applicants submitted that, as members of a minority group, they were not able to defend their rights under Article 1 of Protocol 1 to the Convention. The

European Commission of Human Rights took a strict stance towards the specific positions of the applicants, emphasizing their nationality to the detriment of the specific meaning of being a member of an indigenous community. In the words of the Commission,

> the applicants are Norwegian citizens, living in Norway, and under Norwegian jurisdiction. They have, as other Norwegians, the right to vote and to stand for election to the Norwegian Parliament. They are thus democratically represented in Parliament, although the Lapps have no secured representation for themselves.

The Commission further adopted a limited interpretation of the right to property, stating that the applicants did not appear to have any property rights to the area at issue "in the traditional sense of that concept." Granted, the Commission admitted that there could be an interference with private life, bearing in mind the fact that applicants were members of a minority. However, in the case at issue no violation was found, taking into account that the project of the Norwegian authorities affected only a comparatively small area.

The position of the European Commission in the Alta case, which substantially differs from the approach of the Human Rights Committee in its case law on Article 27 of the ICCPR,[29] evolved over time. As Koivurova has highlighted,[30] a certain evolution can be already seen in *Halvar From against Sweden*,[31] where the Commission found that a measure consisting in the registration of the property of an individual within an elk-hunting area for a Saami village could be permissible in the general interest if it complied with the proportionality principle. The Commission found it to be in the general interest "that the special culture and way of life of the Sami be respected" and it stated that it was clear "that reindeer herding and hunting are important parts of that culture and way of life." Further, even if the case *Könkämä and other 38 Saami villages against Sweden* was considered inadmissible as we have already mentioned in the previous section, the Commission made a very relevant statement in explicitly recognizing that the exclusive hunting and fishing rights claimed by the applicant Saami villages could be regarded as possessions within the meaning of Article 1 of Protocol 1 to the Convention.[32]

Despite this development, a more recent case, *Handölsdale Sami Village against Sweden*[33] makes clear the limitations of the jurisprudential approach of the Strasbourg system to the right to property, already latent in *Könkämä*. In its decision on the admissibility of the application introduced by the Saami village, the ECtHR found that the property interest claimed could not be characterized as an "existing possession" within the meaning of the Court's case law[34] and that the claim to a right to winter grazing on the property at issue was not sufficiently established to qualify as an "asset" that would attract the protection of Article 1 of Protocol 1 to the

Convention.[35] The central role played by the need for national law to recognize the claims remains therefore an element of paramount importance in triggering the protection of the Convention right to property. As Otis and Laurent have rightly put it, the difficulty and the main challenge that is still unresolved by the case law is "whether the Convention imposes an obligation on the state to recognize ancestral title to traditional indigenous lands when, as is the case in Europe, domestic law has still not confirmed pre-colonial title."[36]

The case of *Handölsdale Sami Village against Sweden* also constitutes a paradigmatic example of the challenges that indigenous claims encounter in their attempt to meet the burden and standard of proof when arguing their traditional rights.[37] In this regard, the partly dissenting opinion of Judge Ziemele signals one of the possible paths that may be taken in the future evolution of case law, taking stock of the importance of developments in the legal situation of indigenous peoples in international law and emphasizing the "specific context of the situation and rights of indigenous peoples in so far as it could be relevant to the issue of effective access to court."[38]

Indigenous rights before the Court of Justice of the European Union

The European Union is bound to respect the fundamental rights set out in the Charter of Fundamental Rights of the EU (hereinafter, "the Charter").[39] Additionally, fundamental rights, as guaranteed by the European Convention of Human Rights and by constitutional traditions common to the Member States constitute also general principles of EU law.[40] The Court of Justice of the European Union, despite not being a specialized human rights court, ensures compliance with fundamental rights within the scope of EU law in the framework of the different procedures.[41]

There are different procedures through which the Court of Justice can examine the compatibility with fundamental rights of a national or an EU act affecting Arctic indigenous peoples. For example, in fulfilling their obligations arising from EU law it is not excluded that Member States could adversely affect the rights of individuals belonging to indigenous communities or the interests of the communities themselves. In this event, national courts could refer a preliminary ruling to the European Court of Justice. If a national judge has doubts on the interpretation of an EU act, including its compatibility with fundamental rights, it can also refer a question for a preliminary ruling. However, individuals and private parties do not have a right to have a question referred to the CJEU: this is a prerogative of national judges.

In contrast, the annulment procedure offers private parties the possibility to challenge the legality of EU acts. In this framework, fundamental rights function often as parameters of legality and the Court can be asked to declare the annulment of an EU act for being contrary to these rights.

This procedure has been of particular relevance with regard to the defense of the interests and rights of Arctic indigenous peoples. Inuit individuals and associations representing their interests have brought several actions seeking the annulment of certain EU acts that affect the trade in seal products, claiming that it is a violation of their human rights, among other things. This section takes these cases as a reference to analyze some of the particularities concerning the standing of private persons, which have also affected Inuit individuals and associations representing them, as well as the material approach adopted by the CJEU with regard to the fundamental rights of indigenous peoples.

Standing to institute annulment proceedings

Natural or legal persons are entitled to institute proceedings against EU acts, according to Article 263 TFEU, if the act is addressed to them or concerns them directly and individually, and if the act is a "regulatory act" of direct concern to them and does not entail implementing measures. The third limb contained in the wording of this provision is the result of a modification introduced by the Treaty of Lisbon with the aim of strengthening the legal standing of private parties to challenge EU acts.[42] It is noteworthy that one of the first cases in which the CJEU was invited to interpret the concept of "regulatory acts" under the new provision was a case introduced by several Inuit individuals and associations.

In September 2009, the European Parliament and the Council passed a Regulation on trade in seal products,[43] which contained a general ban on the placing of seal products on the European internal market.[44] Among others, Inuit Tapiriit Kanatami (representing the interests of Canadian Inuit), together with some other Inuit individuals and associations, introduced in January 2010 an application seeking the annulment of this regulation before the General Court. The General Court interpreted that the concept of "regulatory act" is to be understood as covering the acts "of general application apart from legislative acts." Since the challenged regulation was adopted by the co-decision procedure, equivalent to the current ordinary legislative procedure, the General Court established that it constituted a legislative act, therefore, not covered by the third limb of the fourth paragraph of Article 263 TFEU. For this reason, it was necessary to examine whether the applicants were directly and individually concerned. In this regard, the General Court found that even if some applicants were directly affected by the regulation, since they were active in the processing and/or marketing of seal products, they were not individually affected. The fact that the applicants were covered not only by the general prohibition, but also by the exception relating to products of Inuit origin, was not enough to distinguish them individually "in the same way as the addressee of a decision." Therefore, the action for annulment was declared inadmissible.[45] The order of the General Court was confirmed on appeal by the Grand Chamber of the Court of Justice.[46]

In this particular case, this did not deprive the Inuit from the opportunity to challenge the Regulation at issue. Indeed, in August 2010, the Commission adopted an implementing regulation,[47] which was challenged by Inuit Tapiriit Kanatami and other individuals, associations and companies in November of the same year. In order to support their action, the fundamental point of the applicants was to plea the illegality of the basic regulation. Even if the admissibility of the claims was contested by the Council with regard to some applicants, the General Court decided, for the sake of economy of procedure, to dismiss the action on the merits, without a ruling on the issues concerning admissibility.[48] The appeal brought by the applicants against this judgment was equally dismissed on the merits by the Court of Justice,[49] and the admissibility issues regarding legal standing were not analyzed either. Advocate General Kokott made clear in her opinion that since proceedings were directed against the implementing regulation, there were not any fundamental problems of admissibility with regard to the standing to institute proceedings: the Commission Implementing Regulation could be considered of direct concern—at least with regard to those applicants who themselves market seal products and sell them in the internal market—and it could be considered that the implementing regulation required no further implementing measures. Therefore, the conditions of the third limb of the fourth paragraph of Article 263 TFEU could be considered as fulfilled.[50]

However, it is doubtful whether that would be the case concerning an independent application presented by individuals or associations that do not themselves market seal products.

These cases show how Inuit individuals and associations are affected by the same limitations as other private parties and economic actors when it comes to their possibilities to seek annulment of an EU act. The requirements of direct and, most of all, of individual concern, with regard to those acts which are not "regulatory"—that is to say, legislative acts—is difficult to fulfill. Even if in this case the particular situation of the Inuit communities was specifically taken into account in the challenged Regulation, they were still not deemed to be individually affected, since "the prohibition on the placing of seal products on the market laid down in the contested regulation is worded in general terms and applies indiscriminately to any trader falling within its scope."[51] With regard to the requirement of "direct concern" this case shows that even if many of the applicants were affected by the consequences of the regulation in their business activities, only those who were active "in the placing on the market of the European Union of seal products" were considered to be directly affected, since, according to settled case law, these consequences affect only their factual situation, and not their legal situation.[52]

Moreover, even if it can be stated that indigenous peoples and individuals do not face more constraints than other private parties in order to institute annulment procedures, indigenous representative bodies might find it rather difficult to request interim measures successfully when their claim is based on common economic, cultural and social interests. The order of the president of the General Court that examined the application for interim measures presented in the first annulment procedure against the basic regulation establishing the ban on the import and sale of seal products, resorted to established case law, according to which entities governed by public law, who are by their very nature responsible for protecting general economic, social and cultural interests at a national, regional or local level, can make submissions in proceedings for interim measures regarding damage affecting general interests. However, since the applicants were not entities governed by public law, they could not base their claim on the general economic, social and cultural interest of the Inuit in their application for interim measures.[53]

The claims concerning fundamental rights

In the cases that were brought against the Commission Implementing Regulation mentioned above, the applicants relied on a plea of the illegality of the basic regulation by contesting its legal basis and alleging a breach of the principles of subsidiarity and proportionality, and a breach of fundamental rights.

With regard to the principle of proportionality, the applicants claimed that the regulation had disproportionate effects on the Inuit communities. In particular, they considered that the Inuit exception was a dead letter, since Inuit people do not trade seal products by themselves and therefore, they do not have any other option other than to rely on commercial undertakings. However, the General Court considered these allegations "very general in nature and not substantiated."[54] In the same vein, the allegations regarding the right to property and with regard to the right to private life were rejected, for lack of substantiated evidence. Furthermore, with regard to Article 19 of the UN Declaration on the Rights of Indigenous Peoples concerning to the right to be heard, the General Court stated that "it cannot be considered that that declaration can grant the Inuit autonomous and additional rights over and above those provided for by Union law."[55]

In its appeal judgment, the Court of Justice confirmed the judgment of the General Court. Since the appellants had only pleaded the mere possibility of being able to market seal products, there was not a violation of the right to property recognized by Article 17 of the Charter which, according to established case law, does not apply to mere commercial interests or opportunities.[56] Moreover, the applicants only argued breaches of the freedom to conduct a business and of customary law resulting from

Article 19 of UNDRIP before the Court of Justice (and not in first instance). Therefore, the Court of Justice had to declare these grounds inadmissible.

It is doubtful whether these two claims would have led to a substantial examination and to a different result in the first instance judgment. In any case, the fact that they were only put forward in the appeals procedure, together with the lack of substantiation of the other claims related to fundamental rights, does not allow us to reach any definitive conclusions with regard to using the fundamental rights approach when defending indigenous rights before the CJEU, beyond the very limited interpretative role awarded to the UNDRIP.

Conclusion

As anticipated, this brief account of the existing case law is insufficient to reach general and systematic conclusions on the approach of the two European courts to Arctic indigenous rights and interests. If anything, at this stage, it could be considered that in the absence of a substantial body of consolidated case law, only some common problems can be identified.

First, the role of associations in representing Arctic indigenous rights and interests which are collective in nature has encountered some procedural hurdles, such as the impossibility of some associations to fulfill the requirements of having victim status before the ECtHR due to the lack of recognition or exercise of specific competences in the area of the rights at issue. In the same vein, before the CJEU, associations representing Arctic indigenous interests are not regarded as relevant as public actors in the pursuance of public interest with regard to their interest to ask for interim relief.

Second, when it comes to assessing substantive fundamental rights issues, despite the limited developments in the ECtHR in the field of the protection of the right to property and private life, there does not seem to exist a solid recognition of the specificity of indigenous rights that would provide them with a particular level of consideration or differentiated protection. At least at the EU level, it seems that the recognition of the specificity of the interests of Arctic peoples is to be taken into account at the legislative level. At the judicial level this debate is only one episode in the struggle to gain recognition of the need for a specific approach to the protection of the rights of vulnerable groups, particularly in legal reasoning by courts.

Notes

* The views expressed in this chapter are purely personal to the author.
1 Julinda Beqiraj, "Indigenous Peoples' Cultural Identity under EU Law and the ECHR: A Non-Trade Interest or a Human Right?," in *Protecting Vulnerable Groups: The Human Rights Framework*, edited by Francesca Ippolito and Sara Iglesias Sánchez (Oxford: Hart, 2015), 158–79.

2 See in this regard, Rainer Grote, "On the Fringes of Europe: Europe's Largely Forgotten Indigenous Peoples," *American Indian Law Review* 31.2 (2006/2007): 425–43.

3 On this issue, Martin Scheinin, "Indigenous Peoples' Rights Under the International Covenant on Civil and Political Rights," in *International Law and Indigenous Peoples*, edited by Joshua Castellino and Niamh Walsh (Leiden: Martinus Nijhoff, 2005), 3–17. Several cases concerning Arctic peoples in Europe have been decided on the basis of this instrument: *Ivan Kitok* v. *Sweden*, Communication No. 197/1985, July 27, 1988, U.N. Doc. Supp. No. 40 (A/43/40); *Ilmari Länsman et al.* v. *Finland*, Communication 511/1992, October 26, 1994, U.N. Doc. Supp. No. 40 (A/50/40); *Jouni E. Länsman et al.* v. *Finland*, Communication No. 671/1995, October 30, 1996, U.N. Doc. A/52/40, Vol. II; and *Anni Äärelä and Jouni Näkkäläjärvi* v. *Finland*, Communication No. 779/1997, October 24, 2001, UN doc. A/57/40, Vol. II.

4 General Recommendation 23, Rights of indigenous peoples (Fifty-first session, 1997), U.N. Doc. A/52/18, annex V at 122 (1997). See Patrick Thornberry, "The Convention on the Elimination of Racial Discrimination, Indigenous Peoples and Caste/Descent-Based Discrimination," in *International Law and Indigenous Peoples*, edited by Joshua Castellino and Niamh Walsh (Leiden: Martinus Nijhoff, 2005), 17–51.

5 Most importantly, the International Labor Organization Convention No. 169 concerning Indigenous and Tribal Peoples in Independent Countries (also known as the Indigenous and Tribal Peoples Convention), 1989 UNTS 383, adopted on June 27, 1989, and the UN Declaration on the Rights of Indigenous Peoples, adopted by the General Assembly on its 107th plenary meeting, September 13, 2007. On this later instrument, see Karen Engle, "On Fragile Architecture: The UN Declaration on the Rights of Indigenous Peoples in the Context of Human Rights," *European Journal of International Law* 22 (2011): 141–63.

6 On the UN approach to indigenous peoples and the interaction between the different mechanisms, see Rhiannon Morgan, *Transforming Law and Institution: Indigenous Peoples, the United Nations and Human Rights* (Farnham: Ashgate 2011).

7 The UN Permanent Forum on Indigenous Issues is an advisory body to the UN Economic and Social Committee. See http://undesadspd.org/indigenous peoples.aspx, accessed August 10, 2015.

8 The Expert Mechanism on the Rights of Indigenous Peoples was established by the UN Human Rights Council as a subsidiary body by its Resolution 6/36. See www.ohchr.org/EN/Issues/IPeoples/EMRIP/Pages/EMRIPIndex.aspx, accessed August 10, 2015. It substituted the previously existing Working Group on Indigenous Populations, www.ohchr.org/EN/Issues/IPeoples/Pages/WGIP.aspx, accessed August 10, 2015.

9 The Special Rapporteur on the Situation of Human Rights and Fundamental Freedoms of Indigenous Peoples, appointed since 2001 by the Commission on Human Rights (now Human Rights Council). www.ohchr.org/EN/Issues/IPeoples/SRIndigenousPeoples/Pages/SRIPeoplesIndex.aspx, accessed August 10, 2015.

10 See Beqiraj, "Indigenous Peoples' Cultural Identity under EU Law and the ECHR," 146, and the cases reported.

11 See Chapter 12, Soledad Torrecuadrada García-Lozano and Rosa María Fernández Egea, "Environmental Challenges for Arctic Peoples," in *Global Challenges in the Arctic Region: Sovereignty, Environment and Geopolitical Balance*, edited by Elena Conde and Sara Iglesias Sánchez (London: Routledge, 2017).

12 Article 267 Treaty on the Functioning of the European Union (TFEU).

13 Article 263, paragraph 4, TFEU establishes that:

> [a]ny natural or legal person may, under the conditions laid down in the first and second paragraphs, institute proceedings against an act addressed to that person or which is of direct and individual concern to them, and against a regulatory act which is of direct concern to them and does not entail implementing measures.

14 Timo Koivurova, "Jurisprudence of the European Court of Human Rights Regarding Indigenous Peoples: Retrospect and Prospects," *International Journal on Minority and Group Rights* 18 (2011): 3.

15 This last criteria is applied:

> unless respect for human rights as defined in the Convention and the Protocols thereto requires an examination of the application on the merits and provided that no case may be rejected on this ground which has not been duly considered by a domestic tribunal.
>
> (Article 35, paragraph 3.b)

16 On the abundant case law on the concept of "victim," see, for example, David Harris, Michael O'Boyle and Colin Warbrick, *Law of the European Convention on Human Rights* 3rd edn (Oxford: Oxford University Press 2014): 84ff.

17 For a general study of these hurdles before international human rights systems, see Anne van Aaken, "Making International Human Rights Protection More Effective: A Rational-Choice Approach to the Effectiveness of Ius Standi Provisions," *MPI Collective Goods Preprint* 16 (2005), accessed July 7, 2015, http://ssrn.com/abstract=802424.

18 European Commission of Human Rights (EComHR), application no 27033/95, November 24, 1996.

19 European Court of Human Rights (ECtHR), application no 42969/98, January 15, 2005.

20 See, in this regard, Harriet Ketley, "Exclusion by Definition: Access to International Tribunals for the Enforcement of the Collective Rights of Indigenous People," *International Journal on Minority and Group Rights* 8 (2001): 331–68.

21 Elisa Ruozzi, "Indigenous Rights and International Human Rights Courts: Between Specificity and Circulation of Principles," *APSA 2011 Annual Meeting Paper* (2011), accessed July 7, 2015, http://ssrn.com/abstract=1902900.

22 See, generally, UN Sub-Commission on the Promotion and Protection of Human Rights, Indigenous peoples and their relationship to land: Final working paper prepared by the Special Rapporteur, Mrs. Erica-Irene A. Daes, E/CN.4/Sub.2/2001/21, June 11, 2001, accessed July 1, 2015, www.refworld.org/docid/3d5a2cd00.html.

23 Ghislain Otis and Aurélie Laurent, "Indigenous Land Claims in Europe: The European Court of Human Rights and the Decolonization of Property," *Arctic Review on Law and Politics* 4 (2013) 156–80.

24 Article 13, paragraph 1, Convention 169.

25 Article 25 states that:

> indigenous peoples have the right to maintain and strengthen their distinctive spiritual relationship with their traditionally owned or otherwise occupied and used lands, territories, waters and coastal seas and other resources and to uphold their responsibilities to future generations in this regard.

Article 26 has the following wording:

1. Indigenous peoples have the right to the lands, territories and resources which they have traditionally owned, occupied or otherwise used or acquired.

2. Indigenous peoples have the right to own, use, develop and control the lands, territories and resources that they possess by reason of traditional ownership or other traditional occupation or use, as well as those which they have otherwise acquired.

3. States shall give legal recognition and protection to these lands, territories and resources. Such recognition shall be conducted with due respect to the customs, traditions and land tenure systems of the indigenous peoples concerned.

26 See Matthias Ahren, "The Provisions on Lands, Territories and Natural Resources in the UN Declaration on the Rights of Indigenous Peoples, and Introduction," in *Making the Declaration Work: The United Nations Declaration on the Rights of Indigenous Peoples,* edited by Claire Charters and Rodolfo Stavenhagen (Copenhagen: Eks-Skolens Trykkeri, 2009), 212.
27 For this discussion, see Otis and Laurent, "Indigenous Land Claims in Europe."
28 Decision of October 3, 1983, applications no 9278/81 and 9415/81.
29 See on this discussion Timo Koivurova, "Jurisprudence of the European Court of Human Rights Regarding Indigenous Peoples," 11.
30 Ibid.
31 *Halvar From* v. *Sweden,* EComHR (1998), application no 34776/97.
32 EComHR (November 25, 1996), application no 27033/95.
33 Decision as to the admissibility ECtHR February 17, 2009, application no 39013/04.
34 Ibid., Paragraph 51.
35 Ibid., Paragraph 55. The decision found Article 1 of Protocol 1 not to be applicable, and the complaint was therefore rejected as being outside the scope *ratione materiae* of the Convention.
36 Otis and Laurent, "Indigenous Land Claims in Europe," 177.
37 The claims based on the principle of equality of arms and the burden of proof were declared manifestly ill founded. The claim related to the effective access to court in relation to legal costs was rejected on the merits but the Court found a violation of Article 6, paragraph 1 of the Convention in regard to the length of the proceedings in its judgment of March 30, 2010. The complex nature of the cases regarding indigenous claims based on immemorial usage had played a negative role in previous cases when it came to establishing the unreasonable length of procedures. See the decision of the European Commission of Human Rights of January 8, 1993 in *O.B. and others against Norway,* application no 15997/90.
38 Paragraph 5 of the partly dissenting opinion of Judge Ziemele.
39 Article 6, paragraph 1, Treaty on European Union (TEU).
40 Article 6, paragraph 3, TEU.
41 The scope of the Charter of Fundamental Rights of the EU is established in its Article 51, paragraph 1:

the provisions of this Charter are addressed to the institutions, bodies, offices and agencies of the Union with due regard for the principle of subsidiarity and to the Member States only when they are implementing Union law. They shall therefore respect the rights, observe the principles and promote the application thereof in accordance with their respective powers and respecting the limits of the powers of the Union as conferred on it in the Treaties.

42 According to Article 230 of the Treaty on the European Community, private parties not being addressed by the act in question could only challenge it if they were be directly and individually concerned. The CJEU interpreted that:

[p]ersons other than those to whom a decision is addressed may only claim to be individually concerned if that decision affects them by reason of certain attributes which are peculiar to them or by reason of circumstances in which they are differentiated from all other persons and by virtue of these factors distinguishes them individually just as in the case of the person addressed,

which made very difficult in practice for private parties to satisfy this requirement (*Plaumann* v. *Commission*, 25/62, EU:C:1963:17). The gaps in judicial protection arising from this system were famously put forward by the Opinion of Advocate General Jacobs in *Unión de Pequeños Agricultores* v. *Council*, C-50/00 P, EU:C:2002:197, an approach also followed by the General Court in its judgment in *Jégo-Quéré* v. *Commission*, T-177/01, EU:T:2002:112. However, the Court of Justice reversed the judgment of the General Court in its judgment in *Commission* v. *Jégo-Quéré*, C-263/02 P, EU:C:2004:210 and made clear in its judgment in *Unión de Pequeños Agricultores* v. *Council*, C-50/00 P, EU:C:2002:462, that a Treaty reform was necessary to amend the system of judicial review of legality of EU measures of general application.

43 Regulation (EC) No 1007/2009 of the European Parliament and of the Council of September 16, 2009 on trade in seal products, OJ L 286, October 31, 2009, 36–39.

44 The exception to this ban, contained in Article 3 of this regulation, and relating to the seal products resulting from hunts traditionally conducted by the Inuit and other indigenous peoples, will be commented upon in the next section.

45 Order in *Inuit Tapiriit Kanatami and Others* v. *Parliament and Council*, T-18/10, EU:T:2011:419.

46 Judgment in *Inuit Tapiriit Kanatami and Others* v. *Parliament and Council*, C-583/11 P, EU:C:2013:625. The opinion of Advocate General Kokott in *Inuit Tapiriit Kanatami and Others* v. *Parliament and Council*, C-583/11 P, EU:C:2013:21 also went in the same direction.

47 Commission Regulation (EU) No 737/2010 of August 10, 2010 laying down detailed rules for the implementation of Regulation (EC) No 1007/2009 of the European Parliament and of the Council on trade in seal products, OJ L 216, 17.8.2010, 1–10.

48 Judgment in *Inuit Tapiriit Kanatami and Others* v. *Commission*, T-526/10, EU:T:2013:215.

49 Judgment in *Inuit Tapiriit Kanatami and Others* v. *Commission*, C-398/13 P, EU:C:2015:535.

50 Opinion of Advocate General Kokott in *Inuit Tapiriit Kanatami and Others* v. *Commission* (C-398/13 P, EU:C:2015:190), paragraph 26.

51 Judgment in *Inuit Tapiriit Kanatami and Others* v. *Parliament and Council*, C-583/11 P. Granted, the appellants did not argue before the Court of Justice for a more flexible understanding of the "Plaumann formula." See Alexander Kornezov, "Shaping the New Architecture of the EU System of Judicial Remedies: Comment on Inuit," *European Law Review* 39 (2014): 251–63.

52 Order in *Inuit Tapiriit Kanatami and Others* v. *Parliament and Council*, T-18/10, paragraph 75.

53 Order in *Inuit Tapiriit Kanatami and Others* v. *Parliament and Council*, T-18/10 RII, EU:T:2010:329, paragraphs 52 and 53. See, in this regard, Beqiraj, "Indigenous Peoples' Cultural Identity under EU Law and the ECHR," 176.

54 Judgment in *Inuit Tapiriit Kanatami and Others* v. *Commission*, T-526/10, paragraph 98.

55 Ibid., paragraph 112.
56 Judgment in *Inuit Tapiriit Kanatami and Others* v. *Parliament and Council*, C-583/11 P, paragraph 60. The Court also cited the case law of the European Court of Human Rights relating to Article 1 of protocol No 1 to the ECHR according to which "future income cannot be considered to constitute 'possessions' that may enjoy the protection of that article." See paragraph 61.

References

Ahren, Matthias. "The Provisions on Lands, Territories and Natural Resources in the UN Declaration on the Rights of Indigenous Peoples, and Introduction." In *Making the Declaration Work: The United Nations Declaration on the Rights of Indigenous Peoples*, edited by Claire Charters and Rodolfo Stavenhagen, 200–15. Copenhagen: Eks-Skolens Trykkeri, 2009.

Beqiraj, Julinda. "Indigenous Peoples' Cultural Identity under EU Law and the ECHR: A Non-Trade Interest or a Human Right?" In *Protecting Vulnerable Groups: The Human Rights Framework*, edited by Francesca Ippolito and Sara Iglesias Sánchez, 158–79. Oxford: Hart, 2015.

Engle, Karen. "On Fragile Architecture: The UN Declaration on the Rights of Indigenous Peoples in the Context of Human Rights." *European Journal of International Law* 22 (2011): 141–63.

Grote, Rainer. "On the Fringes of Europe: Europe's Largely Forgotten Indigenous Peoples." *American Indian Law Review* 31.2 (2006/2007): 425–43.

Harris, David, Michael O'Boyle and Colin Warbrick. *Law of the European Convention on Human Rights* 3rd edn. Oxford: Oxford University Press, 2014.

Ketley, Harriet. "Exclusion by Definition: Access to International Tribunals for the Enforcement of the Collective Rights of Indigenous People." *International Journal on Minority and Group Rights* 8 (2001): 331–68.

Koivurova, Timo. "Jurisprudence of the European Court of Human Rights Regarding Indigenous Peoples: Retrospect and Prospects." *International Journal on Minority and Group Rights* 18 (2011): 1–37.

Kornezov, Alexander. "Shaping the New Architecture of the EU System of Judicial Remedies: Comment on Inuit." *European Law Review* 39 (2014): 251–63.

Morgan, Rhiannon. *Transforming Law and Institution: Indigenous Peoples, the United Nations and Human Rights*. Farnham, Surrey: Ashgate 2011.

Otis, Ghislain and Aurélie Laurent. "Indigenous Land Claims in Europe: The European Court of Human Rights and the Decolonization of Property." *Arctic Review on Law and Politics* 4 (2013): 156–80.

Ruozzi, Elisa. "Indigenous Rights and International Human Rights Courts: Between Specificity and Circulation of Principles." *APSA 2011 Annual Meeting Paper* (2011). Accessed July 27, 2015, http://ssrn.com/abstract=1902900.

Scheinin, Martin. "Indigenous Peoples' Rights Under the International Covenant on Civil and Political Rights." In *International Law and Indigenous Peoples*, edited by Joshua Castellino and Niamh Walsh, 3–17. Leiden: Martinus Nijhoff, 2005.

Thornberry, Patrick. "The Convention on the Elimination of Racial Discrimination, Indigenous Peoples and Caste/Descent-Based Discrimination." In *International Law and Indigenous Peoples*, edited by Joshua Castellino and Niamh Walsh, 17–51. Leiden: Martinus Nijhoff, 2005.

UN Sub-Commission on the Promotion and Protection of Human Rights. *Indigenous Peoples and their Relationship to Land.* Final working paper prepared by the Special Rapporteur, Mrs. Erica-Irene A. Daes, June 11, 2001, E/CN.4/Sub.2/2001/21. Accessed July 1, 2015, www.refworld.org/docid/3d5a2cd00.html.

Van Aaken, Anne. "Making International Human Rights Protection More Effective: A Rational-Choice Approach to the Effectiveness of Ius Standi Provisions." *MPI Collective Goods Preprint* 16 (2005). Accessed July 7, 2015, http://ssrn.com/abstract=802424.

12 Environmental challenges for Arctic peoples

Soledad Torrecuadrada García-Lozano and Rosa María Fernández Egea

Introduction

The Arctic is a laboratory that illustrates a wide range of problems faced by indigenous peoples in the world. The present chapter, which is divided into two parts, will address some of the challenges that these vulnerable groups are facing nowadays.

The first part deals with the impact that climate change is having on Arctic peoples. Due to global warming, a transformation of their natural habitats can be observed and there is a necessity to adapt to the new realities stemming from this. Also linked to this transformation is the discovery of valuable resources emerging under the melting ice crust of the Arctic that States and private companies are eager to extract, particularly as the indigenous people are cheap and peaceful workers to do the task.

The second part tackles a case study on the trade obstacles concerning seal hunting. This hunting activity has been denounced as being cruel and inhumane, but it is also an essential part of Arctic indigenous peoples' identity. The proposal of introducing an exception to preserve this activity, when conducted by Inuit peoples, has been declared incompatible with international trade laws.

Together with the right to the cultural identity of indigenous peoples, affirmed by the Human Rights Committee in Article 27 of the International Covenant on Civil and Political Rights,[1] the Declaration on the Rights of Indigenous Peoples[2] established the right for "the conservation and protection of the environment" and the correlative duty of States to "establish and implement assistance programs for indigenous peoples for such conservation and protection, without discrimination."[3]

Furthermore, the ILO Convention No. 169 on the Rights of Indigenous and Tribal Peoples establishes in Article 4 the duty of States to adopt "special measures [...] as appropriate for safeguarding the persons, institutions, property, labor, cultures and environment of the peoples concerned."[4] Due to the relative effect of treaties, this convention is only binding for Denmark and Norway, but not for the rest of the Arctic States which are not parties.[5]

The real challenge is how to make the rights—formally recognized for Arctic indigenous peoples in the above-mentioned international instruments—effective, especially when they lack specific monitoring mechanisms except for the Covenant on Civil and Political Rights. In fact, the challenges mentioned above reveal that those rights are not being observed by the international community. In the following pages, we will focus on the main problems that are facing the indigenous peoples of the Arctic, and discuss possible solutions.

The impact of climate change on Arctic peoples

Adaptation to a changing environment

As a result of the special linkage between indigenous peoples and nature,[6] climate change has become a factor that accentuates their vulnerability. This is a common feature of indigenous peoples irrespective of the place, region or continent where they live.

In fact, an indigenous lifestyle is based on respecting nature and "Western" measures to protect the environment often collide with their traditional care for nature. As an example, indigenous peoples criticize the Clean Development Mechanism (CDM) incorporated in the United Nations Convention on Climate Change because it is contrary to their "worldview and philosophy of life." From an indigenous perspective, the CDM is just an excuse for industrialized countries not to reduce their emissions. Also, the mechanism is seen as a "new form of expropriation of our lands and territories and the violation of our rights which would culminate in a new form of colonialism."[7]

Arctic indigenous peoples are aware not only of the existence of climate change, but also of its impact on the determining elements of their traditional ways of life and, consequently, on their cultural identity. This can be illustrated with the examples of nutrition and housing. As for the first, we must take into account that Arctic peoples' diet is based on plants and animals, whose survival depends on the existence of ice. The reduction of the ice layer, that may be anecdotal for some, has produced a substantive change in indigenous peoples' nourishment. This change has generated a remarkable increase of some diseases, such as diabetes, with a high mortality rate when compared with other populations because, in many cases, the illness has not been diagnosed and treated promptly.[8] As far as housing is concerned, igloos not only offer cheap hunting and sheltered lodging but they are also easy to build. With the massive melting of the Arctic, one rarely sees igloos and, in some areas, they have even disappeared.[9]

The environmental deterioration may cause two types of reactions within these human groups. On the one hand, they can decide to change their way of life and leave the traditional lifestyle to adapt to the new reality of a modified habitat; this would hinder the maintenance of characteristics that had existed until that time. This phenomenon, however, is already happening.

On the other hand, they might decide to leave their lands and be relocated elsewhere. This possibility could fit within the obligations inserted in the ILO Convention No. 169, provided that there is a margin for the decision to be made voluntarily. However, since the decision is reduced to whether to "leave or perish," they do not seem to have a real choice in the matter. To consider these human groups as climate refugees and to generalize their relocation is, in our view, not only a paternalist solution but it also indicates a deep ignorance of the indigenous peoples' reality. This easy solution could indeed lead to the physical survival of the group. However, it would mean disobeying the mandate they have received from their ancestors of passing on their lands to future generations in the identical condition that they were received. Moreover, their cultural identity is so closely linked to the land, that before they could even build on their traditions on a newly received land, they would most probably disappear as a group.[10]

Valuable resources and the Western notion of "progress"

Under the melting ice one can find resources of important economic value that States and companies are eager to exploit. These actors are trying to persuade the indigenous peoples,[11] who live in those places to participate in the extraction of those resources.[12] In return, they assure those communities an economic development, according to Western mentality and values, but to the detriment of their respective traditional identities. The quest for those valuable resources contributes to the further reduction of the already weakened layer of Arctic ice crust, with the consequent damage to those who have transformed those dark and cold places into their natural habitats where they have developed their cultural identity.[13]

We are confronted with a vicious circle that is difficult to break. Who can resist extracting diamonds or important sources of oil, even if they know that these activities will produce further environmental deterioration or a reduction in the already diminished ice crust? Still, as a result of these activities, the right to cultural identity of indigenous peoples is being violated and they will lose their cultural characteristics for a progress that is to be understood as the assimilation of Western values. Even so, none of these considerations are enough to resist the immense temptation of exploiting these products and resources that will increase the States' profits or those of large companies.

It should not be forgotten that those who provide content to the terms *progress, development* and *improvement in the quality of life,* are non-indigenous authorities (reiterating these terms over and over again as an instrument of their conviction). And this is all done with a paternalistic approach that base on the belief that it knows what is best for others, even those who are different from us. So, it is not respect for the difference, but rather a new mechanism of assimilation, similar to others that have been used since the fifteenth century. The new mechanism will be applied, even if the group of people that is expected to adapt to the new reality—through vocational training to extract oil—may disagree with the content of the concept of progress on which it is based. That being said, not all indigenous peoples are at the same level of relationship with Western development. For example, there are some Inuit already working in the mining or oil industry as a result of sedentary lifestyles and globalization.[14]

As it was already mentioned, the Arctic is a laboratory for what is happening with indigenous peoples elsewhere. Regardless of the place they live, they share values and principles which are totally different to the Western supreme value: economic growth. Indeed, we all suffer the consequences of the climate changes caused by the development of Western cultures, whose incessant expansion has also lead to the precariousness of the habitats of indigenous groups, together with the use of other instruments of assimilation, that have placed them in situations of maximum vulnerability. Far from being exclusive to the indigenous peoples of the Arctic, this phenomenon is shared with other indigenous peoples who live, for example, in other parts of the American continent.[15]

The training projects that let these groups participate in the objectives and results of this progress are obviously intended to give them access to jobs that will provide them with a decent standard of living, when the prior one becomes more than difficult to maintain. However, the real purpose is not to provide access to the labor market. Rather, it is a way of obtaining workers in places where many would not be willing to go. It is cheaper for the industries since they save the costs that would otherwise be incurred by transfers of labor. It is also easier considering that workers do not usually protest against the eventual loss of cultural identity if they are given opportunities and promises to prosper.

The above-mentioned development can also be understood as a new assimilation mechanism to the extent that "they" are getting closer to "our" ways of life which, on the basis of our consciousness of superiority, we understand as the best possible way to live. But, unlike others that have been used throughout past centuries and considering the confluence between climate change and technological advances, this instrument can be more effective to achieve the desired result: final assimilation.

Possible reparation for human rights violations

An interesting way of providing reparation to human rights violations has already been explored by Arctic indigenous peoples. It was proposed by the Inuit activist Sheila Watt-Cloutier with the support of the Inuit Circumpolar Conference on behalf of all the Arctic regions of the United States and Canada when presenting a petition before the Inter-American Commission on Human Rights against the USA.[16] She held that the USA was responsible for global warming, not only because it was the main emitter (it is estimated that US emissions represent approximately 25 percent of the world's total), but also for refusing to control CO_2 emissions, even though they are aware of its harmful effects.[17] If excessive emissions cause global warming which in turn have severe consequences for the indigenous peoples of the Arctic, a logical solution would be to affirm the responsibility of the USA. Having responsibility means assuming the consequences: to cease the ongoing activities (through the establishment of the necessary mechanisms to control excesses), to provide guarantees of non-repetition and to take care of the repairs. The problem with this argument, however, is the absence of a general reduction obligation for countries that are not parties to the Kyoto Protocol, such as the USA.[18]

Nevertheless, the first hearing was on December 1, 2005. Less than one year later, on November 16, 2006, the Commission denied the request through a letter based on Article 26 of the Regulations of the Commission which sets out the capacity of the Secretariat to control whether all the indispensable requirements for consideration of these requests are met,[19] specifically "the information provided does not enable us to determine whether the alleged facts would tend to characterize a violation of rights protected by the American Declaration."[20]

The Commission's decision was disappointing as it is clear that excessive emissions are incompatible with indigenous rights, and climate change makes it very difficult for indigenous people to maintain their ancestral traditions and leads to their disappearance as culturally distinct groups. Still, the Inter-American system has so far favored the protection of indigenous peoples, as manifested by the judgment in the case of the *Awa Tingni* and subsequent cases.[21] In light of this, there was some hope of the adoption of a more daring decision in the case under consideration too. Yet, such illusion has rapidly perished.

Nevertheless, the hope is not entirely gone. In April 2013, a new application was submitted to the Commission by the Arctic Athabaskan Council on behalf of the Athabaskan peoples of Canada and the United States. The organization filed a new petition against Canada concerning the consequences of black carbon emissions.[22] The reasoning is solid enough: the absence of effective regulation of emissions from black carbon combustion is accelerating the warming of the Arctic and consequently violates the rights of the Athabaskan peoples. It affirms the existence of a clear causal relation between the emissions and the devastating consequences for their cultural survival, requesting that Canada be held responsible. Nevertheless, there are some difficulties with this application, such as the failure to exhaust local remedies and the high procedural expenses to be paid by this vulnerable human group. The Commission has not ruled yet on its admissibility, which will take some years considering the general delay of its proceedings.

The welfare of seals and the Arctic people

The European moral and environmental concerns relating to seal hunt: European legislation

The hunting of seals is of vital importance for the indigenous peoples of the Arctic, including Inuit populations. For centuries, seal hunting has constituted their means of subsistence while also being an essential part of their cultural heritage. Being seal hunter is inseparable from the Inuit identity; but they are not the only ones hunting the various species of seal that live in the Arctic areas. There has been a proliferation of individuals and companies that have used seal hunting as a means of obtaining extra income.

Indeed, seals turn out to be extremely valuable animals because of the multiple products one can obtain from them: meat, oil (omega 3), fat and organs, among others; although the most precious product is their skin, used for the manufacturing of variety of outdoor clothing. However, the difficult environmental conditions of their habitats combined with the animal's characteristics make their capture and killing an arduous task. The combination of geographical and climatological factors, marine environment, ice formations of a volatile nature, very low temperatures, strong winds and large tides do not facilitate the task. Seals have a thick skin, which gives them a very high threshold of endurance to pain without losing consciousness. As a result of these factors, the capture and killing requires methods of such duration and intensity that they are labeled as cruel and inhumane. It is not uncommon that even when injured by gunfire, seals manage to escape by plunging into the icy water resulting in a senseless death as the hunter will not be able to retrieve his prey. All these factors make it virtually impossible to kill seals in a way that avoids pain, distress, fear or other forms of suffering. Still, even if one could decrease the level of cruelty, the geographical area where seals are hunted is so large that it is impossible to effectively control it for all the hunting and killing practices that exist.

These practices have been denounced for years by European society, who particularly have a repugnance to the killing of baby seals for commercial purposes every year in Arctic areas. Indeed, in 1983 the European Community banned the importation for commercial purposes of certain products of white coat pups of harp seals and of pups of hooded seals, or blue backs.[23] In addition, nine Member States had already regulated the trade in seals, prohibiting the marketing of such products within their territories. More recently, the EU decided to go one step further and adopted the Regulation 1007/2009 on trade in seal products,[24] in order to avoid the disturbances and fragmentation of the internal market caused by the different national provisions in this field.[25]

Regulation 1007/2009 prohibits the import and marketing of products derived from seals in the single market, but it also provides some exceptions. The one known as the "Inuit exception" is the most important because it affects a greater amount of products.[26] According to Article 3 (1), the marketing of seal products will be allowed "only where the seal products result from hunts traditionally conducted by Inuit and other indigenous communities and contribute to their subsistence." This rule was introduced so that the economic and social interests of the Inuit would not be undermined, as recognized in recital 14 of the preamble of the given Regulation:

> The hunt is an integral part of the culture and identity of the members of the Inuit society, and as such is recognized by the United Nations Declaration on the Rights of Indigenous Peoples. Therefore, the placing on the market of seal products which result from hunts traditionally conducted by Inuit and other indigenous communities and which contribute to their subsistence should be allowed.

One year later, the Commission adopted Regulation (EU) No. 737/2010 of August 10, 2010, which concerns the implementation of specific trade measures.[27] Among other things, Article 3 specifies the conditions to legally market seal products resulting from Inuit hunting: (1) if there is a tradition of seal hunting in the community; (2) if the products are at least partly used, consumed or processed within the communities according to their traditions; and (3) if seal hunts contribute to the subsistence of the community. Seal products must carry a certificate attesting their origin and the fulfillment of all three conditions in order to be introduced into the European market.

These EU measures introduce, therefore, trade restrictions on seal products based on environmental and moral reasons,[28] affecting the seal industry in Canada and Norway for which the Community market represents an important part of its exports. Unsurprisingly, these two exporting countries filed lawsuits against the EU before the WTO Dispute Settlement Body on the grounds that the EU Regulation contravenes several WTO obligations.

The WTO trade dispute

The WTO is an organization that comprises a series of trade agreements with binding obligations for its parties, among them, the EU and its Member States. Two of those agreements are directly affected by the EU trade restrictions introduced by Regulation 1007/2009: the Agreement on Technical Barriers to Trade Agreement (TBT Agreement) and the General Agreement on Tariffs and Trade (GATT).[29]

The WTO provides for a system of dispute settlement that begins with a phase of consultations and, if they do not succeed, they can request the instauration of an ad hoc group or panel, formed by three arbitrators or panelists that will examine the case and end up with a binding solution for the dispute parties. The panel report can also be appealed before the Appellate Body (AB).

Canada requested consultations on November 2, 2009 and the establishment of a panel on February 11, 2011, which was finally established on March 25, 2011. In turn, Norway requested consultations on November 5, 2009 and establishment of a panel on March 14, 2011, eventually established on April 21, 2011. By virtue of Article 9 (1) of the WTO Dispute Solution Understanding, it was agreed to unify both cases based on their grounds in one panel under the name *European Communities-Measures Prohibiting the Import and Marketing of Products derived from Seals* (DS 400 and 401), which was established on October 4, 2012. The Panel report was circulated to Member States on November 25, 2013. Two months later, the disputing parties appealed the Panel report before the AB, which issued its report on May 22, 2014.

In what follows is a brief analysis of the main findings of the above-mentioned Panel and AB reports.

Discriminatory treatment contrary to WTO obligations

In determining the compatibility of the EU regime with WTO rules, the Panel assessed whether the obligations under the TBT Agreement had been violated. It concluded that the EU regime exceptions introduce a less favorable treatment (de facto discrimination) to the detriment of Canadian and Norwegian products in a manner contrary to Article 2.1 TBT.[30] The AB, however, reversed this Panel consideration[31] holding that it was not the TBT Agreement that was applicable in the case, but the GATT.[32]

In this regard, the complaining parties argued that the EU regime violated Articles I.1 and III.4 GATT, which recognize the rule of most-favored-nation and national treatment rule, respectively. While the principle of non-discrimination is embodied in both rules, the first establishes that any advantage given to products of one country should also be given to the third countries to avoid discrimination. The second rule prohibits granting a less favorable fiscal or regulatory treatment to imported products, placing them at a disadvantage with respect to similar domestic products. In this sense, not every differential treatment will be discriminatory, but only that which results in a protectionist treatment in favor of products of a certain State or of domestic production.

In relation to Article I.1 GATT, both the Panel and the AB affirmed that the European regime infringed this provision because seal products originating in Canada and Norway were not benefiting immediately and unconditionally from the same advantage of access to markets than similar products originating in Greenland.[33] Although the measure is neutral from a formal point of view, in practice the seal products from Greenland benefit almost in its entirety from the "Inuit exception."[34]

Article III.4 GATT requires effective equality of opportunity between imported and similar domestic products. Its infringement was also confirmed with regard to the exception relating to the management of marine resources that introduced a distinction between products and thus modifying the conditions of competition in violation of the national treatment rule. It was held that products from seals hunted in the EU receive more favorable treatment compared with other foreign products, since in Europe seals are only hunted within plans of marine resource management. Again, the exception was seen as producing a de facto discrimination.[35]

Possible justification of the European measures

JUSTIFICATION OF THE EUROPEAN LEGISLATION ACCORDING TO MORAL AND ENVIRONMENTAL GROUNDS

Once a violation of a GATT obligation has been affirmed, it is possible to invoke Article XX GATT, which contains a *numerus clausus* list of exceptions allowing measures that violate other provisions of GATT only when they intend to achieve certain legitimate objectives provided in it.[36]

In the present case, the EU invoked the exceptions contained in paragraph (b) of Article XX GATT concerning measures "necessary to protect the health and the life [...] of animals" as well as in paragraph (a), relating to measures "necessary to protect public morals." However, the Panel and the Appellate Body considered the latter since the main objective of the EU regime was to address concerns of EU public moral regarding the welfare of seals.[37] Both exceptions entail the necessity requirement, that is the "least restrictive measure test" which, according to recent jurisprudence, is weighing a number of factors, such as the relative importance of the interests or values that the contested measure aims to protect, the contribution of the measure to the achievement of the purposes pursued, and the restrictive effects of the measure in international trade.[38] Thus, the EU needed to prove that the trade measure is less restrictive as possible to achieve the objective in question, although in order to do so the complaining parties must identify alternative measures that are reasonably accessible and serve to fulfill the EU goal.[39] Certainly one could think of less restrictive alternatives to a trade embargo—for example, labeling requirements—but it would not be effective enough if what is intended is to avoid the suffering of these animals.[40]

The Panel affirmed that the complaining parties have failed to demonstrate the existence of alternative measures that could effectively achieve the objective of protection set by the EU in its Regulations. The embargo in focus could be justified *a priori* on the basis of a general interest: public moral concerns of the EU related to the welfare of seals.[41] In its report, the AB confirmed that the European action was "necessary" to protect public morals, and, therefore, it could be justified *prima facie* under paragraph (a) of Article XX GATT.[42] For the first time in the WTO history, the argument of animal welfare was accepted as a justification for introducing obstacles to international trade.[43]

THE COMPATIBILITY OF THE INUIT EXCEPTION WITH THE REQUIREMENTS OF THE PREAMBLE OF ARTICLE XX GATT

Once compliance with the specific requirements detailed in each paragraph (see section above) have been verified, it is necessary to establish if trade measures comply with the implementation conditions referred to in the preamble of Article XX. In order to be justified under Article XX, trade measures must not be applied in such a way that constitutes an arbitrary and unjustifiable discrimination or a disguised restriction on international trade. The "Inuit exception" posed the major problems with these conditions.

In its Regulation the EU distinguishes between "non-commercial" hunts, covered by the exceptions, and the rest of "commercial" hunts. According to the EU, both hunts generate considerations of a moral nature and different levels of risk for the well-being of animals. As regards the "Inuit exception," non-commercial seal hunting deserves protection given its importance for the livelihood of these indigenous populations, their cultural identity and their social cohesion. In the view of the complaining parties, the cultural heritage or ethnicity of the hunters do not constitute a legitimate regulatory distinction because it has no connection to the main objective of the EU regime, which is to respond to concerns regarding the welfare of animals. Moreover, they affirm that all hunting activities have commercial dimensions, particularly the Greenland Inuit hunting, which is a very sophisticated and extensive one, well-organized and marketed, and with international scope.

The Panel agreed with the complaining parties on this point, considering that the EU regulation in question did not meet the requirements of the chapeau of Article XX because its practical application to restrict the marketing of seal products—mainly when the hunting was practiced by indigenous communities—meant that a less favorable treatment was introduced to the detriment of Canadian and Norwegian products. The AB reversed the findings made by the Panel in this regard, stating that it is improper to bring the same arguments used to assert the incompatibility of the EU regimen with Article 2.1 TBT and Articles I and III.4 GATT.[44]

According to the preamble of Article XX GATT, one must examine if such discrimination can be justified according to a number of factors, which include the unilateral and extraterritorial character of the measure, whether its application is flexible enough or its purpose is protectionist. In fact, the preamble requirements are meant to prevent abuse of the exceptions and ensure balancing between the different interests in a given case.[45] In the view of the AB, one of the most important factors in the evaluation of arbitrary or unjustifiable discrimination is whether the discrimination rationale is connected with the policy objective with respect to which the measure has provisionally justified in line with the exceptions established in Article XX GATT.[46] The Panel and the AB confirmed that Inuit hunting also causes pain and suffering to seals, since indigenous populations use the same "inhumane" methods to slaughter these animals as those used by commercial hunters. Therefore, the regulatory distinction Inuit/commercial hunting was not seen to be in line with the primary objective of the UE regime which is to prevent seals from a cruel death.[47]

The difficult combination of moral and environmental interests with the interests of the Inuit

While the ban on the importation of products from seals in the territory of the community may well be justified by a general interest (EU public morals concerns regarding the welfare of seals), its exceptions are in tension with GATT obligations. According to the reports referred to below, the protection of Inuit culture and tradition cannot provide a justification for discriminating against foreign products, which are exactly the same from the point of view of the seals' suffering. Nevertheless, it is contradictory that in order to make a measure compatible with WTO rules, an absolute embargo is to be preferred over an exception meant to protect the legitimate needs of indigenous populations.

The EU has already put forward a Regulation to implement the WTO Seal Products Decision, maintaining the "Inuit exception" but modifying it so as to prevent misuse.[48] It is worth noting that the EU has decided to maintain the exception that takes into account the interests of indigenous peoples whose survival and cultural identity may be seriously undermined. In this sense, the Community regulation honors the above-mentioned existing international obligations to protect and recognize indigenous rights as recognized in the ILO Convention No. 169 on the Rights of Indigenous and Tribal Peoples and the United Nations Declaration on the Rights of Indigenous Peoples.

Concluding remarks

This chapter has examined how climate change affects the lives of indigenous peoples in the Arctic. Even though one could think of life-saving solutions for these communities, such as relocation, these measures would mean the end of their cultural identity because of their special relation with nature. At the same time, their decision to stay in the lands received by their ancestors is life-threatening not only because of food and housing shortages, but also because of the emerging economic interests to obtain the precious resources found under the melting ice. These are only some examples of how climate change is heavily affecting human rights of Arctic peoples. The request to make Western countries responsible for climate change in order to repair the damages occasioned to Arctic peoples has failed so far.

We have also analyzed how other international regimes, such as the international trade regime, may have some incidence in preserving cultural identity. It has been pointed out that European trade restrictions of seal products based on environmental and moral concerns challenge an activity that is essential to the Inuit. Aware of its importance for indigenous communities, the European Union introduced an exception to its importation ban only when seals are hunted by Inuit. However, mainly because of this exception, the European regulation is considered incompatible with the trade obligations established in the WTO Agreements. The latter case illustrates how difficult it is to balance commercial interests, environmental needs and the legitimate interests of indigenous populations.

In this sense, there is a need to adopt effective means to turn into reality those rights that so far have only obtained formal recognition. Indigenous rights have to be taken seriously not only by human rights courts, but also in other areas such as environmental protection or international trade. Otherwise, we will lose the richness of cultural diversity provided by indigenous peoples.

Notes

1 Article 27:

> In those States in which ethnic, religious or linguistic minorities exist, persons belonging to such minorities shall not be denied the right in community with the other members of their group, to enjoy their own culture, to profess and practice their own religion, or to use their own language.

2 Resolution (Res.) 61/295, December 10, 2007.
3 Article 29 has the following wording:

> 1 Indigenous peoples have the right to the conservation and protection of the environment and the productive capacity of their lands or territories and resources. States shall establish and implement assistance programs for indigenous peoples for such conservation and protection, without discrimination.

> 2 States shall take effective measures to ensure that no storage or disposal of hazardous materials shall take place in the lands or territories of indigenous peoples without their free, prior and informed consent.

> 3 States shall also take effective measures to ensure, as needed, that programs for monitoring, maintaining and restoring the health of indigenous peoples, as developed and implemented by the peoples affected by such materials, are duly implemented.

4 The text of this international instrument is at: www.ilo.org/dyn/normlex/en/f?p=NORMLEXPUB:12100:0::NO::P12100_ILO_CODE:C169, accessed February 16, 2015.

5 The status of ratifications can be consulted at: www.ilo.org/dyn/normlex/en/f?p=NORMLEXPUB:11300:0::NO::P11300_INSTRUMENT_ID:312314, accessed February 16, 2015.

6 This was recognized by the General Assembly in the preamble of the United Nations Declaration on the Rights of the Indigenous Peoples, noting that it was adopted: "Recognizing that respect for Indigenous knowledge, cultures and traditional practices contributes to sustainable and equitable development and proper management of the environment."

7 This indigenous understanding of the environment was stated in the *Declaration of the First International Forum on Climate Change Indigenous Peoples*, and has been subsequently reiterated in various texts, either produced by these groups (such as the *Quito Declaration* containing the recommendations of the indigenous peoples and organizations facing the process of the UNFCCC of May 6, 2000, www.ciel.org/Publications/QuitoDeclaration.pdf, accessed February 16, 2015; or the *Bonn Declaration* (Third International Forum "Indigenous peoples and local communities on climate change," July 14–15, 2001, www.wrm.org.uy, accessed February 16, 2015); or where they have participated (such as the Report of the third period of sessions of the Permanent Forum for Indigenous Issues, May 10–21, 2004, Doc. E/C19/2004/23, paragraphs 73 to 85, www.un.org/esa/socdev/unpfii/documents/Indigenous_women_UNPFII_session_3.pdf, accessed February 16, 2015).

8 Since the 2007 IWGIA (International Work Group for Indigenous Affairs) Report, alerting on the incidence of diabetes type 2 in the indigenous villages in general and in the Arctic, in particular. See www.iwgia.org/iwgia_files_public ations_files/0306_AI_4_07_Sufrimiento_Social.pdf, accessed February 16, 2015.

9 According to the study published by the National Center for Atmospheric Research of the National Snow and Ice Data Center at the University of Colorado, the Arctic ice crust could disappear seasonally in the next fifteen years which would mean cultural extinction of Arctic peoples.

10 At this point, it is important to remember that, according to United Nations, 5,000 out of 6,000 cultures that exist today are indigenous, see www.un.org/es/globalissues/indigenous, accessed February 16, 2015.

11 There are approximately 4 million indigenous peoples in the Arctic, mainly distributed in four groups: the *Inuit* who live in Alaska, Canada, Greenland and Russia; the *Saami* in Norway, Sweden, Finland and Russia; the *Athabaskan Indians* in Alaska and Canada; the *Aleuts* living in Alaska and Russia, along with other native populations of a smaller composition than the above-mentioned. The UN Fact Sheet on these peoples can be found at: www.un.org/en/events/indigenousday/pdf/Indigenous_Arctic_Eng.pdf, accessed February 16, 2015.

12 A good example is the case of the diamond mines found in the Canadian Arctic territory that echoed in the media, see Dulce Ramos, "El tesoro escondido bajo el hielo del Ártico." *El País,* August 5, 2007: http://elpais.com/diario/2007/08/05/internacional/1186264805_850215.html, accessed February 16, 2015. On Arctic oil, see Patricia Luna, "Explotación de petróleo en el Ártico: ¿necesidad estratégica o campo de minas medioambiental?," *Divulgación y Cultura Científica Iberoamericana,* www.oei.es/divulgacioncientifica/reportajes146.htm, accessed February 16, 2015.

13 It is true that the indigenous peoples have been evolving, just as Western populations have, in the characteristic features of their respective cultural identities. Thus, Canadian Inuit, for example, have abandoned nomadism throughout the twentieth century. See Rafael Pérez Taylor et al., *Antropología del desierto: paisaje, naturaleza y sociedad,* Universidad Nacional Autónoma de México y el Colegio de la Frontera Norte, Mexico City, 2007, 239ff.

14 A summary of the report prepared by the Spanish National Library on the Inuit in: www.bne.es/webdocs/Prensa/Noticias/2013/1004_LosInuit.pdf, accessed February 16, 2015.

15 In this sense, it is enough to take a glance at the case—law on indigenous peoples of the Inter-American Court of Human Rights, see www.corteidh.or.cr/index.php/en, accessed February 16, 2015.

16 On this matter, see Soledad Torrecuadrada, "Medio ambiente y América Latina: los pueblos indígenas," in *Derecho Internacional del Medio Ambiente: una visión desde Iberoamérica*, edited by Francesco Sindico et al. (London: Cameron May, 2011), 522–47; Mireya Castillo Daudí, "Cambio climático y derechos humanos: el asunto de los Inuit ante la Comisión Interamericana de Derecho Humanos," in *Cambio Climático, Energía y Derecho Internacional: Perspectivas de Futuro*, coordinated by Rosa Giles Carnero (Pamplona: Aranzadi, 2012), 207–19.

17 See www.inuitcircumpolar.com (accessed February 16, 2015).

18 On this matter, see Rosa María Fernández Egea, "State Responsibility for Environmental Harm, 'Revisited' within the Climate Change Regime," in *La mise en oeuvre du droit international de l'environnement/Implementation of International Environmental Law*, edited by S. Maljean-Dubois and L. Rajamani (Leiden: Martinus Nijhoff Publishers, 2011), 375–417.

19 Article 28:

> Requirements for the Consideration of Petitions: Petitions addressed to the Commission shall contain the following information:
>
> 1 the name of the person or persons making the denunciation; or in cases where the petitioner is a nongovernmental entity, its legal representative(s) and the Member State in which it is legally recognized;
>
> 2 whether the petitioner wishes that his or her identity be withheld from the State, and the respective reasons;
>
> 3 the e-mail address for receiving correspondence from the Commission and, if available, a telephone number, facsimile number, and postal address;
>
> 4 an account of the fact or situation that is denounced, specifying the place and date of the alleged violations;
>
> 5 if possible, the name of the victim and of any public authority who has taken cognizance of the fact or situation alleged;
>
> 6 the State the petitioner considers responsible, by act or omission, for the violation of any of the human rights recognized in the American Convention on Human Rights and other applicable instruments, even if no specific reference is made to the article(s) alleged to have been violated;
>
> 7 compliance with the time period provided for in Article 32 of these Rules of Procedure;
>
> 8 any steps taken to exhaust domestic remedies, or the impossibility of doing so as provided in Article 31 of these Rules of Procedure; and
>
> 9 an indication of whether the complaint has been submitted to another international settlement proceeding as provided in Article 33 of these Rules of Procedure.

20 See http://graphics8.nytimes.com/packages/pdf/science/16commissionletter.pdf, accessed February 16, 2015.

21 On this matter, see Soledad Torrecuadrada, "Identidad indígena," *Anuario de la Facultad de Derecho de la Universidad Autónoma de Madrid* 17 *Identidad, Derecho y Política* (2013): 544–50.

22 See http://earthjustice.org/sites/default/files/AAC_PETITION_13–04–23a.pdf, accessed February 16, 2015.

23 Council Directive 83/129/EEC of March 28, 1983 concerning the importation into Member States of skins of certain seal pups and products derived there from. OJ L 91 of April 9, 1983.

24 Regulation (EC) No. 1007/2009 of the European Parliament and of the Council of September 16, 2009 on trade in seal products. OJ L 286 of October 31, 2009.

25 That is the reason why, as pointed out by Martínez Pérez, its legal basis is not the environment, but the approximation of laws of the Member States to ensure the free movement of goods, see Enrique Martínez Pérez, "Restricciones comerciales por razones éticas: la prohibición de la Unión Europea a la importación de productos derivados de las focas," *Revista Española de Derecho Europeo* 42 (2012): 36–48.

26 Next to the "Inuit exception" paragraph 2 of Article 3 of the Regulation 1007/2009 includes two other exceptions, allowing the marketing of products derived from seals: "where it is of an occasional nature and consists exclusively of goods for the personal use of travelers or their families" and

> where the seal products result from by-products of hunting that is regulated by national law and conducted for the sole purpose of the sustainable management of marine resources. Such placing on the market shall be allowed only on a non-profit basis. In the two cases, both the nature and the quantity of such goods shall not be such as to indicate that they are marketed for commercial reasons. The little magnitude of products involving these two exceptions, involving a low volume of deaths of seals, explains why the dispute has focused on the "Inuit exception."

27 Commission Regulation (EU) No 737/2010 of August 10, 2010, lying down detailed rules for the implementation of Regulation (EC) No 1007/2009 of the European Parliament and of the Council on trade in seal products (OJ L 216 of August 17, 2010).

28 The ban is based on environmental and moral grounds, as set out in the preamble of the Regulation:

> Seals are sentient beings that can experience pain, distress, fear and other forms of suffering.

(recital 1)

> In response to concerns of citizens and consumers about the animal welfare aspects of the killing and skinning of seals and the possible presence on the market of products obtained from animals killed and skinned in a way that causes pain, distress, fear and other forms of suffering.

(recital 5)

29 In particular, the complaining countries consider that European legislation violates the Articles 2, paragraphs 1 and 2; 5, sections 1, 2, 4 and 6; 6, paragraphs 1 and 2; 7, paragraphs 1, 2, 4 and 5; and 8, paragraphs 1 and 2 of the TBT agreement and the Articles 1.1, III.4 and XI of the GATT. The violation of Article 4.2 of the agreement on agriculture was also invoked, although it was not discussed by the Panel or the AB.

30 A thorough analysis of the Panel report in Sergio Riera Díaz, "Medio ambiente y comercio internacional: el caso de los productos derivados de las focas," in *Revista Jurídica de la Universidad Autónoma de Madrid* 30 (2014): 179–200.

31 The Panel laid down other interesting findings on the compatibility with the TBT Agreement. It affirmed there was no violation of Article 2.2 TBT since the claimant has failed to demonstrate the existence of alternative measures that could efficiently achieve the objective of protection set by the EU in its Regulations; or of Article 5.2 TBT because the EU has not acted in a manner incompatible with the obligation to initiate and finalize procedures for assessment of conformity as quickly as possible. However, the certification system used to verify if the seal products meet the conditions of the exceptions so that they can enter the EU market was considered discriminatory and trade restrictive, in a manner contrary to Article 5.1 TBT.

32 TBT Agreement applies in case of a "technical regulation," what was affirmed by the Panel in case of the given European Regulations (see Panel Report, paragraph 7.85). The AB, on other hand, considered that the UE seal products trade regime did not regulate the "characteristics of a product," which qualifies a norm as "technical regulation" within the meaning of paragraph 1 of annex 1 of the TBT Agreement. Another possibility is if the European regime itself could be considered as a "technical regulation" as it regulates the seal products' processes and production methods (known by the acronym "PPM"). However, the AB declined to rule on this issue because none of the parties had made any observation in this sense. Once again, there was a lost opportunity to clarify this matter.

33 Panel Report, paragraph 7.600 and AB Report, paragraph 5.96.

34 This is due to the fact that 90 percent of Greenland's population is Inuit, while only 5 percent of the seal catches in Canada are done by Inuit peoples. Therefore, while almost all products derived from seals from Greenland can be commercialized and circulate freely among EU Member States, the vast majority of products derived from Canadian seals are being excluded.

35 Panel Report, paragraph 7.608 and AB Report, paragraph 5.116.

36 On the applicability conditions of this provision in environmental matters as well as the relevant jurisprudence, see Rosa María Fernandéz Egea, *Comercio de mercancías y protección del medio ambiente en la OMC* (Madrid: Marcial Pons, 2008), 131ff.

37 Panel Report, paragraph 7.640 and AB Report, paragraph 5.167.

38 AB Report, paragraph 5.169 and the case law cited. In fact, the requisite of necessity required for the exception in paragraph (a) has been conceived on the basis of the same requirement contained in paragraph (b) of Article XX GATT.

39 AB Report, paragraph 5.169, *in fine.*

40 As already explained in recital 12 of Regulation 1007/2009.

41 Panel Report, paragraph 7.639. At this point, the Panel takes up considerations that had been made with respect to Article 2.2 TBT.

42 AB Report, paragraph 5.290.

43 This exception had been previously invoked in the case *China–Measures Affecting Trading Rights and Distribution Services for Certain Publications and Audiovisual Entertainment Products* (WT/DS363) in 2010, but the measure was not considered "necessary" for the safeguarding of public morality. In another case, *United States–Measures Affecting the Cross-Border Supply of Gambling and Betting Services* (WT/DS285) of 2005, an exception similar to the one in paragraph (a) of Article XX GATT was invoked, although, in relation to other WTO trade agreement: the General Agreement on Trade in Services (GATS). On that occasion both the Panel and the AB affirmed that States have some discretion to define

what has to be understood by "public morals" and to determine the level of protection they consider appropriate to safeguard it (see Panel Report from November 10, 2004, paragraph 6,465 and AB Report from April 7, 2005, paragraph 299). In that case, the measure could also be justified *a priori*, but failed to meet the requirements of the preamble.

44 AB Report, paragraph 5.313.
45 AB Report, paragraph 5.297.
46 AB Report, paragraph 5.306.
47 Panel Report, paragraph 7.275 and AB Report, paragraph 5.338. Other compatibility problems of the European measures with the preamble of Article XX GATT were that one could find several ambiguities in the application of the criteria that determine which products can profit from the "Inuit exception" together with the fact that the certifying bodies have wide discretion to interpret those criteria without being controlled. These failures lead to the fact that seals hunted by Inuit peoples in Canada did not benefit from the exception, while other commercial hunting elsewhere did. In addition, the EU was blamed because with regard to the Canadian Inuit, it did not make a "comparable effort" as it did with the Greenlandic Inuit.
48 Article 3 of the Regulation is settled as follows:

> Article 3. Conditions for placing on the market.
>
> 1 The placing on the market of seal products shall be allowed only where the seal products result from hunts conducted by Inuit and other indigenous communities, provided that the following conditions are all fulfilled:
>
>   (a) the hunt has been traditionally conducted by the community;
>
>   (b) the hunt is conducted for and contributes to the subsistence of the community, including in order to provide food and income to support life and sustainable livelihood, and is not conducted primarily for commercial reasons;
>
>   (c) the hunt is conducted in a manner which has due regard to animal welfare, taking into consideration the way of life of the community and the subsistence purpose of the hunt.
>
> See Regulation (EU) 2015/1775 of the European Parliament and of the Council amending Regulation (EC) No 1007/2009 on trade in seal products and repealing Commission Regulation (EU) No 737/2010, February October 6, 2015; OJ L 262/1, October 7, 2015.

References

Castillo Daudí, Mireya. "Cambio climático y derechos humanos: el asunto de los Inuit ante la Comisión Interamericana de Derecho Humanos." In *Cambio Climático, Energía y Derecho Internacional: Perspectivas de Futuro*, coordinated by Rosa Giles Carnero, 207–19. Pamplona: Aranzadi, 2012.

Duyck, Sébastien. "Polar Environmental Governance and Non-state Actors." In *Diplomacy on Ice: Energy and the Environment in the Arctic and Antarctic*, edited by Rebecca Pincus and Saleem H. Ali, 13–40. New Haven, CT: Yale University Press, 2015.

Fernández Egea, Rosa María. *Comercio de mercancías y protección del medio ambiente en la OMC*. Madrid: Marcial Pons, 2008.

Fernández Egea, Rosa María. "State Responsibility for Environmental Harm, 'Revised' within the Climate Change Regime." In *La mise en oeuvre du droit international de l'environnement/Implementation of International Environmental Law*, edited by S. Maljean-Dubois and L. Rajamani, 375–417. Leiden: Martinus Nijhoff, 2011.

Luna, Patricia. "Explotación de petróleo en el Ártico: ¿necesidad estratégica o campo de minas medioambiental?." *Divulgación y Cultura Científica Iberoamericana*, accessed February 16, 2015, www.oei.es/divulgacioncientifica/reportajes146.htm.

Martínez Pérez, Enrique J. "Restricciones comerciales por razones éticas: la prohibición de la Unión Europea a la importación de productos derivados de las focas." *Revista Española de Derecho Europeo* 42 (2012): 25–48.

Nuttall, Mark. *Protecting the Arctic: Indigenous Peoples and Cultural Survival*. Abingdon: Routledge, 1998.

Ørbaek, Jon B., Roland Kallenborn, Ingunn Tombre, Else N. Hegseth, Stig Falk-Petersen and Alf H. Hoel (eds). *Arctic Alpine Ecosystem and People in a Changing Environment*. Berlin: Springer-Verlag, 2007.

Pérez Taylor, Rafael, Miguel Olmos Aguilera and Hernán Salas Quintanal (eds). *Antropología del desierto: paisaje, naturaleza y sociedad*. Mexico City: Universidad Nacional Autónoma de México, 2007.

Ramos, Dulce. "El tesoro escondido bajo el hielo del Ártico." *El País,* August 5, 2007, accessed February 16, 2015, http://elpais.com/diario/2007/08/05/internacional/1186264805_850215.html.

Riera Díaz, Sergio. "Medio ambiente y comercio internacional: el caso de los productos derivados de las focas." *Revista Jurídica de la Universidad Autónoma de Madrid* 30 (2014): 179–200.

Torrecuadrada García-Lozano, Soledad. *Los Pueblos Indígenas en el Orden Internacional*. Madrid: Dykinson, 2001.

Torrecuadrada García-Lozano, Soledad. "Medio ambiente y América Latina: los pueblos indígenas." In *Derecho Internacional del Medio Ambiente: Una visión desde Iberoamérica*, edited by Francesco Sindico, Rosa María Fernández Egea and Susana Borrás Pentinat, 522–47. London: Cameron May, 2011.

Torrecuadrada García-Lozano, Soledad. "Identidad indígena." *Anuario de la Facultad de Derecho de la Universidad Autónoma de Madrid 17 Identidad, Derecho y Política* (2013): 529–59.

13 Climate change and human mobility

The national and international approach to native community relocation in the Arctic

Nuria Arenas-Hidalgo[1]

Introduction

Climate change, and its consequences for the Arctic—in particular melting ice, stronger storms, growing erosion or thawing permafrost—are causing what some term a humanitarian crisis for the Native communities who have lived in the zone for thousands of years. This is a phenomenon that affects their way of life and traditional means of subsistence and, which in extreme cases—especially for people living in coastal areas—prevents them from continuing to live in their habitual locations. As the territories they inhabit shrink in size, these populations are obliged to abandon their natural habitats for safer zones within the State. The States affected have reacted with long-established humanitarian responses to the extreme environmental events, disaster relief and hazard mitigation, but these strategies are not sufficient to protect the community in the face of a rapid deterioration of the environment, and in some zones this is now no longer a viable solution.

In the case of some Native communities in Alaska, the Intergovernmental Panel on Climate Change (IPCC) Fifth Assessment Report has already alerted the world to this problem stating that "accelerated rates of change in permafrost thaw, loss of coastal sea ice, sea level rise and increased weather intensity are forcing relocation of some Indigenous communities in Alaska (high confidence)." The IPCC specifies that "some Alaskan villages such as Shishmaref, Kivalina, and Newtok have already lost critical infrastructures and services, and are becoming unlivable because of permafrost thaw, storm damage, and coastal erosion."[2] A catastrophic climatic event could submerge all the communities within the next fifteen years.[3] In such cases, protection in their place of residence is not possible and community relocation is the only response that can safeguard them from accelerating climate change impacts.

The United States recognized the problem, as stated in the last US Climate Action Report 2014, under the United Nations Framework Convention on Climate Change (UNFCCC):

> The people, lands, and resources of indigenous communities across the United States face an array of climate change impacts and vulnerabilities

that threaten many different Native communities' health, well-being, and ways of life. In parts of Alaska, Louisiana, the Pacific Islands, and other coastal locations, climate change impacts (through erosion and inundation) are so severe that some communities are already undergoing relocation from their historical homelands to which their traditions and cultural identities are tied.[4]

This relocation process is particularly complex for indigenous communities who are especially vulnerable to climate change[5] despite the fact that mobility is not new for Arctic peoples.[6]

This human displacement due entirely to climate events has been termed "climigration,"[7] and it is also connected to other environmentally induced displacement caused by desertification, deforestation, natural catastrophes.... Though environment-induced human mobility has occurred throughout history, it is its scale and intensity in recent times that gives new scope to the phenomenon and has made environment degradation a key factor in determining modern migration. The First Assessment Report of the IPCC in 1990 warned that "the gravest effects of climate change may be those on human migration."[8] The worst-case scenario is that some 200 million people will be displaced in 2050.[9]

The problem lies in the term "climate refugees" or "environmental refugees," which dates back to United Nations Environmental Programme (UNEP) and its categorization of this phenomenon. Twenty years later and thanks to evidence-based studies, there is now greater awareness of the nature of this type of displacement. Studies on the subject tend to eliminate the term "refugee" from the discourse in order to present a new paradigm: environment-induced human mobility (displacement, migration or planned relocation) is not only a question of international protection or safety but can be understood as a *strategy of adaptation* to climate change.[10]

In this study, we analyze the national and international approach to Native community relocation in the Arctic. The first section examines how the USA has responded to the process of relocation of the most affected communities (Kivalina, Shishmaref and Newtok) and the problems identified in that process. The second section looks at how international law has approached this phenomenon, from the first legal instruments established to protect populations against arbitrary displacement—especially in the case of indigenous peoples—to its current consideration of the subject as a community-based adaptation strategy within the framework of international environmental law.

The national approach: governance and institutional challenges for climate-induced relocation in Alaska

Among the indigenous populations that inhabit the Arctic and which are in a process or are in imminent danger of relocation as a consequence of climate change are those that live in Alaska (USA). Some Inuit populations in Canada are deemed to be at future risk.[11] With regard to the indigenous communities in the Russian North or Arctic Scandinavia, the analyses show that these populations are either not at risk of relocation or that the mobility is due to more complex factors on which climate change does not have a direct effect.[12] Hence, this chapter focuses on the study of the problems observed in the relocation process involving some Native communities in Alaska, in particular the three rural villages identified as most critical to relocate: Kivalina, Newtok and Shishmaref.

These communities spent years drawing attention to changes in the ecosystem and the necessity of relocation, however, only in the last decade did governments finally decide to act.[13] In December 2003, the US Government Accountability Office (GAO) issued the first federal government report to document the impact of flooding and erosion on Alaskan Native communities. According to the report, 86 percent (184) of the 213 Alaskan Native villages were affected to some degree by flooding and erosion, with four imminently threatened.[14] By 2009, that number had risen to thirty-one villages, and twelve communities planning to relocate (Kivalina, Newtok, Shishmaref, Shaktoolik, Allakaket, Golovin, Hughes, Huslia, Koyukuk, Nulato, Teller and Unalakleet).[15]

Although in 2005 the US Congress authorized the relocation of specific communities at full federal expense, the relocations did not occur. Instead, the US Army Corps of Engineers (USACE) used these funds to conduct studies to assess the threat and estimate relocation costs for seven at-risk coastal villages and to carry out an Alaska erosion baseline study to coordinate, plan and prioritize responses to erosion in Alaska Native village communities.[16] The Corps completed the assessment of the seven villages in 2006 and the erosion report in 2009.[17]

With the erosion process gathering pace, the State of Alaska officially formed the Alaska Climate Change Sub-Cabinet charged with:

> building the state's knowledge of the actual and foreseeable effects of climate warming in Alaska, developing appropriate measures and policies to prepare communities in Alaska for the anticipated impacts from climate change, and providing guidance regarding Alaska's participation in regional and national efforts addressing the causes and effects of climate change.[18]

The Alaska Climate Change Sub-Cabinet established the Immediate Action Workgroup (IAWG) in 2007. The IAWG was a collaborative multi-disciplinary and intergovernmental workgroup tasked with the responsibility of identifying the immediate needs of the communities imminently threatened by the effects of erosion, flooding, permafrost degradation and other climate change related impacts. The IAWG held numerous meetings with representatives of these communities to develop a strategy to respond to climate change related threats and was instrumental in submitting to the Alaska State Legislature funding recommendations for these communities so that they could receive the necessary financial resources to respond to the changing environment. The IAWG also issued two reports outlining several recommendations to respond to the needs of the imperiled communities located along Alaska's coast and rivers.[19]

The three communities most affected have undertaken a three-pronged relocation process that involved: (1) identification of a new village site; (2) resident voter approval of the relocation site; and (3) documentation to substantiate the need to relocate and the suitability of the relocation site for the community. Despite the similarity of the steps taken by each community to relocate, only Newtok has begun the relocation process.[20]

Kivalina[21] residents first noted coastal erosion in the 1950s, and voted to begin a relocation process in 1992. The community has held five elections related to relocation issues. A special election in 2000 resulted in a majority of voters wishing to move to Kiniktuuraq—located one mile south of the current community site—but there have been disagreements over the new relocation site between Kivalina residents and government agencies and contractors, which has further slowed the relocation. Their experience offers an example of a tribal community attempting to proactively adapt to climate change while being constrained by existing policies—policies that, by their design, have largely channeled assistance and funding towards remaining on the existing settlement rather than relocating.[22]

In the case of Shishmaref,[23] local efforts to relocate the village have been ongoing since the 1970s. During the aftermath of a 1973 storm, extensive planning by local residents and meetings between government representatives and local leaders occurred. These plans did not produce any results and a decision was made by the community to relocate to the mainland, to Nunatuk, six miles south of the existing community. However, in August 1974, the community reversed its position and decided not to relocate but to focus on reinforcing the beachfront to protect the community for another twenty years. During August 1974, 50,000 sandbags were placed along the worst hit areas of Shishmaref protecting homes and retail infrastructures. The protection worked for twenty-four years, however as a result of a 1997 storm, the State of Alaska declared Shishmaref a disaster area and requested federal assistance in relocating thirteen residential homes to higher and more protected areas in the newly plotted residential site on the old airport. Shishmaref residents were unanimous in their refusal to move to Kotzebue because of long-standing difficulties in their relation with the people there would make integration into the community problematic. By the same token, villagers considered Nome to be vice-ridden, exposing people to alcoholism and health problems, in addition to an eventual loss of language and cultural disintegration. The fundamental issues for the people of Shishmaref are continuity of culture as a discrete village on their own land and local control over resettlement decision-making. The villagers of Shishmaref have now officially voted to relocate and have chosen a resettlement site. However, the villagers' plans have been frustrated because it is not clear which agencies are responsible and there is no systematic state or federal strategy for resettlement.[24]

The inhabitants of Newtok[25] voted three times, most recently in August 2003, to relocate to Nelson Island (nine miles from Newtok). The village obtained a title to their preferred relocation site, which they named Mertarvik (in Yup'ik it means "getting water from the spring"), through a land-exchange agreement negotiated with the US Fish and Wildlife Service. In 2006, the Newtok Planning Group, an ad hoc intergovernmental and multidisciplinary working group dedicated to Newtok's relocation and led by the Newtok Traditional Council, began a strategic relocation planning process.[26] Through their efforts, several pioneer infrastructures have been built, including a barge landing, six homes and the foundation for an emergency evacuation center. In 2010, the Alaska Department of Commerce, Community, and Economic Development successfully secured funding from the Federal Coastal Impact Assistance Program for the creation of the Mertarvik Strategic Management Plan. In January 2011, Agnew::Beck Consulting, in partnership with PDC Engineers and USKH Inc., were hired to spearhead the effort. The primary goal of the project is to develop a Strategic Management Plan (SMP) that outlines the community's vision, guiding principles, strategies and timelines for relocation. The process is occurring very slowly, but it is moving forward.[27]

Following recommendations of IAWG, the State of Alaska adopted two programs: the *Alaska Community Coastal Protection Project* designed to increase community resilience of Kivalina and Shishmaref;[28] and the *Alaska Climate Change Mitigation Program* adopted to assist impacted communities in the development of a planned approach to shoreline protection, building relocation and/or eventual relocation of the village (Community Relocation Plans).[29]

From the studies carried out by state agencies and researchers, it can be deduced from the three cases that field analyses have been made by independent experts on the ecological dangers to the zone; state agencies have been involved in the process; the Native communities have been informed of the situation, they have given their consent to relocation and have directly participated in the process. However, the three cases suffer from the same problem: the principal constraint is the lack of a comprehensive governance framework to relocate entire communities. National, state, local and tribal government agencies lack the legal authority and the technical, organizational and financial capacity to implement relocation processes for communities forcibly displaced by climate change.[30] Yet no agency has complete responsibility to relocate the entire public and private infrastructure of a community and rebuild livelihoods in a new location to protect them from climate change induced hazards.[31] Furthermore, few policies and protocols exist to legally move the process forward.[32] Instead, there are multiple agencies with different authorities, norms and responsibilities.[33] The IPCC's Fifth Assessment Report (2014) also drew attention to how the high costs and limitations of government mechanisms are significant barriers to the actual relocation of these communities.[34] Even in the case of Newtok, which has worked for approximately a generation to relocate and has received substantial support from numerous government agencies, statutory and institutional barriers have caused significant delays in the relocation process.[35]

Moreover, the US Global Change Research in the Third National Climate Assessment considers that these shortcomings, to the extent that they hinder any relocation that is absolutely essential, "are causing loss of community and culture, health impacts, and economic decline, further exacerbating tribal impoverishment"[36] In addition, the decision to relocate discourages public investment in improving the living standards of these populations, which makes their situation worse.[37] The IPCC's Fifth Assessment Report (2014) considers that,

> it is now well-documented that the many climate-related impacts on Arctic communities are causing significant psychological and mental distress and anxiety among residents [...] For example, changes in the physical environment (e.g., through thawing permafrost and erosion) that may lead to forced or voluntary relocation of residents out of their villages or loss of traditional subsistence species are causing mental health impacts among Indigenous and other vulnerable, isolated populations [...] Special concern has been expressed by many communities about the unusually high and increasing numbers of suicides in the Arctic, especially among Indigenous youth.[38]

To avoid this situation especially in forthcoming relocations of the rest of the communities affected, scholars have called for measures to be adopted internally as a first step; new federal and state statutes to create what they call "an adaptive governance framework for relocation"[39] (standardized mechanisms or criteria to determine whether and when populations need to be relocated due to environmental change,[40] steps to implement relocation, new governance institutions and funding[41] new post-disaster and hazard mitigation statutory framework...).[42] There thus seems to be some urgency to regulate a specific and holistic framework for climate change induced relocation in Alaska, that covers all the phases in the process and which, leaving some margin of appreciation for each community to regulate its own particular situation, could establish the operational guidance on the matter.

Second, there has also been a call for international action. Scholars consider that no human rights document exists in the USA or internationally that protects communities forced to relocate because of climate change. Protocols to guide community relocation should arguably be rooted in a human rights framework that asserts and protects communities' rights to self-determination, and helps prevent communities from being forced to disband or move from one at-risk location to another.[43] The next section analyzes whether these rights are recognized and what international actions have been undertaken in this respect.

The international approach: planned relocation as an adaptation strategy to climate change

International institutions first analyzed the causal relation between environmental degradation and human movements in 1985, with the United Nations Environmental Programme (UNEP), which began to use the concept of "environmental refugee."[44] Since then, the limited international response has been characterized by the lack of institutions to take responsibility for the issue, and legal instruments that can clarify the regulatory status of environmentally induced displaced people.

There has been indiscriminate use of the term "environmental refugees" or "climate refugees," yet Article 1.A.2 of the 1951 United Nations Convention relating to the Status of Refugees states that the refugee must be outside the country of origin or habitual residence, be lacking in any protection from that State and manifest a well-founded fear of being persecuted for any of the five reasons specified in the Convention (race, religion, nationality, membership of a particular social group or political opinion).[45] Only when environmental degradation is used as a discriminatory policy by the State or when the State prevents assistance or protection from being provided to the victims of environmental disasters with the aim of marginalizing this population for any of the five reasons—noting the importance of individual threat—and when this leads to populations moving across borders, could the 1951 Refugee Convention be cited as a legal instrument for protection.[46] In our case these circumstances do not apply. The response of the State could be ineffectual or uncoordinated but it is not discriminatory or negligent. And above all, the people affected do not need to cross an international border in order to get access to protection.

In fact, the relocation process in Alaska is planned within the State's borders and that means that the State bears the primary responsibility to ensure citizens' well-being. This responsibility is conditioned by international obligations. This international framework lacks a legal instrument that specifically guarantees the right to be relocated as a consequence of climate change. Beyond the fact that the right to be relocated could derive from the general duty to protect, there are certain legal obligations that can be deduced in terms of those normative instruments that were conceived to avoid forced or involuntary displacement within the State: the Guiding Principles on Internal Displacement (IDP Guidelines) is not legally binding but reflects and is consistent with international law;[47] and from others which establish specific rights for indigenous communities: the United Nations Declaration on the Rights of Indigenous Peoples (DRIPS)—signed by the United States on December 16, 2010[48]—and the International Labour Organization (ILO) Convention 169 which is legally binding but to which the USA is not a signatory.[49]

Five principal obligations can be deduced:

First, the right not to be subjected to arbitrary displacement (deduced from Article 12 International Covenant on Civil and Political Rights and in particular for our case: principle 6.2 and 7.2 IDP Guidelines; Article 10 DRIPS and Article 16.1 ILO Convention 169).[50]

Second, relocation is considered an option but only in exceptional circumstances, adopted in cases of emergency, as a last resort to guarantee the survival of the population (principle 6.2.2 IDP Guidelines; Article 16.1 ILO Convention 169).[51]

Third, all relocations must satisfy certain conditions: a free, prior and informed consent of the indigenous peoples and an agreement on just and fair compensation (Article 7.3 c) IDP Guidelines; Article 10 DRIPS; Article 16 ILO Convention 169).[52]

Fourth, in terms of carrying out the relocation, this must occur in a manner that does not violate other human rights (in particular the right to life, dignity, liberty and security); in a way that minimizes the adverse effects of displacement (principle 8 IDP Guidelines); and it must involve the persons to be relocated in the decision-making process, as well as in the planning and management of the actual movements (principle 7.3.d IDP Guidelines).

Finally, relocation includes the right of return to the original lands when the circumstances that forced the relocation cease to apply, and if this is not viable, the State must provide the group affected with lands of quality and legal status at least equal to that of the lands previously occupied by them, as well as any compensation, not for the relocation as such but for the damage that could have been incurred as a result of the relocation (Article 16.4 ILO Convention 169; Article 19 DRIPS).[53]

The relocation processes that affect the Arctic indigenous populations clearly comply with these obligations. Studies have shown that relocation is the only viable option; the populations have been consulted and have even voted on whether to relocate and where; they have set up institutions—especially efficient in Newtok—that involve communities in the decision-making process and management. The only issue absent in these processes is possible compensation. We believe it is unnecessary to establish a human rights instrument that addresses climate-induced population displacement that ensures the right to relocate as a community, as well collective rights to make decisions regarding where and how a community will relocate.[54] There already exist several instruments that guarantee these rights but the potentiality of the instrument proposed must go further in order to set up a specific "action strategy on planned relocation," not only to enshrine rights that we consider to be guaranteed in practice.

Given the direct causal relationship between the environmental consequences of climate change and the need to relocate the Native communities in Alaska, it is important to analyze how the International Environmental Law regulates this issue.

Neither the United Nations Framework Convention on Climate Change (UNFCCC) nor its Kyoto Protocol mention population displacements resulting from climate change. However, with the creation in 2007 of the subsidiary body under the Convention, the "Ad hoc Working Group on Long-Term Cooperative Action under the Convention (AWG-LCA)," a change of attitude has emerged thanks to the efforts of the Inter-Agency Standing Committee (IASC) to raise awareness. As of the Copenhagen Climate Change Conference, the terminology begins to reflect an understanding that human mobility is a continuous adaptation, and with the Tianjin Climate Change Conference a distinction is drawn between the different levels of mobility (regional, national, international), types of displacement (forced, planned, taking the form of a relocation) and types of measures to be adopted (coordination, cooperation or investigation).[55] Paragraph 14 of the Cancun Agreements recognizes *planned relocation as a strategy of adaptation,* which confirms this growing awareness of the issue.

The reference to climate change-induced human mobility appears in the second section of the Cancun Agreements (Paragraph 14.f), in which it:

> invites all Parties to enhance action on adaptation under the Cancun Adaptation Framework, taking into account their common but differentiated responsibilities and respective capabilities, and specific national and regional development priorities, objectives and circumstances, by undertaking, inter alia, the following: f): Measures to enhance understanding, coordination and cooperation with regard to climate change-induced displacement, migration and planned relocation, where appropriate, at the national, regional and international levels.

As a result, climate change-related human mobility ceases to be analyzed as the potential reason for international protection in order to define it as a formula or strategy of adaptation to climate variability. In this context, the planned relocation of Native communities would be a measure for reducing vulnerability and building the resilience of those affected.

From this perspective, planned relocations would be related to: (1) the need to carry out vulnerability and adaptation assessments, including assessment of financial needs of adaptation options; (2) disaster risk reduction strategies (taking into consideration the Hyogo Framework for

Action); and (3) capacity-building for adaptation. Governments must be capable of understanding and foreseeing these changes, formulating legislative and programmatic solutions, applying suitable measures that fit needs and specific circumstances, and supervising and assessing their efficacy. The requirements in terms of creating capacity will differ between countries depending on the form of the environmentally induced migration or relocation that exists in a particular geographic region.

In addition, Paragraph 14.f requires the implementation of an "obligation of understanding, coordination and cooperation," multilevel—national, regional, international—which being defined under the "principle of common but differentiated responsibilities," is conceived in such a way that it is the developed countries that provide adequate, predictable and sustainable financial resources, technology and capacity-building to support the implementation of adaptation action (included planned relocation) in developing countries (paragraph 18, Cancun Agreements). The measures adopted for this issue will be supervised by the Adaptation Committee (paragraph 20 Cancun, Agreements) and will be financed by the Green Climate Fund (paragraph 20, Cancun Agreements). The main advantages laid down in Paragraph 14.f) are of benefit to relocated communities in developing countries, but not to Native communities in the USA.

In fact, the least developed and developing countries are managing environmentally induced migration and planned relocation through National Adaptation Programmes for Action (NAPAs) and National Adaptation Programmes (NAPs).[56] In preparing the NAPAs, countries are to synthesize available information, undertake a participatory assessment of vulnerability, identify key adaptation measures and criteria for prioritizing activities, and select a prioritized short list of activities. An analysis of the NAPAs presented show us that some adaptation activities proposed include assistance for relocation of communities.[57] Developed countries are not called on to present such reports, so the United States is not required to undertake an analysis concerning the relocation of Native communities in Alaska that could be reviewed by the Adaptation Committee. But it is recommended that they do so in their national communications and the mention made in the Sixth National Communication of the United States of America under the UNFCCC is a good example. Nevertheless, there is not a real accountability process for these measures.

The US government has been criticized for not providing these Native populations in Alaska with the necessary financial assistance despite being a developed country. In the case of Kivalina, the community's efforts to obtain relocation costs through US courts failed in 2009 (the community brought an action to recover damages from global warning caused by many of the largest emitters of greenhouse gases in the USA).[58] And we must also consider that most Native US populations face adverse socioeconomic factors such as poverty and lack of resources, so they are already in a more vulnerable situation.[59] This has led some scholars to denounce that indigenous populations have no access to the Green Climate Fund and have called for the creation of an Adaptation Fund through the UNFCCC available to non-State actors and other vulnerable populations regardless of whether they reside in a developed country or not.[60] We do not believe this proposal will prosper. It is difficult enough to raise sufficient voluntary contributions for the Green Climate Fund never mind the setting up of another fund in competition with it, and to which populations in developed countries can accede. Which developed country would pay for the relocation of populations in a world economic powerhouse like the United States?

While it is true that the relocation of these populations is plagued with deficiencies, we believe that the United States could finance it. It is more urgent to create an "action strategy on planned relocation," as an operational guidance, that could be endorsed and reviewed by the Adaptation Committee. We consider it would be more efficient if there were an action strategy as an implementation of the international obligation inferred from Paragraph 14.f Cancun Agreement that could be endorsed by the Adaptation Committee and if competences were designed for it in this area in order to monitor the actions of the States affected. In other words, a flexible and accountable mechanism with an operational guidance that would take into account the basic rights of populations. The Committee has not been assigned this function so far but might request authorization to do so in any future restructuring of the future Paris Climate Agreement.[61] The Arctic Council (where indigenous peoples' organizations have been granted Permanent Participant status) could request it during the current negotiation process.

Despite an official acknowledgement of this formula as an adaptation response, planned relocation continues to be neglected and undeveloped (both technically and theoretically).[62] Some initiatives have been developed for cross-border displacement in the context of natural hazards and climate change,[63] but they do not create legal obligation for States.

Given the lack of political will to establish a legally binding treaty addressing environment-related cross-border displacement or planned relocation, we propose that this "action strategy on relocation" as an operational guidance be designed under the auspices of the UNFCCC. We must bear in mind that although the Cancun Agreements do not amount to an international treaty, but are a decision taken by the Conference of Parties (COP), it contains a road map for the development of UNFCCC obligations, and as such, the States can use it as guidance to design their actions. It is a flexible action framework which functions despite not being legally binding in the sense of classic international law. This action strategy could be designed within this framework to define States' obligations in the case of a planned relocation not only in terms of protectable rights (right to relocation as an exceptional measure, collective rights, free, prior and informed consent, living standards...) but also an operational guidance by which the States inform on whether they possess standardized mechanisms or criteria to determine whether and when populations need to be relocated; whether they have carried out scientific studies to identify climate-related risks and vulnerabilities; whether there exists an adequate post-disaster and hazard mitigation statutory framework; whether evacuation plans have been arbitrated; whether the governance framework and funding mechanisms are adequate (planned relocation should be integrated into national plans and laws relating to land acquisition, climate change adaptation and national action plans); whether there is an operational relocation framework, with clear steps to implement relocation; and whether a community-based and community-guided process has been arbitrated.[64] This would be monitored by the Adaptation Committee regardless of whether these are processes taking place in lesser developed countries or not. It is not sufficient for the affected States to only create an adaptive governance framework for relocation under domestic law, long-term monitoring and evaluation of the objectives and strategies by the Adaptation Committee is also necessary.

The experience of Shishmaref, Kivalina, and in particular Newtok, will be of great value when drawing up this action strategy on planned relocation. The Adaptation Committee could make use of an inventory of good practices for forthcoming relocations in other regions of Alaska, and even in similar processes that take place in other countries across the world.

Conclusions

The Arctic region is particularly vulnerable to the effects of climate change. The phenomenon is affecting the biodiversity of the Arctic, while endangering the living conditions of the region's inhabitants. Accelerated rates of change in permafrost thaw, loss of coastal sea ice, rising sea levels, and more severe weather are forcing the relocation of some Native communities in Alaska. For these villages, protection in place is not possible and community relocation is the only response that can shield them from the impact of accelerating climate change.

According to US government reports, 184 of the 213 Alaska Native villages are affected to some degree by flooding and erosion, with twelve communities planning to relocate (Kivalina, Newtok, Shishmaref, Shaktoolik, Allakaket, Golovin, Hughes, Huslia, Koyukuk, Nulato, Teller and Unalakleet). The communities most affected (Kivalina, Shishmaref and Newtok) have launched a three-pronged relocation process that involved: identification of a new village site; resident voter approval of the relocation site; and documentation to substantiate the need to relocate and the suitability of the relocation site for the community. Despite the similarity of the steps taken by each community to relocate, only Newtok has begun the relocation process.

Of the studies carried out, both by state agencies and researchers, one can conclude that in the three cases independent experts have made an in situ analysis of the ecological dangers threatening the zone; the state agencies have been involved in the process; the Native communities have been informed of the situation, have given their consent to relocation and have directly participated in the process. However, the three cases suffer from the same problem: the principal constraint is the lack of a comprehensive governance framework to relocate entire communities. National, state, local and tribal government agencies lack the legal authority and the technical, organizational and financial capacity to implement relocation processes for communities forcibly displaced by climate change. These problems are slowing down relocations which are urgent and which are causing loss of community and culture, health impacts and economic decline, which further exacerbates tribal impoverishment.

To avoid this situation, especially in terms of the forthcoming relocations of the rest of the communities affected, scholars have called for measures to be adopted internally—new federal and state statutes to create what they call "an adaptive governance framework for relocation." It would appear to be urgent that laws be adopted that enable a legal and holistic treatment specific to climate change-induced relocation in Alaska which tackles all the phases of the process and which, while providing scope for each community to regulate its own situation according to its individual needs, can establish operational guidance on the matter.

The response of international institutions has been poor and uncoordinated. Certain basic obligations have been recognized—especially in relation to indigenous populations—but only indirectly and by means of an international Convention signed by only twenty-two States and a few instruments, none of which are legally-binding (ILO Convention 169, IDP Guidelines and DRIPS). Nevertheless, States tend to assume these obligations in their own national laws. These obligations relate to: the right not to be arbitrarily displaced; the right to be relocated as a last resort; the right to be relocated with the prior, free and informed consent of the indigenous people and an agreement on just and fair compensation; the right to be relocated in a manner that does not violate other human rights; the right to be involved in the decision-making process and management of the movement; the right to be returned to the lands when the circumstances that forced the displacement have ceased to exist, and if not possible, the right to have lands of quality and legal status at least equal to that of the lands previously occupied by them, and compensation.

The relocation processes in Alaska have, by and large, complied with these obligations. However, we believe that there are significant shortcomings that should be resolved by adopting an international instrument to facilitate planned relocation, but within the framework of UNFCCC. We consider that political will is lacking to adopt an international treaty as it is understood in classic international law. As a consequence, the most viable way is to utilize the implementation of legal obligations framed in paragraph 14.f of the Cancun Agreements that consider planned relocation to be an adaptation strategy.

The "action strategy on planned relocation," as an operational guidance, that could be endorsed and reviewed by the Adaptation Committee (through National Adaptation Plans), and designed to define States' obligations ahead of a planned relocation, not only in relation to protectable rights (the right to relocation as an exceptional measure, collective rights, free, prior and informed consent, living standards...) but also an operational guidance by which the States inform on whether they possess standardized mechanisms or criteria to determine whether and when populations need to be relocated; whether they have carried out scientific studies to identify climate-related risks and vulnerabilities; whether an adequate post-disaster and hazard mitigation statutory framework exists; whether evacuation plans have been arbitrated; whether the governance framework and funding mechanisms are adequate (planned relocation should be integrated into national plans and laws relating to land acquisition, climate change adaptation and national action plans); whether there is an operational relocation framework, with clear steps to implement relocation; and whether a community-based and community-guided process has been arbitrated. This would be monitored by the Adaptation Committee regardless of whether these are processes taking place in lesser developed countries or not.

Notes

1 Tenured Professor of Public International Law and International Relations, University of Huelva, CIM, CEI CamBio (Spain). The author has received support of the International Campus of Excellence for Environment, Biodiversity and Global Change: CEI CamBio.
2 IPCC's Fifth Assessment Report:

> In habitats across the Arctic, climate changes are affecting these livelihoods through decreased sea ice thickness and extent, less predictable weather, severe storms, sea level rise, changing seasonal melt/freeze-up of rivers and lakes, changes in snow type and timing, increasing shrub growth, permafrost thaw, and storm-related erosion, which, in turn, are causing such severe loss of land in some regions that a number of Alaskan coastal villages are having to relocate entire communities.
> (Climate Change 2014: Impacts, Adaptation, and Vulnerability (WGII AR5), 1583, 1590)

3 Robin Bronen, "Alaskan Communities' Rights and Resilience," *Force Migration Review* 31 (2008), 30.
4 *United States Climate Action Report 2014*, First Biennial Report of the United States of America, Sixth National Communication of the United States of America under the United Nations Framework Convention on Climate Change (2014), 157.

5 As Section 28.2.4, "Health and Well-being of Arctic Residents," of the Intergovernmental Panel on Climate Change (IPCC) Fifth Assessment Report, states:

> Indigenous communities are especially vulnerable to climate change because of their strong dependence on the environment for food, culture, and way of life; their political and economic marginalization; the social, health, and poverty disparities; and community locations along exposed ocean, lake, or river shorelines. (Ford and Furgal, 2009; Galloway-McLean, 2010; Larsen et al., 2010; Cochran et al., 2013).
>
> (IPCC: WGII-AR5, 1581, accessed May 6, 2016, http://ipcc-wg2.gov/AR5/images/uploads/WGIIAR5-Chap28_FINAL.pdf)

6 According to Elizabeth Ferris, "Migration for livelihoods—whether hunting or reindeer herding—has been central to indigenous ways of life for centuries." Elizabeth Ferris: *A Complex Constellation: Displacement, Climate Change and Arctic People*, Brookings-LSE, Project on Internal Displacement, 2013, 25. This migratory lifestyle changed during the late nineteenth and early twentieth centuries primarily because the US Department of the Interior's Bureau of Education began to develop a formal educational system for the Alaska Native community. The majority of scholars agree that the settlement of the Alaska Native population into permanent communities has affected their ability to adapt to their changing environment. Robin Bronen, *Climate-Induced Displacement of Alaska Natives Communities*, Brookings-LSE, Project on Internal Displacement, 2013, 5.

7 A term coined by Robin Bronen and which is defined as "a specific type of permanent population displacement that occurs when community relocation is required to protect residents from climate-induced biophysical changes that alter ecosystems, damage or destroy public infrastructure, and repeatedly endanger human lives." See Robin Bronen and F. Stuart Chapin III, "Adaptive Governance and Institutional Strategies for Climate-Induced Community Relocations in Alaska", *PNAS*, vol. 110 (2013), 9320.

8 The IPCC Fifth Assessment Report states:

> "Environmental refugees," people displaced by degradation of land, flooding or drought, are becoming a much more significant factor in many developing countries. Even a modest rise in global sea levels could produce tens of millions of such refugees. Population movements from blighted agricultural regions could result in areas where crop productivity may be cut by prolonged drought or temperature stress on vulnerable crops.
>
> ("Human Settlement; The Energy, Transport and Industrial Sectors; Human Health; Air Quality; and Changes in Ultraviolet-B Radiation," in WJ. McG. Tegart, G.W. Sheldon D.C. Griffiths (eds), *Climate Change: The IPCC Impacts Assessment*. Canberra: Australian Government Publishing Service, 1990, 5–10)

9 Frank Laczko and Christine Aghazarm, *Migration, Environment and Climate Change: Assessing the Evidence*, International Organization for Migration, (Geneva: IOM, 2009), 5. Regarding this figure, Susan Martin points out how environmental scholars usually highlight the most alarmist forecasts while migration experts are more skeptical both in terms of numbers and analysis of the situation. Susan F. Martin, "Climate Change, Migration and Governance," *Global Governance* 16 (2010) 397–98.

10 "The Cancun Agreements: Outcome of the Work of the Ad Hoc Working Group on Long-Term Cooperative Action under the Convention": Decision 1/CP. 16 (2011). The Parties to the UNFCCC at COP 16 did not provide an official definition of relocation.

11 In the case of Canada, sea level rise, coastal erosion, permafrost thaw and more active slope processes threaten Inuit cultural sites and limit the potential for new development. Critical infrastructure within these communities will need to be made more resilient to the changing. Physical interventions are being considered in vulnerable communities across the Arctic to protect the infrastructure (moving buildings, raising buildings and installing engineering structures) to provide protection from wave action and permafrost thaw. In extreme situations, the relocation of communities may be inevitable. James D. Ford et al., "Climate Change Policy Responses for Canada's Inuit Population: The Importance of and Opportunities for Adaptation," *Global Environmental Change* 20 (2010): 187. According to Feltmate and Thistlethwaite, communities of Kashechewan and Attawapiskat (Ontario), Tuktoyatuk (Northwest Territories) and Peguis First Nation (Manitoba), may require community relocation with the consent of the aboriginal groups, including their choice of alternative locations. To facilitate community redesign and relocation, the development of an aboriginal climate infrastructure assessment is a necessary first step. This assessment can help evaluate potential infrastructure weakness and inform decision-making about redesigns and potential relocations. Aboriginal groups can invoke the assessment voluntarily to explore redesign or relocation options. See Blair Feltmate and Jason Thistlethwaite, *Climate Change Adaptation: A Priorities Plan for Canada*, University of Waterloo/Intact Financial Corporation, (2012), 14.

12 With regard to the indigenous groups of the Russian North, studies carried out on the Nenets, the Dolgan and Nganasan of the Taimyr Peninsula and the Chukotka-Chukchi and Siberian Yupik illustrate that they are moving for reasons that are more complex than climate change. The Viliui Sakha are not yet in need of relocating due to climate change effects, but considering the current trend of permafrost degradation and increasing precipitation and overall climatic softening, it is possible that they will need to move in the future. Susan A. Crate, *Climate Change and Human Mobility in Indigenous Communities of the Russian North*, Brookings-LSE, Project on Internal Displacement, 2013.

Regarding the indigenous communities in Arctic Scandinavia, the analysis of the environmental and social influences of climate change on Saami migration suggests that climate change itself will have limited impact on migration and is not likely to directly cause displacement. See Ilan Kelman and Marius Warg Naess, *Climate Change and Displacement for Indigenous Communities in Arctic Scandinavia*, Brookings-LSE, Project on Internal Displacement, 2013.

13 The Newtok Traditional Council commissioned the oldest report, which was complete in 1984 and evaluated the Ninglick River's erosion impact on the community. According to the report, the relocation of Newtok is considered an "alternative solution," less expensive than trying to hold back the Ninglick River. Woodward-Clyde Consultants, *Ninglick River Erosion Assessment*, November 29, 1984, 24, accessed May 6, 2016, www.commerce.alaska.gov/web/portals/4/pub/ninglick_river_erosion_assessment_addendum_november_29,_1984.pdf.

14 The Government Accountability Office (GAO): (1) determined the extent to which Alaska Native villages are affected by flooding and erosion; (2) identified federal and Alaska state programs that provide assistance for flooding and erosion and assessed the extent to which federal assistance has been provided to Alaska Native villages; (3) determined the status of efforts, including cost estimates, to respond to flooding and erosion in select villages seriously affected by flooding and erosion; and (4) identified alternatives that Congress may wish to consider when providing assistance for flooding and erosion of Alaska Native villages. GAO, *Alaska Native Villages: Most Are Affected by Flooding and Erosion, but Few Qualify for Federal Assistance* (Washington, DC: Government Accountability Office, 2003), 2.

15 GAO, *Alaska Native Villages: Limited Progress Has Been Made on Relocating Villages Threatened by Flooding and Erosion* (Washington, DC: Government Accountability Office, 2009).

16 In 2005, Congress enacted Section 117 of the Energy and Water Development Appropriations Act of 2005, which authorized the USACE to relocate specific communities at full federal expense (Energy and Water Development Appropriations Act of 2005, Pub. L. No. 108–447, §117, 118 Stat. 2935, 2944–45, 2004). Despite this authority, no community was relocated between 2003 and 2009 when Section 117 authorized these actions. This legislation also appropriated specific funding for the erosion assessments; see Bronen, *Climate-Induced Displacement of Alaska Natives Communities*, 6.

17 USACE, *Alaska Village Erosion Technical Assistance Program: An Examination of Erosion Issues in the Communities of Bethel, Dillingham, Kaktovik, Kivalina, Newtok, Shishmaref, and Unalakleet*, US Army Corps of Engineers (Alaska District, 2006). In the examination, the Corps estimated that the village of Kivalina, as well as Newtok and Shishmaref, would be lost to erosion in ten to fifteen years, estimating the cost of relocation at US$80 million to US$200 million for each village. *Study Findings and Technical Report, Alaska Baseline Erosion Assessment.* US Army Corps of Engineers Alaska District (2009).

18 Administrative Order No. 238 from the Office of the Governor of Alaska. September 14, 2007, accessed May 6, 2016, www.gov.state.ak.us/admin-orders/238.html.

19 IAWG, *Recommendations Report to the Governor's Subcabinet on Climate Change, Alaska Subcabinet on Climate Change*, Immediate Action Workgroup, Juneau, Alaska, (2008). IAWG, *Recommendations Report to the Governor's Subcabinet on Climate Change, Alaska Subcabinet on Climate Change*, Immediate Action Workgroup, Juneau, Alaska, (2009). The last meeting of the IAWG occurred in March 2011 because the Workgroup failed to receive authorization from Governor Parnell or the Subcabinet on Climate Change to continue its work. According to Bronen, the dismantling of the Immediate Action Workgroup creates a tremendous gap for communities faced with climate related threats. Bronen, *Climate-Induced Displacement of Alaska Natives Communities*, 7–18.

20 Bronen and Chapin III, "Adaptive Governance and Institutional Strategies for Climate-Induced Community Relocations in Alaska," 9321. The authors analyze the differences in the relocation process of the three villages.

21 The Village of Kivalina is an Inupiaq Eskimo federally recognized indigenous tribe located on the tip of a thin, six-mile-long barrier reef island in the Chukchi Sea, 128 km above the Arctic Circle. Storm surges and flooding threaten the community as a result of diminished Arctic sea ice and the delay in freezing of the ocean. Between 2002 and 2007, six extreme weather events threatened Kivalina. The state and federal government issued three disaster declarations. Between 2006 and 2009, government agencies spent $15.5 million on erosion-control projects that have failed to protect the community. Bronen and Chapin III, "Adaptive Governance and Institutional Strategies for Climate-Induced Community Relocations in Alaska," 9321–22.

22 Julie Koppel Maldonado et al.: "The Impact of Climate Change on Tribal Communities in the US: Displacement, Relocation, and Human Rights," *Climate Change* 120 (2013): 603; Glenn Gray and Associates, "Situation Assessment: Kivalina Consensus Building Project," July 2010, accessed May 6, 2016, www.relocate-ak.org/wordpress/wp-content/uploads/2012/09/Situation_Assessment_Final_July_20105.pdf.

23 Inhabited for over 4,000 years, the town of Shishmaref is located on a barrier island in the Chukchi Sea, off the western coast of Alaska. Shishmaref depends on the ice surrounding the island for protection, food and water. In recent

decades, Shishmaref has lost 40 percent of the ice that protects it from storm surges reaching the island, and already more than ten homes have had to be evacuated. The Army Corps of Engineers estimated relocation costs to be $100–$200 million. Tribes and Climate Change (2011): "Climate Change: Realities of Relocation for Alaska Native Villages," accessed May 6, 2016, http://www4.nau.edu/tribalclimatechange/tribes/ak_inupiaq_AkRelocation.asp.

24 Elizabeth Marino, "Immanent Threats, Impossible Moves, and Unlikely Prestige: Understanding the Struggle for Local Control as a Means towards Sustainability," in *Linking Environmental Change, Migration and Social Vulnerability*, edited by Anthony Oliver-Smith and Xiaomeng Shen. *UNU-EHS, Munich Re Foundation* (2009), 46.

25 Newtok is a Yup'ik Eskimo village located along the Ninglick River near the Bering Sea in western Alaska. No roads lead to or from the village, which is surrounded by one of the largest river deltas in the world. Wave action and thermal degradation of the permafrost-rich riverbank are causing accelerated rates of erosion. In 2003, the GAO identified Newtok as "an imminently threatened village." Six extreme weather events between 1989 and 2006 exacerbated the rate of erosion. FEMA declared a disaster in five of these events. The State of Alaska spent about $1.5 million to control the erosion between 1983–1989. Despite these efforts, the erosion of the Ninglick River is projected to reach the school, the largest structure in the community, by about 2017. USACE 2008. Bronen and Chapin III, "Adaptive Governance and Institutional Strategies for Climate-Induced Community Relocations in Alaska," 607.

26 The Newtok Planning Group, formed in 2006 by federal, state, regional and village partners, has helped to accelerate the relocation process that the village proactively initiated in 1994. The Newtok Planning Group is unique in Alaska in its multidisciplinary and multijurisdictional structure. The group consists of about twenty-five state, federal and tribal governmental and non-governmental agencies that all voluntarily collaborate to facilitate Newtok's relocation. No similar planning group was implemented to respond to the relocation efforts of Kivalina and Shishmaref. Bronen and Chapin III, "Adaptive Governance and Institutional Strategies for Climate-Induced Community Relocations in Alaska," 9322.

27 *Mertarvik: Nunaullemteggun ikayuqulluta tamamta, assirluta aknirtenritellerkamtenun, nuggtarllemtenun ciunerkamteni: A Community that Builds Together for the Safe and Healthy Future of Newtok.* Relocation Report: Newtok to Mertarvik, August 2011, accessed May 6, 2016, www.commerce.alaska.gov/web/portals/4/pub/mertarvik_relocation_report_final.pdf. Robin Bronen, "Climate-Induced Community Relocations: Creating and Adaptive Governance Framework Based in Human Rights Doctrine," *NYU Review of Law and Social Change* 35 (2011): 373–92.

28 Community resilience is increased through three measures: establishing collaborative organizational structures similar to the Newtok Planning Group; providing a full-time community coordinator (two years); and hiring a contractor to develop a strategic management plan for each community, see "Alaska Community Coastal Protection Project," accessed May 6, 2016, www.commerce.alaska.gov/web/dcra/PlanningLandManagement/AlaskaCommunityCoastalProtectionProject.aspx.

29 See, Alaska Climate Change Impact Mitigation Program (ACCIMP), accessed May 6, 2016, www.commerce.alaska.gov/web/dcra/PlanningLandManagement/ACCIMP.aspx. The Sixth National Communication of the United States of America under the United Nations Framework Convention on Climate Change, submitted in 2014, mentioned this program on page 169. "*United States Climate Action Report 2014*, First Biennial Report of the United States of America, Sixth

National Communication of the United States of America under the United Nations Framework Convention on Climate Change," (2014).

30 T.M.B. Bennett et al., "Indigenous Peoples, Lands, and Resources," *Climate Change Impacts in the United States: The Third National Climate Assessment*, edited by J.M. Melillo, Terese (T.C.) Richmond and G.W. Yohe, *U.S. Global Change Research Program* (2014), 307.

31 Bronen and Chapin III, "Adaptive Governance and Institutional Strategies for Climate-Induced Community Relocations in Alaska," 9320.

32 The suitability of the current post-disaster and hazard mitigation statutory framework has been criticized. The limitations of the Federal Emergency Management Agency (FEMA) are highlighted in GAO (2009). Private contractors also come in for criticism as they are unaccountable to the public. Christine Shearer, "The Political Ecology of Climate Adaptation Assistance: Alaska Natives, Displacement, and Relocation," *Journal of Political Ecology*, vol. 19 (2012): 179.

33 Shearer, "The Political Ecology of Climate Adaptation Assistance: Alaska Natives, Displacement, and Relocation," 177.

34 *IPCC's Fifth Assessment Report*, "Climate Change 2014: Impacts, Adaptation, and Vulnerability," 1590.

35 Bronen, "Climate-Induced Community Relocations," 373–92.

36 T.M.B. Bennett et al., "Indigenous Peoples, Lands, and Resources." According to Maldonado et al.: "Forced relocation is compounded by the current lack of governance mechanisms or budgets to support the communities, which intensifies community impoverishment, negative economic and health impacts, and loss of place, social networks, and culture," Maldonado et al., "The Impact of Climate Change on Tribal Communities in the US," 603.

37 In the years following the decision to relocate, Newtok has seen broad disinvestment from federal and state agencies. This disinvestment was driven by a desire not to waste funds improving and maintaining infrastructure in the existing village when the community intends to move. However, many agencies have since reassessed this policy as evidence suggests that disinvestment has led to poor living conditions and serious public health issues. *Mertarvik, Relocation Report: Newtok to Mertarvik*, 2. This has also occurred in Shishmaref. According to Elizabeth Marino: receiving government aid for housing projects is nearly impossible in the aftermath of the vote for relocation, and residents say that this has caused the out-migration of younger, working-age adults to Nome or Anchorage. Marino, "Immanent Threats, Impossible Moves, and Unlikely Prestige," 46.

38 IPCC WGII AR5: 1583.

39 Bronen, "Climate-Induced Community Relocations," 392–406. Christine Shearer has proposed that relocation policies assist Alaska Natives, and argues that such policies should be merged with existing ones addressing risk mitigation and disasters management. In her opinion, disasters management that prioritizes risk mitigation is arguably a bridge to climate change adaptation. Shearer, "The Political Ecology of Climate Adaptation Assistance," 174.

40 In Alaska, government agencies have proposed using the following indicators: (1) risk to life or safety during storm or flood events; (2) loss of critical infrastructure; (3) threats to public health; and (4) loss of 10 percent or more of residential dwellings. Bronen, "Choice and Necessity: Relocation in the Arctic and South Pacific," *Force Migration Review* 45 (2014): 19.

41 For the key components of governance of climate change adaptation, see Bronen and Chapin III, "Adaptive Governance and Institutional Strategies for Climate-Induced Community Relocations in Alaska," 9323ff.

42 The Federal Emergency Management Agency has several disaster preparedness and recovery programs, but villages often fail to qualify for them, generally

because they may lack approved disaster mitigation plans or have not been declared federal disaster areas, GAO 2009.

43 Maldonado et al., "The Impact of Climate Change on Tribal Communities in the US," 603. Bronen, "Climate-Induced Community Relocations," 394–96.

44 For El-Hinnawi an "environmental refugee" refers to people "who have been forced to leave their traditional habitat, temporarily or permanently, because of a marked environmental disruption (natural and/or triggered by people) that jeopardized their existence and/or seriously affected the quality of their life." Likewise, "environmental disruption" would be "any physical, chemical and/or biological changes in the ecosystem (or the resource base) that render it, temporarily or permanently, unsuitable to support human life." At this time, experts were still trying to call public attention to the problem. The UNEP's Executive Director states, in the preface to this work, that before solutions can be found, the international community needs to recognize that displaced people actually exist. Essam El-Hinnawi, *Environmental Refugees* (Nairobi: United Nations Environmental Programme, 1985), i and 4.

45 Adopted on July 28, 1951 by the United Nations Conference of Plenipotentiaries on the Status of Refugees and Stateless Persons convened under General Assembly Resolution 429 (V) of December 14, 1950. Entry into force: April 22, 1954, in accordance with Article 43. UNTS: No 2545, Vol. 189, 137 (hereinafter 1951 Refugee Convention).

46 See also Walter Kälin, "Conceptualising Climate-Induced Displacement," in *Climate Change and Displacement: Multidisciplinary Perspectives*, edited by Jane McAdam (Oxford and Portland, OR: Hart Publishing, 2010), 88. The scholars who have analyzed the case of Alaska take the same position. See *inter alia*, Robin Bronen, "Forced Migration of Alaskan Indigenous Communities due to Climate Change: Creating a Human Right Response," (2009), accessed May 6, 2016, www.iom.int/jahia/webdav/site/myjahiasite/shared/shared/mainsite/events/docs/abstract.pdf.

47 Guiding Principles on Internal Displacement: E/CN.4/1998/53/Add.2, February 11, 1998.

> For the purposes of these Principles, internally displaced persons are persons or groups of persons who have been forced or obliged to flee or to leave their homes or places of habitual residence, in particular as a result of or in order to avoid the effects of armed conflict, situations of generalized violence, violations of human rights or *natural or human-made disasters*, and who have not crossed an internationally recognized State border. [Italics added].

48 Resolution adopted by the General Assembly A/61/295, September 13, 2007.

49 Treaty adopted in Geneva, 76th ILC session (June 27, 1989). Entry into force: September 5, 1991. Twenty-two ratifications. The first attempt to codify international obligations of States in respect of indigenous and tribal populations was the ILO Indigenous and Tribal Populations Convention No. 107. Although since the adoption of Convention No. 169, Convention No. 107 is no longer open for ratification, it is still in force for eighteen States. The USA is not a signatory.

50 Article 12 ICCPR: liberty of movement and right to choose residence. Subject to the provisions of Article 12, paragraph 3, the right to reside in a place of one's choice within the territory includes protection against all forms of forced internal displacement. Human Rights Committee, General Comment 27 (Article 12), UN Doc CCPR/C/21/Rev.1/Add.9 (1999), paragraph 7. Article 6.2 IDP Guidelines establishes that the prohibition includes displacement in cases of disasters. And principle 9 establishes that special efforts must be made

in the case of indigenous peoples because of their attachment to or dependency on their lands. Article 10 DRIPS: "Indigenous peoples shall not be forcibly removed from their lands or territories." Article 16.1 ILO Convention 169: "the peoples concerned shall not be removed from the lands which they occupy."

51 Article 16.1 ILO Convention169: considers relocation as an exceptional measure. Principle 6.2.2 and 7.2 IDP Guidelines considers this possibility if the safety and health of those affected requires their evacuation. And only after the authorities have ensured that all feasible alternatives have been explored.

52 Take into consideration, in accordance with ILO Convention 169, that the prior free and informed consent is not a *sine qua non* requirement. Article 16.2 of the Indigenous and Tribal Peoples Convention establishes:

> Where their consent cannot be obtained, such relocation shall take place only following appropriate procedures established by national laws and regulations, including public inquiries where appropriate, which provide the opportunity for effective representation of the peoples concerned.

Whatever the case, they must be consulted and consent must be obtained in good faith. The prior and free consultation is to be considered a general principle of international law, and is therefore binding even on States that are not party to the ILO Convention 169. IHR Court: *Kichwa Indigenous People of Sarayaku* v. *Ecuador*. Inter-American Court of Human Rights, Merits and reparations. Judgment of June 27, 2012. Series C No. 245. (*"Sarayaku"*). In contrast, the DRIPS consider that consultation and cooperation are insufficient in terms of getting this consent, and what matters is that consent be informed and freely given. There is no justification for negating the true will of the community. And on compensation, Article 16.5 ILO Convention 169 states: "Persons thus relocated shall be fully compensated for any resulting loss or injury."

53 Soledad Torrecuadrada, "Los derechos indígenas sobre sus territorios y los recursos que se encuentran en ellos." *Cursos de Derechos Humanos de Donostia-San Sebastián, vol. XII: Derechos económicos, sociales y culturales en tiempos de crisis* (Pamplona: Thomson Reuters Aranzadi, 2012), 309–42.

54 This Proposal was formulated by Bronen, "Choice and Necessity, 20.

55 Koko Warner, "Climate Change Induced Displacement: Adaptation Policy in the Context of the UNFCCC Climate Negotiations," *UNHCR*. Legal and Protection Policy Research Series, Division of International Protection (May 2011).

56 Some Plans address the role of the planned relocation as an adaptive strategy, particularly in the context of rising sea levels (Sao Tome and Principle; Samoa; the Solomon Islands; the Maldives; or Tuvalu): See Koko Warner et al., *Integrating Human Mobility Issues within National Adaptation Plans*, UNU-EHS Publication Series, Policy Brief No. 9, (June 2014), 21.

57 Susan F. Martin, "Climate Change, Migration and Adaptation," *Climate Change and Migration*, The German Marshall Fund of the United States, (June 2010).

58 See Kivalina complaint: http://files.ali-cle.org/thumbs/datastorage/skoobe sruoc/source/CN085_Locke-Kivalina%20Complaint_thumb.pdf, accessed May 6, 2016. Neither was the "Petition to the Inter-American Commission of Human Rights Seeking Relief from Violations Resulting from Global Warming Caused by Acts or Omissions of the United States" admitted when submitted by Sheila Watt-Cloutier, with the Support of the Circumpolar Conference, on behalf of All Inuit of the Arctic Regions of the United States and Canada, December 7, 2005. See www.inuitcircumpolar.com/uploads/3/0/5/4/30542564/finalpetitionicc.pdf, accessed May 6, 2016.

59 Bennett et al., "Indigenous Peoples, Lands, and Resources," Chapter 12.

60 Shearer, "The political ecology of climate adaptation assistance: Alaska Natives, displacement, and relocation," 179.

61 Nations concluded the Geneva Climate Change Talks by successfully preparing the negotiating text for the 2015 agreement. The agreement is set to be reached in Paris at the end of 2015 and will come into effect in 2020.

62 Mariya Gromilova, "Revisiting Planned Relocation as a Climate Change Adaptation Strategy: The Added Value of a Human Rights-Based Approach," *Utrecht Law Review* 10.1 (2014): 78.

63 Paragraph 14(f) does not, however, say how exactly climate change-induced displacement should be addressed. This is why UNHCR took the initiative to bring together a group of experts in February 2011 to discuss options for addressing climate-related displacement, internal as well as across borders. The June 2011 Nansen Conference was the next step which should have led to States making a commitment to address the issue at the December 2011 UNHCR Ministerial Meeting to commemorate the Sixtieth and Fiftieth Anniversaries of the UN Refugee and Statelessness Conventions respectively. However, the Ministerial Communiqué adopted on this occasion did not contain any direct reference to cross-border movements triggered by climate-related and other natural disasters. This was no accident but rather the expression of a lack of willingness by a majority of governments, whether for reasons of sovereignty, competing priorities or the lead role of UNHCR in the process. On October 2012 a State-driven approach, the Nansen Initiative, was launched. The Ten Nansen Principles reflect the outcome of the Nansen Conference on Climate Change and Displacement hosted by the government of Norway in Oslo in June 2011. To find out more on the Nansen Initiative, see Walter Kälin (2012): "From the Nansen Principles to the Nansen Initiative," *Force Migration Review*, 41, 2012. Specifically on planned relocation, UNHCR, together with the Brookings Institution and Georgetown University's Institute for the Study of International Migration, organized a consultation on "Planned Relocation, Disasters and Climate Change: Consolidating Good Practices and Preparing for the Future," on March 12–14, 2014, San Remo, Italy: UNHCR, 2014.

64 According to Ten Nansen Principles (X):

> National and international policies and responses, including planned relocation, need to be implemented on the basis of non-discrimination, consent, empowerment, participation and partnerships with those directly affected, with due sensitivity to age, gender and diversity aspects. The voices of the displaced or those threatened with displacement, loss of home or livelihood must be heard and taken into account, without neglecting those who may choose to remain.

References

Bennett, T.M.B., N.G. Maynard, P. Cochran, R. Gough, K. Lynn, J. Maldonado, G. Voggesser, S. Wotkyns and K. Cozzetto. "Indigenous Peoples, Lands, and Resources." In *Climate Change Impacts in the United States: The Third National Climate Assessment*, edited by Jerry M. Melillo, Terese (T.C.) Richmond and Gary W. Yohe, Chapter 12. Washington, DC: U.S. Global Change Research Program, 2014.

Bronen, Robin. "Alaskan Communities' Rights and Resilience." *Force Migration Review* 31 (2008).

Bronen, Robin. "Forced Migration of Alaskan Indigenous Communities due to Climate Change: Creating a Human Right Response," (2009), accessed May 6, 2016, www.iom.int/jahia/webdav/site/myjahiasite/shared/shared/mainsite/events/docs/abstract.pdf.

Bronen, Robin. "Climate-Induced Community Relocations: Creating and Adaptive Governance Framework Based in Human Rights Doctrine." *NYU Review of Law and Social Change* 35 (2011).

Bronen, Robin. *Climate-Induced Displacement of Alaska Natives Communities.* Brookings-LSE, Project on Internal Displacement, January 30, 2013.

Bronen, Robin. "Choice and Necessity: Relocation in the Arctic and South Pacific." *Force Migration Review* 45 (2014).

Bronen, Robin and F. Stuart Chapin III. "Adaptive Governance and Institutional Strategies for Climate-Induced Community Relocations in Alaska." *PNAS* 110 (June 4, 2013).

Crate, Susan A. *Climate Change and Human Mobility in Indigenous Communities of the Russian North.* Brookings-LSE, Project on Internal Displacement, 2013.

El-Hinnawi, Essam. *Environmental Refugees.* Nairobi: United Nations Environmental Programme, 1985.

Feltmate, Blair and Jason Thistlethwaite. *Climate Change Adaptation: A Priorities Plan for Canada.* Climate Change Adaptation Project (Canada), University of Waterloo/Intact Financial Corporation, 2012.

Ferris, Elizabeth. *A Complex Constellation: Displacement, Climate Change and Arctic People.* Brookings-LSE, Project on Internal Displacement, 2013.

Ford, James D. et al. "Climate Change Policy Responses for Canada's Inuit Population: The Importance of and Opportunities for Adaptation." *Global Environmental Change* 20 (2010).

Government Accountability Office. *Alaska Native Villages: Most Are Affected by Flooding and Erosion, but Few Qualify for Federal Assistance.* Washington, DC: Government Accountability Office, 2003.

Government Accountability Office. *Alaska Native Villages: Limited Progress Has Been Made on Relocating Villages Threatened by Flooding and Erosion.* Washington, DC: Government Accountability Office, 2009.

Gromilova, Mariya. "Revisiting Planned Relocation as a Climate Change Adaptation Strategy: The Added Value of a Human Rights-Based Approach." *Utrecht Law Review* 10.1 (January 2014).

Kälin, Walter. "Conceptualising Climate-Induced Displacement." In *Climate Change and Displacement: Multidisciplinary Perspectives,* edited by Jane McAdam. Oxford and Portland, OR: Hart Publishing, 2010.

Kälin, Walter. "From the Nansen Principles to the Nansen Initiative." *Force Migration Review* 41 (2012).

Kelman, Ilan and Marius Warg Naess. *Climate Change and Displacement for Indigenous Communities in Arctic Scandinavia.* Brookings-LSE, Project on Internal Displacement, 2013.

Laczko, Frank and Christine Aghazarm. *Migration, Environment and Climate Change: Assessing the Evidence.* International Organization for Migration, UNU-EHS, the Rockefeller Foundation, 2009.

Maldonado, Julie Koppel et al. "The Impact of Climate Change on Tribal Communities in the US: Displacement, Relocation, and Human Rights." *Climate Change* 120 (2013).

Marino, Elizabeth. "Immanent Threats, Impossible Moves, and Unlikely Prestige: Understanding the Struggle for Local Control as a Means towards Sustainability." In *Linking Environmental Change, Migration and Social Vulnerability,* edited by Anthony Oliver-Smith and Xiaomeng Shen. UNU-EHS, Munich Re Foundation, Source no. 12/2009.

Martin, Susan F. "Climate Change, Migration and Governance." *Global Governance* 16 (2010).

Martin, Susan F. "Climate Change, Migration and Adaptation." *Climate Change and Migration.* The German Marshall Fund of the United States (June 2010).

Shearer, Christine. "The Political Ecology of Climate Adaptation Assistance: Alaska Natives, Displacement, and Relocation." *Journal of Political Ecology* 19 (2012).

Tegart, W.J. McG., G.W. Sheldon and D.C. Griffiths (eds). "Human Settlement; The Energy, Transport and Industrial Sectors; Human Health; Air Quality; and Changes in Ultraviolet-B Radiation." In *Climate Change: The IPCC Impacts Assessment.* Report prepared for Intergovernmental Panel on Climate Change by Working Group II. Canberra: Australian Government Publishing Service, 1990.

Torrecuadrada, Soledad. "Los derechos indígenas sobre sus territorios y los recursos que se encuentran en ellos." *Cursos de Derechos Humanos de Donostia-San Sebastián, vol. XII: Derechos económicos, sociales y culturales en tiempos de crisis.* Pamplona: Thomson Reuters Aranzadi, 2012.

UNHCR. "Planned Relocation, Disasters and Climate Change: Consolidating Good Practices and Preparing for the Future." *UNHCR: The UN Refugee Agency,* San Remo, Italy, 2014.

Warner, Koko. "Climate Change Induced Displacement: Adaptation Policy in the Context of the UNFCCC Climate Negotiations." *UNHCR.* Legal and Protection Policy Research Series, Division of International Protection, 2011.

Warner, Koko et al. *Integrating Human Mobility Issues within National Adaptation Plans.* UNU-EHS Publication Series, Policy brief No. 9, June 2014.

Part IV
Environment and resources

14 Knowledge and natural resources

A crucial connection for local benefits and sustainable Arctic development

Rasmus Gjedssø Bertelsen and
Jens Christian Svabo Justinussen

Introduction: the central role of knowledge for Arctic communities for local benefits and sustainable use of natural resources

Arctic economies are generally natural resource based economies, whether they are indigenous economies largely dependent on living on the land or industrialized economies depending on marine resources, mineral resources or fossil or renewable energy resources.[1] However, the central role of knowledge for Arctic communities to secure local benefits and achieve sustainable development around their natural resources is often overlooked in the literature. This chapter will look at the knowledge–natural resources link for local benefits and sustainable Arctic development. Specifically, the chapter will focus on the Icelandic and Faroese experiences with marine resources, renewable energy resources in geothermal, hydro, tidal and wind power, and offshore oil and gas resources. Iceland and the Faroe Islands are selected because they are examples of very small Arctic societies, which illustrate particularly well how strong human capital can contribute to socio-economic and political-constitutional development.[2]

Renewable biological resources and sustainable harvesting: the case of fisheries management

Both Iceland and the Faroe Islands have and remain deeply dependent on marine resources. The Icelandic economy is deeply dependent on fisheries management policy, and the distribution of the rents from the fisheries is one of the most contentious issues in Iceland politics today. The Faroe Islands are still overwhelmingly dependent on fisheries for exports. The development of the Law of the Sea with economic exclusion zones have posed a particular challenge to the Faroe Islands, as they were cut off from their distant fishing grounds. This Law of the Sea development made the sustainable management of fisheries in the Faroese economic exclusion zone even more important for Faroese socio-economic development.

Iceland: economically efficient, but politically illegitimate fisheries management

Iceland was historically a predominantly agricultural country with some winter fisheries in small open boats. Iceland's industrialization started, as the mechanization of the fishing boats, first with engines and then with the import of the first trawlers in the early years of the 1900s. The great expansion of fisheries had profound social and demographic consequences in Iceland, where much more productive fisheries made centers of population around the coast possible with people leaving rural agricultural communities for urban coastal living. This development was intertwined with Iceland's political and constitutional struggle for greater autonomy within the Kingdom of Denmark: the Althingi assembly had been re-established as a consultative body to the absolutist king of Denmark in 1845, the assembly got legislative and budgetary powers in domestic Icelandic affairs in 1874 while the administration was Danish; Iceland got administrative home rule in 1904; and in 1918, Iceland gained sovereignty as the Kingdom of Iceland, through a personal union of the shared monarch with the Kingdom of Denmark; this union was mutually dissolvable after twenty-five years, and in 1944 Iceland declared the Republic of Iceland.[3]

Fisheries are a renewable resource, which in principle can be harvested indefinitely, if managed sustainably. However, the sustainable total allowable catch is finite and anything beyond that is unsustainable. For Icelandic economic development, it was therefore crucial to ensure this sustainable catch for Icelandic fishermen. This drove the Icelandic policy of expanding its exclusive fishery zone from 4–12 nautical miles (nm) on September 1, 1958. Britain did not initially recognize this limit and sent war ships to protect British fishing from the Icelandic coastguard at considerable expense until Britain accepted the new limit. Iceland expanded its fishery zone to 50 nm on September 1, 1972 again leading to conflict with Britain, who acquiesced in November 1973. The final and most violent Cod War occurred between November 1975 and June 1976, when Iceland expanded its economic exclusive zone to 200 nm in accordance with developing the Law of the Sea. The account of the Cod Wars deserves mentioning in this chapter on knowledge and natural resources to illustrate how a very small state (Iceland) was able to prevail against the opposition of a much greater adversary (Britain) and secure its marine resources through a combination of the superb seamanship of the Icelandic coastguard and the international legal and diplomatic skill of the Icelandic government.[4]

Having secured the monopoly of the Icelandic marine resources, the next challenge to Iceland was to manage these resources in a sustainable and economically optimal way.[5] Unmanaged or poorly managed fisheries can either lead to overfishing or over-investing, which will also be clear from the Faroese experience. It is the sustainable level of biomass, which can be harvested that is the limit. This biomass should be harvested in the most efficient way. However, the limitations for controlling the harvesting of biomass are often not on the biomass (output), but on the efforts to harvesting, typically days at sea (input). If a society seeks to reach sustainable fishing by imposing limits on the harvesting effort, such as days at sea, it can have adverse effects. Limits to the harvesting effort can lead to over-investment in fishing fleets since all fishermen compete to catch as much as possible on the days they are allowed to fish, which can then lead to overfishing and new input limitations on fishing. Iceland was facing a situation where the fishing fleet was in serious financial trouble, which was solved with consecutive devaluations of the Icelandic króna to re-establish profitability, which then contributed to inflation problems in the Icelandic economy.

In 1984, Iceland took up a fisheries management system with individually transferable quotas. The logic is that the Minister of Fisheries, based on the advice of the Icelandic Marine Research Institute, set the total allowable catch for any species every year. In 1984, vessels were allotted relative quotas based on their catches of the three previous years. These quotas are shares of the total allowable catch. The quotas can be rented out or can be sold to others. This system created efficiencies in Icelandic fisheries, as the owners of less competitive vessels sold their quotas to more competitive vessels, leading to a more efficient fleet. Iceland's ability to design and implement a fisheries management system with important efficiencies is a reflection of the level of fisheries economics and policy knowledge in Icelandic academia, government and interest organizations.

However, this quota trade and this efficiency create significant natural resource rents, which first accrued to the owners of the original 1984 vessels and gradually to the quota owners. The trade also created severe socio-economic dislocations with the diminishing of the fleet, the switching around of quotas and the loss of fisheries in some locations. The socially equitable distribution of these fishing rents is a very controversial topic in Icelandic society. There has been and continues to lively debate about the design of the quota system and taxing this fishing rent. There is a clear struggle over economic interests, where large parts of society believe that the fishing rent belongs to the Icelandic nation (legally the marine resources are defined as the property of the nation) and the quota owners who seek to avoid this taxation. The quota system may be biologically sustainable, but it is not politically sustainable, if it is not perceived as legitimate. As long as large parts of the Icelandic populace do not perceive this system as equitable and legitimate, the system will be politically vulnerable. It is therefore important for the long-term credibility and sustainability of the Icelandic fisheries management system that it be designed in a way that is broadly perceived as just and legitimate. Such a democratic solution is highly dependent on relevant knowledge of biology, economics, politics, etc. among a range of stakeholders in Icelandic society.[6]

Knowledge and marine resources in the Faroe Islands

The commercial fishery in the Faroe Islands began in earnest at the end of the nineteenth century. In the early days of the fishery, the main kind of knowledge necessary to successfully harvest the marine resources was traditional knowledge. The skipper had to be able to read the weather, know the likely location of fish, what time of day and year to fish, what techniques to use, etc., to be able to return home safe and with a full hull. Today, progress in fishing technology has made many of these skills obsolete. The main obstacle for fishery in the twenty-first century is no longer how to find and catch the fish, but to figure out how much fish there is and how much to leave in the ocean for next year. While the challenges in the early twentieth century were largely up to the individual fisher, the challenges in the twenty-first century are about how to count the fish in the ocean and how *not* to fish and collectively restrain from the temptation to overfish.[7]

Thus success in commercial fishery is dependent on organized collective scientific effort to gain information and knowledge about the state of the fish stocks. This depends to a large degree on the social and political organization of the industry as a whole, the production of scientifically accurate knowledge about the state of the fish stocks, and a management system that takes these factors into account. Thus the competitiveness of the Faroese fishing industry is dependent upon the human organization of a collective sustainable harvesting of marine resources.

In 1992, the Faroese economy collapsed partly because of over-investment in fishing vessels, and a massive overfishing of limited fish stocks. The economic crises that stemmed from this collective failure to restrain fishery of limited marine resources, led to mass unemployment and the resulting unparalleled emigration of 10 percent of the total population. The following years, a quota system was institutionalized. However, it soon became clear that this system was less than ideal for mixed fishery, where boats catch several species at the same time. While it succeeded in restraining fishery, it led to another problem: counterproductive and wasteful discard.[8]

In 1996, the management system was again revised, and a fishing day system was introduced that regulated the total fishing effort (number of days a boat can fish) instead of the quota system's measurement of output of the fishery (total allowable catch of a certain fish).[9]

The most widely used means to regulate and limit fishery is a form of output regulation, either by catch restrictions or by landing restrictions. Input regulations play a less prominent role, though structural policies play an important role in the EU. Currently the only country that regulates the fishery by input regulation—in this case through a system by which the total fishing effort is limited by a maximum number of allowed fishing days per year—is the Faroe Islands.[10]

The fishing day system, which is not uncontroversial, solves a main problem: the discard problem. Discard is a practice in which unwanted fish (either due to size or "wrong" species) is thrown out, discarded.[11] The lack of discard is a highly underestimated benefit with the Faroese fishing day system. To put this in perspective, it is estimated that on a global scale 6.8 million tons of fish are discarded.[12] The discard rate varies from fishery to fishery but, as a rule of thumb, about 50 percent of the Total Allowable Catch is thrown back to sea. The European Commission reports for discard rates are as high as 90 percent in some cases.[13] These are staggering numbers, and it's worth pondering the implications. It means that in some fisheries 90 percent of the catches are thrown back into the sea, where it rots.

There are two main implications. First the practice eschews the data for actual catches; there are a lot more fish caught than reported, leading to inaccurate fishery assessments. Second, the discard raises a lot of environmental, ethical and moral issues of wasting otherwise excellent food that could be used for human consumption. Thus discard is an enormously problematic practice.

The solution to combating this problem has so far mostly been to make it illegal. However, it is difficult to monitor fishing ships out in the ocean and thus difficult to reign in the practice. The Faroese fishing day system gets around this problem by eliminating the incentive for discard in the first place.[14] The total effort is regulated by limiting the number of fishing days at sea. However, the fishermen are allowed to land all fish they catch during their fishing days. As such, it must be considered a considerable social innovation.

To ensure a sustainable fishery, the number of total fishing days is calculated based on regular estimates of the fish stocks done by marine biologists at the Faroese Marine Research Institute (FMRI) in conjunction with the International Council for the Exploration of the Seas (ICES). The total number of fishing days is decided by a co-management regime, in which the fishing industry, fishery scientists (FMRI and ICES), and the Faroese Ministry of Fisheries jointly recommend an annual upper limit in terms of total number of fishing days. The final decision is made by the *Løgtingið*. This high degree of stakeholder participation in the management system produces a high degree of legitimacy and consent to the system.

To sum up, the Faroese case illustrates an important point: though knowledge is a key, and necessary, factor for the sustainable use of renewable marine resources, it is, however, not sufficient. The institutional set-up is also critical for whether a sustainable practice is achieved. The Faroes are unique in this sense because of their effort-based regulatory system in which fishery is regulated by the number of fishing days, instead of quotas. This has solved the much underappreciated discard problem by eliminating the incentive for discard entirely. As such it must be considered as a major social and organizational innovation.

Knowledge-based industries around renewable energy

The two societies studied in this chapter are noteworthy for the role renewable resources play. These societies have historically depended and developed using renewable resources, and they in the future hold large renewable energy potentials. These renewable energy potentials are important for low-carbon energy systems, which will be increasingly important as the world must address climate change.

Iceland: modernization built on geothermal and hydro energy

Renewable energy resources have played a central role in Icelandic society during the 1900s as Iceland became a modern society with the mechanization of fisheries described above. Throughout its independence struggle and since, Iceland has fought for economic development and diversification as part of that independence. Harnessing renewable resources has from around 1900 been a central part of that history and continues to be so. Iceland has very significant renewable energy resources in the form of hydro and geothermal power. Harnessing these resources is one of the bases of Iceland as a highly developed affluent society today. How Iceland has created globally connected, domestically controlled knowledge-based sectors around these resources is a powerful story of how even very small societies can come to knowledge-wise control their natural resources and derive important benefits from them. It is a story that illustrates well the centrality of local human capital for how societies can derive benefits from their natural resources. There are environmental and esthetical trade-offs from harnessing these hydro and geothermal resources from damming rivers and flooding valleys and from harnessing geothermal active areas causing sound and air pollution. These trade-offs have been the topic of intense Icelandic political debate since the first thoughts of using these resources more than a century ago. These debates are thoroughly described and analyzed in the literature, but are outside the scope of this chapter, except for the fact that knowledge plays a central role informing these debates.

Hydropower: "the white coal"

Around 1900, the energy technology captivating the world was electricity and hydropower to generate this electricity to power the energy-intensive industry of the time, nitrogen-based fertilizer manufacturing. This debate became part of the debate in Iceland on using natural resources for economic development and Iceland's relationship with the outside world.

Strong forces in Icelandic society wanted to harness the Icelandic waterfalls to generate electricity to power fertilizer factories to both earn foreign currency and modernize Icelandic agriculture and economy. Iceland was far from having the capital and technology required. So foreign investors together with Icelandic entrepreneurs invested in water rights and drew up ambitious plans. In the environment of independence politics, this economic development thinking based on foreign investment in natural resources was highly controversial and generated strong political opposition, which led to legislation on the water-rights investment companies being based in Iceland, although the capital was mainly foreign. The First World War and the Great Depression killed these early grand ideas of "putting the waterfalls to work," as the early advocates said. But Icelandic society was knowledge-wise closely connected to the outside world, and individual farmers and local municipalities imported micro-power and small-scale hydropower technology, which electrified Iceland from the bottom up.[15]

Iceland was hard hit by the Great Depression and did not recover before the friendly occupation by Britain from May 10, 1940, who was replaced by the USA on July 8, 1941, which brought much construction and other activity creating employment and consumption. Together with fish exports to Britain (with great losses at sea to German mines and torpedoes), it brought prosperity to Iceland. At the end of the war, Iceland faced the challenge of ensuring continued economic growth and prosperity. Large investments were made in trawlers (the "*nysköpunartogarar*" or innovation trawlers), but the ideas of attracting foreign capital and harnessing hydropower resurfaced. From the late 1940s, great hydrology, glaciology and geology efforts were put into mapping the Icelandic hydropower potential by the new office of the National Director for Electricity (following up on earlier work from the 1910s and onwards carried out by the office of the National Engineer). Here it is important to note that this work was largely done by Icelandic postgraduates of foreign universities or Icelandic graduate students working with international colleagues and advisors supported by the Icelandic government and the United Nations Special Fund.

Iceland had responded to the Great Depression with an exceptionally regulated economy, suspicious of foreign capital. Foreign financed harnessing of hydropower was therefore impossible in the 1940s and 1950s. This regulated economy eventually suffocated itself, and in 1959 the Conservative-Social Democratic "Viðreisnarstjórn" (Restoration) government took power with an agenda of opening up and reforming the economy. A central policy was to attract foreign capital to utilize the hydropower. The Icelandic government negotiated a power-sales agreement with the Swiss aluminum company Alusuisse to build a smelter in Iceland (the red and white painted smelter in Straumsvík before Hafnarfjörður, which visitors pass by in the bus from the international airport in Keflavík to Reykjavík). Financing was secured from the World

Bank, which assisted the Icelandic government in its power-sale negotiations to secure the profitability. The national energy company Landsvirkjun was founded in 1965 to construct the first large-scale hydropower station Búrfellsvirkjun, which was completed in 1969, and sell the power. This power station was designed by the Chicago-based Harza Engineering and largely built by Icelanders.

The Restoration government was replaced in 1971 by a left-wing government critical of foreign capital. But a series of large hydropower stations were built during the 1970s, 1980s and 1990s to supply the greatly expanding domestic electricity demand and the expansion of the Straumsvík smelter. Here, it is central to observe how the Icelandic design component grew bigger and bigger and finally took over completely with the development of human capital and knowledge in Icelandic engineering companies.

A Conservative government in the late 1970s revived the power-intensive industrialization policy and attracted Elkem from Norway to build the ferrosilicon factory at Grundatangi. The next power-intensive industry project was the Columbia Ventures aluminum smelter in Hvalfjörður in 1998. The East Coast of Iceland was hard hit by the strong migration from the rest of Iceland to the capital area, so there was strong political pressure for a large-scale power project to revitalize the region. This led to the first negotiations with Norsk Hydro in the late 1990s. Norsk Hydro withdrew, but was immediately replaced by Alcoa of the USA, who in 2002 agreed with the Icelandic government on a giant 360,000 tonne per year smelter powered by the enormous Kárahnjúkar dam and power station, that doubled Iceland's power generating capacity. The project was environmentally very controversial and attracted the attention of international environmental activists. Kárahnjúkar was the first power station again co-designed with foreign engineering companies for its size and complexity, and built by Portuguese and Chinese workers. So Iceland had come full circle from Búrfellvirkjun in the 1960s designed by Americans and built by Icelanders to Icelanders now occupying the knowledge jobs and employing foreign labor.

Geothermal: lifting the smog over Reykjavík

Iceland's other and even more signature renewable power source is geothermal power of boiling hot water or steam rising from the ground. This water and steam is heated by the intense geological activity caused by the North American and European tectonic plates separating along the Atlantic ridge. This geological activity has been a signature of Iceland since its settlement by Norwegian Vikings in the 800s and 900s AD, who gave Reykjavík its name meaning "Smoky Bay." Icelanders have used the hot streams for bathing and washing ever since. However, early 1900s Iceland was heated by coal and pictures of Reykjavík of the interwar years show a cover of smog over the city, which is difficult to imagine today in one of the cleanest capitals in the world.[16] What changed was the practically nationwide adaptation of geothermal heating of buildings. This transformation was initiated in the early 1930s with the Reykjavík municipal swimming pool and the Austurbæjar-skólinn public school being the first building in Iceland with central heating from geothermal heat.[17]

Since then all areas of Iceland with access to geothermal heat have installed geothermal central heating (there are a few cold areas on the northwest and southeast corners, the farthest from the geologically active rift areas going from the southwest corner of Iceland to the central northern part of the country). Geothermal central heating gives Icelandic households, businesses and institutions access to central heating at very cheap prices compared to other parts of the world relying on heating. Together with the hydropower-based electricity system, geothermal energy reduces Iceland's dependency on fossil fuels to the transport sector and saves Iceland significant sums of foreign currency, which is important for a very small and import-dependent economy.

Also with geothermal power, Icelandic human capital based on quality domestic education, brain circulation and Icelandic attention to technological and other progress abroad has ensured that Iceland early on had access to technology and came to master this technology. The first attention to modern large-scale use of geothermal energy for heating was an article written in 1910 by the prominent Icelandic politician Valtýr Guðmundsson, the first Icelander to earn a doctorate in history, which he did at the University of Copenhagen, where he also became professor. Valtýr Guðmundsson published his article on geothermal heating in the American town of Baise, Idaho, and suggested that Reykjavík could be geothermally heated as well.[18] From the 1930s onwards, Iceland created strong competences and a domestic, globally connected, knowledge-based sector, which exports its knowledge globally. This sector is also largely built on Icelanders who combine Icelandic primary, secondary and vocational or undergraduate education with international postgraduate education.[19] Geothermal knowledge also plays an important in Icelandic development aid. Since 1979, the National Energy Authority of Iceland has hosted the United Nations University Geothermal Training Program which had by 2012 trained 525 engineers and technicians from fifty-three developing and transition countries.

Knowledge and renewable resources in the Faroe Islands

In 1921 about 100 villagers, dignitaries, schoolchildren and engineers were gathered in the local school in Vág, a large fishing village on the Southern Island in the Faroe Islands to watch and celebrate as the light from the first electric light bulb in the Faroe Islands was turned on. "This day is a festival day (festive day) and an important day in Faroese history as well, since the first hydroelectricity power station in the Faroe Islands is being inaugurated."[20] After the speech, Vág's mayor pushed a button, and the lights flooded the classroom in the village school.[21]

Previously, there had been talks about building hydropower in the Faroes since the early 1900s, with no actual results. One attempt was made in Vestmanna by a local businessman, but he lacked social and political support and was never able to complete his project. In 1919, the Faroese Parliament, the *Løgtingið*, commissioned a Norwegian engineer to conduct a survey of the energy potential for hydro in the Faroe Islands. During his time in the Faroes the engineer, Mr. Håkon Blaauw, informed the municipality of Vág that the valley á Botni was an excellent site for a hydropower station given the ample energy in its rivers.

The municipality of Vág was one of the wealthiest villages in the Faroes, and had been a main fishing hub since industrial fishery began in the Faroes in the late nineteenth century. Furthermore, trade had led to frequent exposure to trends and ideas from Europe through business exchanges. In many ways, the village was exceptionally progressive. Most importantly, it was able to mobilize the necessary resources for the investment. Even before the hydropower survey commissioned by the *Løgtingið* was completed, the villagers in Vág had already begun building the hydropower station in á Botni. The same Norwegian engineer, Håkon Blaauw, managed the construction á Botni. The project was a remarkable success. Today, ninety-four years after its inauguration, the hydropower station is still in operation and is an integrated part of the electricity supply of the whole Southern Island.

Thus the modernization of the country and its supply of electricity have, from the beginning, been supplied with renewable energy resources. Shortly after the hydropower station began to lighten up the winters in the Southern Island, a diesel driven electricity plant was built in the northern islands, in Tórshavn.

Birth of an energy giant in a Lilliputian nation

The successful experience with hydropower in Vág soon sparked great interest in developing hydropower in the other villages and towns. Several other villages began to investigate options and, in 1933, Klaksvík, a fishing village in the northern islands also built a hydropower station.

In 1946, all municipalities in the Faroe Islands combined to establish a public energy supply company, SEV, with the purpose of building a countrywide electricity grid and collectively provide the electricity supply. Thus a more comprehensive energy plan was developed that included hydro as a mainstay, but its main source was oil. In 1954, in a project partially funded by the United States' Marshall Plan, a large hydropower station was built in Vestmanna. Today, hydropower supplies about 40 percent of the total electricity consumption in the Faroe Islands.[22]

Wind power

After the 1973 oil shock, renewable energy saw renewed interest in the Faroe. The government's industrial development advisor, Tórmóður Dahl, highlighted the excessive use of energy and the need to reduce the consumption of non-renewable resources when he wrote, "It probably sounds strange, but I am completely convinced, that the oil crisis, which goes through the world today is—after all—the best that could happen."[23] In the wake of the oil shock, oil consumption was rationed, and the dangers of energy dependency became evident. A business in Miðvágur began production of windmills in the hope of profiting from the new market conditions. However, the experiment with wind power was not successful and the production stopped. It took another three decades before wind power began to make a real impact in the Faroe Islands.

In 2003, a private business, Røkt, was granted permission to use SEV's electricity grid, and invested in three 660 kw windmills. These were so successful that SEV, who owns the grid and has a monopoly, itself wanted to invest in several windmills in the following years. This triggered a still ongoing debate about private versus public energy companies. Røkt accused SEV of stifling innovation and entrepreneurship in the energy sector and preventing it from further development of its wind park, while SEV argued that its priority was first and foremost energy security and stability. Furthermore, SEV argued, it was obligated to provide energy to the entire country, and not just for profit. As in many other countries this theme, private versus public energy supply, is highly controversial and continues to rage on as this is being written.[24]

After Røkt clearly demonstrated the feasibility of wind power in the Faroe Islands, in spite of the inhospitable climate featuring frequent storms, SEV decided to invest in its own windmill park and raised thirteen windmills at Húsahagi, just outside Tórshavn. The project is not yet (as of mid-2015) fully completed but will, when all windmills are in full operation, provide a substantial part of total Faroese electricity supply, raising the total share of renewable energy sources (hydro and wind) to 60 percent of the total electricity production.[25]

A crucial part of the wind park at Húsahagi is a new battery system developed by the German wind turbine company, ENERCON, and a new smart grid technology developed by the Danish energy giant, DONG. It is a new way to store energy and distribute energy on the net that minimizes the effect of changing weather conditions—a general problem for most wind parks on the globe. However, if the system works in the harshest of conditions like those found in the Faroe Islands, then the chances are in its favor that it will work in Europe as well. Thus the Faroes has become a renewable energy technology test station as well.

Geothermal

Since there is no volcanic activity in the Faroe Islands—as opposed Iceland—there is no geothermal energy generation in the Faroes. However, the earth stores solar heat in the ground and this heat can be utilized by heat exchange systems. The Faroese Mineral and Energy Ministry, *Jarðfeingið*, has studied the potential this energy source might have for Faroese energy supply. Presently several residential homes are heated by this system and the number of houses heated this way is increasing steadily.[26]

In 2014, one house owner hired a contractor to drill a 200-meter deep hole in the ground for his residential heat exchange system. During this routine operation, they hit a warm water well and hot water, at 26.2 degrees Celsius, gushed out of the ground. This discovery was totally unexpected since, according to our present geological knowledge, there is no volcanic activity in the Faroese underground. Yet, hot water gushes up. Monitoring and tests are being done to see whether the pressure and temperature of the supply stays the same. If so, this might indicate a significant heat source in the underground. As one of the researchers at the Faroese Earth and Energy Directorate said, "it will very difficult for us to explain, and we will have to have an extra phenomenon behind, to be able to explain this heat."[27]

Tidal power

One of the main problems with wind is the varying supply of energy caused by changing weather. Tidal energy, in which ocean currents and tidal patterns are utilized, not only contains massive energy potential, but also a steady and predictable supply. This is very likely to become the future main source of renewable energy in the Faroese, since the country's location in the middle of the Gulf Stream provides an enormously powerful energy source. Researchers at the University of the Faroe Islands are currently involved in mapping the energy potential and the currents, providing the basis for future developments of this sector. Practical experiments are also being done by a private energy company that is currently testing turbines placed on the ocean floor in Vestmannasund (a strait between two islands) where the ocean currents are amongst the strongest.[28]

Educational institutions and renewable energy utilization

An important part of the development of renewable energy in the Faroes has been the Marine College in Tórshavn, which educates officers for the shipping and fishing fleet. Machinists educated at the school staff most of the power stations and are also involved in the new windmill parks. Though the school is not research based, it is nevertheless doing its own tests on solar power systems based at the college in Tórshavn.[29]

A player of increasing importance in Faroese society is the University of the Faroe Islands, which has also conducted research in the field. In 2014, a new Bachelor Program in Renewable Energy Engineering was launched that might bring the Faroes closer to the government's plan to reduce CO_2 emissions.[30]

To sum up, the first light bulb that ever shined in the Faroes was fueled by hydropower. Thus renewable energy has played a central role in the development of the Faroese electricity supply from the beginning. Today about 40 percent of all electricity comes from hydro and wind. This is soon expected to reach 60 percent when the new windmills in Húsahagi are fully operational. One feature of the Faroese case is that renewable energy projects occurred in close cooperation with foreign expertise, and a parallel development of Faroese human capital. Thus the earliest hydropower project was lead by a Norwegian engineer, and the current windmill and smart grid projects are being built and run in close connection with DONG and ENERCON. However, in the twenty-first century, these international knowledge networks are increasingly becoming an integrated part of the work done at the University of the Faroe Islands, which today plays a central role in the research and education in fundamental human capital development, which the utilization of renewable resources depends upon.

Knowledge-based industries around offshore hydrocarbons

The Faroese economic exclusion zone borders the British zone, where oil and gas has been found. The northeast corner of the Icelandic EEZ resembles the Norwegian continental shelf with its rich oil and gas finds geologically. There has therefore especially in the Faroe Islands and more recently in Iceland been great interest in exploring offshore hydrocarbon potentials. Offshore hydrocarbon exploration and production is more challenging capital, knowledge and technology-wise than the marine and renewable energy resources discussed above for very small societies. How the Faroe Islands and Iceland could benefit in sustainable ways from finite resources is a central policy challenge for both nations. The Faroe Islands have almost two decades more experience, which shows the centrality of knowledge to address this policy challenge.

Knowledge and non-renewable energy resources in the Faroe Islands

The Faroe Islands is a dependent territory within the realm of the Kingdom of Denmark. As such, the rights to mineral deposits in the Faroese underground were, until recently, considered Danish. In 1992, a sudden shift in the Danish policy regarding this issue led to a unilateral transfer of all rights to the underground from Copenhagen to the Faroese Government. This started a new era in Faroese economic history. Soon after, a hydrocarbon commission was established to investigate global best practices in oil legislation and administration. At the time the rights to the underground were transferred, there was hardly any oil sector expertise in the Faroes. One of the main goals of the commission was to create a system that deliberately fostered and developed the human capital necessary to benefit from potential hydrocarbon deposits in the Faroese underground.[31]

The resulting legal-administrative framework put in place by the Faroes at the end of the twentieth century was the result of a comprehensive study of the institutional frameworks of the oil industries in Scandinavia, and particularly Norway, but also in Holland and the United States.[32] The framework the Faroese put into practice centered around three pillars:

1   Establishment of a Competence Development Fund (CDF), financed by license holders.
2   All transport to and from offshore rigs should go through a Faroese harbor.
3   Fair and real chance for Faroese labor to participate in oil-related activities by the license holders.

Since the establishment of the framework, the CDF has funneled around 180 million Danish Krone (DKK) into Faroese research and education, and has been instrumental for a wide variety of exploratory activities that have widened the knowledge base in the Faroe Islands. This has included several PhD projects, management educational programs at the local business school, training in offshore trade skills and geological research at the University of the Faroe Islands.[33] The legal requirement that all transport to the offshore rigs pass through a Faroese harbor led to the construction of a new harbor in Skálafjørður that has created an entirely new set of jobs in local communities. Furthermore, it has led to increased air traffic, shipping and related economic activities.

The requirement to offer local businesses a fair chance to participate in the process has given rise to entirely new businesses that have significantly diversified the Faroese economy.[34]

Combined, these core pieces of legislation have led to the creation of a new hydrocarbon related sector in the Faroe Islands. It includes two new oil companies that are engaged in oil production in the UK and Norway, and three offshore supply companies that operate in Norway, the UK, and even in more distant waters such as off the coast of Tanzania and in the Gulf of Mexico. Additionally, there has been more work at the local shipyards, a new recruiting service that leases Faroese labor to the oil industry abroad, IT services, a new harbor, an entirely new Petroleum Administration, increasing geological research at the University of the Faroe Islands, expanded curriculum at the Maritime College to include offshore, and even a Faroese web-based news portal dedicated to hydrocarbon-related news.[35]

All this has been achieved in spite of the fact that no commercially viable deposit has yet been found in the Faroes. Meanwhile, it is estimated that Faroese working abroad in the hydrocarbon sector—mainly in Norway and the UK, but also in Africa and the Gulf of Mexico—are bringing home about 824 million DKK in foreign earnings annually.[36] As such, one could argue that the Faroes is now exporting knowledge and human capital in the oil and gas offshore sector, in spite of the fact that no such deposits have been found in the Faroe Islands.

To sum up, even though no hydrocarbon deposit has yet been dis-covered, the Faroe Islands has benefited substantially from the activities associated with exploration in Faroese waters. A crucial element in these developments has been the intentional and deliberate crafting of the insti-tutional framework in such a way that would maximize the inclusion of Faroese businesses and labor, and develop the human capital necessary to benefit from this sector. This has succeeded to such a high degree that the Faroes is now exporting knowledge in offshore industries, even though no actual commercially viable hydrocarbon has been found.

Iceland

Iceland is embarking on the search for fossil fuels in its exclusive economic zone.[37] The northeast corner of Iceland's EEZ, the Dreki area of the Jan Mayern Ridge is been suspected of holding fossil fuel reserves as it geologic-ally resembles the Norwegian continental shelf, which has produced rich oil and gas finds. The question here becomes to what extent Iceland has been able to build a knowledge-based sector around hydrocarbon exploration and will be able to do so further in the future, and how the human capital and knowledge in Iceland affect the country's ability to possible benefit from this hydrocarbon exploration and possible production.

The demands on knowledge and capital for hydrocarbon exploration and production are even greater than in hydro and geothermal power for a very small state and economy as Iceland. However, we have seen above with the case of the Faroe Islands, how an even smaller society has been able to create a knowledge-based offshore sector working internationally, based on strong human capital, quality local education and knowledge circulation.

The search for hydrocarbons on the Jan Mayern Ridge started in the 1960s and continued in the 1970s. Again we see the value of strong human capital for a very small Arctic society as Iceland, as with the case of hydro and geothermal power. Icelandic scientists collaborated with international scientists in seismic and sediment research. Also concerning offshore hydrocarbon resources, we see the importance of a broad range of know-ledge and human capital from social to natural sciences and technology. With the above-mentioned developments in the Law of the Sea in the 1970s with the 200 nm economic exclusion zone, it was necessary to demarcate the Icelandic and Norwegian economic exclusion zones (the Norwegian zone around the island of Jan Mayern, where Norway had placed a weather station in the 1920s and annexed it in 1929). Iceland and Norway concluded the Jan Mayern agreement in 1981, which gives each side a 25 percent stake in hydrocarbon resources in a zone on the other side of the demarcation line. The agreement is deemed highly advantageous to Iceland and an example of Icelandic diplomatic and international legal skill.

The Continental Shelf committee (Landgrundsnefnd) of the Althingi worked simultaneously to prepare legislation. Seismic testing took place in 1985 after the demarcation line had been settled, but in 1989 the area was not found to be profitable. The Althingi adopted law 13/2001 on search licenses, which was inspired by Norwegian and Faroese experiences. In 2001, an Icelandic-Norwegian consortium (Geysir/Saga) was awarded a search license.

The role of knowledge and human capital for Iceland's development concerning offshore hydrocarbon search is primarily in two domains, a legal and policy domain dominated by parliament and administration, and a natural scientific, technological and commercial dominated by the private sector. In both sectors, strong human capital based on quality domestic education and successful brain circulation is emphasized by interview persons from both government and commercial sector. Especially the links to Norway through Icelanders, who have studied and worked in Norway is brought forward. Norway is a fellow Nordic country with many social and normative similarities with Iceland and with extensive offshore experience from conditions similar to the Dreki area conditions. Familiarity with Norwegian language, authorities, companies, regulations, policies and technologies by Icelandic civil servants or professionals greatly facilitate the transfer of knowledge and experiences from Norway.

The Icelandic legal licensing framework has been developed with legislation in 2009 and revised in 2011 because of poor reception from the industry. The ensuing call resulted in three licenses being awarded to Icelandic-Norwegian (the Norwegian 25 percent stake represented by Petoro) international groups. The first was a consortium of Faroe Petroleum Norge (operator) (67.5 percent), Íslensk Kolvetnis (7.5 percent) and Petoro. The second was Valiant Petroleum (owned by Canadian Ithaca Energy, Inc.) (operator) (56.25 percent), Kolvetni of Iceland (18.75 percent) and Petoro (25 percent). The third application was from the Icelandic company Eykon, which was instructed to find a foreign partner, and partnered with China National Offshore Oil Corporation and Petoro. The partnership of CNOOC and Petoro is extraordinary as it is perhaps the only interface between the Chinese and Norwegian governments under the Chinese diplomatic and political boycott of Norway because of the 2010 Nobel Peace Prize for dissident LIU Xiaobo. The partnership is also highly noteworthy for observing a Chinese national oil company working in the Arctic. The Icelandic companies are owned by a number of Icelandic investors, the Norwegian oil professional Terje Hagevang, and of particular relevance two of the main Icelandic engineering consulting firms, Mannvít and Verkís. The latter shows how technologically leading Icelandic companies are positioning themselves to take part in this possible offshore hydrocarbon adventure.

In light of the technological and especially financial requirements for exploring and producing these hydrocarbon resources, there is also a broad understanding among Icelandic authorities and companies that Icelandic companies will be supporting and servicing foreign oil companies. Icelandic companies are therefore establishing the skills and knowledge to do so. Here as well the legal and policy work, international Icelandic human capital built on quality domestic and successful brain circulation is key. The relatively very extensive foreign educational and professional experience in Icelandic engineering and other companies is highlighted. Again, Norwegian experience is emphasized. As was explained above concerning the Faroe Islands, knowledge may be the export rather than the natural resource itself. Icelandic interviewed people point out that Icelandic companies are looking to prepare themselves to service an area stretching from the rich Norwegian sector to possibilities off Greenland.

Conclusion

Arctic societies are often natural resource-based economies, which pose challenges to deriving local benefits and achieving sustainable development, for instance, because resource rents often leave the community. Iceland and the Faroe Islands are two very small communities in the Arctic that are natural resource-based, but have achieved very high levels of human development and self-government or full independence in the case of Iceland. These two societies suggest a central role for local knowledge and human capital for securing local benefits and sustainable development around natural resources, whether marine resources, renewable energy or hydrocarbons. Marine resources have and continue to play a fundamental role for the two economies, where biologically sustainable, economically efficient and politically legitimate management systems are of central importance. The two societies have come far in this quest, but the Icelandic system suffers from a widespread sense of political illegitimacy, while the Faroese system has struggled with securing economic efficiency. Renewable energy resources have played an important developmental role for both societies. Especially Iceland has very large hydro and geothermal energy resources, which have contributed much to Icelandic modernization over the twentieth century, and Iceland has built a sizeable local, but globally connected, knowledge-based sector around these resources. Hydro and recently wind has contributed significantly to

Faroese power since 1921, which is a technological development based on close technological and commercial ties especially with Norway and Denmark. There are expectations of hydrocarbon resources in the EEZs of both nations, which has however not yet yielded finds. The capital and knowledge requirements are much bigger than the other natural resources discussed, but again the Faroe Islands are demonstrating that knowledge is the key for a very small Arctic community to benefit from these resources.

Notes

1 The chapter acknowledges the central role of traditional knowledge of the Arctic indigenous peoples for sustainable development, though that is beyond the competence field of the authors.

2 This research is part of ongoing research collaboration on knowledge and natural resources in the North Atlantic by Rasmus Gjedssø Bertelsen, Jens Christian Svabo Justinussen and Coco Smits (published or under publication). Bertelsen and Justinussen would like to acknowledge the inspiration and contribution from Smits, who unfortunately could not contribute to this publication. Coco C.A. Smits, Rasmus Gjedssø Bertelsen and Jens Christian Svabo Justinussen, "The Challenges & Opportunities for Arctic Microstates in Developing an Energy Sector: The Role of Human Capital and Knowledge Institutes," *Arctic Yearbook* 3.1 (2014): 1–17, accessed April 9, 2015, www.arcticyearbook.com/images/Arcticles_2014/ Smits_AY2014_FINAL.pdf; Rasmus Gjedssø Bertelsen, Jens Christian Svabo Justinussen and Coco Smits, "Energy as a Developmental Strategy for North Atlantic Microstates in Search of Independence: Creating Knowledge-Based Energy Sectors in Iceland, Faroe Islands and Greenland," in *Handbook of the Politics of the Arctic,* edited by Geir Hønneland and Leif Christian Jensen (Cheltenham: Edward Elgar, 2015, forthcoming); Coco C.A. Smits, Jens Christian Svabo Justinussen and Rasmus Gjedssø Bertelsen, "Oil and Gas Development in the Faroese Islands, Iceland and Greenland: How Local Competence Development Contributes to a Social License to Operate" (paper presented at the Arctic Technology Conference, Copenhagen, March 23–25, 2015), accessed April 12, 2015, www.arctictech nologyconference.org.

3 For a useful introduction to Icelandic history and society, see Jóhannes Nordal and Valdimar Kristinsson (eds), *Iceland, the Republic: Handbook* (Reykjavik: Central Bank of Iceland, 1996).

4 Hannes Jónsson, *Friends in Conflict: The Anglo-Icelandic Cod Wars and the Law of the Sea* (London: C. Hurst, 1982), 240.

5 This academic and policy challenge has been the subject of intense research and policy debate in Iceland, see Þorkell Helgason and Örn D. Jónsson (eds), *Hagsæld í Húfi* [*Prosperity in Danger*] (Reykjavík: Sjávarútvegsstofnun Háskólans: Háskólaútgáfan, 1990), 144; Gísli Pálsson, Ragnar Árnason and Örn D. Jónsson (eds), *Stjórn Fiskveiða Og Skipting Fiskveiðiarðsins* [*Fisheries Management and Distribution of the Fishing Rent*] (Reykjavík: Sjávarútvegsstofnun Háskólans: Háskólaútgáfan, 1992), 110; Stein W. Wallace and Snjólfur Ólafsson (eds), *Nordic Fisheries Management Model: Description and Experience* (Copenhagen: Nordic Council of Ministers, 1994), 105.

6 Svanur Kristjánsson, "Lýðræðisbrestir Íslenska Lýðveldisins: frjálst Framsal Fiskveiðiheimilda [Democratic Failures of the Icelandic Republic: Individually Transferable Quotas]," *Skírnir* 187 (2014): 241–48.

7 Joan Pauli Joensen, "From Peasants to Fisherfolk – the Development of Faroese Fishery Until 1939" (paper presented at a Special Seminar in the Institute of

Social and Economic Research, Memorial University of Newfoundland, September 24, 1992); Joan Pauli Joensen, "Fishing in the 'Traditional' Society of the Faroe Islands," in *A History of the North Atlantic Fisheries: Volume 1, From Early Times to the Mid-Nineteenth Century*, edited by David J. Starkey, Jon Th. Thor and Ingo Heidbrink (Bremen: Verlag H.M. Mauschild GmbH, 2009), 27–48.

8 *Frágreiðing Frá Bygnaðarnevndini – Sambært Avtalu Millum Føroya Landsstýri Og Stjórn Danmarkar Frá 1. Februar 1993*, (Tórshavn: Føroya Landsstýrið, 1993); Jens Christian Svabo Justinussen, *Fanget i Fisken* (Roskilde: Roskilde Universitetscenter, 1999); Lise Lyck, *The Faroese Economy in a Strategic Perspective* (Stockholm: Nordiska institutet för regionalpolitisk forskning, 1997).

9 Søren Eliasen et al. (eds), *Nordic Experience of Fisheries Management*, vol. 579 (Copenhagen: Nordic Council of Ministers, 2009), 84, accessed April 12, 2015, http://norden.diva-portal.org/smash/record.jsf?pid=diva2%3A701979&dswid=1870; Jørgen Løkkegård et al., *Rapport Om Den Færøske Regulering Af Fiskeriet: Færømodellen* (København: Fødevareøkonomisk Institut, 2004), accessed April 12, 2015, http://ifro.ku.dk/english/staff/staffenvironment/?pure=en%2Fpubli cations%2Frapport-om-den-faeroeske-regulering-af-fiskeriet(24ec0a50-a1be-11dd-b6ae-000ea68e967b)%2Fexport.html.

10 Stig S. Gezelius and Jesper Raakjær (eds), *Making Fisheries Management Work: Implementation of Policies for Sustainable Fishing* (London: Springer, 2008), 236; Jesper Raakjær, *A Fisheries Management System in Crisis: The EU Common Fisheries Policy* (Aalborg: Aalborg University Press, 2009), 174.

11 European Commission, *Studies in the Field of the Common Fisheries Policy and Maritime Affairs. Lot 4: Impact Assessment Studies Related to the CFP, Impact Assessment of Discard Reducing Policies* (Brussels: European Commission, 2011); Benoit Mesnil, "When Discards Survive: Accounting for Survival of Discards in Fisheries Assessments," *Aquatic Living Resources* 9.3 (1996): 209–15.

12 Ibid.

13 There are no exact numbers for discards though, and there can be great variation between areas, depending on the type of fishery. The European Commission reports that,

> Discarding occurs in EU fisheries sometimes at high levels, such as: 30–60% for the finfish fishery off the Iberian Peninsula (MRAG, 2007); 50% of the catch in North Sea beam trawl fleets (MRAG, 2007); between 20–98% in the North Sea nephrops trawl fleet (Enever *et al.*, 2009); and 40% of most species through bottom-trawling in North east Atlantic fisheries (STECF, 2006).

> (Ibid.)

14 S.H. Jákupsstovu et al., "Effort Regulation of the Demersal Fisheries at the Faroe Islands: A 10-Year Appraisal," *ICES Journal of Marine Science: Journal Du Conseil* 64.4 (2007): 730–37.

15 The history of hydropower in Iceland and its socio-economic impacts are well set out in his Icelandic literature, which is based on Sigurður Ragnarsson, "Innilokun Eða Opingátt: Þættir Úr Sögu Fossamálsins [Closure or Openness: Elements of the History of the Waterfall Question]," *Saga* 13 (1975): 5–105; Sigurður Ragnarsson, "Fossakaup Og Framkvæmdaáform: Þættir Úr Sögu Fossamálsins. Fyrri Hluti [Waterfall Investments and Planning: Elements of the History of the 'Waterfall Question'. First Part]," *Saga* 14 (1976): 125–82; Sigurður Ragnarsson, "Fossakaup Og Framkvæmdaáform: Þættir Úr Sögu Fossamálsins. Siðari Hluti [Waterfall Investments and Planning: Elements of the History of the 'Waterfall Question'. Second Part]," *Saga* 15 (1977): 125–222; Helgi Kristjánsson, *Birta, Afl Og Ylur: Saga Rafmagnsveita Ríkisins í 50 Ár 1947–1997* [*Light, Power and Heat: The History of the Iceland State Electricity for 50*

Years 1947–1997] (Reykjavík: Rafmagnsveitur Ríkisins, 1997), 172; Helgi M. Sigurðsson, *Vatnsaflsvirkjanir á Íslandi* [*Hydro Power Stations in Iceland*] (Reykjavík: Verkfræðistofa Sigurðar Thoroddsen, 2002), 176; Sveinn Þórðarson, *Afl í Segulæðum: Saga Rafmagns á Íslandi í 100 Ár* [*Power in Magnetic Veins: The Story of Electricity in Iceland in 100 Years*] (Reykjavík: Verkfræðingafélag Íslands, 2004), 259; Pétur H. Ármannsson, "Orkuver Og Arkitektúr [Power Plants and Architecture]," in *Landsvirkjun 1965–2005: Fyrirtækið Og Umhverfi Þess* [*Landsvirkjun 1965–2005: The Company and its Environment*], edited by Sigrún Pálsdóttir (Reykjavík: Hið íslenska bókmenntafélag, 2005), 201–42; Guðmundur Hálfdanarson and Unnur Birna Karlsdóttir, "Náttúrusýn Og Nýting Fallvatna [View of Nature and Utilization of Water Falls]," in *Landsvirkjun 1965–2005: Fyrirtækið Og Umhverfi Þess* [*Landsvirkjun 1965–2005: The Company and its Environment*], edited by Sigrún Pálsdóttir (Reykjavík: Hið íslenska bókmenntafélag, 2005), 165–99; Birgir Jónsson, "Þróun Tækniþekkingar Og Fagvinnu Við Virkjunarframkvæmdir Landsvirkjunar [Technological Development by the Constructions of Landsvirkjun]," in *Landsvirkjun 1965–2005: Fyrirtækið Og Umhverfi Þess* [*Landsvirkjun 1965–2005: The Company and its Environment*], edited by Sigrún Pálsdóttir (Reykjavík: Hið íslenska bókmenntafélag, 2005), 243–66; Gunnar Helgi Kristinsson, "Raforka, Efnishyggja Og Stjórnmálaátök [Electricity, Materialism and Political Strife]," in *Landsvirkjun 1965–2005: Fyrirtækið Og Umhverfi Þess* [*Landsvirkjun 1965–2005: The Company and its Environment*], edited by Sigrún Pálsdóttir (Reykjavík: Hið íslenska bókmenntafélag, 2005), 137–63; Sigrún Pálsdóttir (ed.), *Landsvirkjun 1965–2005: Fyrirtækið Og Umhverfi Þess* [*Landsvirkjun 1965–2005: The Company and its Environment*] (Reykjavík: Hið íslenska bókmenntafélag, 2005), 324; Sigrún Pálsdóttir, "Landsvirkjun: Fyrirtækið, Framkvæmdir Þess Og Hlutverk [Landsvirkjun: The Company, its Constructions and its Role]," in *Landsvirkjun 1965–2005: Fyrirtækið Og Umhverfi Þess* [*Landsvirkjun 1965–2005: The Company and its Environment*], edited by Sigrún Pálsdóttir (Reykjavík: Hið íslenska bókmenntafélag, 2005), 13–110; Sumarliði R. Ísleifsson, *Saga Rafmagnsveitu Reykjavíkur 1921–1998* [*The History of Reykjavik Electricity 1921–1998*] (Reykjavík: Orkuveita Reykjavíkur, 2007), 270; Unnur Birna Karlsdóttir, *Þar Sem Fossarnir Falla: Náttúrusýn Og Nýting Fallvatna á Íslandi 1900–2008* [*Where the Water Falls: Views of Nature and use of Waterfalls in Iceland 1900–2008*] (Reykjavík: Hið íslenska bókmenntafélag, 2010), 307.

16 President of Iceland—Dr. Ólafur Ragnar Grímsson—speaking at Harvard Business School on April 4, 2007 and at Harvard University on September 25, 2007.

17 The history of Icelandic geothermal power and its impact on Icelandic society is set out by the former head of the Geothermal Division of the National Energy Authority of Iceland, Guðmundur Pálmason. See Guðmundur Pálmason (ed.), *Jarðhitabók, Eðli Og Nýting Auðlindar* [*The Book on Geothermal Heating: The Nature and Use of Resources*] (Reykjavík: Hið íslenska bókmenntafélag, 2005), 298.

18 Valtýr Guðmundsson, "Upphitun Bæjar Með Jarðhita [Heating Towns with Geothermal Heat]," *Eimreiðin* 16.1 (1910): 31–32.

19 Ingvar Birgir Friðleifsson, Andrés Svanbjörnsson and Loftur Thorsteinsson, "Icelandic Experience in Transfer of Energy Technology," *Tímarit Verkfræðingafélags Íslands* 69 (1984): 6–10.

20 Poul Andreasen, *Elektrisitetsverkið í Botni* (Tórshavn: Egið forlag, 1996).

21 Ibid.

22 Eiden Müller, *S.e.v. 1954–1979* (Tórshavn: El-felagið SEV, 1979); SEV, *Ársfráðgreiðing Og Ársroknskapur 2012* [*Annual Report and Annual Accounts 2012*] (Tórshavn: SEV, 2012).

23 Tórmóður Dahl, *Ídnaðurin í Føroyum – Quo Vadis?* (Tórshavn: Ídnaðarráðgevin. Ídnaðarstovan, 1974).

24 Ingolf S. Olsen, "Røkt Ætlar at Fleirfalda Vindorkuframleiðsluna ['Røkt' – Name of the Utility Company – Plans to Multiply the Production of Wind Energy]," *Mið & Magn* 10 (2011): 16–21.

25 Týdningarmikið Stig á Grønu Kósini [Important Step in the Green Direction]," SEV, accessed April 11, 2015, www.sev.fo/Default.aspx?ID=196.

26 See, for instance, Jarðfeingið, "Kort Yvir Jarðhitaboringar," accessed November 4, 2015, www.jardfeingi.fo/Default.aspx?pageid=18167.

27 In Faroese: "…tað verður øgiliga ringt hjá okkum at forklára, og vit skulu hava eitt eyka fyribrygdi aftanfyri, fyri at kunna forklára hendan hitan." Ibid.

28 Knud Simonsen and Bárður Á. Niclasen, *On the Energy Potential in the Tidal Streams on the Faroe Shelf* (Tórshavn: University of the Faroe Islands, 2011); Bárður Á. Niclasen and Knud Simonsen, *High Resolution Wave Climate of the Faroe Islands* (Tórshavn: University of the Faroe Islands, 2012).

29 Centre of Maritime Studies & Engineering," Vinnuháskúlin, accessed April 13, 2015, www.vinnuhaskulin.fo/upload/Vinnuháskúlin.pdf.

30 Vinnumálaráðið, *Comprehensive Plan for Electric Energy in the Faroe Islands* (Tórshavn: Ministry of Trade and Industry, 2011).

31 Frederik Harhoff, "Rigsfællesskabet [The Danish Realm]" (Dr. Jur., Københavns Universitet, 1993), 1–578; Bertelsen et al., "Energy as a Developmental Strategy."

32 Oljuráðleggingarnevndin, *Fyrireikingar Til Oljuleiting: Frágreiðing Frá Oljuráðleggingarnevnd Landsstýrisins* (Tórshavn: Oljuráðleggingarnevndin vegna Føroya landsstýri, 1997).

33 Petur Joensen, "Exploration – A Discovery Present," (presentation at the Oil Conference, Tórshavn, June 4, 2013), accessed November 11, 2014, www.foib. fo/; Jan Müller, "Hvat hendir, um vit finna olju [What Happens if We Find Oil?]" (paper presented at "Føroysk Oljuráðstevna á Fólkatingi 21. Februar 2014 [The Faroese Oil Conference at the Danish Parliament, February 21, 2014]," accessed November 23, 2014, www.foib.fo/get.file?ID=12041; "500 Fólk Knýtt at West Hercules [500 People Worked at West Hercules]," Kringvarp Føroya, accessed April 12, 2015, http://kvf.fo/netvarp/sv/2014/08/21/201408 21500folkkittatvesthercules.

34 Bertelsen et al., "Energy as a Developmental Strategy."

35 Ibid.

36 Rakstrarviðurskiftið Gjaldsjavnans [Summary of Current Account]," Hagstova Føroya, accessed November 23, 2014, www.hagstova.fo/fo/hagtalsgrunnur/tjodarroknskapur/gjaldsjavni.

37 This section is based on interviews with key officials at the National Energy Authority of Iceland, the Construction Authority of Iceland, and interested Icelandic companies. Information on oil and gas exploration can be found as well as at the website of the National Energy Authority Orkustofnun: "Oil & Gas Exploration," Orkustofnun, accessed April 9, 2015, www.nea.is/oil-and-gas-exploration/.

References

Andreasen, Poul. *Elektrisitetsverkið í Botni*. Tórshavn: Egið forlag, 1996.

Ármannsson, Pétur H. "Orkuver Og Arkitektúr [Power Plants and Architecture]." In *Landsvirkjun 1965–2005: Fyrirtækið Og Umhverfi Þess [Landsvirkjun 1965–2005: The Company and its Environment]*, edited by Sigrún Pálsdóttir, 201–42. Reykjavík: Hið íslenska bókmenntafélag, 2005.

Bertelsen, Rasmus Gjedssø, Jens Christian Svabo Justinussen and Coco Smits. "Energy as a Developmental Strategy for North Atlantic Microstates in Search of Independence: Creating Knowledge-Based Energy Sectors in Iceland, Faroe Islands and

Greenland." In *Handbook of the Politics of the Arctic*, edited by Geir Hønneland and Leif Christian Jensen. Cheltenham: Edward Elgar, 2015, forthcoming.

Frágreiðing Frá Bygnaðarnevndini – Sambært Avtalu Millum Føroya Landsstýri Og Stjórn Danmarkar Frá 1. Februar 1993. Tórshavn: Føroya Landsstýrið, 1993.

Dahl, Tórmóður. *'Ídnaðurin í Føroyum – Quo Vadis?* Tórshavn: Ídnaðarráðgevin. Ídnaðarstovan, 1974.

Eliasen, Søren, Sten Sverdrup-Jensen, Petter Holm and Jahn Petter Johnsen (eds). *Nordic Experience of Fisheries Management*. Temanord vol. 579. Copenhagen: Nordic Council of Ministers, 2009.

European Commission. *Studies in the Field of the Common Fisheries Policy and Maritime Affairs. Lot 4: Impact Assessment Studies Related to the CFP, Impact Assessment of Discard Reducing Policies*. Brussels: European Commission, 2011.

Friðleifsson, Ingvar Birgir, Andrés Svanbjörnsson and Loftur Thorsteinsson. "Icelandic Experience in Transfer of Energy Technology." *Tímarit Verkfræðingafélags Íslands* 69 (1984): 6–10.

Gezelius, Stig S. "The Problem of Implementing Policies for Sustainable Fishing." In *Making Fisheries Management Work: Implementation of Policies for Sustainable Fishing*, edited by Stig S. Gezelius and Jesper Raakjær, 1–25. London: Springer, 2008.

Gezelius, Stig S. and Jesper Raakjær (eds). *Making Fisheries Management Work: Implementation of Policies for Sustainable Fishing*. London: Springer, 2008.

Guðmundsson, Valtýr. "Upphitun Bæjar Með Jarðhita [Heating Towns with Geothermal Heat]." *Eimreiðin* 16.1 (1910): 31–32.

Hagstova Føroya. "Rakstrarviðurskiftið Gjaldsjavnans." Accessed November 23, 2014, www.hagstova.fo/fo/hagtalsgrunnur/tjodarroknskapur/gjaldsjavni.

Hálfdanarson, Guðmundur and Unnur Birna Karlsdóttir. "Náttúrusýn Og Nýting Fallvatna [View of Nature and Utilization of Water Falls]." In *Landsvirkjun 1965–2005: Fyrirtækið Og Umhverfi Þess [Landsvirkjun 1965–2005: The Company and its Environment]*, edited by Sigrún Pálsdóttir, 165–99. Reykjavík: Hið íslenska bókmenntafélag, 2005.

Harhoff, Frederik. "Rigsfællesskabet." Dr. Jur., Københavns Universitet, 1993.

Helgason, Þorkell and Örn D. Jónsson (eds). *Hagsæld í Húfi [Prosperity in Danger]*. Reykjavík: Sjávarútvegsstofnun Háskólans: Háskólaútgáfan, 1990.

Ísleifsson, Sumarliði R. *Saga Rafmagnsveitu Reykjavíkur 1921–1998 [The History of Reykjavik Electricity 1921–1998]*. Reykjavík: Orkuveita Reykjavíkur, 2007.

Jákupsstovu, S.H., L.R. Cruz, J-J. Maguire and J. Reiner. "Effort Regulation of the Demersal Fisheries at the Faroe Islands: A 10-Year Appraisal." *ICES Journal of Marine Science: Journal Du Conseil* 64.4 (2007): 730–37.

Jarðfeingið. "Kort Yvir Jarðhitaboringar." Accessed April 11, 2015, www.jardfeingi. fo/Default.aspx?pageid=18167.

Joensen, Joan Pauli. "From Peasants to Fisherfolk: The Development of Faroese Fishery until 1939." Paper presented at a "Special Seminar" at the Institute of Social and Economic Research (ISER), Memorial University of Newfoundland, Newfoundland, September 24, 1992.

Joensen, Joan Pauli. "Fishing in the 'Traditional' Society of the Faroe Islands." In *A History of the North Atlantic Fisheries: Volume 1, From Early Times to the Mid-Nineteenth Century*, edited by David J. Starkey, Jon Th. Thor and Ingo Heidbrink, 27–48. Bremen: Verlag H.M. Mauschild GmbH, 2009.

Joensen, Petur. "Exploration: A Discovery Present," Presentation at the Oil Conference in Tórshavn, June 4, 2013. Accessed November 23, 2014, www.foib.fo/.

Jónsson, Birgir. "Þróun Tækniþekkingar Og Fagvinnu Við Virkjunarframkvæmdir Landsvirkjunar [Technological Development by the Constructions of Landsvirkjun]." In *Landsvirkjun 1965–2005: Fyrirtækið Og Umhverfi Þess* [*Landsvirkjun 1965–2005: The Company and its Environment*], edited by Sigrún Pálsdóttir, 243–66. Reykjavík: Hið íslenska bókmenntafélag, 2005.

Jónsson, Hannes. *Friends in Conflict: The Anglo-Icelandic Cod Wars and the Law of the Sea*. London: C. Hurst, 1982.

Justinussen, Jens Christian Svabo. *Fanget i Fisken*. Roskilde: Roskilde Universitetscenter, 1999.

Karlsdóttir, Unnur Birna. *Þar Sem Fossarnir Falla: Náttúrusýn Og Nýting Fallvatna á Íslandi 1900–2008* [*Where the Water Falls: Views of Nature and Use of Waterfalls in Iceland 1900–2008*]. Reykjavík: Hið íslenska bókmenntafélag, 2010.

Kristinsson, Gunnar Helgi. "Raforka, Efnishyggja Og Stjórnmálaátök [Electricity, Materialism and Political Strife]." In *Landsvirkjun 1965–2005: Fyrirtækið Og Umhverfi Þess* [*Landsvirkjun 1965–2005: The Company and its Environment*], edited by Sigrún Pálsdóttir, 137–63. Reykjavík: Hið íslenska bókmenntafélag, 2005.

Kristjánsson, Helgi. *Birta, Afl Og Ylur: Saga Rafmagnsveita Ríkisins í 50 Ár 1947–1997* [*Light, Power and Heat: The History of the Iceland State Electricity for 50 Years 1947–1997*]. Reykjavík: Rafmagnsveitur Ríkisins, 1997.

Kristjánsson, Svanur. "Lýðræðisbrestir Íslenska Lýðveldisins: frjálst Framsal Fiskveiðiheimilda [Democratic Failures of the Icelandic Republic: Individually Transferable Quotas]." *Skírnir* 187, (2014): 241–48.

KVF. "500 Fólk Knýtt at West Hercules." Accessed April 12, 2015, http://kvf.fo/netvarp/sv/2014/08/21/20140821500folkkittatvesthercules.

Løkkegård, Jørgen, Jesper Levring Andersen, J. Bøje, Hans Staby Frost and H. Hovgård. *Rapport Om Den Færøske Regulering Af Fiskeriet: Færømodellen*. København: Fødevareøkonomisk Institut, 2004.

Lyck, Lise. *The Faroese Economy in a Strategic Perspective*. Stockholm: Nordiska institutet för regionalpolitisk forskning, 1997.

Mesnil, Benoit. "When Discards Survive: Accounting for Survival of Discards in Fisheries Assessments." *Aquatic Living Resources* 9.3 (1996): 209–15.

Müller, Eiden. *S.e.v. 1954–1979*. Tórshavn: El-felagið SEV, 1979.

Jan Müller, "Hvat hendir, um vit finna olju? [What Happens if We Find Oil?]" (paper presented at "Føroysk Oljuráðstevna á Fólkatingi 21. Februar 2014 [The Faroese Oil Conference at the Danish Parliament, February 21, 2014]," accessed November 23, 2014, www.foib.fo/get.file?ID=12041.

Niclasen, Bárður Á. and Knud Simonsen. *High Resolution Wave Climate of the Faroe Islands*. Tórshavn: University of the Faroe Islands, 2012.

Nordal, Jóhannes and Valdimar Kristinsson (eds). *Iceland, the Republic: Handbook*. Reykjavik: Central Bank of Iceland, 1996.

Oljuráðleggingarnevndin. *Fyrireikingar Til Oljuleiting: Frágreiðing Frá Oljuráðleggingarnevnd Landsstýrisins*. Tórshavn: Oljuráðleggingarnevndin vegna Føroya landsstýri, 1997.

Olsen, Ingolf S. "Røkt Ætlar at Fleirfalda Vindorkuframleiðsluna." *Mið & Magn* 10 (2011): 16–21.

Orkustofnun. "Oil & Gas Exploration." Accessed April 9, 2015, www.nea.is/oil-and-gas-exploration/.

Pálmason, Guðmundur (ed.). *Jarðhitabók, Eðli Og Nýting Auðlindar* [*The Book on Geothermal Heating: The Nature and use of Resources*]. Reykjavík: Hið íslenska bókmenntafélag, 2005.

Pálsdóttir, Sigrún (ed.). *Landsvirkjun 1965–2005: Fyrirtækið Og Umhverfi Þess* [*Landsvirkjun 1965–2005: The Company and its Environment*]. Reykjavík: Hið íslenska bókmenntafélag, 2005.

Pálsdóttir, Sigrún. "Landsvirkjun: Fyrirtækið, Framkvæmdir Þess Og Hlutverk [Landsvirkjun: The Company, its Constructions and its Role]." In *Landsvirkjun 1965–2005: Fyrirtækið Og Umhverfi Þess* [*Landsvirkjun 1965–2005: The Company and its Environment*], edited by Sigrún Pálsdóttir, 13–110. Reykjavík: Hið íslenska bókmenntafélag, 2005.

Pálsson, Gísli, Ragnar Árnason and Örn D. Jónsson (eds). *Stjórn Fiskveiða Og Skipting Fiskveiðiarðsins* [*Fisheries Management and Distribution of the Fishing Rent*]. Reykjavík: Sjávarútvegsstofnun Háskólans: Háskólaútgáfan, 1992.

Raakjær, Jesper. *A Fisheries Management System in Crisis: The EU Common Fisheries Policy.* Aalborg: Aalborg University Press, 2009.

Ragnarsson, Sigurður. "Innilokun Eða Opingátt: Þættir Úr Sögu Fossamálsins [Closure Or Openness: Elements of the History of the Waterfall Question]." *Saga* 13 (1975): 5–105.

Ragnarsson, Sigurður. "Fossakaup Og Framkvæmdaáform: Þættir Úr Sögu Fossamálsins. Fyrri Hluti [Waterfall Investments and Planning: Elements of the History of the 'Waterfall Question'. First Part]." *Saga* 14 (1976): 125–82.

Ragnarsson, Sigurður. "Fossakaup Og Framkvæmdaáform: Þættir Úr Sögu Fossamálsins. Siðari Hluti [Waterfall Investments and Planning: Elements of the History of the 'Waterfall Question'. Second Part]." *Saga* 15 (1977): 125–222.

SEV. *Ársfráðgreiðing Og Ársroknskapur 2012/Annual Report and Annual Accounts 2012.* Tórshavn: SEV, 2012.

SEV. "Týdningarmikið Stig á Grønu Kósini." *SEV.* Accessed April 11, 2015. www.sev.fo/Default.aspx?ID=196.

Sigurðsson, Helgi M. *Vatnsaflsvirkjanir á Íslandi* [*Hydro Power Stations in Iceland*]. Reykjavík: Verkfræðistofa Sigurðar Thoroddsen, 2002.

Simonsen, Knud and Bárður Á. Niclasen. *On the Energy Potential in the Tidal Streams on the Faroe Shelf.* Tórshavn: University of the Faroe Islands, 2011.

Smits, Coco C.A., Rasmus Gjedssø Bertelsen and Jens Christian Svabo Justinussen. "The Challenges & Opportunities for Arctic Microstates in Developing an Energy Sector: The Role of Human Capital and Knowledge Institutes." *Arctic Yearbook* 3.1 (2014): 1–17. Accessed April 9, 2015, www.arcticyearbook.com/images/Arctcles_2014/Smits_AY2014_FINAL.pdf.

Smits, Coco C.A., Jens Christian Svabo Justinussen and Rasmus Gjedssø Bertelsen. "Oil and Gas Development in the Faroese Islands, Iceland and Greenland: How Local Competence Development Contributes to a Social License to Operate." Paper presented at the Arctic Technology Conference, Copenhagen, March 23–25, 2015.

Þórðarson, Sveinn. *Afl í Segulæðum: Saga Rafmagns á Íslandi í 100 Ár* [*Power in Magnetic Veins: The Story of Electricity in Iceland in 100 Years*]. Reykjavík: Verkfræðingafélag Íslands, 2004.

Þórhallsson, Baldur. "Iceland's External Affairs in the Middle Ages: The Shelter of Norwegian Sea Power." *Stjórnmál Og Stjórnsýsla. Veftímarit* 8.1 (2012): 5–37.

Þórhallsson, Baldur and Þorsteinn Kristinsson. "Iceland's External Affairs from 1400 to the Reformation: Anglo-German Economic and Societal Shelter in a Danish Political Vacuum." *Stjórnmál Og Stjórnsýsla. Veftímarit* 9.1 (2013): 113–37.

Vinnuháskúlin. "Centre of Maritime Studies & Engineering." Accessed April 13, 2013, www.vinnuhaskulin.fo/upload/Vinnuháskúlin.pdf.

Vinnumálaráðið. *Comprehensive Plan for Electric Energy in the Faroe Islands.* Tórshavn: Ministry of Trade and Industry, 2011.

Wallace, Stein W. and Snjólfur Ólafsson (eds). *Nordic Fisheries Management Model: Description and Experience.* Copenhagen: Nordic Council of Ministers, 1994.

15 EU–Greenland relations and sustainable development in the Arctic

Cécile Pelaudeix

Introduction

Greenland and the European Union (EU) have enjoyed a long history of cooperation since the autonomous territory withdrew from the EU in 1985. Greenland, an island with only 57,000 inhabitants, is still part of the Kingdom of Denmark. It has enjoyed political representation in the Danish Parliament, the Folketing, for sixty-two years and was a member of the European Parliament from 1979–1984. Since the Greenland Home Rule Act in 1978,[1] Greenland has exercised legislative and executive power in areas including education, fishing and trade inside the territory. And, since the Act on Greenland Self-Government in 2009, Greenland has exercised jurisdiction in areas including mineral resources.[2] However, Greenland is currently facing major challenges with regard to both economic and social development. The Act on Greenland Self-Government froze Danish subsidies, so Greenland needs to stimulate economic growth in order to balance its budget and to pave the way for independence from Denmark. Gaining independence from Denmark will depend on economic factors and, among other things, the agreement of the Folketing; this political agenda was put forward by the former Greenlandic Government (2013–2014), but it lacks a clear time-frame and an accurate economic and security plan.

As the Arctic is becoming an important geopolitical and geo-economic region, the EU is developing its Arctic policy for which the Union has strengthened its ties with Greenland through various partnerships in addition to the fisheries agreement. The EU is committed to contributing to education and sustainable development, and, in particular, it is interested in securing its supply of raw materials, which are believed to be in plentiful supply in Greenland.[3]

This chapter analyses the relationship between the EU and Greenland with regard to sustainable development. It explores the efforts deployed by the EU institutions on the bilateral level to support cooperation on sustainable development with Greenland and the legal framework that underpins this relationship. The next section analyzes the geo-economic and geostrategic importance of Greenland for the EU from a historical perspective. Part III examines how the increasing relationship with Greenland is reflected in the EU Arctic policy and conversely the extent to which the EU Arctic policy-making process affects the relationship with Greenland. Finally, this chapter discusses the political and legal levers and constraints the EU experiences in developing partnerships on sustainable development with Greenland.

Geo-economic and geostrategic importance of Greenland for the EU

Relations with the EU: historical and political background

After almost 300 years, Greenland officially lost its status as a Danish colony in 1953 with the establishment of the 5th Constitution to become a Danish county, a status that remained at the time, when the Kingdom of Denmark joined the EU in 1972. As such, Greenland could participate in the Constitutional monarchy and was represented by two members of parliament in the Folketing in Copenhagen.[4] One year later, in 1954, Denmark took part in a UN meeting in New York and listed Greenland as a "non-self-governing territory," a qualification perceived by Greenlandic actors as an emphasis on the global stage of Greenland's continued dependence on the Kingdom of Denmark.[5] In 1964, the introduction of new legislation that distinguished between birthplaces created a clear economic division between Greenlanders and Danes in Greenland[6] and questioned their equality. It was at this point that a political party, the Inuit Party, was created. Brøsted and Gulløv (1976) suggest that this initiated a change in the political scene in Greenland as a consequence of the increase in Danish immigration and Danish economic domination.[7]

The decision of the Kingdom of Denmark to join the European Community (EC) in 1972 was another contentious issue for Greenlanders with regard to their ability to control their own fate. The decision was made by a referendum in which both Danes and Greenlanders voted whether or not to join the EC: Greenlanders were concerned about the protection of their fishing rights—over 70 percent of Greenlanders opposed to Greenland membership[8]—but their vote was not considered distinctly from the vote in Denmark. The decision to join the EC, despite Greenlanders' position, was considered an "eye-opener" and even a "wake-up call" by Greenlandic leaders,[9] who subsequently developed their own white paper: a Home Rule commission was established in 1975. In 1982, Greenland held a new referendum on the same issue in which 53 percent of the voters expressed a preference to leave the EC.[10] The withdrawal of Greenland from the EC was governed by a treaty known as the Greenland Treaty, which recognized Greenland as a "distinct community of the Kingdom of Denmark."[11] It was completed in 1985. However, owing to their Danish citizenship, Greenlanders are still EU citizens. Before leaving the EU, Greenland held a seat in the European Parliament: in 1979, Finn Lynge (Siumut party) was elected to the European Parliament (Socialist group) following the first EU elections in Denmark. He was then re-elected in 1984. During his time in the European Parliament, Finn Lynge was a member of the Committee on Agriculture, the Committee on the Environment, Public Health and Consumer Protection, and the Committee on Legal Affairs and Citizens' Rights.

While the Treaty organized the withdrawal of Greenland from the EC, it also established Greenland as one of the EU's overseas countries and territories (OCTs) (Article 3 of the Protocol on special arrangements for Greenland),[12] which laid the foundations for a strong relationship between the EC and Greenland. The OCT association arrangements with the EU are open to countries and territories that depend on EU Member States.[13] These Member States are Denmark, France, the Netherlands and the United Kingdom, and the OCT association arrangements apply to twenty-one countries and territories. Thus Greenland can only benefit from the OCT arrangement by virtue of its sovereign links with Denmark and Denmark's membership of the EU.

Covered by Part IV of the Treaty on the Functioning of the European Union (TFEU), the OCT arrangement aims to promote the economic and social development of the OCTs. The first fisheries agreement—agreed between the EU and the governments of Greenland and Denmark—dates back to 1985: it ensures that Greenland receives compensation for opening Greenlandic waters to the EU fleet.[14] The Greenland–EU fisheries agreements—in force between 1985 and 2006—entitled Greenland to an annual allocation of €42.8 million.

Until December 31, 2006, all EU financial assistance to Greenland (€42.8 million per year) was channeled through the fisheries agreement between the EU and Greenland. However, at some point, the amount of compensation for opening Greenlandic waters to EU fleet was deemed disproportionate.[15] The compensation amount was thus revised, and a separate partnership was established to support sustainable development in Greenland.[16] The Commission issued a Communication in 2002, and the Council agreed Conclusions in 2003 that opened negotiations for an EU partnership with Greenland covering two separate aspects: a Fisheries Agreement adjusted to the real benefit offered to the EU's fisheries industry, and a Partnership Agreement aimed at preserving "the close and lasting links between the partners, while supporting the sustainable development of Greenland."[17] According to the Fisheries Agreement, the owners of vessels concerned were obliged to pay to the Greenlandic authorities a license fee to access its waters:[18] the EU paid Greenland €17.8 million per year between 2007–2013.

Apart from the Fisheries Agreement, the financial assistance of the Partnership Agreement for 2007–2013 amounted to a total of €175 million for the entire seven-year period (€25 million per year). Greenland, on its own initiative, chose to allocate the entire amount to education.[19] Financial assistance from the EU has increased to €217.8 million for the period 2014–2020 (excluding fisheries).

EU–Greenland partnership and Greenland's strategic position in the Arctic arena

Greenland and the EU enjoy close economic and social ties through agreements which rely, as mentioned above, on Greenland being a constitutional part of the Kingdom of Denmark. The EU is Greenland's main trading partner. In 2010, Greenland's exports to the EU (mainly food and live animals) amounted to €331 million (92.7 percent of Greenland's total exports) and Greenland's imports from the EU were valued at €614 million (68.9 percent of Greenland's total imports). Imports from the EU include mineral fuels, machinery and transport equipment (47 percent in total).[20]

In recent years, the geopolitical importance of Greenland has evolved significantly. First, Greenland's territory has abundant mineral resources (ore, rare earth elements and gemstones such as rubies and diamonds) and both offshore and onshore hydrocarbon resources. Second, the emergence of the Arctic as an important geopolitical region in which the EU has various interests makes Greenland a strategic territory.[21] Denmark provides €470 million in economic aid to Greenland each year, which represents approximately 40 percent of Greenland's GDP. Since 2009, the government of Greenland has stimulated the development of extractive industries in order to lessen its economic dependence on Denmark. The expectations related to the development of mineral extractive projects are reflected in the passing of two major pieces of legislation: the Large Scale Act, which aims to facilitate the employment of foreign labor during the construction phase of a mining site, and the repeal of the zero-tolerance policy against exploiting minerals with radioactive elements. Both acts still have to be accepted by Denmark in the parliament, since they affect Denmark's immigration law and Denmark's ratified international obligations; it is still Denmark, as a state, that is responsible for Greenland's activities in the international community.

The Partnership Agreement between the EU, on the one hand, and Greenland and the Kingdom of Denmark, on the other, was renewed for the period 2014–2020. Article 1 of the Partnership acknowledges the geostrategic position of Greenland in the Arctic region, the issues of exploration and exploitation of natural resources, including raw materials, and ensures enhanced cooperation and policy dialogue on these issues.[22] In the context of Greenland's growing strategic importance, the attempt to define areas of support to strengthen sustainable development has given rise to debate, which I will analyze in Part IV of this chapter.

Since 1985, when only the Fisheries Agreement existed, cooperation between the EU and Greenland/Denmark has increased significantly. A specific Partnership for sustainable development has been created and a veterinary control agreement has also been signed. The European Environment Agency (EEA) has also signed two cooperation agreements with Greenland: one with the government of Greenland in 2010 to improve environmental monitoring and data sharing, and another in 2012 with the Ministry of Health to improve the sharing of data and information on the environmental impacts on human health.[23] An agreement was also reached to help Greenland trade its diamonds on the EU market.[24]

These important changes in the relation between the EU and Greenland/Denmark also impact on the EU Arctic policy, which has been in development since 2008. The next section of this chapter analyzes how these changes are reflected in the EU Arctic policy and, conversely, it also examines the extent to which the EU Arctic policy-making process has affected the relationship with Greenland.

The EU Arctic policy and Greenland

Drivers and pillars

The EU Arctic policy was initiated in 2008 in the context of a growing awareness of the global impacts of climate change on international security. Acknowledging the "evolving geo-strategy of the Arctic region," the EU emphasized the need to secure its trade and resources interests.[25] The 2008 report submitted by Solana and Ferrero-Waldner to the European Council suggested that the EU should "develop an EU Arctic policy based on the evolving geo-strategy of the Arctic region, taking into account the access to resources and the opening of new trade routes."[26] Since then, the EU has been developing its Arctic policy, which, in 2016, relies on three pillars: support knowledge (on the environment and climate change); act responsibly with regard to sustainable development; and intensify engagement in terms of international cooperation.[27]

The EP has demonstrated consistent commitment to the protection of the Arctic environment since the 2008 resolution, including the aborted 2009 resolution on an Arctic Treaty, the 2011 EP resolution—which displays a more consistent approach with the Commission and the Council—and the 2014 EP resolution on the EU strategy for the Arctic, which recommends the development of a network of Arctic conservation areas. As far as sustainable development is concerned, the EU has interests in energy as is stated in the seminal document of the EU Arctic policy,[28] in the EP resolution of October 9, 2008 on Arctic governance,[29] and in subsequent documents. Indeed, the EU is dependent on oil and gas imports from Norway and Russia, and it has to diversify its imports of rare earth elements (hereinafter REE).[30]

In 2012, the EU's concept of cooperation in the Arctic arena replaced the concept of governance, which had caused some controversy in the Arctic political arena.[31] Therefore, at this time, the EU ambition to weigh, as a rule-maker or regulator, on the governance of the Arctic region *as a whole* decreased. Nevertheless, since 2012, the EU has continued to develop an environmental policy based on high standards, particularly in light of the 2010 Deepwater Horizon accident, which triggered the need to increase offshore safety: the EU enacted a directive on the safety of offshore oil and gas operations with EEA relevance that came into force on July 18, 2013.[32]

Greenland in the EU Arctic policy

The interest in Greenland in the EU Arctic policy appears in the 2008 Commission Communication as a consequence of several EU Member States and EEA Members having Arctic territories. The Communication states that "additional efforts should be envisaged to make the EU an even more important partner for Greenland in managing its fragile environment and the challenges confronting its population."

The EP resolution 2011 introduces a significantly increased focus on Greenland and expands on the notion of resources.[33] Ever since China placed restrictions on its exports of raw materials and rare earth elements in 2009, EU officials have grown increasingly alarmed at EU dependency on REE imports and the prospects of Chinese investment in Greenland.[34] REEs comprise a set of seventeen chemical elements, which are becoming increasingly important in alternative energy technologies, lifestyle and industry electronics, and the defense industry. Mineral resources are vital for the EU's economy and crucial for industrial production. The EU's reaction to China's restrictions on its exports of REE to ensure supply reliability was threefold: the EU consolidated its raw material strategy in 2011; joined the USA in referring complaints to the WTO;[35] and engaged in enhancing bilateral relations with Greenland, which, with an estimated 9 percent of global REE reserves, is (alongside the Baltic Shield) the major European future supply source.[36] However, the numbers remain uncertain, because other countries, such as the USA, are developing or restarting their REE production.[37] On June 13, 2012, Vice-President and Commissioner for Industry and Entrepreneurship, Antonio Tajani, and Commissioner for Development Cooperation, Andris Piebalgs, traveled to Greenland to make a deal; the EU wished to share exploitation rights to rare earth metal ores in return for technological and environmental mining know-how.[38] On behalf of the EU, they signed a Letter of Intent with Prime Minister Kuupik Kleist, who signed on behalf of Greenland.[39]

The EU's emphasis on Greenland's resources is accompanied by a concern for its environment and the sustainable management of its resources, concern that reflects the EU's environmental policy. The EU's commitment to high environmental protection standards is embedded in the Lisbon Treaty of the Functioning of the European Union (Article 191). As recalled in the joint communication of the Commission and the High Representative in 2012, "the particular emphasis on the protection of the Arctic environment remains the cornerstone of the EU's policy towards the Arctic."[40] In its last resolution (January 2014, Article 56), the EP while underlining the geostrategic importance of Greenland, highlights the need to consider environmental concerns in the promotion of economic development.[41]

In 2014, discussions about the renewal of the Partnership highlighted the EU's expectations with regard to sustainable development and the emphasis on cooperation in the area of raw materials. Another source of concern for the EU was the low representation of EU companies in Greenland in the raw material industry: "Currently ca. 58 percent of exploration companies operating in Greenland are Canadian or Australian companies. The share of EU companies operating in Greenland is only 15 percent (Denmark, Germany, Czech Republic and United Kingdom)."[42] Representatives of ten influential Chinese companies visited Greenland in the summer of 2013 to seek investment opportunities. The Greenlandic Minister of Industry and Mining also paid an official visit to China in November 2013.[43] In December 2014, the Chinese company General Nice Development Limited showed support for London Mining, a company which held a license to exploit iron ore at Isukasia in Western Greenland but which filed for bankruptcy in October 2014.[44] A few months earlier, the Chinese company, China Nonferrous Metal Industry's Foreign Engineering and Construction Co. Ltd. (NFC), one of the world leaders in rare earth processing, signed a Memorandum of Understanding with the Australian company Greenland Minerals and Energy regarding the Kvanefjeld project.

Given that the development of the EU Arctic policy clearly provided an impetus for an intensified partnership with Greenland, it is important to assess the political and legal basis for this cooperation as well as the EU levers and constraints.

EU cooperation levers and constraints

Overseas countries and territories

The cooperation between the EU and Greenland/Denmark mostly takes place within the framework of international cooperation and development. According to the preamble of the 2013 Council decision on the association of the EU's overseas countries and territories (OCTs), "trade and trade-related cooperation between the Union and the OCTs should contribute to the objective of sustainable economic development, social development and environmental protection."[45] However, even though this is mentioned in the preamble, the OCTs association with the EU contains no binding requirement in terms of environmental protection, as specified in Article 3 subsection 5. The European *acquis* does not apply to OCTs either.[46]

The OCTs receive funds from the European Development Fund (EDF). Greenland is not eligible for the EDF but receives funds from the EU's general budget on the basis of the Partnership Agreement between the EU, the Kingdom of Denmark and Greenland. With €217.8 million for the period 2014–2020, Greenland receives a far larger amount than the other OCTs (between €2.4 million for Pitcairn and €29.9 million for French Polynesia).[47]

Areas of cooperation

The Partnership Agreement is complementary to the OCTs arrangement: its renewal in December 2013 led to some discussions about the objectives of the partnership, the EU's authority to manage it, and the extent to which Greenland could influence the choice of the areas of cooperation. In its explanatory statement of the report on the draft Council decision (2014), the EP rapporteur Ricardo Cortés Lastra introduced a question about comitology: which institution has delegation and on which legal basis? The draft Council decision prepared by the Commission suggests that the Act should be approved by the Council according to the procedure for delegated acts (and not implementing acts), according to which the Commission's exercise is under the control of Member States. The Lastra report attempts to reinstate the Commission in its power of delegation.[48] In addition, it is not the ordinary but the special legislation procedure that applies to the Partnership, so the Parliament only has a consultative role. In its final decision, the Council does not take into consideration the suggested amendments: the Council refers to a regulation that establishes rules for financing external action[49] and emphasizes the specific nature of these implementing acts as having a "policy oriented nature" and "financial implications."

Sustainable development, environment and education

A second issue addressed by the Lastra report is environmental protection: as explained above, the EP has consistently shown concern for the environment in its Arctic resolutions. Concerning the Partnership, the EP proposes an amendment on safety, social and environmental standards (number 5) and an amendment on biodiversity (number 9) to ensure that natural resources are exploited on the basis of strict environmental sustainability criteria.[50] The rapporteur also deems that "the Commission's proposal places excessive, and indeed obsessive, emphasis on the exploration and exploitation of Greenland's natural resources," and that this "undermines the desired neutrality of the document."[51]

Concerning the Partnership's focus areas, it is important to remember that the Partnership is a Council decision that presents the EU's interests in developing cooperation with Greenland/Denmark within the framework of the OCTs association. The agreement reflects the importance of some issues from the EU's perspective, but it also gives rise to potential cooperation in a wide range of areas. Policy dialogue and financial cooperation are provided for in a range of areas, including education, natural resources, energy, environment, Arctic issues, the social sector, as well as research and innovation. The Partnership is a financial instrument from which a programming document is elaborated in close consultation with Greenland: the government of Greenland was asked to prepare and submit an indicative Programming Document for the Sustainable Development of Greenland (PDSD) that was consistent with the overall purpose, scope, objectives, principles and policies of the EU. Based on Article 3 of the 2014 Council decision, Greenland deems it has fulfilled this task successfully.[52]

The Prime Minister of Greenland, Kim Kielsen, confirmed the priority given to the education area and the role played by the EU:

> Education helps to create growth [...]. International cooperation is a fundamental prerequisite for the ongoing work of creating a better society in Greenland. A good example is the EU and our partnership agreements, which are also of vital significance to educational initiatives in Greenland.[53]

Industry and entrepreneurship

As explained above, a specific cooperation on raw materials between the EU and Greenland was initiated in June 2012 by representatives of the EU. The objective was "to share exploitation rights to rare earth metal ores in return for technological and environmental mining know-how."[54] The Letter of Intent signed with Greenland proposes four areas of dialogue: (1) geological knowledge; (2) analysis of infrastructure and investment needs related to the exploitation of mineral resources; (3) competence building; and (4) environmental issues related to mining and the social impacts of mining. The dialogue is designed to help achieve the goal of the sustainable development of Greenland as defined in the EU–Greenland partnership.

The Letter of Intent does not create any binding or legal obligations on either side under domestic or international law and has not led to significant results. In its 2014 resolution, the EP expressed concerns about the limited effects of the Letter of Intent on cooperation in the area of mineral resources.[55] The limited results may be due to the fact that the competences of Member States remain paramount in the industrial sector (the EU has only supporting competence with regard to industry) and to the fact that the procedure for the financial support proposed by the EU was very complex because no specific budget was allocated to this cooperation.[56] Cooperation on REE between the EU, Greenland and the Kingdom of Denmark has thus mainly been discussed within the framework of the renewal of the EU–Greenland partnership in 2014 for the period 2014–2020.

Greenland and EU law

Although Greenland has withdrawn from the EU, and although the European *acquis* does not apply to Greenland pursuant to its association with the EU as an OCT, this does not mean that the EU legal order has no impact on Greenland. Indeed, the relationship between Danish, Greenlandic and EU law remains complex. In particular, the extent to which EU environment law may apply to Greenland—as a consequence of Greenland being an integrated part of Denmark and Denmark being a member of the EU—requires investigation. In the following analysis, I consider two sectors: the offshore hydrocarbon activities in the marine areas off the Greenlandic territorial sea and uranium mining.

According to a Danish Royal Order dating back to 1963, the territorial sea of Greenland extends up to three nautical miles seaward.[57] The protection of the marine environment in the internal waters of Greenland is the responsibility of Greenland and is regulated by the Order of the Greenland Parliament number 4 of November 3, 1994 as amended in 2004.[58] On November 16, 2004, Denmark ratified the 1982 United Nation Convention on the Law of the Sea (UNCLOS). Consequently, Denmark is responsible for the marine areas in the EEZ around Greenland: this responsibility is regulated by the Royal Order for the enforcement of the Environmental Protection Act for Greenland of 2004. Indeed, in accordance with the Act on Greenland Self-Government, Greenland exercises authority over the mineral resources but has not taken over responsibility for the protection of the environment in the marine areas beyond three nautical miles. Article 9 subsection 3 of the Mineral Resources Act states: "the rules of the Greenland Parliament Act on the environment do not apply to the continental shelf area and the exclusive economic zone of Greenland insofar as the Marine Environment Act provides otherwise."[59] In addition, the Danish Marine Environment Act in the version passed in 2004 (but not in any subsequent updates) clearly applies to the EEZ of Greenland.[60]

When it comes to the EU, the question arises as to what extent EU Environmental Law covers the EEZ around Greenland. In particular, this includes the Strategy for the marine environment which relies on a Directive (2008/56/EC) that establishes a common framework and objectives for the protection and conservation of the marine environment. This directive was implemented by the above-mentioned Marine Environmental Act, but only in the 2004 version covering Greenland.[61] The question of whether EU law is relevant to the EEZ around Greenland also relates to the Directive of the EP and the Council of June 12, 2013 on the safety of offshore oil and gas operations, which, in the Danish version, does not cover the sea around Greenland.[62] As yet, the Danish Parliament has not considered the specific case of Greenland in its discussions about the incorporation of the EU Directive into Danish law.[63]

Uranium exploitation: international and EU conventions

The exploration and exploitation of uranium has a history in Greenland, but, since the 1980s and until recently, such activities were prohibited in the country.[64] In the past few years, however, Greenland has rediscovered the potential in the production of uranium. The rare earth elements in the Kvanefjeld deposit south of Greenland are bound to uranium, and it is impossible to extract these elements without also extracting the uranium. On the one hand, this could be viewed as a technical and environmental constraint, but, on the other, it presents some added economic value: the presence of uranium in the REE would allow the operating company to be competitive on the international market.[65] In January 2015, Prime Minister Kielsen announced that the new government, formed after the parliamentary elections of November 28, 2014,[66] would support the controversial uranium mining project in Southern Greenland and uphold the repeal of the "uranium zero-tolerance policy," which, after a close fifteen to fourteen vote in the Greenlandic Parliament, was lifted in October 2013 (the common Danish zero-tolerance policy had been in effect since the 1970s).[67]

The regulation of extraction and trade of uranium materials is governed internationally by the Euratom Treaty, which does not apply to Greenland.[68] Among other things, the Euratom Treaty stipulates that Member States should: (a) promote research and ensure the dissemination of technical information; (b) establish uniform safety standards to protect the health of workers and the general public and ensure that these safety standards are enforced. Importantly for Greenland, the Euratom Treaty also obliges Member States to: (e) make certain, by appropriate supervision, that nuclear materials are not diverted to purposes other than those for which they are intended; (h) establish with other countries and international organizations relations that will foster progress in the peaceful uses of nuclear energy.[69]

Article 5 of the Greenland Treaty governing the withdrawal of Greenland from the EC states that the Euratom Treaty should not apply to Greenland.[70] The OCTs association agreement also clearly excludes Greenland from any obligation with regard to uranium:

> The OCTs are fragile island environments requiring adequate protection, including in respect of waste management. In respect of radioactive waste, Article 198 of the Euratom Treaty and the related

secondary legislation provide for this, except with regard to Greenland, to which the Euratom Treaty does not apply. For other waste, it should be specified which Union rules are to apply in respect of the OCTs.

However, in the case of uranium, until recently it was still unclear whether to appeal to Greenland's competence over its own natural resources, as established in the Act on Greenland Self-Government,[71] or whether to appeal to its status as a part of Denmark and, in turn, invoke Danish responsibility under international law. The Act on Greenland Self-Government specifies that:

> Naalakkersuisut [The Greenlandic Government] and the Government [the Danish Government] may agree the fields of responsibility which exclusively concern Greenland's affairs, and which are not referred to in the Schedule, and which may be assumed by the Greenland Self-Government authorities.

This formulation was sufficiently vague to lead to complex legal debates, since Denmark is still the responsible State, according to international law. Indeed, uranium might not only "exclusively concern Greenland," insofar as the use of a nuclear product, in particular its trade, may raise national security issues. The nature of the activities at stake—extraction and export—was debated.

When it comes to the trade of uranium, Denmark retains competence and control capacity by virtue of the security issues at stake. In January 2016, the Governments of Greenland and Denmark signed a set of agreements on cooperation regarding future mining and export of uranium from Greenland. Both parliaments will need to debate forthcoming legislation on safeguards and export controls.[72]

Aarhus convention

The effectiveness of Environmental Law depends on public control and the involvement of the public. The Aarhus Convention (United Nations Economic Commission for Europe Convention on Access to Information, Public Participation in Decision-making and Access to Justice in Environmental Matters)[73] is the most important international agreement on access to environmental information, public participation and access to justice. The Aarhus Convention comprises three pillars that aim to guarantee access to information, public participation, and access to justice in environmental matters. Strictly speaking, the Aarhus Convention is not EU law. Still, the EU applies the Aarhus Convention, and EU Member States are required to implement its provisions by Regulation (EC) No. 1367/2006 of the EP and of the Council of September 6, 2006.[74] The term *environmental information* denotes any available information in written, visual, aural or database form on the state of water, air, soil, fauna, flora, land and natural sites, and on activities or measures that have the potential to adversely affect or protect these (including administrative measures and environmental management programs).[75]

Denmark made a reservation for Greenland, which is starting to be questioned in the Greenlandic parliament (Inatsisartut). In her proposal FM 2014/151, a Member of Inatsisartut, Sara Olsvig, presenting the Inuit Ataqatigiit Party, argues that Greenland should ask the Danish Government to cancel the reservation for Greenland in the Danish ratification of the Convention. A report was submitted to the Government of Greenland in May 2014 and should have been translated into Greenlandic in order to be discussed during the autumn session of 2014 in the Greenlandic Parliament, a session that was canceled due to the celebration of general elections.[76] In June 2014, the government of Greenland proposed amendments to the 2009 Mineral Resources Act in order to reduce public access to documents for the purpose of making decisions pursuant to the Mineral Resources Act and to remove the right to appeal decisions made by the Minister. A Member of Inatsisartut, Naaja Nathanielsen, wrote an open letter to the former Minister for Industry and Minerals requesting explanations regarding the two amendments.[77]

Conclusion

Greenland is a strategic partner for the EU in the Arctic. Although it has withdrawn from the Union, Greenland, being part of the Kingdom of Denmark, is still linked to the EU through the Overseas Countries and Territories association. Over the past years, the EU has intensified its links with Greenland: in addition to the fisheries sector, which remains the largest trade sector between the EU and Greenland, cooperation is developing through a growing number of agreements, as well as the Partnership for sustainable development. A number of constraints and levers for the EU to contribute to sustainable development in Greenland and areas of common interest have appeared. The balance between economic development and environmental protection has led to debates in the EU institutions. However, EU institutional consistency has by no means been challenged. Some constraints have also appeared concerning EU competitiveness in the industry of raw materials in terms of economic diplomacy in a sector where Member States retain competence.

To support its interests with regard to sustainable development, the EU has several levers: a long-standing cooperation with Greenland in the education sector, expertise in technology, know-how and strong environmental standards. Apart from its valuable cooperation in the education sector, these levers have not been fully utilized. As Greenland is currently developing extractive industries, difficult challenges remain in terms of protecting the environment. Current instruments of cooperation, such as the OCTs partnership, are not binding with regards to environmental protection. The legal complexity of the relationship between EU, Danish and Greenlandic law needs further consideration. The incorporation of EU law into Danish law is one important question. Also considering the relationship between Greenland and Denmark, some environmental issues—such as the case of offshore hydrocarbon activities and uranium extraction and trade—remain complex.

A clarification of the legal nexus between Greenland, Denmark and the EU would enable a more consistent and responsible cooperation framework between the EU and Greenland. In addition to the current focus on education, a contribution to the diversification of the Greenlandic economy, which is characterized by an extreme specialization in fisheries and high hopes for hydrocarbons and raw materials, would undoubtedly help strengthen long-standing ties between the EU and Greenland.

Notes

1 Act No. 577 of November 29, 1978, The Greenland Home Rule Act.
2 Bent Ole Mortensen, "The Quest for Resources – the Case of Greenland," *Journal of Military and Strategic Studies* 15.2 (2013): 93–128.
3 European Commission, Memo 12–428 EU, Brussels, June 13, 2012.
4 Constitutional Act of Denmark, June 5, 1953. Part IV, §28.
5 Aqqaluk Lynge, "Autonomy in Action: Inuit and the Case of Greenland," Presentation at the Symposium on "The Right to Self-Determination in International Law," The Hague, September 29–October 1, 2006.
6 Robert Petersen, "Colonialism as Seen by a Former Colonized Area," *Arctic Anthropology* 32. 2 (1995): 118–26.
7 Jens Brøsted and Hans Christian Gulløv, "Recent Trends and Issues in the Political Development of Greenland," adapted from a presentation at the *XLII Congrès International des Américanistes*, Paris, September 1976.
8 Fernando Garcés de Los Fayos, *Greenland: The Challenge of Managing a Key Geostrategic Territory*. 2014 In Depth Analysis (European Parliament: Policy Department, Directorate-general for external policies), 20.
9 Lynge, "Autonomy in Action."
10 Garcés de Los Fayos, *Greenland*.
11 Treaty amending, with regard to Greenland, the Treaties establishing the European Communities. Signed on March 13, 1984 (1985) OJ L 29/1.
12 Ibid.
13 Council Decision 2001/822/EC of November 27, 2001 on the association of the overseas countries and territories with the European Community ("Overseas Association Decision"), entry into force December 2, 2001, OJ L 314 of November 30, 2001, amended 2007/249/EC, entry into force April 26, 2007, OJ L 109 of April 26, 2007.
14 European Commission, DG MARE, Fisheries partnership agreement. European Council, Council Regulation, (EC) No 753/2007 of June 28, 2007 on the conclusion of the Fisheries Partnership Agreement between the European Community on the one hand, and the Government of Denmark and the Home Rule Government of Greenland, on the other hand. OJ L 172, June 30, 2007.

15 Garcés de Los Fayos, *Greenland*, 20.
16 Council Decision of July 17, 2006 on relations between the European Community on the one hand, and Greenland and the Kingdom of Denmark on the other (Text with EEA relevance) (2006/526/EC). OJ L 208, of July 29, 2006, 28–31.
17 Council Decision 2014/137/EU of March 14, 2014 on relations between the European Union on the one hand, and Greenland and the Kingdom of Denmark on the other. OJ L 76 of March 15, 2014, 1–5.
18 This concerns eleven EU Member States: Denmark, Germany, Estonia, France, Ireland, Spain, Lithuania, Latvia, Poland, Portugal and the UK.
19 Garcés de Los Fayos, *Greenland.*
20 European Commission, Directorate General for Trade, "European Union, Trade in Goods with Greenland."
21 Security issues including the role of the USA and NATO are not covered in this chapter. See Ulrik P. Gad, "Greenland: A Post-Danish Sovereign Nation State in the Making," *Cooperation and Conflict* 49.1 (2014): 98–118.
22 European Council, Council Decision 2014/137/EU of March 14, 2014 on relations between the European Union on the one hand, and Greenland and the Kingdom of Denmark on the other. OJ L 76 of March 15, 2014, 1–5.
23 Cooperation Agreement between the Government of Greenland and the European Environment Agency, 2010. Cooperation Agreement between the Ministry of Health in Greenland and the European Environment Agency, 2012.
24 European Parliament and European Council, Regulation (EU) No 257/2014 of the European Parliament and of the Council of February 26, 2014 amending Council Regulation (EC) No 2368/2002 as regards the inclusion of Greenland in implementing the *Kimberley* Process certification scheme. OJ L 84, March 20, 2014, 69–71.
25 Javier Solana and Benita Ferrero-Waldner, "Climate Change and International Security." Paper from the High Representative and the European Commission to the European Council, S113/08, March 14, 2008.
26 Ibid.
27 European Commission and High Representative, Joint communication to the European Parliament and the Council, JOIN (2016) 21 final. Council Conclusions on the Arctic of June 20, 2016.
28 Solana and Ferrero-Waldner, "Climate Change and International Security."
29 European Parliament Resolution of October 9, 2008 on Arctic governance.

> Article 8 calls on the Commission to include energy and security policy in the Arctic region on its agenda, and to propose, in particular, in its expected communication on the region, suitable subjects and joint working procedures for the EU and the Arctic countries in the fields of climate change, sustainable development, security of energy supply and maritime safety.

> Article 11 emphasises the external aspects of energy policy and the role of the Arctic in the formulation of the Energy Policy for Europe (EPE), as proposed by the March 2007 European Council.

30 Cécile Pelaudeix, "China's Interests in the Arctic and the EU's Arctic Policy: Towards a Proactive EU Foreign Policy?," *The Yearbook of Polar Law* 7.1 (2015): 128–50.
31 Cécile Pelaudeix and Thierry Rodon, "The EU Arctic Policy and National Interests of France and Germany: Internal and External Policy Coherence at Stake," *Northern Review* 37 (Fall 2013): 57–85.
32 Directive 2013/30/EU of the European Parliament and of the Council of June 12, 2013 on safety of offshore oil and gas operations and amending Directive 2004/35/EC Text with EEA relevance. OJ L 178, June 28, 013, 66–106.

33 European Parliament resolution of January 20, 2011 on a sustainable EU policy for the High North.
34 Pelaudeix, "China's Interests in the Arctic and the EU's Arctic Policy."
35 World Trade Organization. *Dispute Settlement: Dispute DS394.* "China, Measures Related to the Exportation of Various Raw Materials." Appellate Body Report circulated on January 30, 2012. On July 2, 2009, the European Community requested to join the consultations. On July 6, 2009, Canada, Mexico and Turkey also requested to join the consultations. Subsequently, China informed the Dispute Settlement Body that it had accepted the requests of Canada, the European Community, Mexico and Turkey to join the consultations.
36 According to the US Geological Survey of 2010, Greenland's share of the overall REE resources amounts to 3.44 percent and, if one includes the latest project figures, Greenland's shares of global REE resources could amount to 9.16 percent. See European Commission, *Greenland's Raw Materials Potential and the EU Strategic Needs.* Memo 12–428. Brussels, June 13, 2012. Also, Peter Thagesen and Ingeborg Ørbech, *Kina mister monopol på sjældne jordarter.* Dansk Industri Indsigt. February 2012; Bent Ole Mortensen, "The Quest for Resources."
37 USGS, Rare Earths Statistics and Information. Molycorp rare earth production in the fourth quarter of 2014 at its Mountain Pass, California facility increased year-on-year and nearly doubled that of the preceding quarter. In MCP, "Rare Earth Production Rises in Q4 at Molycorp's Mountain Pass Facility," February 2, 2015.
38 European Commission, Greenland's raw materials potential and the EU strategic needs, MEMO, Brussels, June 13, 2012.
39 Commission Decision (C[2012] 3777) of June 8, 2012 on the signature of a Letter of Intent between the European Union and Greenland on cooperation in the area of mineral resources. Ares (2015)3073447.
40 European Commission and High Representative, Joint communication to the European Parliament and the Council. JOIN(2012) 19 final.
41 European Parliament resolution of March 12, 2014 on the EU strategy for the Arctic (2013/2595[RSP]) P7_TA(2014)0236.
42 DG GROW. DG Enterprise and Industry has been renamed DG GROW (Directorate-General for Internal Market, Industry, Entrepreneurship and SMEs).
43 Garcés de Los Fayos, *Greenland.*
44 Government of Greenland, *New Strong Force Behind London Mining Greenland A/S,* Government website, January 8, 2015.
45 Council Decision 2013/755/EU of November 25, 2013. OJ L 76 of March 15, 2014, 1–5.
46 Instead, the detailed rules and procedures for the Association are provided by the Council Decision 2013/755/EU on the Association of the OCTs with the European Union which was adopted on November 25, 2013.
47 European Commission, International cooperation and development, "OCT – EU relations in detail." Accessed July 1, 2015, https://ec.europa.eu/europeaid/regions/overseas-countries-and-territories-octs/oct-eu-relations-detail_en.
48 European Parliament, Report on the draft Council decision on relations between the European Union on the one hand, and Greenland and the Kingdom of Denmark on the other (Lastra Report) (12274/13_C7–0237/2013_2011/0410 [CNS]).
49 Regulation (EU) No. 236/2014 of the European Parliament and of the Council of March 11, 2014 laying down common rules and procedures for the implementation of the Union's instruments for financing external action. OJ L 77, March 15, 2014, 95–108.
50 European Parliament, Lastra report.

51 European Parliament legislative resolution of February 5, 2014 on the draft Council decision on relations between the European Union on the one hand, and Greenland and the Kingdom of Denmark on the other (12274/2013–C7–0 237/2013–2011/0410[CNS]) (Special legislative procedure – consultation).

52 Article 3 (1) in the Council Decision (2014/137/EU).

53 Kim Kielsen, New Year's Address, January 8, 2015. Accessed February 14, 2015, http://arcticjournal.com/press-releases/1240/new-years-reception-greenland-representation.

54 European Commission, Greenland's raw materials potential and the EU strategic needs, MEMO, Brussels, June 13, 2012.

55 European Commission, Commission Decision (C[2012] 3777) of June 8, 2012 on the signature of a Letter of Intent between the European Union and Greenland on cooperation in the area of mineral resources. Ares (2015)3073447.

56 Interviews conducted by the author with EU officials: DEVCO (May 14, 2014), DG GROW (May 12, 2014) and with the Greenland representation to the EU (May 15, 2014).

57 Order No. 191 of May 27, 1963 on the Delimitation of the Territorial Sea of Greenland. The Royal Regulation No. 2 of May 21, 2004 also establishes the jurisdiction of Greenland within three nautical miles from the coast.

58 Order No. 4 of November 3, 1994 as amended in 2004 of the Greenland Parliament.

59 Act No. 7 of December 7, 2009 of the Greenland Parliament on mineral resources and mineral resource activities (the Mineral Resources Act).

60 As put in force by Order No. 1035/2004 (Act on the Protection of the Marine Environment 1993).

61 Directive 2008/56/EC of the European Parliament and of the Council of June 17, 2008 establishing a framework for Community action in the field of marine environmental policy (Marine Strategy Framework Directive). OJ L 164 of June 25, 2008, 19–40.

62 Directive 2013/30/EU of the European Parliament and of the Council of June 12, 2013 on safety of offshore oil and gas operations and amending Directive 2004/35/EC. OJ L 178, June 28, 2013, 66–106.

63 Ellen Margrethe Basse, "Lovforslaget til gennemførelse af Offshore-sikkerhedsdirektivet følger ikke direktivets intentioner," *Altinget*, November 27, 2014, accessed February 14, 2015, www.altinget.dk/artikel/ny-lovgivning-skaber-forvirring.

64 "In 1980, 4,200 tons of material from Kvanefjeld was brought to Risø to be tested for the extraction of uranium." See Mortensen, "The Quest for Resources."

65 John Mair, "The Kvanefjeld of the Future – New, Attractive Jobs for Greenland," *Greenland Minerals and Energy*, originally published in *Sermitsiaq*, November 14, 2014, accessed February 14, 2015, http://gme.gl/en/kvanefjeld-future-new-attractive-jobs-greenland-0.

66 Former Premier Aleqa Hammond had to step down after allegation of misuse of public funds.

67 Kim Kielsen, New Year's Address, January 8, 2015.

68 Denmark signed the Convention on Nuclear Safety, but made a reservation for Greenland. The Convention commits participating States operating land-based nuclear power plants to maintain a high level of safety by setting international benchmarks to which States would subscribe. *Convention on Nuclear Safety*, adopted in Vienna on June 17, 1994. The reservation for Greenland was accepted on November 13, 1998.

69 The consolidated version of the Treaty establishing the European Atomic Energy Community, which entered into force on March 25, 1957, and represents binding primary law for all EU Member States. See Rasa Ptasekaite, "The

Euratom Treaty v. Treaties of the European Union: limits of competence and interaction," SSM Report number: 2011: 32, July 2011.
70 Treaty amending, with regard to Greenland, the Treaties establishing the European Communities.
71 Act on Greenland Self-Government No. 473 of June 12, 2009.
72 The agreements on uranium mining and export can be accessed at: http://um.dk/da/nyheder-fra-udenrigsministeriet/newsdisplaypage/?newsID=EB9E3E18-9441-489C-93D3-3253DECC4423.
73 Aarhus Convention, signed on June 25, 1998, UNTS, vol. 2161, 447.
74 Regulation (EC) No.1367/2006 of the European Parliament and of the Council of September 6, 2006 on the application of the provisions of the Aarhus Convention on Access to Information, Public Participation in Decision-making and Access to Justice in Environmental Matters to Community institutions and bodies. Entered into force on September 28, 2006. OJ L 264 of September 25, 2006.
75 Ellen Margrethe Basse, *Environmental Law in Denmark* (Alphen aan den Rijn and Zuidpoolsingel: Kluwer Law International, 2013).
76 Ellen Margrethe Basse, "Juridisk responsum om den gældende grønlandske lovgivning vurderet til y setaf Århus konventionen," Report to the Government of Greenland, May 18, 2014.
77 Letter from Naaja Nathanielsen to Minister Jens-Erik Kirkegaard from June 27, 2014. Under the new government of Kim Kielsen, the administration of the mineral resources area has been restructured. Government of Greenland, "New Structure Related to Administration of the Mineral Resources Area," February 9, 2015.

References

Basse, Ellen Margrethe. *Environmental Law in Denmark.* Alphen aan den Rijn and Zuidpoolsingel: Kluwer Law International, 2013.

Basse, Ellen Margrethe. "Lovforslaget til gennemførelse af Offshore-sikkerhedsdirektivet følger ikke direktivets intentioner." *Altinget,* November 27, 2014. Accessed February 14, 2015, www.altinget.dk/artikel/ny-lovgivning-skaber-forvirring.

Basse, Ellen Margrethe. "Juridisk responsum om den gældende grønlandske lovgivning vurderet til y setaf Århus konventionen." Report to the Government of Greenland, May 18, 2014.

Brøsted, Jens, and Hans Christian Gulløv. "Recent Trends and Issues in the Political Development of Greenland," adapted from a presentation at the *XLII Congrès International des Américanistes.* Paris, September 1976.

Gad, Ulrik P. 2014. "Greenland: A Post-Danish Sovereign Nation State in the Making." *Cooperation and Conflict* 49.1 (2014): 98–118.

Garcés de Los Fayos, Fernando. *Greenland: The Challenge of Managing a Key Geostrategic Territory.* 2014 In Depth Analysis (European Parliament: Policy Department, Directorate-general for external policies). Accessed February 14, 2015, www.europarl.europa.eu/thinktank/en/document.html?reference=EXPO-AFET_SP%282014%29522332.

Government of Greenland, "New Structure Related to Administration of the Mineral Resources Area." February 9, 2015. Accessed February 14, 2015, www.nuna-law.com/sites/default/files/Newsletter_9-feb-2015.pdf.

Government of Greenland, "New Strong Force behind London Mining Greenland A/S." Government website, January 8, 2015. Accessed February 14, 2015, http://naalakkersuisut.gl/en/Naalakkersuisut/News/2015/01/080115-London-Mining.

Kielsen, Kim. New Year's Address, January 8, 2015. Press release. Accessed February 14, 2015, http://arcticjournal.com/press-releases/1240/new-years-reception-greenland-representation.

Lynge, Aqqaluk. "Autonomy in Action: Inuit and the Case of Greenland," presentation at the Symposium on "The Right to Self-Determination in International Law." The Hague, September 29–October 1, 2006. Accessed February 14, 2015, http://unpo.org/downloads/AqqalukLynge.pdf.

Mair, John. "The Kvanefjeld of the Future – New, Attractive Jobs for Greenland." Greenland Minerals and Energy, originally published in *Sermitsiaq*, November 14, 2014. Accessed February 14, 2015, http://gme.gl/en/kvanefjeld-future-new-attractive-jobs-greenland-0.

Mortensen, Bent Ole. "The Quest for Resources – The Case of Greenland," *Journal of Military and Strategic Studies* 15.2 (2013): 93–128.

Nathanielsen, Naaja. Letter to Minister Jens-Erik Kirkegaard, June 27, 2014.

Pelaudeix, Cécile. "China's Interests in the Arctic and the EU's Arctic Policy: Towards a Proactive EU Foreign Policy?." *The Yearbook of Polar Law* 7.1 (2015): 128–50.

Pelaudeix, Cécile and Thierry Rodon. "The EU Arctic Policy and National Interests of France and Germany: Internal and External Policy Coherence at Stake." *Northern Review* 37 (Fall 2013): 57–85.

Petersen, Robert. "Colonialism as Seen by a Former Colonized Area." *Arctic Anthropology* 32.2 (1995): 118–26.

Ptasekaite, Rasa. "The Euratom Treaty v. Treaties of the European Union: Limits of Competence and Interaction." SSM Report number: 2011:32, July 2011. Accessed February 14, 2015, www.stralsakerhetsmyndigheten.se/Publikationer/Rapport/Avfall-transport-fysiskt-skydd/2011/201132/.

Solana, Javier and Benita Ferrero-Waldner. "Climate Change and International Security." Paper from the High Representative and the European Commission to the European Council, S113/08, March 14, 2008.

Thagesen, Peter and Ingeborg Ørbech. *Kina mister monopol på sjældne jordarter.* Dansk Industri Indsigt. February 2012.

The Danish Ecological Council. "Recent Developments in the Uranium Debate in Greenland." Website article. October 15, 2013. Accessed June 14, 2015, www.ecocouncil.dk/releases/articles-pressreleases/chemicals-and-climate/2226-recent-developments-in-the-uranium-debate-in-greenland.

USGS (US Geological Survey), Rare Earths Statistics and Information. Accessed June 14, 2015, http://minerals.usgs.gov/minerals/pubs/commodity/rare_earths/mcs-2015-raree.pdf.

16 The effectiveness of current regulatory models of gas flaring in light of black carbon emissions reduction in the Arctic

Daria Shapovalova

Introduction

As the Arctic is warming twice as fast than the rest of the world,[1] the international community has a growing concern over the consequences for the Earth's climate system and further implications on security.[2] Scientists agree that Black Carbon (BC) is the second most important (after CO_2) human emission in terms of its effect on climate change. While efforts to reduce black carbon cannot replace long-term mitigation of CO_2,[3] immediate reductions in BC emissions could lower the rate of Arctic warming over the next few decades.[4]

BC, a particulate matter "formed through the incomplete combustion of fossil fuels, biofuel, and biomass," warms the Earth by absorbing heat in the atmosphere and by reducing the albedo (the ability to reflect sunlight) of snow and ice.[5] In the Arctic, BC sources include open burning, diesel vehicles and electricity generation.[6] Until recently, it was not believed that the oil and gas sector was responsible for a large share of BC emission in the High North.[7] However, the latest studies show that the share of hydrocarbons sector has been underestimated.[8]

During oil production, the gas contained in the reservoirs comes out to the surface. When not utilized or injected in the grid, such gas is "generally flared or vented."[9] Recent studies reveal that around 42 percent of BC in the Arctic comes from associated petroleum gas (APG) flaring during oil and gas production within the region.[10] The Arctic States, acting together through the Arctic Council, recognize the challenges presented by climate change and are working on its mitigation through joint research and non-binding legislation.[11]

Regulation of APG flaring by individual Arctic States has undergone substantial changes in the recent years.[12] However, States are using different models of APG regulation. Whereas the policy goals are usually similar (increase in APG utilization rate/emissions reduction), the mechanisms chosen to achieve these goals vary.

Despite numerous hurdles[13] and current low oil price, oil companies do not lose interest in Arctic oil.[14] As global warming frees more Arctic Ocean surface areas from ice for further oil exploration and production, it is crucial to take action to create a special regime for oil and gas in the High North to ensure the adoption of elevated environmental and technical standards for operation in this fragile region.

The present chapter aims at testing the effectiveness of two legal models for APG flaring regulation (Russian and Norwegian models) in the Arctic as a means to achieve BC emissions reduction. To this end, the first section presents an overview of the actions taken collectively by the Arctic States with regards to BC. The second section analyzes the regulatory models for gas flaring in Norway and Russia. Finally, the third section offers a proposal for the improvement of the effectiveness of BC regulation in the Arctic by introducing a common gas-flaring regime in the region.

For the purposes of the present chapter, the effectiveness of a regulatory model is measured with the help of three criteria: (1) whether it is successful in achieving substantial[15] reductions in the volumes of BC emitted in the Arctic via gas flaring; (2) whether such reductions can be made in the nearest decades; and (3) whether it is consistent with the relevant national and international legal framework. As noted above, immediate substantial reductions in BC emissions can slow down the Arctic warming in the nearest decades. Thus, the fulfillment of the chosen criteria would help achieving the goals of a number of Arctic related documents.[16] When applying these criteria it is essential to take into account the presence of the causal link between the regulatory instruments and the desired effects. The persuasive demonstration of such a causal link is one of the most crucial and difficult aspects of regime effectiveness evaluation, according to Young.[17] Additionally, it is important to bear in mind the issue of regime interplay, which in this chapter has twofold nature: international–national interplay and soft law–hard law interplay.

International efforts in BC emissions reduction in the Arctic

From the standpoint of international law, the Arctic is seen as any other ocean surrounded by continents. It does not enjoy the special environmental protection mechanisms as does the Antarctic[18] and is governed primarily by domestic legislation of the Arctic States, the United Nations Convention on Law of the Sea (UNCLOS)[19] and other relevant international environmental agreements.[20] The vulnerability of ice-covered marine areas to pollution, however, has been acknowledged by being granted a separate UNCLOS provision. Article 234 contains a so-called "Arctic clause" allowing a coastal State to adopt special regulations for the protection of marine environment from pollution within its Exclusive Economic Zone (EEZ),

> where particularly severe climatic conditions and the presence of ice covering such areas for most of the year create obstructions or exceptional

hazards to navigation, and pollution of the marine environment could cause major harm to or irreversible disturbance of the ecological balance.[21]

Additionally, the Polar Code, recently adopted by the International Maritime Organization (IMO) will present a new environmental framework for the shipping activities in the polar regions.[22] This document will be the first international agreement to set binding rules for shipping in the Arctic, however, leaving oil and gas drilling out of the scope.[23]

Environmental protection of the Arctic was the issue that first brought the Arctic States together to establish Arctic Environmental Protection Strategy (AEPS) in 1991. Prior to the AEPS there have been occasional cases of cooperation on environmental matters between the Arctic States, such as the 1973 Polar Bear Conservation Agreement,[24] and the 1911 Fur Seals Agreement.[25] AEPS further transformed into the Arctic Council, which was established in 1996[26] as a high level intergovernmental forum of the Arctic States.[27] The Arctic Council is usually described as a "soft law regime,"[28] as it does not have the power to take binding decisions as an international organization.

In 2007, Geir Hønneland and Olav Stokke from the Fridtjof Nansen Institute published a study of the Arctic regime effectiveness which included a number of case studies. When assessing the effectiveness of the Arctic Council, Hønneland and Stokke found that the Council is most effective in the areas where it "enjoys niche advantages,"[29] such as environmental monitoring, encouraging Arctic States to take common stand on hazardous pollutants, and "capacity enhancement in certain areas."[30] As for a normative contribution, the authors have concluded that the Council is rather "limited."[31] However, the assessment was conducted in 2007 and in the recent years the Council has been strengthening its authority by hosting the adoption of two binding treaties.[32] Also, with regards to BC, the Council's work on the matter started after the study had been published.

The Arctic Council first acknowledged Short Lived Climate Forcers (SLCFs)[33] in 2009 during a Ministerial Meeting in Tromsø by creating a Task Force on SLCFs and charging it with a task: "to identify existing and new measures to reduce emissions of these forcers and recommend further immediate actions that can be taken and to report on progress at the next Ministerial Meeting." In 2009, the task was refined to focus on BC due to its "unique role"[34] in the Arctic. After publishing two reports, the Task Force was restructured into the Task for Action on BC and Methane (TFABCM).[35] In 2013, during a Ministerial Meeting in Kiruna, the Council recognized that the reduction in BC emissions "could slow Arctic and global climate change and have positive effects on health"[36] and made national BC emissions inventories "a matter of priority."[37] TFABCM so far held six meetings[38] and is due to deliver a report to the Council in 2015.[39]

The Arctic States then agreed to draft a Framework for Enhanced Action to Reduce Black Carbon and Methane Emissions. Such framework document was intended to "represent a political commitment" and not to impose any binding obligations on its signatories.[40] It was decided that the document would avoid setting any quantitative targets until 2017, even though just two months prior to this decision during the 5th meeting of the TFABCM "most [participants] indicated a preference for a quantitative vision."[41] Instead, the Framework would "send a strong political signal in the form of an ambitious, politically aspirational collective vision." The decision not to set a common BC emission reduction target, even in a non-binding document, could be argued to be a step back. However, it could also be justified by the absence of proper BC emissions reporting inventories in large emitter-States, such as the Russian Federation.[42]

Finally, in April 2015 at the Council's Ministerial Meeting, the Framework for Action on BC and Methane Emissions Reductions was adopted.[43] It was noted that this document marks "the first time that Arctic nations have formally agreed to work together to mitigate climate change [...] sending a hugely important political message that climate change mitigation can be organized regionally as well as globally."[44] The implementation of the Framework will be assessed by the Expert Group once every two years with first results coming in 2017.

It must be noted that the Arctic Council is not the only institution concerned with BC.[45] In 2012, the Gothenburg Protocol to the Convention on Long-Range Transboundary Air Pollution[46] was updated to include $PM_{2.5}$, or particulate matter with diameter equal or less than 2.5 micrometer of which BC is a component.[47] However, while all the Arctic States are Parties to the CLRTAP, Canada, Russia and Iceland have not ratified the Protocol. Out of eight Arctic States only four European countries have agreed to $PM_{2.5}$ reduction goals. With Canada, Russia and the USA out of the picture, the biggest polluters in the Arctic are left outside the jurisdiction of the Protocol or do not have binding reduction obligations under it.

Regulation of gas flaring: Russian polluter pays v. Norwegian zero tolerance

As most of the oil resources lie within the Exclusive Economic Zones of the Arctic littoral States[48] it is, ultimately, national regulations that define the legal framework applicable to companies in the process of obtaining exploration and production licenses and the actual operation, especially in the absence of any international binding rules for Arctic oil and gas.

Gas flaring during oil production is usually regulated under the framework of air pollution in a State's legislation. Alternatively, these rules can be found in the requirements for oil and gas development process.

Generally, we could distinguish such approaches to regulating pollution as: technical prescriptions (making use of certain technologies obligatory); emission standards (specifying the pollutant amounts which may be released from specific installations); and quality standards (standards relating to the quality of the environmental media into which emissions are released, usually framed as limit values for pollutant concentration).[49] When it comes to gas flaring, various models for pollution control are used by different States. For instance, Norway takes a "zero tolerance" approach to flaring, combining the prohibition of any flaring unless specifically permitted for the safety purposes, and the carbon tax providing financial incentives to implement new technologies. On the other hand, Russia adopts a "polluter pays" approach and allows companies to flare 5 percent of its AGP, fining them for any excessive flaring. It is interesting to compare flaring policies of these two States given that Norway and Russia are Arctic neighbors, two of the biggest oil producers in the region, both members of the top fifteen world oil exporter countries.

The Russian Federation

In Russia, the development of the Arctic region has been high on the State's agenda in the past years. Along with the necessity of the maritime delimitation, resource extraction and socio-economic development of the region, the need for environmental protection improvement has been highlighted. However, the primary focus is on oil spill preparedness and response and the clean-up of the existing pollution rather than emissions to air. The issue of black carbon pollution appears to be left out of the Arctic priorities list.

Not only does Russia hold the largest Arctic territory among the Arctic States and the biggest share of hydrocarbons,[50] it also is the biggest gas flaring country in the world.[51] Therefore, if there is a solution for the Arctic BC problem, Russian participation is essential to its success.

The regulatory regime of gas flaring in Russia has undergone some major changes in the recent years. The new decree regulating gas flaring was introduced in 2013.[52] It was created with the goal of "reducing air pollution and greenhouse gas emissions."[53] However, the decree is designed not to cut flaring volumes but to increase utilization rates. Decree 1148 prescribes that 95 percent of all the APG at the installation be utilized. If the flaring volume exceeds 5 percent of the total APG produced, the company is obliged to pay a fine. The major difference between Decree 1148 and its predecessor[54] is the multiplying rate used to calculate the fine. Whereas the rate used in the old decree was 4.5, in the Decree 1148 the fines are set to be multiplied by twelve for 2013 and twenty-five for 2014 and consecutive years.[55] Where the metering equipment is absent at the installation, the multiplying rate becomes 120,[56] however, it remains unclear how the final fine would be calculated in the absence of emissions data. This model of pollution regulation is not new for Russian environmental legislation. The "polluter pays" principle is clearly established by Article 16 of the Environmental Protection Law.[57] After Decree 1148 entered into force, the amount of fines paid by oil companies for polluting the environment have substantially increased. For example, Gazprom reports fine increases from under 140 million rubles in 2009 to almost 2 billion in 2013.[58]

The Deputy Minister of Environment Nikolay Popov has commented that such a drastic increase in fines is justified by the lack of economic incentive for companies to invest into AGP utilization systems before the introduction of higher fines.[59] However, such approach has its critics too. Skolkovo Energy Centre has criticized such a one-sided regulation, using only financial instrument as a "stick." They have suggested that this approach can lead to the closure of the fields where utilization of the APG is simply not feasible (for example, remote fields).[60] The Decree, however, also contains a number of flexibility mechanisms.

While imposing comparatively large fines on the oil companies, the Decree's effectiveness for BC emissions reduction in the Arctic region might be undermined by a number of reasons. First and foremost, the present approach to gas flaring in Russia is based on a post-emission fine mechanism. Carbon Limits reports that: "to date there have been no license revocations due to failure to fulfill APG utilization rates, despite reported widespread non-compliance with APG utilization conditions specified in license agreements."[61] To effectively target the problem, the preventive approach should be taken, requiring companies to apply the best available technology to avoid flaring rather than "buying a right to flare."

Second, by virtue of Russian law only State oil companies operate on the Arctic shelf in Russia.[62] Doubts arise about whether real financial incentives exist for such companies to reduce flaring. Such State companies get substantial financial support from the State and with the lack of transparency of such processes it is hard to assess if fines indeed motivate companies to implement new technologies for gas flaring elimination.[63]

Third, the utilization rate is counted in total for all the company's installations,[64] meaning that while it can have a rather high utilization rate in the locations where it is convenient to utilize APG in the isolated locations (where most of the Arctic installations are) the utilization rate can be much lower and the company would still have an acceptable overall rate. Due to the unavailability or absence of the infrastructure, the inability of grid injection and the harsh climate conditions, it is possible that companies would continue to burn off the AGP in remote oil fields and level the overall rate by utilizing AGP more efficiently in more convenient locations.[65]

To further explore the regime interplay between international instruments to eliminate air emissions/gas flaring and Russian new regulations, it would be useful to try to establish the causal link between a certain regime or regulation and the positive outcome. The establishment of such link between the Arctic Council Offshore Oil and Gas Guidelines and the introduction of new national legislation is rather difficult. Not only are the Guidelines non-binding, the air emissions section is not very detailed and only calls for the regulation of APG flaring.[66] When it comes to the establishment of such a link with other international regimes, the most obvious one would be the United Nations Framework Convention on Climate Change (UNFCCC) regime influence. Despite dropping out of UNFCCC Kyoto Protocol 2nd commitment period, Russia pledged to reduce its greenhouse emissions by 25 percent from its 1990 level by 2020. Such claims, made by the Russian representative at the Conference of Parties to UNFCCC in Doha,[67] have been supported by the recent legislation adopted, reinforcing the commitment and creating a plan of steps that need to be taken to achieve the target.[68] Moreover, within the Framework of the Kyoto Protocol 1st commitment period near to twenty-five of the Joint Implementation Projects were directed at efficient utilization of the APG.[69] It would also be fair to suggest that the World Bank Global Gas Flaring Reduction Partnership (GGFR) Programme made its contribution to the process. Russia is a member of the Partnership and hosted a rather successful gas flaring reduction project in Khanty-Mansiisk Autonomous Okrug.[70]

The effectiveness of the Russian new APG legislation remains to be seen. However, as the regulated unit is not the volumes of flared gas, but rather the utilization rate, even in the event of success, the volume of emissions might not reduce. With growing production volumes, even if utilization grows, the emission volumes may grow as well. It is therefore advisable, that at least for the Arctic-related projects the emissions standards approach be used, rather than the utilization rate.

Norway

Norway is a country with long-standing oil development traditions. One of the largest exporters of crude oil,[71] Norway, through its state company Statoil has been operating in cold Arctic waters for decades. The country's Pollution Control Act is aimed at maintaining the satisfactory quality of the environment.[72] Generally, environmental pollution in Norway is regulated with a preventive approach: all pollution is prohibited,[73] unless specifically permitted by the Act itself[74] or by the relevant authorities.[75] That is not to say that Norway does not employ polluter-pays principle at all. Chapter 8 of the Pollution Control Act is covering compensation for pollution damage. The liability for environmental damage, however, is not limited to the financial.[76] In some instances of willful or negligent environmental damage, criminal liability can also be imposed.[77]

The same principle applies to the gas flaring. Back in 1971, the Norwegian government adopted their so-called "10 Oil Commandments," principles on which oil-related policies were to be built. One of these commandments prescribes that "flaring of exploitable gas on the Norwegian Continental Shelf must only be allowed in limited test periods."[78] In 1997, a zero-discharge target was established for the petroleum activities.[79] According to the Norwegian Petroleum Ministry, the main rule is that "no environmentally harmful substances may be released, neither added chemicals nor naturally occurring chemical substances that could harm the environment."[80]

The Norwegian Petroleum Act stipulates that the "burning of petroleum in excess of the quantities needed for normal operational safety shall not be allowed unless approved by the Ministry."[81] Each gas flaring application is dealt with by the Ministry on a case-by-case basis ensuring that the best available techniques (BAT) are used on an installation and that all the possible measures to avoid flaring are taken.[82] In this way, the issue of flaring is dealt with on the planning phase and development plans are only approved if they contain an acceptable solution for the APG.[83] The use of the BAT, though not set out as an obligation in the Pollution Control Act is imposed on Norway by the EU Pollution Control Directive.[84]

Additionally, the financial incentive to reduce flaring is also used for the petroleum sector in Norway. In 1991, a CO_2 tax for petroleum activities was introduced, which largely "contributed to development and use of technology."[85] Moreover, since 2008, the petroleum sector has been part of the Kyoto Protocol emission quota system for greenhouse gases.[86]

Through the combination of a preventive approach and financial incentives, Norway has established an exemplary regime for reducing gas flaring. The "Norwegian mode" for gas flaring is seen as one of the best in the world[87] and is being exported to other States.[88] The targets set by the authorities were rather ambitious, but "combined with a close dialogue with companies and a certain level of flexibility in implementation,"[89] they seem to have produced rather effective results. Norwegian oil installations produce less than half amount of CO_2 than an average oil producing country.[90]

Improving the effectiveness: a better solution for flaring in the Arctic?

The Arctic ecosystem is seen by the scientific community as a rather unique and fragile one for a number of reasons. The Arctic is unique in that many of its landscapes and seascapes are pristine;[91] its ecosystem, flora and fauna are very distinctive.[92] The Arctic is not uninhabited, like the Antarctic. The Circumpolar North is a home to over 4 million people,[93] many of whom are indigenous communities that remain linked to their lands and waters, and depend on subsistence.[94] In a global context, the Arctic is a "significant component of the diversity of life on Earth."[95]

There are, however, no special binding oil and gas development standards to provide special protection to the Arctic ecosystem. The possibility of adopting a binding treaty to regulate the Arctic has been a subject of heated debate over the last decade. Some believe that a conclusion of such a document is absolutely necessary for the protection of the Arctic environment,[96] others believe that "there is already a binding regime in the Arctic—UNCLOS" and the focus should be on the implementation of the existing obligations and "engaging the general public, business, politicians and governments."[97] The necessity of providing elevated environmental protection to the region in light of hydrocarbons development has been stressed in the EU Offshore Oil and Gas Directive.[98] The Arctic States themselves have declared their satisfaction with the present international framework and did not express a need in a new binding Arctic regime.[99]

To tackle the problem of BC, a group of commentators argue for the adoption of a rather specific document, "an Arctic regional agreement on black carbon" which "would complement and advance implementation of commitments under CLRTAP."[100] This approach has its advantages: because black carbon is a short-lived pollutant, it "tends to have more localized effects" and a regional agreement could be more effective in the Arctic context.[101]

This idea will be "half-way" realized by the soon to be published TFABCM Framework Document on BC. However, as mentioned above, such document is not intended to become a binding agreement. As gas flaring represents such a large share of BC emissions in the Arctic, it is possible that taking actions to reduce emissions from this particular practice could be an effective first step in combating BC.

Arctic oil and gas exploration and production is fully regulated by Arctic States' national legislation. There are no regional binding treaties on the matter.[102] Even though "the Arctic Council structure poses challenges to regulating the issue of short-lived climate forcers,"[103] it would be possible to continue the Council's trend of adopting binding treaties under its auspices and work on a binding gas flaring treaty.[104] This could be the first step in leveling the playing field of the environmental policies for Arctic oil and gas, creating a common set of rules for oil production in the Arctic that would represent the highest environmental standards.

Arctic oil and gas exploration and production is fully regulated by Arctic States' national legislation. There are no regional binding treaties on the matter. Even though "the Arctic Council structure poses challenges to regulating the issue of short-lived climate forcers,"[105] it would be possible to continue the Council's trend of adoption of binding treaties under its auspices and work on a binding gas flaring treaty. This could be the first step in leveling the playing field of the environmental policies for Arctic oil and gas, creating a common set of rules for oil production in the Arctic that would represent the highest environmental standards. In the latest BC and Methane Framework, the Council acknowledges the important role of the private sector in "reducing emissions, developing new technologies, and sharing best practices that will lower emissions, especially in key sectors like transportation and oil and gas development."[106]

The adoption of an Arctic-wide treaty on gas flaring with a reference to BC reduction could be an effective short-term global warming solution for a number of reasons. First, it would raise awareness on the BC issue and provide an incentive for States to take actions domestically. Second, it would facilitate further research on BC sources and effects, creating national inventories. Additionally, the agreement could potentially include a provision allowing other States to join. Should such measure indeed bring substantial reduction in BC emissions in the region, that could "buy time" for the international community to adopt and implement a successful CO_2 reduction treaty. Finally, a binding BC treaty could generally improve cooperation in the Arctic and strengthen the Arctic Council as an institution. The results of past regime effectiveness research are not definitive on whether global environmental treaties are more effective when non-binding.[107] Nevertheless, there are examples of binding solutions bringing good results. For example, recent findings suggest that the ozone hole above the Arctic was avoided due to the Montreal Protocol, which phased out ozone-depleting chemicals.[108]

The purpose of the treaty should lie in ensuring a uniform approach to the gas flaring in the Arctic which could be based on the Norwegian "zero tolerance" scheme in which flaring should generally be prohibited, unless specifically permitted by the relevant national authorities. The essential elements of a proposed treaty should include, among others:

1   monitoring of emission volumes, sources and effects, which can be done with the assistance of the AMAP;
2   transparency provisions obliging all States to make flaring data and environmental impact statements public;
3   BAT provisions obliging States to ensure that companies are only allowed to operate when they are using BAT even if they come with higher costs;
4   technology transfer between the Arctic States;
5   the representatives of the petroleum industry should be consulted during the negotiation process.

Conclusions

In 2015, the United States started its chairmanship at the Arctic Council. With the recent developments in the US Arctic and environmental policies[109] and the Obama Administration's focus on climate change, it is fair to suggest that this Council will be ready to take firm action on climate change. The adoption of an Arctic gas flaring treaty could be facilitated by using Offshore Guidelines and the Framework Document on BC as the basis for the future document. Moreover, the working gas flaring policy model is already present and just needs to be modified to address national peculiarities. As India and China, large emitters, are now observers to the Arctic Council, they are influenced by the Council processes and could potentially participate in future agreements. There is still undoubtedly a question on whether certain Arctic States would agree to a binding treaty, especially between States currently experiencing political and diplomatic tensions. It is important to note here that amidst the present conflicts between the USA and Russia over the situation in Ukraine and annexation of Crimea,[110] the Arctic Council activities have not been disrupted.[111]

Substantial reductions of BC emissions in the Arctic could have an immediate effect and provide the international community with so much needed time to negotiate a strong climate treaty under the UNFCCC framework. Routine gas flaring, the largest source of BC, is not only an unnecessary waste of a valuable resource but also an obsolete practice that needs to be eliminated. The effectiveness of current gas flaring policies and practices vary across the Arctic and the only way to stop routine flaring is to adopt the best preventative practices across the region. Even though the Arctic Council is a soft law institution, it has the capacity to take the first step in imposing the best environmental standards on the Arctic oil industry.

Notes

1 National Oceanic and Atmospheric Administration, Arctic Report Card 2014, accessed May 6, 2016, www.arctic.noaa.gov/reportcard/.
2 Arctic Climate Impact Assessment, *Impacts of a Warming Arctic* (Cambridge: Cambridge University Press, 2004); United Nations General Assembly Resolution 63/281(2009) A/RES/63/281.
3 The World Bank and the International Cryosphere Climate Initiative (ICCI), *On Thin Ice: How Cutting Pollution Can Slow Warming and Save Lives* (The World Bank, 2013), xvii.
4 Tami C. Bond et al., "Bounding the Role of Black Carbon in the Climate System: A Scientific Assessment," *Journal of Geophysical Research: Atmosphere* 118.11 (2003): 5380; Arctic Council Task Force on Short-Lived Climate Forcers (TF SLCF), *Recommendations to Reduce Black Carbon and Methane Emissions to Slow Arctic Climate Change* (2013), 2; World Bank and ICCI, *On Thin Ice*, 2.
5 United Nations Environmental Programme and World Meteorological Organization (UNEP and WMO), *Integrated Assessment of Black Carbon and Tropospheric Ozone* (2011), 274.
6 Arctic Council TF SLCF, *Recommendations*, 6.
7 Ibid.
8 World Bank and ICCI, *On Thin Ice*, 57; Andreas Stohl et al., "Black Carbon in the Arctic: the Underestimated Role of Gas Flaring and Residential Combustion Emissions," *Atmospheric Chemistry and Physics* 13 (2013): 8833.
9 Carbon Limits, *Best Practices for Reduction of Methane and Black Carbon from Arctic Oil and Gas Production* (2012), 3, accessed August 16, 2015, www.carbonlimits.no/PDF/Best%20Practices%20for%20the%20reduction%20of%20black%20carbon%20and%20methane.pdf.
10 Stohl et al., "Black Carbon in the Arctic."

11 Arctic Council, Protection of the Arctic Marine Environment (PAME), Arctic Offshore Oil and Gas Guidelines (adopted April 29, 2009) section 6.3; Arctic Council Secretariat, Kiruna Declaration of the 8th Ministerial Meeting of the Arctic Council (May 15, 2013).

12 For example, the Russian Federation introduced a new Decree 1148 on the Calculation of Fines for Emissions to Air Formed through Flaring or Venting of Associated Petroleum Gas (November 8, 2012); Alberta Energy Regulator has released Directive 060 on Upstream Petroleum Industry Flaring, Incinerating, and Venting (May 1, 2014).

13 For example, in 2014, a US court ruled against Shell, halting the offshore drilling due to the unsatisfactory environmental impact statement (*Native Village of Point Hope* v. *Jewell*, 44 ELR 2001, N 12–35287 [9th Circuit Court of Appeal 2014]). Additionally, Russian Arctic oil production is hit by Western sanctions prohibiting Western companies from selling, supplying, transferring or exporting technology to Russian companies for the purposes of oil development in the Arctic (Council Regulation [EU] 833/2014 of July 31, 2014 Concerning Restrictive Measures in View of Russia's Actions Destabilising the Situation in Ukraine [2014] OJ L 229/1–11 Article 3, annex II); Executive Order 13662 Blocking Property of Additional Persons Contributing to the Situation in Ukraine 79 (56) C.F.R. 16169 (March 24, 2014).

14 "Shell Resumes Arctic Drilling but Cuts $15bn from Global Investment," *BBC News*, January 29, 2015, accessed February 20, 2015, www.bbc.com/news/business-31034870; Trude Pettersen, "First Winter Shipment of Oil from Yamal," *BarentsObserver*, February 20, 2015, accessed February 25, 2015, http://barentsobserver.com/en/energy/2015/02/first-winter-shipment-oil-yamal-20-02.

15 "Substantially" in the present context means near 90 percent reduction. This figure is based on the policy goals of the Arctic States such as 95 percent in Russian Federation, and on the past experience: for example, in Alberta, Canada a 70 percent reduction in gas flaring was achieved between 1996 and 2003 due to the policy change, in Norway, about 90 percent, according to Arctic Council TF SLCF, *Recommendations*, 8.

16 For example, "to provide means for promoting cooperation, coordination and interaction amongst the Arctic States [...] in particular, issues of sustainable development and environmental protection in the Arctic," Declaration on the Establishment of the Arctic Council, section 1a (Ottawa Declaration, signed September 19, 1996); "[...]sustainable socio-economic development," Russian Federation 2014 Arctic Zone Development Strategy Objective.

17 Oran R. Young, "Evaluating the Success of International Environmental Regimes: Where Are We Now?" *Global Environmental Change* 12 (2002): 73.

18 Protocol on Environmental Protection to the Antarctic Treaty (signed October 4, 1991; entered into force January 14, 2008), *ILM* 30 (1991): 1455.

19 United Nations Convention on Law of the Sea (UNCLOS, signed December 10, 1982; entered into force November 16, 1994), *UNTS* (1833): 3.

20 Among others, Convention on Biological Diversity (signed June 5, 1992; entered into force December 29, 1993), *UNTS* (1760): 79; Convention on Long-Range Transboundary Air Pollution (CLRTAP, signed November 3, 1979; entered into force March 16, 1983), *UNTS* (1302): 217. Part of the Arctic marine environment is covered by the Convention for the Protection of the Marine Environment of the North-East Atlantic (OSPAR Convention, signed September 22, 1992; entered into force March 25, 1998), *UNTS* (2354): 67.

21 Article 234 UNCLOS. See Joe Borg, Member of the European Commission Responsible for Fisheries and Maritime Affairs, "The Arctic: a Matter of Concern to Us All," Speech delivered at the conference "Common Concern for the Arctic," Ilulissat, September 9, 2008.

22 The draft Polar Code was approved by the IMO's Marine Environment Protection Committee (MEPC) on October 20, 2014, adopted with further amendments in May 2015, and will enter into force by January 2017. IMO MEPC 67th Session Briefing 32 (2014).

23 The IMO first addressed shipping in Arctic ice-covered waters in 2002 by adopting relevant Guidelines. The latest edition of Guidelines for Ships Operating in Polar Waters was approved by the IMO Resolution A.1024 (26) from December 2, 2009. Recently, the IMO has reportedly agreed to include BC definition in the Polar Code: "IMO Progress on Black Carbon in Arctic 'Welcome but Long Overdue'," *Transport and Environment*, January 23, 2015, accessed February 25, 2015, www.transportenvironment.org/press/imo-progress-black-carbon-arctic-%E2%80%98welcome-long-overdue %E2%80%99.

24 Agreement on the Conservation of Polar Bears (signed November 15, 1973; entered into force May 26, 1976) *UST* (27): 3918.

25 On the earlier steps in international law and environment in the Arctic, see Donald R. Rothwell, "International Law and the Protection of the Arctic Environment," *International and Comparative Law Quarterly* 44.2 (1995): 280.

26 Ottawa Declaration.

27 Canada, Denmark, Finland, Iceland, Norway, the Russian Federation, Sweden and the United States of America.

28 Donald R. Rothwell, "Polar Opposites: Environmental Discourses and Management in Antarctica and the Arctic," in *Environmental Discourses in Public and International Law*, edited by Brad Jessup and Kim Rubenstein (Cambridge: Cambridge University Press, 2012), 355 and 367.

29 Olav S. Stokke and Geir Hønneland (eds), *International Cooperation and Arctic Governance: Regime Effectiveness and Northern Region Building* (London: Routledge, 2007), 182–83.

30 Ibid., 183.

31 Ibid., 182.

32 Agreement on Cooperation on Aeronautical and Maritime Search and Rescue in the Arctic (signed May 12, 2011; entered into force January 19, 2013); Agreement on Cooperation on Marine Oil Pollution, Preparedness and Response in the Arctic (signed May 15, 2013). Yuval Shany, when assessing the effectiveness of international courts, argued that the analysis of the first years of a court's functioning "may fail to accurately capture delayed instances of goal attainment" as it could still be in its phase of trial and error. The same "time-frame" argument could be used for assessing the effectiveness of the Arctic Council. Yuval Shany, *Assessing the Effectiveness of International Courts* (Oxford: Oxford University Press, 2014), 23.

33 The main short-lived climate forcers are BC, methane, tropospheric ozone and some hydrofluorocarbons.

34 Arctic Council TF SLCF, *Progress Report and Recommendations for Ministers* (2011), 1.

35 Kiruna Declaration.

36 Ibid.

37 Ibid.

38 Arctic Council TFABCM, *6th Meeting Summary Report* (Tromsø, November 17–18, 2014).

39 Kiruna Declaration.

40 Arctic Council TFABCM, *6th Meeting Summary Report*.

41 Arctic Council TFABCM, *5th Meeting Summary Report* (Iqaluit, September 29–October 1, 2014).

42 Anna Vinogradova, "Anthropogenic Black Carbon Emissions to the Atmosphere: Surface Distribution through Russian Territory," *Atmospheric and Oceanic Optics* 27 (2014): 1059–65 [in Russian].

43 Arctic Council, *Enhanced Black Carbon and Methane Emissions Reductions: An Arctic Council Framework for Action*, Annex 4 to the SAO Report to the Ministers, Iqaluit Ministerial Meeting, April 24, 2015.

44 Chief Michael Stickman of the Arctic Athabaskan Council quoted in Heather Exner-Pirot, "Arctic Council Ministerial – Winners and Losers," *Alaska Dispatch News*, April 29, 2015, accessed August 17, 2015, www.adn.com/article/20150429/arctic-council-ministerial-winners-and-losers.

45 For further discussions on international cooperation efforts for research on BC effects and reduction recommendations, see World Bank and ICCI, *On Thin Ice*, 212; Lindsey Griffith, *The Last Climate Frontier: Leveraging the Arctic Council to Make Progress on Black Carbon and Methane. Policy Prescriptions for Making the U.S. Chairmanship of the Arctic Council Count on Key Climate Variables* (Clean Air Task Force, 2014), 6, 10–11.

46 Protocol to the 1979 Convention on Long-Range Transboundary Air Pollution to Abate Acidification, Eutrophication and Ground-Level Ozone (Gothenburg Protocol, signed November 30, 1999; entered into force May 17, 2005), *UNTS* (2319): 81.

47 Executive Body of the CLRTAP, Decision 2012/2 Amendment of the Text of and Annexes II to IX to the 1999 Protocol to Abate Acidification, Eutrophication and Ground-Level Ozone and the Addition of New Annexes X and XI ECE/EB.AIR/111/Add.1.

48 Donald L. Gautier et al., "Assessment of Undiscovered Oil and Gas in the Arctic," *Science* 324.5931 (2009): 1175.

49 Gertrude Lube-Wolff, "Efficient Environmental Legislation – On Different Philosophies of Pollution Control in Europe," *Journal of Environmental Law* 13 (2001): 80–81 as quoted in Jane Holder and Maria Lee, *Environmental Protection, Law and Policy: Text and Materials* 2nd edn (Cambridge: Cambridge University Press, 2007), 363. A similar classification can be found in Richard MacRory, *Regulation, Enforcement, and Government in Environmental Law* 2nd edn (Oxford: Hart Publishing, 2014), 135.

50 Gautier et al., "Assessment of Undiscovered Oil and Gas in the Arctic."

51 Global Gas Flaring Reduction (GGFR), *Flaring Estimates by Satellite Observations* (GGFR, 2012), 2. However, Russian data sources usually claim figures around 20 percent lower than those provided by GGFR and the World Bank. That could be attributable to a "combination of overestimates from satellite-based data sources and underreporting in national statistics" according to *Carbon Limits Associated Petroleum Gas Flaring Study for Russia, Kazakhstan, Turkmenistan and Azerbaijan* (Report for EBRD, *Carbon Limits*, 2013), 17.

52 Government of the Russian Federation, Decree No. 1148, "On the Calculation of Fines for the Emissions to Air Formed through Flaring and (or) Venting of Associated Petroleum Gas" (signed November 8, 2008; entered into force January 1, 2013) [in Russian].

53 Ibid., preamble.

54 Government of the Russian Federation, Decree No. 7, "On Measures to Stimulate Reduction of Emissions to Air Formed through Flaring of Associated Petroleum Gas" (signed January 8, 2009, not in force) [in Russian].

55 Russian Federation, Decree No. 1148, Article 2.

56 Ibid., Article 5.

57 Federal Law of Russian Federation No. 7-FZ, "On Environmental Protection" (signed January 10, 2002), *Sobranie Zakonodatel'stva Rossiiskoi Federatsii* 2 (2002): 133, Article 6.

58 Gazprom, Environmental Report 2013 (Gazprom, 2013), 16 [in Russian].
59 Nikolay Popov, Speech at the opening of the Regional Conference of Europe and Central Asia "Experience of the RF Government and Oil Companies in Efficient Use of APG" (Surgut, May 31, 2013).
60 Skolkovo Energy Center, *Utilization of Associated Petroleum Gas: Problem of 2012* (2012), 2, 23 [in Russian].
61 Report for EBRD, *Carbon Limits*, 20.
62 Federal Law of Russian Federation No. 23–95–1, "On Mineral Resources" (signed February 21, 1992), *Sobranie Zakonodatel'stva Rossiiskoi Federatsii* 10 (1995): 823, Article 9 [in Russian].
63 Lars P. Lunden and Daniel Fjaertoft, *Government Support to Upstream Oil and Gas in Russia: How Subsidies Influence the Yamal LNG and Prirazlomnoe Projects* (WWF/IISD/Sigra Group/GSI, 2014).
64 Russian Federation, Decree No. 1148, Article 11.
65 Report for EBRD, *Carbon Limits*, 20–21; WWF, *Analytical Report on Economic and Environmental Effects of Gas Flaring in Russia* (WWF, 2013), 35 [in Russian].
66 Arctic Offshore Oil and Gas Guidelines.
67 Statement of the Advisor to the President of the Russian Federation, Special Representative of the President of the Russian Federation on Climate Change, Mr. Alexander Bedritskiy, to the 18th Conference of the Parties to the UNFCCC, Doha. Qatar. December 6, 2012, accessed August 17, 2015, http://unfccc.int/resource/docs/cop18_cmp8_hl_statements/Statement%20by%20Russia%20%28COP%20%29.pdf.
68 President of Russian Federation, Order No. 752, "On Greenhouse Gas Emissions Reduction" (signed September 30, 2013); Government of the Russian Federation, Decree No. 504-r establishing the Plan of Measures for the Achievement by 2020 Reduction in Greenhouse Gas Emissions to 75 percent of the year 1990 Level (April 2, 2014).
69 KPMG and WWF, *Problems and Perspectives of Associated Petroleum Gas Utilization in Russia*, Annual Review 4, 24–26 [in Russian].
70 "Igniting Solutions to Gas Flaring in Russia," The World Bank, November 12, 2013, accessed February 20, 2015, www.worldbank.org/en/news/feature/2013/11/12/igniting-solutions-to-gas-flaring-in-russia.
71 United States Energy Information Administration, accessed February 21, 2015, www.eia.gov/countries/index.cfm?topL=exp.
72 Act No. 6 Concerning Protection against Pollution and Concerning Waste (Norwegian Pollution Control Act, signed March 13, 1981), section 7.
73 Ibid., section 1.
74 For example, ordinary pollution from fisheries, agriculture and forestry. Ibid., section 8.
75 Norwegian Pollution Control Act, section 11. See also, Hans C. Bugge, "General Introduction," in *IEL Environmental Law*, edited by Deketelaere Kurt et al. (Alphen aan den Rijn: Kluwer Law International, 2014), 20.
76 Norwegian Pollution Control Act, Chapter 8.
77 Ibid., Chapter 10.
78 As quoted in Norwegian Ministry of Petroleum and Energy, *An Industry for the Future – Norway's Petroleum Activities* (Report to the Storting, 2011), 8.
79 Storting (Norwegian Government) White Paper No. 58 (1996–1997).
80 Norwegian Ministry of Petroleum and Energy, *An Industry for the Future*, 24.
81 Act No. 72 Relating to Petroleum Activities (Norwegian Petroleum Act, signed November 29, 1996) section 4–4.
82 "Comparison of Associated Gas Flaring Regulations: Alberta and Norway," The World Bank, accessed February 21, 2015, http://siteresources.worldbank.org/EXTGGFR/Resources/578068–1258067586081/Alberta_Norway_regulations_comparison.pdf.

83 Ibid.
84 Not being a European Union (EU) Member State, Norway is still bound by some EU legislation through its participation in the European Economic Area (EEA) Agreement. Directive 2008/1/EC of January 15, 2008 Concerning Integrated Pollution Prevention and Control (2008) OJ L 24/8.
85 Act No. 72 Relating to Tax on Discharge of CO_2 in the Petroleum Activities on the Continental Shelf (signed December 21, 1990); Norwegian Ministry of Petroleum and Energy, *An Industry for the Future*, 121.
86 Norwegian Ministry of Petroleum and Energy, *An Industry for the Future*, 25.
87 Gulzhan Nurakhmet, "Gas Flaring And Venting: What Can Kazakhstan Learn From The Norwegian Experience?," *CEPMLP Annual Review 10*, accessed August 17, 2015, www.dundee.ac.uk/cepmlp/gateway/?news=28103.
88 The Norwegian Government and the World Bank have issued a report on standards of gas flaring to be adopted in the countries participating in Gas Flaring Reduction Initiative. The World Bank, *A Voluntary Standard for Global Gas Flaring and Venting Reduction* (2004).
89 Report for EBRD, *Carbon Limits*, 39.
90 Antony T. Buller, *Compatibility between Norwegian Petroleum Activities and Environmental Stewardship: A Case for Boosting Mainstream Petroleum Research Funding* (OG21, 2009), 10.
91 Conservation of Arctic Flora and Fauna (CAFF), *Arctic Flora and Fauna: Status and Conservation* (2001), 256.
92 Ibid., 45, 256; Thor S. Larsen, "The Uniqueness of the Arctic," *GRID-Arendal*, accessed August 17, 2015, www.grida.no/publications/et/at/page.aspx.
93 Arctic Human Development Report (Stefansson Arctic Institute, 2004), 27.
94 CAFF, *Arctic Flora and Fauna*, 256.
95 Ibid., 45. See also, K.I. Johnsen et al., *Protecting Arctic Biodiversity* (UNEP, GRID-Arendal, 2010).
96 Scott G. Borgerson, "Arctic Meltdown: The Economic and Security Implications of Global Warming," *Foreign Affairs* 87.2 (March–April 2008), accessed August 17, 2015, www.foreignaffairs.com/articles/arctic-antarctic/2008–03–02/arctic-meltdown; Melissa A. Verhaag, "It is Not Too Late: The Need for a Comprehensive International Treaty to Protect the Arctic Environment," *Georgetown International Environmental Law Review* 15 (2003): 555–81.
97 Hans Corell, "Reflections on the Possibilities and Limitations of a Binding Legal Regime," *Environmental Policy and Law* 37.4 (2007): 321–24.
98 Directive 2013/30/EU of June 12, 2013 on Safety of Offshore Oil and Gas operations and Amending Directive 2004/35/EC (2013) OJ L 178/66, recital 52. In negotiations of the Directive even the possibility of banning Arctic offshore drilling was discussed.
99 The Ilulissat Declaration (May 27–29, 2008).
100 Martin Williams and Erika Rosenthal, "Time for Leadership on Black Carbon," *WWF The Circle* 1 (2013): 21.
101 Dennis Clare, Kristina Pistone and Veerabhadran Ramanathan, "Getting Rid of Black Carbon a Neglected but Effective Near-Term Climate Mitigation Avenue," *Georgetown Journal of International Affairs* 11.2 (2010): 99, 103.
102 Except for bilateral agreements between Russia and Norway, for example. In 2009, the Arctic Council issued Arctic Offshore Oil and Gas Guidelines, which represent a set of non-binding principles and recommendations, and do not create any new rules.
103 Griffith, *The Last Climate Frontier*, 52.
104 Young noted that: "a regime that links actors that share a tradition of effective cooperation in other issue areas […] is more likely to succeed than a similar arrangement that must build bridges among antagonistic actors." Oran R. Young, "Evaluating the Success of International Environmental Regimes," 75.

105 Griffith, *The Last Climate Frontier.*
106 Arctic Council, *Enhanced Black Carbon.*
107 See Jon B. Skjærseth, Olav S. Stokke and Jørgen Wettestad, "Soft Law, Hard Law, and Effective Implementation of International Environmental Norms," *Global Environmental Politics* 6.3 (2006): 104.
108 Martyn P. Chipperfield et al., "Quantifying the Ozone and Ultraviolet Benefits Already Achieved by the Montreal Protocol," *Nature Communications* 6 (2015): 7233.
109 For example, the recent withdrawal of nearly 10 million acres in the US Arctic from oil leases. "Interior Department Announces Draft Strategy for Offshore Oil and Gas leasing," Department of Interior Press Release, January 27, 2015, accessed August 17, 2015, www.doi.gov/news/pressreleases/interior-department-announces-draft-strategy-for-offshore-oil-and-gas-leasing.cfm.
110 Julian Borger, "US and Russia in Danger of Returning to Era of Nuclear Rivalry," *The Guardian*, January 4, 2015, accessed August 17, 2015, www.theguardian.com/world/2015/jan/04/us-russia-era-nuclear-rivalry.
111 There was only one episode of Canada skipping an Arctic Council meeting. "Canada to Skip Arctic Council Meeting in Moscow," *CTV News*, April 15, 2014, accessed August 17, 2015, www.ctvnews.ca/canada/canada-to-skip-arctic-council-meeting-in-moscow-1.1777444.

Bibliography

Arctic Climate Impact Assessment. *Impacts of a Warming Arctic.* Cambridge: Cambridge University Press, 2004.
BBC News. "Shell Resumes Arctic Drilling but Cuts $15bn from Global Investment." January 29, 2015. Accessed February 20, 2015, www.bbc.co.uk/news/business-31034870.
Bond, Tami C. et al. "Bounding the Role of Black Carbon in the Climate System: A Scientific Assessment." *Journal of Geophysical Research: Atmosphere* 118.11 (2003): 5380–5552.
Borg, Joe. "The Arctic: A Matter of Concern to Us All," Speech delivered at the conference "Common Concern for the Arctic." Ilulissat, September 9, 2008.
Borger, Julian. "US and Russia in Danger of Returning to Era of Nuclear Rivalry." *The Guardian*, January 4, 2015. Accessed August 17, 2015, www.theguardian.com/world/2015/jan/04/us-russia-era-nuclear-rivalry.
Borgerson, Scott G. "Arctic Meltdown: The Economic and Security Implications of Global Warming." *Foreign Affairs* 87.2 (March–April 2008). Accessed August 17, 2015, www.foreignaffairs.com/articles/arctic-antarctic/2008–03–02/arctic-meltdown.
Boyle, Alan, and Christine Chinkin. *The Making of International Law.* Oxford, New York: Oxford University Press, 2007.
Bugge, Hans Cristian. "General Introduction." In IEL Environmental Law, edited by Deketelaere Kurt et al., 15–66. Alphen aan den Rijn: Kluwer Law International, 2014.
Buller, Anthony T. *Compatibility between Norwegian Petroleum Activities and Environmental Stewardship: A Case for Boosting Mainstream Petroleum Research Funding* (OG21, 2009).
Chipperfield, Martyn P. et al., "Quantifying the Ozone and Ultraviolet Benefits Already Achieved by the Montreal Protocol." *Nature Communications* 6 (2015).

Clare, Dennis, Kristina Pistone, and Veerabhadran Ramanathan. "Getting Rid of Black Carbon A Neglected but Effective Near-Term Climate Mitigation Avenue." *Georgetown Journal of International Affairs* 11.2 (2010): 99–107.

Corell, Hans. "Reflections on the Possibilities and Limitations of a Binding Legal Regime." *Environmental Policy and Law* 37.4 (2007): 321–24.

CTV News. "Canada to Skip Arctic Council Meeting in Moscow." April 15, 2014. Accessed August 17, 2015, www.ctvnews.ca/canada/canada-to-skip-arctic-council-meeting-in-moscow-1.1777444.

Department of Interior Press Release. "Interior Department Announces Draft Strategy for Offshore Oil and Gas Leasing," January 27, 2015. Accessed August 17, 2015, www.doi.gov/news/pressreleases/interior-department-announces-draft-strategy-for-offshore-oil-and-gas-leasing.cfm.

Exner-Pirot, Heather. "Arctic Council Ministerial – Winners and Losers." *Alaska Dispatch News*, April 29, 2015, accessed August 17, 2015, www.adn.com/article/20150429/arctic-council-ministerial-winners-and-losers.

Gautier, Donald L. et al., "Assessment of Undiscovered Oil and Gas in the Arctic." *Science* 324.5931 (2009): 1175–79.

Griffith, Lindsey. *The Last Climate Frontier: Leveraging the Arctic Council to Make Progress on Black Carbon and Methane. Policy Prescriptions for Making the U.S. Chairmanship of the Arctic Council Count on Key Climate Variables.* CleanAir Task Force, 2014.

Hof, Andries F., Michel G.J. Den Elzen and Detlef P. van Vuuren. "Environmental Effectiveness and Economic Consequences of Fragmented versus Universal Regimes: What Can We Learn from Model Studies?" *International Environmental Agreements: Politics, Law and Economics* 9.1 (2009): 39–62.

Holder, Jane, and Maria Lee. *Environmental Protection, Law and Policy: Text and Materials* 2nd edn. Cambridge: Cambridge University Press, 2007.

Jessup, Brad and Kim Rubenstein (eds). *Environmental Discourses in Public and International Law.* Cambridge: Cambridge University Press, 2012.

Larsen, Thor S. "The Uniqueness of the Arctic." *GRID-Arendal,* accessed August 17, 2015, www.grida.no/publications/et/at/page.aspx.

Levy, Marc A. "European Acid Rain: The Power of Tote-Board Diplomacy." In *Institutions for the Earth: Sources of Effective International Environmental Protection,* edited by Peter M. Haas, Robert O. Keohane and Marc A. Levy. Cambridge, MA and London: MIT Press, 1993.

Lube-Wolff, Gertrude. "Efficient Environmental Legislation – On Different Philosophies of Pollution Control in Europe." *Journal of Environmental Law* 13 (2001): 79–89.

Lunden, Lars P. and Daniel Fjaertoft. *Government Support to Upstream Oil & Gas in Russia: How Subsidies Influence the Yamal LNG and Prirazlomnoe Projects* (WWF/IISD/Sigra Group/GSI 2014).

MacRory, Richard. *Regulation, Enforcement, and Government in Environmental Law* 2nd edn. Oxford: Hart Publishing, 2014.

McGrath, Chris. *Does Environmental Law Work? How to Evaluate the Effectiveness of an Environmental Legal System.* Saarbrucken: Lambert Academic Publishing, 2010.

Møller, Hans Skotte. *Nordic Workshop on Action related to Short-lived Climate Forcers.* Copenhagen: TemaNord, 2012.

Muir, Derek C.G. and Cynthia A. de Wit. "Trends of Legacy and New Persistent Organic Pollutants in the Circumpolar Arctic: Overview, Conclusions, and Recommendations." *Science of the Total Environment* 408 (2010): 3044–51.

National Oceanic and Atmospheric Administration. Arctic Report Card 2014. Accessed February 20, 2015, www.arctic.noaa.gov/reportcard/.

Norwegian Ministry of Petroleum and Energy, *An Industry for the Future – Norway's Petroleum Activities.* Report to the Storting (2011).

Nurakhmet, Gulzhan. "Gas Flaring And Venting: What Can Kazakhstan Learn From The Norwegian Experience?." *CEPMLP Annual Review* 10, accessed August 17, 2015, www.dundee.ac.uk/cepmlp/gateway/?news=28103.

Pettersen, Trude. "First Winter Shipment of Oil from Yamal." *BarentsObserver*, February 20, 2015. Accessed February 25, 2015, http://barentsobserver.com/en/energy/2015/02/first-winter-shipment-oil-yamal-20-02.

Popov, Nikolay. Speech at the opening of the Regional Conference of Europe and Central Asia "Experience of the RF Government and Oil Companies in Efficient Use of APG." Surgut, May 31, 2013.

Rothwell, Donald R. "International Law and the Protection of the Arctic Environment." *International and Comparative Law Quarterly* 44.2 (1995): 280–313.

Rothwell, Donald R. "Polar Opposites: Environmental Discourses and Management in Antarctica and the Arctic." In *Environmental Discourses in Public and International Law*, edited by Brad Jessup and Kim Rubenstein, 355–75. Cambridge: Cambridge University Press, 2012.

Saladin, Claudia. "The LRTAP POPs Protocol and its Relevance to the Global POPs Negotiations." *Center for International Environmental Law.* Accessed August 17, 2015, www.ciel.org/Publications/LRTAPPOPsProtocolGlobal.pdf.

Shadian, Jessica M. *The Politics of Arctic Sovereignty: Oil, Ice, and Inuit Governance.* London and New York: Routledge, 2014.

Shany, Yuval. *Assessing the Effectiveness of International Courts.* Oxford: Oxford University Press, 2014.

Skjærseth, Jon B., Olav S. Stokke and Jørgen Wettestad, "Soft Law, Hard Law, and Effective Implementation of International Environmental Norms." *Global Environmental Politics* 6.3 (2006): 104–20.

Skolkovo Energy Center, *Utilization of Associated Petroleum Gas: Problem of 2012* (2012) [in Russian].

Sprinz, Detlef E. and Carsten Helm. "The Effect of Global Environmental Regimes: A Measurement Concept." *International Political Science Review* 20.4 (1999): 359–69.

Stohl, Andreas et al. "Black Carbon in the Arctic: The Underestimated Role of Gas Flaring and Residential Combustion Emissions." *Atmospheric Chemistry and Physics* 13 (2013): 8833–55.

Stokke, Olav S. "Examining the Consequences of Arctic Institutions." In *International Cooperation and Arctic Governance: Regime Effectiveness and Northern Region Building*, edited by Olav S. Stokke and Geir Hønneland, 13–27. London: Routledge, 2007.

Stokke, Olav S. "The Interplay of International Regimes: Putting Effectiveness Theory to Work." *The Fridtjof Nansen Institute (FNI) Report* 14 (2014): 1–35.

Stokke, Olav S. and Geir Hønneland (eds). *International Cooperation and Arctic Governance: Regime Effectiveness and Northern Region Building.* London: Routledge, 2007.

Storting (Norwegian Government) White Paper No. 58 (1996–1997).

Transport and Environment. "IMO Progress on Black Carbon in Arctic 'Welcome but Long Overdue'," January 23, 2015. Accessed February 25, 2015, www.transport environment.org/press/imo-progress-black-carbon-arctic-per centE2 per cent80 per cent98welcome-long-overdue per centE2 per cent80 per cent99.

United Nations Environmental Programme and World Meteorological Organization, *Integrated Assessment of Black Carbon and Tropospheric Ozone* (2011).

United States Energy Information Administration. Accessed February 21, 2015, www.eia.gov/countries/index.cfm?topL=exp.

Verhaag, Melissa A. "It is Not Too Late: The Need for a Comprehensive International Treaty to Protect the Arctic Environment." *Georgetown International Environmental Law Review* 15 (2003): 555–81.

Vinogradova, Anna. "Anthropogenic Black Carbon Emissions to the Atmosphere: Surface Distribution through Russian Territory." *Atmospheric and Oceanic Optics* 27 (2014): 1059–65 [in Russian].

Williams, Martin and Erika Rosenthal. "Time for Leadership on Black Carbon." *WWF The Circle* 1 (2013): 1–28.

Wilson, Simon et al. "Trends in Stockholm Convention Persistent Organic Pollutants in Arctic Air, Human Media and Biota." *AMAP Technical Report* 7 (2014): 1–62.

The World Bank. *A Voluntary Standard for Global Gas Flaring and Venting Reduction.* 2004.

The World Bank and the International Cryosphere Climate Initiative. *On Thin Ice: How Cutting Pollution Can Slow Warming and Save Lives.* The World Bank, 2013.

The World Bank. "Comparison of Associated Gas Flaring Regulations: Alberta and Norway." Accessed February 21, 2015, http://siteresources.worldbank.org/EXTGGFR/Resources/578068-1258067586081/Alberta_Norway_regulations_comparison.pdf.

The World Bank. "Igniting Solutions to Gas Flaring in Russia." November 12, 2013. Accessed February 20, 2015, www.worldbank.org/en/news/feature/2013/11/12/igniting-solutions-to-gas-flaring-in-russia.

WWF. *Analytical Report on Economic and Environmental Effects of Gas Flaring in Russia.* WWF 2013 [in Russian].

Young, Oran R. "Evaluating the Success of International Environmental Regimes: Where Are We Now?" *Global Environmental Change* 12.1 (2002): 73–77.

Part V

Geopolitical and security challenges

17 From cylinder to sphere

The impact of climate change in the Arctic beyond the Polar Circle

Ángel Gómez de Ágreda

Introduction

The two single most misleading truths are statistics and maps. You can tell (or sell) a thousand stories with a single spreadsheet or a custom-made map. And it really matters very little what the truth is when you are the one deciding on the units and the scale. Units and projections constitute a specific mindset on which we build our ideas and narratives. And we make them fit the model, for it is far more comfortable to distort the data than to change the scenario against which they are set.

Regardless of what we want to think of ourselves, most of us who live in the mild medium latitudes are used to thinking about the globe as a cylinder more than a sphere. We have learned to disregard both the "upper" and the "lower" end of the planet as something beyond our reach.

The very visualization of the way Mercator[1] produced his projection of Earth so that it could be seen on a two dimensional plane suffices to illustrate our mindset.

Mercator basically inserted the globe inside a cylinder tangential to it at the Equator, put a light at the center of the earth and depicted what was projected on the inner surface of the cylinder. After "opening up" the cylinder, he obtained a graphic representation of the better part of Earth in which both poles would never be shown as their projection runs parallel to the surface of the cylinder.

In practical terms, Mercator was representing not only most of the inhabited land mass, but was also highlighting, much like Lambert's conical projection, the medium latitudes where the dominant powers lay. Mercator's projection was useful for navigational purposes and it only left out barren, unexplored, unexploited and unexploitable land and sea masses.

It was not until commercial aviation begun using polar routes that geographers paid some attention to whatever happened beyond the Polar Circle. Climate change and the melting of the polar ice caps are changing that for good.

Receding ice in the Arctic regions will impact many aspects of our lives within the next few years and decades. Most of the consequences of climate change in the Arctic have already been discussed, mostly one at a time. I intend to highlight the most profound of the geopolitical changes it will have, a change we most likely have not even considered as we did not realize how biased our view was: the change in the paradigm from a "cylindrical" Earth to a spherical one.

Passages and routes: a new "string of pearls"?

The concept of the Global Commons and its links with security and defense was recently reintroduced by Dr. Dick Bedford and a few others working at NATO's Allied Command Transformation (ACT) in Norfolk, Virginia.[2] Though widely known and researched by lawyers and economists around the world, its importance for military operations was only highlighted at the beginning of the present decade along with the inclusion of cyberspace to the list of fighting domains.[3]

The history of human conflict is the history of the fight for resources, the fight for markets and the fight for the routes which interconnect those resources and the production and consumption centers. Globalization does not change the concept itself, but it certainly modifies the scale and the scope of the struggle.

The ability of the Arctic to contribute additional resources—and, therefore, to stimulate the greed of nations and corporations—is discussed later in this chapter. The value of the Arctic communities to constitute a worthy market will depend on their future development. However, the role of the Northern and Northwest Passages can already be estimated if we look at and compare them with other routes currently in use or just being developed.

Possession of a resource means little in today's cooperative and highly interdependent economies. Let us take the case of Iran and its vast hydrocarbon resources. The embargo imposed by the international community on both its exports and access to the necessary equipment to transform crude oil into usable fuel and other products has had one of the larger producers in the world importing diesel fuel and gasoline.

Thomas P. Barnett,[4] in his famous map, divides the world between the so-called functioning core and the non-integrated gap. While there could be some disagreement about the exact boundary between both worlds, and even admitting the fact that this boundary may shift over time, Barnett's message still holds: the world is divided between those economies which are intertwined and inter-dependent and those which are close to irrelevant on a global scale. It does not matter how large an economy is, what matters is how much it is linked to others.

In order to realize the preponderance of routes over nodes, it is useful to bear in mind how civil societies are configuring themselves these days. Most economists are talking about the incoming "age of abundance," meaning that resources will cease to be scarce as technology is able to create more wealth than we can use.

It will not be production that will really matter in the next few decades but distribution of the wealth we have produced at a very low marginal cost per unit.[5] Therefore, it will be the control over the routes upon which goods are being distributed which will define the power of the nations.[6] The not-so-subtle competition for outposts along the Indian Ocean is proof that most nations understand the relevance of trade and the autonomy of their own fleets as something of paramount importance.

The race for the trade routes in the Indian Ocean can be seen in a number of recent developments ranging from military missions and deployments to a discreet, yet constant, expansion of China's logistic locations in what has been called the String of Pearls.[7]

The String of Pearls is the modern equivalent to the supply stations all navies throughout history have set up for logistic purposes along their main routes. It is not very different from what the Portuguese or the British did when they mastered the Indian Ocean. Even though some like to describe these states as a chain of military facilities, they are really only capable of offering merchant fleet logistic services.

Yet, the mere fact that the largest trading nation today has gone through all the complex process of arranging the diplomatic, operational, logistic, financial and other agreements with a number of scattered countries along the shores of the Indian Ocean highlights the importance they have for the stability of its own system. Indeed, the survival of the political system in China very much depends on the ability of the Chinese Communist Party to perform in the economic arena.

To some extent this could be also said of many other regimes. Trade, as we explained before, is the lifeline of today's economies. Safeguarding the routes has become vital in order to gain access to the resources that will, in due course, guarantee that one is able to distribute its manufactured goods.

Arguably, the opening of the Northern Route along the coast of Russia will not only provide an alternative and shorter way for Chinese (and Japanese, Korean and Taiwanese) products but will, in the process, redesign the geopolitical landscape of the whole of what Sir John Mackinder called the Heartland.[8]

If often overlooked, this is likely to become the most significant issue associated with the receding ice cap in the Siberian Arctic. The Northern coast will no longer be both unassailable and unusable. This is the rough equivalent to a continental shift to the South, that is, to continents moving south as a whole. The hard-learned lessons of the Indian Ocean should shed some light on the problem of dealing with an ice-free Arctic.

Mackinder's approach to geostrategy emphasizes the continental character of the Heartland and both its strength and its weakness. Being out of the direct reach of naval powers, whoever occupied the area which mostly constitutes modern Russia was relatively safe from invasion. Its lines of communication, relying on land routes, were not as efficient as sea lanes but they were also difficult to intercept. For the British geographer, a unified power in the Eurasian heartland would be able to dominate the world.

The whole construction of this scheme is based on the cylindrical view of Earth which disregards the poles as "out-of-bounds." The same approach, or more precisely a fairly similar one, is taken by Samuel Huntington[9] and Zbigniew Brzezinski,[10] who have shaped US and Western strategy for the last decades.

There are a number of other relevant factors which will affect the outcome of this new situation. Present-day Russia will cease benefiting from the strategic depth that allowed her to resist Napoleon or Hitler if her northern flank is open. On the other hand, she will be allowed access to the open ports she has coveted for a long time.

Later in this chapter, we will discuss some of the other relevant factors mentioned. In any case, a great deal of geopolitical change is to be expected with the opening of the Northern Route.

The overwhelming influence the United States has upon Canada will likely somewhat diminish the importance of the Northwest Passage. However, both the American and European continents are likely to see the northern regions take on a more relevant role in both economic and political terms.

As we see, beyond the significance for the economy that the opening of the Northern Route may have, its mere existence as a passage and as a way for a foreign military force to eventually threaten Mackinder's heartland bears an even deeper geopolitical significance.[11]

Indeed, there are also sociological implications to this new scenario. As a territory open to the global seas, Russia, or whoever controls that region, is likely to gradually shift into a more commercially oriented society.[12] Alternatively, it might also become even more suspicious of foreigners and regard the disadvantage of losing the protection of the ice as more important than the positive features already mentioned.

One way or another, the receding ice caps along the Eurasian North will have an impact on the entire continent and the world as a whole, which goes far beyond the current domains of ice. It is not an overstatement to say that the mere fact that Russia loses its frozen border to the north will dramatically change the geostrategic landscape as we know it today, and as we have known it for the best part of human history.

Rising tides, sinking islands: redrawing the maps?

Another trend that is often seen when talking about climate change is that of dealing with the different aspects as non-related issues. Climate is a system and, therefore, an interlinked set of phenomena. It is impossible to draw an accurate image of the consequences of any individual change without relating it to the rest.

A global redistribution of water resources is under way. Most experts will agree that the overall amount of water will remain relatively stable. In fact, climate change is not so much about a quantitative modification of weather conditions as about a redesign in the patterns that govern it. The focus has to be put on "change" more than on "weather," as change is what triggers conflict. The need to re-adjust to the new conditions will generate winners and losers as any change does. Only this time, since weather is something global, the scope of that change will also be planet-wide.

One of the redistributive processes happening as I write this chapter is the meltdown of part of the largest water reserve on Earth: glaciers and polar ice caps. Water in the solid state is being liquefied and poured into the oceans.

The first thought might be that the most important impact of the ensuing sea level rise would happen in the vicinity of the polar region. Closer scrutiny will lead to a different conclusion. The consequences of these new water inputs will be felt most in places closer to the Equator, notably the Indian Ocean.

Rising sea levels have been sufficiently covered in thousands of lectures, articles and books to allow us to move into further-reaching implications—further, at least from the geopolitical point of view.

For humanitarian reasons, the most devastating effects will follow the flooding of some of the largest deltas and estuaries of the main rivers worldwide. Sought after for human settlement since ancient times, these include some of the most dense and prosperous concentrations of human habitation, not to mention some of the richest agricultural terrains.

Whereas the loss of terrain could be mitigated with a massive resettlement of the population somewhere further from the coast, with only a marginal impact in terms of migration and the generation of refugees, the imbalance caused by the flooding on food production for certain countries would likely lead to a very significant redistribution of the population in nations such as Bangladesh.

As forecast today, rising sea levels in the Mediterranean or the China Sea will have a particular impact where the Nile or Yangtze rivers meet the seas. However, the largest of the impacts is expected in the mouths of the Ganges, in Bangladesh. The best crop land is only slightly above the level of the Indian Ocean, whose rise would not only flood the cities where millions live, but would also cover fertile ground and increase the saltiness of aquifers nearby.

Scarce attention has been paid to this issue. If, in addition to the loss of arable land, the sea water affects the aquifers, most significantly in the vicinity of Cairo in Egypt, the threat to sustainability of densely populated regions of the world will be even greater.

While the Arctic States are mostly concerned with the development of new opportunities which will open up along their shores, the same process that creates these benefits will generate countless challenges in many other places.

It seems appropriate at this stage to emphasize the need to find the synergies between demand and supply which will occur almost simultaneously as climate conditions shift. Instead of reverting to subsidies, charity or even stabilizing military campaigns, careful planning could pair surpluses and deficits in both human and other resources in what could be a win–win solution.

As change will happen irrespective of human action henceforth, a pragmatic approach would be to steer that change instead of being passive and reactive. Would it not make much more sense to identify and analyze the populations likely to migrate and anticipate suitable destinations where their potential could be useful?

The Government of the Maldives has shown such foresight but clearly it is insufficient. The authorities have been consistently buying property abroad to resettle the population of the archipelago, which is expected to become uninhabitable within a short period of time as the sea level rises. Pure and simple relocation will, in all likelihood, induce a number of secondary problems, as was the case with the native people of the island of Diego Garcia, the largest in the Chagos archipelago.[13]

The forced resettlement of the population of the Diego García atoll in the Indian Ocean followed the construction of a military airstrip by the British. The airfield is a key facility for both the United Kingdom and the United States and it has served as a launching platform for many raids into Afghanistan or Iraq, to name a few. The entire civilian population of the archipelago, numbering several hundred families, around one thousand persons, was evicted almost forty years ago mostly to Mauritius or to the metropolis.

As of March 2014, Her Majesty's Government was still seeking a solution for the expatriates. The possible return of the refugees could be jeopardized by the threat of rising sea levels and the legal reforms which imposed a ban on fishing around the islands.

Lessons to be drawn from this man-made migration include the need to carefully study the skills and the needs of the outgoing population and to find a suitable location for them, preferably as a community, that they can agree to. Poor planning and lack of generosity will inevitably trigger a chain reaction or a vicious circle that will lead to chaos.

Yet, as important as these consequences are from the standpoint of geopolitics, some of the most intense current international law litigation cases will also be deeply affected by submerging lands. Again, looking beyond the mere loss of land and possible human implications, there is reason for concern on how this will affect power relationships in the near future.

Indeed, the complete disappearance of territories which are today considered islands under the United Nations Convention on the Law of the Sea (UNCLOS) will have a heavy impact on the determination of coastal states' rights regarding territorial waters and Exclusive Economic Zones (EEZs).

Likewise, shifting coast lines will result in differences in the adjudication of these waters to one or another nation, as the formula used to establish the dividing line is reliant on the coast line at high tide. A glance at the length and complexity of current disputes suffices to imagine a world with constantly changing baselines.

Certainly, most of the disputes could and probably will be solved without resorting to international tribunals. That in itself does not mean there will be a seamless transition from present-day boundaries to the hypothetical new ones. And neither does it mean that the few remaining conflicts will not have a huge impact on international relations.

A case study could be made of the present-day disputes in the East China Sea and the South China Sea. Remote uninhabited islands, islets and atolls are coveted by most coastal nations in the Western Pacific for the sake of their value as providers of an EEZ and, therefore, access to either submerged resources or passages along key logistic routes.

In both these cases, there is no local population that might be affected by rising sea levels and no possible disappearance or large reduction of the island's territory.[14] Quite on the contrary, several regional powers are settling their nationals on every acre of land to use human habitation as leverage in a future legal dispute. In one case, a cargo ship grounded on a reef is being used as quarters for a mostly isolated military community that even has to smuggle their supplies across a rival blockade.

Far beyond (or below) is South Korea's submerged rock of Ieodo (Socotra), home to the Ieodo Ocean Research Station. This facility is built on a rock that is fifteen feet below sea level and is the object of a dispute between South Korea and China. The rock "surfaced" in the news when Beijing established an Air Defense Identification Zone (ADIZ) which included it.

Rising sea levels caused by melting Arctic ice have the potential for changing the landscape of the South China Sea. While the dispute between China and Japan over the Senkaku/Diaoyu Islands is largely unaffected by this, lower lying islands coveted by Vietnam, the Philippines, Brunei, Indonesia and both continental China and Taiwan risk disappearing altogether.

What do we make of the claims made by all these nations today? How is sovereignty over thousands of square miles of sea and rights over its resources affected? More to the point, how palatable will these changes be for claimant nations?

Once again, we cannot fully study the implications Arctic melting will have in this region. While geostrategic issues will likely be the most relevant, they are by no means the only ones affected. The Chinese and others are trying to mitigate the impact of rising sea levels in the South China Sea with vast engineering projects which attempt to expand and protect the surface terrain.

Woody Island may be the best known example of an atoll which has come to more than double its original size to accommodate an airstrip and several military facilities. More of these rocks and islets are either being artificially elevated or enlarged to allow their habitation and an eventual change in their status.

The Arctic's influence on the South China Sea is not only a question of disappearing islands, but also in its role as the busiest sea lane linking the East and the West. China's String of Pearls, the chain of logistic facilities along the route followed by its merchant vessels in the Indian Ocean, as already mentioned, is proof of the importance of these waters. Not only is the South China Sea one of the key segments of that string, but also the most challenging.

Around 60 percent and 80 percent of both energy and raw materials feeding the large manufacturing economies of the Far East transit through the South China Sea. The importance of maintaining freedom of navigation in these waters can hardly be overstated. Hence the fierce disputes among coastal nations for ownership of the land features in it.

A visit to Singapore's port and the view of the Strait of Malacca suffices to show the relevance of this passage. Huge projects, such as the Kra Canal in Thailand or pipelines across Myanmar linking the Indian Ocean and Southern China, are being implemented or designed to help guarantee China's free access to supplies and markets in South Asia and Africa.

The opening of the Northern Route will, on the one hand, significantly reduce the importance of the Strait of Malacca and the South China Sea providing an alternative and shorter route, if not for supplies, for markets in Western Europe. On the other hand, much of the tension and interest devoted to the String of Pearls and the southern route is likely to be transferred to the northern one.

We are likely to witness a race to gain access to port facilities along the Siberian coast similar to the one that we are seeing in the Indian Ocean. Land communications between China and Western Europe, like the train which ran from China to Spain in December 2014 for the first time in history, will add to the shrinking of the Eurasian continent in terms of traveling time.

Never mind political union, if Mackinder lived today, he would be warning about the geostrategic consequences of open and free markets within the core of Eurasia. Physical or political interdiction of the routes which might allow for this union would be the logical—and historically most likely—response to it.

The disappearance of some insular territories and shifting baselines will no doubt result in disputes well beyond the Arctic Circle. Climate change calls for a comprehensive approach to international law and a flexible and cooperative new design of international relationships, because climate change itself knows no boundaries.

An end to rivers without an end?

We have already discussed several different ways in which geography is relevant to the development of power and the creation of nations. In fact, geography dictates that there are regions in the world which are and will always be crossroads at which civilizations tend to crash. Change the name of the different actors involved, but clashes appear to be present at such places as the Balkans or Palestine.

If you draw straight lines on a map between the different regional powers, the area contained in the resulting parallelogram is likely to be a contested one. Take the Russian, Persian and Ottoman empires, under whichever name they adopted throughout history, and the intersection of the lines joining them is where the Caucasus lies. For all three, this is and will be a region of special interest.

Likewise, as already defined even before Alfred T. Mahan's work on the influence of maritime power, a handful of choke points are the only vital areas needed to be controlled to gain mastery of the seas. There are sixteen traditional such points which have proved resilient to changing political situations.

Our new world, defined as a sphere versus the unconscious notion of a cylinder, might not dramatically change the definition of these vital passages, but is certainly going to affect the importance of each of them.

Communications rank among the top priorities upon establishing a settlement, and sea lanes and fluvial arteries are the most efficient ways to deliver goods to your customers or to ship raw materials home. Of course, that is provided both you and your customer have access to appropriate ports.

Stratford's Chairman, George Friedman, highlighted the importance of the Mississippi-Missouri river basin, along with the coastal waters of the United States, in the economic development of the nation.[15] Furthermore, he pointed out how this fact has steered the geopolitics of the USA throughout history.

He argues that:

> (t)he Greater Mississippi Basin together with the Intracoastal Waterway has more kilometres of navigable internal waterways than the rest of the world combined. This waterway runs through the American Midwest, which is also the world's largest contiguous piece of farmland. The U.S. Atlantic Coast possesses more major ports than the rest of the western hemisphere combined.

Having established this fact, he reasons that it was this circumstance which gave the US economy the boost to become a world power.

Of course, there is much more in Friedman's work which is also important in understanding the role of the United States in modern history, but this point seems of particular relevance now. If you take Germany's river system and compare it with an aerial photograph of Europe at night, it is easy to infer that the "engine of Europe" is also built upon the banks of its rivers.

It may be unnecessary to remind the reader how the earliest civilizations were also established along main fluvial arteries. Be it China, Egypt or Mesopotamia, the mortar which kept these empires together was prepared with the water of such rivers as the Yellow River, the Tigris, the Euphrates or the Nile.

Yet, the eventuality of opening up vast regions in Siberia to global trade, while undoubtedly positive for the region as a geographical entity, might not be so for the nation that currently exerts sovereignty over those territories. Much like the wealth in many African nations has come to be known as the "curse of resources,"[16] the same might well happen to Russia.

Indeed, both President Putin and his predecessor at the Kremlin, the incumbent Prime Minister Dmitri Medvedev, have repeatedly urged the colonization of the Arctic region to little or no avail.

With a declining population, which is a full 10 percent lower today than that living in Russia at the break-up of the Soviet Union, it is almost impossible to populate and exploit most of the area beyond the Urals.

And yet, history reminds us that the discovery of new opportunities rarely fails to attract scores of people who see it as an improvement over their former way of life. Regardless of how harsh the conditions may be, where there is a chance, there is a will to take advantage of it.

There remains little doubt of who are the prime candidates to occupy the empty spaces which will become profitable, as rivers provide an easy and effective route for raw materials and commodities alike.

If not towards the Arctic region itself, the opening of sea lanes for communications along the Northern Route will probably signal the starting point of a new race to the west, only this time it will be to the north.[17]

How Russia, the countries of origin of potential immigrants and the international community as a whole will manage this exodus remains uncertain. Moscow's grip on Siberia, while centuries old, is not to be taken for granted.

Much ado about resources?

When talking about incoming opportunities in the Arctic region as ice recedes, the most recurrent topic is the fight for resources. Energy ranks among the first, if not the prime resource which is going to trigger a competition in the North.

While there are lots of proven reserves which will become technically exploitable within the next decades, it is too much to expect that the energy mix will remain unchanged for that long.

Industry does not respond very rapidly to changes triggered by efficiency, and fiscal policies are unlikely to deter the use of fossil fuels in many nations, except when other more powerful nations exert pressure. Nonetheless, both of these factors, combined with the availability of more easily accessed and more sustainable indigenous types of fuel, will alter the mix and make Arctic fuel prohibitive for the most part.

The events unfolding as we write reinforce the idea that the development of new technologies have already pushed further into the future the date in which the exploitation of gas and fuel in the Arctic becomes widely profitable. Chances are technology will continue to provide fuel at cheaper prices than those we can expect when drilling has to occur in such adverse conditions.

Fuel prices have dropped significantly since the arrival of shale oil and gas from the USA began impacting supplies worldwide. A more efficient use of existing wells also contributed to an increased global production. In fact, regardless of the limited amounts coming from places such as Libya, Iran or a war-torn Iraq, or even the sanctions are imposed on Russia, there is no shortage of fuel in the markets.

OPEC countries might be contributing to achieve lower crude prices in a mid-term effort to defeat shale oil and gas companies, which depend on higher prices to remain profitable.

Still, oil and gas eventually coming from Arctic wells is likely to have an even higher price tag, but this will depend on the state of art of technology at that time, as we cannot rule out a disruptive technology appearing within the next few years.

As long as cheaper resources remain available and communications or accessibility to the goods is unimpeded, there will be very few reasons to drill new wells. Of course, drilling in disputed waters is even less likely unless there is a political intent behind the occupation of those areas.

Concurrently, we are likely to witness quite a rapid shift from fossil fuels to other more environmentally friendly ones. While this is not going to affect many developing nations which have either recently industrialized and, therefore, have just spent their resources in soon-to-be obsolete plants or are at the bottom of the research and development list, more advanced nations will reduce their use of petroleum products.

This is, in fact, already happening. For many reasons, nations are relying more and more on indigenous clean energy even when fuel prices remain competitive.

Energy security is as much about securing access to resources as it is about getting the most efficient deal possible. Yet, given the chance of investing in classic sources or gaining the upper hand in new technologies, we will see a number of the players opting for the latter. States will surely have a say in the choice companies make, if only by shifting the subsidies from one source to another. Public opinion will, no doubt, also be of importance in the information society of the twenty-first century.

A bearish fuel market will deter the exploitation of most fuel sources in nations which are likely to be at the cutting edge of technology in renewable sources. Although it may be safe for Russia, the rest of the Arctic nations will find it far more appealing to focus on new technologies than to risk going very far down the slope in emissions.

There are, however, a number of minerals which will still be profitable to exploit.[18] In all likelihood, there will be a few which will become strategic either as new materials are developed or as others become scarce in other locations.

It goes far beyond the scope of this chapter to dig into the details of current profitability or to explore the crystal ball in search for future markets. Recent history is quite clear in showing our inability to forecast what the trend of tomorrow will be. Technology is moving far too quickly and in too many directions to allow for an accurate guess. But we can still be sure that changes will take place and the Arctic will be one of the guest stars.

Safety and security challenges

What happens if the Arctic does not stay in the Arctic?

There are multiple implications of the effects of climate change in the Arctic beyond the ice. We have explored just a few of them here. The bottom line is: The Arctic is of interest to all of us. This assessment looks far beyond the environmental issues involved,[19] it also has to do with changes in living conditions worldwide.

Most sovereignty lawsuits currently focus on issues which will only have an impact, if they do at all, in a distant future, when conditions are likely to be very different from today. There are just a handful of disputes regarding access and proprietary rights over resources or territory which might represent a clear and present problem.

From a global perspective this means that the focus should be on cooperation and on the identification and mitigation of geopolitical changes rather than on litigation over resources whose importance will likely diminish over time. Still, most of those resources lie in undisputed territories of strong and mostly well-governed states.

A reasonable assumption would be that most of the problems derived from climate change in the Arctic will take place somewhere else. In all likelihood, they will also have a global scope and demand a coordinated effort by the international community to make the best of them, not just to adapt to their consequences.

This is a relevant point. Changes are not intrinsically good or evil, they are just changes. In all catastrophes there are those who end up being better off than when they started. While this is usually done at the expense of others, we face a unique situation in which the drama is unfolding at such a pace and our technology is in such an advanced state that we are able to foresee the most enduring changes and should try to take advantage of them as much as possible.

We know we are going to see a replica of the String of Pearls further north. The actors may be different but the importance of shipping lanes has not varied throughout history and is not likely to do so within the next few decades. A search for a win–win outcome should commence as of today to try to avoid competition among the stakeholders being harsher than needed while we improve cooperative mechanisms.

Opening up Arctic waters to commerce implies a dramatic shift in our vision of the planet. This is implied in the title of this chapter, we are moving from a cylindrical interpretation of our environment towards a spherical one.

The reader has probably already dedicated some thought to the meaning of this change. Let us put it this way, with this shift in our vision everything becomes closer. The globalization process that began with the discovery of the Americas by Spain more than five centuries ago is reaching its apex with the advent of global communication via the internet and the effects of climate change in the Arctic.

Whatever you may want to define as a comprehensive domain, there are only two true issues that cut across the full spectrum of topics: Climate change and cyberspace. These are the only ones with enough reach and depth to influence all other aspects of life on Earth.

I have repeatedly argued that both topics will call for a similar approach when defining their governance. Likewise, by no means will current legal solutions be able to cover such borderless issues. It is difficult to envisage an arrangement like the United Nations Convention on the Law of the Sea (UNCLOS)[20] being applied either to climate change or cyberspace.

UNCLOS took decades of negotiations to be drafted and implemented. Yet, almost half of a century after beginning work, the United States has still failed to ratify the agreement, making it a far less credible tool. With UNCLOS we were also moving in "charted waters," if you will allow the pun. We have been dealing with maritime aspects of life for millennia and the seas are just the same now as they were then. This all becomes different when dealing with these two new global domains.

The environment affected by climate change will be different next year and, what is even more relevant, the rate of change will be ever greater for the foreseeable future. Cyberspace is also evolving at lightning speed. Whatever we design to regulate both these will have to be done fast and will have to be flexible enough to adapt to shifting conditions.

One of the main problems when dealing with both climate change and cyberspace is that they do not remain within their own confines but, quite to the contrary, affect all other aspects of life. We have seen, as an example, the influence of rising sea levels on the definition of territorial waters.

As a consequence, it will be difficult to legislate on these aspects without a more profound shift in our governance model worldwide. How can we pretend to create an overall good governance model if we base the design on laws that were created for much more limited domains, especially when the issues often cut across many different areas?

A global world needs global rules, a code of conduct which will include the full spectrum of interactions taking place in the twenty-first century. Failure to do so is not an option. Interconnected societies worldwide are already living in this new reality.

The Arctic might be the paradigm of these challenges. Widely defined as an empty space due to its small population and geographical vastness, changes happening beyond the Arctic Circle will come to affect the whole planet. Its management or mismanagement will impact on billions of people worldwide and should, therefore, be conducted with a wider view than local gains or losses.

Notes

1 Mercator was a Flemish cartographer and mathematician. He developed a new projection which represented sailing courses of constant bearing as straight lines.

2 Maj. Gen. Mark Barrett, Dick Bedford, Elizabeth Skinner and Eva Vergles, *Assured Access to the Global Commons*. (Norfolk: NATO Supreme Allied Command Transformation, 2011), accessed July 21, 2015, www.alex11.org/wp-content/uploads/2013/01/aagc_finalreport_text.pdf; also Dick Bedford and Paul Giarra, "Securing the Global Commons," *The RUSI Journal* 155.5 (2010): 18–23.

3 This idea, however, is far from new. Alfred T. Mahan, the key naval strategist of all times, had it as the hub of all his studies in his classic *The Influence of Sea Power upon History, 1660–1783*, first published in 1890 by Little, Brown and Company, Boston. The identification of sixteen key choke points whose control allows denying access to global markets is behind the rational for the existence and deployment of the fleets of major sea powers in the last few centuries.

4 Thomas P.M. Barnett, *The Pentagon's New Map* (New York: Berkley Trade, 2005). See also the blog of Barnett at: http://thomaspmbarnett.com/.

5 Jeremy Rifkin, *The Zero Marginal Cost Society: The Internet of Things, the Collaborative Commons, and the Eclipse of Capitalism* (New York: Palgrave Macmillan Trade, 2014), accessed July 22, 2015, http://digamo.free.fr/rifkin14.pdf.

6 I am far less confident than Dr. Rifkin regarding the implications of 3D printing. I expect some sort of raw materials trade to be essential for decades to come.

7 For an up-to-date vision of the String of Pearls concept, see Virginia Marantidou, "Revisiting China's 'String of Pearls' Strategy: Places 'with Chinese Characteristics' and their Security Implications," *Issues and Insights* 14.7 (Honolulu, HI: Pacific Forum CSIS, 2014), accessed July 22, 2015, http://csis.org/files/publication/140624_issuesinsights_vol14no7.pdf.

8 Halford John Mackinder, "The Geographical Pivot of History." *The Geographical Journal* 23 (1904): 421–37. The same article can be found as well in Halford John Mackinder, *Democratic Ideals and Reality: A Study in the Politics of Reconstruction* (Washington, DC: National Defense University Press, 1996), 175–94.

9 Samuel P. Huntington, "The Clash of Civilizations?," *Foreign Affairs* (Summer 1993), accessed July 22, 2015, www.foreignaffairs.com/articles/48950/samuel-p-huntington/the-clash-of-civilizations.

10 Zbigniew Brzezinski, *The Grand Chessboard: American Primacy and Its Geostrategic Imperatives* (New York: Basic Books, 1997).

11 There is a full military strategy being developed around the Arctic by many different nations (not all of them Arctic States). See Chief of Naval Operations, *U.S. Navy Arctic Roadmap 2014–2030*, (Washington, DC: Department of the Navy, 2014), accessed July 22, 2015, https://info.publicintelligence.net/USNavy-Arctic Roadmap.pdf.

12 Dmitry Gorenburg, "Russian Interests and Policies in the Arctic," *War on the Rocks*, August 7, 2014, accessed July 22, 2015, http://warontherocks.com/2014/08/russian-interests-and-policies-in-the-arctic/.

13 John Vidal, "Chagos Islands: UK Experts to Carry Out Resettlement Study," *The Guardian*, March 13, 2014, accessed July 22, 2015, www.theguardian.com/world/2014/mar/13/chagos-islands-uk-experts-resettlement-study.

14 Gemima Harvey, "Sinking States: Climate Change and the Pacific," *The Diplomat*, May 22, 2014, accessed July 22, 2015, http://thediplomat.com/2014/05/sinking-states-climate-change-and-the-pacific/.

15 George Friedman, "The Geopolitics of the United States, Part 1: The Inevitable Empire," *STRATFOR Global Intelligence*, July 4, 2014, accessed July 22, 2015, www.stratfor.com/analysis/geopolitics-united-states-part-1-inevitable-empire#axzz3NrtRPgCj.

16 Jeffrey D. Sachs and Andrew M. Warner, "Natural Resource Abundance and Economic Growth," *NBER Working Paper* No 5398 (Cambridge, MA: National Bureau of Economic Research, 1995).

17 The right assets are being quickly developed to gain and maintain access to these routes. An arms race has already started on the design and construction of ice-breakers among mayor powers. See Milosz Reterski, "Breaking the Ice," *Foreign Affairs Magazine*, December 11, 2014, accessed July 22, 2015, www.foreignaffairs.com/articles/142516/milosz-reterski/breaking-the-ice. Also, Mia Bennet, "Full Steam Ahead for Asian Icebreakers in the Arctic this Summer," *Alaska Dispatch News*, July 14, 2014, accessed July 22, 2015, www.adn.com/node/1616956.

18 Genevieve Wanucha, "The Unprecedented Policy Issues Emerging as Melting Sea Ice Opens Up New Opportunities for Deep-Sea Mining," *PHYS.org*, June 19, 2014, accessed July 22, 2015, http://phys.org/news/2014–06-unprecedented-policy-issues-emerging-sea.html#jCp.

19 Most certainly, environmental issues cannot be neglected. While sovereignty issues remain unsolved, the Arctic needs a code of conduct to prevent its fragile equilibrium from being shattered. See Karl Mathiesen, "Polar Code Agreed to Prevent Arctic Environmental Disasters," *The Guardian*, November 21, 2014, accessed July 22, 2015, www.theguardian.com/environment/2014/nov/21/polar-code-agreed-to-prevent-arctic-environmental-disasters?CMP=EMCENVEML1631.

20 The text of the UNCLOS can be consulted at: www.un.org/depts/los/convention_agreements/texts/unclos/unclos_e.pdf.

References

Barnett, Thomas P.M. *The Pentagon's New Map*. New York: Berkley Trade, 2005.

Barrett, Mark, Dick Bedford, Elizabeth Skinner and Eva Verges. *Assured Access to the Global Commons*. Norfolk: NATO Supreme Allied Command Transformation, 2011. Accessed July 21, 2015, www.alex11.org/wp-content/uploads/2013/01/aagc_finalreport_text.pdf.

Bedford, Dick and Paul Giarra "Securing the Global Commons." *The RUSI Journal* 155.5 (2010): 18–23. Doi: 10.1080/03071847.2010.530500.

Bennet, Mia. "Full Steam Ahead for Asian Icebreakers in the Arctic this Summer." *Alaska Dispatch News*, July 14, 2014. Accessed July 22, 2015, www.adn.com/node/1616956.

Brzezinski, Zbigniew. *The Grand Chessboard: American Primacy and Its Geostrategic Imperatives*. New York: Basic Books, 1997.

Chief of Naval Operations. *U.S. Navy Arctic Roadmap 2014–2030*. Washington, DC: Department of the Navy, 2014. Accessed July 22, 2015, https://info.publicintelligence.net/USNavy-ArcticRoadmap.pdf.

Friedman, George. "The Geopolitics of the United States, Part 1: The Inevitable Empire." *STRATFOR Global Intelligence*, July 4, 2014. Accessed July 22, 2015, www.stratfor.com/analysis/geopolitics-united-states-part-1-inevitable-empire#axzz3NrtRPgCj.

German Advisory Council on Global Change (WBGU). *Climate Change as a Security Risk*. London and Sterling, VA: Earthscan, 2008. Accessed July 22, 2015, www.wbgu.de/fileadmin/templates/dateien/veroeffentlichungen/hauptgutachten/jg2007/wbgu_jg2007_engl.pdf.

Gorenburg, Dmitry. "Russian Interests and Policies in the Arctic." *War on the Rocks*, August 7, 2014. Accessed July 22, 2015, http://warontherocks.com/2014/08/russian-interests-and-policies-in-the-arctic/.

Harvey, Gemima. "Sinking States: Climate Change and the Pacific." *The Diplomat*, May 22, 2014. Accessed July 22, 2015, http://thediplomat.com/2014/05/sinking-states-climate-change-and-the-pacific/.

Huntington, Samuel P. "The Clash of Civilizations?." *Foreign Affairs* (Summer 1993). Accessed July 22, 2015, www.foreignaffairs.com/articles/48950/samuel-p-huntington/the-clash-of-civilizations.

Kuertsen, Andreas. "Russian Sanctions, China and the Arctic." *The Diplomat*, January 3, 2015. Accessed July 22, 2015, http://thediplomat.com/2015/01/russian-sanctions-china-and-the-arctic/.

Mackinder, Halford John. "The Geographical Pivot of History." *The Geographical Journal* 23 (1904): 421–37.

Mackinder, Halford John. *Democratic Ideals and Reality: A Study in the Politics of Reconstruction*. Washington, DC: National Defense University Press, 1996.

Mahan, Alfred T. *The Influence of Sea Power upon History, 1660–1783*. Boston, MA: Little, Brown and Company, 1890.

Marantidou, Virginia. "Revisiting China's 'String of Pearls' Strategy: Places 'with Chinese Characteristics' and their Security Implications." *Issues and Insights* 14.7 (Honolulu, HI: Pacific Forum CSIS, 2014). Accessed July 22, 2015, http://csis.org/files/publication/140624_issuesinsights_vol. 14no7.pdf.

Pen, Karl. "Polar Code Agreed to Prevent Arctic Environmental Disasters." *The Guardian*, November 21, 2014. Accessed July 22, 2015, www.theguardian.com/environment/2014/nov/21/polar-code-agreed-to-prevent-arctic-environmental-disasters?CMP=EMCENVEML1631.

Reterski, Milosz. "Breaking the Ice." *Foreign Affairs Magazine*, December 11, 2014. Accessed July 22, 2015, www.foreignaffairs.com/articles/142516/milosz-reterski/breaking-the-ice.

Rifkin, Jeremy. *The Zero Marginal Cost Society: The Internet of Things, the Collaborative Commons, and the Eclipse of Capitalism*. New York: Palgrave Macmillan Trade, 2014. Accessed July 22, 2015, http://digamo.free.fr/rifkin14.pdf.

Sachs, Jeffrey D. and Andrew M. Warner. "Natural Resource Abundance and Economic Growth." *NBER Working Paper* No. 5398. Cambridge, MA: National Bureau of Economic Research, 1995.

Vidal, John. "Chagos Islands: UK Experts to Carry Out Resettlement Study." *The Guardian*, March 13, 2014. Accessed July 22, 2015, www.theguardian.com/world/2014/mar/13/chagos-islands-uk-experts-resettlement-study.

Wanucha, Genevieve, "The Unprecedented Policy Issues Emerging as Melting Sea Ice Opens Up New Opportunities for Deep-Sea Mining." *PHYS.org*, June 19, 2014. Accessed July 22, 2015, http://phys.org/news/2014-06-unprecedented-policy-issues-emerging-sea.html#jCp.

18 Security challenges in the Arctic

Rob Huebert

Introduction

It is nearly impossible to watch the news or read a newspaper without finding some mention of the Arctic.[1] This has not always been the case though. For a long time, the Arctic was viewed by most as an inaccessible and forbidding location of stark beauty and extreme climate. However, this was not true for those who call the Arctic home, such as the Inuit or other indigenous populations whose numbers have always been smaller than the rest of the world's population. Throughout the centuries, there were many efforts, predominately by European explorers, to "find" the Northwest Passage—of course the Inuit would point out that it was never lost—in the 1800s and 1900s. Even though there was submarine traffic in the region during the Cold War, most of the Arctic remained rather unexplored by the "southerners" in the region. Thus, we may conclude that for a long time this area of the Earth maintained its existence in splendid isolation from the rest of the international system.

All of this is now changing. The world began to take notice of the transforming Arctic early in the 1990s when climate change resulted in an increasingly dramatic melting of the sea ice covering the Arctic Ocean.[2] But this is not the only change occurring within the region. New resources were both discovered and exploited, prompting many to see this zone as a new source of resources. Most pertinent to the current analysis was its transformation from a region of superpowers' tension during the Cold War to one of increasingly promising cooperation. Any of these variables supposes a significant transformation, but taken in their entirety, these changes—climate, resource development and geopolitics—point to a transformation of epic proportions. Therefore, it is not surprising that the Arctic is now a region of increasing interest worldwide.

But what makes the region so interesting also makes it very confounding, as it simply refuses to remain still. Every time we believe the region has finally been comprehended, new events further transform the world's understanding of it. Hence, the purpose of this chapter is to address one of the most dynamic elements of the region: the *geopolitical security*. The

Arctic location between two of the most powerful states in the international system means that it has always been at the center of any discussion of international security. Throughout the Cold War it remained one of the most important operational theaters for both the Soviet Union and the United States, and their allies. It played a central role in the maintenance of deterrence, and would have been one of the most critically important regions for conflict had war broken out.[3] Following the end of the Cold War there was significant hope that this region could be transformed into an area of international cooperation and peace.[4] Significant efforts were made to bring the former adversaries together. For over a decade these efforts appear to have been successful. However, in the mid-2000s, while Russia was starting to determine a new direction for its overall security and defense policy, new security challenges began to develop as various countries began to recognize the potential of the Arctic. While there are still strong avenues of cooperation, there are also growing points of tension within the region.

How then can this complex geopolitical region be understood? To answer this question, the chapter will examine the evolving nature of international security within the circumpolar north. At the heart of this transformation lays the increasingly vigorous debate as to what the Arctic will look like in security terms as it transforms further.[5] There is no question whatsoever that a new Arctic security environment is being formed on a global basis. But what will it look like? Will it provide for continuance of the peaceful cooperation that characterized the 1990s and early 2000s or will it resemble more complicated relations that contain elements of both cooperation and conflict, characteristic of the current political environment in the region?

A transforming Arctic

There is a wide range of processes developing in the Arctic. Each of them is very powerful and each of them interacts with the rest. In some instances, this interaction provides for mutually reinforcing trends, while, in others, they counteract each other. For example, as climate change makes the maritime region more accessible for resource development, there will be an increased level of exploitation of oil and gas resources. As these resources are being developed, they will contribute to the ongoing causes of climate change, thereby further increasing the warming trends that allow their original exploitation. On the other hand, as more resources become available, there will be a greater international interest in benefiting from them. This could conceivably create tensions that make it difficult for the ongoing exploitation of these resources, thereby decreasing its level. Thus, it is very difficult to understand how these transformations will continue to interact over time. But the question remains: what are the main transformational factors?

Climate change

Undoubtedly, at the head of the list of transformational forces is climate change. It was within the Arctic that some of the most pronounced early signs of climate change were detected. Prior to the 1990s, few imagined the possibility of an Arctic Ocean without ice cover. However, it soon became apparent to most observers that the incipient climatic changes represented something more than just a seasonal variation. By the early 2000s it had become evident that not only was the Arctic being affected by worldwide temperature increases, but also that the region was the most significantly affected area of the earth. As part of the cooperation movements that were then prevalent in the region, the Arctic Council organized an extensive multi-year, multinational and multidisciplinary study of the impacts of climate change.[6] It was found that there was almost no aspect of the Arctic that was not being affected by the rising temperatures. However, the one finding that attracted the most significant international attention pertains to the melting of the permanent ice cover.

As we know, much of the Arctic is an ocean: a fact that is often contrasted with the Antarctica, which is a continent. The Arctic Ocean has remained ice covered for as long as human observation has existed. Ice cores have suggested that this region may have been open waters at some points of this prehistoric time-frame but this is thought to be well before the time of human civilization.[7] The initial studies in the late 1990s suggested that the Arctic Ocean would become ice free in summer sometimes towards the end of the 2000s, possibly around 2090.[8] This estimation is now considered to be wrong. Current scientific studies of the rate of ongoing melting in the region point towards an ice free Arctic in the mid-2020s to 2030s.[9] It is expected that the ocean will refreeze in the winter months, but this ice is known as first-year ice as opposed to the multi-year or permanent ice cover that now exists in the Arctic. Multi-year ice has many different properties from first-year ice, the most important being that multi-year ice is considerably denser and therefore harder than first-year ice and tends to be thicker. Therefore, any form of navigation through such ice is much more difficult and often impossible even for the most powerful ice-breakers, let alone any other vessels—with the exception of submarines that can travel under the ice, and, of course, this is limited specifically to the nuclear-powered submarines. Thus, a melting ice covers means the possibility of increased maritime traffic.[10]

The impacts also go beyond maritime navigation. Climate change is transforming the entire way of life of the indigenous populations that had been able to flourish in this region for eons. There is a very significant impact on their traditional knowledge for hunting and fishing. Some have argued that the impacts of climate change may be so severe as to end the traditional way of life that has endured for thousands of years.[11]

Likewise, the flora and fauna of the region are also being dramatically affected. There is a growing concern that one of the most enigmatic symbols of the Arctic—the polar bear—may face a dire future.[12] New species such as killer whales have also been moving further into the Arctic region as sea ice recedes.[13] This represents a very significant transformation of the apex predator of the region as more killer whales enter the region and the polar bear pollutions face increasing pressures. There is also a growing debate regarding the possibility that fish populations from southern latitudes may move northward.[14] While there is considerable disagreement within the scientific community as to whether or not this will occur, the prospects of a new fishery region has already attracted considerable attention from the international fishing nations.[15]

Resources

As the Arctic is physically transformed due to the impacts of climate change, there has also been considerable attention given to both existing and potential resource development. The Arctic is seen by some as a treasure trove of new resources.[16] Whether or not the arctic does become a "treasure trove" remains to be seen, but there have been significant projects on the road for the last decade or so.[17] For example, the discovery of diamonds in the Canadian north has resulted in the development of four mines in the Northwest Territories resulting in Canada becoming the world's third largest producer of diamonds.[18] However, the resources that have garnered the greatest attention are the new oil and gas discoveries. The US Geological Survey released in 2008 suggested that 13 percent of all undiscovered oil in the world and 30 percent of all natural gas may be located in the Arctic region.[19] This study has provoked considerable responses.[20] Nevertheless, there had been extensive efforts from Russia, Greenland, United States and Canada to find these new resources offshore. However, to date only Russia's efforts have been successful and the country has actually begun to produce oil from its Arctic reserves.

These unfortunate results have not disheartened the belief that the Arctic region is the last major gold rush for the discovery of oil.[21] Within this debate, it has been recognized that the Arctic would become particularly sensitive for environmental challenges if the oil and gas exploitation in the region proceeds on the expected scale. Should an accident—similar to the Deepwater Horizon disaster in the Gulf of Mexico—occur in the region, there is a very limited ability to respond to such a threat.[22] Therefore, there are ongoing debates suggesting that it is way too dangerous to develop Arctic's natural resources should they be found.[23] Still, the Russians have been producing since 2013, and both the American and Danish governments have given every indication of supporting its development if ever found within their waters. Currently, an even more significant challenge has been created as a result of the falling oil prices: brought about by a large number of factors, the price of oil is at a very low rate which has made some to question the economic rationale for developing Arctic oil.[24]

Geopolitics

This is the third major transformation of force that is changing the very nature of how the Arctic region fits into the greater international system. As mentioned earlier, the challenges presented by the Arctic regarding both distances, climate and lack of infrastructure has meant that there has been limited international interest and engagement within the region. This is now changing as the international community has become significantly more interested in the region and equally important have been developing the means by which to engage with it. The main focus of international interest in this region has traditionally been in regards to economics and security. But even in these two instances the effort required to engage in this region has been so substantial that few have been able to do so from the south. The indigenous populations are the exception who have flourished in the region.

During the Cold War era, the Soviet Union and the Americans with the assistance of its allies were able to develop weapons systems that were able to engage under and over the permanent ice. As a result, the Arctic became one of the most dangerous geopolitical flashpoints between the two sides.[25] It became critically important in the maintenance of the deterrence system, and should that system collapse, the Arctic would have been one of the most important geographic locations for the aerospace war.

When the Cold War ended, some of the most immediate impacts on the Arctic were the efforts to improve international cooperation between the Soviet Union and the other Arctic States. This is demonstrated by the creation of the Arctic Environmental Protection Strategy (AEPS) and its successor organization the Arctic Council.[26] One of the most important intentions behind the creation of both organizations was to allow for the inclusion of the USSR/Russia in cooperation with the other Arctic States.[27]

The second major change that occurred was an immediate reduction of all military activity in the region. The Soviet forces that were deployed in the region were either eliminated or simply rusted out. Specifically the Soviet Cold War navy deteriorated into oblivion. This meant that the large number of nuclear-powered submarines simply rusted out of existence. Paradoxically, this created a new environmental security threat to the region. Since the Soviet Union/Russia did not have the resources at the time to properly dispose of its nuclear-powered submarines, the danger arose that these vessels could create a major nuclear environmental disaster should any of the reactors experience a meltdown. To this end, the United States and Norway created a body to assist the Russians in the decommissioning of their submarines in a safe manner.[28] Known as the Arctic Military Environmental Cooperation (AMEC), it eventually became supported by the G8 Member States to assist the Russians, by providing extensive resources and for the decommissioning.

Ultimately the period between 1989 to about 2006 can easily be characterized as one of the most cooperative periods in the circumpolar region. It is during this time period that the Arctic region was transformed from being a location with little international cooperation into one where cooperation became the new norm. To a very large degree this cooperation was driven by a desire of the other Arctic States to ensure that the new Soviet Union/Russia did not fall back into the uncooperative behavior that characterized its policies during the Cold War. As such, it was Finland that pioneered an initiative with Canadian assistance to create a multi-body entity that would provide a forum for cooperation between Russia and the rest of the Arctic States. The Arctic Environmental Protection Strategy (AEPS) became a means by which Russia, United States, Canada, Finland, Sweden, Norway, Iceland and Denmark (for Greenland) met to discuss shared environmental concerns regarding the Arctic. It was presumed that the cooperation on environmental issues would be relatively easy to facilitate. This assumption of course proved to be incorrect in that the Arctic environment was not a pristine and simple region, but the assumption at least allowed the eight countries to cooperate together.[29] This strategy was formally accepted in 1991. It was followed by a Canadian initiative to create a body that would expand beyond its environmental concerns. In 1996, Canada successfully negotiated the creation of the Arctic Council.[30] Building on the successes of the AEPS, the Arctic Council has now become one of the most important fora for international cooperation in the region. Following on the innovation of the AEPS, it continued the practice of including special representation for the northern indigenous peoples. It has also become very popular with non-Arctic States including countries such as China, Japan and India as observer members.[31] More importantly, it has produced a number of groundbreaking report's that have mobilized an international understanding of the region. The *Arctic Climate Impact Assessment* played a pivotal role in alerting the international community to the dangers of climate change.[32] The Council has recently moved into the process of creating new international agreements that go beyond simply producing reports. It has now created a treaty on Search and Rescue in the Arctic.[33]

Much of the success of the AEPS and the Arctic Council was the result of the spirit of cooperation that existed between all eight of the Arctic States. While the Russian government found itself in dire economic straits after the collapse of the USSR, it still adopted a policy of cooperation. The other seven Arctic States attempted to engage the Russians more closely and cooperatively. In particular, the Americans and the Norwegians and, subsequently, the Canadians, provided extensive funding to allow for the safe decommissioning of their extensive Cold War submarine fleet. Equally important was the fact that Russia's scientists and government officials were allowed to interact directly with their Western counterparts.

There were also clear signs of better cooperation between the Arctic States on a bilateral basis. The Russians and Norwegians were able to resolve their long-standing maritime boundary dispute in the Barents Sea.[34] This disagreement had existed for over forty years, but the two sides were able to come to a settlement in 2010. There were also multilateral cooperative efforts. In 2008, the five coastal Arctic States—United States, Canada, Norway, Denmark (on behalf of Greenland) and Russia—met in Ilulissat (Greenland) to agree to settle peacefully all of their potential conflicts regarding their extended continental shelves under the terms of the United Nations Convention on the Law of the Sea.[35]

In short, the period between the end of the Cold War towards the end of the 2000s can clearly be seen as a period of cooperation and collaboration regarding the Arctic region. Most analysts on this basis came to regard the potential of conflict in the region as highly improbable if not impossible. However, while these very important acts of cooperation were occurring, there have also been forces at work that introduced significant complexity into the region with regard to security. Perhaps the most confusing element of these forces is that most of this has very little to do with the Arctic but rather is occurring within the Arctic. The key issues revolve around the key security requirements of Russia and United States. Both of these states have begun to take actions in the Arctic to support their core defense policy requirements. It is the geopolitical imperatives of these two countries that are acting to fundamentally change the nature of security within the region.

Russian geopolitical considerations

Russia security policy in the 2000s focused on several key requirements. First and most importantly, Russian defense policy made the maintenance and support of what they termed nuclear stability the most important priority of the Russian State. In the West, this is more commonly understood as the support of nuclear deterrence. While the end of the Cold War caused many observers to assume that the need to maintain nuclear deterrence policies was no longer required, all other major nuclear powers did maintain their nuclear deterrent as the ultimate protection of their states.[36] Russia made this explicit through their Security Council policy titled *Russia's National Security Strategy to 2020.*[37] This document explains that the security of the Russian State will ultimately depend on convincing any potential enemy that it will utilize its nuclear weapons before it surrenders to any military attack. The assumption is that the knowledge of this commitment means that any potential adversary will not attack in the first place.

In order to give meaning to this, as a priority the Russian State has also commenced a significant rebuilding of the maritime element of its deterrent forces. As mentioned previously, the end of the Cold War resulted in a virtual elimination of the entire Russian submarine fleet. Very few submarines survive from this period and those that did were allowed to significantly deteriorate.[38] In order to address the need to rebuild its submarine forces, the Russian governments introduced the State Programme of Armament (*Gosudarstvennaya Progmma razvitiya Vooruzheniy*) outlining their intention for rebuilding their forces beginning in 2007.[39] This was an ambitious document and significant elements of the program were not fulfilled.[40] But the one area where the Russians have maintained the effort to advance was in regard to the modernization and expansion of their submarine forces.[41] In the period that follows, the Russians have dedicated significant effort and resources to modernizing their existing fleet that survived at the end of the Cold War, comprised primarily of their Delta III and Delta IV SSBN submarines. They have also introduced a new class of nuclear missile carrying submarines—the Borei class (Project 955). They have built three; three more are being built and they plan to build another two, making a total of eight by 2020.[42] There have been problems with the missile that the submarines are to carry, but the Russians remain determined to remedy these difficulties and to have these submarines fully operational.[43] An examination of their actual deployments demonstrates that the preferred location can be found in their northern fleet operational locations. Some of their nuclear missile carrying nuclear-powered submarines (SSBNs) have been based in the Pacific, but these tend to be their older and less capable submarines.

The Russians also revived their long-range bomber patrols in August 2007.[44] Prior to this, they had ceased almost all of their bomber patrols following the end of the Cold War. However, not only have they reinstituted these patrols, but they have also increased both their numbers and complexity.[45] They have recently attached fighter escorts to these patrols that had been deployed across the Arctic.[46] There are some indications that these patrols are intended to provide signaling and that a second objective is to provide for operational training. There have been some unconfirmed reports that they have in fact been carrying nuclear weapons. Another unconfirmed story revolves around the short-lived military council that brought together the eight chief of defense staffs of the Arctic States.[47] There have been suggestions that a request was made to the Russian chief of defense staff during one of their meetings that the Russians provide prior notification of these bomber patrols. Even during the period prior to Russian intervention in Ukraine, and in a period of good relationships, the Russians were said to have refused to provide such notification.

The Russians have also been re-establishing a series of military bases along the northern sea route.[48] Officially, this is being done to improve and facilitate Russian search and rescue capabilities in an area where they are hoping to encourage an increase in maritime traffic. Some observers wonder whether these bases are not in fact also being modernized to improve the Russian military capabilities that are occurring within the entire region. These bases will provide a significantly improved ability for the Russian Air Force to provide protection for its maritime forces. All these activities—the modernization and expansion of their submarine forces; the reinstitution and maintenance of their long-range bomber patrols; and the modernization and expansion of their northern bases— are expensive and require considerable effort on the part of the Russian armed forces. There should be little doubt that when considered as a whole, they signify a very important priority of the Russian government.

The second major Russian defense policy pertains to their concerns regarding NATO expansion. The Russian Government has always been concerned about the expansion of NATO eastward. Even during the Yeltsin Government, the Russians could not understand why there was a need to maintain the alliance let alone encourage its expansion when the Cold War was over.[49] These concerns have grown under the Putin–Medvedev administration. The Russian defense policy documents also highlight their concern over the expansion of NATO towards their borders.[50] When identifying the main external danger, the first is related to:

> the desire to endow the force potential of the North Atlantic Treaty Organization (NATO) with global functions carried out in violation of the norms of international law and to move the military infrastructure of NATO member countries closer to the borders of the Russian Federation, including by expanding the bloc.[51]

While Western NATO leaders do not believe that their decisions to welcome eastern European states into the alliance threaten Russia, the Russians do not share this view. There are indications that in 2008 part of the Russian decision to militarily intervene in Georgia was influenced by the Georgian declarations that they were planning to seek membership in NATO.[52] While the evidence is still inconclusive, the link between the concerns of NATO expansion and Russian military intervention into neighboring states was made much more explicit during the Ukrainian crisis. In April 2014, when asked about the Russian decision to use military force to seize the Crimean peninsula with its naval bases Putin responded, "[w]hen the infrastructure of a military bloc is moving toward our borders, it causes us some concerns and questions. We need to take some steps in response."[53] In effect, this was a linkage to NATO expansion as explicit as it is possible to make.

The Russian decision to use both direct and indirect military force against Ukraine has had two major impacts on Arctic security. First, the Russian decision has resulted in direct action that has cooled relations between the Russians and the other Arctic States. Several Arctic States including Canada, Norway and the United States have imposed sanctions against officials and business leaders with direct interest to activities in the

Arctic.[54] Some countries such as Canada have also limited diplomatic exchanges regarding the Arctic as an indication of their opposition to Russian action.[55] The Icelandic government "postponed" its turn to host the eight Arctic chief of defense staff meeting.[56] There have been some efforts, principally led by the Americans, to separate their displeasure over Russian intervention and the Arctic through multilateral proceedings such as the recently held Glacier conference in Alaska in September 2015. However, it remains clear that relations between Russia and the other Arctic States have yet to return to their high points of the early 2000s.

The Russian intervention has also had another direct impact on Arctic security that relates directly to the issues surrounding NATO. Following the Russian intervention and the response of the Western states, Russia has begun to intensify military activities in and around the other Arctic States. Both Sweden and Finland have reported increased military activities that have been either directly or indirectly attributed to the Russians.[57] Some observers have suggested that this increased military activity has been meant as a display to dissuade the governments of Finland and Sweden from likewise considering membership in NATO.[58] This action may produce the opposite effect. While it is impossible at this point in time to know for certain whether either the Finnish or Swedish governments are in fact preparing to seek full membership, there are clear indications that both are seriously considering the option. This was made clear in Sweden in 2012. Swedish Defense officials began publicly speaking of the inability of Sweden to defend itself. These officials included the Finnish Commander-in-Chief Sverker Göranson, who did not specifically point to the Russians as the main threat. However, this idea was implicit within his statements. What was particularly telling was that right after the Swedish military leaders had gone public with their concerns, the Secretary General of NATO Anders Fogh Rasmussen publicly stated that only full members of NATO were entitled to the collective security protection provided by Article 5 of the North Atlantic Treaty.[59] The fact that the secretary general felt it necessary to make such a statement and had received the concurrence of the alliance members to do so is telling. Clearly, NATO was suggesting in no uncertain terms that Sweden needed to think about seeking full membership.

If Sweden and/or Finland do seek membership, there is little doubt that this will further hurt relations between Russia and the other Arctic States. If both of the "neutrals" were to join NATO, it would mean that seven out of eight members of the Arctic Council would belong to NATO. Well, it is entirely understandable why the governments of Finland and Sweden would feel that it is in their individual interest to join NATO to protect their national security. It is equally understandable how Russia would come to view this as an effort to encircle its borders with an alliance of states whose interests are not in keeping with Russian interests.

Ultimately, the point of tensions and the dynamics of these tensions between Russia and the other Arctic States do not originate in the Arctic, nor do they represent conflict about the Arctic. But they do ultimately affect the relationships that have been developed throughout the period of good cooperation in the region. Given the Russian core policies of the development and protection of its nuclear deterrent and its concerns regarding NATO expansion, it is unavoidable that the Russians will see a necessity to build up their military forces in the Arctic region. With the build-up of such forces when there are other tension points within the international system between the Russians and other Western states, it is almost inevitable that the Arctic will become involved.

American geopolitical considerations

The other part of the equation which further complicates the Arctic security environment are the actions taken by the Americans for the protection of their core security requirements. Following the terrorist attacks of September 2001, along with the recognition that there is an increasing possibility of both terrorist organizations and states hostile to the United States acquiring nuclear tipped missiles, there has been a continued importance attached to American capabilities to defend against missile attacks against the United States (referred to as the defense of the homeland). Once again, the military decisions taken by one of the major powers in the Arctic region have absolutely nothing to do with the conflict or challenges in the Arctic region but they place significant military forces in the region. One of the most important American anti-ballistic missile bases is found in Alaska in a location called Fort Greely. Located close to the Canadian border, this base was almost decommissioned following the end of the Cold War. It is partly through the political efforts of Alaskan politicians that this base has been maintained as an experimental location. Some have suggested that this was simply to satisfy the political need to reduce the downsizing that was occurring following the end of the Cold War. However, the base became the location where the Americans began to develop their ground-based midcourse interceptors following their withdrawal from the Anti-Ballistic Missile (ABM) treaty with Russia.[60] What began as an experimental location was soon transformed into the operational deployment of the bulk of their interceptors. They currently have twenty-six interceptors based in silos at this location. But following one of the continuing and improving missile launches on the part of the North Koreans, it was announced that fourteen more interceptors were to be added to the Fort Greely base.

The Alaska base is said to provide the best geographic location to protect against a launch of missiles from Asia towards the United States. The only other base that has these interceptors is located at Vandenberg Air Force Base in California. The Americans, however, only deployed four interceptors at this base. This suggests that they see limited utility in the California location. It is clearly in the Alaskan base where they see the best location to protect against a possible North Korean attack. The development of the

American ABM capabilities in Alaska has nothing to do at this point in time with Arctic security. But the problem that arises is that in the long term it may provide the means of defending against attacks from other countries in that location. The Russian government has noted its concerns that the American efforts to improve its ABM capabilities in general and specifically in Alaska may ultimately be directed against Russia.[61] Regardless of whether this is the case, what it does create is concerns on the Russian side that the Americans are in the long term attempting to develop a means to destabilize the Russian nuclear deterrent. The Russians are concerned that the Americans will ultimately develop the technology that allows them to defend against a large number of incoming missiles. The American position remains that the missiles in both Alaska and California are limited to only defending against a small-scale attack and that it would be impossible for them to defend against a large-scale attack. This means from an American perspective, that the Russian nuclear deterrent remains. From the Russian perspective the concern is that American technological capabilities will advance to the point where they will be able to defend against large-scale attacks and therefore render the Russian deterrent inoperable.

The Americans have also taken steps to publicly note that their attack submarines (SSN) are also resuming their patrols in the Arctic waters. While it is not known with any certainty whether the Americans had in fact reduced or eliminated Arctic patrols of their attack submarines, senior American naval officials had testified in Congress that at the end of the Cold War they did not see a necessity to maintain an Arctic capability and their newer classes of attack submarines. At the end of the Cold War, questions began to arise regarding the cost of the Seawolf class submarines that were just beginning to replace the Los Angeles class attack submarines. With the collapse of the Soviet Fleet, the necessity for continuing to build the Seawolf was challenged. As a result the American navy re-examined its requirements for a new class of attack submarines. The driving feature of what has become known as the Centurion project was cost reduction. The Americans wanted to reduce the cost of the submarines while retaining a core combat capability. As a result the navy was required to find avenues to reduce the cost of the proposed new class of submarines. A General Accounting Office (GAO) Report to the Secretary of Defense, commented that this was to be achieved by being slower and "less capable in diving depth and Arctic operations."[62] The logic was that the Russian threat was not as extensive as a Soviet threat had been and that it was unlikely that there would be a renewed effort to contend with the submarine threat in the Arctic region.

However, once the submarines (now known as the Virginia class) began construction, the vessels were given the capabilities necessary to operate in the Arctic region. The first Virginia class submarine in the Arctic was the USS *Texas* which entered the region to conduct initial cold water and under ice testing for the class in the fall of 2009.[63] The first operational deployment of Virginia class submarines occurred in 2011. Various Virginia class submarines have been used in the American scientific expeditions to the Arctic region that utilize American submarines (known as ICEX). While these exercises do provide for important scientific study of the region, they are also a convenient means of ensuring that observers are aware of American submarine capabilities in the Arctic region. When the USS *New Hampshire* entered the ice-covered waters of the Arctic with the Seawolf class submarine USS *Connecticut*, there were several photo opportunities to ensure that the world knew that the submarines are now operating in the region. In 2014, the USS *New Mexico* became the first Virginia class to surface at the North Pole.[64] Ultimately, this demonstrates that the American submarine force has retained its Arctic capabilities. While it cannot be proven, it seems more than coincidental that the American Navy began to showcase its capabilities of all of its attack submarines to operate in the Arctic at a time when the Russian Fleet had also renewed activity in the region. The challenge that will develop over time is that as the Russians move to improve their nuclear deterrent by renewing their maritime deterrent, they will need to take into account the American ability, through their attack submarines, to threaten that deterrent. Taking into consideration that Russian defense leaders already suspect that many of the American efforts to develop an ABM capability is really directed against them in the long term, this continued American ability to threaten their submarine force will undoubtedly lead to countermeasures to protect those assets.

The last strategic consideration that will influence the actions of both the American and Russian political defense leaders is the new arrival of China as a participant in the Arctic region. Initially China has limited its efforts to become an important participant through diplomatic, scientific and economic initiatives.[65] The Chinese ice-breaker began to visit the Arctic region in 1999 and the Chinese have been very active in developing a long-term and extensive scientific research program for the Arctic. However, in the fall of 2015, a Chinese naval task force comprising of three warships and two auxiliary vessels sailed as far as the southern section of the Bering Strait.[66] In that same year and also for the first time, Chinese vessels made an official port visit to Denmark, Finland and Sweden. What will be interesting to monitor will be development of future Chinese submarine development.[67] Will the Chinese begin to give these vessels the capabilities to operate in Arctic waters? Given the secrecy surrounding the construction of Chinese naval vessels, and particularly their submarines, it is impossible to know if this is intended. However, what is known is that since the beginning of the 2000s, the Chinese Navy has embarked upon an extensive program of new submarine construction.[68] If the Chinese do provide for some Arctic capabilities in the future, having Chinese submarines operating in the Arctic will significantly complicate the strategic operating environment for both the Americans and the Russians.

Conclusion

Ultimately, a focus on the changing geopolitics of the region demonstrates a rapidly changing environment. Clearly both Russia and the United States have made major strategic decisions based on their core security requirements that are having a major impact on the Arctic region. Both countries are not engaging upon this new activity in anticipation of a conflict over the Arctic or its resources. Rather, the increasing military activities of both countries in this region are caused by factors that are beyond the Arctic region. Nevertheless, the geopolitical imperatives that have been driving this transformation of the military environments in the region are ultimately felt when other points of conflict harm relations between Russia and the other Arctic States. This is why many observers correctly point out that the Arctic remains by itself a region of peace and cooperation. If it were able to remain completely isolated from the geopolitical events and factors beyond its borders, there is little doubt that it could retain its title as one of the most cooperative regions of the international system. Unfortunately, as the Arctic continues its dramatic transformation, it is becoming more and more connected to the greater international system. Thus, events that are seemingly distant and unrelated to the Arctic are increasingly having a bearing on the alternate determination of the region security. Furthermore, the geopolitical position of Russia and the United States inevitably means that the region will always feel the impact of the larger security relationship that exists between those two major powers.

None of this suggests that conflict is predetermined in the region because of these geopolitical realities. But the existence of these factors needs to be borne in mind in any consideration of the future security environment of the region. The region cannot be thought of in isolated terms. For better or for worse, it is now part of the greater international security environment. Any effort to pretend otherwise is simply to engage in wishful thinking.

Notes

1 There are lots of electronic services that focus exclusively on the Arctic. For example, *Arctic Update* maintained by the US Arctic Research Commission, or the *Arctic Journal*, among many others.

2 There has been an increasingly dizzy array of stories—including many cover stories—on the issue. See, for example, "Who Owns the Arctic," *Time Magazine*, October 1, 2007; "Gold Rush: The Race to Tap a Melting Arctic's Riches," *Newsweek*, July 6, 2015; "The Vanishing North: What the Melting of the Arctic Means for Trade, Energy and the Environment," *The Economist*, June 19, 2012.

3 Richard Compton-Hall, *Submarine vs Submarine: The Tactics and Technology of Underwater Confrontation* (Toronto: Collins, 1988), 79–85.

4 Michael Byers, *Who Owns the Arctic? Understanding Sovereignty Disputes in the North* (Vancouver: Douglas and McIntyre, 2009).

5 Alun Anderson, *After the Ice: Life, Death, and Geopolitics in the New Arctic* (New York: Smithsonian Books, 2009); Charles Emmerson, *The Future History of the*

Arctic (London: The Bodley Head, 2010); Shelagh D. Grant, *Polar Imperative: A History of Arctic Sovereignty in North America* (Vancouver: Douglas and McIntyre Publishers, 2011); Roger Howard, *The Arctic Gold Rush: The New Race for Tomorrow's Natural Resources* (London and New York: Continuum, 2009); Richard Sale and Eugene Potapov, *The Scramble for the Arctic: Ownership, Exploitation and Conflict in the Far North* (London: Frances Lincoln, 2010).

6 Susan Joy Hassol, *Impacts of a Warming Arctic: Arctic Climate Impact Assessment* (Cambridge: Cambridge University Press, 2004).

7 Willi Dansgaard et al., "Evidence for General Instability of Past Climate from a 250-kyr Ice-Core Record," *Nature* 364.6434 (1993): 218–20.

8 Hassol, *Impacts of a Warming Arctic.*

9 Julienne Stroeve and Dirk Notz, "Insights on Past and Future Sea-Ice Evolution from Combining Observations and Models," *Global and Planetary Change* 135 (2015): 119–32.

10 The Protection of the Arctic Marine Environment Working Group, Arctic Marine Shipping Assessment Report (Arctic Council, 2009).

11 Tristan Pearce et al., "Inuit Vulnerability and Adaptive Capacity to Climate Change in Ulukhaktok, Northwest Territories, Canada," *Polar Record* 46.2 (2010): 157–77.

12 Ian Stirling and Claire L. Parkinson, "Possible Effects of Climate Warming on Selected Populations of Polar Bears (Ursus maritimus) in the Canadian Arctic," *Arctic* (2006): 261–75. There are analysts who fear that a loss of the sea ice may result in dramatic reductions, if not the elimination, of most or even all of the polar bear populations.

13 Jeff Higdon and Steven H. Ferguson, "Loss of Arctic Sea Ice Causing Punctuated Change in Sightings of Killer Whales (Orcinus orca) Over the Past Century," *Ecological Applications* 19.5 (2009): 1365–75.

14 Natalie Sopinka, "Fisheries on the Move as Oceans Heat Up," *Fisheries* 40.1 (2015): 32–35.

15 Min Pan and Henry P. Huntington, "A Precautionary Approach to Fisheries in the Central Arctic Ocean: Policy, Science, and China," *Marine Policy* 63 (2016): 153–57.

16 "The Emerging Arctic," *Council on Foreign Relations,* accessed December 7, 2015, www.cfr.org/polar-regions/emerging-arctic/p32620#!/?cid=otr_marketing_use-arctic_Infoguide.

17 Geneviève King Ruel, "The (Arctic) Show Must Go On: Natural Resource Craze and National Identity in Arctic Politics," *International Journal* 66.4 (2011): 825–33.

18 Government of Canada, "Diamonds," *Natural Resources Canada – Canadian Minerals Yearbook (2009),* last modified May 15, 2013, accessed December 7, 2015, www.nrcan.gc.ca/mining-materials/markets/canadian-minerals-yearbook/2009/8464.

19 US Geological Survey, *Circum-Arctic Resource Appraisal: Estimates of Undiscovered Oil and Gas North of the Arctic Circle,* July 2008, accessed December 7, 2015, http://energy.usgs.gov/GeneralInfo/EnergyNewsroomAll/TabId/770/ArtMID/3941/ArticleID/1023/Undiscovered-Gas-Resources-in-the-Alum-Shale-Denmark-2013.aspx.

20 Andreas Østhagen, "Arctic Oil and Gas: Assessing the Potential for Hydrocarbon Development in the Polar Region," *The Arctic Institute,* April 16, 2013, accessed December 6, 2015, www.thearcticinstitute.org/2013/04/arctic-oil-and-gas-hype-or-reality.html.

21 Ed Struzik, "Oil Drilling in Arctic Ocean: A Push into Uncharted Waters," *Yale Environment* 360, June 8, 2015, accessed December 6, 2015, http://e360.yale.edu/feature/oil_drilling_in_arctic_ocean_a_push_into_uncharted_waters/2882/.

22 National Research Council, *Responding to Oil Spills in the US Arctic Marine Environment* (Washington, DC: The National Academies Press, 2014).

23 Tim Donaghy, "Why Cleaning up an Arctic Oil Spill would be Impossible," *Greenpeace,* January 15, 2015, accessed December 6, 2015, www.greenpeace.org/usa/cleaning-arctic-oil-spill-impossible/.

24 Alexis Arthur, "Does Arctic Drilling have a Future with Sub $50 Oil?" *OilPrice,* August 24, 2015, accessed December 6, 2015, http://oilprice.com/Energy/Crude-Oil/Does-Arctic-Drilling-Have-A-Future-With-Sub-50-Oil.html.

25 John Gaddis, *The Cold War: A New History* (New York: Penguin Press, 2005); Barry Posen, "Inadvertent Nuclear War? Escalation and NATO's Northern Flank," in *Strategy and Nuclear Deterrence,* edited by Steven E. Miller (Princeton, NJ: Princeton University Press, 1984), 85–112.

26 Rob Huebert, "New Directions in Circumpolar Cooperation: Canada, the Arctic Environmental Protection Strategy, and the Arctic Council," *Canadian Foreign Policy Journal* 5.2 (1998): 37–57.

27 Oran R. Young, "Governing the Arctic: From Cold War Theater to Mosaic of Cooperation," *Global Governance* 11.1 (2005): 9–15.

28 Seven Sawhill, "Cleaning-up the Arctic Cold War Legacy: Nuclear Waste and Arctic Environmental Cooperation," *Cooperation and Conflict* 35.1 (2000): 5–36.

29 David VanderZwaag, Rob Huebert and Stacey Ferrara, "The Arctic Environmental Protection Strategy, Arctic Council and Multilateral Environmental Initiatives: Tinkering While the Arctic Marine Environment Totters," *Denver Journal of International Law and Policy* 30.130 (2001): 131–72.

30 John English, *Ice and Water: Politics, Peoples, and the Arctic Council* (Toronto: Allen Lane, 2013).

31 Whitney Lackenbauer, "Canada and the Asian Observers to the Arctic Council: Anxiety and Opportunity," *Asia Policy* 18 (2014): 22–29.

32 Hassol, *Impacts of a Warming Arctic.*

33 Svein Vigeland Rottem, "A Note on the Arctic Council Agreements," *Ocean Development and International Law* 46.1 (2015): 50–59. The text of the *Agreement on Cooperation on Aeronautical and Maritime Search and Rescue in the Arctic* (Nuuk, Greenland, May 12, 2011) can be found at: www.arctic-council.org/index.php/en/about/documents/category/20-main-documents-from-nuuk#, accessed December 6, 2015.

34 Luke Harding, "Russia and Norway Resolve Arctic Border Dispute," *The Guardian,* September 15, 2010, accessed December 6, 2015, www.theguardian.com/world/2010/sep/15/russia-norway-arctic-border-dispute. The text of the *Treaty between the Kingdom of Norway and the Russian Federation concerning Maritime Delimitation and Cooperation in the Barents Sea and the Arctic Ocean* (Murmansk, Russia, September 15, 2010) can be found at: www.regjeringen.no/upload/SMK/Vedlegg/2010/avtale_engelsk.pdf, accessed December 6, 2015.

35 Klaus Dodds, "Flag Planting and Finger Pointing: The Law of the Sea, the Arctic and the Political Geographies of the Outer Continental Shelf," *Political Geography* 29.2 (2010): 71–72.

36 Ray Acheson, "Modernization of Nuclear Weapons: Aspiring to 'Indefinite Retention'?" *Bulletin of the Atomic Scientists* 68.5 (2012): 88–95.

37 Decree No. 537 of the President of the Russian Federation *"Russia's National Security Strategy to 2020"* [Стратегия национальной безопасности Российской Федерации до 2020 года], May 12, 2009, accessed December 7, 2015, http://rustrans.wikidot.com/russia-s-national-security-strategy-to-2020.

38 For one of the best sources on the Russian Northern Fleet, see Aleksandr Nikitin, Igor Kudrik and Thomas Nilsen, "The Russian Northern Fleet," *Bellona Report* 2 (2006), accessed December 7, 2015, www.bellona.org/subjects/1140451462.29.

39 Marcel De Haas, *Russia's Foreign Security Policy in 21st Century: Putin, Medvedev and Beyond* (London: Routledge, 2010): 89–90.

40 Martin Russell, *Russia's Armed Forces: Reform and Challenges* (Brussels: European Parliamentary Research Service, 2015), accessed December 6, 2015, www.europarl. europa.eu/RegData/etudes/IDAN/2015/554213/EPRS_IDA%282015%295542 13_EN.pdf.

41 "Submarines," RusNavy.com, 2013, accessed December 7, 2015, http://rusnavy. com/nowadays/strength/submarines/.

42 "3rd Russian Borei-Class Nuclear Sub Raised its Colors," *RT*, December 19, 2014, accessed December 6, 2015, www.rt.com/news/214155-russia-submarine-vladimir-monomakh/.

43 Franz-Stefan Gady, "Confirmed: Russia's Deadliest Sub Test Fires 2 Ballistic Missiles," *The Diplomat*, November 18, 2015, accessed December 6, 2015, http://thediplomat.com/2015/11/confirmed-russias-deadliest-sub-test-fires-2-ballistic-missiles/; "Bulava Missile Test History," The Russian Strategic Nuclear Forces, December 23, 2012, accessed December 7, 2015, http://russianforces.org/navy/slbms/bulava.shtml.

44 "Russia Restarts Cold War Patrol," *BBC News*, August 17, 2007, accessed December 6, 2015, http://news.bbc.co.uk/2/hi/europe/6950986.stm.

45 Sam LaGrone, "West: NORAD Head says Russia Increasing Arctic Long Range Air Patrols," *USNI News*, February 10, 2015, accessed December 6, 2015, http://news.usni.org/2015/02/10/west-norad-head-says-russia-increasing-arctic-long-range-air-patrols.

46 Michael Winter, "Russian Bombers increase Flights near US Airspace," *USA Today*, August 17, 2014, accessed December 6, 2015, www.usatoday.com/story/news/world/2014/08/07/russia-bombers-arctic/13746681/.

47 Randy Boswell, "Military Leaders from Arctic Countries to Meet in Canada," *Nunatsiaq Online*, April 4, 2012, accessed December 6, 2015, www.nunatsiaqonline.ca/stories/article/65674military_leaders_from_arctic_countries_to_meet_in_canada.

48 "Putin: Russia to Reopen Soviet-Era Arctic Military Base," *Reuters*, September 16, 2013, accessed December 6, 2015, www.reuters.com/article/us-russia-arctic-idUSBRE98F0VX20130916#rXyzGkPDVP4M1Eg5.97; "Russians in the Arctic: The Prize of a Presence," *Stratfor Global Intelligence*, November 28, 2015, accessed December 6, 2015, www.stratfor.com/analysis/russians-arctic-prize-presence.

49 Roger Cohen, "Yelstin Opposes Expansion of NATO in Eastern Europe," *New York Times*, October 2, 1993, accessed December 6, 2015, www.nytimes.com/1993/10/02/world/yeltsin-opposes-expansion-of-nato-in-eastern-europe.html.

50 Office of the Russian President, *The Military Doctrine of the Russian Federation*, February 5, 2010, accessed December 7, 2015, http://carnegieendowment.org/files/2010russia_military_doctrine.pdf.

51 Ibid., 3.

52 Denis Dyomkin, "Russia says Georgia War Stopped NATO Expansion," *Reuters*, November 11, 2011, accessed December 6, 2015, http://in.reuters.com/article/idINIndia-60645720111121.

53 "Putin says Annexation of Crimea Partly a Response to NATO Enlargement," *Reuters*, April 17, 2014, accessed December 6, 2015, www.reuters.com/article/2014/04/17/us-russia-putin-nato-idUSBREA3G22A20140417#V2oG8F5 3OTi8AxG7.97.

54 "International Sanctions during the Ukrainian Crisis," Wikipedia, accessed November 27, 2015, https://en.wikipedia.org/wiki/International_sanctions_during_the_Ukrainian_crisis.

55 Margo McDiarmid, "Arctic Council Tensions Threaten Environment as Canada Exits Chair," *CBC News*, April 24, 2015, accessed December 6, 2015, www.cbc.ca/news/politics/arctic-council-tensions-threaten-environment-as-canada-exits-chair-1.3045975.

56 Ekaterina Klimenko, "Russia and the Arctic: An End to Cooperation?." *Stockholm International Peace Research Institute*, March 15, 2015, accessed December 6, 2015, www.sipri.org/media/newsletter/essay/mar-15-russia-and-the-arctic.

57 Lizzie Dearden, "Full List of Incidents involving Russian Military and NATO since March 2014," *Independent*, November 10, 2014, accessed December 6, 2015, www.independent.co.uk/news/world/europe/full-list-of-incidents-involving-russian-military-and-nato-since-march-2014-9851309.html.

58 "Russia Warns Sweden and Finland against NATO Membership," *DefenseNews*, June 12, 2014, accessed December 6, 2015, http://archive.defensenews.com/article/20140612/DEFREG01/306120040/Russia-Warns-Sweden-Finland-Against-NATO-Membership.

59 "Sweden Can't Count on Help from NATO," *The Local*, January 14, 2013, accessed December 6, 2015, www.thelocal.se/20130114/45608.

60 US Department of State, "Statement by the White House Press Secretary, Announcement of Withdrawal from the ABM Treaty," Office of the Press Secretary, December 13, 2001, accessed December 7, 2015, http://2001–2009.state.gov/t/ac/rls/fs/2001/6848.htm.

61 Robert Burns, "US to Beef up Missile Defense against North Korea," *Alaska Journal of Commerce*, May 21, 2013, accessed December 6, 2015, www.alaskajournal.com/Alaska-Journal-of-Commerce/March-Issue-4–2013/US-to-beef-up-missile-defense-against-North-Korea-/.

62 General Accounting Office (GAO), *New Attack Submarine: More Knowledge Needed to Understand Impact of Design Changes*, April 30, 1998, accessed December 7, 2015, www.gpo.gov/fdsys/pkg/GAOREPORTS-NSIAD-98–38/pdf/GAOREPORTS-NSIAD-98–38.pdf.

63 "USS Texas Completes Historic First for Virginia Class," Commander Submarine Forces US Pacific Fleet, October 30, 2009, accessed December 7, 2015, www.csp.navy.mil/archived_news/Oct09/release_09054.shtml.

64 Julian Barnes, "Cold War Echoes under the Arctic Ice," *Wall Street Journal*, March 25, 2014, accessed December 6, 2015, www.wsj.com/articles/SB10001424052702304679404579461630946609454.

65 Linda Jacobson and Jinchao Peng, "China's Arctic Aspirations," *SIPRI Policy Paper* 34 (2012).

66 Phil Stewart, "Five Chinese Ships in Bering Sea as Obama visits Alaska," *Reuters*, September 2, 2015, accessed December 6, 2015, www.reuters.com/article/us-usa-china-military-idUSKCN0R22DN20150902#9kWwvRRTioiF1p3Q.97.

67 Shannon Tiezzi, "China's Navy Makes First-Ever Tour of Europe's Arctic States," *The Diplomat*, October 2, 2015, accessed December 6, 2015, http://thediplomat.com/2015/10/chinas-navy-makes-first-ever-tour-of-europes-arctic-states/.

68 Thomas Harding, "Chinese Nuclear Submarines Prompt 'New Cold War' Warning," *London Daily Telegraph*, May 3, 2008, accessed December 6, 2015, www.telegraph.co.uk/news/politics/local-elections/1920917/Chinese-nuclear-submarines-prompt-new-Cold-War-warning.html.

References

Acheson, Ray. "Modernization of Nuclear Weapons: Aspiring to 'Indefinite Retention'?" *Bulletin of the Atomic Scientists* 68.5 (2012): 88–95.

Anderson, Alun. *After the Ice: Life, Death, and Geopolitics in the New Arctic*. New York: Smithsonian Books, 2009.

Arthur, Alexis. "Does Arctic Drilling have a Future with Sub $50 Oil?" *OilPrice*, August 24, 2015. Accessed December 6, 2015, http://oilprice.com/Energy/Crude-Oil/Does-Arctic-Drilling-Have-A-Future-With-Sub-50-Oil.html.

Barnes, Julian. "Cold War Echoes under the Arctic Ice." *Wall Street Journal*, March 25, 2014. Accessed December 6, 2015, www.wsj.com.

Boswell, Randy. "Military Leaders from Arctic Countries to Meet in Canada." *Nunatsiaq Online*, April 4, 2012. Accessed December 6, 2015, www.nunatsiaqonline.ca/stories/article/65674military_leaders_from_arctic_countries_to_meet_in_canada.

Burns, Robert. "US to Beef up Missile Defense against North Korea." *Alaska Journal of Commerce*, May 21, 2013. Accessed December 6, 2015. www.alaskajournal.com.

Byers, Michael. *Who Owns the Arctic? Understanding Sovereignty Disputes in the North.* Vancouver: Douglas and McIntyre, 2009.

Cohen, Roger. "Yelstin Opposes Expansion of NATO in Eastern Europe." *New York Times*, October 2, 1993. Accessed December 6, 2015, www.nytimes.com/1993/10/02/world/yeltsin-opposes-expansion-of-nato-in-eastern-europe.html.

Commander Submarine Forces US Pacific Fleet. "USS Texas Completes Historic First for Virginia Class," October 30, 2009. Accessed December 7, 2015, www.csp.navy.mil/archived_news/Oct09/release_09054.shtml.

Compton-Hall, Richard. *Submarine vs Submarine: The Tactics and Technology of Underwater Confrontation.* Toronto: Collins, 1988.

Council on Foreign Relations. "The Emerging Arctic." Accessed December 7, 2015, www.cfr.org/polar-regions/emerging-arctic/p32620#!/?cid=otr_marketing_use-arctic_Infoguide.

Dansgaard, Willi, S.J. Johnsen, H.B. Clausen, D. Dahl-Jensen, N.S. Gundestrup, C.U. Hammer, C.S. Hvidberg et al. "Evidence for General Instability of Past Climate from a 250-kyr Ice-Core Record." *Nature* 364.6434 (1993): 218–20.

De Haas, Marcel. *Russia's Foreign Security Policy in 21st Century: Putin, Medvedev and Beyond.* London: Routledge, 2010.

Dearden, Lizzie. "Full List of Incidents involving Russian Military and NATO since March 2014." *Independent*, November 10, 2014. Accessed December 6, 2015, www.independent.co.uk/news/world/europe/full-list-of-incidents-involving-russian-military-and-nato-since-march-2014-9851309.html.

Dodds, Klaus. "Flag Planting and Finger Pointing: The Law of the Sea, the Arctic and the Political Geographies of the Outer Continental Shelf." *Political Geography* 29.2 (2010): 57–126.

Donaghy, Tim. "Why Cleaning Up an Arctic Oil Spill would be Impossible." *Greenpeace*, January 15, 2015. Accessed December 6, 2015, www.greenpeace.org/usa/cleaning-arctic-oil-spill-impossible/.

Dyomkin, Denis. "Russia says Georgia War Stopped NATO Expansion." *Reuters*, November 11, 2011. Accessed December 6, 2015, http://in.reuters.com/article/idINIndia-60645720111121.

Emmerson, Charles. *The Future History of the Arctic.* London: The Bodley Head, 2010.

English, John. *Ice and Water: Politics, Peoples, and the Arctic Council.* Toronto: Allen Lane, 2013.

Gaddis, John. *The Cold War: A New History.* New York: Penguin Press, 2005.

Gady, Franz-Stefan. "Confirmed: Russia's Deadliest Sub Test Fires 2 Ballistic Missiles." *The Diplomat*, November 18, 2015. Accessed December 6, 2015, http://thediplomat.com.

General Accounting Office (GAO). *New Attack Submarine: More Knowledge Needed to Understand Impact of Design Changes.* April 30, 1998. Accessed December 7, 2015, www.gpo.gov.

Government of Canada. "Diamonds." *Natural Resources Canada – Canadian Minerals Yearbook (2009).* Last modified May 15, 2013. Accessed December 7, 2015, www.nrcan.gc.ca.

Grant, Shelagh D. *Polar Imperative: A History of Arctic Sovereignty in North America.* Vancouver: Douglas and McIntyre Publishers, 2011.

Harding, Luke. "Russia and Norway Resolve Arctic Border Dispute." *The Guardian,* September 15, 2010. Accessed December 6, 2015, www.theguardian.com.

Harding, Thomas. "Chinese Nuclear Submarines Prompt 'New Cold War' Warning." *London Daily Telegraph,* May 3, 2008. Accessed December 6, 2015, www.telegraph.co.uk.

Hassol, Susan Joy. *Impacts of a Warming Arctic: Arctic Climate Impact Assessment.* Cambridge: Cambridge University Press, 2004.

Higdon, Jeff and Steven H. Ferguson. "Loss of Arctic Sea Ice Causing Punctuated Change in Sightings of Killer Whales (Orcinus orca) Over the Past Century." *Ecological Applications* 19.5 (2009): 1365–75.

Howard, Roger. *The Arctic Gold Rush: The New Race for Tomorrow's Natural Resources.* London and New York: Continuum, 2009.

Huebert, Rob. "New Directions in Circumpolar Cooperation: Canada, the Arctic Environmental Protection Strategy, and the Arctic Council." *Canadian Foreign Policy Journal* 5.2 (1998): 37–57.

Jacobson, Linda and Jinchao Peng. "China's Arctic Aspirations." *SIPRI Policy Paper* 34 (2012).

King Ruel, Geneviève. "The (Arctic) Show Must Go On: Natural Resource Craze and National Identity in Arctic Politics." *International Journal* 66.4 (2011): 825–33.

Klimenko, Ekaterina. "Russia and the Arctic: An End to Cooperation?." *Stockholm International Peace Research Institute,* March 15, 2015. Accessed December 6, 2015, www.sipri.org.

Lackenbauer, Whitney. "Canada and the Asian Observers to the Arctic Council: Anxiety and Opportunity." *Asia Policy* 18 (2014): 22–29.

LaGrone, Sam. "West: NORAD Head says Russia Increasing Arctic Long Range Air Patrols." *USNI News,* February 10, 2015. Accessed December 6, 2015, http://news.usni.org.

McDiarmid, Margo. "Arctic Council Tensions Threaten Environment as Canada Exits Chair." *CBC News,* April 24, 2015. Accessed December 6, 2015, www.cbc.ca/news/politics/arctic-council-tensions-threaten-environment-as-canada-exits-chair-1.3045975.

National Research Council. *Responding to Oil Spills in the US Arctic Marine Environment.* Washington, DC: The National Academies Press, 2014.

Nikitin, Aleksandr, Igor Kudrik and Thomas Nilsen. "The Russian Northern Fleet." *Bellona Report* 2 (2006). Accessed December 7, 2015, www.bellona.org.

Office of the Russian President. *The Military Doctrine of the Russian Federation.* February 5, 2010. Accessed December 7, 2015, http://carnegieendowment.org.

Østhagen, Andreas. "Arctic Oil and Gas: Assessing the Potential for Hydrocarbon Development in the Polar Region." *The Arctic Institute,* April 16, 2013. Accessed December 6, 2015, www.thearcticinstitute.org.

Pan, Min and Henry P. Huntington. "A Precautionary Approach to Fisheries in the Central Arctic Ocean: Policy, Science, and China." *Marine Policy* 63 (2016): 153–57.

Pearce, Tristan, Barry Smit, Frank Duerden, James D. Ford, Annie Goose and Fred Kataoyak. "Inuit Vulnerability and Adaptive Capacity to Climate Change in Ulukhaktok, Northwest Territories, Canada." *Polar Record* 46.2 (2010): 157–77.

Posen, Barry. "Inadvertent Nuclear War? Escalation and NATO's Northern Flank." In *Strategy and Nuclear Deterrence*, edited by Steven E. Miller, 85–112. Princeton, NJ: Princeton University Press, 1984.

The Protection of the Arctic Marine Environment Working Group. *Arctic Marine Shipping Assessment Report.* Arctic Council, 2009.

Rottem, Svein Vigeland. "A Note on the Arctic Council Agreements." *Ocean Development and International Law* 46.1 (2015): 50–59.

Russell, Martin. *Russia's Armed Forces: Reform and Challenges.* Brussels: European Parliamentary Research Service, 2015. Accessed December 6, 2015, www.europarl.europa.eu.

The Russian Strategic Nuclear Forces. "Bulava Missile Test History." December 23, 2012. Accessed December 7, 2015, http://russianforces.org.

Sale, Richard and Eugene Potapov. *The Scramble for the Arctic: Ownership, Exploitation and Conflict in the Far North.* London: Frances Lincoln, 2010.

Sawhill, Seven. "Cleaning-up the Arctic Cold War Legacy: Nuclear Waste and Arctic Environmental Cooperation." *Cooperation and Conflict* 35.1 (2000): 5–36.

Sopinka, Natalie. "Fisheries on the Move as Oceans Heat Up." *Fisheries* 40.1 (2015): 32–35.

Stewart, Phil. "Five Chinese Ships in Bering Sea as Obama visits Alaska." *Reuters,* September 2, 2015. Accessed December 6, 2015, www.reuters.com.

Stirling, Ian and Claire L. Parkinson. "Possible Effects of Climate Warming on Selected Populations of Polar Bears (Ursus maritimus) in the Canadian Arctic." *Arctic* (2006): 261–75.

Stratfor Global Intelligence. "Russians in the Arctic: The Prize of a Presence," November 28, 2015. Accessed December 6, 2015, www.stratfor.com.

Stroeve, Julienne and Dirk Notz. "Insights on Past and Future Sea-Ice Evolution from Combining Observations and Models." *Global and Planetary Change* 135 (2015): 119–32.

Struzik, Ed. "Oil Drilling in Arctic Ocean: A Push into Uncharted Waters." *Yale Environment* 360, June 8, 2015. Accessed December 6, 2015, http://e360.yale.edu.

Tiezzi, Shannon. "China's Navy Makes First-Ever Tour of Europe's Arctic States." *The Diplomat,* October 2, 2015. Accessed December 6, 2015, http://thediplomat.com.

US Department of State. "Statement by the White House Press Secretary, Announcement of Withdrawal from the ABM Treaty." *Office of the Press Secretary,* December 13, 2001. Accessed December 7, 2015, http://2001-2009.state.gov.

US Geological Survey. *Circum-Arctic Resource Appraisal: Estimates of Undiscovered Oil and Gas North of the Arctic Circle.* July 2008. Accessed December 7, 2015, http://energy.usgs.gov.

VanderZwaag, David, Rob Huebert and Stacey Ferrara. "The Arctic Environmental Protection Strategy, Arctic Council and Multilateral Environmental Initiatives: Tinkering While the Arctic Marine Environment Totters." *Denver Journal of International Law and Policy* 30.130 (2001): 131–72.

Wikipedia. "International Sanctions during the Ukrainian Crisis." Accessed November 27, 2015, https://en.wikipedia.org/wiki/International_sanctions_during_the_Ukrainian_crisis.

Winter, Michael. "Russian Bombers increase Flights near US Airspace." *USA Today,* August 17, 2014. Accessed December 6, 2015, www.usatoday.com.

Young, Oran R. "Governing the Arctic: From Cold War Theater to Mosaic of Cooperation." *Global Governance* 11.1 (2005): 9–15.

19 Geopolitical dynamics in the Arctic

Actors and global interests

Taisaku Ikeshima

Introduction

Numerous studies and environmental organizations report that the melting of Arctic ice due to global climate change is opening the door for the frequent use of the Northern Sea Route (NSR), which will bring about a revolutionary change in the distribution of goods and trade between European and Asian countries in particular.[1] One may also add to this the related possibility of the potential use of the North West Passage (NWP) along the Canadian coast.[2] However, it may still be too early to realize this optimistic view in practice. A recent report on the sharp decrease in vessels passing the NSR in 2014 cast a shadow over the optimistic perspective towards the future use of the NSR and offshore drilling of natural resources, such as oil and natural gas, in the Arctic.[3] Nevertheless, the value of the Arctic has attracted global attention in many ways and for various reasons. The most straightforward reason for this is, probably, that the Arctic is the last unknown territory of the globe open to wishful thinking regarding energy development and resource exploitation, along with the development of a navigational route, such as the NSR. One cannot, therefore, over stress the geopolitical significance of the Arctic.[4] During the Cold War, the United States and the Soviet Union confronted each other over the North Pole, with their intercontinental ballistic missiles ready to launch. Geopolitically, territorial and maritime disputes over some land and islands in the Arctic are not, in fact, so major as to have a huge impact on maintaining the peace and stability of the region.[5]

Human beings have already learned a lesson in the case of the other polar area, the Antarctic, where the Antarctic Treaty System (ATS), including the Antarctic Treaty (AT), has effectively functioned as a legally binding framework for more than half a century. As researchers often disagree on the issue of Arctic governance and its legal structure,[6] there may be no comprehensive legal institution to govern all the matters that arise in the Arctic region. Though the Arctic Council (AC), which is a "high level forum,"[7] has been functioning as the de facto regional mechanism for nearly two decades, one cannot easily analogize a treaty system

equivalent to the ATS to the situation of the Arctic, due to the fundamental differences in these two polar areas. Basically, the five coastal states
in the Arctic Ocean, among others, do not need any other permanent
legal structure than the United Nations Convention on the Law of the Sea
(UNCLOS), as we will see below. Now that the issues of governance and
order in the Arctic region have reached global significance, it seems more
meaningful to speak of the similarities between these two poles than of
differences and contradictions. At least, we all know that the Antarctic case
is, doubtlessly, the successful one, no matter what one may have seen in
terms of its governance and order-making process. If the goal of good governance and order in the Arctic region is to maintain peace and security
for its regional sustainable development as well as global interests, the
lessons that human beings learned through the ATS, the UNCLOS, and
other similar governance structures will also be of great help in the case of
the Arctic, which is almost the last "common space" on Earth where the
competing interests of the concerned states and stakeholders in and
around the region have not yet been settled.[8]

This chapter discusses the various actors and their roles in the Arctic
region and considers the interests of the various actors in the Arctic. The
Arctic is a unique place where traditional geopolitical notions such as *state-
as-actor* and *state interest* become obsolete and where contemporary geopolitical considerations are necessary. Through these two points of discussion,
this chapter seeks to clarify the geopolitical dynamics in the Arctic region,
where the non-traditional, diverse interplay of politics, economy and society
has gradually and specifically emerged and developed against the backdrop
of the globalized world.

Various actors

The Arctic region is geographically a maritime area mainly covered by ice.
In the Arctic, therefore, the main actors are the five coastal states, or the
"Arctic Five," that is, Canada, Denmark (representing Greenland),
Norway, Russia and the United States. They are the coastal states that exercise jurisdiction and control over their maritime space and resources off
the coasts. However, there remain three non-coastal but still Arctic States
that also have significant historical and geographical interest: Finland,
Iceland and Sweden. These eight actors, often called the "Arctic Eight,"
consult, negotiate and cooperate through the AC,[9] which is not an international organization under international law but a de facto consultative
machinery among the Arctic Eight, plus observer states and non-state
interested actors.

It is nevertheless unsurprising that the interests of the Arctic Five do
not necessarily overlap with those of the Arctic Eight. The maritime area
of the Arctic, though mostly frozen and covered by sea ice, is governed by
the Law of the Sea, whose main part is nowadays represented by UNCLOS.

All the Arctic coastal states, except for the USA, are the contracting parties to UNCLOS. The US government is of the opinion that the customary law rules reflected in UNCLOS apply to the Arctic maritime area.[10] Only the Arctic Five agreed and declared in the 2008 Ilulissat Declaration that there is "no need to develop a new comprehensive international regime to govern the Arctic Ocean"[11] because the Law of the Sea, including UNCLOS, applies to maritime space. The coastal states' interest in the governance of the maritime space in the Arctic is not necessarily the same as those of the non-coastal states.[12] It is here worth taking a closer look at some specific aspects of the Arctic coastal states, or the Arctic Five. These are certainly the stakeholders in the Arctic region, and the most directly concerned states in the region. However, the geographical and demographical factors differ considerably even among these five states, and the Arctic Five have different geographical and economic backgrounds, in particular.

With respect to the shipping route in the Arctic Ocean, the NSR along Russia's long coastline[13] and the NWP through Canada's convoluted coastline of islands[14] are economically beneficial but are also a source of environmental and security concern. Canada probably has more interest in the protection of the regional environment and ecosystem in the Arctic. Russia's incomparably lengthy coastline inevitably has given a heavy burden of coastal security vis-à-vis not only other opposite Arctic coastal states but also the transit flag states, even in the post-Cold War era. The United States, in accordance with its Arctic strategy and policy,[15] seeks to defend its national interests in the Arctic for security, commercial and scientific purposes. Geographically, Alaska is the only US state whose coastline faces the Arctic Ocean, and the USA, under its National Strategy, needs to put a particular stress on its consultation and coordination with Alaska Natives. Besides the freedom of navigation (FON), which is the highest priority of the USA in the sea,[16] the US Arctic policy and strategy necessarily stresses international cooperation due to the limits of direct interest in the region and of national budgets.[17] But, obviously, the FON means different things for different states. Here a conflict arises over the interpretation of the FON between the Arctic coastal states and other shipping states.

Norway's geographical location[18] with the position of the Svalbard Islands in the Arctic will be of significant benefit to its economic development, since the future perspective of oil and gas development in the Barents Sea will certainly decide the Norwegian relations with the two major factors: first, Russia as a neighboring energy power to compete with over territorial mapping strategies with respect to gas and oil development in the High North; and second, its environmental policy making to mitigate the impact of climate change.[19] For Norway, at the same time, its bilateral security relations with Russia are most important, while the rise of Asian countries such as China and Japan will highly affect the Norwegian economy through energy resource development in the Arctic.[20]

Denmark's interest is principally represented by its remote island territory, Greenland, whose Autonomous Government's prime minister "strongly hopes to become independent from Denmark" after promoting the development of mineral resources and oil off its coast and harnessing enough economic power for independence.[21] Greenland, which has enjoyed its detachment from the European Commission (EC) fisheries policy, is opening its doors to foreign investment from, for example, China and Japan. This might be of concern not only for its mainland, Denmark, but also for the AC. Offshore drilling for oil around the coasts of Greenland is an ongoing project and will provide an opportunity for economic growth and the enhancement of Greenland's autonomy if it is allowed to continue.[22] By doing so, the minority island government of Greenland may be able to unburden itself of its heavy dependence on subsidies from the mainland government of Denmark. Greenland's independence will also require a clear and solid plan for its own foreign and security autonomy. Economic development in the Arctic may take a new and unexpected turn, too.

It is already unproductive to spotlight only states as actors or players in the Arctic. The Arctic region is a maritime but frozen space surrounded by the very thinly populated coasts of the Arctic Five. Demographic density varies from state to state in the Arctic region.[23] There are indigenous peoples living in the region.[24] The Antarctic continent does not have any indigenous people, and the geographical features and locations of the nearest coastal states in the Antarctic are entirely different from those in the Arctic.

The Arctic region is therefore unique, particularly because non-state actors are also permitted to join the AC as Permanent Participants (PP). There are six entities representing indigenous peoples living in and around the Arctic: the Aleut International Association (AIA), the Arctic Athabaskan Council (AAC), the Gwich'in Council International (GCI), the Inuit Circumpolar Council (ICC), the Russian Association of Indigenous Peoples of the North (RAIPON) and the Saami Council. They are important players not because they are admitted to the AC forum but because they are the directly concerned parties in Arctic matters in terms of their actual life therein. It may be said that the AC cannot operate without the voice of these PPs, as their intentions and thoughts must be taken into account in the process of consultation and discussion.[25]

The traditional idea of geopolitics views national states as the main actors,[26] but this does not fully cover the scope of the current situation in the Arctic region. The state-centered concept of geopolitics does not grasp the reality of the presence of indigenous peoples in the Arctic. These indigenous peoples, whose living space, or *lebensraum*, may go beyond or straddle state boundaries, send representatives to the AC through the six entities mentioned above. In fact, these peoples are historically the individuals who lead lives and conduct activities such as fisheries and hunting in the Arctic region.[27]

Within the category of the AC observer status,[28] moreover, are some developed European states and Asian states that show interest in advancing the development of peaceful and stable governance of the Arctic. From Europe come France, Germany, Italy, Poland, Spain, the Netherlands and the United Kingdom. It is obvious that major economic powers in Europe are among those that have been admitted as observers of the AC.[29] The Asian states are China, India, Japan, Singapore and South Korea. Each has significant influence in the world economy.[30] The NSR will be an important maritime route for transportation of their goods and energy resources mainly because of the character of the NSR as a "short cut" between European countries and Asian countries.[31]

Singapore and South Korea will have more interest in the use of the NSR, as they are famous for their trade interests and the position of their ports as hubs. China and India, in particular, are the so-called newly rising powers, largely as a result of the size of their populations and their geographical territoriality. They may be seen as stakeholders in Arctic matters because they intend to participate in the process of decision-making and law-making in any region where global interests are affected. In this sense, the sea lane for trade through the Arctic matters more for those who utilize trade than for those who see goods pass by their coasts. In other words, NSR trade may not bring about significant economic profit for the Arctic States, whose geographical location is, like a passer-by, just along the route, without any relevance to it. Rather, their coastal environments and ecosystems may be negatively impacted from the navigation and transit caused by the commercial ships and vessels mainly of non-Arctic States. Except for Singapore, all observer states in the AC, also as consultative states of the Antarctic Treaty, have left ample achievements in terms of polar observation and research with economic power and potential.[32]

Among others, China, as a rising power, has attracted the attention of the Arctic States as well as the world because the Arctic coastal states see China's activities around the polar areas as threatening peace and stability in the area.[33] Mass media has recently reported that, on behalf of this country, a Chinese buyer of real estate has a strong intention to purchase plots of land in some countries in the Arctic region, particularly in the several years' time.[34] Some observers may see China's active economic expansion in the region as an aggressive transformation of the local life and communities.[35] However, these views may be too one-sided and prejudiced by the current common misperceptions regarding China's assertive standpoints in and around the South China Sea and the East China Sea.[36] A simple analogy of the case of Southeast and East Asia does not apply to the current situation of the Arctic region. China's active Arctic policy has become fruitful through its scientific and economic cooperation with Norway, Canada and Iceland, for instance. This is mainly because these Arctic countries have reasonable domestic demands for China's economic and technological power. Rather, China's incorporation into the political framework, such as through the AC, by way of cooperation will be mutually beneficial to China and the AC Member States, so that they will be able to ease possible tensions and enhance trust in the region.

A Chinese admiral of the People's Liberation Army Navy stated in 2010 that the North Pole and its surrounding area do not belong to any state but are "the common wealth of the world people."[37] This statement, which has a meaningful and universal value, did not attract as much global attention as the planting of a Russian flag on the deep seabed of the Arctic pole by Russian politicians, including Mr. Artur Chilingarov, in 2007. As is seen in the UNCLOS negotiations between 1973 and 1982, one may, here again, recall the conflicts between the coastal states, who claim the maximum maritime interests through their creeping jurisdiction over the space and its resources, and those who are left behind with nothing but their legitimate interest in the name of the community. The Chinese statement mentioned above is more politically and legally meaningful than the Russian action because the former is likely to represent a legitimate act in a political and diplomatic scene of negotiation over rule-making, while the latter action is as a legally outdated and hollow act of chauvinism that may only lead to an unnecessary conflict in the region.

From the viewpoint of the current economic conditions of the world, China, as a "returning power," is and will be, inevitably, involved in the process of governance and order-making in the Arctic region.[38] Even with the power shift that is taking place gradually in the world, from US unipolar order to a more fluid and diverse order with newly rising powers such as China and India, it would not be of merit to the stable and balanced development of Arctic governance to unnecessarily exaggerate China's activities in the Arctic region or one-sidedly distort the real state of Arctic affairs.

Globalization and global interests

Global climate change is a major double-edged sword, presenting drastic change leading to future possible economic opportunities in the Arctic, on the one hand, and dynamic degradation of the Arctic environment and ecosystem, on the other. Though the Arctic Ocean is geographically remote from the rest of the world's maritime areas, it is observed that it is not completely separate—rather, all oceans are ecologically and environmentally interconnected.[39] Global climate change and its potential effects present the international community with much reason to be concerned by Arctic matters that may affect the world environment, ecosystem and natural resources.[40] In other words, the world has realized that it has a community interest in a peaceful and stable situation in the Arctic region as a whole, since global environmental problems have brought about the concept of "common concern" with legal significance.[41] This interest may also be called a public interest of the international community.

On the other hand, the states which are engaged in any activities are responsible for their conduct in relation with the international community as a whole. This notion of global responsibility has been gradually emerging, since a series of international conferences on environment and development have taken place over recent decades.[42] Nowadays, matters of global concern such as human rights or environmental protection can entitle any country to intervene in the process of decision-making and law-making. The melting of Arctic ice due to global climate change gives the so-called micro states in the middle of the Pacific Ocean a significant voice on the environmental and ecological conditions of the Arctic Ocean because these states, micro or powerful, will be greatly influenced by these natural conditions irrespective of their geographical location, north or south.

The notion of public interest in the international community[43] can give the non-Arctic States, in particular, good reason to intervene in the discussion and decision-making on the regime operation and on governance of the region. Those actors able and motivated to pay attention to matters outside their region, that is to say, newly rising states such as China[44] and India,[45] are concerned with this process in the Arctic. In turn, it can also be said that, without consent of the community as a whole, the Arctic Five and other Arctic States would not easily take action that may influence the community and public interest in the Arctic region.

If and when the transportation of goods and products between Europe and Asia through the NSR becomes more common, this route, which actually comprises several different variations of routes through the region, will possibly be of almost the same value as the sea lanes that go through the Malacca-Singapore straits, the Red Sea, the Suez Canal, the Gibraltar Strait and other important places. Theoretically speaking, the value of the straits will depend on the quantity and substance of the goods and products that pass through them. In this sense, oil and natural gas, among other products, will be the major factors that determine the preciousness of the routes for transportation. Transportation routes on the sea, or "sea lanes," are also regarded as important resources in common use in the international community. Because of the nature and function of these transportation resources, public interest in the shipping routes is part of the basic infrastructure of the international community. The more frequently the sea routes are used by more countries, the more likely the routes will garner public interest.

Thus, more and more non-Arctic States may find opportunities to get involved in the use of routes such as the NSR in the future, as the number of states along the shipping routes grows. This trend towards the expansion of the actors and stakeholders interested in the Arctic region through the sea routes will enlarge the circle of the members who will be concerned with the order and governance of the region. The economic factor will be a major driving force in the emergence and development of the idea of global concerns and interest in the Arctic.

The Arctic region, which may sometimes arguably be called one of the Global Commons, is not directly governed by the United Nations (UN), but, in fact, the UN indirectly has relevance for the regional order through the application and interpretation of the relevant treaties, which have been adopted in the UN and whose operation is conducted through UN-affiliated bodies such as the International Maritime Organization (IMO).[46] In this sense, the interest in the Arctic region is within the scope of the global concern and interest covered by the UN architecture.[47] The Arctic Five, among others, are in agreement with each other on the application of the Law of the Sea, including UNCLOS, to the Arctic Ocean, and they intend to exclude the possibility of establishing a new comprehensive legal framework to govern the region.

There exists a portion of the high seas in the Arctic Ocean, although the majority of the water belongs to the territorial waters and the exclusive economic zone (EEZ) of the coastal states. The coastal states of the Arctic Ocean have the continental shelf under the water column of their EEZ and may extend the outer limit of their continental shelf under certain UNCLOS regulations as well as under the recommendation of the Commission on the Limits of the Continental Shelf (CLCS).[48] The coastal states undoubtedly have the power to control the maritime space and its resources, in the sense that they have jurisdiction and control over the maritime space and its resources under UNCLOS rules.[49] As regards the deep seabed, or the "Area," and its resources under the Arctic Ocean, however, the UN and the International Seabed Authority (ISA) are in charge of the governance and regulation of the activities therein under UNCLOS.[50] The "Area" and its resources in the Arctic region are also the Common Heritage of Mankind (CHM),[51] whose rights "are vested in mankind as a whole, on whose behalf the Authority shall act."[52] Therefore, the certain space and its resources are under the realm of the UN's control and management, because the UN and its affiliated bodies such as the CLCS and the ISA are, under the notion of CHM and relevant rules of international law, entitled to act on behalf of humankind as a whole, although the notion of humankind and its scope are still theoretically vague and left open to some interpretation. Here, again, arise the viewpoints of public interest and matters of public concern.

The more reasons arise, the more complicated the situations surrounding the Arctic will become. The globalization of the Arctic by giving the states concerned the grounds to commit themselves to governance of the Arctic region would be likely to invite more players into the order-making and decision-making process of the region. Rising states such as China and India will not miss this chance to join in the process of governance and order in the Arctic region, since their economic power inevitably accompanies their political and diplomatic capability in many international scenes. For example, the "Group of Seven" states (G7)—an informal forum of the seven major industrial states, Canada, France, Germany, Italy, Japan, the United Kingdom and the United States[53]—has been less influential in world politico-economy than the "Group of Twenty" (G20)—a group of major advanced and emerging market economies, to which China and India belong. Non-Arctic States, including rising powers, will have more and more opportunities to take part in the development plans and projects of the natural resources and transportation routes in the Arctic region against the growth of their economic development.

These significant actors will have practically no reason to be excluded from Arctic governance or order-making. On the contrary, they will have more reasons to commit themselves to the process and the consequences of the regional order and governance. In this sense, these actors will easily have legitimacy to intervene in the process. In addition, what accelerates their involvement in the regional order-making is the pretext for them to claim their standing in the process. These legitimate interests may be "global commons," "global concerns," "Common Heritage of Mankind" (CHM), and other similar concepts that tend to attract attention and appeal to many people in the world.[54] Non-Arctic States are likely to gain the legitimacy to get involved in Arctic affairs in the name of global interests: they are not excluded from Arctic politics by the Arctic States.

This sequence of state of affairs in the Arctic is also inevitable and common in the similar case of the Antarctic. The ATS was obliged to leave the ancient regime of the closed diplomatic conference of limited elite members in order to become more democratic and transparent, particularly after the severe criticism that followed the successful adoption of the final text of UNCLOS in 1982.[55] The 1980s was a good period for the ATS to be modernized and democratized, as Antarctica was designated as a "natural reserve" under the 1991 Environmental Protocol to the Antarctic Treaty, and the ATS was dedicated to its environmental protection without the risk of endangering its nature and ecosystem, thanks to a general prohibition on mineral exploitation activities for half a century.[56] Human actors recall what they have seen before in world politics. The globalization of the Arctic is not a negative phenomenon but an inevitable consequence in a globalized world where various players and actors are interrelated and interdependent irrespective of their geographical location.

What is currently specific to Arctic affairs is that there is always room for coordination and cooperation between the Arctic States, or the Arctic Five more precisely, and non-Arctic States with politico-economic power due to the potential conflict of legitimate interests that each group claims in the Arctic region. Legitimate interests in the Arctic region may surpass geopolitical interests when the former are principally claimed by participants in the name of global interest and/or global concerns. Certainly, the Arctic Five, in particular, are keenly aware of these claims and arguments in the light of what they have learned in the historical development of the rule-making process in the fields of the Law of the Sea, the ATS, environmental issues, and so on. The tug of war between the Arctic States and non-Arctic States is one of the most significant aspects of Arctic geopolitics.

Conclusion

This chapter has explored how geopolitical dynamism evolved in and around the Arctic region, in terms of, first, the various actors involved in the process of governance and order-making in the Arctic and, second, the emergence and function of the global interest and concerns in the region. The first and second aspects are interrelated. This relationship will be more enhanced and accelerated in the near future as a result of the dynamic changes in the globalized world.

Regarding the first aspect, the traditional idea of geopolitics tends to highlight the relations between states while paying much less attention to non-state actors, such as indigenous peoples and international organizations. However, the contemporary situation in the Arctic does not merit a simple juxtaposition of the state–state relationship in the almost closed local region of the Arctic Ocean; rather, it also represents the actual life of the indigenous peoples in the region. Moreover, the actors are not limited to the states in the local region. The states concerned are not only the coastal states in the Arctic Ocean but also include states that are geographically remote but remain concerned and involved for various reasons. The stakeholders in the development of Arctic mineral resources and its maritime transportation routes are the Arctic Eight, including the Arctic Five and other non-Arctic States, which are represented by Asian states with the economic capability to take part in the development of maritime routes and natural resources in the Arctic region. Interest in the Arctic region is not only regional but also global.

In this sense, a geographical standpoint to classify the user-states of Arctic resources is not necessarily helpful to grasp the whole situation of the movement of actors, stakeholders and other beneficiaries in the current globalized community. This aspect is rather a natural reflection of the globalization of the world's politico-economic situation, in which the G20 has more accurately represented the interest of the globalized economy than the G7 has. The world has seen the geopolitical dynamism of various actors in the Arctic region, although the major stakeholders may still be the states which are directly and deeply concerned with the use and development of the region.

This first observation regarding the actors leads us to the second point, that the globalized participants in Arctic development explain not only their own interest in the region but also their grounds, or pretexts, to act on behalf of the community. Needless to say, the Arctic Five, or the Arctic Eight, are the directly concerned states in the Arctic region because of its geographical location. However, global climate change and its environmental impact on the global community will inevitably bring the Arctic region to the world's attention.

The notion of global interest or public interest in the international community arises in and permeates the agenda of global diplomatic fora.

The Arctic issues of today are not confined within the regional framework of governance but can be regarded as matters of public concern. Arctic matters are therefore both regional and global. The AC, which is still functioning as a de facto forum of the Arctic region, will be obliged to take into consideration and work on behalf of public interest as well, in order to become legitimate and responsible for Arctic governance. The AC is currently vested with the trust to manage the governance and order-making of the Arctic region against the background of geopolitical dynamics and the rise and development of the notion of public interest in the region.

Notes

1 For academic analysis of the shipping routes in the Arctic Ocean, see Willy Østreng et al., *Shipping in Arctic Waters: A Comparison of the Northeast, Northwest and Trans Polar Passages* (Heidelberg: Springer, 2013).
2 For a Canadian point of view, see Franklyn Griffiths, Rob Huebert and P. Whitney Lackenbauer, *Canada and the Changing Arctic: Sovereignty, Security, and Stewardship* (Waterloo, ON: Wilfrid Laurier University Press, 2011).
3 See, for example, Trude Pattersen, "Northern Sea Route Traffic Plummeted," *BarentsObserver*, December 16, 2014, accessed December 26, 2014, http://barents observer.com/en/arctic/2014/12/northern-sea-route-traffic-plummeted-16–12; The Associated Press, "Number of Ships Transiting Arctic Waters Falls in 2014," *New York Times*, January 5, 2015, accessed January 15, 2015, www.nytimes.com/aponline/2015/01/05/us/ap-us-arctic-shipping.html?_r=0.
4 For geopolitical viewpoints in the Arctic, see Lassi Heininen, "Northern Geopolitics: Actors, Interests and Processes in the Circumpolar Arctic," in *Polar Geopolitics?: Knowledges, Resources and Legal Regimes*, edited by Richard C. Powell and Klaus Dodds (Cheltenham: Edward Elgar, 2014), 241–58.
5 For security issues, see James Kraska (ed.), *Arctic Security in an Age of Climate Change* (Cambridge: Cambridge University Press, 2011).
6 For the views in favor of a possible Arctic Treaty, see Donald Rothwell, "The Arctic in International Affairs: Time for a New Regime?," *The Brown Journal of World Affairs* XV.1 (2008): 248–51. For contrary views, see Alf Hakon Hoel, "Do We Need a New Legal Regime for the Arctic Ocean," *International Journal of Marine and Coastal Law* 24 (2009): 443–56; Oran R. Young, "Arctic Governance – Pathways to the Future," *Arctic Review on Law and Politics* 1.2 (2010): 180–84.
7 See the Ottawa Declaration of September 19, 1996, paragraph 1.
8 For the concepts and ideas of international spaces and common interests, see Rüdiger Wolfrum, "Common Interests in the Ocean," in *Science Diplomacy: Antarctica, Science, and the Governance of International Spaces*, edited by Paul Arthur Berkman et al. (Washington, DC: Smithsonian Institution Scholarly Press, 2011): 281–85; Oran R. Young, "Governing International Spaces: Antarctica and Beyond," in *Science Diplomacy: Antarctica, Science, and the Governance of International Spaces*, edited by Paul Arthur Berkman et al. (Washington, DC: Smithsonian Institution Scholarly Press, 2011): 287–94.
9 For its origin and historical background, see E.T. Bloom, "Establishment of the Arctic Council," *American Journal of International Law* 93.3 (1999): 712–22.
10 The US government observes the UNCLOS "as reflective of customary international law and practice." See "Law of the Sea Convention," National Oceanic and Atmospheric Association (NOAA) Office of General Counsel, accessed

December 30, 2014, www.gc.noaa.gov/gcil_los.html; Secretary of Defense, "Arctic Strategy," US Department of Defense, November 2013, 10, accessed August 4, 2015, www.defense.gov/pubs/2013_Arctic_Strategy.pdf.

11 See the Ilulissat Declaration of May 28, 2008.

12 This can also apply to security matters in the Arctic. See Lassi Heininen, "Arctic Security – Global Dimensions and Challenges, and National Policy Responses," *The Yearbook of Polar Law* 5 (2013): 93–115.

13 For the geographical features and historical background of the NSR, see Nataliya Marchenko, *Russian Arctic Seas: Navigational Conditions and Accidents* (Berlin: Springer, 2012), 1–25.

14 For the detailed legal analysis of the NWP, see Donat Pharand, *Canada's Arctic Waters in International Law* (Cambridge: Cambridge University Press, 1988), 187–243.

15 For US Arctic strategy and policy, see "National Strategy for the Arctic Region," May 2013, accessed August 18, 2015, www.whitehouse.gov/sites/default/files/docs/nat_arctic_strategy.pdf; "US Coast Guard Arctic Strategy," May 2013, accessed August 18, 2015, www.uscg.mil/seniorleadership/DOCS/CG_Arctic_Strategy.pdf; "Implementation Plan for National Strategy for Arctic Region," January 2014, accessed August 18, 2015, www.whitehouse.gov/sites/default/files/docs/implementation_plan_for_the_national_strategy_for_the_arctic_region_-_fi....pdf; and "The United States Navy Arctic Roadmap for 2014 to 2030," February 2014, accessed August 18, 2015, www.navy.mil/docs/USN_arctic_roadmap.pdf.

16 See James Kraska, *Maritime Power and the Law of the Sea: Expeditionary Operations in World Politics* (Oxford: Oxford University Press, 2011), 8–9; 397–98.

17 See Ronald O'Rourke, "Changes in the Arctic: Background and Issues for Congress," June 2, 2015, Congressional Research Service, R41153, accessed August 18, 2015, www.fas.org/sgp/crs/misc/R41153.pdf.

18 But there remains a risk of being a mere pass point in terms of shipping goods between European and Asian countries, when and if the NSR comes into full use.

19 See Berit Kristoffersen, " 'Securing' Geography: Framings, Logics and Strategies in the Norwegian High North," in *Polar Geopolitics?: Knowledges, Resources and Legal Regimes*, edited by Richard C. Powell and Klaus Dodds (Cheltenham: Edward Elgar, 2014), 131–48.

20 See Rolf Tamnes, "Arctic Security and Norway," in *Arctic Security in an Age of Climate Change*, edited by James Kraska (Cambridge: Cambridge University Press, 2011), 56–62.

21 See Kosuke Terai, "Strengthening Economic Power for Independence," *Nikkei*, April 11, 2015, 3, in Japanese (print version); electronic version, accessed August 18, 2015, www.nikkei.com/article/DGXLASGM31H21_R10C15A4NNE000/.

22 For the issue of Greenland's independence and autonomy, see Jeppe Strandsbjerg, "Making Sense of Contemporary Greenland: Indigeneity, Resources and Sovereignty," in *Polar Geopolitics?: Knowledges, Resources and Legal Regimes*, edited by Richard C. Powell and Klaus Dodds (Cheltenham: Edward Elgar, 2014), 259–76.

23 See Laurence Smith, *The New North: The World in 2050* (London: Profile Books, 2012), 172–74.

24 For the issue of indigenous peoples in the Arctic region, see Michael Byers, *International Law and the Arctic* (Cambridge: Cambridge University Press, 2013), 216–44.

25 See Hannah Strauss and Nuccio Mazzullo, "Narratives, Bureaucracies and Indigenous Legal Orders: Resource Governance in Finnish Lapland," in *Polar Geopolitics?: Knowledges, Resources and Legal Regimes*, edited by Richard C. Powell and Klaus Dodds (Cheltenham: Edward Elgar, 2014), 295–312.

26 See, for example, Saul Bernard Cohen, *Geopolitics: The Geography of International Relations* 2nd edn (London: Rowman & Littlefield Publishers, 2009), 25 and 47.
27 See Shelagh D. Grant, *Polar Imperative: A History of Arctic Sovereignty in North America* (Vancouver: Douglas & McIntyre, 2010), 404–34.
28 See Arctic Council, "4.3 Observers," in *Arctic Council Observer Manual for Subsidiary Bodies*, 2, accessed August 2, 2015, www.arctic-council.org/index.php/en/about-us/arctic-council/observers.
29 For a view on EU's Arctic policy, see Fernando Garcés de los Fayos, "Arctic Governance: Balancing Challenges and Development," DG EXPO/B/PolDep/Note/2012_136, Directorate-General for External Policies of the Union, June 2012, accessed August 3, 2015, www.europarl.europa.eu/RegData/etudes/briefing_note/join/2012/491430/EXPO-AFET_SP%282012%29491430_EN.pdf. For a view on the AC as a "state-centric body," however, see also Philip E. Steinberg and Klaus Dodds, "The Arctic Council after Kiruna," *Polar Records* 51.1 (2015): 108–10.
30 For non-Arctic States, see Taisaku Ikeshima, "Arctic States and Asian States for Arctic International Governance and Security: A Japanese View-point," *Transcommunication* 2 (2014): 81–89.
31 See Willy Østreng, "Geopolitics and Power Constellations in the Arctic," in *Shipping in Arctic Waters: A Comparison of the Northeast, Northwest and Trans Polar Passages*, edited by Willy Østreng et al. (Heidelberg: Springer, 2013), 47–82.
32 See the official website of the Secretariat of the Antarctic Treaty, "Parties" section, accessed January 15, 2015, www.ats.aq/devAS/ats_parties.aspx?lang=e.
33 For the issue of China's activities in the Arctic, see Linda Jakobson, "China Prepares for an Ice-Free Arctic," *SIPRI Insights on Peace and Security*, No. 2010/2, March 2010; Aldo Chircop, "The Emergence of China as a Polar-Capable State," *Canadian Naval Review* 7.1 (2011): 9–14; Linda Jakobson and Jingchao Peng, "China's Arctic Aspirations," *SIPRI Policy Paper* 34, November 2012; Taisaku Ikeshima, "China's Interests in the Arctic: Threat or Opportunity?," *Transcommunication* 1 (2013): 73–83.
34 See, for example, Andrew Higgins, "A Rare Arctic Land Sale Stokes Worry in Norway," *New York Times*, September 27, 2014, accessed December 15, 2014, www.nytimes.com/2014/09/28/world/.
europe/a-rare-arctic-land-sale-stirs-concerns-in-norway.html?_r=0; "Arctic Land Sale Stokes Fears in Norway," *Australian Financial Review*, October 4, 2014, accessed December 15, 2014, www.afr.com/news/world/asia/arctic-land-sale-stokes-fears-in-norway-20141003-jlm17.
35 See, for example, James Kraska, "The New Arctic Geography and U.S. Strategy," in *Arctic Security in an Age of Climate Change*, edited by James Kraska (Cambridge: Cambridge University Press, 2011), 257–58; Lee Willett, "Afterword: A United Kingdom Perspective on the Role of Navies in Delivering Arctic Security," in *Arctic Security in an Age of Climate Change*, edited by James Kraska (Cambridge: Cambridge University Press, 2011): 295–96.
36 See Ikeshima, "China's Interests in the Arctic," 78. For the issue of the South China Sea dispute, see Taisaku Ikeshima, "China's Dashed Line in the South China Sea: Legal Limits and Future Prospects," *Waseda Global Forum* 10 (2014): 17–50.
37 See "Rear Admiral: China Cannot 'Miss a Position' to Develop the Arctic Ocean," *China News*, March 5, 2010, in Chinese, accessed January 15, 2015, www.chinanews.com/gn/news/2010/03–05/2154039.shtml.
38 It is maintained that China is not only a "rising power" but also a "returning power." For this point of view, see Ikeshima, "China's Dashed Line in the South China Sea," 36–38; Ikeshima, "China's Interests in the Arctic," 79–80.

39 For the notion of common concern and its relations with the environment and global climate change, see Patricia Birnie, Alan Boyle and Catherine Redgwell, *International Law & the Environment* 3rd edn (Oxford: Oxford University Press, 2009), 128–35, 338–39.

40 See Sundhya Pahuja, "Conserving the World's Resources?," in *The Cambridge Companion to International Law*, edited by James Crawford and Martti Koskenniemi (Cambridge: Cambridge University Press, 2012), 398–420.

41 See Birnie et al., *International Law & the Environment*, 129–30.

42 See the 1972 Stockholm Conference on Environment and Development, and the 1992 Rio Conference on Environment and Development, to name a few.

43 For the concept of public and community interest, see Isabel Feichtner, "Community Interest," in *Max Planck Encyclopedia of Public International Law (MPEPIL)*, MPEPIL 1677, 2007, accessed August 18, 2015, http://opil.ouplaw.com.ez2.wul. waseda.ac.jp/view/10.1093/law:epil/9780199231690/law-9780199231690-e167 7?rskey=yyTjLt&result=1&prd=EPIL; Wolfrum, "Common Interests in the Ocean," 281–85 (mainly for the world ocean in general, including Antarctica, though); Taisaku Ikeshima, "The Stable Use of Global Commons and Role of the United Nations," in *The United Nations Studies: Global Commons and the United Nations* 15, edited by The Japan Association for United Nations Studies (Tokyo: Kokusaishoin, 2014), 21–28 (in Japanese).

44 For China's argument, see Ikeshima, "China's Interests in the Arctic," 78–79.

45 For India, its experience as a consultative party in the Antarctic Treaty system can be a strong driving force for polar diplomacy. See Østreng, "Geopolitics and Power Constellations in the Arctic," 76.

46 The IMO has adopted the so-called "Polar Code" (International Code for Ships Operating in Polar Waters) both in its Maritime Safety Committee (MSC) (MSC. 285 [94]) and in its Marine Environment Protection Committee (MEPC) (MEPC 264 [68]). The Polar Code is applicable to both the Arctic and Antarctic maritime areas. See the IMO's website: www.imo.org/en/Media Centre/HotTopics/polar/Pages/default.aspx, accessed May 20, 2015. Therefore, the UN has bearing upon these areas through being an affiliated organ.

47 See Ikeshima, "The Stable Use of Global Commons and Role of the United Nations," 40–41.

48 See Articles 55, 76 and Annex II of UNCLOS. For the recommendations given by the CLCS, see the home page of the UN at www.un.org/Depts/los/clcs_new/commission_submissions.htm, accessed January 20, 2015.

49 See, for example, Article 81 of UNCLOS, which provides for the offshore drilling on the continental shelf.

50 See Part XI of UNCLOS.

51 See Article 136 of UNCLOS.

52 See Article 137 (2) of UNCLOS.

53 The G7 was renamed the G8 after Russia joined in 1998. However, Russia's membership has been tentatively suspended due to the sanction in the Ukraine crisis of 2014.

54 See Ikeshima, "The Stable Use of Global Commons and Role of the United Nations," 25–28.

55 See the so-called "Mahathir's speech," at the UN General Assembly on September 29, 1982, UN Doc. A/37/PV, 17–18.

56 For more details on the historical background, see Taisaku Ikeshima, *The Antarctic Treaty Regime and International Law: Accommodation of Interests in the Territory, Resources, and Environment* (Tokyo: Keio University Press, 2000), 234–38; 275–78 (in Japanese).

References

The Associated Press. "Number of Ships Transiting Arctic Waters Falls in 2014." *New York Times*, January 5, 2015, accessed January 15, 2015, www.nytimes.com/aponline/2015/01/05/us/ap-us-arctic-shipping.html?_r=0.

Birnie, Patricia, Alan Boyle and Catherine Redgwell. *International Law & the Environment* 3rd edn. Oxford: Oxford University Press, 2009.

Bloom, E.T. "Establishment of the Arctic Council." *American Journal of International Law* 93.3 (1999): 712–22.

Byers, Michael. *International Law and the Arctic*. Cambridge: Cambridge University Press, 2013.

Chircop, Aldo. "The Emergence of China as a Polar-Capable State." *Canadian Naval Review* 7.1 (2011): 9–14.

Cohen, Saul Bernard. *Geopolitics: The Geography of International Relations* 2nd edn. London: Rowman & Littlefield, 2009.

Feichtner, Isabel. "Community Interest." In *Max Planck Encyclopedia of Public International Law (MPEPIL)*, MPEPIL 1677, 2007, accessed August 18, 2015, http://opil.ouplaw.com.ez2.wul.waseda.ac.jp/view/10.1093/law:epil/9780199231690/law-9780199231690-e1677?rskey=yyTjLt&result=1&prd=EPIL.

Garcés de los Fayos, Fernando. "Arctic Governance: Balancing Challenges and Development." DG EXPO/B/PolDep/Note/2012_136, June 2012. Directorate-General for External Policies of the Union. Accessed August 3, 2015, www.europarl.europa.eu/RegData/etudes/briefing_note/join/2012/491430/EXPO-AFET_SP%282012%29491430_EN.pdf.

Grant, Shelagh D. *Polar Imperative: A History of Arctic Sovereignty in North America*. Vancouver: Douglas & McIntyre, 2010.

Griffiths, Franklyn, Rob Huebert and P. Whitney Lackenbauer. *Canada and the Changing Arctic: Sovereignty, Security, and Stewardship*. Waterloo, ON: Wilfrid Laurier University Press, 2011.

Heininen, Lassi. "Arctic Security – Global Dimensions and Challenges, and National Policy Responses." *The Yearbook of Polar Law* 5 (2013): 93–115.

Heininen, Lassi. "Northern Geopolitics: Actors, Interests and Processes in the Circumpolar Arctic." In *Polar Geopolitics?: Knowledges, Resources and Legal Regimes*, edited by Richard C. Powell and Klaus Dodds, 241–58. Cheltenham: Edward Elgar, 2014.

Higgins, Andrew. "A Rare Arctic Land Sale Stokes Worry in Norway." *New York Times*, September 27, 2014, accessed December 15, 2014, www.nytimes.com/2014/09/28/world/europe/a-rare-arctic-land-sale-stirs-concerns-in-norway.html?_r=0.

Hoel, Alf Hakon "Do We Need a New Legal Regime for the Arctic Ocean." *International Journal of Marine and Coastal Law* 24 (2009): 443–56.

Ikeshima, Taisaku. *The Antarctic Treaty Regime and International Law: Accommodation of Interests in the Territory, Resources, and Environment*. Tokyo: Keio University Press, 2000.

Ikeshima, Taisaku. "China's Interests in the Arctic: Threat or Opportunity?." *Transcommunication* 1 (2013): 73–83.

Ikeshima, Taisaku. "Arctic States and Asian States for Arctic International Governance and Security: A Japanese View-point." *Transcommunication* 2 (2014): 81–89.

Ikeshima, Taisaku. "China's Dashed Line in the South China Sea: Legal Limits and Future Prospects." *Waseda Global Forum* 10 (2014): 17–50.

Ikeshima, Taisaku. "The Stable Use of Global Commons and Role of the United Nations." In *The United Nations Studies: Global Commons and the United Nations* 15, edited by The Japan Association for United Nations Studies, 21–56. Tokyo: Kokusaishoin, 2014.

Jakobson, Linda. "China Prepares for an Ice-Free Arctic." *SIPRI Insights on Peace and Security*, No. 2010/2, March 2010.

Jakobson, Linda and Jingchao Peng. "China's Arctic Aspirations." *SIPRI Policy Paper* 34, November 2012.

Kraska, James (ed.). *Arctic Security in an Age of Climate Change.* Cambridge: Cambridge University Press, 2011.

Kraska, James. *Maritime Power and the Law of the Sea: Expeditionary Operations in World Politics.* Oxford: Oxford University Press, 2011.

Kraska, James. "The New Arctic Geography and U.S. Strategy." In *Arctic Security in an Age of Climate Change,* edited by James Kraska, 244–66. Cambridge: Cambridge University Press, 2011.

Kristoffersen, Berit. "'Securing' Geography: Framings, Logics and Strategies in the Norwegian High North." In *Polar Geopolitics?: Knowledges, Resources and Legal Regimes,* edited by Richard C. Powell and Klaus Dodds, 131–48. Cheltenham: Edward Elgar, 2014.

Marchenko, Nataliya. *Russian Arctic Seas: Navigational Conditions and Accidents.* Berlin: Springer, 2012.

O'Rourke, Ronald. "Changes in the Arctic: Background and Issues for Congress." August 4, 2014, Congressional Research Service, R41153, accessed August 18, 2015, www.fas.org/sgp/crs/misc/R41153.pdf.

Østreng, Willy. "Geopolitics and Power Constellations in the Arctic." In *Shipping in Arctic Waters: A Comparison of the Northeast, Northwest and Trans Polar Passages,* edited by Willy Østreng et al., 47–82. Heidelberg: Springer, 2013.

Østreng, Willy et al. *Shipping in Arctic Waters: A Comparison of the Northeast, Northwest and Trans Polar Passages.* Heidelberg: Springer, 2013.

Pahuja, Sundhya. "Conserving the World's Resources?" In *The Cambridge Companion to International Law,* edited by James Crawford and Martti Koskenniemi, 398–420. Cambridge: Cambridge University Press, 2012.

Pattersen, Trude. "Northern Sea Route Traffic Plummeted." *BarentsObserver,* December 16, 2014, accessed December 26, 2014, http://barentsobserver.com/en/arctic/2014/12/northern-sea-route-traffic-plummeted-16-12.

Pharand, Donat. *Canada's Arctic Waters in International Law.* Cambridge: Cambridge University Press, 1988.

Rothwell, Donald. "The Arctic in International Affairs: Time for a New Regime?" *The Brown Journal of World Affairs* XV.1 (2008): 241–53.

Smith, Laurence. *The New North: The World in 2050.* London: Profile Books, 2012.

Steinberg, Philip E. and Klaus Dodds. "The Arctic Council after Kiruna." *Polar Records* 51.1 (2015): 108–10.

Strandsbjerg, Jeppe. "Making Sense of Contemporary Greenland: Indigeneity, Resources and Sovereignty." In *Polar Geopolitics?: Knowledges, Resources and Legal Regimes,* edited by Richard C. Powell and Klaus Dodds, 259–76. Cheltenham: Edward Elgar, 2014.

Strauss, Hannah and Nuccio Mazzullo. "Narratives, Bureaucracies and Indigenous Legal Orders: Resource Governance in Finnish Lapland." In *Polar Geopolitics?: Knowledges, Resources and Legal Regimes,* edited by Richard C. Powell and Klaus Dodds, 295–312. Cheltenham: Edward Elgar, 2014.

Tamnes, Rolf. "Arctic Security and Norway." In *Arctic Security in an Age of Climate Change*, edited by James Kraska, 47–63. Cambridge: Cambridge University Press, 2011.

Terai, Kosuke. "Strengthening Economic Power for Independence." *Nikkei*, April 11, 2015, 3, in Japanese (print version); electronic version, accessed August 18, 2015, www.nikkei.com/article/DGXLASGM31H21_R10C15A4NNE000/.

Willett, Lee. "Afterword: A United Kingdom Perspective on the Role of Navies in Delivering Arctic Security." In *Arctic Security in an Age of Climate Change*, edited by James Kraska. Cambridge: Cambridge University Press, 2011.

Wolfrum, Rüdiger. "Common Interests in the Ocean." In *Science Diplomacy: Antarctica, Science, and the Governance of International Spaces*, edited by Paul Arthur Berkman et al., 281–85. Washington, DC: Smithsonian Institution Scholarly Press, 2011.

Young, Oran R. "Arctic Governance – Pathways to the Future." *Arctic Review on Law and Politics* 1.2 (2010): 164–85.

Young, Oran R. "Governing International Spaces: Antarctica and Beyond." In *Science Diplomacy: Antarctica, Science, and the Governance of International Spaces*, edited by Paul Arthur Berkman et al., 287–94. Washington, DC: Smithsonian Institution Scholarly Press, 2011.

20 Changing foreign policy roles in the changing Arctic

Michał Łuszczuk[1]

Introduction

"There is not one Arctic. There are many Arctics."[2] This statement, at first glance rather surprising for many people living south of the Circumpolar Circle, is actually fully justified, and for many reasons. The Arctic is a very heterogeneous region, and proves to be so in many ways. For instance, many parts of the region have dissimilar climate and weather conditions; they possess a diverse set of social and political norms, rules, regulations and legal systems; and they also vary in terms of population density, economic potential and infrastructure. What is more, they have numerous and often divergent interests. However, even if we agreed to think of the Arctic as "a multi-form place, rather than as everything south of the North Pole,"[3] we should also remember that "there are no politically and geographically innocent definitions of the Arctic."[4] This is especially true in regard to the discussions about international politics and international relations in the High North.

Following from this, several perspectives or discourses have arisen on the importance of the Arctic for world politics and on the region's exceptional geopolitical and geostrategic functions. First, for several decades in the twentieth century, the region was perceived as a quasi-colonial periphery sparsely inhabited by indigenous peoples and "as a vast reserve of natural resources and military space for the performance of sovereignty, national security and economic interests of the Arctic states."[5] Then, during the Cold War period, this perspective became even more established, supplemented by the general approaches to the industrialized, militarized and environmentally damaged borderlands of the two superpowers. A geopolitical thaw came to the Arctic in the late 1980s, when international cooperation and activities oriented towards region building were initiated not only by the Arctic States, but also by non-state entities, such as organizations representing the indigenous peoples of the Arctic and/or international non-governmental organisations.[6] At the beginning of the twenty-first century, the image of the Arctic is transforming once again. The processes and repercussions of globalization and modernization as well as the myriad consequences of climate change are reshaping the Arctic and opening up this region to the gradually expanding activities of the various stakeholders. This raises concerns about the region's future. Issues such as territorial claims, prospective commercial shipping through the Arctic seas, hydrocarbon and mineral resource exploitation, ecological threats and increased political activities relating to the Arctic have transformed the region into a significant arena of global politics.

How to interpret this transformation from the International Relations perspective, and how to better understand what is actually taking place in the region?[7] Is the Arctic nowadays primarily a place of competition, self-interest, hard security and military build-up?[8] Or is it—following (neo) liberal arguments—a prime example of close cooperation supporting the important roles played by several increasingly mature and fully grown international institutions? The position presented by the English School is that these diverging perceptions are complementary. And on the contrary, maybe the Arctic is actually a post-sovereign space that requires a very unconventional understanding, different to what (neo)realism, (neo)liberalism or the English School are capable of providing?[9] In what follows, the International Relations (IR) perspective is supported by foreign policy analysis and role theory is applied to reconsider the current developments taking place in the Arctic region.

The purpose of this study is to provide a preliminary interpretation of the main types of international roles played both by the Arctic and the non-Arctic States: an interpretation based in equal measure on official policy documents and existing analysis presented in other publications.[10]

The chapter is divided into four main sections. Following these introductory comments, the second section constitutes a brief presentation of role theory and an explanation of its basic assumptions. The third section provides an overview of the roles of the Arctic States as well the roles of the non-Arctic States. The final section offers conclusions focused on the question of what kind of developments can be expected in the near future in terms of the roles of the states involved in the region.

Role theory

As mentioned previously, starting with the argument that agency and structure can be perceived as "mutually constitutive and co-determined,"[11] this chapter focuses on the policies of the Arctic and non-Arctic States towards the Arctic region through the theoretical lens of role theory. According to L. Aggestam, "role provides an essential link between agent and structure, as they incorporate the manner in which foreign policy is both purposeful and shaped by institutional contexts."[12] From this point of view role conception, role expectations and role performance should be treated as the three independent variables of the analysis, setting up a framework in which the dynamic tension between the vision of self-representation and the realistic interpretation (covering the understanding and acknowledgement of the other actors) jointly define the scope of possible actions.[13] It is usually understood that role conception refers to self-image and identity, role expectations to structure and norms prescribing behavior, and role performance to agency.[14]

Roles usually involve patterns of expected or even favorable behaviors. Role conceptions contain both an actor's own views and ideas about its place, position and advantageous performance vis-à-vis others in a given situation or in a social environment and the assumptions, or role prescriptions, of other actors, as communicated through language and action.[15] Role performance should be defined as the actual policy behavior of the given actor in this social context. It is worth noting that while an actor's role conception appears to be stable and consistent, in reality, it is very often revised and adjusted through confrontations with others' expectations, needs and behaviors. This means that in such situations, the "anticipated attributes of a social role are constantly in a process of interpretation by the role beholder at the same time as external expectations are shaped by the actor's role performance."[16] An actor's foreign policy, while being predominantly motivated by internal (domestic or inter-institutional) ideas and processes, is also to a certain extent adjusted in response to others' expectations and reactions through adaptation processes. Thanks to processes stemming from the socialization game, usually resembling the characteristics of the learning process, others' role expectations (prescriptions) referring to actor characteristics and to a given social context contribute to the development of specific international roles. As Bengtsson and Elgström explain,

> third-party understandings of an actor and its roles form a part of an intersubjective international structure that helps shape the practices of this actor; in a dynamic fashion, it is the recognition by others that impact on future role performance, in turn affecting future recognition.[17]

In the Arctic theater: roles of Arctic and non-Arctic actors

The Arctic has always required from the people an extraordinary determination in both defining and achieving the objectives of their engagement in a region characterized by such harsh and demanding conditions. The traditional livelihoods of all Arctic indigenous peoples, the heroic discoveries of many European and the North American explorers, even most of today's activities conducted north of the Arctic Circle have been established in strict compliance with elementary guidelines and consistent, historically grounded rules. To some extent, this approach also applies to the political dimension of the human presence in the Arctic, whether it is a question of the domestic (national, regional or local) policy or of various forms of international relations. This pattern can also be identified in the process of growing engagement among numerous states in establishing their credentials as players of note in Arctic geopolitics in the first decades of the twenty-first century.

How do these patterns influence role performance by the states that are stakeholders in Arctic affairs? It could be assumed that they stabilize existing roles and keep them deeply rooted in previous experiences. In reality, as was noted in the introduction to this chapter, the international relations within the Arctic region as well as its international or global significance have evolved several times throughout the twentieth century. Every development of this nature has also entailed a change in the scale and/or the manner of engagement of the individual states in Arctic affairs, and eventually in the chosen and performed roles.[18]

It is well recognized that over the last few years, many states, both Arctic and non-Arctic, have begun to reassert or reinvigorate their claims and interests in the North, usually manifesting their strategies (Arctic role conceptions) and/or implementing their "Arctic policies" (Arctic role performance).[19] As was explained,

> the Arctic has become anything but another important chessboard for playing out and defending national interests. Both Arctic and sub-Arctic actors are in the process of (re)discovering their Arcticness, and the presence of this notion increasingly influences strategic considerations of global and regional actors.[20]

Unsurprisingly, these steps are not only focused on manifesting, in different ways, these actors' presence in the region, but also refer to the various functional aspects of the main developments taking place in the region, namely, the challenges connected with providing sustainable development, comprehensive security, effective governance mechanisms, with mastering research cooperation or environmental management focused on hydrocarbons and shipping projects. Of course, there are distinct differences between the approaches presented by the Arctic and non-Arctic players, stemming primarily from their geographical position determining the historical background and legal status within the Arctic borders as well as the scope of sovereign competencies.[21]

These differences, combined with the same set of new circumstances and challenges taking place within the Arctic, bring three main types of declared Arctic roles: leaders, partners and newcomers, which are respectively the roles of the Arctic States, the non-Arctic States that were Arctic Council observer states before 2013, and the non-Arctic States, which joined the Arctic Council in 2013. It should be emphasized, however, that within each of these main types there is a variety of "specializations," which will be explained in what follows.

Leaders

What, then, are the specific roles of the Arctic States that perceive, position and promote themselves as leaders in the Arctic? First, it should be highlighted that the aspiration to become a leader among the Arctic States is usually driven by two contradictory needs: first, to confirm their "Arcticness," and second, to differentiate and individualize. While the first demand is rather obvious and common (in each of the region states' strategies one may find such self-concepts or even self-definitions as "Arctic nation," "Arctic States"),[22] the commitment to the "exceptionality" of the leadership is more complicated. As Nabers suggests,

> First, leadership as a role is essentially relational, hence situated in a complex structure of differential relationships. Second, leadership may have particular "objective" sources; this may involve translating relative power capabilities into bargaining leverage, but not necessarily. Materially weaker states sometimes act as brokers to gain support for salient solutions, which is to suggest that objectivity is always discursively constituted. Third, leadership involves the continuous contestation over different representations that we can call politics. It requires communication and social interactions, and thereby serves as a constant reminder that role can never be thought of without identity.[23]

These three issues can be easily identified when analyzing the Arctic States and their policies. As Heininen points out, "a common feature in all the strategies is that the Arctic states would like to remain leading actors in the Arctic, and to be recognised as such by extra-territorial parties."[24] Taking into consideration that among the eight Arctic States who are members of the Arctic Council, there are states with very different potentials, capabilities, histories, and perspectives on the Arctic region and the developments taking place there, it is not particularly difficult to identify their unique "Arctic identities" as well as areas of their expertise and specialization as Arctic leaders.

In the case of Russia—the largest of the five littoral states of the Arctic Ocean—this would be the role of a leading Arctic power, which primarily derives from the size of the Russian Arctic and the "hydrocarbon factor."[25] The activities and declarations made by Russian presidents and governments since 2008 suggest that the importance of the Arctic to Russia lies primarily in its rich energy deposits, strategically important metals and minerals, as well as in the political control it affords over the Northern Sea Route.[26] With that said, in the current geopolitical situation—hallmarked by the political tensions between the West and Russia concerning the latter's role in the geopolitical crisis in Ukraine in 2014 and 2015, as well the significant drop in world oil market prices in 2014 and early 2015—the current prospects for Russia's effective engagement in this role seem to be rather problematic.

A very interesting role can be attributed to the United States, a state that could be deemed a "global Arctic leader." This has been captured in Steinberg's comment on the dominant perspective of US interests and role in the Arctic region: "The United States is an 'Arctic nation' simply because it has strategic interests there."[27] This approach also seems to be advocated by Rosenberg, Titley and Wiker, who point out, that the development of the US Arctic policy and its effective chairmanship in the Arctic Council (2015–2017) will "improve US credibility as a global leader in Arctic affairs and inform and shape the nation's Arctic ethos, policy and investments for decades to come."[28] It should also be highlighted that although in 2009 the USA was called a "reluctant Arctic power,"[29] the government has since gradually (re)formulated its policy approach towards the region. It is now not only more developed, but also more focused on the maritime dimension of regional cooperation and, in particular, on the importance of the Arctic Council (which is related to the US Chairmanship of the Arctic Council in 2015–2017).

In the case of Canada, it should be highlighted that the government in Ottawa defined the state not only as an Arctic power, but also as a responsible Arctic nation "taking a robust leadership role in shaping the stewardship, sustainable development and environmental protection of [...] [the] Arctic region."[30] A closer look at the official documents in Canada, however, supports the idea that Canada actually still plays the role of a "leader in exercising Arctic sovereignty," which means that the state focuses most of its potential and political resources on providing (and demonstrating) its abilities to protect Canadian Arctic sovereignty, to protect its northern territories and boundaries.[31] Regardless of the fact that this approach has a lot in common with the idea of the Canadian identity and nationalism,[32] its implementation is still problematic and criticised for its lack of consistency and effectiveness.[33]

Considering in turn, the role of Norway as an Arctic leader, this leadership seems to be exercised in two interlinked, but also somewhat contradictory domains: on the one hand, environmental protection, and on the other, of hydrocarbon extraction.[34] Calling Norway a leader in energy security and environmental security is related to the efforts of the governments in Oslo to support an image of Norway as an environmentally conscious energy provider, even when most of this energy comes from oil and gas extraction.[35] What is also interesting is that this leadership is partially a function of some of the roles played by Norway in Arctic affairs as portrayed by E. Wilson Rowe, specifically, the role of a leading "knower" of the High North, the role of a provider of information, and the role of a "convenor."[36]

According to the Kingdom of Denmark's Arctic strategy, the Kingdom perceives itself as a "leader in Arctic cooperation" responsible for "promoting an open and inclusive dialogue in bilateral relations."[37] While the organization of the Ilulissat meeting in 2008 indicated, in fact, a slightly different approach, that conference, as M. Nuttall argues also provided evidence of Denmark's ability to behave as "a major global player in the international politics of the circumpolar North as a member of an exclusive group of Arctic costal states."[38] Denmark's Arctic role is, however, more complicated, especially due to its links with Greenland[39] (itself perceived as a "near-state"[40]), and the Faroe Islands (also pursuing their own Arctic roles).[41]

The issue of inventing its Arctic role in relation to geographical factors is also important in the case of Iceland.[42] Though not fully recognized as a coastal state and bearing limited economic potential, Iceland seeks its chance in playing the role of a "leading hub for maritime business in Arctic," particularly for trade with partners from the Far East, as well in connecting US/Canadian services with European services.[43] In fact, "Iceland has long taken Arctic economics seriously and has been interested in exploiting its position not just by encouraging new investments and facilities on its land, but by active commercial engagement."[44]

Finland's role as a "leading expert on Arctic issues" is primarily predicated on "knowledge in the fields of winter shipping, sea transport and shipbuilding technology."[45] It is also worth noting that Finland's government openly expresses its special determination to properly define the state's position in Arctic affairs: "Arctic issues play an important part in Finland's foreign policy and international role and in its efforts to create a unique country brand."[46]

In the case of Sweden, it is more difficult to identify its specialization as a leader in Arctic issues and affairs. According to the Swedish strategy, "efficient, multilateral cooperation on the Arctic is a main priority for Sweden." Moreover,

> Sweden has a natural interest in the favourable current situation being consolidated and the entire Arctic region being driven by a positive political, economic and ecological dynamic. In bilateral and multilateral contexts, Sweden should stress the importance of an approach based on security in its broadest sense and that the use of civil instruments is preferable to military means.[47]

These arguments may suggest that Sweden would be interested in playing the role of an advocate of Arctic cooperation, and its engagement during the Swedish chairmanship of the Arctic Council (2012–2013) is a good indication of such an approach.

Partners and newcomers

As regards the non-Arctic States, it is proposed here to distinguish two general types of roles that are associated with them. First, the role of a partner, a role declared by several of the "older" European Arctic Council observers (France, Germany, the Netherlands, Poland, Spain and the UK). Second, the role of a newcomer, which is usually assigned to the Asian states (China, India, Japan, Republic of Korea and Singapore) that were (along with Italy) accepted as the Arctic Council's observers during the Ministerial Meeting in Kiruna in 2013.

One of the main differences between these two types of roles is that "partners" are actual roles that have been individually specified and promoted by the states, while the role of a "newcomer" is not explicitly defined, but rather only generally expected by the Arctic community and its leaders. Further, while the "partners" eagerly provide evidence of their long-standing and substantive engagement in the Arctic region (although not all of them have published official Arctic policy documents), the newcomers usually restrain themselves from declaring or issuing any official policy statements and spotlight only the motives of their interests in the region.

In the official document presenting Germany's Arctic policy, it is mentioned that Germany is "a partner with vast expert knowledge in the areas of research, technology and environmental standards,"[48] and furthermore, it "is seeking to more strongly and creatively put this know-how to use."[49] Similarly, even if the British government's official statement describes the UK's involvement in the Arctic without using the word "partner," it suggests that such a role, coupled with support for the Arctic community, remains a core tenet of its engagement in the Arctic region.[50] This interpretation is supported by the clear suggestion presented in a report drafted by the House of Lords, where the following passage appears:

> By dint of its combination of Arctic proximity, history, skills, knowledge and research, its competitive advantage in applicable business sectors, and its own international standing, the UK should be positioned as the premier partner for Arctic states and other interests in Arctic co-operation: the Government should adopt this as its ambition in Arctic affairs.[51]

What is interesting is that the first of the "old" observers to the Arctic Council—the United Kingdom and Germany—presented their overall Arctic policy documents in fall 2013, just a few months after the Ministerial Meeting in Kiruna. As Śmieszek and Kankaanpää suggest, these steps and their timing should be considered in the context of both "the increasing geopolitical and geoeconomic relevance of the region" as well as the expected implementation of the revised AC Rules of Procedure, adopted during the ministerial session in Nuuk in 2011.[52] According to Graczyk and Koivurova, "the formulation and wording of [the Nuuk] criteria also imply that external actors' (foreign) policy statements [...] play a significant role in the way Arctic states consider applications for observer status."[53] In light of the international roles theory, such criteria actually resemble patterns of expected or even favourable behaviours.

While France is still finalizing its polar strategy, Spain and the Netherlands choose a rather moderate strategy in presenting only the scientific dimension of their presence and interests in the Arctic. Poland constitutes a distinct case, where the country has not issued any comprehensive documents or current research plans in regard to the Arctic. As Polish experts explain, "Poland, as one of [the] stakeholders in the Arctic, cannot remain indifferent to the ongoing changes there, not only because it shares in the responsibility for those changes, but also because Poland will increasingly feel their consequences."[54]

As mentioned already, an analysis of the newcomers' roles confirms that they are roles that are expected rather than precisely defined (aside from the Nuuk criteria for the Arctic Council observers). The drivers and interests of these stakeholders with respect to the Arctic slightly differ. However, research on climate change and its consequences, expected changes to the global energy and minerals markets, new transport routes and developments in polar shipping, as well as geopolitical considerations remain issues of concern for them all.[55] The suggestion that their individual expectations and expertise in polar issues could transform into more specific Arctic roles in the coming years seems to be reasonable. If this does happen, it will allow us to classify them as new partners.

Conclusions

While there are several studies that conduct a detailed examination of the approaches, strategies, policies or even declarations issued by all states involved in the Arctic region, there is still a possibility—or perhaps even a need—to provide more comparative studies that aim to identify similarities and differences between them.[56] Role theory offers an interesting possibility for a reinterpretation of the behaviors of all players involved in Arctic affairs. Referring to the concept of a state and/or nation's "Arctic identity" and states' "Arctic self-perception" helps to understand the choices made by the decision-makers in the realm of foreign policy in different Arctic and non-Arctic countries. At the same time, paying attention to the relational aspect of foreign policy exposes the dynamic character of national Arctic policies across the board. Especially interesting in this context is the transformation of the roles of individual states, which is closely related to changes in the international environment, as well as domestic factors. Taking into consideration that the intensity of international relations in the Arctic, as well as predictions about further economic development in the region have been scaled down in recent years, it can be implied that the presented types of roles and their performance will be the same in the next three to five years. However, since the Arctic is still so unique an environment, even small-scale transformations of international rules pertaining to this region should be scrutinized as they occur.

Notes

1 This chapter has been drafted within the scope of research supported by a National Center for Science post-doctoral fellowship under the grant: DEC-2011/04/S/HS5/00172.

2 Børge Brende, "The Arctic: Major Opportunities – Major Responsibilities," speech of the Norwegian Minister of Foreign Affairs Mr. Børge Brende delivered at American University Washington College of Law in Washington, DC, November 14, 2013, accessed May 18, 2015, www.norway.org/News_and_events/Embassy/Text-of-FM-Brendes-Speech-The-Arctic-Major-Opportunities–Major-Responsibilities/#.VOHRFi79wsc.

3 Charles Emmerson, "Transcript: Opening up the Arctic: Prospects, Paradoxes and Geopolitical Implications," unpublished manuscript, 3, July 17, 2012, accessed December 15, 2014, www.chathamhouse.org/sites/files/chatham-house/public/Meetings/Meeting%20Transcripts/170712arctic.pdf.

4 Lassi Heininen, "Northern Geopolitics: Actors, Interests and Processes in the Circumpolar Arctic," in *Polar Geopolitics? Knowledges, Resources and Legal Regimes*, edited by R.C. Powell and K. Dodds (Cheltenham: Edward Elgar, 2014).

5 Ibid., 242.

6 Oran R. Young, "The Structure of Arctic Cooperation: Solving Problems/Seizing Opportunities," paper prepared at the request of Finland in preparation for the fourth conference of Parliamentarians of the Arctic Region, Rovaniemi, August 27–29, 2000, and the Finnish chairmanship of the Arctic Council during the period 2000–2002, unpublished manuscript, last modified November 12, 2014, accessed May 7, 2015, www.arcticparl.org/files/static/conf4_sac.pdf.

7 Mikkel R. Olesen, "Cooperation or Conflict in the Arctic: A Literature Review," *Working Paper* 8 (unpublished manuscript: Danish Institute for International Studies, last modified December 20, 2014), accessed May 7, 2015, www.diis.dk/files/media/images/publications/covers/wp2014–08_runge-olesen_for_web_0.pdf.

8 Frederic Lasserre, Jérôme Le Roy and Richard Garon, "Is There an Arms Race in the Arctic?," *Journal of Military and Strategic Studies* 14.3/4 (2012): 1–56.

9 Robert W. Murray, "Conclusions: Arctic Politics Moving Forward," in *International Relations and the Arctic: Understanding Policy and Governance*, edited by Robert W. Murray and Anita Dey Nuttall (Amherst, NY: Cambria Press, 2014), 625.

10 Alyson J. Bailes and Lassi Heininen, *Strategy Papers on the Arctic or High North: A Comparative Study and Analysis* (Reykjavík: Institute of International Affairs – Centre for Small State Studies, 2012); Robert W. Murray and Anita D. Nuttall (eds), *International Relations and the Arctic: Understanding Policy and Governance* (Amherst, NY: Cambria Press, 2014); Andris Sprūds and Toms Rostoks (eds), *Perceptions and Strategies of Arcticness in Sub-Arctic Europe* (Riga: Latvian Institute of International Affairs, 2014).

11 Alexander Wendt, *Social Theory of International Politics*, Cambridge Studies in International Relations 67 (Cambridge and New York: Cambridge University Press, 1999), 184.

12 Lisbeth Aggestam, "Role-Identity and the Europeanisation of Foreign Policy: A Political-Cultural Approach," in *Rethinking European Union Foreign Policy*, edited by Ben Tonra and Thomas Christiansen (Manchester and New York: Manchester University Press, 2004), 82.

13 Michael Charokopos, "Asserting a Leading Role for the European Union in International Aviation: When Aspirations Meet Reality," *International Journal: Canada's Journal of Global Policy Analysis* 70.1 (2015): 42, accessed December 15, 2014, doi:10.1177/0020702014563109.

14 Marijke Breuning, "Role Theory Research in International Relations: State of the Art and Blind Spots," in *Role Theory in International Relations: Approaches and Analyses*, edited by Sebastian Harnisch, Cornelia Frank and Hanns W. Maull (London: Routledge, 2011), 22.

15 Rikard Bengtsson and Ole Elgström, "Conflicting Role Conceptions? The European Union in Global Politics," *Foreign Policy Analysis* 8.1 (2012): 94, accessed May 7, 2015, doi:10.1111/j.1743–8594.2011.00157.x.

16 Ibid.

17 Ibid.

18 Dirk Nabers, "Identity and Role Change in International Relations," in *Role Theory in International Relations: Approaches and Analyses*, edited by Sebastian Harnisch, Cornelia Frank and Hanns W. Maull (London: Routledge, 2011).

19 Bailes and Heininen, *Strategy Papers on the Arctic or High North*; Michał Łuszczuk (ed.), *Arktyka na początku XXI wieku: Między współpracą a rywalizacją* (Lublin: Wydawnictwo Uniwersytetu Marii Curie-Skłodowskiej, 2013).

20 Norbert Beckmann-Dierkes, Andris Sprūds and Toms Rostoks, "Introduction," in *Perceptions and Strategies of Arcticness in Sub-Arctic Europe*, edited by Andris Sprūds and Toms Rostoks (Riga: Latvian Institute of International Affairs, 2014), 9.

21 Per E. Solli, Elana Wilson Rowe and Wrenn Yennie Lindgren, "Coming into the Cold: Asia's Arctic Interests," *Polar Geography* 36.4 (2013): 253–70, accessed May 7, 2015, doi:10.1080/1088937X.2013.825345; House of Lords, "Responding to a Changing Arctic," Select Committee on the Arctic, Report of Session 2014–15, unpublished manuscript, accessed May 7, 2015, www.publications.parliament. uk/pa/ld201415/ldselect/ldarctic/118/118.pdf; Oran R. Young, "Listening to the Voices of Non-Arctic States in Arctic Ocean Governance," in *The Arctic in World Affairs: A North Pacific Dialogue on the Future of the Arctic* (2013 North Pacific Arctic Conference Proceedings), edited by Oran R. Young, Jong Deog Kim and Yoon Hyung Kim (Seoul: Korea Maritime Institute; Honolulu, HI: East-West Center, 2013).

22 Bailes and Heininen, *Strategy Papers on the Arctic or High North*.

23 Dirk Nabers, "Identity and Role Change in International Relations," 91.

24 Heininen, "Northern Geopolitics," 253.

25 Lassi Heininen, Alexander Sergunin and Gleb Yarovoy, "Russian Strategies in the Arctic: Avoiding a New Cold War" (Valdai Discussion Club, unpublished manuscript, last modified December 12, 2014), accessed December 20, 2014, http://vid-1.rian.ru/ig/valdai/arctic_eng.pdf; Arild Moe, "Potential Arctic Oil and Gas Development: What are Realistic Expectations?," in *The Arctic in World Affairs: A North Pacific Dialogue on the Future of the Arctic (2013 North Pacific Arctic Conference Proceedings)*, edited by Oran R. Young, Jong Deog Kim, and Yoon Hyung Kim (Seoul: Korea Maritime Institute; Honolulu, HI: East-West Center, 2013); Gleb Yarovoy, "Russia's Arctic Policy," in *International Relations and the Arctic: Understanding Policy and Governance*, edited by Robert W. Murray and Anita Dey Nuttall (Amherst, NY: Cambria Press, 2014).

26 Marlène Laruelle, *Russia's Arctic Strategies and the Future of the Far North* (New York: M.E. Sharpe, 2014); Katarzyna Zysk, "Military Aspects of Russia's Arctic Policy: Hard Power and Natural Resources," in *Arctic Security in an Age of Climate Change*, edited by James Kraska (Cambridge: Cambridge University Press, 2011); Barbora Padrtova, "Russian Military Build-Up in the Arctic: Strategic Shift in the Balance of Power of Bellicose Rhetoric Only?," *Arctic Yearbook* (2014): 415–33.

27 Philip E. Steinberg, "U.S. Arctic Policy," in *International Relations and the Arctic: Understanding Policy and Governance*, edited by Robert W. Murray and Anita Dey Nuttall (Amherst, NY: Cambria Press, 2014), 181.

28 Elizabeth Rosenberg, David Titley and Alexander Wiker, "Arctic 2015 and Beyond. A Strategy for U.S. Leadership in the High North," *Policy Brief*, Center for a New American Security, December 2014, accessed January 16, 2015, www. cnas.org/sites/default/files/publications-pdf/CNAS_ArcticHighNorth_policy-brief_RosenbergTitleyWiker.pdf, 11.

29 Rob Huebert, "United States Arctic Policy: The Reluctant Arctic Power," *The School of Public Policy (SPP) Briefing Papers* 2.2 (2009): 1–27, accessed May 7, 2015, www.policyschool.ucalgary.ca/sites/default/files/research/sppbriefing-huebert online.pdf.

30 "Statement on Canada's Arctic Foreign Policy: Exercising Sovereignty and Promoting Canada's Northern Strategy Abroad," Department of Foreign Affairs and International Trade (2010), accessed December 12, 2014, www.inter national.gc.ca/arctic-arctique/arctic_policy-canada-politique_arctique.aspx? lang=eng.

31 Ibid.; Franklyn Griffiths, Robert N. Huebert and P. Whitney Lackenbauer, *Canada and the Changing Arctic: Sovereignty, Security, and Stewardship* (Waterloo, ON: Wilfrid Laurier University Press, 2011).

32 Rob Huebert, "Canadian Arctic Security: Shifting Challenges," in *International Relations and the Arctic: Understanding Policy and Governance*, edited by Robert W. Murray and Anita Dey Nuttall (Amherst, NY: Cambria Press, 2014).

33 Heather Exner-Pirot, "The Canadian Arctic Council Ministerial – What to Expect," *Eye on the Arctic*, April 15, 2015, accessed May 7, 2015, www.rcinet.ca/ eye-on-the-arctic/2015/04/15/the-canadian-arctic-council-ministerial-what-to-expect/.

34 Kjersti Kræmmer, "The Norwegian Arctic: Energy, Economy, and the Environment: A Discourse Analysis of Norwegian Policy in the High North" (Edinburgh: University of Edinburgh, 2013), accessed May 7, 2015, www.academia.edu/ 4718263/The_Norwegian_Arctic_Energy_Economy_and_the_Environment.

35 Leif C. Jensen and Geir Hønneland, "Framing the High North: Public Discourses in Norway after 2000," *Acta Borealia* 28.1 (2011): 37–54, accessed May 7, 2015, doi:10.1080/08003831.2011.575659.

36 Elana Wilson Rowe, "Arctic Hierarchies? Norway, Status and the High North," *Polar Record* 50.1 (2014): 72–79, accessed May 7, 2015, doi:10.1017/S003224741 200054X.

37 Denmark, Greenland and the Faroe Islands, "Kingdom of Denmark Strategy for the Arctic 2011–2020" (unpublished manuscript, 2011), last modified February 9, 2015, accessed May 7, 2015, http://um.dk/en/~/media/UM/ English-site/Documents/Politics-and-diplomacy/Greenland-and-The-Faroe-Islands/Arctic%20strategy.pdf, 55.

38 Mark Nuttall, "Territory, Security and Sovereignty: The Kingdom of Denmark's Arctic Strategy," in *International Relations and the Arctic: Understanding Policy and Governance*, edited by Robert W. Murray and Anita Dey Nuttall (Amherst, NY: Cambria Press, 2014), 273.

39 Damien Degeorges, "Denmark, Greenland and the Arctic: Challenges and Opportunities of Becoming the Meeting Place of Global Powers" (unpublished manuscript: Royal Danish Defence College, 2013), accessed May 7, 2015, http://forsvaret.dk/fak/publikationer/briefs/documents/denmark-greenland-and-the-arctic.pdf.

40 Nils Wang and Damien Degeorges, "Greenland and the New Arctic: Political and Security Implications of a State-Building Project" (unpublished manuscript: Royal Danish Defence College, 2014), accessed May 7, 2015, http:// forsvaret.dk/FAK/eng/publications/Documents/Greenland%20and%20the% 20New%20Arctic.pdf.

41 Alyson J. Bailes and Beinta í. Jákobsstovu, "The Faroe Islands and the Arctic: Genesis of a Strategy," *Veftímaritið Stjórnmál og stjórnsýsla* 9.2 (2013): 531–48, accessed May 7, 2015, doi:10.13177/irpa.a.2013.9.2.14.

42 Klaus Dodds and Valur Ingimundarson, "Territorial Nationalism and Arctic Geopolitics: Iceland as an Arctic Coastal State," *The Polar Journal* 2.1 (2012): 21–37, accessed May 7, 2015, doi:10.1080/2154896X.2012.679557.

43 Adele Airoldi, *The European Union and the Arctic: Developments and Perspectives 2010–2014* (Nordic Council of Ministers, 2014), 29, accessed May 7, 2015, https://books.google.pl/books?id=s1zXBQAAQBAJ; "Breaking the Ice: Arctic Development and Maritime Transportation. Prospects of the Transarctic Route – Impact and Opportunities," Icelandic Government (unpublished manuscript, 2007, last modified January 20, 2015), accessed May 7, 2015, www.mfa.is/media/Utgafa/Breaking_The_Ice_Conference_Report.pdf.

44 Alyson J. Bailes and Margret Cela, "Iceland – A State within the Arctic," in *International Relations and the Arctic: Understanding Policy and Governance*, edited by Robert W. Murray and Anita Dey Nuttall (Amherst, NY: Cambria Press, 2014), 361.

45 Lassi Heininen, "Finland as an Arctic and European State: Finland's Northern Dimension (Policy)," in *International Relations and the Arctic: Understanding Policy and Governance*, edited by Robert W. Murray and Anita Dey Nuttall (Amherst, NY: Cambria Press, 2014), 333.

46 "Finland's Strategy for the Arctic Region 2013. Government Resolution on 23 August 2013," *Finnish Prime Minister's Office Publications* 16 (unpublished manuscript): 8, last modified January 18, 2015, accessed May 7, 2015, http://vnk.fi/documents/10616/334509/Arktinen+strategia+2013+en.pdf/6b6fb723–40ec-4c17-b286–5b5910fbecf4.

47 "Sweden's Strategy for the Arctic Region," Swedish Ministry for Foreign Affairs, Department for Eastern Europe and Central Asia (unpublished manuscript, 2011), accessed January 20, 2015, www.government.se/content/1/c6/16/78/59/3baa039d.pdf, 23.

48 Auswärtige Amt, "Guidelines of the Germany Arctic Policy: Assume Responsibility, Seize Opportunities" (unpublished manuscript, 2013), accessed May 7, 2015, www.bmel.de/SharedDocs/Downloads/EN/International/Leitlinien-Arktis politik.pdf?__blob=publicationFile, 1.

49 Ibid., 13.

50 HM Government, "Adapting to Change: UK Policy Towards the Arctic" (unpublished manuscript, 2013), accessed December 20, 2014, www.gov.uk/government/uploads/system/uploads/attachment_data/file/251216/Adapting_To_Change_UK_policy_towards_the_Arctic.pdf.

51 House of Lords, "Responding to a Changing Arctic," 94.

52 Małgorzata Śmieszek and Paula Kankaanpää, "Observer States' Commitments to the Arctic Council: The Arctic Policy Documents of the United Kingdom and Germany as Case Study," in *The Yearbook of Polar Law* Vol. 6, edited by Gudmundur Alfredsson and Timo Koivurova (Leiden: Brill/Martinus Nijhoff, 2015).

53 Piotr Graczyk and Timo Koivurova, "A New Era in the Arctic Council's External Relations? Broader Consequences of the Nuuk Observer Rules for Arctic Governance," *Polar Record* 50.3 (2013): 225–36, accessed May 7, 2015, doi:10.1017/S0032247412000824.

54 Michał Łuszczuk et al. "Poland's Policy Towards the Arctic: Key Areas and Priority Actions," *Policy Paper* 11.113 (unpublished manuscript: The Polish Institute of International Affairs, 2015), 1, accessed May 7, 2015, www.pism.pl/files/?id_plik=19746.

55 Uttam Kumar Sinha and Jo Inge Bekkevold, *Arctic: Commerce, Governance and Policy* (London: Routledge, 2015).

56 Ian G. Brosnan, Thomas M. Leschine and Edward L. Miles, "Cooperation or Conflict in a Changing Arctic?," *Ocean Development and International Law* 42.1/2 (2011): 173–210, accessed May 7, 2015, doi:10.1080/00908320.2011.543032.

References

Aggestam, Lisbeth. "Role-Identity and the Europeanisation of Foreign Policy: A Political-Cultural Approach." In *Rethinking European Union Foreign Policy*, edited by Ben Tonra and Thomas Christiansen, 81–98. Manchester and New York: Manchester University Press, 2004.

Airoldi, Adele. *The European Union and the Arctic: Developments and Perspectives 2010–2014.* Nordic Council of Ministers, 2014. Accessed May 7, 2015, https:// books.google.pl/books?id=s1zXBQAAQBAJ.

Amt, Auswärtige. "Guidelines of the Germany Arctic Policy: Assume Responsibility, Seize Opportunities." Unpublished manuscript, 2013. Accessed May 7, 2015, www. bmel.de/SharedDocs/Downloads/EN/International/Leitlinien-Arktispolitik. pdf?__blob=publicationFile.

Bailes, Alyson J. and Margret Cela. "Iceland – A State within the Arctic." In *International Relations and the Arctic: Understanding Policy and Governance*, edited by Robert W. Murray and Anita Dey Nuttall, 347–79. Amherst, NY: Cambria Press, 2014.

Bailes, Alyson J. and Lassi Heininen. *Strategy Papers on the Arctic or High North: A Comparative Study and Analysis.* Reykjavík: Institute of International Affairs, Centre for Small State Studies, 2012.

Bailes, Alyson J. and Beinta í. Jákobsstovu. "The Faroe Islands and the Arctic: Genesis of a Strategy." *Veftímaritið Stjórnmál og stjórnsýsla* 9.2 (2013): 531–48. Accessed May 7, 2015, doi:10.13177/irpa.a.2013.9.2.14.

Beckmann-Dierkes, Norbert, Andris Sprūds and Toms Rostoks. "Introduction." In *Perceptions and Strategies of Arcticness in Sub-Arctic Europe*, edited by Andris Sprūds and Toms Rostoks, 9–16. Riga: Latvian Institute of International Affairs, 2014.

Bengtsson, Rikard and Ole Elgström. "Conflicting Role Conceptions? The European Union in Global Politics." *Foreign Policy Analysis* 8.1 (2012): 93–108. Accessed May 7, 2015, doi:10.1111/j.1743-8594.2011.00157.x.

Brende, Børge. "The Arctic: Major Opportunities – Major Responsibilities." Speech of the Norwegian Minister of Foreign Affairs, Mr. Børge Brende delivered at American University Washington College of Law in Washington, DC, November 14, 2013. Accessed May 18, 2015, www.norway.org/News_and_events/Embassy/Text-of-FM-Brendes-Speech-The-Arctic-Major-Opportunities-Major-Responsibilities/#. VOHRFi79wsc.

Breuning, Marijke. "Role Theory Research in International Relations: State of the Art and Blind Spots." In *Role Theory in International Relations: Approaches and Analyses*, edited by Sebastian Harnisch, Cornelia Frank and Hanns W. Maull, 16–35. London: Routledge, 2011.

Brosnan, Ian G., Thomas M. Leschine and Edward L. Miles. "Cooperation or Conflict in a Changing Arctic?." *Ocean Development and International Law* 42.1/2 (2011): 173–210. Accessed May 7, 2015, doi:10.1080/00908320.2011.543032.

Charokopos, Michael. "Asserting a Leading Role for the European Union in International Aviation: When Aspirations Meet Reality." *International Journal: Canada's Journal of Global Policy Analysis* 70.1 (2015): 40–62. Accessed May 7, 2015. doi:10.1177/0020702014563109.

Degeorges, Damien. "Denmark, Greenland and the Arctic: Challenges and Opportunities of Becoming the Meeting Place of Global Powers." Unpublished manuscript, Royal Danish Defence College, 2013. Accessed May 7, 2015. http://forsvaret. dk/fak/publikationer/briefs/documents/denmark-greenland-and-the-arctic.pdf.

Denmark, Greenland and the Faroe Islands. "Kingdom of Denmark Strategy for the Arctic 2011–2020." Unpublished manuscript, last modified February 9, 2015. Accessed May 7, 2015, http://um.dk/en/~/media/UM/English-site/Documents/ Politics-and-diplomacy/Greenland-and-The-Faroe-Islands/Arctic%20strategy.pdf.

Department of Foreign Affairs and International Trade. "Statement on Canada's Arctic Foreign Policy: Exercising Sovereignty and Promoting Canada's Northern Strategy Abroad." Unpublished manuscript, 2010. Accessed December 12, 2015, www.international.gc.ca/arctic-arctique/arctic_policy-canada-politique_ arctique.aspx?lang=eng.

Dodds, Klaus and Valur Ingimundarson. "Territorial Nationalism and Arctic Geopolitics: Iceland as an Arctic Coastal State." *The Polar Journal* 2.1 (2012): 21–37. Accessed May 7, 2015, doi:10.1080/2154896X.2012.679557.

Emmerson, Charles. "Transcript: Opening up the Arctic: Prospects, Paradoxes and Geopolitical Implications." Unpublished manuscript, last modified December 15, 2014. Accessed May 7, 2015, www.chathamhouse.org/sites/files/chatham-house/public/Meetings/Meeting%20Transcripts/170712arctic.pdf.

Exner-Pirot, Heather. "The Canadian Arctic Council Ministerial – What to Expect." *Eye on the Arctic,* April 15, 2015. Accessed May 7, 2015, www.rcinet.ca/eye-on-the-arctic/2015/04/15/the-canadian-arctic-council-ministerial-what-to-expect/.

Finnish Prime Minister's Office. "Finland's Strategy for the Arctic Region 2013. Government resolution on 23 August 2013." *Prime Minister's Office Publications* 16. Unpublished manuscript, last modified January 18, 2015. Accessed May 7, 2015, http://vnk.fi/documents/10616/334509/Arktinen+strategia+2013+en.pdf/ 6b6fb723-40ec-4c17-b286-5b5910fbecf4.

Graczyk, Piotr and Timo Koivurova. "A New Era in the Arctic Council's External Relations? Broader Consequences of the Nuuk Observer Rules for Arctic Governance." *Polar Record* 50.3 (2013): 225–36. Accessed May 7, 2015, doi:10.1017/ S0032247412000824.

Griffiths, Franklyn, Robert N. Huebert and P. Whitney Lackenbauer. *Canada and the Changing Arctic: Sovereignty, Security, and Stewardship.* Waterloo, ON: Wilfrid Laurier University Press, 2011.

Harnisch, Sebastian, Cornelia Frank and Hanns Maull (eds). *Role Theory in International Relations: Approaches and Analyses.* London: Routledge, 2012.

Heininen, Lassi. "Finland as an Arctic and European State: Finland's Northern Dimension (Policy)." In *International Relations and the Arctic: Understanding Policy and Governance,* edited by Robert W. Murray and Anita Dey Nuttall, 321–48. Amherst, NY: Cambria Press, 2014.

Heininen, Lassi. "Northern Geopolitics: Actors, Interests and Processes in the Circumpolar Arctic." In *Polar Geopolitics? Knowledges, Resources and Legal Regimes,* edited by R.C. Powell and K. Dodds, 241–59. Cheltenham: Edward Elgar, 2014.

Heininen, Lassi, Alexander Sergunin and Gleb Yarovoy. "Russian Strategies in the Arctic: Avoiding a New Cold War." Unpublished manuscript, last modified December 12, 2014. Accessed May 7, 2015, http://vid-1.rian.ru/ig/valdai/arctic_eng.pdf.

HM Government. "Adapting To Change: UK Policy Towards the Arctic." Unpublished manuscript, 2013. Accessed December 20, 2014, www.gov.uk/government/

uploads/system/uploads/attachment_data/file/251216/Adapting_To_Change_UK_policy_towards_the_Arctic.pdf.

House of Lords. "Responding to a Changing Arctic." Select Committee on the Arctic, Report of Session 2014–15. Unpublished manuscript. Accessed December 20, 2014, www.publications.parliament.uk/pa/ld201415/ldselect/ldarctic/118/118.pdf.

Huebert, Rob. "United States Arctic Policy: The Reluctant Arctic Power." *The School of Public Policy (SPP) Briefing Papers* 2.2 (2009): 1–27. Accessed May 7, 2015, www.policyschool.ucalgary.ca/sites/default/files/research/sppbriefing-huebertonline.pdf.

Huebert, Rob. "Canadian Arctic Security: Shifting Challenges." In *International Relations and the Arctic: Understanding Policy and Governance*, edited by Robert W. Murray and Anita Dey Nuttall, 131–63. Amherst, NY: Cambria Press, 2014.

Icelandic Government. "Breaking the Ice: Arctic Development and Maritime Transportation. Prospects of the Transarctic Route – Impact and Opportunities." Unpublished manuscript, 2007, last modified January 20, 2015. Accessed May 7, 2015, www.mfa.is/media/Utgafa/Breaking_The_Ice_Conference_Report.pdf.

Jensen, Leif C. and Geir Hønneland. "Framing the High North: Public Discourses in Norway after 2000." *Acta Borealia* 28.1 (2011): 37–54. Accessed May 7, 2015, doi:10.1080/08003831.2011.575659.

Kræmmer, Kjersti. "The Norwegian Arctic: Energy, Economy, and the Environment: A Discourse Analysis of Norwegian Policy in the High North." Edinburgh: University of Edinburgh, 2013. Accessed May 7, 2015, www.academia.edu/4718263/The_Norwegian_Arctic_Energy_Economy_and_the_Environment.

Laruelle, Marlène. *Russia's Arctic Strategies and the Future of the Far North*. New York: M.E. Sharpe, 2014.

Lasserre, Frederic, Jérôme Le Roy and Richard Garon. "Is There an Arms Race in the Arctic?" *Journal of Military and Strategic Studies* 14.3/4 (2012): 1–56.

Łuszczuk, Michał (ed.). *Arktyka na początku XXI wieku: Między współpracą a rywalizacją*. Lublin: Wydawnictwo Uniwersytetu Marii Curie-Skłodowskiej, 2013.

Łuszczuk, Michał, Piotr Graczyk, Adam Stępień and Małgorzata Śmieszek. "Poland's Policy Towards the Arctic: Key Areas and Priority Actions." *Policy Paper* 11 (113). Unpublished manuscript: The Polish Institute of International Affairs, 2015. Accessed May 7, 2015, www.pism.pl/files/?id_plik=19746.

Moe, Arild. "Potential Arctic Oil and Gas Development: What are Realistic Expectations?" In *The Arctic in World Affairs: A North Pacific Dialogue on the Future of the Arctic (2013 North Pacific Arctic Conference Proceedings)*, edited by Oran R. Young, Jong Deog Kim and Yoon Hyung Kim, 227–51. Seoul: Korea Maritime Institute; Honolulu, HI: East-West Center, 2013.

Murray, Robert W. "Conclusions: Arctic Politics Moving Forward." In *International Relations and the Arctic: Understanding Policy and Governance*, edited by Robert W. Murray and Anita Dey Nuttall, 623–29. Amherst, NY: Cambria Press, 2014.

Murray, Robert W. and Anita D. Nuttall (eds). *International Relations and the Arctic: Understanding Policy and Governance*. Amherst, NY: Cambria Press, 2014.

Nabers, Dirk. "Identity and Role Change in International Relations." In *Role Theory in International Relations: Approaches and Analyses*, edited by Sebastian Harnisch, Cornelia Frank and Hanns W. Maull, 74–92. London: Routledge, 2011.

Nuttall, Mark. "Territory, Security and Sovereignty: The Kingdom of Denmark's Arctic Strategy." In *International Relations and the Arctic: Understanding Policy and Governance*, edited by Robert W. Murray and Anita Dey Nuttall, 263–90. Amherst, NY: Cambria Press, 2014.

Olesen, Mikkel R. "Cooperation or Conflict in the Arctic: A Literature Review." *Working Paper* 8. Unpublished manuscript: Danish Institute for International Studies, last modified December 20, 2014. Accessed May 7, 2015, www.diis.dk/files/media/images/publications/covers/wp2014-08_runge-olesen_for_web_0.pdf.

Padrtova, Barbora. "Russian Military Build-Up in the Arctic: Strategic Shift in the Balance of Power of Bellicose Rhetoric Only?." *Arctic Yearbook* (2014): 415–33.

Rosenberg, Elizabeth, David Titley and Alexander Wiker. "Arctic 2015 and Beyond. A Strategy for U.S. Leadership in the High North." *Policy Brief*, Center for a New American Security, December 2014. Accessed January 16, 2015, www.cnas.org/sites/default/files/publications-pdf/CNAS_ArcticHighNorth_policybrief_RosenbergTitleyWiker.pdf.

Sinha, Uttam K. and Jo I. Bekkevold. *Arctic: Commerce, Governance and Policy.* London: Routledge, 2015.

Śmieszek, Małgorzata and Paula Kankaanpää. "Observer States' Commitments to the Arctic Council: The Arctic Policy Documents of the United Kingdom and Germany as Case Study." In *The Yearbook of Polar Law* Vol. 6, edited by Gudmundur Alfredsson and Timo Koivurova. Leiden: Brill/Martinus Nijhoff, 2015: 375–97.

Solli, Per E., Elana Wilson Rowe and Wrenn Yennie Lindgren. "Coming into the Cold: Asia's Arctic Interests." *Polar Geography* 36.4 (2013): 253–70. Accessed May 7, 2015, doi:10.1080/1088937X.2013.825345.

Sprūds, Andris and Toms Rostoks (eds). *Perceptions and Strategies of Arcticness in Sub-Arctic Europe.* Riga: Latvian Institute of International Affairs, 2014.

Steinberg, Philip E. "U.S. Arctic Policy." In *International Relations and the Arctic: Understanding Policy and Governance*, edited by Robert W. Murray and Anita Dey Nuttall, 166–90. Amherst, NY: Cambria Press, 2014.

Swedish Ministry for Foreign Affairs, Department for Eastern Europe and Central Asia. "Sweden's Strategy for the Arctic Region." Unpublished manuscript, 2011. Accessed January 20, 2015, www.government.se/content/1/c6/16/78/59/3baa039d.pdf.

Wang, Nils and Damien Degeorges. "Greenland and the New Arctic: Political and Security Implications of a State-Building Project." Unpublished manuscript,: Royal Danish Defence College, 2014. Accessed May 7, 2015, http://forsvaret.dk/FAK/eng/publications/Documents/Greenland%20and%20the%20New%20Arctic.pdf.

Wendt, Alexander. *Social Theory of International Politics.* Cambridge Studies in International Relations 67. Cambridge and New York: Cambridge University Press, 1999.

Wilson Rowe, Elana. "Arctic Hierarchies? Norway, Status and the High North." *Polar Record* 50.1 (2014): 72–79. Accessed May 7, 2015, doi:10.1017/S003224741200054X.

Yarovoy, Gleb. "Russia's Arctic Policy." In *International Relations and the Arctic: Understanding Policy and Governance*, edited by Robert W. Murray and Anita Dey Nuttall, 191–233. Amherst, NY: Cambria Press, 2014.

Young, Oran R. "The Structure of Arctic Cooperation: Solving Problems/Seizing Opportunities." Paper prepared at the request of Finland in preparation for the fourth conference of Parliamentarians of the Arctic Region, Rovaniemi, August 27–29, 2000, and the Finnish chairmanship of the Arctic Council during the period 2000–2002. Unpublished manuscript, last modified November 12, 2014. Accessed May 7, 2015, www.arcticparl.org/files/static/conf4_sac.pdf.

Young, Oran R. "Listening to the Voices of Non-Arctic States in Arctic Ocean Governance." In *The Arctic in World Affairs: A North Pacific Dialogue on the Future of the*

Arctic (2013 North Pacific Arctic Conference Proceedings), edited by Oran R. Young, Jong Deog Kim and Yoon Hyung Kim, 275–303. Seoul: Korea Maritime Institute; Honolulu, HI: East-West Center, 2013.

Young, Oran R., Jong D. Kim and Yoon H. Kim (eds). *The Arctic in World Affairs: A North Pacific Dialogue on the Future of the Arctic (2013 North Pacific Arctic conference proceedings)*. Seoul: Korea Maritime Institute; Honolulu, HI: East-West Center, 2013.

Zysk, Katarzyna. "Military Aspects of Russia's Arctic Policy: Hard Power and Natural Resources." In *Arctic Security in an Age of Climate Change*, edited by James Kraska, 85–106. Cambridge: Cambridge University Press, 2011.

21 The role(s) of China in the Arctic

Regional governance and foreseeable challenges

François Perreault

Introduction

From 2006 to 2013, a political tug-of-war on Arctic governance took place through the use of discourse, regional and national policies, active diplomacy, and investments in commercial opportunities, scientific endeavors and military capabilities.[1] Powerful "outsiders" questioned the Arctic's status quo and, as a result, the political tug-of-war process underscored latent and explicit power disparities in the region.

The *who* and *what* should govern the region were the main fault lines between the Arctic and non-Arctic States, but amongst the Arctic Council's permanent members, there were also differences of opinions on how the region should be governed. A delicate balance needed to be established between including/excluding and the idea of internationalizing/regionalizing.

The political tug-of-war culminated in the Arctic Council's institutional enlargement of May 15, 2013, when the Arctic States granted Italy and five Asian States, China, India, Japan, Singapore and South Korea, observer status.

China was one of the powerful "outsiders" questioning the region's legal status quo and by default, the regional balance of power. Among all observer States, old and new, China stands out as it is the only one overtly seeking global power status. This simple fact is extremely important. It not only has ramifications for China's Arctic interests and perceived regional role(s), but it also echoes loudly on the political radar of other Arctic stakeholders, sometimes influencing some of their regional policies.

This chapter looks at the region from a somewhat realist and social constructivist point of view. States, power disparities, hierarchies, statuses and role perceptions, are at the center of the analysis. Specifically, the chapter looks at China's Arctic interests, its perceived regional role(s)/desired statuses, and the impact of those on the Arctic States' policies and regional governance.

The next section provides a brief overview of China's regional interests in the economic, environmental and political spheres. Further, in a separate section, we focus on China's and the Arctic States' perceived regional roles and desired statuses. The following one addresses the impact of roles, statuses, power disparities and hierarchies, on the evolution of regional policies and governance between 2006 and 2013. The chapter ends with a discussion on foreseeable challenges.

China's Arctic interests

New economic pressures are slowly connecting the region's natural resources to global markets.[2] Resource exploitation (oil, gas and minerals), offshore fishing and the promise of new commercial shipping routes through Russia's Northern Sea Route (NSR) and Canada's North West Passage (NWP) are naturally attracting commercial investments to the region. The economic interests of coastal States, large corporations and non-Arctic States are merging quite well, and the likelihood of seeing national strategic interests collide in the economic sphere is currently very small. The melting ice caps are also connecting the region's physical changes to the future livelihood of Southern countries. People often refer to the Arctic as the world's canary in the coal mine, and so the interconnectedness of the world's climate has rightly given the impulse to countries that can afford it to push for extensive polar science research programs. International collaboration in this sphere is significant and often transcends the highs and lows of international relations.

Related to the economic and environmental appeal are States' political interests in regard to regional governance: how to use and manage the Arctic's resources, regulate shipping and protect the environment.

The legal and political system governing the Arctic forms a complex interplay between international, regional and national institutional bodies. The Arctic Council is considered the central governing institution that plays the role of a knowledge builder, capacity enhancer and a stimulator for stronger international regulatory provisions.[3] Inside and outside the Arctic Council, within this complex governance system, bilateral and regional agreements, as well as regulatory regimes are currently being discussed, developed and adopted.[4] Non-Arctic States naturally want to be included in the discussions preceding any groundbreaking decisions that could affect international law and the regulation of what China and other non-Arctic States see as global commons.

Economic interests: shipping and energy security

Russia's NSR is likely to become more important to China's economic development in the near future. In 2013, 286,000 tons of cargo or 21 percent of the NSR traffic did depart from or arrived in Chinese ports.[5] By 2020, between 5–15 percent of China's international trade might transit the NSR.[6] Some Chinese analysts are projecting up to $120 billion in saving.[7] Shipping lanes are indeed a cornerstone of China's economy. To put things in perspective, the Middle Kingdom has twelve of the world's top fifty container ports, with ten in the top twenty, and seven in the top ten.[8] It also has two of the world's top ten global container fleet operators.[9] In practical terms, though, the NSR is still not experiencing high international traffic. In 2014, only thirty-one vessels crossed both Western and Eastern NSR boundaries,[10] and in 2013 only thirty traversed the route with cargo. These extremely low numbers show that the NSR is currently not competing against other international shipping lanes. In fact, it is still used primarily "as a domestic supply and export route for Russia."[11] Economic interests drive China's growing involvement in the North. Commercial shipping aside, resource exploitation, such as oil, gas and minerals are also crucial to China's economy, which is dependent on the importation of energy, raw material and international exports. Moreover, energy security is a question of national security and regime maintenance to China, and the Arctic has lots to offer in terms of resource exploitation and importation through bilateral economic cooperation with resource rich Arctic States. For example, in May 2014, Gazprom agreed to supply China National Petroleum Corporation with 38 billion cubic meters of gas per year for thirty years starting in 2018. The deal is worth $400 billion dollars. A number of pipelines are being built to deliver gas from Siberia and Yakutia to China.[12] In the same vein, the NSR could become, with time and sufficient infrastructure investments, an important energy corridor between China (Asia), Russia and Europe.

Environmental and scientific interests

The 1920 Treaty regulating the Archipelago of Svalbard, Norway, gave China the opportunity to open its first Arctic research base on Ny-Ålesund in 2004, even though it does not own any territory in the region. It became a member of the research town's Science Managers Committee one year later. China did join the International Arctic Science Committee in 1997 and has since made six expeditions to the region (1997, 2003, 2008, 2010, 2012 and 2014). It also helped create the Asian Forum for Polar Science in 2004 with Japan, South Korea, India and Malaysia. China has an extensive polar science program, although the Arctic receives only about one-fifth of the research funds.[13] The largest share goes to its Antarctic Program where China has made thirty-one expeditions and runs two-year-round research stations, one inner land summer station and one camp.[14]

China genuinely wants to understand the negative and positive effects of a warming Arctic on its climate. Since every climate effect and corresponding weather phenomenon are connected, China needs to prepare for, among other things, the likelihood of potential extremes, more droughts, more floods, more typhoons, or a changing hydrographic system with the melting of the Tibet glaciers, and the impact that this could have on its rivers and lakes. International collaboration in this sphere is significant, and since China is an emerging economic superpower, it can afford to push for extensive polar science research programs. Its people-to-people connections are growing. Conferences on the Arctic are being hosted in China, and international academic exchanges and collaborations with the Arctic States are multiplying. For example, the China-Nordic Arctic Research Center (CANRC) was established in December 2013. It is currently composed of eleven member institutes, six from Nordic States and five from China. Moreover, among others, the Chinese Academy of Meteorological Sciences, the Chinese Research Academy of Environmental Sciences, the Ocean University of China and the Polar Research Institute of China have all joined the University of the Arctic, which is a cooperative network of universities, colleges and research institutes working on the North.

China's active diplomacy in the region through scientific research reflects its growing economic and political power. Since it is overtly seeking global power status, science is an extremely useful platform for track two diplomacy. Increasing China's soft power in the region is important to gain more influence and help reduce the China Arctic threat perception that has naturally permeated the Arctic (or the perceptions of certain Arctic States' elected officials, academics and policy makers) due to its incredible rapid growth and greater political assertiveness.

Political interests

The Arctic is a necessary adjunct to China's overall strategic posture. As it seeks global power status, it wants to be perceived as a responsible international stakeholder by participating in a number of international and regional organizations. Getting a seat on the Arctic Council was thus one of China's main political objectives in the North from 2006–2013.

During that time, China increased its diplomatic ties with all of the Arctic States, but specifically with the smaller Nordic countries through scientific research and resource diplomacy. The Nordic countries eventually voiced their support for China's observer status, which contrasted Canada and Russia, who remained reluctant until the night the decision was being taken. They were both uneasy about granting China greater political influence in the region (more on this in Section IV).

Now that China has received observer status, its main political objective is to keep its status and gain a bigger say in Arctic affairs by being a good circumpolar stakeholder and a friendly northern partner. Resource-oriented diplomacy will dominate, but China will certainly continue to collaborate actively in polar science research and the working groups of the Arctic Council.

According to Feng Gao, head of the Chinese delegation in Kiruna 2013, China's official goals are to reduce its knowledge gap by understanding the region in terms of natural science, political and legal environment. It wants to protect the region's natural environment and then work with the international community to ensure a sustainable use of its resources. In fact, China would like to portray itself as being interested mainly in research and environmental protection.[15]

Two political principles linked to China's foreign policy now seem to be guiding its strategy in the North: avoid confrontation at all cost[16] and advance incrementally.[17] In doing so, the Middle Kingdom wants to increase its soft power in order to reduce the China Arctic threat perception and hopefully gain more influence.

Roles and statuses in the Arctic

Role perception is understood here as a *subjective self-understanding of a state's position in the international system*,[18] its desired status relative to others. A State's regional or international status is formed and sustained when others recognize it. It means nothing if it is unacknowledged by other States.[19]

Seeking status and respect is among other factors that shape States' behavior and their foreign policy. In the Arctic, role perceptions, power disparities, statuses and hierarchies still matter a lot.[20] In fact, several countries involved in Arctic governance, among others, Canada, China, Norway and Russia, are seeking recognition and standing in the region, and the world, through their official regional discourses, policies and actions. Analyzing their different role perceptions helps identify the power disparities and hierarchies at work in the North, which are important as they will continue to define regional governance even within the consensual Arctic Council.

Arctic States' role perceptions

Russia wants to regain its great power position in the international system, as well as its status as a global naval power and energy superpower.[21] The Arctic plays a crucial role in this strategy as it is an important piece of its internal economic and social policies. Around 20 percent of Russia's GDP is Arctic related. The Arctic is also a major component of its foreign and defense policy. Its Northern Fleet—Russia's largest—is stationed there, maintaining and guaranteeing most of its global strategic nuclear deterrence and capabilities, and boasting the world's largest and most powerful ice-breaker fleet.[22]

Russia defines itself as a *leading Arctic power*. It is also perceived by the other coastal states (at least by their regional practitioners) as a *regional great power*.[23] Russia has indeed a de facto predominant role in the Arctic because of the sheer size of its land mass above the Arctic Circle, its available resources, level of economic activity, large human population, and good military and civilian polar capabilities, especially its sea capabilities.[24] It is also a de facto gatekeeper in the East, where it controls Asia's access to the Arctic through the NSR.

The region's legal status quo and the status quo in the regional balance of power are important to Russia's overall strategy.[25] Russia wants to maintain a peaceful Arctic that favors cooperation and fosters economic growth. In order to do this, it has created a "highly cooperative Arctic brand" for itself,[26] which is sometimes put in peril because of extraregional conflicts, such as the Georgian crisis in 2008 and the current Ukraine crisis.

Canada also favors the legal status quo for Arctic governance, and its subjective self-understanding of its position in the international system has changed over the years. For more than a decade now, Canada has wanted to move away from its middle power status to be perceived as a major power in the world's hierarchy, and to be recognized for its self-proclaimed emerging role as an energy superpower.[27]

Like Russia, the Arctic plays a crucial role in this strategy where Canada also sees itself as a *leading Arctic power*, owning more than a third of the region's territory and resources. It is not clear if it is also perceived as a *regional Arctic power* by others. Canada is a large Arctic coastal State, and the sheer size of its land mass and amount of resources are significant.

Again similarly to Russia, the region is intrinsically linked to its national and international identity, and its nation-building discourse. But where Canada shares Russia's distinction as an Arctic giant in terms of land mass, its human population is low and dispersed; its North is lacking basic infrastructure and economic development, and its military and civilian capabilities in the region are not optimal, even though in discourse and official defense strategies exercising and protecting Canada's sovereignty in the Arctic is identified as a strategic prerogative. For these reasons, commentators and politicians frequently perceive foreign threats to their Northern region, especially to their North West Passage.[28]

Like Canada and Russia, Norway also defines itself as a *leading Arctic State*. It wants to lead through knowledge and science, and it sees itself as a *convener* and *bridge-builder*. Others also seem to perceive Norway as fulfilling those roles in the region.[29]

Indeed, Norway is a de facto convener in Ny-Ålesund, Svalbard, where forty-one States have equal rights to open up scientific bases and exploit natural resources. In fact, due to the 1920 Treaty, Norway has become a vital component in Asia's Arctic expansion.[30]

Norway also fulfilled its convener role when it used its extensive knowledge of the Arctic to convince the European Union to get rid of some of its most "controversial" Arctic policies in 2008–2009.[31] Among other things, the EU parliamentarians were calling for an international negotiation round to create an Arctic Treaty. It could be said that because of its perceived role as a leading Arctic State and information provider, Norway went on to change the EU's position with success.

Its bridge-builder role in the region is linked to its relationship with Russia and also to its new regional relationship with China. The Ukraine crisis has, of course, complicated Norway's bilateral relationship with Russia, which has always included a deterring and containing element, even when relations are on good standing. For Norway, its High North is the most important strategic priority of its foreign policy, especially regarding commercial and societal opportunities, and Russia is its principal actor and preoccupation.

Although Norway is a small country, it is a coastal state with important oil and gas, fishery and shipping industries. For a small country, it has a rather large role in the region. It can even be argued that it has "created a central niche for itself in the politics of the North,"[32] and that it is "trailing only Russia in global Arctic significance."[33]

The United States is currently the sole superpower in the Arctic, but unlike Canada, Norway and Russia, it has not made any claims of leadership in the region. Nevertheless, it is still viewed by the other Arctic States as a *regional great power*.[34]

The United States is a coastal State by means of Alaska. Contrary to the last decades when the Arctic was not on its political radar, the USA now has an increased interest in the region. It sent Secretaries of States to the last two Arctic Council's Ministerial meetings in 2011 and 2013, and it will hold the chairmanship for two years starting in 2015. The internationalization of the region and its eastern shift, especially with China in the mix, has most likely helped heighten the United States' Arctic interests.

The Kingdom of Denmark is also a coastal State by means of Greenland, which could achieve full independence in the future, leaving Denmark without any territory above the Arctic Circle—the Faroe Islands being a little below at 62 degrees north of the equator. Denmark does not have any status claims in the North. However, it was Denmark that decided to invite its counterparts and host the Ilulissat Conference in 2008. This coastal State-only meeting created a dichotomy between the five coastal States, the Arctic Five, and the other three founding members of the Arctic Council, the non-littoral States.

The Arctic Five club (A5) confers a higher status on its members in relation to Arctic affairs.[35] This points to our *first hierarchy* and *power disparity* at work in the North. The five coastal States claim ultimate power and legitimacy in any governance process pertaining to the Arctic. They even asserted their dominance in the region by issuing the Ilulissat Declaration in 2008, reminding the world that they are the only ones to have exclusive rights over all of the landscape and internal and historical waters by means of their sovereignty, sovereign rights and jurisdiction.

Finland, Iceland and Sweden are founding members of the Arctic Council, but they cannot issue such claims as they are non-littoral states. It can even be argued that outside of the institution, in specific issue areas related to the Arctic Ocean, their power and legitimacy are not significantly higher than, among others, the new Asian observers.[36] Needless to say, all three non-littoral Arctic States see the A5 process as potentially undermining the centrality of the Arctic Council and their predominant roles within it as permanent Member States. They are, of course, concerned about being left out of important regional discussions that can affect their interests as Arctic States.

Iceland does not claim any leadership role in the region, but it has a vision of becoming an *Arctic Singapore*, eventually striving economically due to its strategic location as the new northern shipping routes gain in importance. It views the exclusive A5 process as contrary to its interests. In response, Iceland started to brand itself as a *regional coastal State* connected to the Arctic Ocean by the Greenland, Norwegian and Barents seas. It started to remind everyone that it is "the only country located entirely in the Arctic region."[37] It also successfully branded itself as "a meeting place for Arctic debate."[38]

In fact, it created a new global and more inclusive regional forum called the Arctic Circle. That the Prime Minister of Iceland announced the new forum's creation just before the Arctic Council Ministerial Meeting in May 2013 seems to have been a calculated move to put some political pressure on the A5 members to accept new observers, and to stress the importance of the Arctic Council's centrality in light of a potential institutional enlargement, which Iceland naturally favored. Internationalizing the Arctic calls for a more inclusive process as oppose to the A5 exclusiveness.

Finland responded to the A5 process by issuing an updated Arctic Strategy in August 2013 that surprisingly called for an Arctic Council Treaty. It seems that this was also a calculated political move to protect its interests. A treaty-based Council would help all its permanent members (coastal or not) to preserve their privileged position and maintain their power and influence on regional governance.[39] Similarly to Iceland, Finland wants the Arctic Council to remain relevant.

Finally, Sweden also criticized the A5 process. In its 2011 Arctic Strategy issued by the Prime Ministers' office, it explicitly called for more inclusion in order to maintain the Arctic Council's status as the central governing institution.[40]

China's role perceptions

China is an emerging superpower. It is establishing itself as a global naval power to be reckoned with, and it is recognized as a global economic power. It wants to restore and heighten its status within the world's hierarchy by participating in regional issues worldwide. The Arctic is a "convenient location to demonstrate this new status"[41] and thus a necessary adjunct to China's overall strategic posture or grand strategy.

As mentioned above, Canada, Norway and Russia are all seeking recognition and standing in the Arctic, but Canada and Russia also have global ambitions. Since geography confers them with a de facto elevated status in the region—they are both coastal states with significant land mass above the Arctic Circle—they are using the Arctic to try and heighten their importance in the world's hierarchy. Their official regional discourses, policies and actions over the last two decades are a reflection of that desire.

Unlike Canada and Russia, geography does not give China a de facto elevated status in the region, and so Chinese academics and policy makers have started to label their country as a "near Arctic State."[42] By means of geography, China labeled as such can more easily be linked to the region's environmental changes and economic development,[43] which is important if it wants to be seen as a legitimate Arctic stakeholder.

China's global ambitions and desired international status have had a direct link to its perceived regional roles over the years. Because China is a global power, it believes it has the responsibility "to provide public goods in Arctic governance," which it argues should be globally governed.[44] It also believes to have positively affected "the interactions between Arctic and non-Arctic States in relations to Arctic governance."[45]

In practical terms, as a global economic power, China can have a significant impact on regional development and by the same token heighten its political influence in the region. Some Chinese academics argue that China should develop its regional identity as a "public goods provider" by investing in infrastructure projects within the Arctic States at subnational levels.[46]

Indeed, China seems more than willing to invest in big infrastructure and exploitation projects, and "influence, if not lead the direction of Arctic development."[47] That said, China is not the only one willing to do this as building infrastructure and capabilities seem to "form a crucial part of Northeast Asian Arctic activities and polar identity building."[48]

Regional governance

Several countries involved in Arctic governance are indeed seeking recognition and standing in the region and the world. Their different role perceptions impact their behaviors and, in turn, highlight the power disparities and hierarchies at work in the North. The evolution of regional governance is a reflection of those dynamics.

Power disparities and hierarchies

We have seen that there are a perceived status and role distinction between the coastal and non-littoral states. Three of the five coastal states have made claims to a leadership role in the region. The other two that have not are the United States and Denmark. The former is the world's superpower, which essentially means it has a large role to play in the Arctic regardless of any status claim. The latter initiated the A5 process, which of course explicitly exposed a previously latent hierarchy amongst the permanent Member States of the Arctic Council. The five coastal states have since claimed ultimate power and legitimacy over anyone else in the region, pushing aside, so to speak, the three non-littoral Arctic States that cannot legitimately voice a similar claim to power.

Other power disparities at work in the region reflect the different hierarchies within the Arctic Council itself. As a high level intergovernmental forum, the permanent Member States—the Arctic Eight—are the dominant players. The Permanent Participants (PPs) represented by six indigenous peoples' organizations also have a predominant role with full consultation rights in negotiations and decisions, but they do not have final decisional powers like the Arctic States.

The PPs' full consultation rights are not explicitly extended to the observers. Hence, there is yet another status distinction between the permanent members—the Arctic States and PPs—and the observers—the non-Arctic stakeholders. However, even though the PPs have full consultation rights within the Arctic Council, observer States have sometimes "been granted greater influence in the working groups at the PPs' expense."[49]

In fact, there is a latent if not explicit power disparity between all non-State stakeholders (including the PPs) and the countries involved in regional governance within the Arctic Council, but especially in other international fora that have an interest in the North. The international system and its institutions are still largely dominated by States.

This brings to focus the power disparities and complex hierarchies between the institutions involved in the Arctic governance. As mentioned previously, the legal and political system governing the region forms a complex interplay between international, regional and national institutional bodies.

The Arctic Council is considered the central governing body, and it does have a "degree of power through the studies it conducts,"[50] but depending on the issue area, different institutions will dominate or control the process and outcome. In reality, "the Arctic Council is only one of many international bodies in the larger institutional complex governing the Arctic," and this includes narrower and broader institutions.[51]

The Northern Sea Route Administration—a Federal State Institution in Russia—has the mandate to organize navigation in the water area of the Northern Sea Route. The A5 group has recently reached an agreement outside of the Arctic Council related to commercial fishing. These are two examples of narrower institutions. It is most likely that national institutions and intergovernmental agreements will dominate or control the process and outcome of any issue areas the coastal States perceive to be related to their sovereign rights.

UNCLOS, the favored legal framework of all the Arctic States, and the International Maritime Organization (IMO), where the Polar Code is being created to regulate international shipping in the region, both fall into the category of broader institutions. These international institutions will dominate or control the process and outcome of many issue areas related to the Arctic Ocean. China and the other observers have a legitimate voice within these broader institutions.

Nevertheless, the Arctic Council has been the driver of discussions on resource development, shipping and environmental protection in the region since 1996. As a soft law and consensual intergovernmental body, its degree of power is limited, but its perceived central role resides in the fact that it was created by the Arctic States themselves, of which five coastal states have ultimate power and legitimacy to control the outcomes of any regional governance processes within the Arctic Council and, it could be argued, within whatever broader institutions that decide to focus on the region. The A5 power and legitimacy derives from their "state's recognised sovereignty over land, internal waters and the territorial sea, and from its sovereign rights to natural resources in its exclusive economic zones (EEZ) and continental shelves."[52]

The political tug-of-war on Arctic governance

Today, the Arctic States have to deal with powerful non-arctic stakeholders, like China, who firmly believe they have a right to be included in regional governance. In 2013, the regional states decided to include six new observers on the Arctic Council, but only after a delicate balance between including/excluding and internationalizing/regionalizing had been established.

Between 2006 and 2013, a political tug-of-war on Arctic governance took place through the use of discourse, national and regional policies, active diplomacy, and investments in commercial opportunities, scientific endeavors and military capabilities. China was part of this tug-of-war process.

In fact, because of its global status and regional role perceptions, China's views on who and what should govern the Arctic echoed loudly on the political radar of other Arctic stakeholders, sometimes influencing their policies and causing concerns about the vitality of their own regional role perceptions and statuses. China definitely had an impact on the recent evolution of regional governance and Arctic policies, but so did several other non-Arctic stakeholders, such as the European Union who, through its parliamentarians, controversially proposed to launch international negotiations to create an Arctic Treaty.

The evolution of the political tug-of-war on Arctic governance that eventually led to the institutional enlargement of May 15, 2013 followed two distinct phases. The first one, reactionary in nature, saw powerful non-Arctic stakeholders—through their national media, military and elected officials, policy makers and scholars—make controversial policy recommendations and advocate hawkish stance in regards to their countries' regional roles. The phase is characterized by a fundamental lack of regional knowledge. It is thus a learning and policy-making phase for China and many non-Arctic States (and the EU) who were interested in obtaining observer status on the Arctic Council.

During this reactionary phase, there were unrestrained public discussions on the subject of Arctic governance in China. Academics, policy makers and military officials discussed China's role to safeguard and defend the Arctic's global commons, as well as the rights of non-Arctic States. Among other things, they attached significant military value to the region. They talked about the importance of controlling the Arctic routes, and about the possibility that the Arctic States would form an alliance that would be contrary to their country's rights and interests. Some argued that no states should have sovereignty rights over the region and that the use of force could not be ruled out. Most agreed that China should not remain neutral and that it needed to play a big role in the Arctic because of its global significance.[53]

For many people outside of China, these voices represented the official positions of the Chinese state. Their controversial and sometimes hawkish positions naturally helped foment the China Arctic threat perception, or the media-infused fear of Chinese and Asian activities in the region.

China was not the only country involved in this tug-of-war process on Arctic governance, but its emerging global significance does have an important effect on how others perceive its foreign policy behavior. Hence, after its observer application was deferred a second time in May 2011, Chinese scholars and military officials became more restrained in public.

The second phase of the political tug-of-war, which started in and around 2009 and 2011, is characterized by a more tempered and diplomatic approach. Everyone involved—the Arctic States, the EU, China, Germany, Japan and other non-Arctic stakeholders—finally agreed that the Arctic Council should keep its central role and that regional governance processes should proceed within the legal status quo, with UNCLOS as the main framework.

The Arctic States proceeded with policy changes that directly affected the positions of non-Arctic stakeholders and greatly influenced the start of the second phase. In fact, in order to receive observer status, the "outsiders" needed officially to accept the legal status quo and the positions expressed in the Ilulissat Declaration of the Arctic Five.

Of course, the regional states also needed to come to a consensus about internationalizing the Arctic and including new observers on the Council. There were real differences among them. For example, the A5 process is a clear expression of a preference for exclusivity and the continued regionalization of issues.

In various ways, the Nordic countries played a big role in pressuring wary States (Canada and Russia) to accept a more inclusive and international process and allow for the May 15, 2013 Arctic Council Enlargement. Iceland created the inclusive and international Arctic Circle that some viewed at the time as a potential competitor to the Arctic Council. Norway, who defines itself as a leading Arctic State, initiated strong bilateral relationships with China and many non-regional States through knowledge-sharing activities and scientific collaborations, effectively acting as a *convener* and *bridge-builder* for the region. Moreover, all of the Nordic countries officially supported China's application before the 2013 Arctic Council Ministerial Meeting.

China's unintended regional roles

During the first phase of the political tug-of-war, powerful outsiders like China and the EU questioned the legal status quo, and the sovereignty and interests of certain coastal States. In doing so, they fulfilled unintended regional roles as institutional enablers and unofficial policy makers.

China (and other outsiders) helped strengthened the resolve of the Arctic Five to control all potential outcomes in the region. With international pressure mounting, as powerful outsiders advocated controversial positions on regional governance and seeked to fulfill certain regional roles, the five coastal States decided to institutionalize an exclusive forum in order to protect their interests and keep everyone out of sovereignty issues and boundary disputes in the Arctic Ocean.[54]

The Ilulissat Conference and its Declaration were an institutional and policy response to counter claims that the coastal States could not cooperate, or that governance in the Arctic Ocean was deficient. It was a way to keep the international community at bay.

The Ilulissat Declaration is a historical component of Arctic cooperation,[55] but it is also a clear departure from the modus vivendi of governing the region through consensus, evidently showing a definite power disparity and hierarchical structure within the regional governance processes.

China (and other outsiders) also seem to have created the urgency to end certain border disputes. In fact, in 2010, Russia and Norway decided to settle their competing claims in the Barents Sea. Some argue that external pressures were one of the main motivation to settle the forty-year-old disagreement. With non-Arctic actors, such as China and the EU, seeking more influence in the region, Russia would have decided that settling outstanding disputes with other Arctic States was in its long-term interests.[56]

Moreover, during the political tug-of-war on regional governance, China (and other outsiders) also unintentionally "forced" the Arctic States to enact certain policies within the Arctic Council to preserve the status quo. For example, the Nuuk observer rules were created in 2011 in response to the permanent members (Arctic States and PPs) wariness of an increasing number of observers applicants. The rules contain a set of political requirements that observers must meet to keep their permanency. In fact, the Nuuk Observer rules are meant to pressure outsiders (China and the EU) to change any of their positions that might challenge the supremacy of the Arctic States.

Today, existing observers "are being evaluated on the basis that they are not seen as a challenge to Arctic states' and PPs' regional interests,"[57] essentially re-enforcing the permanent members' status—PPs included—within the Arctic Council. "Outsiders" also need to accept the legal status quo officially.

The leading States behind the Nuuk Observer rules were Canada and Russia. Russia did not want to grant political influence to China or the EU. They saw them as powerful enough to challenge the regional balance of power and affect the efficiency of the Arctic Council.[58] Russia also had a serious bias against China's observer application. It saw Beijing and other Asian States as potential challengers to its status and influence.[59] Canada, who frequently perceives foreign threats to its Northern region, especially to its North West Passage, was also highly suspicious of China's interests in the North.[60] It also does not want anyone to challenge its status and influence in the region.

Hence, the new observer rules were a way for Canada and Russia to keep the Arctic States in control of regional governance in the eventuality of an Arctic Council enlargement. In a way, the Nuuk Observer rules were part of a pre-emptive policy tool and perhaps "a postponement strategy designed to mask real differences among the Arctic States."[61]

Needless to say, during the political tug-of-war, China had to embark on an active diplomacy strategy in the economic and scientific sphere to "dispel suspicion and burnish its credentials as a non-threatening, unobtrusive 'joiner' in the Arctic politics."[62] Several Chinese military officials, policy makers and academics had already voiced controversial opinions on regional governance and China's role in the region, which did not help Beijing's case, especially with Canada and Russia.

Moreover, in 2011, Iceland denied the Chinese billionaire Huang Nubo the purchase of a large parcel of land on the basis of a national law. Even if it was based on a national law that the current government is said to be reviewing, the China Arctic threat theory permeated many analyses in which Nubo was somehow tied to Beijing's grand strategy to buy all the region's resources and set up military bases in the Arctic. Furthermore, China's state-own corporations' increasing interests in Greenland's mineral resources was also (and still is) viewed as a way for Beijing to gain lots of political leverage in a "soon to be" independent country.

China needed to reassure regional states of its benign intentions, so it turned to Norway, the region's bridge-builder and convener. Beijing established joint polar research programs with Oslo and opened a formal dialogue on Arctic issues. Scientific research is a great platform to help dispel suspicions, and in the Arctic scientific collaboration often transcends the highs and lows of international relations. A few years later the

China-Nordic Arctic Research Centre opened its doors, and Beijing is now a major scientific partner of all the smaller Nordic countries.

China also looked to the Nordic countries to collaborate in the economic spheres. Beijing even signed a free trade agreement with Iceland in April 2013 after six years of negotiations. Then again, the likelihood of seeing national strategic interests collide in the economic sphere is currently very small. Even with the China Arctic threat theory alive and well, Canada and Russia are collaborating actively with China's state-owned corporations in the oil, gas and mineral sectors. In fact, all the Asian states, but specifically China, offer much-needed investment capital and export markets for the resource-rich Arctic States.

Of course, the issue of governance is more political than economic. The Arctic States, especially the coastal states, believe that by virtue of their geography, they (and the permanent participants) should be the ones who decide how best to use and manage the Arctic's resources, regulate shipping and protect the environment.

In the end, the Arctic Council enlargement of May 15, 2013 was possible because of the establishment, during the political tug-of-war process, of a delicate balance between including and excluding, and internationalizing and regionalizing. Norway is said to have been a major broker at the Ministerial Meeting in Kiruna,[63] as well as the United States, even if some US officials shared Canada's and Russia's bias towards granting more political influence to China.[64]

Foreseeable challenges

There are several hierarchies as well as latent and explicit power disparities in the Arctic. Furthermore, role perceptions influence regional stakeholders' behavior and policies. Although a delicate balance seems to have been established in the region, there are still foreseeable challenges. In fact, the dynamics of power disparities, hierarchies and perceived regional role(s)/desired statuses will continue to affect the evolution of regional governance.

The Arctic Five and the delicate balance

There will be a continued regionalization of most issues through the Arctic Five process. In February 2014, again in Greenland, the five coastal States decided unilaterally to temporary prohibit commercial fishing in the high seas of the central Arctic Ocean.[65]

It is foreseeable that the three non-littoral States will have to be on the sidelines while decisions are taken that could affect international law and the regulation of what China and other non-Arctic States see as global commons. Besides, the observers (among them, China) will have no choice but to "observe" as the coastal states control the process and outcome of most issue areas they consider to be in their sovereign interests (such as environment, maritime security, mineral exploration, oil and shipping).

This state of affairs could trigger another political tug-of-war on regional governance in the near future. This time, it could play out within broader institutions, where China and others have power and legitimacy. Having said that, actively involving the observers in the Arctic Council working groups might positively affect their positions within these global institutions[66] and avoid political discontent.

The challenge will be to keep the established delicate balance alive and well in the region. To do so, the coastal states, particularly Canada and Russia, will need to try and put geopolitical issues aside. They will need to collaborate actively in the economic and scientific spheres with China and other non-Arctic stakeholders to share regional knowledge, and at the same time gather their support for Arctic initiatives within the broader institutions involved in Arctic governance.

New geopolitical factors

Putting geopolitical issues aside is easier said than done. In fact, there is a foreseeable China challenge linked to larger geopolitical factors.

As China continues its upward path to superpower status, its political influence will increase worldwide, and this includes its influence in the circumpolar region. The challenge is global in nature, but China's increasing interests in the region makes it also an Arctic challenge.

In the economic sphere, China's state-owned corporations will continue to invest more capital in the region. Beijing will argue that the investments are solely business matters, but it will be hard sometimes for others to entirely decouple them from its global ambitions. China's involvement in the Arctic Economic Council might help dispel suspicions, but, of course, the fact that most Arctic States are ready to accept much needed investment capital, certainly will.

The biggest foreseeable China challenge will be extra-regional. How Beijing decides to handle its maritime issues in its neighborhood will have a direct impact on its political status in the North. China's unilateral and military actions in the East and South China Sea are at odds with what it advocates in the Arctic.[67] There are similarities between the maritime disputes in the Circumpolar North and Asia, such as the presence of natural resources and the desire to exploit them, but there are also many differences with the most crucial one being the use of UNCLOS.[68]

As the East and South China Sea disputes evolve, reciprocity will become an important concept in the North, as Arctic States might choose to deny China certain maritime freedoms that China would have decided to deny them off its coast.[69] It is also likely that China would be stripped of its observer status if a future maritime conflict involved US treaty allies.

Extra-regional conflicts: Ukrainian crisis

Tomorrow, a potential East or South China Sea conflict might have a small impact on regional governance. China's and other Asian States' observer status could be suspended. There would also be a decreased Asian involvement in the Arctic Council proceedings because of a much more pressing matter. Be that as it may, the immediate and most pressing Arctic governance challenge does not come from Asia, but from Eastern Europe.

The annexation of Crimea by Russia in March 2014 has had and will continue to have repercussions in the Arctic. The Ukraine crisis has put seven of the Arctic Council permanent Member States in a serious diplomatic row with the eighth member who has a de facto predominant role in the region.

Its impacts are numerous. They include, among other repercussions, boycotts of certain working meetings, freezing of funds from workshops, reduction of government-to-government contacts and meetings, the cancellation of the 2014 Annual Chiefs of Defence meeting between the Member States, the Arctic Security Forces Roundtable without Russia's participation, an increased pressure to include the Arctic on NATO's official agenda, sanctions on Russia's state-controlled oil companies Rosneft and Gazprom, reciprocal sanctions and bans on imported Arctic products, and a recent military readiness across the Baltics and in the Arctic.

In the past, the Arctic Council has often been a theater for cooperation even when extra-regional conflicts divided its permanent members. During the 2008 Russo-Georgian War, there was a continued regional collaboration, almost business as usual. During the more recent Syrian conflict, the Arctic Council provided for a low-key forum to discuss matters unofficially.

Unfortunately, the Ukrainian crisis is probably the region's biggest test since the end of the Cold War. Hopefully, there are enough issue areas in the region that can be depoliticized to keep fostering the numerous transnational people-to-people connections. Geopolitical issues should not trump developmental needs in the region. The Arctic States need to put its people(s) ahead of extra-regional issues, but this too is easier said than done.

Notes

1 The author first addressed this political tug-of-war process in a 2014 joint research paper edited and published by the Spanish Ministry of Defence. See Elena Conde Pérez and François Perreault, *Security and Defence Dossiers 66 – Geopolitics of the Arctic. Two Complementary Visions. Spain – Singapore*, edited by Spanish Institute for Strategic Studies (Madrid: Ministerio de Defensa, Secretaría General Técnica, 2014), 1–63.
2 Lawson Brigham, "The Changing Arctic: New Realities and Players at the Top of the World," *Asia Policy* 18 (2014): 5–13, accessed January 25, 2015, doi:10.1353/asp. 2014.0029.

3 Olav Schram Stokke, "Asian Stakes and Arctic Governance," *Strategic Analysis* 38.6 (2014): 770–83, accessed January 25, 2015, doi:10.1080/09700161.2014.952946.

4 For example, the Agreement on Cooperation in Aeronautical and Maritime Search and Rescue in the Arctic (2011); the Cooperation on Marine Oil Pollution Preparedness and Response in the Arctic (2012); the establishment of a permanent secretariat in Tromsø (2013); the recent Agreement between the coastal States (Arctic Five) to Adopt Interim Measures to Deter Unregulated Fishing (2014); the establishment of the Arctic Economic Council (2014); ISO 19906, the Petroleum and Natural Gas Industries: Arctic Offshore Structures; the Polar Code via the International Maritime Organization (IMO); the recent and future resolutions of Jurisdictional and Maritime Boundary Disputes, such as the bilateral agreement between Norway and Russia in 2010, the potential agreement to split Hans Island between Canada and Denmark, and the future agreement in the Beaufort Sea between Canada and the United States. Finally, the continental shelf claims via the United Nation Convention on the Law of the Sea (UNCLOS).

5 Malte Humpert, "Arctic Shipping: An Analysis of the 2013 Northern Sea Route Season." *Arctic Yearbook* (2014): Briefing Notes. Accessed May 6, 2016, www.arcticyearbook.com/index.php/briefing-notes2014.

6 Katarzyna Zysk, "Asian Interests in the Arctic: Risks and Gains for Russia," *Asia Policy* 18 (2014): 34, accessed January 25, 2015, doi:10.1353/asp.2014.0038; James Kraska, "Asian States in U.S. Arctic Policy: Perceptions and Prospects," *Asia Policy* 18 (2014): 18, accessed January 25, 2015, doi:10.1353/asp.2014.0032.

7 Shiloh Rainwater, "Race to the North: China's Arctic Strategy and its implications," *Naval War College Review* 66.2 (2013): 70.

8 "Top 50 Container Ports," WorldShipping.org, accessed January 25, 2015, www.worldshipping.org/about-the-industry/global-trade/top-50-world-container-ports. Source data: The Journal of Commerce annual top 50 World Container Ports, Lloyd's List annual Top 100 Ports, AAPA World Port Rankings and individual port websites.

9 "Alphaliner top 50 Global Container Fleet Operators," JOC.com, accessed January 25, 2015, www.joc.com/maritime-news/container-lines/alphaliner-top-50-global-container-fleet-operators. Source: Alphaliner.

10 "Northern Sea Route Information Office," accessed January 25, 2015, www.arctic-lio.com/node/225.

11 Humpert, "Arctic Shipping," Briefing Notes.

12 "Russia and China sign Framework Agreement on Gas Supplies via Western Route," Gazprom, accessed January 13, 2015, www.gazprom.com/press/news/2014/november/article205898/; "Gazprom and CNPC agree on Power of Siberia Border Crossing," Interfaxenergy, accessed February 15, 2015, http://interfaxenergy.com/gasdaily/article/15269/gazprom-and-cnpc-agree-on-power-of-siberia-border-crossing.

13 Linda Jakobson and Jingchao Peng, "China's Arctic Aspirations," *SIPRI Policy Paper* 34 (2012): 19.

14 For more information, see the Chinese Arctic and Antarctic Administration website: www.chinare.gov.cn/en/.

15 Aki Tonami, "The Arctic Policy of China and Japan: Multilayered Economic and Strategic Motivations," *The Polar Journal* 4.1 (2014): 112–13, doi:10.1080/2154896X.2014.913931.

16 Ibid., 108.

17 Andrea Beck, "China's Strategy in the Arctic: A Case of Lawfare?" *The Polar Journal* 4.2 (2014): 306–18. doi:10.1080/2154896X.2014.954886.

18 Alexander Wendt, *Social Theory of International Politics* (Cambridge: Cambridge University Press, 1999).

19 Elana Wilson Rowe, "Arctic Hierarchies? Norway, Status and the High North," *Polar Record* 50.252 (2013): 72, accessed January 25, 2015, doi:10.1017/S003224 741200054X.

20 Ibid.

21 Barbora Padrtova, "Russian Military Build-Up in the Arctic: Strategic Shift in the Balance of Power or Bellicose Rhetoric Only?," *Arctic Yearbook 2014* (2014): 1–19; Lassi Heininen, "State of the Arctic Strategies and Policies: A Summary," *Arctic Yearbook 2012* (2012): 2–46; Charles Emmerson, *The Future History of the Arctic* (New York: PublicAffairs, 2010).

22 Padrtova, "Russian Military Build-Up in the Arctic," 5–6.

23 Wilson Rowe, "Arctic Hierarchies?," 74–76. Elana Wilson Rowe administered "two sets of qualitative, semi-structured interviews with representatives (primarily civil servants) of the five Arctic coastal states" mainly on Norway's role in the Arctic, but also on others' role perceptions and claims to regional status. She proceeded with one set (twelve interviews) in 2007, and another set (nineteen interviews) in 2011. They were all conducted in Oslo, Moscow, Washington, DC and Copenhagen.

24 For a good list of Russia's sea capabilities, see Padrtova, "Russian Military Build-Up in the Arctic," 18.

25 Zysk, "Asian Interests in the Arctic," 33; Tom Røseth, "Russia's China Policy in the Arctic," *Strategic Analysis* 38.6 (2014): 844, accessed January 25, 2015, doi:10.1080/09700161.2014.952942.

26 Marlène Laruelle, "Continuing Cooperation Patterns with Russia in the Arctic Region," *Wilson Center Polar Initiative Policy Brief Series* (2014): 3.

27 François Perreault, "The Arctic Linked to the Emerging Dominant Ideas in Canada's Foreign and Defence Policy," *The Northern Review* 33 (2011): 47–67.

28 Canada's North West Passage and Russia's Northern Sea Route, which they both claim as internal waters, are contested mainly by the United States who argues that the straits should be considered international straits and open to transit passage, which means foreign ships can pass through without obtaining prior permission and foreign submarine can sail submerged. China has yet to weigh in on the debate.

29 Wilson Rowe, "Arctic Hierarchies?."

30 Adam Grydehøj et al., "The Globalization of the Arctic: Negotiating Sovereignty and Building Communities in Svalbard, Norway," *Island Studies Journal* 7.1 (2012): 113–14.

31 Njord Wegge, "The EU and the Arctic: European Foreign Policy in the Making," *Arctic Review on Law and Politics* 3.1 (2012): 6–29; Wilson Rowe, "Arctic Hierarchies?."

32 Wilson Rowe, "Arctic Hierarchies?," 76.

33 Leiv Lunde, "The Nordic Embrace: Why the Nordic Countries Welcome Asia to the Arctic Table," *Asia Policy* 18 (2014): 40, accessed January 25, 2015, doi:10.1353/asp. 2014.0020.

34 Wilson Rowe, "Arctic Hierarchies?," 76.

35 Ibid., 74.

36 Stokke "Asian Stakes and Arctic Governance," 773.

37 Heininen, "State of the Arctic Strategies and Policies," 14.

38 Lunde, "The Nordic Embrace," 42.

39 Wilson, "An Arctic Council Treaty? Finland's Bold Move," *Arctic Yearbook 2014* (2014): 2.

40 Ibid., 4.

41 Gang Chen, "China's Emerging Arctic Strategy," *The Polar Journal* 2.2 (2012): 370, accessed January 25, 2015, doi:10.1080/2154896X.2012.735039.

42 Kai Sun, "Beyond the Dragon and the Panda: Understanding China's Engagement in the Arctic," *Asia Policy* 18 (2014): 48, accessed January 25, 2015, doi:10.1353/asp. 2014.0023.

43 Nong Hong, "Emerging Interests of Non-Arctic Countries in the Arctic: A Chinese Perspective," *The Polar Journal* 4.2 (2014): 280, accessed January 25, 2015, doi:10.1080/2154896X.2014.954888.

44 Ye Jiang, "China's Role in Arctic Affairs in the Context of Global Governance," *Strategic Analysis* 38.6 (2014): 915, accessed January 25, 2015, doi:10.1080/0970 0161.2014.952938.

45 Ibid.

46 Chen, "China's emerging Arctic strategy," cited in Mia Bennett, "North by Northeast: Toward an Asian-Arctic Region," *Eurasian Geography and Economics* 55.1 (2014): 87, accessed January 25, 2015, doi:10.1080/15387216.2014.936480.

47 Tonami, "The Arctic Policy of China and Japan," 106.

48 Bennett, "North by Northeast," 73.

49 Matthew Willis and Duncan Depledge, "How We Learned to Stop Worrying about China's Arctic Ambitions: Understanding China's Admission to the Arctic Council, 2004–2013," *The Arctic Institute Center for Circumpolar Security Studies*, September 22, 2014, accessed January 25, 2015, www.thearcticinstitute.org/2014/09/092214-China-arctic-ambitions-arctic-council.html.

50 Olya Gayazova, "China's Rights in the Marine Arctic," *The International Journal of Marine and Coastal Law* 28 (2013): 76, accessed January 25, 2015, doi:10.1163/157118085–12341264.

51 Stokke, "Asian Stakes and Arctic Governance," 778.

52 Ibid., 772–73.

53 Some examples are: Admiral Zhuo Yin stated that "the Arctic belongs to all people of the world and no states should have sovereignty over it"; "the current scramble for the sovereignty of the Arctic among some nations has encroached on many other countries' interest"; "China must play an indispensable role in Arctic exploration as we have one-fifth of the world's population" (Gordon Chang, "China's Arctic Play," *The Diplomat*, March 9, 2009). Li Zhenfu stated that "whoever has control of the Arctic route will control the new passage of world economics and international strategies" and that the Arctic "has significant military value." Guo Peiqing, professor at the Ocean University of China argued that China cannot remain neutral in Arctic affairs because it is on the verge of becoming a global power, and that there is a possibility of an alliance forming between the Arctic States. Senior Colonel Han Xudong stated that the use of force in the Arctic cannot be ruled out. (Linda Jakobson, "China Prepares for an Ice-Free Arctic," 6–7.)

54 Valur Ingimundarson, "Managing a Contested Region: The Arctic Council and the Politics of Arctic Governance," *The Polar Journal* 4.1 (2014): 187, accessed January 25, 2015, doi:10.1080/2154896X.2014.913918.

55 Joël Plouffe, "Canada's Tous Azimuts Arctic Foreign Policy," *The Northern Review* 33 (2011): 79.

56 Ingimundarson "Managing a Contested Region," 187.

57 Piotr Graczyk and Timo Koivurova. "A New Era in the Arctic Council's External Relations? Broader Consequences of the Nuuk Observer Rules for Arctic Governance," *Polar Record* 50.254 (2013): 234, accessed January 25, 2015, doi:10.1017/S0032247412000824.

58 Zysk, "Asian Interests in the Arctic," 33.

59 IBID., 33–36; Hong, "Emerging Interests of Non-Arctic Countries in the Arctic," 282.

60 Hong, "Emerging Interests of Non-Arctic Countries in the Arctic," 283.

61 Ingimundarson, "Managing a Contested Region," 191.

62 Chen, "China's emerging Arctic strategy," 368.
63 Lunde, "The Nordic Embrace," 40.
64 Kraska, "Asian States in U.S. Arctic Policy," 20.
65 Government of Canada website, accessed February 27, 2014, http://news.gc.ca/web/article-en.do?nid=819859.
66 Stokke, "Asian Stakes and Arctic Governance," 781.
67 Kraska, "Asian States in U.S. Arctic Policy," 21.
68 Ian Storey, "Arctic Lessons: What the South China Sea Claimants can Learn from Cooperation in the High North," *ISEAS Perspective* 65 (2013): 1–9.
69 Gayazova, "China's Rights in the Marine Arctic."

References

Beck, Andrea. "China's Strategy in the Arctic: A case of Lawfare?." *The Polar Journal* 4.2 (2014): 306–18. Accessed January 25, 2015, doi:10.1080/2154896X.2014.954886.

Bennett, Mia M. "North by Northeast: Toward an Asian-Arctic Region." *Eurasian Geography and Economics* 55.1 (2014): 71—93. Accessed January 25, 2015, doi:10.1 080/15387216.2014.936480.

Brigham, Lawson. "The Changing Arctic: New Realities and Players at the Top of the World." *Asia Policy* 18 (2014): 5–13. Accessed January 25, 2015, doi:10.1353/asp. 2014.0029.

Chang, Gordon. "China's Arctic Play." *The Diplomat*, March 9, 2009. Accessed January 25, 2015, http://thediplomat.com/2010/03/chinas-arctic-play/.

Chen, Gang. "China's Emerging Arctic Strategy." *The Polar Journal* 2.2 (2012): 358–71. Accessed January 25, 2015, doi:10.1080/2154896X.2012.735039.

Conde Pérez, Elena and Perreault, François. *Security and Defence Dossiers 66 – Geopolitics of the Arctic. Two Complementary Visions. Spain-Singapore*, edited by the Spanish Institute for Strategic Studies. Madrid: Ministerio de Defensa, Secretaría General Técnica, 2014, 1–63.

Emmerson, Charles. *The Future History of the Arctic.* New York: PublicAffairs, 2010.

Gayazova, Olya. "China's Rights in the Marine Arctic." *The International Journal of Marine and Coastal Law* 28 (2013): 61–95. Accessed January 25, 2015, doi:10.1163/157118085–12341264.

Graczyk, Piotr and Koivurova, Timo. "A New Era in the Arctic Council's External Relations? Broader Consequences of the Nuuk Observer Rules for Arctic Governance." *Polar Record* 50.254 (2013): 225–36. Accessed January 25, 2015, doi:10.1017/S0032247412000824.

Grydehøj, Adam et al. "The Globalization of the Arctic: Negotiating Sovereignty and Building Communities in Svalbard, Norway." *Island Studies Journal* 7.1 (2012): 99–118.

Heininen, Lassi. "State of the Arctic Strategies and Policies: A Summary." *Arctic Yearbook 2012* (2012): 2–46.

Hong, Nong. "Emerging Interests of Non-Arctic Countries in the Arctic: A Chinese Perspective." *The Polar Journal* 4.2 (2014): 271–86. Accessed January 25, 2015, doi:10.1080/2154896X.2014.954888.

Humpert, Malte. "Arctic Shipping: An Analysis of the 2013 Northern Sea Route Season." *Arctic Yearbook 2014*: Briefing Note.

Ingimundarson, Valur. "Managing a Contested Region: The Arctic Council and the Politics of Arctic governance." *The Polar Journal* 4.1 (2014): 183–98. Accessed January 25, 2015, doi:10.1080/2154896X.2014.913918.

Jakobson, Linda and Peng, Jingchao. "China's Arctic Aspirations." *SIPRI Policy Paper* 34 (2012): 1–36.

Jakobson, Linda. "China Prepares for an Ice-Free Arctic." *SIPRI In-Sights on Peace and Security* (2010): 1–16.

Jiang, Ye. "China's Role in Arctic Affairs in the Context of Global Governance." *Strategic Analysis* 38.6 (2014): 913–16. Accessed January 25, 2015, doi:10.1080/09 700161.2014.952938.

Kraska, James. "Asian States in U.S. Arctic Policy: Perceptions and Prospects." *Asia Policy* 18 (2014): 14–21. Accessed January 25, 2015, doi:10.1353/asp. 2014.0032.

Laruelle, Marlène. "Continuing Cooperation Patterns with Russia in the Arctic Region." *Wilson Center Polar Initiative Policy Brief Series* (2014): 1–4.

Lunde, Leiv. "The Nordic Embrace: Why the Nordic Countries Welcome Asia to the Arctic Table." *Asia Policy* 18 (2014): 39–45. Accessed January 25, 2015, doi:10.1353/asp. 2014.0020.

Padrtova, Barbora. "Russian Military Build-Up in the Arctic: Strategic Shift in the Balance of Power or Bellicose Rhetoric Only?." *Arctic Yearbook 2014* (2014): 1–19.

Perreault, François. "The Arctic Linked to the Emerging Dominant Ideas in Canada's Foreign and Defence Policy." *The Northern Review* 33 (2011): 47–67.

Plouffe, Joël. "Canada's Tous Azimuts Arctic Foreign Policy." *The Northern Review* 33 (2011): 69–94.

Rainwater, Shiloh. "Race to the North–China's Arctic Strategy and its Implications." *Naval War College Review* 66.2 (2013): 62–82.

Røseth, Tom. "Russia's China Policy in the Arctic." *Strategic Analysis* 38.6 (2014): 841–59. Accessed January 25, 2015, doi:10.1080/09700161.2014.952942.

Stokke, Olav Schram. "Asian Stakes and Arctic Governance." *Strategic Analysis* 38.6 (2014): 770–83. Accessed January 25, 2015, doi:10.1080/09700161.2014.952946.

Storey, Ian. "Arctic Lessons: What the South China Sea Claimants can Learn from Cooperation in the High North." *ISEAS Perspective* 65 (2013): 1–9.

Sun, Kai. "Beyond the Dragon and the Panda: Understanding China's Engagement in the Arctic." *Asia Policy* 18 (2014): 46–51. Accessed January 25, 2015, doi:10.1353/asp.2014.0023.

Tonami, Aki. "The Arctic Policy of China and Japan: Multilayered Economic and Strategic Motivations." *The Polar Journal* 4.1 (2014): 105–26. Accessed January 25, 2015, doi:10.1080/2154896X.2014.913931.

Wendt, Alexander. *Social Theory of International Politics.* Cambridge: Cambridge University Press, 1999.

Wegge, Njord. "The EU and the Arctic: European Foreign Policy in the Making." *Arctic Review on Law and Politics* 3.1 (2012): 6–29.

Willis, Matthew and Duncan Depledge. "How We Learned to Stop Worrying about China's Arctic Ambitions: Understanding China's Admission to the Arctic Council, 2004–2013." *The Arctic Institute Center for Circumpolar Security Studies*, September 22, 2014. Accessed January 25, 2015, www.thearcticinstitute. org/2014/09/092214-China-arctic-ambitions-arctic-council.html.

Wilson Rowe, Elana. "Arctic Hierarchies? Norway, Status and the High North." *Polar Record* 50.252 (2013): 72–79. Accessed January 25, 2015, doi:10.1017/S003224741200054X.

Wilson, Page. "An Arctic Council Treaty? Finland's Bold Move." *Arctic Yearbook 2014* (2014): Commentary.

Zysk, Katarzyna. "Asian Interests in the Arctic: Risks and Gains for Russia." *Asia Policy* 18 (2014): 30–38. Accessed January 25, 2015, doi:10.1353/asp.2014.0038.

22 Chinese Arctic science diplomacy

An instrument for achieving the Chinese dream?

Rasmus Gjedssø Bertelsen, Li Xing and Mette Højris Gregersen

Introduction

XI Jinping has made "the Chinese Dream" the motto of his administration, as previous Chinese leaders had very important policy mottos as "peaceful rise" and "peaceful development." The Chinese Dream entails both national glory and individual prosperity. Here we will focus on the dream of Chinese national greatness in the context of Chinese Arctic policy. We will use China's ambitions to participate in Arctic political, economic and scientific affairs as a case of China's aspirations to be an accepted major power in politics, business and science.

The chapter will look at how China uses science diplomacy as an instrument of soft power policy to reach goals in Arctic affairs of access, participation and recognition as a legitimate stakeholder. We will analyze top science as a marker of great power status. The chapter will also trace how China enters the Arctic through science; how China creates an image of a legitimate Arctic stakeholder through science; how China builds relations with Arctic nations and wider through science. Likewise, the chapter will consider how Arctic nations work with Chinese Arctic science in order to accommodate and integrate China in the Arctic.

The chapter shall be considered consonant with the existing debate within the International Relations and International Political Economy theories on the rise and accommodation of China in the international system. The Arctic is a useful sub-region to study these events as the Arctic is dominated by the status quo powers from the West and Russia. The case of science diplomacy gives the opportunity to explore a broader power concept in power transition and to explore transnational instruments in the management of the rise and accommodation of a new power.

The Arctic is characterized by relatively intense international scientific activity and cooperation, especially compared to the small and sparse populations. The role of science in the political, economic and transnational relations of the Arctic is therefore a valid and interesting topic, which has received attention in a West–USSR/Russia context.[1] Antarctic science diplomacy has received much more attention.[2] However, the political and diplomatic function of Arctic science concerning the new Asian participants in Arctic affairs has not been explored.

This chapter argues that Arctic science diplomacy plays an important role both for China and for the Arctic States in managing the rise of China and its aspirations in the Arctic. This region is just another region where status quo powers and rising China must handle an international system under transformation, taking in consideration the economic and political rise of China. The argument of this chapter is that China as well as the Arctic States uses science (diplomacy) skillfully in this process. Arctic States use scientific collaboration with China to integrate and socialize China into the Arctic and its institutions in a non-conflictual way. Equally, China uses its Arctic research and participation in research collaboration as a way to enter the region in a way, which is non-provocative and does not raise fears and concerns among Arctic States. The success of this approach is clear from the general acceptance and welcome of China's scientific role in the Arctic. Arctic science is one of the few topics China will communicate with Norway about in its diplomatic boycott of Norway after the 2010 Nobel Peace Prize to Chinese dissident LIU Xiaobo. These successes stand out in contrast to the strong opposition and suspicion even rumors of Chinese investments in energy and mineral resources in the region raise. Prime examples of such suspicions are the speculations surrounding China's new and bigger embassy in Reykjavík,[3] the plans of Chinese property developer HUANG Nubo to develop an ecotourism resort in northeast Iceland,[4] or the controversies in Denmark about possible Chinese investments in Greenlandic minerals. The latter controversy led to a 2013 *New York Times* op-ed "No, Greenland does not belong to China" by Martin Breum and Jørgen Chemnitz refuting these speculations.[5]

The chapter first introduces the topic of China as a rising power in International Relations and International Political Economy and the relevance of Chinese Arctic policy. Then the concepts of science diplomacy and the soft power of science diplomacy are introduced and Chinese Arctic science diplomacy is described using these concepts.

China foreign policy calculation and the Arctic nexus

The world is undergoing a great transformation in International Relations and International Political Economy brought about by the rise of China. China's rise has created a spillover effect and impact on all global issues, security, environment, balance of power, world order, among others and some issues are in close connection with the Arctic region, such as ecosystem, transportation and energy. What we are witnessing today are two sides of the same coin: great power rivalry, on the one side, and a process of process of waxing and waning or a state of flux and reflux, on the other side, in which China/other emerging powers and the US-led existing powers are intertwined in a constant process of shaping and reshaping the world order in the nexus of national interest, regional orientation, common political agenda, political alliance and potential conflicts.

The current debate on the relationship between China as one of the key emerging powers and the US-led existing world order has largely centered on whether China is to be seen as either a "status quo" or "revisionist" power in relation to the established "rules of game." Many of China's foreign policy orientations and behaviors are perceived to be revisionist vis-à-vis the defined rules, norms, values and systems by international institutions, such as the International Monetary Fund, the World Bank and the World Trade Organization. It is based on these established rules, norms, values and systems that China is often assessed to be a challenger, a destabilizer or a supporter of the existing world order.

Recently, the concept of "the Chinese Dream" has become a new word in the International Relations vocabulary, a concept with profound meanings that the whole world—including China itself—is trying to deconstruct and demystify. On the level of International Relations and world order, whether the rise of China represents a hegemonic project in the form of presenting an alternative development model has been subject to worldwide debate. It can be argued that the Chinese dream represents China's main aspiration for economic and political rise, which must be interpreted and understood beyond the narrow definition of "rise" in terms of modernization or rejuvenation. The essence of the Chinese Dream is a desire to tell the world that China—as a catch-up state—is able to provide an alternative to the existing liberal world order[6] and that its successful development in the past three decades is a possible model for others.[7]

Moreover, the Chinese Dream literally seems to come from China, but it belongs to the world: China and the rest of the world are a "community of common destiny." Beijing's economic performance and its policies on finance, currency, trade, security, environment issues, resource management, food security, raw material and commodity prices are bearing worldwide implications and are increasingly seen as connecting with the economies of millions of people outside China's boundaries. China's shifts in supply and demand can cause changes in prices, hence leading to adjustment in other countries. Beijing's energy-driven foreign policies are unavoidably having a serious impact on resource-rich regions, including the Arctic region.

Notwithstanding, the Arctic region is a very interesting case/laboratory to study the emergence of "a new world order." In other words, the Arctic is an emerging international stage to watch how international actors—the existing and the rising powers—are maneuvering to increase their stakes in bilateral and multilateral ways to shape the development direction of an "Arctic order." What makes the Arctic region interesting for International Relations and International Political Economy is the fact that the Arctic has been the "backyard" of the status quo powers of the USA, Russia (in an Arctic context), Canada and the small Nordic states. So the Arctic is a region where the status quo powers must decide how to manage the interest of rising powers, especially that of China, in their "backyard." Against this background, it is not difficult to understand the reason why the Arctic is becoming one of the centers of world political, economic and security gravity. Currently the Arctic is receiving vastly increasing international attention for a number of reasons: climate change, resource and transportation potential, and political-economic globalization.

China is closely following the evolution of the Arctic affairs and is playing an increasingly active role in Arctic-related scientific, political, transnational and economic relations. China's growing presence in the Arctic is seen as linking with Beijing's Arctic interest for potentially undiscovered resources as well as alternative ocean transportation routes. Driven by its shortage of energy resources and facing the recurrent problems with its maritime transport in the Indian Ocean, China, as an emerging stakeholder but without a formal place or role in the Arctic political and legal set-up, is perceived to be struggling to find ways to safeguard its rights to the access to Arctic resources and maritime transport route (reflected in its bid for Arctic Council observer status). Chinese foreign policy calculation and action, in the eyes of Western mainstream media, is going to generate a huge impact on the agenda of global geopolitics and geoeconomics in the Arctic region in the years to come.

Defining itself as a "near-Arctic state,"[8] Chinese foreign policy makers deem China to be a natural participant and stakeholder in the Arctic. China has been given observer's status in the Arctic Council, which has also created anxieties among the existing council members, mainly Canada and even Russia, about the possible challenges which might emerge from China's engagement in Arctic affairs. Consequently, the existing Arctic Council members (Canada, Kingdom of Denmark, Finland, Iceland, Norway, Russia, Sweden and the USA) have to relate to this Asian giant, either willingly or unwillingly. China's interest in the Arctic, apart from political and economic calculations, is also driven by climate change concern as Arctic climate change affects Asian weather patterns and therefore agriculture and food security.

China is one of the emerging powers that mostly depend on global supply of energy, raw materials and global ocean transportation because it is the world largest trading nation. China is also among the rare countries that define energy to be their "national security" concerns—a priority in foreign policy making process.

The "unique" strength of Arctic geoeconomic potential makes Beijing interested in taking a share of Arctic energy, raw materials and new shipping routes. The Arctic will therefore be a new dimension of the relationship between the Arctic States and China as well as other Asian stakeholders. This situation may give especially the small Nordic states privileged scientific, political and economic nexus to the rising and existing Asian powers.

The Nordic states have a natural presence in the Arctic and a central position in Arctic governance (sovereignty and Arctic Council membership), which is one of the important characteristic of the Arctic seen from all perspectives: International Relations, International Political Economy, security and global governance. The role of the Arctic in relations with China as a rising power is therefore an important question of foreign policy, transnational relations and economic development of the Nordic countries and other Arctic States. As some scholars point out "now, even though the Arctic is not a foreign policy priority, China's growing interest in the region raises concern—even alarm—in the international community about China's intentions."[9]

In order to reduce the global anxiety to China's Arctic policy, China has been trying to decrease what is perceived to be significant geoeconomic calculation, by prioritizing science diplomacy in Arctic and Antarctic research, that is, scientific exploration and research collaboration. In the past two decades, China conducted five Arctic and twenty-eight Antarctic expeditions. Its scientific research position was further strengthened by the installation of the Arctic Yellow River Station as an attempt to pursue ecological and environmental monitoring. China reached an agreement with Finnish company Aker Arctic Technology to embark a second ice-breaker in 2014 that is the second one after the MV *Xuě Lóng*.[10] Furthermore, Beijing's policy objective has been to increase its representatives taking part in the Arctic-related international cooperation in scientific research, such as joining the Arctic Science Committee (1996), hosting the Arctic Science Summit Week (2005), joining the Ny-Ålesund Science Managers Committee (2005), International Polar Year (IPY) (2007–2008).

It is clear that "scientific diplomacy" alone will not seem to be enough to ensure China's permanent member state seat in the most influential and important Arctic organization, the Arctic Council. But still, scientific diplomacy is the most resilient and receptive approach to the Arctic policy formation and to minimize the "myth and misperception" of China's Arctic motivation.[11] Chinese statistics reveal that China's Arctic policy focuses on Arctic exploitation in cooperation with Arctic States while international law and Arctic governance are considered as a good platform for China's involvement in Arctic affairs.[12] In a word, China's long-term Arctic policies are aimed to not provoke misperceptions and negative responses from the Arctic States while at the same time struggling to position itself not to be excluded from the rightful access to the Arctic stakes. Linda Jakobson predicted the centrality of Chinese Arctic science diplomacy for China's integration into Arctic affairs in her 2012 report "China's Arctic Aspirations" recommending that: "China must rely on diplomatic cooperation and the positive impact of scientific engagement and investments to promote its interest in the Arctic."[13]

Science diplomacy as an instrument of soft power

The political and diplomatic role of science is not well understood outside circles of researchers and practitioners of the field, so we will introduce in some detail the concept of science diplomacy and how it relates to the concept of power in International Relations.

What the exact definition of science diplomacy is and what is to be included in this has yet to be determined in academia. Currently various definitions exist emphasizing different aspects. The idea of science diplomacy is not new. Research communities and governments have over time engaged in activities that could have been considered acts of science diplomacy, but were not identified as such.[14] A well-known example of this is the scientific exchanges during the Cold War between the USA and the Soviet Union that helped open up an alternative channel of communication between the two and in this way aided the mending of political relations overall.[15] Following a renewed interest in the possibilities of science diplomacy, new efforts are being made to work towards a definition. While underlining that the concept of science diplomacy is still fluid, in 2010 the Royal Society proposed a general definition of science diplomacy which was referred to at the National Academies Workshop in 2012, suggesting participants' acknowledgement of its usefulness.[16] This general definition stated that the term "science diplomacy" may be applied to: "the role of science, technology and innovation in three dimensions of policy: informing foreign policy objectives with scientific advice, facilitating international science cooperation, using science cooperation to improve international relations between countries."[17]

Each of these dimensions of policy specifies an observed link between science and diplomacy thereby clarifying the goal/outcome of this relationship. Accordingly, we can say that there are three "types" of science diplomacy: "science in diplomacy," "diplomacy for science" and "science for diplomacy," which are all potentially termed "science diplomacy."[18] Because there is no determined definition, the term "science diplomacy" is at times used as a catch-all for any interaction of policy and science and the three-sided definition thus requires further clarification. First, "science in diplomacy" describes situations where science is used to inform on issues of diplomatic concern thereby ensuring that diplomats, institutions and other decision makers and policy makers have access to legitimate and respected scientific advice, as well as the capacity to understand the scientific and technical information presented to them. Second, "diplomacy for science" relates to the facilitation of international scientific cooperation for the advancement of science and achievement of specific scientific goals or projects that require the participation of multiple countries in order to, for example, cover the cost of these and ensure sufficient investments. Finally, "science for diplomacy" refers to the use of science, through scientific cooperation, to improve (international) relations between countries, particularly in cases where these relations are weak, strained or otherwise challenged.[19]

It is particularly "science for diplomacy" that is of interest here. The basic idea of this type of science diplomacy is that international scientific cooperation can help bridge cultural gaps based on "shared scientific understanding": a shared foundation of scientific values (rationality, transparency and universality) that are considered to be universal and, in this way, giving "science" a special capacity for advancing communication and cooperation.[20] In this way, the sharing of scientific information between research communities, and the scientific cooperation between these in general, may create a parallel communication track between countries. This communication track runs alongside official governmental discourse and communication and may deliver diplomatic results even if this was not the original intent or main purpose of the communication.[21]

This phenomenon has been described in academia as *track one* and *track two* diplomacy.[22] Track one diplomacy represents the traditional and narrow approach to diplomacy in which only states and states' representatives can be considered diplomatic actors, suggesting that diplomacy can only occur in official relations between states. The second track is the broad, multilateral and, at times considered, informal approach to diplomacy. Here several actors may be involved in the diplomatic relation such as citizen groups, non-governmental organizations, academic experts and other "non-state actors" or civil society stakeholders.[23] Davidson and Montville, who coined the term, suggests that track two diplomacy holds great potential to aid the goals of the official track one diplomacy. They recognized that this type of track two diplomatic interactions need not be limited to "enemies," but could also be used to improve already established and amiable relations and is considered "strategically optimistic."[24] Davidson and Montville explained that this inherent characteristic is due to the underlying assumption: "that actual or potential conflict can be resolved or eased by appealing to common human capabilities to respond to good will and reasonableness," such as is the case with scientific and cultural exchanges.[25] The presentation of the tracks of diplomacy reveals the diplomatic potential of science (the people and activities included in this) in this way suggesting that the scientific community right down to the individual scientist can be seen as having a degree of diplomatic agency. However, the government (and policy makers) has a prominent role as well when it comes to science diplomacy. Chaimovich explained this as follows: "science diplomacy is done by the state, and while science can be a tool for diplomacy, it is part of a government's policy."[26] The scope of actors of science diplomacy can thus be unclear. The problem with this lack of clarity arises when trying to determine which cases are a matter of scientific cooperation (global science cooperation) and which are a matter of science diplomacy. While the two are closely related, they are not the same. The difference between these lies in the potential political motivations for the use of scientific engagement: the former entails an apolitical purpose (such as advancing science and working on issues of common concern), the latter however denotes potential governmental interference through the word "diplomacy," that is, the pursuit of national agendas through science and thus a politicization of science. The term "science diplomacy" may carry negative connotations which could interfere with the reception of scientific engagement in some countries and interfere with goals both apolitical and otherwise.[27]

The power potential of Chinese science (diplomacy)

In 1990, Joseph S. Nye published the book *Bound to Lead* in which he presented his theory on the existence of "soft power," which he further developed in his 2004 book *Soft Power: The Means to Success in World Politics.*[28] Since then his take on power cultivation including the concepts of "soft power" and "smart power" have become highly influential in the world of IR and are of particular relevance to a country's diplomatic efforts.[29] Nye defines soft power as "the ability to get preferred outcomes through the co-optive means of agenda-setting, persuasion and attraction."[30] China is one country that has been particularly fascinated by the potential of this new type of power. The Chinese government has made significant efforts to cultivate its soft power and through this (attraction, persuasion and agenda-setting) attempted to convince the world of its peaceful and non-revisionist intentions to assure a more amiable international structural environment.[31] These soft power cultivation efforts include attempted cultivation of resources such as Chinese culture (e.g., through broadcasting, Confucius Institutes, the 2008 Olympics), the Chinese economic model (the Beijing Consensus) and its foreign policy through the promotion of state-level cooperation agreements based on the idea of mutually beneficial and equal relationships.[32] In this context, it is worth considering the potential of "science" as a power resource and of "science diplomacy" as a strategy of soft power cultivation which may aid China in its overall soft power endeavor.

The diplomatic "ability" of science within the type "science for diplomacy" is, among others, ascribed to the "soft power of science"; "its attractiveness and influence both as a national asset, and as a universal activity that transcends national interest." This is based on the idea that the "soft power of science" interacts with all levels of diplomacy in International Relations.[33] The basic premise of observing the soft power (and following smart power) implications of science for diplomacy, is the assessment of this as both an instrument (implying agency) but also a strategy of the state.[34] This strategy may be used to improve relations with other countries and the process of this can be examined based on a relational conceptualization of power. The identification of a state's use of such a strategy is depended on a pronounced conceptualization of power as a matter of "power with" implying intention of co-optive behavior (essential for the conversion of power resources into soft power outcomes) thus providing the foundation for soft power cultivation. In the soft power cultivation strategy, "science for diplomacy" science is considered the primary resource, but may be further integrated into a national smart power strategy alongside other soft power cultivation strategies such as those based on culture.[35]

The capacity of Chinese science

The rise of China has led to an impressive economic growth over the last three decades among others, as a result of Deng Xiaoping's policies of "economic reform and opening up" that was first implemented back in the late 1970s.[36] Since then, Chinese foreign policy has embraced a more active international role, referred to as China's "new" diplomacy. Within this, Chinese foreign policy strategy has thus evolved from being strategy of "reaction" and "bringing in" (foreign interest and investments) to a proactive strategy of "going out," beginning in the early twenty-first century.[37] The need for, and incentive behind, the Chinese strategy of going out can in part be explained by the continuously expanding energy need of the Chinese society which is created by the economic and societal progress; exemplified, among others, by its demand for oil which is predicted to double by 2030 to over 16 million barrels a day.[38] Chinese foreign and open door policy furthermore entails a substantial focus on international science and technology cooperation and exchange. A strategic use of science and scientific cooperation would primarily be based on the quantity of Chinese science. As a result of the rapid economic growth, China has been able to dedicate significant funds to improve the national level of science and technology.[39] The research and development (R&D) intensity of China has, in fact, tripled since 1998.[40] The primary focus of the Chinese government has been on developing the country's internal capacity for R&D and innovation, encouraging, among others, technological advance in the industrial sectors to move up the ladder towards an increase in high technology exports.[41] A particular rapid increase in R&D spending can be observed from the year 2000 to 2012 where spending on this area rose from US$10.8 billion to US$168 billion.[42] The R&D spending in 2012, at 1.9 percent of GDP, meant that China had surpassed the EU in R&D intensity[43] and if these growth trends continue China is on line to overtake the USA (to which it is still second in actual R&D spending) in about ten years.[44] However, there have been questions on the quality and credibility of Chinese science, a factor which may undercut soft power cultivation efforts, as the Chinese research community has faced challenges with academic misconduct involving plagiarism and corruption cases.[45] Nonetheless, the focus on science and technology is becoming a key part of China's vision for the future of achieving "innovation based and harmonious (social, economic and environmental) development."[46] The "National Medium- and Long-term Program for Science and Technology Development (2006–2020)" published by the Chinese government further reflects the ambition of China to become a global leader in science and innovation and thus aspires to increase the R&D spending to 2.5 percent of GDP by 2020.[47] As China is fast developing its R&D capacity, China is constantly looking for new cooperation partners who may contribute to achievement of national goals and the fulfillment of XI Jinping's Chinese Dream, among others, in the Arctic. With the enormous science capacity that China has, considering "science" as a potential soft power resource in the same vein as culture that holds the potential of furthering both domestic and foreign policy goals is an interesting prospect.

Chinese science diplomacy in the Arctic

In the case of the Arctic, we have seen an increase in Chinese Arctic scientific activities since 2007. These include an increase in funding for polar research and polar expeditions, reflected also in an increase in the frequency of the Chinese National Arctic Research Expeditions (CHINARE). There have been a total of six Arctic research expeditions, which took place in 1999, 2003, 2008, 2010, 2012 and 2014.[48] In 2012, the Chinese ice-breaker *Xuě Lóng* became the first Chinese vessel to conclude a voyage across the Arctic Ocean.[49] However, Chinese Arctic activities and interests, including those of Chinese commercial actors, have at times been met with opposition and worry with regards to China's intentions, as exemplified in the introductory paragraph. The media focus on resource extraction, territorial rights and the energy sector led to a narrative of an international and competitive Arctic "Gold" Rush in the High North[50] to which the Chinese Arctic interests were seen to be part of. This may have had a harmful effect on China's reputation in the Arctic. According to a public opinion survey, in 2011, China was considered the least attractive partner in dealing with Arctic issues by the Arctic Eight which was in large part found to be due to its assertive discourse on China's rights in the Arctic Ocean.[51] However, since China received its second deferral of decision on its application for permanent observer status in 2011 by the Arctic Council, the assertive statements pertaining to rights and resource exploitation have been replaced with a focus on science, co-optive behavior and climate change. This development reflects the recommendations by Linda Jakobson, in her 2012 report "China's Arctic Aspirations," as stated above; in particular the positive impact of scientific engagement.[52] The "positive impact" mentioned refers to the soft power of science as discussed above and has proved itself a highly useful strategy in China's effort to improve its relations with the Arctic countries, particularly the Nordic countries, and establish itself as an active Arctic stakeholder. In May 2013, China obtained its observer status in the Arctic Council and has since then maintained an active stance on Arctic research and Arctic issues in general.

China's achievement of observer status did not mark finality in the Chinese Arctic efforts. On the contrary, they are continuing to pursue an Arctic research agenda that could be considered a "science for diplomacy" strategy, which can be illuminated by Chinese actions indicating the use of science for diplomatic purposes. A well-known instrument for science for diplomacy is the pursuit and following creation of science cooperation agreements between two or more countries or unions which has often, historically, been perceived as symbolizing improving political relations.[53] China has engaged in scientific cooperation worldwide. As of 2006, China had a total of 152 science and technology agreements with other countries and regions.[54] In the Arctic, China has scientific agreements with and has explored joint research ventures with all of the Arctic Eight. Most recently, China and Canada held talks on possible collaboration on Arctic research.[55] An important point in this respect was that the $7 million of yearly research funding that the Canadian government has pledged for their own high Arctic research station in Cambridge Bay, was considered by Jin Huijun, Deputy Director of China's State Key Laboratory of Frozen Soil Engineering to be "grossly insufficient" for working in the North. Huijun pointed to the fact that with China's Arctic research budget rising 10 percent a year, a scientific Arctic cooperation between the two countries could give Canadian Arctic research more resources thereby making it an attractive prospect.[56] This use of science to create attraction through co-optive behavior is exactly what a science for diplomacy strategy that aims to produce soft power entails. From a Chinese perspective a win–win situation would thus arise as a key element of the suggested cooperation would be the possible construction of a permanent Chinese research outpost/observatory facility in the Northwest Territories where long-term research data can be collected.[57]

In this way, Chinese scientists are looking establish a physical presence in the Arctic. This is similar to China's cooperative plans to expand the aurora observatory in Karholl, Iceland known as the China-Iceland Joint Aurora Observatory. Here, the Chinese side is investing an estimated 300 million ISK to the construction and maintenance of the project according to a report by RUV.[58] China already has its "Yellow River" research station on Norway's Svalbard archipelago opened in 2004. On this occasion, former president HU Jintao wrote in a letter commenting its scientific research stations that: "The three stations have not only provided a crucial platform for China's polar scientific research, but also opened important windows for scientific exchanges with other countries."[59] Building collaborative research stations is one way that China enters the Arctic through the strategic use of science. Even so, suggesting that China uses its science strategically does not negate the fact that China also has a genuine interest in working with climate change research in the Arctic. The implications of Arctic climate change on Chinese ecological systems, food security and following domestic economic development remain important.[60] However, since this early statement by HU Jintao, it seems that China has realized the value of opening up track two communications to build relations with the Arctic nations.

This is particularly notable with China's approach to the Nordic states. In December 2013, the Polar Research Institute of China (PRIC) established the China-Nordic Arctic Research Center (CNARC), which provides a platform for academic cooperation to increase knowledge of the Arctic and to promote cooperation between Nordic and Chinese scientists for sustainable development of a global China and the Nordic Arctic.[61] The creation of new research institutions such as CNARC, including the establishment of educational scholarships, encourage networking and scientific partnerships between track two contacts, is considered an additional instrument of a science for diplomacy strategy. This initiative by the PRIC is important as it is the link between Chinese policy makers and Chinese academia on polar affairs. It is China's principal research institution for polar affairs, and is governed by the Chinese Arctic and Antarctic Administration (CAA), which is in turn subordinate to the State Oceanic Administration (SOA).[62] The common denominator in these examples is the utilization of track two (diplomacy) contacts in a research capacity, which are considered highly relevant, particularly in cases where track two contacts act within the framework of government policy. Institutions such as CNARC cultivate relationships between researchers and can convert the resource of science into potential soft power outcomes.

A basic characteristic of the power conversion strategy "science for diplomacy" is that it must seek to produce soft power and thus utilize the co-optive power behaviors associated with this. This intent is often reflected in foreign policy and relevant activities of official representatives. China has yet to publish an official Arctic policy so articulated strategic intent of producing soft power in an Arctic context is difficult to determine. Therefore one must turn to observing indicators of strategic action, such as the use of the instruments above. Soft power through science is not the only power that China is pursuing and exercising in the Arctic. China's Science for diplomacy strategy is part of a wider and multifaceted strategy where it functions as one soft power element in China's national smart power strategy. This overall strategy may relate to how several types of power are designed at national level to interact and allow us to consider whether any of the other types interfere/undercut the soft power efforts related to "science for diplomacy." In an Arctic context, China is also utilizing its economy to produce soft power, such as in the case of its free trade agreement with Iceland, and the immense economic capability is naturally what underlies the quantity aspect of Chinese science. The use of economy alongside science through co-optive behavior for soft power outcomes is not necessarily confrontational as long as the behavior chosen by the agents builds towards the same narrative. The Chinese Arctic narrative revolves around mutually beneficial partnerships with shared interest in climate change and scientific exchange and may have been chosen to frame China's image in the Arctic. Jakobson explains: "By advocating a focus on climate change, Chinese scholars strive to circumvent the sensitivity of Arctic resources and sovereignty issues [...] Climate change cooperation provides China with opportunities to partner with other states on the Arctic agenda."[63] The image of China as a non-threatening Arctic actor, which is a main outcome of its science based soft power activities, will thus depend on its ability to continue its usage of co-optive soft power behaviors in the Arctic. According to Nye, the successfulness of a soft power cultivation strategy will depend on the opinion of the intended subject and therefore any utilization of hard power behaviors, threatening or coercing, may seriously undermine China's narrative and desire to be considered a legitimate Arctic stakeholder.

Conclusion: Arctic science diplomacy, rising China and managing power transition

The rise of China (and to less extent other rising powers) and its effects on the international political and economic system, the balance of power, the relative distribution of power, global governance and security are some of the main topics of International Relations and International Political Economy research today. This scholarly question translates into a central policy question for both the status quo powers of the international system and China and the other rising powers of how to navigate and manage this power transition. In light of the poor historical record of peaceful systemic changes and power transitions,[64] prudent statecraft in the decades ahead is of great importance.

These international systemic changes are also very relevant in an Arctic context. Before the Ukraine crisis between the West and Russia, the newly found interest of Asia (and especially of China) in the Arctic was the predominant topic in Arctic international politics research. The emerging interest of China and other Asian states in the Arctic, which was recognized with the Arctic Council observer status of China, India, Japan, Singapore and South Korea in May 2013, should be seen as an instance of these greater international systemic power transitions and globalization. It is important for Arctic international politics research to see the Arctic as part of the international political and economic system and Arctic policy as part of the foreign policies of Arctic and outside states. The Arctic is a region traditionally of the exclusive interest of status quo powers of the international system, the USA, Russia (concerning the Arctic), the small Nordic states and more peripherally European great powers as Britain, France and Germany and a few other European states as the Netherlands, Poland, Spain and Italy who have been Arctic Council observer states for some time (Italy being the latest addition). The Arctic is therefore a laboratory for how status quo powers can respond to rising power asking for a role in regional governance and how status quo and rising powers can manage this situation. The Arctic Council decision to admit the five Asian states as observers demonstrates a policy of integration and socialization of rising powers into existing institutions of the status quo powers, which is in line with, for instance, China's WTO membership.

Both status quo and rising powers must deploy a range of power instruments to manage these transition processes. Here we have focused on Arctic science diplomacy deployed by China and reciprocally by Arctic States. Chinese possible economic, political and security ambitions in the Arctic raise much suspicion (as also evidenced in, for instance, Africa). In contrast, China's scientific engagement with Arctic States progresses harmoniously, including Arctic research stations in Svalbard, Norway, and upcoming in Iceland and Sweden. China's willingness to continue Arctic science collaboration with Norway during its diplomatic–political boycott of Norway is particularly noteworthy. We therefore propose the argument that science diplomacy plays a central role in the integration of a rising China into the Arctic, which has historically been the exclusive preserve of status quo powers. China uses science diplomacy in the meaning of science for diplomacy as a means to enter the Arctic in a non-provocative way, and the Arctic States reciprocally use science diplomacy as a means to integrate and socialize China as an Arctic stakeholder in a non-confrontational way. The lessons seem to indicate that science diplomacy could be a useful instrument to manage the rise of China in other regions of the world and functional areas of the international system.

Notes

1 Paul Arthur Berkman, "Stability and Peace in the Arctic Ocean through Science Diplomacy," *Science & Diplomacy* 3.2 (2014), accessed July 24, 2015, www.science diplomacy.org/perspective/2014/stability-and-peace-in-arctic-ocean-through-science-diplomacy.

2 Paul Arthur Berkman et al. (eds), *Science Diplomacy: Antarctica, Science, and the Governance of International Spaces* (Washington, DC: Smithsonian Institution Scholarly Press, 2011).

3 Didi Kirsten Tatlow, "China and the Northern Rivalry," *New York Times*, October 5, 2012, accessed July 24, 2015, http://rendezvous.blogs.nytimes.com/2012/10/05/china-and-the-northern-great-game/.

4 Andrew Higgins, "Teeing Off at the Edge of the Arctic? A Chinese Plan Baffles Iceland," *New York Times*, March 22, 2013, accessed July 24, 2015, www.nytimes.com/2013/03/23/world/europe/iceland-baffled-by-chinese-plan-for-golf-resort.html?smid=tw-share.

5 Martin Breum and Jørgen Chemnitz, "No, Greenland does not Belong to China," *New York Times*, February 20, 2013, accessed July 24, 2015, www.nytimes.com/2013/02/21/opinion/no-greenland-does-not-belong-to-china.html.

6 Shaun Breslin, "Understanding China's Regional Rise: Interpretations, Identities and Implications," *International Affairs* 85.4 (2009): 817–35.

7 Nicola Spakowski, "National Aspirations on a Global Stage: Concepts of World/Global History in Contemporary China," *Journal of Global History* 4.3 (2009): 475–95.

8 "10 May 2012: China Defines itself as 'Near-Arctic State', Says SIPRI," Stockholm International Peace Research Institute, accessed April 3, 2015, www.sipri.org/media/pressreleases/2012/arcticchinapr.

9 Linda Jakobson and Jingchao Peng, *China's Arctic Aspirations* (Stockholm: Stockholm International Peace Research Institute, 2012), accessed December 20, 2012, http://books.sipri.org/product_info?c_product_id=449.

10 It was built in 1993 at Kherson Shipyard in Ukraine, and it was originally converted from an Arctic cargo ship to a polar scientific research and resupply vessel.
11 Ping SU and Marc Lanteigne, "China's Developing Arctic Policies: Myths and Misconceptions," *Journal of China and International Relations* 3.1 (2015).
12 Ping SU and Xing LI, "Defining China's Arctic Interest in the Background of Arctic Exploitation Risks," (forthcoming).
13 Jakobson and Peng, *China's Arctic Aspirations*, 1–23.
14 National Research Council, *U.S. and International Perspectives on Global Science Policy and Science Diplomacy* (Washington, DC: National Academies Press, 2012), accessed April 5, 2015, www.nap.edu/catalog/13300/us-and-international-perspectives-on-global-science-policy-and-science-diplomacy; The Royal Society and AAAS, *New Frontiers in Science Diplomacy: Navigating the Changing Balance of Power* (London and Washington, DC: The Royal Society; AAAS, 2010), accessed April 5, 2015, https://royalsociety.org/policy/publications/2010/new-frontiers-science-diplomacy/.
15 National Research Council, *U.S. and International Perspectives*, i–60.
16 Ibid.
17 Royal Society and AAAS, *New Frontiers in Science Diplomacy*, 1–34.
18 Ibid.
19 Ibid.; National Research Council, *U.S. and International Perspectives*, i–60.
20 John Vogler, "Environmental Issues," in *The Globalization of World Politics: An Introduction to International Relations*, edited by John Baylis, Steve Smith and Patricia Owens (Oxford: Oxford University Press, 2008), 350–68; Royal Society and AAAS, *New Frontiers in Science Diplomacy*, 1–34; National Research Council, *U.S. and International Perspectives*, i–60.
21 Royal Society and AAAS, *New Frontiers in Science Diplomacy*, 1–34.
22 William D. Davidson and Joseph V. Montville, "Foreign Policy According to Freud," *Foreign Policy* 45 (1981–1982): 145–57.
23 Ibid.; "Diplomacy," in *The SAGE Glossary of the Social and Behavioral Sciences*, edited by Larry Sullivan (Thousand Oaks, CA: SAGE Publications, 2009), 154–55; Geoffrey Allen Pigman, "Soft Power Diplomacy," in *Encyclopedia of Global Studies*, edited by Helmut K. Anheier and Mark Juergensmeyer (Thousand Oaks, CA: SAGE Knowledge, 2013), accessed April 5, 2015, http://m.knowledge.sagepub.com/mobile/view/globalstudies/n494.xml.
24 Davidson and Montville, "Foreign Policy According to Freud," 145–57.
25 Ibid.
26 National Research Council, *U.S. and International Perspectives*, i–60.
27 Ibid.
28 Joseph S. Nye Jr., *Bound to Lead: The Changing Nature of American Power* (New York: Basic Books, 1990), 307; Joseph S. Nye Jr., *Soft Power: The Means to Success in World Politics* 1st edn (New York: PublicAffairs, 2004), 191.
29 Joseph S. Nye Jr., *The Future of Power* (New York: PublicAffairs, 2011), 300.
30 Ibid.
31 Pauline Kerr, Stuart Harris and Yaqing Qin (eds), *China's "New" Diplomacy: Tactical Or Fundamental Change* (New York: Palgrave Macmillan, 2008); Mingjiang Li (ed.), *Soft Power: China's Emerging Strategy in International Politics* (Lanham, MD: Lexington Books, 2009), 275; Nye, *The Future of Power*, 300.
32 Mingjiang, Li. *Soft Power*, 275; Nye, *The Future of Power*, 300; Craig Hayden, *The Rhetoric of Soft Power: Public Diplomacy in Global Contexts* (Plymouth: Lexington Books, 2012).
33 Royal Society and AAAS, *New Frontiers in Science Diplomacy*, 1–34; National Research Council, *U.S. and International Perspectives*, i–60.
34 Mette Højris Gregersen, "Science Diplomacy: Examining the Power of Science" (MSc thesis, Aalborg University, 2014).

35 Ibid.
36 Xing Li, "Introduction: The Rise of China and the Capitalist World Order: The 'Four China' Nexus," in *Rise of China and the Capitalist World Order*, edited by Xing Li (Farnham: Ashgate, 2010), 1–24; Nye, *The Future of Power*, 300.
37 Kerr et al., *China's "New" Diplomacy*; Zhiqun Zhu, *China's New Diplomacy: Rationale, Strategies and Significance* 2nd edn (Farnham: Ashgate, 2013), 282.
38 Ibid.
39 Arthur Sweetman and Jun Zhang, "Crossing the River by Touching the Stones: An Introduction to China's Remarkable Thirty Years of Reform and Opening Up," in *Economic Transitions with Chinese Characteristics: Thirty Years of Reform and Opening Up* Vol. 1, edited by Arthur Sweetman and Jun Zhang, (Montreal: McGill-Queen's University Press, 2009), 1–10; KMPG, "Innovated in China: New Frontier for Global R&D," *KPMG*, August 2013, accessed April 5, 2015, www.kpmg.com/CN/en/IssuesAndInsights/ArticlesPublications/Newsletters/China-360/Documents/China-360-Issue11–201308-new-frontier-for-global-R-and-D.pdf.
40 Richard van Noorden, "China Tops Europe in RD Intensity," *Nature* 505 (2014): 144–45, accessed April 5, 2015, www.nature.com/news/china-tops-europe-in-rd-intensity-1.14476.
41 Sweetman and Zhang, "Crossing the River by Touching the Stones," 1–10.
42 "Scientific Research. Looks Good on Paper: A Flawed System for Judging Research is Leading to Academic Fraud," *The Economist*, September 28, 2013, accessed April 5, 2015, www.economist.com/news/china/21586845-flawed-system-judging-research-leading-academic-fraud-looks-good-paper; Noorden, "China Tops Europe in RD Intensity," 144–45.
43 Ibid.
44 KMPG, "Innovated in China."
45 GUO Jiaxue, "Academic Corruption Undermining Higher Education: Yau Shing-Tung," *China Daily*, June 2, 2010, accessed April 5, 2015, www.chinadaily.com.cn/hkedition/2010–06/02/content_9919871.htm; Nye, *The Future of Power*, 300; Timothy Beardson, "China Needs a Culture of Creative Innovation," *China Daily*, June 30, 2014; "Scholars Suggest Academic Cleanup," *Xinhua*, accessed April 5, 2015, http://news.xinhuanet.com/english/china/2014–01/27/c_133078615.htm; Yu Xie, Chunni Zhang and Qing Lai, "China's Rise as a Major Contributor to Science and Technology," *Proceedings of the National Academy of Sciences of the United States* 111.26 (2014): 9437–42, accessed April 5, 2015, www.pnas.org/content/111/26/9437.abstract.
46 Bengt-Åke Lundvall et al., "China's System and Vision of Innovation: An Analysis in Relation to the Strategic Adjustment and the Medium- to Long-Term S&T Development Plan (2006–20)," *Industry and Innovation* 16.4–5 (2009): 369–88.
47 KMPG, "Innovated in China."
48 "Chinese Arctic and Antarctic Administration," Chinese Arctic and Antarctic Administration, accessed April 5, 2015, www.chinare.gov.cn/en/.
49 Jakobson and Peng, *China's Arctic Aspirations*, 1–23.
50 Roger Howard, *The Arctic Gold Rush: The New Race for Tomorrow's Natural Resources* (London and New York: Continuum, 2009), 259.
51 Ekos Research Associates Inc, *Rethinking the Top of the World: Arctic Security Public Opinion Survey* (Toronto: Munk-Gordon Arctic Security Program, 2011); James Kraska (ed.), *Arctic Security in an Age of Climate Change* (Cambridge: Cambridge University Press, 2013), 342.
52 Jakobson and Peng, *China's Arctic Aspirations*, 1–23.
53 Royal Society and AAAS, *New Frontiers in Science Diplomacy*, 1–34.

54 "International Cooperation in Science and Technology," China.org.cn, accessed April 5, 2015, http://china.org.cn/english/features/Brief/193306.htm.
55 Nathan Vanderklippe, "Chinese Scientists Look to Canadian Arctic for Research Outpost," *The Globe and Mail*, March 18, 2015, accessed April 5, 2015, www.theglobeandmail.com/report-on-business/industry-news/energy-and-resources/chinese-scientists-dream-of-arctic-research-outpost-in-the-north/article23527009/.
56 It is to be noted that as of March 2015, the Chinese actors have yet to make a formal proposal for the Canadian government. Ibid.
57 Ibid.
58 "300 Milljónir í Norðurljósarannsóknir [300 Million [ISK] for Northern Lights Research]," RÚV, accessed April 5, 2015, www.ruv.is/frett/300-milljonir-i-nordurljosarannsoknir; "About AO," China-Iceland Joint Aurora Observatory, accessed April 5, 2015, http://karholl.is/en/um-ao.
59 "Yellow River Station Opens in Arctic (China Daily, July 29, 2004)," *China.org.cn*, accessed April 5, 2015, www.china.org.cn/english/2004/Jul/102431.htm.
60 Jakobson and Peng, *China's Arctic Aspirations*, 1–23.
61 "Background," China-Nordic Arctic Research Center, accessed April 5, 2015, http://cnarc.info/index.php/organization.
62 Jakobson and Peng, *China's Arctic Aspirations*, 1–23.
63 Ibid.
64 John J. Mearsheimer, *The Tragedy of Great Power Politics* (New York: W.W. Norton, 2001), 555.

References

Beardson, Timothy. "China Needs a Culture of Creative Innovation." *China Daily*, June 30, 2014.

Berkman, Paul Arthur. "Stability and Peace in the Arctic Ocean through Science Diplomacy." *Science & Diplomacy* 3.2 (2014). Accessed July 24, 2015, www.sciencediplomacy.org/.

Berkman, Paul Arthur, Michael A. Lang, David W.H. Walton and Oran R. Young (eds). *Science Diplomacy: Antarctica, Science, and the Governance of International Spaces*. Washington, DC: Smithsonian Institution Scholarly Press, 2011.

Breslin, Shaun. "Understanding China's Regional Rise: Interpretations, Identities and Implications." *International Affairs* 85.4 (2009): 817–35.

Breum, Martin and Jørgen Chemnitz. "No, Greenland does Not Belong to China." *New York Times*, February 20, 2013. Accessed July 24, 2015, www.nytimes.com/2013/02/21/opinion/no-greenland-does-not-belong-to-china.html.

China Internet Information Center. "Yellow River Station Opens in Arctic (China Daily, 2004/07/29)." Accessed April 5, 2015, www.china.org.cn/english/2004/Jul/102431.htm.

China.org.cn. "International Cooperation in Science and Technology." Accessed April 5, 2015, http://china.org.cn/english/features/Brief/193306.htm.

China-Iceland Joint Aurora Observatory. "About AO." Accessed April 5, 2015, http://karholl.is/en/um-ao.

China-Nordic Arctic Research Center. "Background." Accessed April 5, 2015, http://cnarc.info/index.php/organization.

Chinese Arctic and Antarctic Administration. "Chinese Arctic and Antarctic Administration." Accessed April 5, 2015. www.chinare.gov.cn/en/.

Davidson, William D. and Joseph V. Montville. "Foreign Policy According to Freud." *Foreign Policy* 45 (1981–1982): 145–57.

The Economist. "Scientific Research. Looks Good on Paper. A Flawed System for Judging Research is Leading to Academic Fraud." September 28, 2013.

Ekos Research Associates Inc. *Rethinking the Top of the World: Arctic Security Public Opinion Survey.* Toronto: Munk-Gordon Arctic Security Program, 2011.

Gregersen, Mette Højris. "Science Diplomacy: Examining the Power of Science." MSc thesis, Aalborg University, 2014.

Guo, Jiaxue. "Academic Corruption Undermining Higher Education: Yau Shing-Tung," *China Daily*, June 2, 2010. Accessed April 5, 2015, www.chinadaily.com.cn/hkedition/2010-06/02/content_9919871.htm.

Hayden, Craig. *The Rhetoric of Soft Power: Public Diplomacy in Global Contexts.* Plymouth: Lexington Books, 2012.

Higgins, Andrew. "Teeing Off at the Edge of the Arctic? A Chinese Plan Baffles Iceland." *New York Times*, March 22, 2013. Accessed July 24, 2015, www.nytimes.com/2013/03/23/world/europe/iceland-baffled-by-chinese-plan-for-golf-resort.html?smid=tw-share.

Howard, Roger. *The Arctic Gold Rush: The New Race for Tomorrow's Natural Resources.* London and New York: Continuum, 2009.

Jakobson, Linda and Jingchao Peng. *China's Arctic Aspirations.* Stockholm: Stockholm International Peace Research Institute, 2012. Accessed December 20, 2012, http://books.sipri.org/product_info?c_product_id=449.

Kerr, Pauline, Stuart Harris, and Qin Yaqing (eds). *China's "New" Diplomacy: Tactical Or Fundamental Change.* New York: Palgrave Macmillan, 2008.

KMPG, "Innovated in China: New Frontier for Global R&D." *KPMG*, August 2013, accessed April 5, 2015, www.kpmg.com/CN/en/IssuesAndInsights/ArticlesPublications/Newsletters/China-360/Documents/China-360-Issue11-201308-new-frontier-for-global-R-and-D.pdf.

Kraska, James (ed.). *Arctic Security in an Age of Climate Change.* Cambridge: Cambridge University Press, 2013.

LI, Xing. "Introduction: The Rise of China and the Capitalist World Order: The 'Four China' Nexus." In *Rise of China and the Capitalist World Order*, edited by Xing Li, 1–24. Farnham: Ashgate, 2010.

Lundvall, Bengt-Åke, Gu, Shulin Liu Ju, Sylvia Schwaag Serger, and Franco Malerba. "China's System and Vision of Innovation: An Analysis in Relation to the Strategic Adjustment and the Medium- to Long-Term S&T Development Plan (2006–2020)." *Industry and Innovation* 16.4–5 (2009): 369–88.

Mearsheimer, John J. *The Tragedy of Great Power Politics.* New York: W.W. Norton, 2001.

Mingjiang, Li (ed.) *Soft Power: China's Emerging Strategy in International Politics.* Lanham, MD: Lexington Books, 2009.

National Research Council. *U.S. and International Perspectives on Global Science Policy and Science Diplomacy.* Washington, DC: National Academies Press, 2012. Accessed April 5, 2015, www.nap.edu/catalog/13300/us-and-international-perspectives-on-global-science-policy-and-science-diplomacy.

Noorden, Richard van. "China Tops Europe in RD Intensity." *Nature* 505 (2014): 144–45. Accessed April 5, 2015, www.nature.com/news/china-tops-europe-in-rd-intensity-1.14476.

Nye, Joseph S., Jr. *The Future of Power.* New York: PublicAffairs, 2011.

Nye, Joseph S., Jr. *Soft Power: The Means to Success in World Politics* 1st edn. New York: PublicAffairs, 2004.

Nye, Joseph S., Jr. *Bound to Lead: The Changing Nature of American Power.* New York: Basic Books, 1990.

Pigman, Geoffrey Allen. "Soft Power Diplomacy." In *Encyclopedia of Global Studies*, edited by Helmut K. Anheier and Mark Juergensmeyer. Thousand Oaks, CA, SAGE Knowledge, 2013. Accessed April 5, 2015, http://m.knowledge.sagepub.com/mobile/view/globalstudies/n494.xml.

RÚV. "300 Milljónir í Norðurljósarannsóknir [300 Million [ISK] for Northern Lights Research]." Accessed April 5, 2015, www.ruv.is/frett/300-milljonir-i-nordurljosarannsoknir.

Spakowski, Nicola. "National Aspirations on a Global Stage: Concepts of World/Global History in Contemporary China." *Journal of Global History* 4.3 (2009): 475–95.

Stockholm International Peace Research Institute. "10 May 2012: China Defines itself as 'Near-Arctic State,' Says SIPRI." Accessed April 3, 2015, www.sipri.org/media/pressreleases/2012/arcticchinapr.

SU, Ping and Marc Lanteigne. "China's Developing Arctic Policies: Myths and Misconceptions." *Journal of China and International Relations* 3.1 (2015).

SU, Ping and Xing LI. "Defining China's Arctic Interest in the Background of Arctic Exploitation Risks." (forthcoming).

Sullivan, Larry (ed.). "Diplomacy." In *The SAGE Glossary of the Social and Behavioral Sciences*, 154–55. Thousand Oaks, CA: SAGE Publications, 2009.

Sweetman, Arthur and Jun Zhang. "Crossing the River by Touching the Stones: An Introduction to China's Remarkable Thirty Years of Reform and Opening Up." In *Economic Transitions with Chinese Characteristics: Thirty Years of Reform and Opening Up*, Vol. 1, edited by Arthur Sweetman and Jun Zhang. 1–10. Montreal: McGill-Queen's University Press, 2009.

Tatlow, Didi Kirsten. "China and the Northern Rivalry." *New York Times*, October 5, 2012, accessed July 24, 2015, http://rendezvous.blogs.nytimes.com/2012/10/05/china-and-the-northern-great-game/.

The Royal Society and AAAS. *New Frontiers in Science Diplomacy: Navigating the Changing Balance of Power*. London and Washington, DC: The Royal Society; AAAS, 2010. Accessed April 5, 2015, https://royalsociety.org/policy/publications/2010/new-frontiers-science-diplomacy/.

Vanderklippe, Nathan. "Chinese Scientists Look to Canadian Arctic for Research Outpost." *The Globe and Mail*, March 18, 2015.

Vogler, John. "Environmental Issues." In *The Globalization of World Politics: An Introduction to International Relations*, edited by John Baylis, Steve Smith and Patricia Owens, 350–68. Oxford: Oxford University Press, 2008.

Xie, Yu, Chunni Zhang and Qing Lai. "China's Rise as a Major Contributor to Science and Technology." *Proceedings of the National Academy of Sciences of the United States* 111.26 (2014): 9437–42. Accessed April 5, 2015, www.pnas.org/content/111/26/9437.abstract.

Xinhua. "Scholars Suggest Academic Cleanup." Accessed April 5, 2015, http://news.xinhuanet.com/english/china/2014-01/27/c_133078615.htm.

Zhiqun, Zhu. *China's New Diplomacy: Rationale, Strategies and Significance* 2nd edn. Farnham: Ashgate, 2013.

Index

63039148R00266